£12.00

FURNESS AND THE INDUSTRIAL REVOLUTION

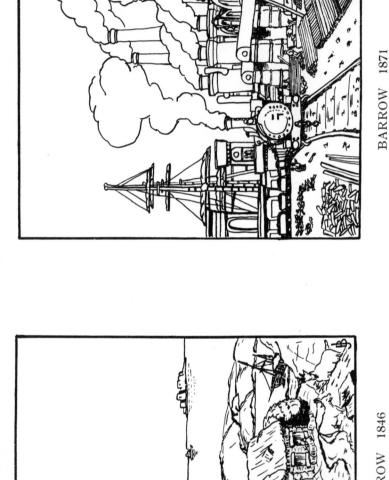

BARROW 1871

BARROW 1846

The transformation of the village of Barrow ; copied from the plinth of the Ramsden monument, Barrow-in-Furness (1872) by Miss J. Bramhall.

FURNESS
AND THE
INDUSTRIAL REVOLUTION

AN ECONOMIC HISTORY OF FURNESS (1711 – 1900)
AND THE TOWN OF BARROW (1757 – 1897)
WITH AN EPILOGUE

by
J. D. Marshall

MICHAEL MOON
AT THE BECKERMET BOOKSHOP
BECKERMET, CUMBRIA
and also at 41, 42 ROPER STREET, WHITEHAVEN CUMBRIA.

First edition 1958
Reprinted 1981

AUTHOR'S NOTE FOR THE 1981 REPRINT

I am glad to have another opportunity of thanking all those who helped to produce this book in the first instance, including the Barrow Town Council. Mr Moon's enterprise in producing this reprint is also to be commended. Although the publisher has been obliged to leave the text as it is, further basic corrigenda are to be found on the page before the index. I do not believe that geographer colleagues are 'dull'; otherwise, there is little to add.

J. D. Marshall

March, 1981.

ISBN. 0 904131 26 2

Reprinted in Great Britain by
THE MOXON PRESS LTD
Ben Rhydding, Ilkley
West Yorkshire

CONTENTS

Chapter   *Page*

LIST OF ABBREVIATIONS   x

INTRODUCTION   xiii

PART ONE

FURNESS INDUSTRY AND SOCIETY
BEFORE THE RAILWAY AGE.

I FURNESS IN THE EARLY EIGHTEENTH CENTURY : A
   GENERAL SURVEY   1
      Introductory : The Furness District   1
      Parochial and other divisions   3
      The People of Furness, 1700—50   4
      Land tenure, customs, and types of agriculture   8
      Stability of the population   14
      Trade, industry and population   15

II THE RISE OF THE FURNESS CHARCOAL IRON
   INDUSTRY   19
      The establishment of blast furnaces   19
      Further progress of the industry   29

III THE SLATE, COPPER AND TEXTILE INDUSTRIES OF
    FURNESS IN THE LATE EIGHTEENTH AND EARLY
    NINETEENTH CENTURIES   42
      Slate   42
      Copper   47
      Textiles   49

IV FURNESS AGRICULTURE AND WOODLAND INDUSTRIES,
    1746—1850   55
      The eighteenth century   55
      Land reclamation and enclosure   63
      Agricultural developments to the year 1850   70

V ROADS AND SHIPPING, 1760—1840   82
      Roads   82
      Shipping and the Ulverston Canal   85

VI THE POPULATION OF FURNESS, 1700—1831   97
      Population constancy and immigration   104
      Emigration from the district   109
      The mechanics of local population increase   112
      Public health and social conditions   115

VII   SOCIAL ORGANISATION : LOCAL GOVERNMENT, THE
      POOR LAW, SCHOOLS, AND OTHER INSTITUTIONS   127
          Local Government   127
          Pauperism and the new Poor Law   132
          Education   143
          Eminent Men   151
          Social Institutions   156
VIII FURNESS SOCIETY BEFORE THE RAILWAY AGE   159
          Clergy and people   159
          Relaxations   165

                         PART TWO

             VICTORIAN YEARS : TRANSPORT, TOWNS
                        AND METAL.

IX   THE GENESIS OF THE FURNESS RAILWAY   171
          The general background   171
          The construction of the railway   176
          The Earl of Burlington — a biographical note   184
X   RAILWAY AND IRONFIELD, 1846—61 (I)   187
          Effects and fortunes of the F. R., 1846—50   187
          The trade in iron ore   191
          Barrow harbour and village   197
XI   RAILWAY AND IRONFIELD, (II)   202
          H. W. Schneider and the discovery of the Park
              deposits   202
          The further development of the ironfield   204
          The Furness Railway and the ore trade   209
          Local railway politics in the 'fifties   212
          W. H. Schneider and Furness iron-smelting   220
          Individuals in local history   224
XII   POPULATION AND SOCIAL CHANGE, 1841—61   227
          Anticipation of population growth   227
          The population of N. Lonsdale to 1861   234
          Further aspects of social change   240
XIII IRON, STEEL AND RAILWAY PROGRESS, 1861—70   249
          The Hindpool works   249
          The expansion of local ironmaking   254
          Iron mining in the 'sixties   257
          Railway development in the 'sixties   258
          Port and passengers   272
          The F. R. directors in the 'sixties   278

XIV SOCIAL ORGANISATION AND URBAN GROWTH :
BARROW AND DISTRICT IN THE 'SIXTIES 281
Barrow and the railway influence 281
Local government and misgovernment 288

XV WORKMEN AND TOWNSMEN IN THE 'SIXTIES 307
Social conditions and the trade unions 311
Further light on the social conditions 320
Beerhouses, temperance and churches 325
The townsman's politics 334

XVI THE OVERCROWDED YEARS, (I) : CAPITAL, LABOUR
AND INDUSTRIAL DEVELOPMENT, 1870—3 336
Capital 336
Labour 353

XVII THE OVERCROWDED YEARS, (II) : LOCAL GOVERN-
MENT IN BARROW AND DISTRICT, 1870—4 367
The separation of Barrow 367
Administrative problems 371
Institutions 378

XVIII YEARS OF ANTI-CLIMAX 380

XIX TOWN AND COUNTRY, 1870—1900 407

EPILOGUE 425

ILLUSTRATIONS

Fig. No.		Page
1. Furness parochial areas		xix
2. Manorial map of Furness		xx
3. Economic Geography		xxi
4. The Furness charcoal-iron industry, 1711—1800		xxii
5. Graph of baptisms, burials and marriages		101
6. Plan of Barrow in 1856		230
7. Plan of Barrow in 1866		231
8. Plan of Barrow in 1885		232
9. Mines and works : end of 19th Century		256

Barrow 1846 and 1871 .... *Frontispiece*
Holograph bill for some Romney portraits .... *between* 96 & 97
At Conishead Bank .... do.
The end of the over-sands route near Ulverston .... do.
Dalton market place in the early nineteenth century .... do.
Ulverston market place in the late eighteenth century .... do.
Bill of lading for Whitriggs iron ore .... do.
Greenodd as a Furness port .... do.
Sir John Barrow's cottage at Dragley Beck, Ulverston .... do.
Sir James Ramsden as King Midas .... *facing* 169
Barrow's rulers in the title of *Barrow Vulcan* .... do.
An opposition cartoon 170
The first Furness Railway cottages at Salthouse, Barrow *between* 224 & 225
The Barrow Mechanics' Institute and School .... do.
Travelling by the over-sands route in the pre-railway era .... do.
Urswick — a typical Furness village .... do.
The Leven Viaduct, 1857 .... do.
Dalton Court Leet, c. 1900 .... do.
Hindpool — Job Bintley's pipe-dream .... do.
Abbots Wood, Furness Abbey .... do.
The 7th Duke of Devonshire .... do.
Henry William Schneider .... do.
Sir James Ramsden .... do.
J. T. Smith .... do.
Abbey Road, Barrow-in-Furness .... do.
Barrow Ironworks, 1874 .... do.
Robert Hannay .... do.
Alexander Brogden .... do.
Joseph Richardson .... do.
Lord Frederick Cavendish .... do.
Inside Barrow Jute Works, 1874 .... *between* 320 & 321
At the Theatre, Barrow .... do.
Barrow Flax and Jute Works in the 'eighties .... do.
Furness Railway Company Offices at Barrow .... do.
The original F. R. Station at St. George's Square, Barrow ..... do.
The former Royal Hotel, Strand, Barrow .... do.
Part of the former Town Hall, Market and Police Offices .... do.
Haematite Company furnaces, 1874 .... do.
Model housing, 1884 style ; flats at Old Barrow .... do.
Barrow's first steam tram, 1884 .... do.
The Buccleuch Dock, Barrow .... do.
The Liner " *City of Rome* " .... do.
Cattle sheds and shipping in the Barrow docks, mid-'eighties ..... do.

TABLES

No.   *Page*

1. Total tonnages of the ships belonging to North-western ports 32
2. Buccleuch mines in Furness, ten-yearly averages of annual outputs 35
3. Wages in the 18th Century Furness Iron Industry 40
4. Land Tax Assessments 57
5. Improvements at Salthouse, Plain Furness 76
6. Land Utilisation in parts of Furness 77
7. Approximate Agricultural Wage-Levels in Furness, 1809—50 80
8. Shipping based upon Ports ; Tonnages 87
9. Vessels entered and cleared outwards with cargoes at Customs House, Ulverston 91
10. Vessels inward and outward : coastal trade only 93
11. Duke of Buccleuch's mines, Plain Furness 93
12. Baptisms and Burials of Furness and Lonsdale 98
13. Distances of places of origin of marriage partners 105
14. Distribution of burial ages 119
15. General trends in expenditure on the Furness poor 134
16. Educational establishments in Furness and Cartmel 145
17. Estimate of educational provision in Furness parishes or townships 148
18. Ulverston Canal Traffic, 1839—49 187
19. Iron Ore firms, pits and outputs in Furness, 1849 194
20. Furness Haematite Production 206
21. Profits of a Furness haematite firm, 1857—61 208
22. Furness Railway and the Ore Trade 209
23. Value of Annual Traffic per mile 210
24. Decennial rates of population growth in Furness and Cartmel, 1801—61 235
25. Birthplaces of Inhabitants, Ulverston(e) District, 1861 239
26. Average cost for ton of Hindpool haematite pig (1862) compared with cost of Backbarrow charcoal furnace (1747) 250
27. Average yearly dividends of Furness Railway, 1858—73 259
28. F. R. Receipts and Expenditure, 1860—70 260
29. Barrow's Industrial Basis in 1867 275
30. Statistics of Dalton Co-operative Society, 1861—70 310
31. (a) Furness Railway receipts and expenditure etc., 1869—76 337
    (b) F. R. traffic deriving from iron and steel industries 337
    (c) F. R. traffic deriving from non-basic industries 338
32. Estimated loss of population in Furness villages etc., 1861—70 354
33. The population growth of Barrow-in-Furness and Dalton 355
34. Borough of Barrow-in-Furness ; numbers of workpeople by firms and occupations, 1871—2 356

Antiquities, 1774 and 1805.　　Thomas West, *Antiquities of Furness,* 1774 ; 1805 edition of the same, ed. William Close, with a supplement by Close.

Autobiography　　*The Autobiography of William Stout,* ed. J. Harland, 1851, (supplemented by a copy of the original manuscript, by courtesy of Dr. W. H. Chaloner).

Backbarrow MSS.　　Account ledgers of the Backbarrow Iron Company at Barrow-in-Furness Public Library.

Barfoot & Wilkes　　John Barfoot and Peter Wilkes, *Universal British Directory,* Vol. IV, 1794.

Barrow P. L.　　The Local Collection, Barrow-in-Furness Public Library.

B. Her.　　The *Barrow Herald,* first published as a weekly newspaper on Jan. 10th, 1863.

B. M.　　*British Museum.*

B. N. F. C.　　*Barrow Naturalists' Field Club, Proceedings O. S. and N. S.,* 1877 to date.

B. T.　　*Bishop's Transcript* (parish register).

B. T. C. Mins.　　*Minutes* of the Barrow-in-Furness Town Council (1867—), used by courtesy of the Town Clerk, Mr. W. Lawrence Allen.

B. Times　　*Barrow Times,* newspaper published 1866–71.

C. & W.　　*Cumberland and Westmorland Antiquarian and Archaeological Society ; Transactions, Old Series and New Series,* 1874 to date.

Chet. Soc.　　Publications of the Chetham Society, 1844—

Dir. Mins. (F.R.)　　*Directors' Minutes* of the Furness Railway (MS), viewed by courtesy of the British Transport Commission.

Dir. Mins. Jt. Cttee.　　*Directors' Minutes* of the Furness Railway— Midland Railway Joint Committee, by courtesy of the above.

Dir. Mins. (S. D. & L. U.)　　*Directors' Minutes* of the South Durham and Lancashire Union Railway, by courtesy of the British Transport Commission.

Dir. Mins. (U. & L.)　　*Directors' Minutes* of the Ulverston and Lancaster Railway, by courtesy of the British Transport Commission.

D.N.B.　　*Dictionary of National Biography.*

Duddon Accts.	*Account books* of the Duddon Ironworks (MS) 1750—1775, at the Lancashire Record Office, Preston.
Ec. H. R.	*The Economic History Review.*
E. I. I. F.	Alfred Fell, *The Early Iron Industry of Furness* (1908).
F. P. & P.	Joseph Richardson, *Furness Past and Present* (2 vols., 1880).
Gent. Mag.	*The Gentleman's Magazine.*
G. L.	Day Book and General Account Ledger of the Backbarrow iron partnership (1713—15), at the King's College Library, Newcastle, (transcript at Barrow Public Library).
Hawkfield Farm Accts.	*MS. account books* of the Hawkfield Farm, Urswick, Lancashire (1810—25), in the Local Collection of the Barrow Public Library.
Hist. Soc. L. & C.	*Historic Society of Lancashire and Cheshire* Transactions, 1849 to date.
H. M. C. Fleming.	*Historical Manuscripts Commission, Twelfth Report, Appendix, Part 7, The Manuscripts of S. H. Le Fleming, Esq., of Rydal Hall,* 1890.
Holker MSS.	Documents of the families of Lowther of Holker and Cavendish of Holker at the Lancashire Record Office : viewed (with other material in these archives) by courtesy of the County Archivist, Mr. R. Sharpe France, and the Clerk of the Peace for Lancashire.
Itinerary.	William Close, *An Itinerary of Furness and the Environs etc.* (MS), transcript by Thomas Alcock Beck, 1835 ; with misc. notes of Close transcribed by Beck, and original notes on population by Close. At the Manchester Reference Library.
J. I. S. I.	*Journal of the Iron and Steel Institute.*
Kendall MSS.	*MS. notes* of the late William Barrow Kendall, at the Barrow Public Library, with further material privately loaned ; by courtesy of Mr. J. L. Hobbs and Mr. H. Kendall.
Lancs. P. R. Soc.	*Lancashire Parish Register Society.*
Lancs. R. O.	*The Lancashire Record Office.*
L. & C.	*Lancashire and Cheshire Antiquarian Society* ; *Transactions,* 1883 to date.
Mannex.	P. Mannex & Co., *Directory and Topography of North Lancashire District* (Preston, 1866).
Mills v. Muncaster.	A collection of documents, relating to customs, land tenure and mining rights, compiled for the purpose of a lawsuit ; at the Barrow Public Library.

Min. Stats. U.K.	*Mineral Statistics of Great Britain* (1854—).
Mins. U. C. Co.	*Minutes* of the Ulverston Canal proprietors (1793—), by courtesy of the British Transport Commission.
Mins. Ulv. Gdns.	The *Minutes* of the Ulverston Board of Guardians (1836—), at the Lancashire Record Office.
MS. Diary.	The *MS diary* of William Cavendish, 2nd Earl of Burlington and 7th Duke of Devonshire (1808—1891), by courtesy of Mr. Francis Thompson, M.A., Librarian and Archivist, Chatsworth House.
Parson & White	William Parson & William White, *History, Directory and Gazetteer of the Counties of Cumberland and Westmorland with . . . Furness and Cartmel,* 1829.
Pennant	Thomas Pennant, *Tour in Scotland* (Chester, 1774) ; passages relating to Furness.
Port Inspections	*MS. Volumes, Inspections of Ports : Reports, for the Commissioners of Customs,* at H.M. Customs & Excise Library, King's Beam House, London ; by courtesy of Mr. R. C. Jarvis.
Proc. Inst. C. E.	*Proceedings of the Institution of Civil Engineers.*
Proc. Inst. Mech. E.	*Proceedings of the Institution of Mechanical Engineers.*
Proc. N. of E. Inst. M. & M. E.	*Proceedings of the North of England Institute of Mining and Mechanical Engineers.*
Public Charities	*The Public Charities of the Hundred of Lonsdale North of the Sands* (Ulverston, 1852) ; a reprint of the Report of the Charity Commissioners, Jan., 1820, with additional particulars.
Rec. Man. Muchland.	A private transcript, by the late Mr. Edward Walker, of the proceedings of manorial courts held at Torver, within the Manor of Muchland, Plain Furness, from the 16th to the 18th centuries ; used by courtesy of Mr. J. L. Hobbs.
Ulv. Adv.	The *Ulverston Advertiser* (first known as *Soulby's Ulverston Advertiser*), published as a weekly newspaper by Stephen Soulby at Ulverston, (1848—).
Wadham Diary.	The *MS. diary* of Edward Wadham (1828—1913), mineral agent to the Duke of Buccleuch from 1851 ; by courtesy of Mr. H. A. Slater, F.S.I., and Boughton Estates Ltd.

INTRODUCTION

This work is an attempt to describe the effects of the Industrial Revolution on the people of an isolated area of Lancashire. It deals with their changing ways of life and with the industries in which they worked.

It is well known that enormous changes took place in Britain between the middle of the eighteenth century and the middle of the nineteenth ; but we sometimes forget that this vast transformation of society is still going on. We live in the middle of it, and are not aware of the forces around us until we receive some salutary reminder—an encounter with radio-active milk or vegetables, for instance. On the other hand, those who are able to unfold in their minds the major events of one or two generations can be in no doubt that significant changes have come over the lives of British citizens. It is in the nature of things that we see their significance afterwards.

Although the narrative in these pages commences at the year 1711, remoteness in time does not mean lack of relevance. Industrial revolutions are happening in other parts of the world ; and yet more will have to happen, under wise and far-seeing guidance, if this world is to remain at peace. Historians and economists are deeply concerned with such problems, or should be if they are not completely insulated from the demands of the present. It is terribly important that we should look back into the past, driven by deep curiosity and a sense of urgency, to discover what lessons it has to teach us and to revalue our achievements and analyse our mistakes.

This book is a modest enough contribution to the careful and detailed exploration of our industrial past. In order that it could be of any value at all, it had to sift and assemble the results of research into many aspects of Furness (and also English) history, to show their interconnections and significance, and to indicate the sources of information on which the story is based. I would ask members of the public not to be put off by the footnotes which pile up on nearly every page. They are merely the sleepers and permanent way on which the narrative runs, and a few of them are actually entertaining. Nevertheless, one does not normally gaze down at the track ; would-be local historians may find an occasional useful tip there, and they may help fellow-students to test the validity of my own arguments and to further their own researches. That is their chief justification.

The story, then, begins in 1711 with the establishment of a water-powered blast furnace by a group of men associated with the first Abraham Darby. Afterwards Furness played a modest enough part in the iron-smelting revolution which produced the basic raw material of modern industry ; it helped to roof the houses of new and growing towns and to provide those towns with food, and to supply human beings for " mechanical employments ". Yet the great majority of the local population were not aware of significant change—any more than are millions of people today. They cheered when the tiny Ulverston Canal was opened, and they refused to send their children to work in local cotton mills. Furness inhabitants also increased in numbers, as did people in other parts of Britain in the eighteenth century ; as jobs multiplied, so did individuals who could fill those jobs. I have devoted a good deal of attention to Furness people of the pre-railway age, if only because one of the major problems which excites present-day economic historians is that of the probable effect of industrialisation upon the ordinary countryman or citizen. Was the latter materially better off when he went to the towns ? Was he more or less healthy than we have been led to believe ? It is the writer's opinion—based on some evidence duly set forth—that the eighteenth century northcountryman could be physically and morally superior to his town-dwelling descendants. This, I know, contradicts some notions fashionably held by professional historians here and there. Fashion, however, is irrelevant to the search for truth.

Part II deals with the more dramatic and violent upheavals of the mid-nineteenth century ; with the establishment of a local railway system, the consequent expansion of iron-mining in Furness and the phenomenally rapid growth of the town of Barrow between 1857 and 1875. An Industrial Revolution, in the most literal sense, was upon the district at last ; and, as its story is revealed in detail, it becomes possible to compare two distinct periods. We see that in both the eighteenth and nineteenth centuries the district was in fact " colonised ". The eighteenth century Furness ironmasters performed such colonisation on a very limited scale, and as is shown in these pages, they cannot have imported many workpeople into the peninsula ; but they took advantage of cheap labour and abundant raw materials, and organised some aspects of the economic life of the neighbourhood to suit their purposes. Anything they did, or forgot to do, the Furness Railway Company and its associates did much more thoroughly a century later. There were, of course, vast differences in scale, detail and organisation. The men of 1711 had difficulty in obtaining skilled workers, but seem to have had no problem in getting labourers ; the railway colonisers, on the other hand, had much difficulty in obtaining workmen of almost any kind in sufficient numbers for their purposes. The dominating powers of both periods were obliged to provide housing and other amenities for their workers, and, because the former were operating in an undeveloped district, they were in each case forced to enter into activities which had little direct connection with the main industries of the locality.   The early ironmasters entered into general trade and banking, and the men of the railway age into several major industries as well as town and dock-building.

The coastal position of the district was of course decisive, and brought it a thriving economic life which would have been exceptional a few miles inland.   Whether in modest (eighteenth century) fashion, or in spectacular (nineteenth century) style, its development was aided by techniques, labour and capital from afar.   So many external forces affected Furness economic history that it would be difficult to write a really parochial account.   One can enumerate some of them ;   a Quaker group of businessmen in the west of England, demands for ore and iron in the south-west, a growing coastal shipping trade in the eighteenth and nineteenth centuries, the existence of fuel reserves in Scotland, merchant capital in Lancaster, Liverpool or Bristol, steelmaking in Sheffield, the competition and policy-making of great railway companies, developments in copper-mining in South Australia and the North American rail market ;   and, ultimately, the development of the Gilchrist-Thomas process which struck at the non-phosphoric ore trade.   To this list one can of course add the increasing use of Spanish haematite.   The major industrialist of the area, the 7th Duke of Devonshire, had estates all over England and was one of the most successful of mid-Victorian aristocratic investors, while H. W. Schneider had coalmines in Wales and a tin mine in Cornwall as well as extensive investments in Mexico and South Australia.

One learns to appreciate, even more keenly than is customary, that the Industrial Revolution was a revolution in transport more than anything else.   Before the manufacture of goods could take place in factory or works, raw materials (cotton, iron, iron ore and coal) had to be brought together from considerable distances and the finished products carried away in bulk to faraway markets.   The history of the comparatively small Furness Railway system adds emphasis to the point ;   and if yet more is needed, the story of Barrow should provide it.

Barrow was not only a railway and steelmaking town.   It was also a planned one.   That is to say, it was tidily and generously laid out, like another great industrial stronghold of rather similar parentage and date—namely, Middlesbrough.   To this extent, I think that the planned aspect of Barrow's character was a product of certain forces and ideas of that time.   It would be quite unhistorical to write as though its fine main thoroughfares emanated solely from the genius of James Ramsden, and the spirit of an age pervades its layout.   There is a preoccupation with size, space and vast achievement ;   does it not appear in other lands in the twentieth century.   The Lord Bishop of Carlisle, admiring the shining new town in 1872, confessed that he was " thoroughly a nineteenth century man." Even more so was James Ramsden himself. Personally a not very sympathetic character, he carried within him the urge to transform a dull little shipping place into a city before he reached old age. Was this colossal egotism—for, after all, one can have a well laid-out barracks, and even enlightened men spoke of industrial " armies "—or the drive towards a new Jerusalem? Perhaps it does not matter : in spite of the religiosity of that time, its values, like those of the bustling and not untypical Richard Potter, were liable to overlook the possible inundation of the Holy Places.

Potter—so his daughter Beatrice Webb tells us—regarded workmen as so many units of labour. Likewise economists and ecomonic historians often forget that they are writing about human beings, and the writer has not been immune from temptations to do the same. By way of amends, I have tried to show the human, as well as the economic, problems of employers and workmen ; not only achievements in terms of building, manufacture and output of goods, but the tensions and dislocations of a rapidly growing society. The activities of the captains of industry who carried vast responsibilities are subjected to close analysis and some criticism, but it should be noted that most of this criticism is not mine. It is contemporary, and I have merely ventured an occasional moral aside. Amplifiers of public opinion like medical men, demographers, directory writers, professional satirists and newspaper editors, growing ever more critical of father-figures who appeared to abnegate their social responsibilities, could flay industrialists into palliative action of some kind. Those who are complacent in their attitude to civil liberties might care to note that some Victorian editors exercised a freedom and savagery of comment which is almost unknown in local editorial chairs these days. Whatever the case, local studies of " the entrepreneur doing good " are of limited use unless they show the individual being influenced by, as well as influencing, social opinion and development.

A certain amount of space is devoted to those factors which influenced the quality of life for the many : rents, wages, trade union activity, sickness, death, working hours, migration, pauperism, unemployment. I only wish that much more material of this type could have been set down. It seems futile to argue, as many historians do nowadays, that early industrialism brought " betterment " of various kinds, until we know far more about its social effects. Opinions can be of little account unless we have evidence at our disposal, and until that evidence is properly presented. This, of course, means being quite clear what to look for in the history of an industrial area, and although students and colleagues may be rightly critical of my own approach, I hope that (whether influenced or not by the matter here presented) they will be still more critical of past and future effusions in the field of close-focus economic history.

The late Sir John Clapham wrote scornfully of historians who ignored quantities. We must all be indebted to him for the reminder, and my statistical jottings, which are kept or inserted in the text for purposes of precision, are usually relevant to what is said in the narrative. Figures, of course, must always be distrusted, but the reader should not ignore the general tendencies shown by them on that account. For the rest, human beings are not ciphers or totalities or averages, or even balls on an economic pin-table ; it happens that through the use of quantities we can sometimes understand man-in-society a little more clearly. It is for the reader to assist in the imaginative re-creation of the past, and to help to put the living flesh on statistical bones, at the same time properly suspecting those who affect to perform all such re-creation for him.

Regarding the work as a whole ; for exposition badly rendered, unsupported or unsound assertions and errors of judgment or distortion of the truth, there can be no excuse. For other sins of omission or commission there may be an explanation. Although many—perhaps most—historians must firmly believe that their work is written in the worst possible circumstances, this book was not compiled in strictly ideal conditions ; its building up encountered grimmer problems than exhaustion, and its progress was assisted by few of the aids to study which are normally granted to research students.

It follows that *Furness and the Industrial Revolution* would never have seen the light of day, in its present form at least, but for the help of other people. I earnestly hope that the very real sacrifices of my wife and family have been worth while, and if this book is not imbued with complacency, this is perhaps the result of natural annoyance that innocent people anywhere should have to suffer for the misdeeds of others ! During the work of research and enquiry over a number of years, I have been generously sustained by two colleagues, Mr. F. Barnes, B.A., F.L.A., Chief Librarian of Barrow-in-Furness, and Mr. J. L. Hobbs, Furness historian and antiquary. If this work has any scholarly virtues, then they have a hand in the achievement, even though they are not in any way responsible for the handling of the facts and advice that they have placed at my disposal. Dr. S. Pollard, of the University of Sheffield, was investigating some aspects of local mid-Victorian history when I was drafting out parts of this work, and I have been fortunate indeed to have his assistance, especially in the analysis of the voluminous diaries of the 7th Duke of Devonshire. It is impossible to overvalue, too, the stimulus of a penetrating and able mind. After working independently for some time, we found ourselves in substantial agreement on certain major aspects of local history ; the few disagreements that are expressed in these pages, therefore, are of little account. Professor G. P. Jones provided helpful information and advice in demographic matters, as well as encouragement. This type of assistance was all the more deeply appreciated because London University does not normally provide advisers for its externally registered research students.

Numerous fellow-students have troubled themselves greatly to provide items of information, and I have done my best to acknowledge their help in specific footnotes. Those whose kindness is not so acknowledged include Mrs. Isobel Ross and Dr. A. Raistrick, both of whom offered assistance and encouragement at an early stage of the enquiries, while further expressions of gratefulness are made to Mr. T. N. E. Smith, F.L.A., and to the staffs of the Lancashire Record Office, the Nottingham Reference Library and the Barrow Public Library.

Mr. E. Whiteside's maps not only perform the task they are intended to perform—that of giving precise geographical and economic information—but they have none of the dullness that usually issues from professional geographers.

Finally, the responsibility for the publication of this book has been taken by the Barrow-in-Furness Library and Museum Committee. I hope that it is worthy of their act of public enterprise, which (through the patience, skill and co-operation of the printers, Messrs. James Milner of Barrow) makes it possible to offer a substantial volume to the reading public, without subsidy, at a price between one-half and one-third of that which would be demanded by a commercial publisher. It should be added that the Chief Librarian of Barrow not only assisted in the provision of research material, but undertook the infinitely more onerous work of seeing the book through the press.

The Committee desires, by this action, to focus attention on the industrial achievements of the area, which has contributed so largely to Britain's economic and military strength. One thing is certain ; Furness people, like occupiers of less developed " colonies," deserve the fullest benefits from the Industrial Revolution which they have assisted in such great measure. But these benefits—and our continued existence—will not be ensured without clear and unsentimental thought. I have striven, I do not know how successfully, to infuse such qualities of thought into this book. It sees the light of day at a grim time.

A substantial part of this work was originally accepted by the University of London as a thesis for the degree of Doctor of Philosophy. Parts of the text have been re-written, and several chapters have been extensively revised or added. The work of research was assisted, during part of the author's studies, by a grant (in aid of travelling expenses) from the University of London Central Research Fund.

June 20th, 1958.   J. D. M.

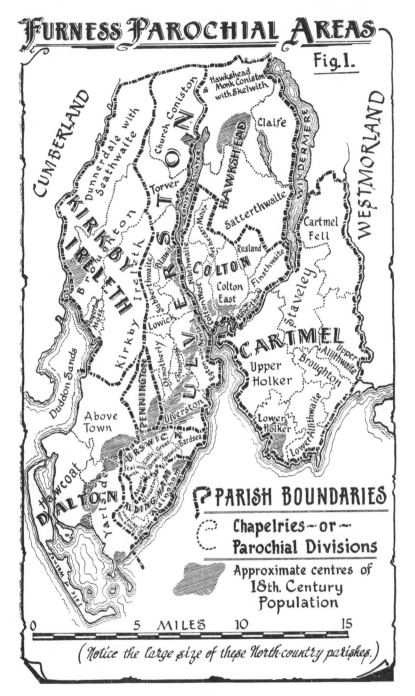

FURNESS PAROCHIAL AREAS

Fig. 1.

PARISH BOUNDARIES

Chapelries ~or~
Parochial Divisions

Approximate centres of
18th. Century
Population

0   5 MILES 10   15

(Notice the large size of these North-country parishes.)

MANORIAL MAP of FURNESS

Fig. 2.

BARONY OF KENDAL

BARONY OF EGREMONT

MANOR OF MUNCASTER

MANOR OF MILLOM

MANOR OF CARTMEL

SKELWITH

✝HAWKSHEAD

2

CONISTON✝

✝SEATHWAITE

3

4

TORVER

SATTERTHWAITE

✝HAWKSHEAD

SAWREY

1

RUSLAND

FINSTHWAITE

5

WOODLAND

6

BLAWITH

BROUGHTON

7

8

COLTON

LOWICK

9

MILLOM

KIRKBY IRELETH

11

EGTON

10

12

PENNINGTON

ULVERSTON

13

CARTMEL

IRELETH

LINDAL

14

15
DALTON

URSWICK

BARDSEA

16

17

ALDINGHAM

DENDRON

WALNEY

Reference to MANORS & Owners circa 1860.

1. **HAWKSHEAD** — Duke of Buccleuch.—
2. **CONISTON** — General Le Fleming.—
3. **DUNNERDALE** WITH SEATHWAITE — Major Rawlinson.—
4. **TORVER** — Crown.—
5. **BROUGHTON** — S. Sawrey.—
6. **BLAWITH** — Duke of Buccleuch.—
7. **SUBBERTHWAITE** — appendage of 5.—
8. **KIRKBY.** — Duke of Devonshire.—
9. **LOWICK** — Mrs. Gaskarth.—
10. **EGTON** with **NEWLAND** — Duke of Buccleuch.—
11. **OSMOTHERLEY** — leased to the tenants for 999 years.—
12. **PENNINGTON** — Baron Muncaster.—
13. **ULVERSTON** — Duke of Buccleuch.
14. **PLAIN FURNESS** — Duke of Buccleuch.
15. **DALTON**
16. **BOLTON** with **ADGARLEY** — Earl of Derby.—
17. **MUCHLAND** — Crown.

13, 14 and 17 — *Court Leet.*

KEY to COPYHOLD ESTATES of PLAIN FURNESS.

i Tenement of SOUTHEND
ii Hamlet of BIGGAR
iii Hamlet of NORTH SCALE
iv Tenement of NORTHEND
v Hamlet of COCKEN
vi Hamlet of BARROW HEAD
vii Hamlet of SALTHOUSE
viii Roose House
ix Hamlet of ROOSECOTE
x RAMPSIDE
xi NEWBARNS
xii HAWCOAT
xiii Marsh Grange
xiv IRELETH
xv Ireleth Park
xvi SCALEBANK and MARTON
xvii Vill. of LINDAL
xviii Hamlet of NEWTON
xix Hamlet of STANK
xx NEWTOWN etc.
xxi BRIDGEGATE, Park House etc.
xxii SOWERBY Lodge
xxiii ORMSGILL
xxiv HINDPOOL
xxv OLD BARROW
xxvi BILLINGCOTE
xxvii Stewnor Bank and Park
xxviii Standish Cote
xxix Ancient Freehold Estate

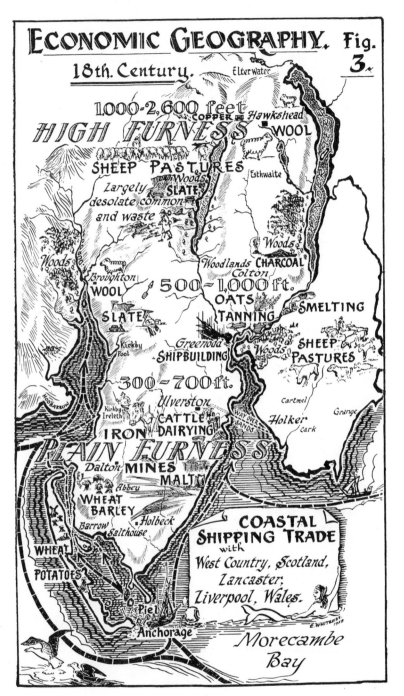

ECONOMIC GEOGRAPHY. Fig. 3.

18th. Century.

Elter Water

1000-2,600 feet
COPPER Hawkshead

HIGH FURNESS
WOOL

SHEEP PASTURES
Largely desolate common and waste
Woods SLATE
Esthwaite

Woods

Woods

Woodlands CHARCOAL
Colton

500~1,000 ft.
Broughton
WOOL
OATS
TANNING
SMELTING

SLATE

Greenodd Woods SHEEP PASTURES

300~700ft.
Kirkby Pool
SHIPBUILDING

HODBARROW

Kirkby Ireleth
Ulverston
WAY OVER SANDS
Cartmel
Grange

CATTLE DAIRYING
Holker
cark

PLAIN FURNESS
IRON
Dalton MINES
MALT

Abbey
WHEAT BARLEY

Barrow Holbeck
Salthouse

WHEAT
POTATOES

Piel
Anchorage

COASTAL SHIPPING TRADE
with
West Country, Scotland,
Lancaster,
Liverpool, Wales.

E. WHITEFIELD
1918

Morecambe Bay

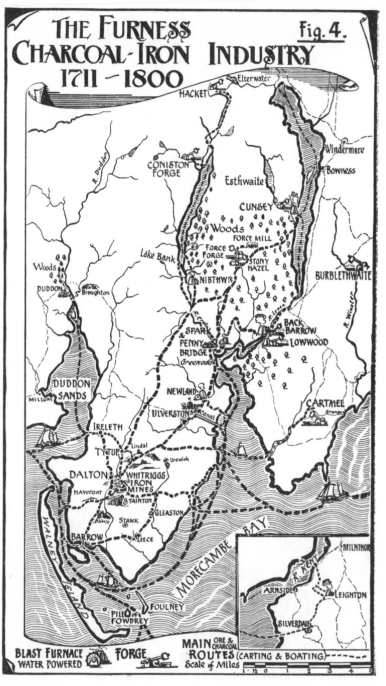

THE FURNESS CHARCOAL-IRON INDUSTRY 1711-1800

Fig. 4.

Elterwater

HACKET

CONISTON FORGE

R. Duddon

Esthwaite

Windermere

Bowness

CUNSEY

Woods

FORCE MILL

Force FORGE

Lake Bank

STONY HAZEL

Woods

BURBLETHWAITE

DUDDON

Broughton

NIBTHWTE

R. Leven

SPARK & PENNY BRIDGE

Greenodd

BACK BARROW

LOWWOOD

R. Winster

DUDDON SANDS

MILLOM

NEWLAND

ULVERSTON

Canal

CARTMEL

Grange

IRELETH

Lindal

TYTUP

Urswick

DALTON

WHITRIGGS IRON MINES

HAWCOAT

STAINTON

GLEASTON

Abbey

STANK

BARROW

Leece

WALNEY ISLAND

MORECAMBE BAY

MILNTHOR

R. KENT

ARNSIDE

LEIGHTON

SILVERDALE

PILE of FOWDREY

FOULNEY

BLAST FURNACE WATER POWERED — **FORGE** — **MAIN** ORE & CHARCOAL **ROUTES** (CARTING & BOATING)
Scale of Miles   1 ½ 0 1 2 3 4 5

xxii

PART ONE

Furness Industry and Society before the Railway Age.

Tho' smelting fires flame in the vale,
And iron mills benight the mead,
And — (black the air, like Colebrookdale) —
Furness be furnace fells indeed :

Yet why should every sapling fall,
To build those smouldering charcoal fires
Why is the axe laid loose on all   —
Hide, sods, the forest's funeral-pyres !

Charles Farish,   *The Minstrels of
Winandermere,*   (1811).

CHAPTER I

FURNESS IN THE EARLY EIGHTEENTH CENTURY : A GENERAL SURVEY

INTRODUCTORY : THE FURNESS DISTRICT

Lonsdale, the northernmost Hundred of the County of Lancaster, contains two parts known respectively as Lonsdale North, and Lonsdale South of the Sands. These parts are completely separated by the estuary of the River Kent and by the extensive sandy wastes of Morecambe Bay, that portion lying to the north being known as Furness and Cartmel.[1] Lonsdale South of the Sands contains the town of Lancaster, but Furness and Cartmel, that area of the county traditionally known as " over sands ", appears geographically as an outlier of the Cumbrian region or land-mass.

Furness proper lies between the Duddon[2] and Leven estuaries ; and owing to these deep indentations it assumes the form of a peninsula. Its administrative boundaries, however, reach deeply into the Lakeland hills after passing along the western bank of Lake Windermere. The greatest length of the Furness area, from Wrynose Mountain to the island of Walney at its south-western extremity, is about 30 miles, and its breadth from Windermere to the River Duddon is about 13 miles. The area of Furness and Cartmel together, subject to any minor boundary changes which may have been made over the period covered by this study, may be taken at rather over 162,000 acres for the purposes of demographic and other calculation, or some 250 square miles. Cartmel, originally a single parish of nearly 60 square miles, is separated from Furness by the River Leven.

The distinctive geographical features of Furness have naturally affected its history. Isolated by river and mountains to the north-west and north, by Windermere to the east, and by sea and sands to the south, it can be treated as a complete unit in the historical as well as in the geographical or administrative senses. While the two portions of Lonsdale have long been connected by a passage over the Morecambe Bay sands[3] (thereby explaining the Furness allegiance to Lancashire rather than to Cumberland), and in more recent times by a railway along the coastline, trade and social movement have been impeded by the Cumberland mountains ; trade routes to

---

[1]For an outline of the relevant historical geography, *vide V.C.H. Lancs.*, VIII, 1-3. [2]Familiar enough to tourists, this river attained fame through the *Duddon Sonnets* of Wordsworth. [3]*Op. cit.*, 3.

the Cumberland interior have been few and poor. Before the nineteenth century, Furness trade and rural industries, in so far as they were carried on by means of land transport, responded more to the markets of Kendal and Lancaster than to those of any town beyond the northern mountains ; and by the eighteenth century they reacted still more sensitively to the demands of iron-dealers and traders in western Lancashire, Wales, and the south-west. Much aided by its sea-girt position, the district became an exporter of iron, iron ore and slate, while copper-mining had become established at Coniston in the sixteenth and seventeenth centuries. The rapid becks of the neighbourhood were used to drive fulling mills, to work mechanical hammers and furnace bellows, and perhaps also to wash and prepare ore ; and the lakes of Coniston and Windermere, far from being internal impediments, became thriving waterways. Walney Island, nearly ten miles in length, and serving as a barrier against the westerly gales from the Irish sea, gave protection to the deep anchorage of Piel and later to the small port of Barrow.

Furness itself is divided into two portions, High Furness or Furness Fells—the hilly region, with an altitude of 500 to 1,000 feet east, north and west of Coniston Lake—and Plain or Low Furness in the south. Both are distinctive, the first consisting mainly of moorland given over in the eighteenth century to sheep-farming and the cultivation of coppice woods, and the second being characterised by undulating foothills (of 250 to 750 feet) and coastal lowland suitable for stock-raising and arable farming. In Plain Furness more land was available for the purposes of husbandry, and in consequence the population of the district, comparatively sparse throughout the period of recorded history, was more thickly settled there.

Both districts were endowed with mineral wealth, the neighbourhood of Dalton-in-Furness containing rich deposits of iron ore which were known and worked from the Middle Ages.[1] Slate and copper, found primarily in the Coniston locality, had, ultimately, far less influence on the economic development of the district. Slate-quarrying was, however, an important High Furness industry from the mid-eighteenth century onwards, the Silurian green slate of Coniston and the blue slate of Kirkby-in-Furness commanding a wide market. A belt of carboniferous limestone extending across the middle of the Plain Furness peninsula provided building material and flux for the eighteenth-century charcoal furnaces, while a fringe of New Red Sandstone at its foot provided–as at Hawcoat quarries– a further source of stone for building, the characteristic results of which are to be seen in the masonry of Furness Abbey and in

[1]There is evidence of Iron Age working of this metal at Urswick Stone Walls, not far from Dalton-in-Furness.

2

numerous farmhouses of that locality.[1] The deposits of the
haematite iron ore, now largely worked out, were found in " sops "
or pockets in the carboniferous limestone ; their richness and extent
was but barely appreciated in the eighteenth century, and only
fully understood after the numerous trials and surveys of the nineteenth.[2] Glacial clays, forming the surface deposits of the lowland
areas of Plain Furness (including Walney Island and the Barrow
neighbourhood) provided a soil suitable for wheat-growing, and
enabled the latter to become recognised, in the late eighteenth
century, as one of the few wheat districts of Lancashire.

The main eighteenth-century market town of Furness,
Ulverston, was equidistant from the outlying areas of both Plain
and High Furness, drawing commerce—and perhaps also population
—from both. Roads and lanes converged upon it,[3] the produce of
a wide district was sent to its market, and it became a centre of
the social and economic life of the peninsula. The smaller market
towns or villages of the area were Dalton (its main town during the
period of the overlordship of Furness Abbey), Hawkshead, the
market for the fell parishes, and Broughton-in-Furness, which had
little importance before about 1760. Of these places Ulverston was
by far the largest, and approached 3,000 in population by the time
of the 1801 Census, a figure which is apt to minimise rather than to
exaggerate its importance. It became the chief town of a considerable region, the nearest market centres of any consequence
being Lancaster, Kendal and Whitehaven. Cartmel had a small
market in the village of that name.

PAROCHIAL AND OTHER DIVISIONS

Furness and Cartmel were divided into nine parishes ; Dalton,
Aldingham, Kirkby Ireleth, Pennington, Ulverston, Urswick,
Colton, Hawkshead and Cartmel. Since these nine parishes shared
between them an area of some 250 square miles, it will be seen that
their respective areas were unusually large. One parish, as at
Dalton, Ulverston, Cartmel and Hawkshead, might embrace several
divisions, townships, villages or chapelries. The parish of Ulverston
occupied the western side of Furness for a distance of nearly 17
miles, and contained nine separate townships and four chapelries,
those of Lowick, Blawith, Torver and Church Coniston. Dalton,
with an area of some 27 square miles, contained the divisions of
Dalton Proper (i.e. Dalton township), Hawcoat including

[1]For a recent study, *vide* Dunham, K. C., and Rose, W. C. C., *Permo-Triassic
Geology of Cumberland and Furness, Proc. Geological Association*, 1949. [2]The
iron ore is believed to be an original constituent of the sandstone of the locality;
op. cit., 27-8. [3]For eighteenth-century roads, *vide A map of the liberty of
Furness in the County of Lancaster as survey'd by Wm. Brasier 1745 & copied by
T. Richardson,*1772, given as frontispiece to *Antiquities*, 1774.

Walney, Yarlside and Above Town ; but these were not called townships but were traditionally known as bierleys or quarters, [1] containing one or several hamlets. The manorial administration of earlier times seems to have had little direct connection with parochial divisions as finally established, and one parish might contain several manors or traces of manors. [2] The general historical drift is clear enough, however ; manorial administration (a matter of some local importance until quite recent days) was imposed on remote and scattered settlement units, mother churches were established when the district was very sparsely peopled, chapels were founded in several parts of the district by the monks of Furness and Conishead, and around their sites the later " chapelries " appeared. The process of sub-division went on as population increased ; finally, the chapelry areas were often coterminous with the " manors " of the district distinguishable between the sixteenth and nineteenth centuries, although a manor might still overlap into other parishes or parochial sub-districts. [3] The subject is a complex one, and requires far more study than it has hitherto received. It is only mentioned here because it has some bearing on the subject of local government, discussed elsewhere in these pages. [4]

The parochial areas were exceptionally large because the district was, on the whole, a thinly settled and infertile one. Until the middle of the nineteenth century, nevertheless, its inhabitants were mainly concerned with agricultural pursuits, and their affairs were controlled by vestries and manorial courts. Reference is made elsewhere in this study, to these bodies and to the districts over which they held sway. The typical organ of local government was the closed or select vestry consisting of twenty-four, twelve or six sidesmen, controlling an entire parish (as at Dalton and Cartmel), or devolving its authority, as in the extensive parish of Ulverston. [5] Manorial administration, which was equally important, was carried on side by side with that of the vestry. Before this is discussed further, it is necessary to make a brief survey of the eighteenth-century population of Furness and its occupations.

THE PEOPLE OF FURNESS, 1700-50

About two-thirds of the people of the district had, at this period, some sort of direct stake in the land. This generalisation is based upon three types of evidence ; (a) the total number of

[1]Walney was not a separate bierley. The term was mediaeval, and was used during the overlordship of Furness Abbey. [2]Cf. the map of Furness manors by Mr. Wilson Butler in C. & W. XXVI (NS), 323. [3]Viz., Torver, a chapelry of Ulverston, was a bailiwick of the Manor of Muchland. The rest of this manor, covering mainly the Aldingham district, was several miles away; Rec. Man. Muchland. The large parish of Kirkby Ireleth contained several manors, while Hawkshead, containing several chapelries or sub-divisions, was one manor. [4]See pp. 127-32 below. [5]See pp. 128-9 below.

4

properties rated in the land tax assessments for given divisions, compared with the total estimated population of those divisions, (b) the recurrence of agricultural occupations in parish registers and lists of wills, and (c), other occupations mentioned in these sources and their degree of connection or non-connection with the land.

While the properties rated for land tax can be counted with some exactitude, population estimates and their safety are notoriously a matter for controversy. All that can be said here is that numerous parish registers for the locality have been analysed systematically, and that it is clear beyond much doubt that the population of Furness—or at least three-fifths of it—rose at a rate corresponding roughly to authoritative estimates for the country as a whole.[1] In six parishes[2] which were subjected to this analysis, the 1801 Census population was 6,145 ; and according to calculations based upon the rates of baptism and burial in these parishes, their population in 1740 was of the order of 4,500. In 1746, the total number of properties rated for land tax[3] in all divisions of these parishes was 569. The ratings varied from a few pence to several pounds, but more than seventy per cent of them were for properties of under ten shillings' assessment. There can be no doubt that an unspecified number of local people held land in more than one parish or division, and to that extent the following calculations are weakened.

As a further stage, it is necessary to relate not total population to holdings, but total families to the latter. The relationship of baptisms to marriages in these parishes shows that couples in the district customarily produced four children.[4] Of these, at least one customarily died.[5] We can safely take five as the size of the average Furness family in 1740 ; hence, rather over 900 families dwelt in the six parishes in that year. If the outlying divisions of Leece, Gleaston and Dendron are included in one of these parishes, Aldingham, the total number of rated properties was not 569, but 651 ; but if we subtract those over the 600 mark as parcels of land in different divisions but held by the same person, the ratio of three families to two rated properties emerges as a fairly convincing one. If one of these parishes—the sparsely populated chapelry of Torver, near the foot of Coniston Water—is brought into closer focus, it is found that even in the first half of the nineteenth century, it never supported more than 263 people, and that in 1801 it had 182. The

[1]See p. 102 below.   [2]Dalton (excluding Walney), Aldingham, Kirkby Ireleth (excluding Broughton, which was a separate chapelry), Broughton, Torver and Colton.   [3]*Land Tax Assessments, N. Lonsdale*, 1746—list in *Holker MSS.*, collection of documents at the Lancs. R.O. The divisions of Leece, Gleaston and Dendron, which were in Aldingham parish, are excluded. The Aldingham population figure allowed for here is probably a slight under estimate.   [4]See p. 112 below.   [5]See p. 103 below.

1740 estimate is 137; yet in 1746 it had 37 separate properties the bulk of them rated at from two to five shillings, and if the names in the tax list are any guide, almost all in the hands of different persons.

A list of wills, pertaining to the Archdeaconry of Richmond and proved between 1748 and 1792,[1] tells a rather similar story. Six hundred and two of these are wills of individuals belonging to the Furness Deanery (many of them to the parishes already dealt with) ; and their bare particulars were extracted because they give the occupations of the persons concerned. The result of this labour shows that 269 or nearly 45 per cent. were those of " yeomen ", and a further 101, or 17 per cent., those of " husbandmen ". Here again, roughly two-thirds of the total (all of whom were males in this sample) thereby had a direct interest in the land.

The parish registers, on the whole, are far less helpful in the matter of occupations. That of Broughton-in-Furness Chapel[2] is especially helpful in that it refers to the latter consistently between 1721 and 1740. In these years 195 occupations are stated, of which 155 are entered as "yeo" (viz., in the burial register). The Bishop's Transcript[3] shows some variations, classing several tradesmen as yeomen, and in a few cases " yeoman " and " husbandman " were used interchangeably. Here it seems that the percentage of land-holders may have been higher than in the other examples, a supposition which is strengthened by the land tax figures.[4]

These figures, of limited enough statistical value, serve only to underline what would in any case be fairly obvious, viz. that Furness was a primarily agrarian district in the eighteenth century. But many of the rated holdings were so small that their occupiers or owners cannot have obtained a very satisfactory living by means of husbandry alone. In the case of the parish of Aldingham, it is poss-ible to make a rough but indicative estimate of the average size of the holding. Unlike most of the other parishes of Furness, this one contained a very high proportion of arable or fertile land ; according to the Tithe Commutation Survey of 1846, no fewer than 3257 acres out of 4459 were classed as arable.[5] In 1746 there were 229 separately rated properties in all divisions of the parish, giving an average size of less than 20 acres. One hundred and nineteen of these were rated at under 1s., and were plainly occupied by cottagers or smallholders. Fifteen were rated at between 10s. and £1.[6] The

[1]Fishwick, H. (ed.), *A List of the Lancashire Wills proved within the Archdeaconry of Richmond . . . from 1748 to 1792* (1891). [2]*Lancs. P. R. Soc.* [3]Quoted in *Lancs. P. R. Soc.* transcript (ed. Dickinson), and at *Lancs. R. O.* [4]The est. population in 1740 was about 600 (see also Prof. G. P. Jones's estimate in *C. & W.* (NS), LIII, 140) and the total number of properties, 135. [5]See p. 77 below. [6]The name of one of the 10s.—£1 occupiers, James Goad, appears against the description " yeoman " in *Richmond Wills*, cited.

average assessment was 3s. 3d. Not all of the parish was in the hands of separate or private occupiers, and there were township or open fields at Dendron,[1] one of its divisions ; but the 1846 survey shows that there was then very little woodland (63 acres) or waste. The Tithe Commutation plan for Dendron, Leece and Gleaston,[2] all within the parish in the eighteenth century, shows a mass of tiny holdings, closes and crofts of one or two furlongs in length, a great many of them in narrow strips up the sides of valleys, with a number of common " dales " in Dendron's " Deep Meadows " and in Leece Mosses.

Aldingham was in Plain Furness, a comparatively fertile district ; but parishes like Broughton and Torver contained much bare moorland and fell country, and in these cases there is a complication, for many of the High Furness land occupiers enjoyed common grazing rights for their sheep on the fells, and also shared town fields in the valley bottoms. Accordingly, calculations based on average assessments would be misleading. The owners of small sheep flocks[3] would sell their wool to local dealers and in the Kendal or other regional markets, and the husbandman or yeoman of the area, according to an interesting if perhaps not wholly reliable account of Wordsworth,[4] set his family on the spinning and preparation of woollen yarn. Although some arrangement of this kind must have been common in High Furness, there were other occupations ancillary to agriculture or sheep-raising ; weaving, tanning, smith-work, swill basket-making, carpentry, fulling, innkeeping, walling, general labour and the boating and carting of ore, slate and charcoal. In the neighbourhood at large, the extraction of iron ore, slate and copper gave employment to several hundreds later in the eighteenth century, and as the population increased, the numbers of mariners and town tradesmen became larger also. The use of the title of " yeoman " in a parish register may in fact conceal the person who followed a more or less specialised industrial or other non-agricultural occupation.

References to non-agricultural pursuits occur irregularly in these sources ; besides the 156 Broughton yeomen or husbandmen who were buried in 1721-40, one labourer, six shoemakers or cordwainers, one weaver, two fullers or dyers, four wallers, five carpenters, a hooper, a collier, a blacksmith, two millers and fifteen small tradesmen or shopkeepers of various kinds (including a petty chapman,

[1]See p. 12 below. [2]Copy of plan, 1848, by John Bolton, in *B.N.F.C.*, XVII (1909), facing p. 243. [3]For the most valuable data on the possessions and wealth of typical yeomen of the region, *vide* the Rev. Dr. C. Moor's paper, " Statesman Families at Irton " in *C. & W.* (NS), X, 148 sqq. The average number of sheep owned here in the late 17th and early 18th centuries seems to have been about 35. [4]*Guide to the Lakes* (Malvern facsimile edn. 1945), 80; " The family of each man, whether estatesman or farmer, formerly had a twofold support . . . "

mercers, tailors and butchers) were also interred—thirty-nine persons in all. In the Torver chapel registers for 1711-40, a series of somewhat similar references may be found, viz. two tanners, a shearman, a shoemaker, a butcher, a saddletree maker, a cordwainer, a tailor and a slater.[1] In 1746 a blacksmith, William Jackson, paid 2s. 10d. land tax on a property in Torver. It may be added that although Torver was in the area of coppice woodland, no " colliers " or charcoal-burners are mentioned in this period.

The Archdeaconry will list[2] shows that none of these occupations was predominant, and that in fact sailors were most numerous in the district after yeomen and husbandmen. Here the small but growing town of Ulverston is left out of account ; the parish register of Ulverston,[3] a treasure-house of information on occupations later in the century, does not often mention the latter in this period, but such references as are made between 1700 and 1740 relate most frequently to mariners. Otherwise the trades mentioned are those which could be expected in a market town and port combined ; smith, saddler, wright, brazier, mercer, rope-maker, waller, apothecary, tanner, weaver, carpenter, milner, butcher, mason, and attorney. A shipcarpenter appears in 1735, and two physicians occur in 1728 and 1729 respectively ; evidently there was some organised care for public health at this date. The population of Ulverston,[4] however, accounted for perhaps one-seventh of that of Furness, and the certainty remains that the great majority of the people of this district were indeed connected with husbandry in some intimate fashion.

LAND TENURE, CUSTOMS, AND TYPES OF AGRICULTURE

The occupiers of land were partly customaryholders or copyholders owing allegiance to one or other of the manorial courts, but in some cases enjoying a certainty of tenure amounting almost to freehold. Customs varied from manor to manor, and exhibited some complexity. Thus, the profits of the Manor of Ulverston, which was sold to the Duke of Montagu in 1736 and which afterwards descended to the Dukes of Buccleuch and Queensberry (the lords being in each case non-resident), included free customary, encroachment, hen, greenhew and shearing rents, and " the fines of customary tenants upon every alienation by death or purchase of the tenant ",[5] the size of the fine varying from estate to estate. In other manors, distinctive customs obtained ; at Pennington,[6] Kirkby Ireleth,[7] Broughton,[8] Lowick,[9] and Church Coniston.[10]

---

[1]*Lancs.P.R.Soc.*   [2]*Op. cit.*   [3]Ed. Bardsley and Ayre (1886).   [4]In 1754 Ulverston was a " small neat . . . town, but no corporation, nor is there a justice of the peace in it. They have a handsome market-house . . . There is a great trade here in corn, especially oats, chiefly for exportation, and they weave some camlets, and serges " ; *Dr. Pococke's Travels (Camden Soc.)*, II, 1.   [5]*Antiquities* 1774, 46.   [6]*Op. cit.*, 168.   [7]*Op. cit.*, 167-8.   [8]*Op. cit.*,213.   [9]*Op. cit.*, 169.   [10]*V.C.H. Lancs.*, VIII, 367.

Those of Kirkby Ireleth seem to have been onerous, and included a fine of ten years' rent for petty larceny, while no person could let his land without the lord's permission (viz. for a period of more than seven years) ; it is doubtful, however, how far these conditions were imposed in the deed. [1] At Broughton-in-Furness the conditions were comparatively reasonable, and only 20d. was paid on admission to an estate, as against 16 years' quit-rent on admission at Pennington.

In the district as a whole, the fines were certain and fixed in amount. In return, the yeoman customaryholder is said to have enjoyed security of tenure. The effect of the customs, and the aim of the manorial courts, was to prevent undue sub-division of estates and to keep them in the occupation of the same families. Descent on intestacy was to the eldest daughter or nearest other female relative in default of male. [2] A typical entry in the records of the Torver Court Baron for the Manor of Muchland (1738) [3] is :
" We present John Fleming Deceased and find Willm Fleming his Son next Heir of Ye Yearly Rent of 5s 1½d." A man might surrender his holding, and as far as can be ascertained, there was nothing to prevent its sale ; but the incomer had to pay his fine.

The yeoman customaryholders of this area and other parts of Cumbria were later known as " statesmen ", but the term was not peculiar to the region. Nor, apparently, was it used much, if at all, in the written records of the eighteenth century. [4] It is clear that these small landholders were common in Furness, save in the bailiwicks of Nibthwaite, Colton, Haverthwaite, Satterthwaite, and Sawrey (i.e. Claife), which were bought free of manorial customs in 11 James I, and which were almost certainly all freehold land at the end of the eighteenth century. [5] The larger estates had their tenant farmers, and may have had numerous leaseholders for lives —the latter were common in Lancashire in the reign of George III [6]—while it was stated in the early nineteenth century that Crown land in Plain Furness had been held on thirty-year leases. [7] At the same period it was revealed that Lord George Cavendish did not grant any at all, that the Braddylls of Conishead granted seven to nine-year leases, and that few were granted in the Hawkshead area. [8] Comparatively small landholders could of course

<hr>

[1] At the Court Baron of the Manor of Kirkby Ireleth, March 8th, 1744, William Middleton, on the death of his father, took the messuage and tenement of Fellyeat at the Customary Finable Rent of 7s. 2d. per year, plus a halfpenny Intack Rent ; but he also had to pay eight and a half years' arrears of rent, £3 0s. 11d., and nine years' Intack Rent, 4½d : *Barrow P.L.*, MSS. Z 380/1 and Z 380/2. The courts seem to have been held infrequently here, and it was apparently accepted that tenants would make intakes on the fell-sides. [2] Butler, Wilson, *C. & W. XXVI* (NS), 324. [3] *Rec. Man. Muchland*, Court Baron, February 9th, 1738. [4] *O.E.D.*, *s.v.* statesman ; use of the term occurs in 1787 (Norfolk) and 1794 (Westmorland, Derbys.). It appears in the *Ulverston P.R.* in 1803. [5] Cf. *Gent. Mag.*, LXXIII, Pt. II (1803), 1202. [6] Dickson ,R. W., *Agric. of Lancs.* (1815), 94. [7] *Ibid.* [8] *Op. cit.*, 142.

purchase customary estates and let parcels to others ; an interesting but not very satisfactory indicator of the degree of letting and sub-letting in the mid-eighteenth century occurs in the 1746 land tax lists, which in four divisions of High Furness distinguish the " occupiers " separately. Hence, Colton had 7 out of 40 taxees classed in this way, Hawkshead 5 out of 78, and Claife 19 out of 59. It is a point of some importance that there was a noticeable tendency to engrossment of some estates during the century,[1] and it is evident that there was a growing traffic in renting, letting and purchase of land ; but it is equally certain that the latter never took a violent turn. The yeoman customaryholders were removed by attrition, not catastrophe.

The following examples may be indicative of the state of affairs in given times and in particular parts of the district, during the eighteenth century. Between 1705 and 1710, Lord Molyneux, who had bought Mary Anderton's customary lands at Bardsea, acquired other customary holdings there—" divers parcels which were formerly customary or copyhold of the Manor of Bardsea ". In 1748 an Ulverston yeoman, John Dodson, was buying up dales and parcels in the town fields at Bardsea ; and nine years later another Ulverston inhabitant was selling land in the same place to Dodson. Evidently such buying and selling of township or other lands was widespread ; to such effect that in the Cartmel divisions of Staveley and Upper Allithwaite, a one-third proportion or less of all fields and closes were the property of owner-occupiers[2] by the end of the century.

Perhaps the majority of Plain Furness tenant farmers were to be found on an estate owned by the Lowthers of Holker to 1755, and later by the Cavendish family.[3] This estate was known, in the local idiom, as the " Manor " of Furness, and contained 34 tenants in 1707-08 ; the total annual rent roll at that period was about £800, and six farms paid more than £50 p.a. rental, chiefly in the Hawcoat-Gleaston area.[4] This was by far the largest agricultural estate in the district, and the number of tenants within it did not vary greatly during the century, although the rentals had increased considerably by 1786.[5] The Lowther and Cavendish property in Plain Furness was diffused over the divisions of Hawcoat, Above Town, Yarlside, Dalton, Leece, Holbeck, Upper and Lower Aldingham, Dendron, Gleaston, Stainton and Adgarley.[6] In Cartmel there were also extensive properties in the same ownership,[7] the

[1]See p. 57 below. [2]C. &W. (NS), XX (1920), 154 ff. ; and The Surveyor's Book of William Pearson (MS), with the Cartmel enclosure documents at Lancs. R. O. [3]Bouch, C. M. L., in C. & W. (NS), XLIV, 100 sqq., for the Lowthers. [4]Holker MSS., Rentals and Accounts, Lancs. R. O. [5]The total " Manor " rent roll had swelled to £1297 by 1786-7 ; Rentals and Accounts. [6]Land Tax Assessments, 1746. [7]Rentals and Accounts ; Land Tax Assessments.

total in Furness and Cartmel amounting to perhaps five thousand acres. Other and smaller estates, in or before 1746, were in the hands of the Duke of Montagu (in Dalton), the Wilson and Braddyll family (in Bardsea), and among other manorial lords, the Sawreys of Broughton ; in High Furness were woodland estates belonging to the Taylors of Finsthwaite, the Rawlinson and Sandys families, and the Machells of Haverthwaite. Each of these certainly had its scattering of tenant farmers or lessees, but of all the estates or demesnes mentioned, only that of the Duke of Montagu was rated at more than £5 for land tax.

Hence, all in all, the total number of tenant farmers cannot have been a large one. The characteristic tiller of the soil or sheep-raiser of these years was still the yeoman or statesman.

Agriculture seems to have been generally backward ; so much so that Thomas Pennant, visiting the district in 1772, remarked of the inhabitants of Plain Furness that they had " but recently applied themselves to husbandry ", going on to say that " till within these twenty years even the use of dung was scarcely known to them ".[1] In 1773 Thomas West was equally disparaging ; he observed that " One general obstacle to improvement and advancement of agriculture in Furness, is the mixed lands or township fields . . . domestic oeconomy calls for the improvement of every acre ; this can never be done, where there is common of pasture, by which every man has it in his power to prevent his neighbour's industry ".[2] W. B. Kendall, an antiquary who made elaborate studies of a number of Plain Furness hamlets, wrote that in the first half of the century " the land was neither drained, cleared, or manured " ; the breeds of sheep, horses and longhorn cattle were alike poor, and oats was the main cereal cultivated.[3]

West's reference to township fields may serve to draw attention to the systems of agriculture practised by the yeomen and husbandmen of the area. The latter lived and worked in small, sometimes scattered, but nevertheless coherent communities of cultivators and sheep-raisers. In Plain Furness these communities consisted, in numerous instances, of a handful of customaryholders or freeholders living in a hamlet and using one or several township fields in common.[4] In High Furness the unit was a scattering of sheepfarms with a few arable fields privately held, and in certain instances a township field or fields in addition to the moorland common. Only in Plain Furness is there any evidence that the township fields were consistently used for arable purposes, and here the land

---

[1]*Pennant*, 26.   [2]*Antiquities* 1774, xxiii.   [3]Kendall, *Salthouse*, *B.N.F.C.* VI (*NS*), 33.   [4]See pp. 12-13 below. The strips or dales were part and parcel of the freehold or leasehold estates, and were exchanged only for consolidation purposes.

was divided into strips (by means of reeans or reins) and held in scattered parcels. The methods by which crop rotation was carried out are obscure ; the field-arrangements may originally have had some affinities with run-rig, but in the Dalton district certain imprints were left upon local agriculture by the monks of Furness Abbey, and the units of cultivation here were in several cases former granges. W. B. Kendall has reconstructed what may have been a three-field system in one of these Abbey granges, the hamlet of Salthouse, but only two large field areas are visible in his valuable survey-map of the hamlet.[1] Dendron, in the nearby parish of Aldingham, had two town fields in the early eighteenth century, both containing dales or intermixed strips belonging to small occupiers and to " Lords or Ladies of the Manor ", and " one called the North Field ". The method of tilling them up to 1714 was to pasture one for three years and to plough or mow the other. Around these fields were pieces of common meadow and waste.[2] The Furness Abbey Rental of 1537 mentions two fields of almost equal size at Bolton-with-Adgarley, but only two of the Bolton tenants had holdings in both fields ; clearly no proper rotation of crops could be effected here.[3] The run-rig or Celtic system is usually regarded as consisting of an infield-outfield arrangement,[4] and the name " Infield " occurs in a few Plain Furness hamlets.[5] Otherwise there is no clear evidence that any fixed pattern of field arrangements had lasted to the early eighteenth century ; the hamlet of Askam seems to have had one large town field to the south of the settlement, while P. V. Kelly has shown that at Newbarns there were twelve tenements with parcels scattered over no fewer than six town fields, these being apparently used both for pasture and arable " in the course of a rotation ".[6] It should be added that each of the hamlets mentioned was situated in a part of Furness where much arable farming was possible, and which later grew wheat and barley in some quantity as well as the perpetual oats crops associated with the region.

Early in the nineteenth century the tenement-holders of Biggar, on Walney Island, are found meeting annually in accordance with long-established practice to decide how the cultivation of the riggs, or arable parcels in the town fields, should be arranged, and whether they should plough the field to the north or the south of the hamlet.[7]

---

[1]Kendall, *op. cit.*, Map. 2 and pp. 27-9. [2]Humphris, Rev. A., *Dendron, B.N.F.C. XVII*, 247-8.
[3]*Chet. Soc. LXXVIII* ; a " Dalton Feld " is also mentioned here, p. 612. [4]Cf. Clapham, *Econ. Hist. Modern Britain*, I, 23-5, 137. [5]Viz., at Roose, Cocken and Hindpool. Near, Middle and Far Infield, in the Tithe Commutation Survey of the Hindpool district (1843), suggest that a town field had been carved into several portions at Hindpool. I am indebted to Messrs. J. L. Hobbs and J. Melville for information here. [6]Bainbridge, T. H., *C. & W.* (NS), XLIII, 88-90, with map ; Kelly, *Newbarns, B.N.F.C. V* (NS), 19 sqq. [7]Pearson, H. G., *C. & W. XI* (NS), 191 and 185 sqq.

Similar methods seem to have prevailed elsewhere in the same neighbourhood.[1]

These Plain Furness town fields were generally small, and they cannot compare with the extensive open arable fields of Midland England ; but the hamlet or agricultural unit was also diminutive, and might consist of between four and sixteen tenants. The Askam field, still intact in 1842, consisted of 34 strips or dales of about one acre each and averaging one to two furlongs each. Arable and meadow dales were then intermixed.[2] In other Plain Furness hamlets individualism asserted itself in the mid-eighteenth century, and the " tenants " or customaryholders arranged their holdings in more concentrated form at Hawcoat (1731), Salthouse (1734) and Cocken (1741).[3] Urswick landholders may have exchanged dales as early as 1725.

High Furness also had its town fields; but since there was little arable husbandry here, they were of less importance, save in the sense that owners of stock found common hay dales of considerable value. Church Coniston had a common hayfield near the lake, and probably other common dales at Heathwaite and Little Arrow.[4] The Manor of Broughton and Subberthwaite had as many as six town hay or other fields, used for hay and pasture ;[5] there is a fragment of evidence that a common field at Subberthwaite was used for arable as well as grazing.[6] According to the Tithe Award of 1849, there were two common fields in Great Langdale,[7] and the hamlet of Torver had its town field or fields in the valley bottom near the church ; a manorial court of 1738 orders that " no Person or Persons that has any right in the Meddow commonly called Torver Meddows put in any more (beasts) then their proper stint that is to say for every half acre one Beast or Stand during ye time between ye 29 September and ye 11th November Yearly upon pain of forfeiture of 3s. 4d, every default ".[8] Each owner of a sheep flock in High Furness seems also to have had a " heaf " or section of moorland for grazing purposes ; but it is tradition which speaks here, and the writer knows of little documentary evidence on the subject.

[1]Cf. *B.N.F.C.* (OS), XII, 36 and (NS), VI, 41 (Cocken) ; and (OS), XIII, 44 (North Scale).   [2]Bainbridge, *loc. cit.*   [3]Kendall, *op. cit.*, 26.   [4]Porter, R. E., in C. *&* W., XXIX (1929), 273-7.
[5]Butler, Wilson, C. *&* W. *XXIX*, 293 sqq.   [6] *Op. cit.*, 301 ; in a Broughton manor court of 1659 it was ordered that several tenants of Subberthwaite shall " yearly stint the high field equally that is to say the beasts for one aker after they have gotten their corn . . ."   [7]Simpson, G. M., C. *&* W. *XXIX*, 272.
[8]*Rec. Man. Muchland*; cf. Ellwood, T., *The Reeans of High Furness*, C. *&* W. (O.S.) XI, 1891, 365.

In sum, it is fairly clear that agriculture, the basis of life for the majority of the people of Furness, was communally organised in many parts of the district, and in this respect it differed little from the open-field husbandry of central England. In other respects—types and rotation of crops, and heavy reliance on the sheep—it doubtless differed profoundly. [1]

STABILITY OF THE POPULATION

As might be expected, Furness people did not, in the seventeenth and early eighteenth centuries, move far from their native parishes, where the same family stock names occur again and again in the registers. Many of these surnames were certainly not peculiar to the district, [2] and for that reason it is most dangerous to base any estimates of mobility upon them. All that can be said is that families tended to stay in one neighbourhood and to ramify exceedingly, with the result that Aldingham swarmed with Gardiners, Fells and Simpsons, Pennington with Fells, Torver with Atkinsons and Parkes, the Crake Valley with Kirkbys and Redheads, and Church Coniston with Flemings and Dixons. The names of Taylor, Holme, Coward, Fell, Grave, Jackson, Postlethwaite, Towers and Wilson took pride of place at Ulverston from Tudor times, and H. S. Cowper [3] has shown that at Hawkshead Braithwaites, Rigges, Walkers, Satterthwaites and Knipes were the dominant clans, while Taylors proliferated at Finsthwaite, Colton and Penny Bridge. From time to time common names disappear from the registers of a particular parish, suggesting that the plague, failure in business or the non-appearance of male heirs had disposed of given families for the time being; but even in a township like Ulverston, where there was some commerce and social movement, 122 separate surnames entered in the registers for the years 1545-56 had about 90 survivors throughout the eighteenth century and until 1812, viz. they were appearing regularly to that date. Most of these surnames were fairly common in Furness as a whole, where about 150 names were especially favoured by the population in the seventeenth and eighteenth centuries. As is shown elsewhere, [4] individual parishes could show a steady turnover of stock names, but those which disappeared were often likely to be numerous in the immediate vicinity. A thorough statistical treatment, [5] which would be a work of considerable magnitude, is not hazarded here.

---

[1]Nothing is said here of the origins of Furness and Cumbrian field-systems; for an interesting critique, *vide* Graham, T. H. B., *C. & W.* (NS), X, esp. pp. 129-34. This study is especially critical of Dr. Slater's views on Cumbrian agriculture. [2]E.g., certain names like Atkinson, Jackson and Harrison were common where Englishmen breathed; others, like Hirdson, Grave, and Keen, were common in Furness and less so in nearby parishes. [3]Cowper, *Hawkshead* (1898), 199-201.

[4]See p. 105 below. [5]Professor Jones's treatment, *loc. cit.*, and the late E. J. Buckatzsch in *Population Studies*, 5 (1951-2), pp. 66-7.

14

There was certainly some emigration from the district in the eighteenth century,[1] and it is likely that there was inward movement from adjoining parts of Cumberland and Westmorland. It is interesting to record, meanwhile, that Atkinsons, Parkes, Wilsons and Flemings could remain dominant in a small moorland hamlet like Torver for the major part of two centuries, and probably much longer,[2] this in spite of the fact that other less common names disappeared frequently.

Several Furness parish registers do not begin to show an influx of obviously non-local or non-regional names until about 1760.[3] From this time a leavening of the local clans may have commenced in earnest, and before it, the evidence of the registers points to the truth of Canon C. W. Bardsley's view of the Furness population, that " to have emigrated twelve or fifteen miles seems to have been the limit of their ambition ".[4] The manorial customs, the favourable conditions of border tenure,[5] and the slow economic development of the region, undoubtedly worked against radical change and noticeable movement of the people.

TRADE, INDUSTRY AND POPULATION

Trade and industry are great redistributors of population, and since neither underwent any great change or grew to any importance in Furness before 1700, people had little incentive to come into the district. The latter had been touched by far-reaching enterprise in Tudor times, when the establishment of copper-mining by the Company of Mines Royal at Keswick and Coniston led to the settlement of German miners in High Furness,[6] and when supplies of charcoal were obtained by its industrialists from the woodlands of that area. This industry, however, was temporarily eclipsed by the time of the Civil War, and in other fields of activity, like iron manufacture, very limited progress was made ; a number of bloomery forges were established in the seventeenth century at Cunsey, Hacket, Coniston, Force in Rusland[7] and possibly other places, but the capitals involved were evidently small and outputs

[1]See pp. 109-11 below.   [2]In a manor court of 1585 the " Libri tenents " of Torver included a Fleming, an Atkinson and a Wilson, while the homagers included seven Atkinsons and a Parke (rendered as " Pke ") ;   *Rec. Man. Muchland* ; cf. published P.R., *Lancs. P. R. Soc.*   [3]See pp. 105-9 below. [4]*Chronicles of Ulverston*, 22.   [5]*Vide* Gatey, G., *C. & W. Assn. for the Advancement of Lit. and Science*, XI, 1885-6, 1 sqq.; and for a more recent commentary, Campbell, Mildred, *The English Yeoman* (1942), 149-53.   [6]Cf. Davies, " The Records of the Mines Royal and the Mineral and Battery Works ", *Ec.H.R.*, VI, 2, 209 sqq. ;   Collingwood, W. G., *Elizabethan Keswick* (1916), *passim* ; and genl. acct. in Rhys Jenkins, *Trans. Newcomen Soc.*, XVIII, 1937-8, 233-4, 228-9.
[7]By William Wright, the Fells of Swarthmoor and the Flemings of Coniston;   *E.I.I.F.*, var. refs., and Ross, Isabel, *Margaret Fell, Mother of Quakerism* (1949), 266 sqq.

equally so. The Dalton and Plain Furness iron ore mines, long known, were not exploited on any appreciable scale, and only a little haematite was exported in the seventeenth century. There was some slate-quarrying in the Coniston district towards the end of the latter.[1] In the late seventeenth and early eighteenth centuries a few enterprising local families, together with outside capitalists, showed interest in the production of iron and the mining of copper ; and in the field of iron-smelting there began a new phase of progress. This subject is discussed at some length below.[2] In 1709, when all the local iron was made " in the Bloomery way ",[3] quantities of it were being sold in Lancaster and probably much further afield.

The lives of local people were inevitably affected by this industry. It tended to stimulate the digging and raising of ore by small partnerships, to enliven rural industries like swill-making and saddle-tree-making, to divert the attention of yeomen towards the transport of ore and charcoal, and to awaken their interest in the preservation and use of the woodlands. From this time onward the local population, as reflected in the parish registers, tended to increase unmistakeably if slowly, and although the blast furnaces and forges of the eighteenth century employed a relatively small number of workers, economic activity spread outwards from the charcoal iron industry like ripples in a pool. The exportation of pig and bar iron attracted shipping and stimulated the building of small vessels on local shores ; the number of mariners increased ; and trade channels were established or developed.

On the other hand, there is no satisfactory means of tracing a direct connection between industrial or commercial development and population growth. By 1673 disastrous and persistent epidemics of the bubonic plague, a feature of local as well as of national history, had ceased to take their toll in Furness and Cartmel. These epidemics had played a big part in keeping down the numbers of the local inhabitants,[4] and epidemics afterwards, of diseases other than the plague, were comparatively less serious. This subject, a highly important one to the student of population problems, cannot here be given the treatment that it deserves ; local eighteenth-century mortality-waves are dealt with separately,[5] but a wider and more exhaustive comparison of epidemics in this

[1]In 1689 and 1693 slaters are mentioned in the Coniston parish registers, and slate was being sent from Piel Harbour in 1688 ; *vide* Willan, T. S., *The English Coasting Trade*, 1600-1750, 187, citing *K. R. Port Books* 1448/6. [2]Chap. II below, *passim.* [3]Stout, *Autobiography*, 80. [4]E.g., in 1631 Dalton lost 480 people and did not recover for half a century, as shown in its registers ; cf. Postlethwaite, G., *Lugubrious Lines on the Destructive and Violent Plague in Dalton* (1631), *Barrow P. L.*, and *M.S. notes* by William Close on the Dalton registers (in *Itinerary*). In Hawkshead, epidemic years occur in 1612, 1623, 1636 and 1668-72 ; Cartmel was visited by the plague in 1623 and 1670. [5]Pp. 140-2 below.

period with those of the plague era might well throw much light on the apparent tendency of the population of the most remote districts to climb in the late seventeenth and early eighteenth centuries. [1] The probable stimulants to population growth are so many and so complex that they are discussed separately, in so far as they may have obtained in this locality. [2]

The present study deals, in essentials, with the history of Furness after 1711. In that year two charcoal iron companies established ambitious enterprises in the neighbourhood, thereby making an energetic attempt to exploit its natural resources of mineral and woodland. The main ironmaking areas of England were suffering from a fuel famine. Accordingly the woodlands of Furness acquired a new value ; the district had potential supplies of charcoal as well as much water-power. Meanwhile, the coastal shipping trade of the western and north-western districts of England and Wales was slowly increasing, and it was more easy to send bar iron or merchandise from Piel or Ulverston to Bristol than it was to transport heavy goods a few miles inland. The coastal position of Furness profoundly affected its history throughout the eighteenth and nineteenth centuries, although the district did not experience anything approaching an " industrial revolution " until long after the central and southern areas of Lancashire had been transformed. Until the eighteen hundred and fifties it remained a remote and isolated district, hardly recognisable to the experienced or knowledgeable visitor as a part of Lancashire. This must be kept in mind when the more intimate details of its economic history are examined. It was hardly an important district, save in the sense that it contributed to the greater changes which were taking place elsewhere. It had no port accommodating vessels from the colonies, like Lancaster ; it had no coal, like West Cumberland ; it was one of the most sparsely populated areas of the County Palatine ; and it was, in short, like a great many rural or coastal areas of England. Herein, although possessing its peculiarities, it may well be representative.

It has sometimes been pictured as a lesser Black Country in the eighteenth century. [3] These pictures are almost certainly exaggerated. While the crash of the forge hammers at Coniston

---

[1]Slack, Miss M., *Some Aspects of Economic History in the Parish Records . . of North-West Yorkshire* (M.A. thesis in the University of Leeds), contains interesting data, and shows an increasing excess of baptisms over burials from 1700 onwards in many parishes of Airedale and Wharfedale. The excess was greatest in parishes with small industries. [2]See Chap. VI, *passim.*

[3]Contemporaries like Thomas Gray (*Journal*) and the Rev. S. Stebbing Shaw were impressed by the sound of a forge or the activity of ore-carting later in the century ; but the verses quoted on the title-page of Part I above are typical hyperbole in the style of the period.

or Backbarrow may have disturbed the peace of many a husbandman or shepherd, its furnaces could have been hidden from sight behind the smallest clump of trees, and only the green spaces of fallen coppice woods would have suggested to the traveller that something unusual was afoot. It remained a peacefully " backward ". area, colonised by a few ironmasters and their workers. That was undoubtedly the appearance. In the following pages, some attempt is made to penetrate beneath it.

CHAPTER II

THE RISE OF THE FURNESS CHARCOAL
IRON INDUSTRY

THE ESTABLISHMENT OF BLAST FURNACES

Although the water-powered blast furnace may have been used in England from mediaeval times, the method of smelting iron in pre-eighteenth century Furness was more primitive, and there is no reference to any advanced mode of working in the district before 1711. In that year, as is now generally known,[1] a partnership of Staffordshire and Cheshire ironmasters entered Furness in search of new supplies of charcoal, thus following the migratory tendency which the then desperate fuel shortage brought about. Local ironmasters, who had up to that time smelted their iron " in the Bloomery way ", reacted by forming a rival enterprise.[2] This enterprise became known as the Backbarrow Company, and was for a number of years one of the most highly-organised iron firms in the north. Comparatively little is known about its founders, who erected blast furnaces in the district, and whose enterprise was rewarded by a long period of profitable working ; the undertaking—in changed ownership—surviving the general introduction of coke-smelting in other parts of England.

The two iron companies of 1711 did more than bring success to their founders ; they inaugurated an important phase of eventful ironmaking activity in Furness, leading to the erection of more furnaces and a considerable expansion of local trade in pig and bar iron and haematite ore. The original stimulus, an increasing national demand for iron wares made keener by the " drying up " of Swedish sources of supply, was strengthened by the needs of wartime as well as those of peace. In consequence the woodlands, becks, easy water transport, rich haematite and coastal position of Furness almost immediately acquired an enhanced value. Several factors seem to have prevented a more rapid expansion of the smelting industry than in fact took place ; the monopolistic—or duopolistic—grip of the firms which succeeded in getting a footing in the district, the small capitals involved, and the difficulty of organising iron-making in an undeveloped district. In the last-mentioned respect the native ironmasters, members of the local

[1]*E.I.I.F.*, 207.   [2]That there was early rivalry between the local ironmasters and the incomers is satisfactorily established ; see pp. 20-1 below. The exact details of the story, however, are not known, and William Rawlinson and John Machell, two of the Furness ironmasters, had been engaged in bloomery-smelting previously. Alfred Fell, whose authority is used in the above statement, either had access to sources which have now disappeared or was indulging in guesswork.

19

squirearchy (one of them, rather surprisingly in this connection, was also a Quaker) enjoyed an obvious advantage.

The ironmasters from elsewhere, Edward Hall of Cranage furnace near Holmes Chapel in Cheshire, and Daniel and Thomas Cotton of " Doddlepool, Cheshire ",[1] built a smelting furnace by Cunsey Beck, near the western shore of Lake Windermere, at some time in 1711. Hence their local undertaking became known as the Cunsey Company or Edward Hall and Co. Their incursion was resented by the already established ironmasters, the chief of whom were William Rawlinson of Graythwaite and John Machell of Hollow Oak. It seems that the last-mentioned were obliged to take partners and to form a new and more ambitious company, known as William Rawlinson and Co. or the Backbarrow Company. The Backbarrow partners caused a blast furnace to be built at the place of that name, and were forced to abandon their primitive methods of smelting and to reorganise or rebuild their forges.[2]

The origins of the Backbarrow partnership extended back into the history of Quakerism. Three of its four members appear to have been Friends,[3] two of them, William Rawlinson and Stephen Crossfield, having been definitely of this persuasion, and John Olivant probably so. The fourth, John Machell, was evidently orthodox in religion[4] and belonged, like Rawlinson, to the landed gentry of the neighbourhood. Rawlinson's father, Thomas (1627-1689), was a convert of George Fox, and had acted as bailiff for Force Forge in High Furness, formerly owned by the Fells of Swarthmoor. Margaret Fell of this family became the wife of George Fox and a great figure in the propagation and defence of Quakerism.[5] William Rawlinson (1664-1734) was brought up as a Friend, and in about 1690 he married Margery Goldney of Chippenham, of a family of affluent West India merchants based on Bristol.[6]

---

[1]*E.I.I.F.*, 192, 207, 209, 265 ; Dr. W. H. Chaloner, *Ec. Hist. R.*, II, 2, 1949, p. 186, has suggested that " Doddlepool " may signify Doddlespool Hall, N.W. Staffs., about a mile from Doddington furnace in Cheshire. Cotton was a cousin of the Yorkshire Cottons, also ironmasters, and therefore, in the view of Mr. R. L. Downes, was probably of the Presbyterian-Baptist connection. The Cottons were using haematite ore at the Vale Royal furnace, Cheshire, at the commencement of the 18th century.

[2]For light on the tension between the companies, cf. letter repr. by Chaloner, *op. cit.*, 186-7. Darby I visited Furness in 1712 ; the Backbarrow refinery was built in that year on the site of a bloomery forge, Coniston forge was reconstructed in 1713, and Hacket forge in 1715 ; *E.I.I.F.*, 195-8, 253. [3]Gaythorpe, H., *Swarthmoor Meeting House* (1910), 41, & register of burials ; Satterthwaite, E. J., *Records of Friends' Burial Ground at Colthouse* (1914), 21 ; *Penrith M.H. Registers*, for reference to an " Olivent " in 1719—Olivant was " of Penrith "—by courtesy of the Clerk of Penrith Friends' Meeting. [4]The Machells appear with regularity in the parish registers of Colton ; for pedigree, Bardsley, *op. cit.*, 90-3. [5]Ross, Isabel, *Margaret Fell, passim.* [6]Foster, *Lancashire Families*, s.v. *Rawlinson of Graythwaite* ; Raistrick, *Quakers in Science and Industry* (1950), 324-5.

Rawlinson later appears as a friend or acquaintance of one of the most notable of all Quakers, Abraham Darby I, who worked in Bristol between 1700 and 1709. Much of the trade of the Furness ironmasters was with the Severn ports, and in 1719 Thomas Goldney, then a kinsman [1] of William Rawlinson, became a partner in the Coalbrookdale ironworks. [2] It is not difficult to see, therefore, why Darby showed some interest in the affairs of the Backbarrow Company. Religious ties gave the Furness Quakers a direct contact with such leading iron merchants as the Champions of Bristol, [3] who, after about 1712, handled much of their iron for resale; and it may not be without significance that William Stout, the prominent and astute Quaker merchant of Lancaster, was purchasing produce of the bloomeries of Rawlinson and Machell several years before that date. [4] Accordingly it is by no means certain that the formation of the Backbarrow Company was solely due to the incursion of Edward Hall and Co., although the latter may have caused the necessary decision to be made.

The surviving documents of the Backbarrow Company show that soon after its establishment it had an extensive trading organisation, and that it worked through a group of Quaker dealers in Bristol, Lancaster, Warrington and Whitehaven. William Rawlinson appears as the main intermediary and the moving force in the partnership, although Machell, a landowner in the Backbarrow district, had apparently offered the company land there on which to build their first blast furnace. [5] The original capital of the company was £6000, of which Rawlinson and Machell each had a one-third share, and Olivant and Crossfield a one-sixth share respectively. The two former partners undertook much of the administrative work, Rawlinson being the manager of the firm at a salary of £60 *per annum* ; his sons Thomas (1687-1739), William (1692-1760), Goldney (1695-1767) and Job (1698-1760) afterwards took some part as they reached responsible age. Although the Rawlinsons were Quakers, they were also country gentry of some standing, [6] and combined the attributes of the Quaker tradesman with the prestige of persons of more exalted rank. In this way they were equally at home in commerce and in the delicate negotiations involved in dealings with local landowners and woodowners,

---

[1]William Rawlinson's third son was christened Goldney Rawlinson. [2]Raistrick, *loc. cit.*, [3]*Vide* Raistrick, *op. cit.*, 191, for the family relationships, and Latimer, *Annals of Bristol in the 18th Century*, 289, 362, 368, for a few references ; also Raistrick, *Two Centuries of Industrial Welfare*, 95, 101, showing that a Bristol Quaker group may have been connected with copper mining at Caldbeck, Keswick and Coniston in the late 17th century.
[4]*Autobiography*, *loc. cit*. [5]*G.L.* (*Day Book* etc. of the Backbarrow Co., 1713-15), fol. 120. The Co. rented the site from Machell in 1713. [6]*V.C.H. Lancs*, VIII, 382, and Foster, *loc. cit.* William Rawlinson (1608?-80), the grandfather of the Backbarrow ironmaster, was a prominent Parliamentarian soldier.

the " country " of contemporary idiom. Official prejudice against the Friends cannot have counted for much in this district, and Machell, whose descendants obtained a controlling interest in the company, was fortunate in his partners.

The Company developed rapidly between 1711 and 1720. By September, 1715, the Backbarrow furnace had completed three blasts with a total output of 1718 tons 18 cwt. About half of the pig iron then made went to the company forges at Backbarrow, Force, Cunsey and Coniston, these refining a total of 648 tons of bar iron at the same period.[1] In about 1713 the firm made arrangements for the erection of a second blast furnace at Leighton near Arnside;[2] and in October, 1714, it acquired a large wood at the same place for £1115,[3] the Leighton furnace venture (viz., preparations and erection) costing the company a further £759 by 1715.[4] The Backbarrow furnace had cost £550.[5] According to Alfred Fell, the profits of the company in 1716 were £3850 " from all sources ",[6] but since the surviving records of the undertaking are incomplete it is not possible to verify this statement.[7] The firm's journal for 1713-15 is a record of vigorous activity in many fields ; expenditure of all kinds was comparatively heavy, and it is difficult to believe that the revenue did not justify it.

In 1717 came the prohibition of trade with Sweden : " The King of Sweden," announced William Stout, " seizes all the ships he meets with in the Baltic Sea, and all commerce with Sweden (being) interrupted, has caused their iron to advance here from £16 to £24 a ton : which has induced this country to build furnaces here to run iron, which ... brings a great benefit to the north part of this county (Furness) where mines and coals are plentiful, and labour cheap."[8] The success of the Leighton furnace demonstrates the truth of Stout's remarks. Between November 9th, 1717, and October 30th, 1718, the period of a complete blast, the recorded book profit of that furnace was £1965 or about 53s. 6d. on every ton of iron produced, the total cost of production per ton being 80s. 5d. Out of this figure 5s. 7d. went on wages ; charcoal was 36s. 6½d., ore 29s. 10d., and the expenses on limestone, peat and sundries were negligible.[9] Charcoal delivered to Backbarrow furnace in 1715 was about 27s. 6d. a dozen sacks, haematite ore being 14s. 3d. a ton at the furnace itself.[10] Leighton was easily

---

[1]*G.L.*, fol. 380 ; the combined pig output of Lancashire, Cheshire and Yorkshire is given as 4300 tons in 1717, the Coalbrookdale furnaces producing about 200 t.p.a. early in the century ; Court, *The Rise of Midland Industry*, 171-7, for these and other data.   [2]*G.L.*, fols. 163, 170, 172, 179, 182, 187-8, 213, 219, 224, 234, 235 etc.   [3]This wood became an important source of revenue : *G.L.*, fols. 187-8, 190, 207, 222, 240, 340.   [4]*G.L.*, fol. 406.   [5]*G.L.*, fol. 282.   [6]*E.I.I.F.*, 238.   [7]Numerous ledgers of the iron companies of Furness were destroyed during Alfred Fell's lifetime ; cf. *E.I.I.F.*, 275, for an allusion.   [8]*Autobiography*, 93.   [9]*E.I.I.F.*, 238.   [10]*G.L.*, 364.

reached across the Leven and Cartmel sands from the Dalton ore mines,[1] while the Backbarrow partners had of course taken the precaution of purchasing Leighton Wood in 1714, thereby securing nearby supplies of charcoal.

Although Rawlinson and his colleagues had not welcomed the Cunsey adventurers, tension between the two companies did not last for very long. It was soon understood that competitive hunting for charcoal woods would only raise the price of fuel, and following the advice of Abraham Darby I[2] a price-fixing arrangement was made between the partnerships in or soon after 1712. Each firm was apportioned a quota of charcoal which was exceeded upon payment of a penalty proportionate to the excess.[3] In this way the companies established an oligopoly over the " country ", the suppliers of woodlands and fuel, and the local ironmasters of later years made combinations of similar type. Haematite ore was more easily obtained than charcoal, and there is little indication of squabbling over " mine " (ore) or iron mining sites. Earlier prospectings for haematite in the Dalton district had revealed so many suitable sites that between 1712 and 1718 five or more pits were being utilised there.[4] The Backbarrow Company used ore from Adgarley and Crossgates, and in 1714 the two partnerships were jointly working a mine at Heaning Wood,[5] thereby making their collaboration more intimate still. There were obvious advantages in sharing mining equipment and labour, particularly when two furnaces had to be supplied. Soon afterwards, however, the Backbarrow Company obtained further mining leases in anticipation of the needs of Leighton furnace.[6]

The fuel problem was never solved with ease. By 1715 the Backbarrow partners were drawing their supplies of charcoal from an area of perhaps 150 square miles, and were reaching out as far as Troutbeck and Borrowdale for this fuel.[7] The lake and river valleys of High Furness were thickly wooded, but the ground suitable for coppice growth was necessarily limited, for much of the bare and elevated moorland was suitable only for sheep pasture, and local proprietors had to learn the art of systematic and scientific wood cultivation. Hall and the Cottons wisely situated their furnace within a short distance of Lake Windermere, and were thereby able to take advantage of the means of communication offered by this great natural waterway. The Backbarrow furnace was not far from

---

[1]Ore was carried from " ffurness-side of the Sands to Leighton shore " (1714) at 2s. 6d. a ton ; *G.L.*, 241. [2]Chaloner, *loc. cit.* [3]*E.I.I.F.*, 142. [4]At Tytup, Marton, Hills, Crossgates, Heaning Wood and Adgarley ; *E.I.I.F.*, 32-8, 63. [5]*G.L.*, 249, 404 ;*E.I.I.F.*, 38. In 1715 a gin was made at Leighton for use at Crossgates ; 128 feet of elmwood were used and nearly 1½ cwt. of iron, with 12 ft. of oak timber. It was carried to Crossgates in six carts ; *G.L.*, 249.

[6]At Tytup (1714), Crossgates (1714) and Adgarley. [7]*G.L.*, 11, 369.

the Crake and Rusland valleys, with their sheltered sides, and was fairly easily approachable from Lake Windermere *via* Newby Bridge. Much of the Backbarrow fuel came down Windermere by the " Long " and " Short " voyages—viz., from points above or below Rawlinson Nab on the west bank of the lake—and about 500 boatloads of charcoal were brought by these routes to feed the second blast of the Backbarrow furnace.[1] Both ore and charcoal frequently had to be carried about ten miles to the point of production, but the ore routes from Dalton to the eastern Furness shores and thence up the Leven by boat, were in general easier. In either case the use of water transport was an incalculable advantage to the ironmasters, and the relative ease of the former largely, though not entirely, explains the prolonged existence of the Furness charcoal iron industry.[2]

But keenly as the local yeomanry and landowners responded to the strengthened demand for fuel, coppice ground was used in a rotation of twelve to fifteen years, and the woodlands were far from inexhaustible. It is a feature of the local economic history of the period that after prolonged bursts of iron-smelting activity, ironmasters sought new supplies of fuel in Scotland. They controlled Furness charcoal prices ; but they could not hasten the growth of the vital woods. The control exerted jointly by the iron firms, however, had its roots in the peculiar problems and advantages encountered by the companies when they established their undertakings in an undeveloped district. Competition for fuel might not have ruined them in the circumstances, particularly when the demand for pig and bar iron was strong, but it would certainly have reduced their profits. They were in the position of colonisers, importing their skilled labour and taking advantage of cheap local labour ;[3] not only were they woodowners, furnace-owners and forgemasters, but they became bankers, general dealers and timber salesmen as well. In this way the Backbarrow Company became an industrial unit of some complexity and integration.[4]

It is now clear that the tendency to careful organisation owed not a little to Quaker ironmasters and iron dealers. It was on the advice of Abraham Darby I that the Furness charcoal " pool " was originally established, and a Quaker trading network, of which the Backbarrow partners took full advantage, extended throughout the west of England. This, again, was a matter of circumstance. The Friends, who still felt the impact of legal disability and of the official attitude to dissent, had been driven more and more into

[1]*G.L.*, 98, 294. [2]Another factor was the richness of Plain Furness haematite, which made for cheaper smelting. [3]Stout, *Autobiography*, 93 : " coals (in Furness) are plentiful, and labour cheap " (1717). [4]Cf. Mr. Lipson's comments, *Econ. History of England*, I, 164-5.

trade and industry, while religious practice cemented their associations, friendships and intermarriages. Hence much of the iron produced by the Backbarrow undertaking passed through Quaker hands, primarily (in 1713-20) those of Nehemiah Champion of Bristol, Samuel Milner of Bewdley, Joseph Titley of Warrington, Robert Dowthwaite of Whitehaven, and William Stout of Lancaster.[1] By 1723 the Champions stood in some family relationship to the Rawlinsons of Graythwaite,[2] and, as has been seen, the latter were related by marriage to the Goldneys of Bristol. This brief sketch of family connections is by no means complete,[3] a consideration which is hardly surprising when it is remembered that George Fox himself had married into a prominent Furness family. The Friends, generally faithful to their religious organisation, were certainly not sectarian in business when sober counsel dictated, nor were individuals among them afraid to meet the worldly demands of society at large.[4]

Although Furness Quaker influence appears to have waned later in the century, it was dominant in local industry in the decisive years 1711-30. The Backbarrow Company, judged in terms of its mines, furnaces and forges, was a more powerful firm than that of the Cunsey partners; but it nevertheless continued to collaborate with the latter, and actually had a forge at Cunsey,[5] while in 1720 the two companies acquired joint control of a forge at Stony Hazel in Rusland,[6] deepening their intimacy yet again. Recently discovered evidence suggests that Hall and his Cunsey colleagues were Catholic or Presbyterian;[7] and this possibility should occasion no surprise, for John Machell of Backbarrow was, in the light of similar evidence, an orthodox churchman, and it is plain already that religious differences were not allowed to hinder the activities of business. The pattern of collaboration which was thus established, satisfying the demands of self-interest and profitable ironmaking, was reproduced at several stages in the later history of the local charcoal iron trade, and the more orthodox ironmaking gentry of the neighbourhood learned their lesson well.

[1]*G.L.*, 101, 105, 113, 167, 380 ; *Bar Iron Ledger, Backbarrow Co.* (1713-18), Barrow P.L., fols. 65, 79, 164, 171, 180, 188. [2]*Backbarrow MSS.*, *MS letter*, 23.3.1722/3, where William Rawlinson addressed Nehemiah Champion as " Esteemed Kinsman ". [3]The following examples may be indicative. Esther Rawlinson, William Rawlinson's niece, married Thomas Titley of Warrington in 1732 ; Anthony Wilson, whose sister Dorothy married Robert Dowthwaite, was a leading wood agent of the Backbarrow Company, while earlier a William Wilson of the same ramifying family was married to an Ann Stout. Light on the families mentioned, including the Milners, is to be found in the *Meeting House Registers* of Bewdley and Warrington (transcript material and information by courtesy of Mrs. Alice Parker and Mr. Leslie Richardson), and in Foster, *Wilson of High Wray and Kendal*, priv. printed pedigree, Friends' House Library, London, and *Lancashire Families*, pedigree handbook by the same genealogist. [4]Cf. Raistrick, *Quakers in Science & Industry*, 61-5 ; Latimer, *op. cit.*, 75. [5]*G.L.*, 97. [6]*E.I.I.F.*, 206. [7]Inf. by courtesy of Mr. R. L. Downes. Hall's name appears in a list of recusants.

Abraham Darby's connection with William Rawlinson naturally brings to the fore the topic of coke-smelting, which was then (1712) the subject of experiment on the part of the former. Following a visit to Furness in that year, Darby wrote to Rawlinson that " I had some other things in vew in youer parts moore than making iron in the common way and with common fuell, but did partly forget it at coming away, and partly the season, being first day (i.e. Sunday), was unfit for buisnes of that nature." [1] He even raised the question of a possible partnership with Rawlinson and his colleague, proposing to take a royalty of " one 8th part of the neet profets " which might accrue from the use of the new process, " as I think thear is not the least dought but by it you may save £700 per annum ". [2] But there is no evidence that the Backbarrow and other local iron companies ever used the coke-smelting process during the eighteenth century, and references to the importation of pit-coal for coking in the district are notable by their absence, [3] although this fuel was of course used for domestic and other purposes in the locality, and there was no difficulty in obtaining it from White-haven vessels. [4] At that time, charcoal-smelting was very profit-able to the Backbarrow partners, and as happened in the case of a great Furness steel company over a century and a half later, easy profits were apt to check the course of technical advance. [5] Rawlin-son and his fellow-investors evidently preferred the known to the unknown, and there the matter may have rested.

But these men were by no means unenterprising. The intricate organisation of the local iron industry must have absorbed all their energies ; unable to confine themselves to the supervision of the furnaces and forges, and without the assistance of a large clerical staff, they ranged over the countryside in search of wood purchases and leases, superintended the transport of ore and charcoal, visited customers and merchants, organised fisheries and food supplies for workmen, chartered vessels or arranged for their construction, went to immense trouble to obtain the material for the erection of Leighton furnace, and in the cases of Rawlinson

[1]Chaloner, *loc. cit.* [2]*Loc. cit.* I am indebted to Dr. W. H. Chaloner for the loan of a photo-facsimile of this valuable letter, the copy being listed in Nat. Lib. Wales, MSS. 10823. [3]One of the few references to coal importation occurs in *G.L.*, fol. 219, and is typical : " For the charge of coal from White-haven to burn lime for furnace building . . . . £1 17. 0." This coal went (1715) to Leighton. [4]Cf. Jarvis, R. C., *C. & W.* (NS), XLVII, 1948, 144-9, where it is shown that by 1728-9 fairly large quantities of coal were being delivered at Rampside, Penny Bridge, Milnthorpe and Grange. Much of the Milnthorpe coal went to Kendal, and was used in connection with tanning and textiles. The absence of easily available coking coals may have discouraged Rawlinson, but there is no evidence that he even experimented. [5]The reference is to the Barrow Haematite Steel Co. ; *vide J.I.S.I.*, 1876, 13-28. This firm was slow in adopting the use of molten iron direct from the furnace for steel production in converters, but " the decrease in the price of iron and steel had sharpened the Barrow wits . . . " (Schneider, *op. cit.*, 28).

and Machell, left the district on long journeys to see their agents in Bristol and Bewdley and to obtain skilled workmen from the south-west.[1] Nor does it follow that they were deaf to the advice of Quaker technicians elsewhere ; Dr. Raistrick has written that " the Quaker potters of Bristol, the brass-founders of Bristol and Birmingham, the ironmasters of Furness and those of Sheffield, and the great group of ironmasters of South Wales, are all illustrative of . . . close attention to technical research ".[2] In 1714, three years before the death of the first Abraham Darby, the Backbarrow partners were sending the former samples of haematite and local copper ore, the consignment passing through the hands of Samuel Milner,[3] who for his part arranged for the shipment of forgemen to Furness.[4] Darby, meanwhile, had carried on careful experiments in sand-moulding, and it may be no accident that in 1721 skilled " potters " were brought into Furness, and that the production of cast ironwares was commenced at Leighton.[5] Little is known of the techniques used by local ironmasters ; naturally enough the Backbarrow partners had a high opinion of their own wares, and in 1723 William Rawlinson is found remarking of his company's iron pigs that " . . . a right working ym in our way requires skill and care which too few workmen are Masters of . . . ".[6]

A rapidly expanding enterprise often requires capital for investment over and above that obtained from its net profits. There is no reason to suppose that the four Backbarrow partners were exceptionally wealthy men when their company was formed ; and the Quaker merchant Nehemiah Champion of Bristol soon afterwards made them a loan of £2000,[7] doubtless as a means of securing one of his most important sources of bar and pig iron. Other and smaller sums were invested by local gentry and merchants before 1715 or in that year. One John Pattison received 6 per cent. on a £400 loan ; Sir William Fleming, the squire of Coniston, lent the firm £107 ; and the company owed William Shaw £227 in principal and interest, while " Lawyer " Gibson, the firm's legal agent in Lancaster, lent the partners £134 in 1713.[8] On one occasion the sum of £100 was borrowed from a creditor for two weeks only, and the small sum representing 5 per cent. annual

[1]G.L., fols. 17, 68, 103, 105, 107, 113, 139, 147, 155, 157, 161, 170-9, 220, 250; other illustrative references are scattered throughout the journal entries in this volume. [2]Raistrick, A., Two Centuries of Industrial Welfare, 95. [3]G.L., 143, 313. [4]G.L., 319, 321. [5]E.I.I.F., 239. The sources of Fell's information have not been traced, and it is probable that the relevant letters or accounts are now destroyed or diffused. There is no reason to doubt the correctness of his statement. [6]MS. Letter dated 3/mo : 23d, 1722, Rawlinson to Champion; the reference was apparently to refining : " . . . here is no sale for any pigs: all the way we have of disposing of them is to work ym in small quantities among our other pigs . . ." [7]The premium on this loan is mentioned in Profit and Loss Account, G.L., 411. [8]Ibid., and G.L., 314, 358.

interest was refunded.[1] At this stage the company was not disposed to act as a banker *per se*, but it eventually became a repository for small savings accumulated by local persons. Meanwhile, the financial difficulties of the Backbarrow partnership were manifold, and grew with its increasing trade; bills of exchange, the instruments of credit used and received by its faraway agents, were often dishonoured,[2] and the collection of a mass of debts from local customers always offered difficulty. Nevertheless it continued to flourish, and by 1728 William Rawlinson's eldest son, Thomas, was in a position to invest £7000 in the erection of a new furnace near Loch Garry in Inverness-shire on behalf of the Backbarrow Company.[3] The total capital of the latter was £16,000 in 1749.[4]

Until well into the second half of the century, this undertaking was the largest in Furness in terms of capital, furnaces and forges.[5] By 1750, however, several other firms had entered the field, and the charcoal iron industry of the locality started upon a new phase of expansion. Between 1711 and 1736 no new firms appeared and the hegemony of the Backbarrow and Cunsey partnerships remained undisturbed ; but reliable information regarding this period is scarce. The bold attempt to establish a branch of the Backbarrow enterprise in the wilds of Scotland, conceived in about 1727 and ending in disaster in 1736, was itself indicative of the growing difficulty of obtaining charcoal supplies " at home ". Alfred Fell estimated that the average annual quantity of charcoal supplied to the Backbarrow and Cunsey companies between 1715 and 1730 was 1270 dozens,[6] and the consequent effect upon the standing growth of coppice woodland, in that period of fifteen years, must have been considerable. In 1725 William Stout was remarking upon the " great advance of charr coals and the iron mine ",[7] and it is known that Thomas Rawlinson and his colleagues were drawn to Scotland by the bait of cheap charcoal ; 15s. 6d. a dozen at their Loch Garry furnace,[8] compared with 27d. 6d. at Backbarrow in 1715.[9] The Backbarrow Company thought it worth while to freight Furness haematite to Invergarry, and went to considerable trouble to import workmen into Scotland and to buy the favours of Highland landowners and officials.[10] The over-liberal expenditure of the quixotic Thomas Rawlinson, together

---

[1]*Ibid.* [2]E.g.; " 1714—Dec. 29. Wm. Rawlinson is Dr to Nehemiah Champion the sum of £582.11.0—wch sum is the ballance of a pcell of Bills . . . to the value of £952.11.0—pt of the Sd bills being returned to the value of £370.0.0." (Entry in *G.L.*)
[3]*E.I.I.F.*, 388. [4]*E.I.I.F.*, 260. [5]The company's forges in 1713-15 were at Force, Cunsey, Coniston and Backbarrow ; the ground for another at Hacket, Little Langdale, was rented by the firm, and this forge was afterwards used until c.1744, the others being used fairly regularly in the first half of the century. *G.L.*, 97, 359 ; *E.I.I.F.*, 191-2, 196, 200, 203, 209, 253. [6]*E.I.I.F.* 135-6. [7]*Autobiography*, 107. [8]*E.I.I.F.*, 354. [9]*G.L.*, 364. [10]*E.I.I.F.*, 351-3, 355, 360-3.

with the administrative difficulties inherent in such an undertaking, doomed the Invergarry project to an early failure.[1]   Here a speculation may be permitted ; while there is no certainty that the adoption of coke-smelting in Furness, in a time when the process was untested and scarcely known, might not have brought serious difficulties in its train, it is difficult to escape the conclusion that the acceptance of Darby's advice might in the end have saved the company much trouble.

FURTHER PROGRESS OF THE INDUSTRY

The subsequent progress of the local iron industry may be dealt with briefly.   In 1718 the number of Cunsey partners had been increased by the addition of William Rea, an experienced ironmaster of " Monmouth ", Edward Kendall of Stourbridge, and Ralph Kent of Kinderton in Cheshire.[2]   Richard Ford of Middlewich (b. 1697)[3] came to Cunsey to manage the company's enterprise in 1722, and remained there until 1735, when he built a new furnace at Nibthwaite in the Crake Valley with Thomas Rigg as partner.[4] The firm of Richard Ford and Co. was the progenitor of the better known Newland Company, ultimately the last considerable charcoal iron concern to remain in England.   Meanwhile, the management of the Cunsey firm passed into the hands of William Latham, of Austrey in Warwickshire, and under his direction the Duddon furnace was built in 1736.[5]   The Kendalls, who were probably relatives of the Lathams, retained their interest in the Cunsey enterprise, and were afterwards closely associated with the Latham family in the working of this new furnace (which stood a short distance to the N.W. of Duddon Bridge on the Lancashire and Cumberland boundary).

There was then no further erection of furnaces until 1747-9, when three more were erected in the district, bringing the total number to eight.   In 1747 Richard Ford was joined by Michael Knott of Rydal, William Ford of Grizedale, and James Backhouse of " Jolliver Tree " (July Flowertree), Finsthwaite, this new partnership taking on the construction of a smelting furnace at Newland near Ulverston.[6]   Meanwhile, the Rawlinsons and Machells had become the sole proprietors of the Backbarrow Company's furnaces and forges in 1731 ; but the original leading partner and manager, William Rawlinson, died in 1734, and his son Job went into partnership with William Crossfield of Cartmel, George Drinkall of Rusland, and Isaac Wilkinson of Backbarrow (the father of the great ironmaster John Wilkinson) to form the Lowwood Company (1747), which built a furnace at Lowwood near

---

[1]*E.I.I.F.*, 388-9.   [2]*E.I.I.F.*, 265-9.   [3]*E.I.I.F.*, 269 ; this Ford was apparently no relative of the Richard Ford of Coalbrookdale.   [4]*E.I.I.F.*, 269-70.   [5]*E.I.I.F.*, 215, 265-6.   [6]*E.I.I.F.*, 270.

the Leven Estuary, and about a mile from the Backbarrow furnace. [1]
But this company was short-lived, and soon afterwards passed into
the hands of the Sunderlands, landed gentry from the Halifax
district. [2]

One further company was then formed to complete the list of
local partnerships called into being by the demand for charcoal iron ;
this was an equally short-lived enterprise which had the aim of
building a furnace at Penny Bridge, in the Crake Valley, and formed
by a group of woodowners who wished to be independent of the
ironmasters' monopoly of smelting.   In 1749 it was absorbed into
the Backbarrow undertaking, which remained, for practical purposes,
in the hands of the Machells of Hollow Oak. [3]   In this year the Backbarrow Company controlled three furnaces—Backbarrow, Penny
Bridge, and Leighton—and the Cunsey Company, two, the Newland
Company having two furnaces at Newland and Nibthwaite.   But
'he Duddon Company (which paraded under a number of differing
titles[4]) was now firmly established, and almost immediately afterwards the effective hegemony over local smelting passed to the
Newland, Duddon and Backbarrow Companies.   The Cunsey
furnace was leased to the Backbarrow Company in 1750 and was
dismantled a few years later, while that at Nibthwaite ended its
career in 1755.   The Leighton furnace was sold to the Halton
Company of the Lancaster district in the same year. [5]   Five local
furnaces then remained in use for several decades longer ; in the
case of the Duddon and Newland smelting furnaces, through much
of the nineteenth century, or even, as at Backbarrow, into the
twentieth.

It is very doubtful whether there were ever more than six
charcoal furnaces simultaneously in blast in the Furness district,
and it is therefore important not to over-emphasise the magnitude
of the industry at any particular period.   It is also far from clear
what caused the erection of new furnaces in 1735-6 ; as Professor
T. S. Ashton has shown, [6] the period 1725-38 was one of relative
buoyancy in the national iron trade, and it may be that the Cunsey
men took advantage of the embroilment of the Backbarrow partners
in Scotland by forming offshoot enterprises as the occasion offered.
Local material on trade conditions is scanty, William Stout referring
to 1721 as a bad year (owing to the bursting of the South Sea
Bubble), [7] and 1723 seems also to have been a slack period as
affecting pig iron sales. [8]   1725 was a good year, and the disastrous
harvests of 1728-9 brought a general decline in trade as well as high

[1]*E.I.I.F.*, 266-9.   [2]For pedigree, Bardsley, *op. cit.*, 97.   [3]*E.I.I.F.*,
260-3.   [4]E.g., Hall, Kendall & Co., Latham & Co., William Latham & Son,
Jona. Kendall & Co., Kendall, Latham & Co.   [5]*E.I.I.F.*, 209-10.   [6]Ashton,
T.S., *Iron and Steel in the Industrial Revolution*, Chap. VI. [7]*Autobiography*, 99.
[8]See p. 27 above, f.n. 6.

mortality in the villages ; 1730-2 brought a recovery, but by 1739-40 trade was again bad.[1] There is some evidence that abundant harvests stimulated commerce.[2] According to a table of pig iron prices at Backbarrow compiled by Alfred Fell,[3] these prices were at their lowest level for the eighteenth century (£5 16s. per ton) during the seventeen hundred and thirties, but climbed to a peak of £7 10s. during the following decade and a half. His account of the erection of local iron furnaces, upon which this section of the narrative is based, is therefore entirely consistent with his price tables, and it would seem that the late 'forties and early 'fifties of the century constituted a boom period in north-western iron-making, a supposition which is borne out by shipping figures.[4] The rapid local expansion of 1746-50 was undoubtedly connected with the growing demand for cast and refined iron wares of all kinds, associated equally with the needs of the home, the needs of war and war preparation, and the requirements of the colonial shipping trade and home textile industries. Gun-making and the manufacture of shot were commenced in Furness in 1745,[5] and in 1744 the Backbarrow Company was making box-irons, sad-irons, fire-grates, heaters, cast-iron ballusters, loom stoves and pans, skillet and possnet handles, hatters' basins and Guinea kettles ; the company's sales of such goods amounted to the value of £5500 in that year.[6] Pots and pans were sent to the West Indies, evidently passing through the port of Lancaster,[7] while in 1750 Furness bar iron was being sold in Liverpool and was used in the manufacture of anchors, chains and other shipbuilding requirements. The Backbarrow exports of cast goods remained large in 1752-3, and 19,000 pieces (made from 190 tons of pig) were cast at that works in 1752, and 23,500 pieces in the following year.[8]

The commencement of the Seven Years' War appears to have affected the local iron trade unfavourably. The following shipping figures (Table 1) are to be taken in conjunction with movements of iron prices and particulars of furnace-building in the neighbourhood. Backbarrow pig fell in value from £7 10s. a ton to £6 10s. between 1755 and 1760,[9] but prices recovered in the early 'sixties. The shipping tonnages give no indication of the export trade of Furness, but they are valuable in showing general trends in the north-west :

---

[1]*Autobiography*, 107, 123, 138. [2]Cf. Ashton, T.S., *An Economic History of England : The Eighteenth Century*, 60-61. Stout is very definite in this matter. [3]*E.I.I.F.*, 237. [4]See p. 32 below. [5]After experiments by the Backbarrow Co. had failed ; *E.I.I.F.*, 245-6. [6]*E.I.I.F.*, 239. [7]*E.I.I.F.*, 239. [8]*Op. cit.*, 239-40. [9]*Op. cit.*, 237.

Table 1 [1]

Total tonnages of ships belonging to north-western ports.

F = trading to foreign ports. C = trading coastwise.

T = total tonnages of port. Fishing vessels included in Totals for Whitehaven.
N.B.—In 1717 " above forty sail " belonged to Piel (Furness) and the creeks of Leven and Kent sands, and in the period 7th May, 1737 to 10th May, 1738, 231 ships visited Furness shores. [2]

	Whitehaven			Piel (Furness)			Lancaster			Liverpool (Coastal only)
	F.	C.	T.	F.	C.	T.	F.	C.	T.	
1709	4285	243	4604	(Prob. included			693	211	904	592
1716	6325	735	7140	with Lancaster,			614	296	910	1090
1723	7285	449	7814	or incomplete).			375	197	572	1180
1730	9327	354	9761	—	1115	1115	462	203	665	1871
1737	10,528?	402	11,010	—	1142	1142	451	159	610	1916
1744	16,985	420	17,485	—	1124	1124	986	274	1260	2120
1751	17,832	504	18,416	—	1421	1421	1992	281	2273	2030
1758	20,198	785	21,133	369	338	707	1920	470	2390	1794
1759	19,676	694	20,520	256	435	691	2200	510	2710	1595
1763	21,895	1212	23,450	190	534	724	2205	560	2765	—

The growth of the shipping tonnages of Whitehaven, Lancaster and Liverpool cannot be discussed here ; but it will be seen that the Piel (Furness) figures for coastal vessels compared not unfavourably with those of the better-known ports. [3]

Much of the trade of the Furness iron firms was carried on with traders and industrialists in those districts reached by the Severn and Stour, and in the area behind Liverpool. Some surviving records of the Duddon ironworks throw light on this subject. In the year 1750 the Duddon furnace had been in blast for 17 weeks, and,

[1] *B.M., Addl. MSS.* 11255, *An Account of the Tonnages of all Ships and Vessels belonging to each respective Port in England* etc., compiled by Sir William Musgrave for the Commissioners of Customs. [2] Jarvis, R. C., *C. & W. (NS)*, XLVII, 1948, 154, q. *Lancaster Letter Book,* 18.5.1717; *E.I.I.F.*, 316. The ships used at least ten local places of anchorage.

[3] The annual shipping fluctuations (home-based tonnages) for all Furness vessels in the 'fifties were as follows : 1751, 1421 tons ; 1752, 1338 tons ; 1753, 1360 tons ; 1754, 1322 tons ; 1755, 1309 tons ; 1756, 2482 tons (probably the peak figure for the century) ; 1757, 1720 tons ; 1758, a drop to 707 tons ; 1759, 691 tons ; and 1760, a mere 628 tons. In 1772, when the Ulverston and Piel tonnage was 1200, Thomas West (*Antiquities*, 1805, 16) estimated that about 70 ships belonged to Ulverston. These vessels were obviously very small, 15 to 20 tons each. Pennant, *Tour in Scotland*, 1774, 25, wrote that there were " formerly about 150 " vessels based on Ulverston, but that the sailors " now go to Liverpool for employ ". He obtained his information from Henry Kendall of the Duddon Company. It should be added that Furness trade was not purely in iron ; bark for tanning, staves and laths, and agricultural produce also entered into it. But haematite export became more and more important.

The growth of Lancaster and Liverpool, due partly to the colonial and slaving trades, affected Furness. In 1745 Lancaster was trading to the West Indies with hardware (*vide* Ray, James, *Rebellion*, 1750 ed., 129, 192-4), and Furness farmers were growing beans for use as food for the negroes on slave vessels (Pennant, *loc. cit.*).

of its output, 107 tons of pig went to Chepstow. Small quantitites of bar iron, refined at the Duddon Company's Spark Forge, were being sent to Liverpool, or further south, and the firm also sent about 250 tons of haematite ore to Frodsham in Cheshire.[1] But it is clear from these records that there was a good market for bar iron in the immediate region.

In 1750 the Furness iron companies were still working in close liaison in order to keep the local woodowners at bay, and the Penny Bridge episode of 1748 may serve to illuminate the general tendency. In that year, 180 local woodowners agreed to supply charcoal only to the proprietors of a newly-erected furnace at Penny Bridge, the price of the fuel to be based on Bristol pig prices. Their motive was that of wrecking the main companies' controlling influence over the prices of charcoal ; but soon afterwards the newly recon- stituted Backbarrow Company[2] purchased the new furnace and brought this apparently quite justifiable scheme to nothing. There were bitter recriminations, controversy raging in the district ; but the ironmasters' hand gripped firmly.[3] The proprietors of the estab- lished furnaces maintained a front which was difficult to break, and their collaboration extended into many fields. In 1750 the Back- barrow, Penny Bridge and Duddon concerns were sharing ore from the Plumpton mines ; the Duddon Company rented a wharf at Crane House from James Machell of the Backbarrow Company, and had the rental of a former Backbarrow forge at Coniston ; bar iron went to the Nibthwaite furnace from the Duddon Company's forge at Spark Bridge, a small lot being sent to the Lowwood Company ; and there are indications that charcoal was resold by or exchanged between companies.[4] When the Duddon partners required special fitments in the form of castings, a hammer and an anvil they obtained them from the Nibthwaite firm,[5] and in 1772 the Duddon concern shared land at Nibthwaite with the Newland Company, obtained ore by arrangement with the Lowwood Company, shared boats with other firms, and borrowed supplies of fuel from them.[6] In 1753 the Backbarrow and Halton companies agreed to share the cost of any woods offered for sale, and in 1756 the local ironmasters met together to agree that " no bar iron at home be sold under £19, at Liverpool £17 per ton ".[7] This last arrangement amounted to exploitation of the local consumer, for, as has been shown, the market for bar iron in the immediate neighbourhood was

---

[1]*MS. Account Books of the Duddon Ironworks*, Lancs. R.O., DDX 192/1, fols. 1-59, 81, 87, 113-4.
[2]For the company constitution of 1749, *vide E.I.I.F.*, 260-1 ; the Machells remained in control. [3]*Vide* a surviving copy of the *Penny Bridge Wood Articles*, Barrow P.L., and *E.I.I.F.*, 145-7, and Appx. E. A century later, a local oligopoly, this time over the transport of ore, was exerted by the Furness Railway directors, who came to control the affairs of the district. [4]*Duddon Accts.*, 1750, fols. 41, 58, 70, 79, 88, 96, 98. [5]*Ibid.*, 113. [6]*Duddon Accts.*, 1772-5 (DDX 192/4), fols. 4, 23, 61. [7]*E.I.I.F.*, 254.

by no means inconsiderable. In 1781 the Newland, Lowwood and Backbarrow companies made an agreement whereby all the charcoal in Lancashire, Westmorland and Cumberland was to be divided into three equal shares at an initial price of 36s. a dozen, and whereby any company getting less than its share was to have the difference made up in the following season. The Duddon ironworks accounts show that prices not far removed from this one were paid in the early 'seventies, and it may be concluded that the ironmasters were successful in keeping fuel prices at a relatively low level. [1]

Cheap charcoal did not mean adequate supplies of fuel. Once again Furness ironmasters established enterprises in Scotland. The Newland partners obtained woods at Bunawe, or Bonaw, in Argyllshire in 1752, and built the Lorn furnace there in the following year. [2] Ore was sent to Scotland from Furness, and a regular shipping connection was established, aiding the settlement of Scots people in Ulverston and other parts of the district. [3] The Newland experiment stimulated the Duddon Company to act in similar fashion and to set up a furnace at Goatfield, near Inverary. In this second instance, there is evidence that the initial arrangements to buy land or erect a furnace took place before 1755, for in that year the Duddon firm made reference to Goatfield in its accounts. [4] A date on the lintel of the furnace (which was situated near the shore of Loch Fyne) has shown that 1775 may have been the original date of erection, and according to Fell, no ore was shipped to Inverary until 1777. [5] The Lorn and Goatfield furnaces remained in use during the closing decades of the century, and the first-named continued in work until 1874. Hence, the Duddon and Newland partnerships succeeded in their Highland enterprises where the Backbarrow group had failed miserably.

The nature of the local iron trade changed steadily in the second half of the century. Charcoal-smelting survived in the district when it was becoming a curiosity elsewhere. Up to the time of the Napoleonic Wars a number of iron firms were able to remain in being, but the total " make " of the district was not large. The Cunsey furnace was demolished in 1750, and the furnaces at Nibthwaite, Penny Bridge and Lowwood were similarly treated in 1775, 1780 and 1785 respectively. [6] In 1788 it was reported that the Backbarrow, Newland, Leighton, Duddon and Halton furnaces were in use in the district, but that only two were in blast, while four forges were at work. [7] Since Halton lay outside Furness, only

---

[1]For the agreement, *E.I.I.F.*, 142-4.   In 1772-3 prices at the Duddon works varied from 30s. (a very low price, scarcely above the 1713 level) to 42s. ; *Duddon Accts.*, 1772-5, fols. 10, 185.   [2]Full account in *E.I.I.F.*, 391-414. [3]See p. 105 below.   [4]*Duddon Accts.*, 1755, fol. 6 : " pd John Wilkinson & Partner draw'g up Hearth at Duddon and Carrying down to Landing 3 Sows for Goatfield. £2.—2.—0 ".   [5]*E.I.I.F.*, 412.   [6]*E.I.I.F.*, 208-22.   [7]*E.I.I.F.*, 311-2.

four of the eight furnaces of 1750 then remained. But ironmaking elsewhere was expanding rapidly, and the national output rose from about 19,000 tons in 1720 to an estimated 68,000 tons in 1788, when charcoal furnaces were producing about one-fifth of the total. [1] In 1806 the output had risen to 260,000 tons ; but in 1803 the Furness contribution was only 2700 tons, [2] an almost negligible figure. Of the eleven charcoal furnaces in blast in 1806, three or four belonged to North Lancashire, which was ultimately to have the monopoly of charcoal-smelting, albeit in the hands of a single firm, the Newland Company.

Although the Furness iron trade was by-passed by the coke-smelting revolution, its main companies had not perished by 1806 because the demand for haematite ore, as well as for haematite pig for specialised uses, enabled them to benefit. The exportation of haematite became a major preoccupation of local ironmasters, and this trend is clearly reflected in the output figures for the Duke of Buccleuch's mines from the year 1743 [3] onwards. These ore pits, situated primarily at Whitriggs ("the Peru of Furness"), Lindal Moor, Lindal Cote and Crossgates, were in the Dalton area :

Table 2

Buccleuch mines in Furness, ten-yearly averages of annual outputs

Decade	Annual Average	Decade	Annual Average
1743-50	2818 tons	1781-90	12,491 tons
1751-60	5277 tons	1791-00	11,220 tons
1761-70	6810 tons	1801-10	9258 tons
1771-80	9802 tons	1811-20	4310 tons

These figures give only a general indication of the total ore output of the district, and may represent about 60 per cent. of it throughout the decades covered. Thus, at Stainton mine in the royalty of the Lords George and Frederick Cavendish, 4633 tons were raised in 1787 and 7000 tons in 1793, [4] suggesting that the Furness output approached 20,000 tons in the peak years before the date last-mentioned. Not all of this quantity was sold, for large stocks accumulated at the pits in the 'nineties, and in 1793 the Backbarrow Company had as much as 17,000 tons in hand. [5] Shortly before 1780 " the richest ore (was) found in immense

[1]Ashton, *op. cit.*, Appx. B, 235-6. Scrivenor, *History of the Iron Trade* (1854), 87-8. [2]*Gent. Mag.*, 1803, II, 929 (article on *Colton*) ; Scrivenor, *op. cit.*, 99. [3]The calculations of Edward Wadham, quoted by Lord E. Cavendish, account of the local iron trade in *Barrow Times*, 27.7.1878. Wadham was the mineral agent to the Duke of Buccleuch, and had access to the relevant documents.
[4]*Backbarrow MSS.*, General Ledger, 1787 (Barrow P.L.) ; cf. *E.I.I.F.*, 97-8. [5]In December, 1798, the Backbarrow Co.'s total accumulated ore stocks at Whitriggs amounted to 19,703 tons ; *Backbarrow MSS*, Ledger 103, fol. 482. *Vide* also *E.I.I.F., loc. cit.*

quantities " at a pit in Adgarley ; " one hundred and forty tons ",
said West, " have been raised at one shaft in twenty-four hours ". [1]
" New iron works " were then being carried on under the old
workings, and iron ore was being exported " in great quantities "
from Ulverston. [2] The horse gin, rag-and-chain pump and pick
and gad were the tools commonly employed, and in 1792 labourers
were paid 1s. 6d. a day for the heavy work of " teeming " water.
Timbered bell-pits or levels were wrought in the case of the shallower
mining, but shafts 40 to 45 yards in depth had been sunk early in
the following century. [3] Four men, with assistants on the surface,
could raise about 14 tons of ore a day at 2s. 3d. to 2s. 6d. a ton ;
but in 1809 they had to pay for their own tools, and for the maintenance of the horse at the gin. [4] These men often worked under
sub-contractors, and the wage of the miner cannot be computed
with certainty, for in 1795 one man was paid 1s. a ton " for
raising 50 tons ore " ; and as early as 1774 the ore was sold at 11s.
to 12s. a ton after all expenses (mining, royalty and carriage) were
paid. [5] According to Alfred Fell, the mining operations of the
Backbarrow Company at Whitriggs, for a period of 17 years prior
to 1766, gave a profit amounting to £1200 only, or less than £80
a year. [6] In 1774, however, the tonnage profit was at least 2s. [7]
and the saleable Furness output during the two decades following
must have brought an annual income of not less than £1500 to the
ironmasters. In 1778 the profit on Backbarrow pig-iron was just
over 37s. a ton [8] at the furnace, and even when any further expenses
are taken into account, the trade in haematite alone was hardly as
lucrative as this ; but it is evident that the latter was becoming a
most useful " standby ".

In about 1774 the Backbarrow Company was beginning to
export ore " in considerable quantity " to Chepstow and Cardiff,
and it has been stated that the declining iron industry of the Forest
of Dean used haematite exclusively. [9] The Duddon Company
was sending it to Cheshire in 1750, [10] and the ironmasters of South
Yorkshire are known to have used Furness ores from time to time. [11]
By 1790 local firms were offering small lots of haematite pig to
south-western and Cheshire buyers as bait, in order that they might
obtain orders for iron ore. [12] At the end of the century, John Wilkinson of Brymbo and Bersham was one of the most notable of the

[1]West, *Guide to the Lakes* (1780 ed), 40. [2]*Op. cit.*, 35, 40. [3]*Backbarrow
MSS.*, Ledger, 1792, fol. 545 ; E.I.I.F., 84, 87 ; Dickson, R. W., *Agriculture of
Lancs.* (1815), 73-4, which gives the best contemporary account (c.1809) of local
mining. [4]Dickson, *loc. cit.* [5]*Backbarrow MSS.*, Gen. Ledger, April, 1795 ;
Antiquities (1774), 17.
[6]E.I.I.F., 87. [7]*Antiquities*, 1774, *loc. cit.* [8]Cost table, E.I.I.F.,
236. [9]E.I.I.F., 92, 319 ; Jenkins, Rhys, *Trans. Newcomen Soc.*, VI, 1 sq.
[10]See p. aa above. [11]Baker, H. G., *Trans. Newcomen Soc.*, XXIV (1943-5),
114. [12]E.I.I.F., 311.

Backbarrow Company's ore customers, and the great ironmaster (whose father had worked at Backbarrow, and whose country residence at Castle Head lay in the immediate region) obtained some quantities of haematite pig from the same source.[1] Among other well-known iron firms to receive local haematite or pig-iron were Jonathan Walker and Co. of Rotherham (ore), John Cockshutt of Wortley Ironworks (pig), and William Lewis of Pentyrch Works, Cardiff (pig). Thomas Eyton of Bodvary Forge, Denbigh, bought pig and plates ; John Miers of Neath, John Hayton of Giveraylt Wire Mill, and William and John Smalley of Dolgelly bought pig-iron from Backbarrow ; while Messrs. Gaskell and Bell of Dovey furnace, Robert Thompson of " Abby Tintern " and James Davies and Co. of Upper Redbrook (Mon.) were purchasers of Stainton or Whitriggs ore, as were Harford, Partridge and Co. of Monmouth.[2] The quantities involved were never large, but the local produce had widely recognised uses for special purposes. Between one-third and one-half of the haematite from Furness pits was still taken by the ironmasters of the district, and the Duddon partners were using local ores in their " Argyll " (Goatfield) furnace in Scotland,[3] while the Newland Company, who in 1799 acquired an important new mining concession in the parish of Pennington,[4] appear to have used Furness haematite exclusively at their Bonaw furnace. By about 1809, when Dickson was making his agricultural survey of Lancashire, the produce of the local mines was " shipped for Wales, Carron and other places ",[5] and in 1807, 11,202 tons of haematite were sent from the port of Ulverston.[6]

These particulars will show that although the Furness iron-masters were left behind by the coke-smelting revolution, they nevertheless aided its progress and working ; firms throughout Britain were fully alive to the value of the haematite as a mixing component, and Dickson commented that it sometimes yielded " sixteen or seventeen hundredweights of metal to the ton, and the worst ten or twelve ".[7] It was therefore advantageous to transport the ore over long distances, and it was no accident that towards the end of the eighteenth century the town of Ulverston improved its sea approaches by the construction of a short canal and elongated harbour, and the Newland Company adapted the small port of Barrow—a point now within the great modern town of that name—by building an ore quay there to facilitate the work of loading vessels.[8] During the wartime and immediate post-war

[1]*Backbarrow MSS.*, Gen. Ledger and Journal, 1798-9, and do., 1800-1, Barrow P.L. (Z. 196).
[2]*Backbarrow MSS.*, loc. cit.   [3]*Loc. cit.*   [4]In the royalty of Lord Mun-caster, lord of the manor of Pennington ;   *Mills v. Muncaster*, Barrow P.L.
[5]*Op. cit.*, 74.   For Cumberland export to Carron, *vide V.C.H. Cumberland*, II, 89,
[6]*An Account of the Imports, Exports and Coastways Supplies of the Port of Ulverston*, Anno. 1807, repr. Dickson, *op. cit.*, 630.   [7]*Op. cit.* 73.   [8]*Vide* pp. 88-9 below.

years, however, the trade is believed to have suffered badly,[1] and the commerce of Ulverston and district did not improve until the late eighteen hundred and twenties.

There can be no doubt that the increasing demand for iron engendered by the Industrial Revolution enabled a technically backward local industry to survive long after coke-smelting had become general, although, as has been implied elsewhere in these pages,[2] the district's resources of mineral, woodland, water-power and water transport were important factors in this survival. The district produced few ironmasters, technicians or capitalists of note; the great ironmaster John Wilkinson received some early training at Backbarrow,[3] but after William Rawlinson had gone to his grave in 1734,[4] and after the main enterprises had become firmly established, local ironmaking remained in the hands of a few families. The " Gentlemen Ironmasters " of Furness were exactly what that title implied; landed gentry and members of the squirearchy who tended their furnaces, forges and coppice woods much as representatives of the same social class, in other parts of England, tended their farms.[5] Local records[6] throw an occasional fitful light on their more intimate activities. The Newland Company (later, Harrison, Ainslie and Co.) was the only eighteenth-century enterprise of the neighbourhood to last throughout the nineteenth century, and to play a part in the flurry of action which marked the middle years of the latter. The proprietors of this firm, however, rose to local importance and affluence as ore merchants, although their charcoal furnaces remained in use through the period covered by this study. The Backbarrow furnace was acquired by them in 1818, and the Duddon furnace in 1828,[7] after which dates the companies of those names ceased to exist.

---

[1]Cavendish, Lord E., *loc. cit.*; "In 1804 a long period of slackness seems to have set in, and there was no great recovery until 1825 . . . there must have been many at that time who thought that the Furness iron trade would never recover ".
    [2]See p. 24 above.   [3]*E.I.I.F.*, 214; *vide* also Dickinson, H. W., *John Wilkinson, Ironmaster* (1914), for a fuller story.   [4]William Rawlinson's death may have marked the end of the Quaker influence in local ironmaking; his eldest son Thomas, the Invergarry adventurer, " conformed to the established church "; Foster, note in genealogy of *Rawlinson of Graythwaite* etc., *Lancs. Families.*   [5]The Knotts of Rydal and Coniston (Newland Co.) were 16th century tradespeople who had risen into the ranks of the gentry; Armitt, M.L., *Rydal*, 341. The Machells, extensive landowners (MS. *Land Tax Assessments*, 1746, 1790-) were squires and justices in the Colton district and in Cartmel; pedigrees, Bardsley, *op. cit.*, 119-20. Their firm showed " a want of enterprise " towards the end of the 18th century; *E.I.I.F.*, 264-5. The Harrisons of Coniston Waterhead were also considerable landowners; Brydson, A. P., *Two Lakeland Townships*, 104n., and *Land Tax Assessments*.   [6]E.g., journal entries in *Backbarrow MSS.*, Ledger E., 1795 (Barrow P.L.); the *Diary of Edward Jackson*, 1775 (ed. Casson, T. E.), *C, & W.* (NS), XL, 1940; and Fell, John, in *C. & W.* (OS), XI, 368 sqq. The last-named sources tell something of the social life of the ironmaster-landowners, as do a few quotations in *E.I.I.F.*, Pt. IV, I, *The Masters.*   [7]*E.I.I.F.*, 209.

This study is concerned less with the biographies of individual industrialists than with the effect of ironmaking upon the local economy and upon local people in general. The introduction of large-scale charcoal-smelting after 1711 necessarily stimulated many small trades and industries. The iron furnaces themselves did not normally require the labours of more than a dozen men apiece ; but the work of carting and mining haematite, preparing and transporting charcoal, and shipping pig and bar iron, naturally occupied many more. Owners of parcels of woodland sold not only charcoal, but staves, shafts and props for the mines ; carpenters and saddletree makers made carts and transport gear, and large numbers of swill baskets were required for the furnaces ; tanners, who purchased bark from the coppice plantations, produced bellows-hides for forge and furnace and the leather for harness ; and small vessels were locally built by ship carpenters. For every dozen men employed at furnaces and forges, many scores were affected by the working of the latter. This process, or its effects, should not be exaggerated, for there was no marked or traceable influx of population into the district before about 1760,[1] when the iron industry had passed its peak ; but it is clear beyond doubt that more jobs or livelihoods were provided for a slowly growing population.[2] It also seems fairly certain that population growth and economic development were in some way interrelated. The small farmer or yeoman was able to add to his income by carting ore,[3] and the able-bodied labourer might have been able to earn a little more in woodland or mining occupations than would formerly have been possible. A slowly rising standard of living must have meant, in numerous cases, longer lives for children and adults.

This being said, there is no evidence that the vigorous exploitation of the Furness woodlands and mineral deposits brought " prosperity " to more than a small section of the local populace. William Stout wrote that North Lancashire was benefiting from the improvement of the iron trade in 1717, but that labour was " cheap ". Accordingly the ironmasters and woodowners seem to have enjoyed most of the benefits. There was always a keen demand for skilled forgemen and good head furnacemen, and these were aristocrats of labour, worthy to be imported long distances and given comparatively high rates of pay. In 1715 an unskilled worker received 7d. to 10d. a day,[4] and a craftsman carpenter 1s.[5] Thereafter local wages certainly did not rise as Dr. Gilboy has shown

[1]See pp. 105-9 below.   [2]For estimates of population growth, see p. 100 below.   [3]E.I.I.F., 302 ; " At the time when all the furnaces were working, large sums were paid for cartage of ore, iron and charcoal, and this important branch of the trade was one of considerable profit to the persons by whom the work was done, especially the farmers . . . A farm or piece of land, with so much carting guaranteed to the tenant, always brought in a high rent ".
    [4]Entries in G.L. and Account Book of the Leighton furnace, Backbarrow MSS., Barrow P.L.   [5]G.L. and Acct. Book cited.

wages to have risen in the country at large,[1] although there was an improvement at the end of the century. It should be added that the ironworkers tended to live in colonies near their workplaces (sometimes, it would appear, in company-owned cottages), that they received some perquisites, if only in the form of ale, and that some truck payment was made by the Backbarrow Company early in the century.[2]

Table 3.

Wages in the 18th Century Furness Iron Industry.[3]

Key: Fr. = founder. K. = keeper. F., 1st F., 2nd F. = filler, first filler or second filler. B.S. = bridge server.

Occupations are given as entered in account books.

Leighton Furnace, 1715	Duddon Ironworks 1750	1775	Backbarrow Furnace 1791	1795	1800	1801
Fr. 21s. 6d.	Fr. 13s.	K. 12s.	Fr. 10s. 6d.	Fr. 10s. 6d.	Do.	12s.
K. 12s.	K. 10s.	K. 11s.	—	1st F. 8s.	9s.	10s. 6d.
1st F. 7s.	1st F. 8s.	1st F. 7s.	F. 7s.	1st F. 8s.	9s.	10s. 6d.
2nd F. 5s. 4½d.	? 7s.	B.S. 11s.	F. 7s.	2nd F. 7s. 6d.	9s.	10s. 6d.
	2nd F. 5s. 6d.		F. 7s.			
			B.S. 8s.			
General labour at furnaces. Leighton, 1715 5s. to 6s. 4½d.	Do. Duddon 1750 6s.	Do. Duddon 1775 6s.	General labour in the Ulverston district, 1772 1s. 2d. to 1s. 6d. per diem.			General labour at ore mines, 1792 C. 1s. 6d. per diem.

[1]Gilboy, E. W., *Wages in Eighteenth Century England*, 182; " Selecting 9d. as the base, median wages for the whole country rose practically 133 per cent. from 1700 to 1790. One third of the rise took place in the first 30 years of the century, and wages then remained the same for the next 30. It was in the last 30 that the greater part of the upward swing occurred." [2]Var. refs. in *G.L.* [3]Figs. from *Acct. Book of the Leighton Furnace*, entries for 1715; *Duddon Accts.*, 1750, fol. 93 (17 weeks' blast); 1775, fol. 69 (two blasts of 20 and 24 weeks, 1775-6); *Backbarrow Acct. Book*, 1792, fol. 494, jnl. entry, Nov. 1791; and *E.I.I.F.*, 295, who gives further examples from volumes which are now presumed to be missing.

These lagging wage-rates are not altogether a symptom of a dying or declining industry ; the Duddon wages of 1750, a year when the industry was flourishing, show little improvement over those paid at Leighton in 1715. In the second half of the century several furnaces were demolished, and there was presumably no shortage of suitably skilled men. The slow rise of the Backbarrow wages for the 'nineties was attributed by Alfred Fell to the " dearness of provisions ",[1] and he may well be right, but it should be added that in 1792, Furness quarrymen could earn as much as £50-£60 a year,[2] more than twice the income of the furnace fillers. It would seem, on the whole, that the ironmasters got away lightly in the matter of labour costs, and that their activities did little to raise wage-levels in the district.

To sum up : the Furness charcoal iron industry, aided by Quaker investment, collaboration and possibly technical knowledge, made great strides between 1711 and 1718, and further great advances between about 1746 and 1756. Its chief proprietors learned the art of combination against the woodowners. They disposed of their pig and bar iron to merchants in the Severn ports, who doubtless resold it to industrialists in South Wales and the south-west Midlands ; but as charcoal became more expensive, and national competition keener, they were obliged to export haematite for mixing with poorer-quality ores. After its early progress, the local industry tended to stagnate, and to be run on traditional lines by established families of gentry. Only one of the eighteenth-century firms survived into the mid-nineteenth century. Nevertheless, Furness played its small part in paving the way for greater developments elsewhere, although its workpeople were not paid very high wages by the ironmaster " colonisers " of this hitherto undeveloped district.

[1]*E.I.I.F.*, 295.   [2]See p. 43 below.

CHAPTER III

THE SLATE, COPPER AND TEXTILE INDUSTRIES OF FURNESS IN THE LATE EIGHTEENTH AND EARLY NINETEENTH CENTURIES

1. SLATE

By the time of the Napoleonic Wars, the slate-quarrying industry of High Furness ranked next in importance to the haematite ore and iron trades of the district. In 1807, 11,202 tons of iron ore and 682 tons of pig and bar iron were exported coastwise through the Ulverston Canal, and 11,372 tons of slate,[1] the latter coming mainly from quarries in the neighbourhood of Kirkby-in-Furness. There were numerous quarries at Coniston and Tilberthwaite, which sent their slate through the small port of Greenodd on the River Leven, and consequently the output of the whole district, in peak years, must have been considerably higher than the export figure given. More men were employed in slate-getting than in mining iron ore or in working at iron furnaces, and the former occupation became a comparatively well-paid one in the conditions of wartime and industrial expansion in south Lancashire and the Midlands. It had more influence upon the movements of people within the district than did ironmaking,[2] in the sense that it led to new settlement near the quarries.

This industry owed much of its progress to geographical position. Although the Silurian blue and green slates, of Coniston and Kirkby respectively, were of high quality and were suitable for a variety of roofing and other purposes, the fragile produce could best be carried by sea. Kirkby lay on the coast, and the quarry-occupiers of Coniston could reach the shipping of the Leven estuary *via* Coniston Water and the Crake Valley.

Slate was sent from Furness shores in the late seventeenth century, and it is likely that work in the quarries continued in the first half of the eighteenth. By about 1750 most of the known quarries at Tilberthwaite, Coniston, Gaitswater (above Torver and due W. of Coniston) and Walna Scar were in working condition.[3] In that year the Kirkby quarries are also mentioned.[4] An estimate of 1772 indicated that about 2000 tons of slate *per annum* went through Greenodd—from the Coniston district—and a separate estimate of 1774 stated that a further 2000 tons passed through

---

[1]Dickson, *loc. cit.* [2]See especially p. 102 below. [3]See p. 16 above, f.n. 1 ; Collingwood, W. G., in *Memorials of Old Lancashire*, II, 179. [4]*Duddon Accounts*, 1750, fol. 86 ; " By Slate from Kirkby, 1000. £0. 10. 0 ".

Kirkby or Broughton-in-Furness *en route* to the sea. A total output of about 4000 tons may not be far wide of the mark ; the principal slate quarries of Coniston were then worked by the firm of William Rigge and Son, which alone sent away 1100 tons a year. The slate raised in the Coniston neighbourhood was carried to Greenodd at 6s. 10d. to 7s. 10d. a ton,[1] showing that the carters and boatmen, who carried iron, charcoal and birch besoms, had here an additional source of business and income.

In 1771 Lord John Cavendish purchased the Manor of Kirkby Ireleth from Lord Mulgrave,[2] thus making an important extension to the Cavendish estates in Furness ; and in 1773 the former was party to the purchase of slate quarries at Longlands in Kirkby.[3] Some twenty years later the fortunes of the Furness slate industry can be followed through the reports of Lord John's agent or steward, J. N. Robinson. Robinson wrote to his master in 1792 in the following terms : " The farmers of Slate Quarries are getting large quantities of slates, and the demand for them is so great, that there are scarce any on hand, I have had many applications to open new Quarries, which I have refused, as the present Quarries employ all the labourers in the neighbourhood at high wages. Some of those who are expert at riving and chopping slates making £50 or £60 a year each . . . Some of the farmers of those Quarries co'd well afford to make large advances in their rents, particularly for some of the Quarries on the Common of pasture which are eight in number, and the rent about £10 a year each . . . "[4]

Until about 1794 these quarries were thriving. In 1792 the best slates (known, according to Holt[5] and later writers, as " London " quality) were selling at between £3 and £4 a thousand ; the second best grade (" country " quality) at £2 10s. to £3 ; and the inferior types, or " tom " slates, at 30s. to £2 a thousand.[6] Since the Duddon ironworks proprietors had paid only 10s. for a thousand Kirkby slates in 1750, it is clear that both price and demand had increased greatly. As has been implied, the quarry sites at Kirkby were rented out to farmers or contractors, and in 1793 the profits of these persons were stated to be about double the rents paid. The half-yearly total rent accruing to Lord John Cavendish between Christmas, 1792 and midsummer, 1793 was £166 19s. 1d. In the latter year Thomas Rigge of Hawkshead (the son of the William Rigge alluded to above) transferred his activities from Coniston—" having been turned out of his farm of the mines of Conistone belonging to Sir Michl. le Fleming "—to Kirkby, where he was " glad to engage a quarry ".[7]

[1]*Antiquities*, 1774, 212 ; *Pennant*, 30. [2]*Antiquities*, 1774, 246. [3]*Holker MSS* : Deed of lease and release, 11/12 Mar., 1773 ; Lancs. R.O. [4]*Holker MSS.*, letter of J. N. Robinson to Lord J. Cavendish, 1.10.1792. [5]Holt, John, *Agric. Lancs.* (1794), 10. [6]*MS. letter*, Robinson to Cavendish, 26.10.92. [7]*MS. letters*, 14.1, 4.4.1793, 13.1.1794.

At this time, much of the Kirkby slate was carried coastwise to Liverpool and Scotland, some of it going round the coast to Hull and entering into competition with the produce of Yorkshire and Derbyshire quarries.[1] In 1794, however, this trade was faced with a severe rebuff. Pitt's wartime government announced its intention of imposing a tax of 10s. a ton on slates carried coastwise. Thomas Rigge, as the leading slate merchant of the district, reacted rapidly and wrote to Lord John Cavendish urging him to communicate the protests of the quarry occupiers to the Speaker of the House of Commons. In 1795 it was complained that the duty of £20 for every £100 of the value of all slates carried coastally (imposed by an Act of 34 Geo. III and taking effect from 5th July, 1794), was causing " almost a total stagnation in the trade " ; the sales of slate had become " a mere trickle ". Rigge and his colleagues memorialised Pitt and attempted to interest Wilberforce in their plight, pointing out the injustice of a tax which put exporting quarries at a disadvantage compared with those situated inland. These protestations met with little immediate result, and in 1796 the local slate merchants had discharged " more than half their workmen, and have great quantities of slates on hand which they cannot sell ".[2]

It is thus clear that the stringencies of wartime affected the district badly, and, as is shown below, the quarrymen themselves liked neither Pitt nor the counter-revolutionary war which threatened them with pauperism or conscription. Between 1750 and 1794, however, the local extractive industries, haematite and slate, had made considerable strides. In the boom year of 1793 work was commenced on the excavation of the Ulverston Canal, planned in anticipation of an increasing ore and slate export, and its promoters discussed the construction of a road from Kirkby-in-Furness to the canal itself.[3] William Close, in his 1805 edition of West's *Antiquities of Furness,* claimed that the total slate output of the district was then about 25,000 tons *per annum,* [4]a figure which may be accepted as credible if it is assumed that the quarries had recovered their trade in the early years of the new century. They had certainly done so by 1809-10, when the agricultural reporter R. W. Dickson visited Furness ; but here again, the word " prosperity " is not to be used lightly, for if wages and other incomes were rising, so were prices, and the quarrymen were apt to be turbulent.

[1]*Holker MSS.* ; *Memorial of Slate Merchants* (1795) ; *MS. letter,* Robinson to Lord J. Cavendish, 21.2.1794.
[2]*Holker MSS.* : Robinson to L.J.C., 10.2., 21.2.1794 ; Rigge to L.J.C., 3.3.1794 ; Robinson to L.J.C., 6.2.1795, 14.3.1795 ; Rigge to Cavendish, 30.6, 25.12.1795 ; Cavendish to Rigge (undated) ; *Memorial, cit.* [3]*Mins.* U.C. Co. (Minutes of the Ulverston Canal Co.), 4.6.1798, 10.11.1802. [4]*Antiquities,* 1805, Close's Supplement, 411.

The industry suffered badly between 1794 and 1801 ; and in 1800, according to the Lakeland antiquary Alexander Craig Gibson (1813-74), the quarrymen and miners of High Furness took part in a bread riot which seems unusually large in scale even by eighteenth-century standards. Quarrymen from Yewdale, Tilberthwaite, Coniston, Torver and Kirkby marched upon the town of Ulverston and emptied the stocks of warehouses, distributing flour to local womenfolk and acting throughout in a disciplined and organised fashion. Their object, wrote Gibson, was " not spoliation but warning ".[1] A similar body of quarrymen and others soon after-wards organised an anti-conscription demonstration, Ulverston being once more the scene of the excitement. The magistrates, who were sitting to arrange the militia ballot for the year, were put to flight ; but not before one of their number had been suspended head downwards through an open window by his ankles. A leading demonstrator carried a club carved with the likeness of a head and entitled " Charley Fox the Peace Maker ". Gibson's account of this event suggests that the large bodies of organised workpeople then employed in quarrying had discarded some of the insularity of the peasant dalesman, and were showing a clearcut attitude to political developments.[2]

R. W. Dickson's account of Furness quarrying, published a few years later, shows that a large labour force was working in the former in about 1809. There were three quarries on Kirkby Moor, at one of which was installed an iron railway for running the slates down to a wharf, and several others on Gawthwaite Moor ; going further into High Furness, at least seven quarries were to be seen at Tilberthwaite, three of which belonged to the firm of Woodburn and Coward.[3] At one of the Kirkby quarries the work was highly organised, and three teams of men were at work, the first raising the stone, the second splitting it, and the third dressing the slates, which were sold in the three grades already mentioned.[4] " The quarry-men here," observed Dickson, " get from 3s. to 4s., and sometimes 5s. a day." They had " constant work ". The occupiers of the quarries of Lord George Cavendish (viz. at Kirkby) paid 10s. a ton royalty on the best slates, 8s. on the second best, and 6s. on the " toms ". " This heavy tonnage rate," went on Dickson, " seems to have had the effect of lessening the demand for this kind of slate in other parts of the kingdom very much : and Mr. Woodburn jun. observed, that in consequence of it, the Welsh and other slate dealers had been able to undersell them."[5] In Tilberthwaite, Sir Daniel Fleming exacted only 3s. 4d. a ton royalty on the best slates, and 2s. on the seconds, while at Gawthwaite " they do not pay a tonnage

[1]*Hist. Soc. L. & C.*, XXI, 1869, 49. Gibson obtained the details of this story from one or more of the participants, many years after the riot had taken place. [2]*Op. cit.*, 51-9. [3]Dickson, R. W., *Agric. of Lancashire* (1815), 74-7. [4]Dickson, *op. cit.*, 74. [5]*Op. cit.*, 76.

duty on the quantity of slate raised, but pay a certain stipulated rent for the liberty of the royalty ".[1] At other Tilberthwaite quarries, the liberty of working them was " paid for to Tilberthwaite ", as there was no manor, " at the rate from £100 to £150 per annum ".[2]

Dickson provided little else of statistical or other interest ; prices of the slate (the precise year being omitted) ran from 40s. to 50s. a ton, and one quarryman in Tilberthwaite could raise " nearly a ton of slate per day, when the metal falls out well, for which he is paid from 2s. 6d. to 3s. 6d."[3] These estimates show, firstly, that the prices of the best grades of slate had not risen greatly since 1794, when best green slates had been sold at 42s. to 45s. a ton,[4] and, secondly, that royalties in Cavendish property, as sometimes happened subsequently, were apt to bulk large in the costs of slate and haematite merchants.[5] Thirdly, wages do not appear to have risen since the commencement of the French wars, but were still remarkably high in comparison with agricultural wages.

A directory of 1818 stated that at Hawkshead Mr. Thomas Rigge, " a most respectable merchant ", worked the principal quarries in that district (i.e. Coniston), and had " several sloops constantly employed in the carriage of it from Penny Bridge . . . to almost every principal seaport town in England and Ireland, whence it is forwarded into the inland counties by the canals . . . lately a quantity of it has been shipped to the West Indies ".[6]

The rapid town-building of the Industrial Revolution was a major stimulus to local quarrying, which remained an important occupation in High Furness through much of the nineteenth century. In 1828 there were at least thirteen firms in occupation of eighteen Furness quarries, scattered through the fells as far as Seathwaite, and in that year some 10,000 tons of their produce passed through the Ulverston Canal.[7] But shipping records for 1832 show that more than half as many ships left " Ireleth and Angerton " (probably Kirkby Pool, the anchorage for slate vessels taking on the metal from Kirkby quarries) as left the port or canal of Ulverston,[8] and much of the Coniston slate went through Greenodd on the Leven.

---

[1]*Loc. cit.* [2]*Op. cit.*, 77. [3]*Loc. cit.* [4]*Holker MSS.*, letter, Robinson to Lord J. Cavendish, 10.2.1794. [5]The Cavendish family owned iron mines at Stainton, from which they drew royalties of 1s. 6d. in the ton in the 18th century ; *Backbarrow MSS.* It should be added that this was the charge imposed by the Buccleuch or Montagu families at the Dalton mines.
[6]*Universal British Directory* (1818 ed., editors n.s. but probably a re-edition of Barfoot and Wilkes, 1794 ; copy in Lancs. R.O.), s.v. *Hawkshead.* The dating of this commentary is dubious, for Rigge had been turned out of his Coniston quarries in 1793 or earlier. [7]*Parson and White* (Directory, 1829), 721, 728. [8]*MS. Abstracts, Inspections of Ports* etc. (*Port Inspections*), s.v. *Lancaster*, fol. 342 ; H.M. Customs & Excise Library, London. See also p. 93 below.

Hence the total output of the district was probably still in excess of 20,000 tons. In 1831, " 200 labourers, 20 years of age " were employed " in the slate quarries of Leathwaite (*sic*) and Low and Middle Quarter " in the parish of Kirkby Ireleth, and " about 100 " at Church Coniston, Lowick, Osmotherley, Satterthwaite and Torver. [1]

Such figures seem puny enough when compared with the great numbers of workpeople and volumes of produce in the industrialised areas not many miles away. But two to three tons of slate roofed a cottage or house ; and it is probable that in this great age of economic development, five to ten thousand houses each year, throughout England, were covered with the results of Furness industry.

2. COPPER

In the sixteenth and seventeenth centuries the Company of Mines Royal worked copper mines at Keswick and Coniston, this industry suffering a severe blow at the time of the Civil War. In 1687 there was some attempt to re-start the mining, [2] and some ten years later a partly Quaker group known as the Royal Mines Copper (1697) took over the sites and leases of the old Mines Royal at Caldbeck, Keswick and Coniston. [3] In 1709, however, there was little or no activity in this field at Coniston. [4] Eighteenth century references to the industry are scanty, and contemporary writers make few allusions to it. On the other hand, it is likely that the Bristol Brass and Copper Company of 1705, with which the Champions were connected, [5] obtained some of its supplies from Coniston ; and in 1714 the Backbarrow Company sent a small quantity of copper ore to Abraham Darby I through their agent Samuel Milner, the consignment going *via* Penny Bridge to Chepstow. [6]

Thereafter the industry appears to have been prosecuted on a small scale and in fluctuating fashion, a further reference occurring in 1758 when the Macclesfield Copper Company (Charles Roe and

---

[1]*Census of* 1831, *Enumeration Abstracts*, notes, p. 292. *The Land Tax Assessments* (Lancs. R.O.), list for Kirkby Ireleth, 1831, shows that there were eight quarry occupiers at Kirkby in 1830-1, paying rentals of £34 to £187 *per annum*.
[2]*H.M.C., Fleming (MSS.* of S. H. Le Fleming Esq., of Rydal Hall (1890)), 12*th Rept.*, Appx., Pt. VII, 1954-, 202 ; *vide* also Collingwood, W. G., *The Keswick and Coniston Mines in* 1600 *and later*, in *C. & W., XXVIII*, 1928, p. 3. [3]Raistrick, A., *Trans. Newcomen Soc.*, XIV, 1934, 128. [4]Collingwood, *op. cit.*, 4. [5]Latimer, *Annals of Bristol in the* 18*th Century*, 66-7, 289, 362, 368 ; Raistrick, *Quakers in Science and Industry*, 191. [6]*Backbarrow MSS., G.L.*, 143, 313, 353, e.g. "Samuel Milner Dr to Acct of the Furnace in the sum of £16 for fft of 20 tuns of Copper Oar from Penny Bridge to Chepstow at 16 s. per tun."

partners) took the lease of a mine at Coniston from Sir Michael le Fleming. Between 1758 and 1767 a total of 904 tons of ore was raised at this mine, Sir Michael receiving a royalty of one-twelfth, amounting to £376. The Macclesfield partners, however, seem to have encountered drainage difficulties, and laid out a large sum on making a sough or level. In 1759, meanwhile, Anthony Tissington of Alfreton was the lessee of " copper and other mines in Tilberthwaite " and copper and lead mines in the manors of Hawkshead and Egton-cum-Newland, acquiring at the same time the right to build a quay and warehouse at Greenodd[1] (near Penny Bridge, and at the mouth of the River Crake). But although Coniston copper, like the local resources of coppice woodland, attracted men of business from afar, these activities brought little in the way of striking result, and after his visit to the district in 1772 Pennant commented that the Furness copper trade was in a state of decline.[2] The Macclesfield Copper Company of Charles Roe and colleagues appears to have undertaken little local mining between 1770 and *circa* 1792. At this last date the company had lost an important source of copper ore supply at the Parys Mine in Anglesey. Accordingly there is evidence of renewed activity at Coniston in 1792, over 283 tons of ore being held in stock there by the Macclesfield partnership ; but three years later this company offered to surrender its lease of the mine because it " has for some time past been so unproductive that it has been determined to discontinue the working ".[3]

Soon afterwards, however, there were further attempts to win the local ore, and it is unlikely that the mines ceased working altogether. Dickson reproducing information obtained *circa* 1809, remarked that Furness copper had been met with " only in two or three places, and not very abundantly even in these ". The oldest mine was at Coniston, and there were others at Muckle Gill and Hartriggs, the Muckle Gill mine having been " established about five years " by the Cheadle (Staffs.) firm of Watkins, Borrow and Atkinson, whose workmen raised about two and a half tons of ore a week. The ore was washed and stamped on the spot, and sent into Staffordshire " to be reduced into metal, and formed into wire and sheets for coppering the bottoms of ships ". Twelve to fifteen men were employed underground, and eight or ten on the surface, the miners themselves working a six-hour day. Of the surface-workers, the ore-breakers received 13s. a ton, the box-men 1s. 6d. a day, and boy workers 8d. a day. The Coniston mine, regarding which Dickson seems to have collected little information, was " managed in much the same manner ", and the produce " sometimes sent to Cheadle ".[4]

[1]*E.I.I.F.*, 307. [2]*Pennant*, 30. [3]Collingwood, *op. cit.*, 31-2; for Roe, *vide* Chaloner, W. H., *L. & C.*, LXII, 1950-1, and LXIII. [4]Dickson, *op. cit.*, 71.

These particulars indicate that a relatively small labour force was employed in the copper-mining industry of High Furness between 1758 and 1809 ; and mining in Coniston did not assume important dimensions until about 1835, when the firm of Barratt developed it considerably, and when migrants from a distance began to move into that district. [1]

3. TEXTILES

During the eighteenth century every Furness parish had its scattering of domestic textile workers. In High Furness, the spinning of woollen yarn for the Kendal and local markets entered into the domestic economy of many yeoman households ; [2] but although the labours of women and children enabled such families to subsist more satisfactorily than would have been possible had they been purely dependent upon agriculture, there is little evidence of any marked specialisation of the textile trades in the district. In 1754, Ulverston weavers were producing their " camlets and serges ", [3] but the weaving colony there was not large. [4] At Broughton-in-Furness, less than twenty years later, the principal commodity brought to the market was " woollen yarn spun by the country people ", the annual return on the sale of this article being over £4000 per annum. [5] Farther into the fell district, the families of Hawkshead statesmen engaged in " a considerable manufacture of woollen yarn, spun by hand . . . the principal part of which was sold in the Hawkshead market to the Kendal manufacturers ", [6] and at Ambleside in 1772 the inhabitants were " much employed in knitting stockings for Kendal market ; in spinning woollen yarn, and in making thread to weave their linsies ". [7]

Pennant, perhaps significantly, made no reference to Furness textile industries after his visit to the neighbourhood in 1772, and at about the same time West asserted that in Ulverston and environs, imported clothes had supplanted home-made or locally manufactured clothes. [8] The number of weavers in Ulverston did however greatly increase after 1780, [9] a possible result of the

[1]See pp. 139, 222 below.   [2]Wordsworth, *Guide to the Lakes* (1945 ed.), 80 ; " The family of each man, whether *estatesman* or farmer, formerly had a twofold support ; first, the produce of his lands and flocks ; and secondly, the profit drawn from the employment of the women and children, as manufacturers ; spinning their own wool in their own houses (work chiefly done in the winter season), and carrying it to market for sale . . . . "   [3]*Dr. Pococke's Travels* (Camden Soc.), II, 1.   [4]Fourteen weavers were married at the Ulverston parish church between 1755 and 1780, out of 328 other persons whose occupations were given in the marriage records.   [5]*Antiquities*, 1774, 212.   [6]Apparently retrospective statement in Baines, *Lancashire*, 1836, 11, 674 ; *vide* also *Universal British Directory*, 1818, 247.
[7]*Pennant*, 36.   [8]*Antiquities*, 1774, 22.   [9]The Ulverston marriage registers for the period 1781-1806 suggest that weavers had then become the most numerous handicraftsmen, with 48 entries out of 419 for all other trades and professions. They had a colony in Ratten Row ; bap. & bur. registers, Ulverston P.R. (*op. cit.*).

establishment of factory industry elsewhere, and a reflection of the needs of a growing local population. During the half century before that date, there are comparatively few references to other Furness textile trades and occupations ; isolated chapmen occur at Broughton and Hawkshead, and the occupation of " flaxman " appears in Ulverston, which was developing a small linen industry. [1] By about 1790, however, when Barfoot and Wilkes were compiling their *Universal British Directory*, the manufactures of the latter town included " cotton, check, canvas and hats ". [2] By that time at least four small cotton-spinning factories had been established in Ulverston.

The date of appearance of the earliest Furness textile factory has not been satisfactorily ascertained, although the year 1781 has been suggested. [3] In or about 1782 there were cotton mills at Backbarrow (near the site of the smelting furnace) and at Cark-in-Cartmel, the former one having been rebuilt from the ruins of a corn and paper mill standing on the bank of the River Leven. By 1790 the firm of Birch, Robinson and Walmsley had " two large cotton mills " at Backbarrow, and individuals bearing these names were among the early subscribers to the Ulverston canal project. [4] The Cark cotton mill was built by James Stockdale " about the year 1782 " together with cottages, workshops, engine houses, tail and other races, " and no fewer than nine bridges or archways, destroying entirely the rural appearance of the village . . . " [5] Stockdale, who was John Wilkinson's brother-in-law, [6] was in correspondence with James Watt in 1785 regarding the erection of a large steam engine, [7] and his local-historian-grandson, the author of *Annals of Cartmel*, implied that a Watt engine was in fact installed at the Cark Mill. [8] The 1790 Directory of Barfoot and Wilkes, however, indicated that the mill at Cark was operated by the firm of " Thackeray and Co." ; [9] and, in the words of Professor Ashton, " Thackeray, of Manchester, was one of the most determined of pirates, and, in addition to the engine in his own works, had constructed another for James Stockdale . . . " [10] In other words, the latter, far from installing a steam engine of Watt's design, set up one which infringed the Scots engineer's patent, and Boulton and Watt were obliged to use the services of a spy or spies in order to

[1]Ulverston and Broughton, P. Registers. (*cit.*) ;   Handlist of *Richmond Wills*, 1748-92.   [2]Barfoot, J., and Wilkes, P., *Universal Brit. Directory*, IV (1794), 633 ; several of their references to Ulverston merely reproduce Pennant's material.   [3]White, Wm., *Furness Folk and Facts*, 83, which states that a cotton manufacture was started at Ulverston by Col. C. L. Mordaunt in 1781.
[4]*Barfoot & Wilkes*, 1790 ed., II, s.v. *Cartmel* ;   *Subscription Agreement* of Ulverston Canal Co., 29th Oct., 1792, repr. in Park, *Some Ulverston Records*, 18-9.   [5]Stockdale, *Annals of Cartmel*, 385.   [6]*Cartmel P.R.* ; William Wilkinson, the brother of John, married a Miss Stockdale.   [7]*Op. cit.*, 207.   [8]*Ibid.*   [9]*Barfoot & Wilkes, loc. cit.*   [10]*Iron and Steel in the Industrial Revolution*, 81, n. 1, quoting material from *Boulton and Watt MSS*.

" have Thackeray fast also " in the course of an episode which seems little less than fantastic.[1] None of the other cotton mills in the district used steam power until well into the following century.

The Ulverston cotton manufactories of 1789-90 were owned or operated respectively by William Briggs, William Warhurst,[2] John Kavanagh, and one Swindell, and at least two of these mills were old fabrics originally used for corn-grinding or leather manufacture. By 1799 the largest Ulverston mill was owned by William Warhurst, Joseph Procter, Robert Sandys and Joseph Green (all of that town) together with John Strickland of Rusland, who are mentioned as " partners in the manufacture of cotton " ; it stood at Lund Beck, and was later known as the Low Mill. In 1806 it was a four-storey building of 30 by 11 yards, with a wing twenty feet square ; water-driven, it had some 4700 spindles on 22 mules, with stretching and drawing frames and other gear.[3] It was perhaps typical of the smaller northern mills of the period. In that year the firm of Warhurst, Procter, Sandys and Co. had owned and were selling off two smaller mills in the Ellers, Ulverston, one of which had 2500 spindles on 27 spinning jennies, and the second a mere 13 jennies of 104 to 106 spindles each.[4] The Warhurst partnership, which included a number of local persons, had therefore operated a relatively ambitious little enterprise.

The much larger factory establishment at Backbarrow was offered for sale in 1807, when it was stated to be " now used for the spinning of Cotton, Flax and Tow". The premises consisted of three mill buildings, each equipped with a water wheel and four storeys high, of workshops for joiners, clock-smiths (who turned their skill to textile machine repair) and blacksmiths, an apprentice-house capable of accommodating 200, offices, a manager's house, and no fewer than " 80 comfortable substantial dwellings for the People employed in the above Works ".[5] This sizeable industrial colony became, less than ten years later, notorious for its ill-treatment of factory children. The rapid growth of the Backbarrow colony, " its inhabitants supported by employment at an iron-furnace and two cotton mills "[6] is reflected in the Colton parish registers and in the 1811 census particulars for Haverthwaite and Finsthwaite.[7] The mill property also included over 140 acres of arable and pasture land, as well as a small farm at Brow Edge, half a mile from the

---

[1] I am also indebted to Dr. W. H. Chaloner for independently supplied particulars. [2] Given as " Warris " by *Barfoot & Wilkes*
[3] *Lancaster Gazette*, advt. of sale, 4.1.1806 ; deeds of 11th & 12th Feb., 29th Mar., 1806, transcr. Park, *op. cit.*, 39-40. [4] *Loc. cit.* [5] *Notice of Sale*, 6.7.1807, Walker Collection of Advertisements now in possession of Mrs. Waghorn, Force Forge, Rusland (by courtesy of Mr. J. L. Hobbs). [6] Close, (MS.) *Itinerary* of Furness, fol. 67, [7] See p. 111 below, and Census of 1811, Abstract of Answers and Returns, p. 153.

works ; and the proprietors became improving agriculturalists, developing land reclaimed from the waste by the Cartmel enclosure of 1796-1809. [1]

One of the small factories in the Ellers, Ulverston, was sold to a flax-spinning partnership in 1806, and by 1813 it was owned by James Stockdale and others, being then purchased by Fell, Burton, and Co., bankers and flax spinners. [2] Meanwhile, another mill appeared at Penny Bridge before 1815, [3] making a total of seven such works in Furness and Cartmel in that year. Dickson, in writing of the district, confined himself to the remark that at Ulverston (c.1809) " there are large manufactures for the working of flax, as well as for making checks, in each of which a great number of persons are employed at the rate, in good times, of eighteen shillings a week " [4]. The size of the labour force employed cannot be estimated with accuracy, but it almost certainly did not exceed 500 persons as relating to the textile mills and establishments large and small (viz., in Furness and Cartmel together). Child apprentices had been used at the Backbarrow mill for some time before the 1816 *Committee on Child Employment* made its report, but numerous adults worked in the mills, as Dickson implies and the Ulverston parish registers testify. [5]

The story of the ill-treated children of the Backbarrow mills is now a well-known one. [6] One hundred and forty " apprentices " were working there in 1805, [7] and 111 in February, 1814, during the ownership of Messrs. Birch, Robinson and Walmsley. Between these two dates the work was irregular ; and the children, drawn from workhouses at Whitechapel, Liverpool and Brighton, were on at least one occasion turned astray to fend for themselves and to beg their way to their former parishes after the masters had " stopped payment ". Even so, if half the evidence can be believed, the children were little better off when working in the mills than when they were starving in comparative freedom. Working hours in 1816 were from 5 a.m. to 8 p.m. with a total time of one hour for meals ; but if the water supplied by the River Leven was insufficient to work two of the mills, then a night shift was introduced in one of them. There were no seats in the buildings, and according to the evidence of John Moss, a former apprentice master, several children had become crippled as a result of their labours. William Travers, the manager of the mill, who had worked there for " above thirty years ", said that he had " seen the children not very well off at

[1]Notice of sale, *cit.*, and Dickson, *op. cit.*, 281, 480. " Birch and Robinson " were still the proprietors in c.1809.
[2]Park, *op. cit.*, 50. [3]*Parl. Papers*, 1816, *III* ; *Sel. Cttee. on Children in Manufactories*, 184. This was at the site of the former Penny Bridge furnace, and was small. It became a bobbin mill. [4]Dickson, *op. cit.*, 629-30. [5]There are 46 references to cotton-spinners in the Ulverston P.R., 1801-10. [6]Cf. Hammond, J. L., & B., *The Town Labourer*, I, 148 sqq. [7]*Sel. Cttee., cit.*, 182 ; *MS. Minutes, Incorp. Guardians, Brighton, Sussex*, June 3-18, 1805, quoted by Webb, *Eng. Poor Law History*, Pt. 1, 202.

times", but attacked the character of Moss and his wife; he did not however succeed in rebutting much of the former employee's evidence. It may well be that Moss, angered by what he had seen, laid on the black strokes heavily enough, but Travers did not deny the length of the hours worked, nor that the children had been turned adrift to beg at a time of slack trade. Several witnesses forwarded written testimony that the chidren were " well treated ",[1] and it was claimed (for instance) that they received some education —but regarding this subject more is said elsewhere in these pages.[2] According to the incumbent of Finsthwaite, only six of the apprentices (out of about 150) died in seven years, and if this was true it cannot be said that the juvenile death-rate was abnormally high. On the other hand, the manufacturers had no reason to slaughter their charges wantonly.

About twenty children of local families also worked at the Backbarrow mills. These families were " very poor people and mostly Irish ", and the parents' complaints of the long hours worked were unavailing, if indeed any person did object to the magistrates. The Penny Bridge mill did not work such long hours " by an hour and more in a day ",[3] and it is plain enough that even at this late date, local people did not suffer their own children to work in the mills if they could avoid it. Apprentice labour was cheap and manageable, and the successive proprietors at Backbarrow[4] showed partiality to it for the reasons given. The mere fact that the use of apprentices persisted for several decades at certain mills shows that shortage of adult workers does not in itself explain the popularity of the system.[5]

Little or nothing is known of conditions in the Ulverston cotton mills. The manufactures of flax and cotton were still flourishing there in 1828, when Philip Hartley acquired the Low Mills, and when there were small factories at Beckside, Lowick Green and Spark Bridge. There were also four firms which manufactured linen in Ulverston in 1828, as well as three which manufactured checks and ginghams.[6] By 1836, when Baines published an edition of *The History of Lancashire*, two of the Ulverston mills were said by him to derive " their motion from the combined power of water and steam ", these being the Hartley mills alluded to. The industry,

---

[1]*Sel. Cttee.*, 182-3, 286 sqq.   [2]See p. 149 below.   [3]*Sel. Cttee*, 184-5.
[4]Until about 1812, the firm of Birch, Robinson and Walmsley ; for a number of years thereafter, Ainsworth, Catterall and Co. ; in 1837, Thomas and William Ainsworth. For details, Park, *Some Ulverston Records*, p. 7, 24-5.   [5]*Vide* the fragmentary *Colton Poor Law Accounts* (MS.), 18.6.1836, at Barrow P.L. and *Mins. Ulv. Gdns.* (MS), 7.4.1842, which indicates that overseers and Guardians were regarded as suppliers of cheap labour at these late dates. It should be added that many adult workers had then been employed at local mills for some decades, and the lack of trained hands surely cannot be advanced as an excuse by the most vehement anti-Hammondite.   [6]*Parson and White* (Directory) 1829, 721, 725-9.

however, was still a small one.   According to the Census returns of 1831, 207 persons in Furness and Cartmel (including 99 at Colton or Backbarrow, 38 in Ulverston, and 35 in Upper Holker) were employed in manufacture or machine-making,[1] and in 1835 there were four cotton mills in the Ulverston district employing 474 persons.[2]

The appearance of the local textile factories owed much to the availability of water-power in the form of the Lund and Newland becks at Ulverston, and the rivers Crake and Leven ; but these enterprises never struck very deep roots.   They could flourish in the water-wheel era, but when the nearness of coal supplies became a condition of the successful use of steam, this branch of industry, like that of charcoal iron-smelting, was by-passed.   By 1861 only one firm of cotton-spinners was left in Ulverston.[3]   A number of the small High Furness flax and cotton mills were turned over to the manufacture of bobbins during the early and middle decades of the nineteenth century, taking advantage of demand in Lancashire and Yorkshire.[4]

[1]*Census of* 1831, Enumeration Abstract, Vol. I (1833), pp. 291-2. [2]White, William, *op. cit.*, 83.   [3]Mannex, P., *Directory of N. Lancs* (*Mannex*), 1866, 408 ; *Census of* 1861, Occupation Tables, Vol. II, 645, when 166 Furness females were employed in cotton manufacture, evidently at the Ellers Mill of Messrs. Hartley in Ulverston.   [4]*Mannex*, 1866, 400 (Egton-cum-Newland), 432 (Satterthwaite), 437 (Colton), 438 (Nibthwaite).   For the early demand for bobbins, and alder poles for drying cotton yarn, *vide* Dickson, *op. cit.*, 437, 441, 443.

CHAPTER IV

FURNESS AGRICULTURE AND WOODLAND INDUSTRIES, 1746-1850

1. THE EIGHTEENTH CENTURY

During the late eighteenth and early nineteenth centuries, the agriculture of Plain Furness was devoted primarily to the production of wheat, oats, barley and potatoes, while that of High Furness was concerned mainly with the care of woodlands and the raising of sheep. The growing markets in other parts of Lancashire and the north led to increased exportation of produce from both parts of the district. High Furness, however, reacted notably to the demands of the iron industry, by the enclosure and cultivation of coppice woods, and here the market was a purely local one. But ships which came to local shores to take away bar or pig iron, and iron ore, did not necessarily restrict their cargoes to these goods, and the produce of the woodlands was not all turned into charcoal. Much of this produce, in the form of timber, poles, laths and hoops, was sent to external markets. In consequence, many a bare and unpromising piece of fell territory became comparatively valuable land, rewarding the labours of the more affluent yeomen and landowners with a steady income. Plain Furness, by contrast, was a fertile area on which fairly good cereal crops could be grown, and high farming there made considerable progress during the first half of the nineteenth century, until its agriculture was in the vanguard of that in Lancashire as a whole. Lancashire standards were not of course outstandingly high, but there was more progressive farming in the county than is sometimes realised.[1]

Throughout the period under review, the district was *par excellence* one of the small yeoman (or statesman) and farmer, occupying thirty to forty acres of land. As has been shown, large landowners were few, and there was little change in the sizes or ownership of the main landed estates between 1750 and 1850 ; nor was there much extensive enclosure of commons, save in the sense that there was always an element of private (or non-parliamentary) enclosure of arable field and fell. Superficially, therefore, there are few signs of any of the "catastrophic" changes in agriculture which are commonly associated with this period. But at its commencement, and for many years afterwards, at least two-thirds of the population of Furness had some sort of stake in the land as cottagers,

---

[1]Cf. the agricultural reports of Holt, Dickson, Garnett, Rothwell and Binns, all cited elsewhere in these pages.

yeomen and small farmers, [1] and therefore any change in the balance of the various landowning or land-occupying grades becomes a matter of some consequence. As the eighteenth-century population of the district increased, [2] so, inevitably, there was greater competition for land and smallholdings ; as trade and industry extended the market for produce, and as there were more mouths to feed, so there would be a tendency to enlarge the area under cultivation ; and land itself increased considerably in value, [3] making it more and more difficult for the husbandman to acquire new parcels of land and stock of his own.

Furness, which received many immigrants of its own after about 1760, [4] was one of the rural areas of Lancashire which supplied the industrial towns with people, and it is therefore tempting to suggest that an original stimulus to the recruitment of town labourers was what one eminent historian [5] has called " the demographic upsurge ", or comparative over-population of the countryside. This, however, over-simplifies what was really a complex process, for the countryside, as in the case of North Lonsdale, West Cumberland and many of the Yorkshire dales, had its own small industries, and population tended to rise where these were well established. [6] The failure of these industries, together with any concentration of farming territory in fewer hands (not necessarily those of very large landowners), would play a part in uprooting country families. In much of the north of England, too, we are dealing not with the squire-tenant relationships of many a Midland parish, but with what was still in part a peasant economy without very great differentiation in the sizes of estates. But just as the study of agrarian life in the middle ages has been known to gain by the convenient division of the mediaeval peasantry into social classes or economic classifications—lower, middle and upper—so, in this case, we can talk of cottagers or smallholders, husbandmen and small yeomen, and the more affluent landholders.

Furness land tax assessment lists indicate that the numbers of cultivators or woodland occupiers did not increase greatly during the second half of the eighteenth century, but that any change in landholding by social groups was in the direction of an increase in the numbers of smallholders and cottagers with parcels of five acres or less ; mainly persons in or near towns and villages, but not invariably so situated, who were certainly not solely dependent on

---

[1]See pp. 4-6 above. [2]For an analysis, *vide Chapter Six* below. [3]See pp. 58, 68 below. [4]See especially p. 105 below. [5]Dr. J. D. Chambers, in discussion with the writer. [6]*Vide* for instance Miss M. Slack's thesis on population in the Yorks. dales (*cit.*, p. 113) ; " it was in the industrial parishes that the baptisms rose sharply in the eighteenth century ", e.g. Addingham, Bolton Abbey (small textiles), Keighley and Kildwick (small textiles and mixed trades), and Lindale and Bentham. Miss Slack shows evidence of immigration in Gargrave, Clapham, Ingleton and Thornton-in-Lonsdale (*ibid.*). For Furness, particularly Dalton and Kirkby Ireleth, see *Chapter Seven* below.

husbandry for a livelihood.   At the other end of the scale (a very modest one, it will be noticed, with only two estates assessed at over £5), a scattering of larger yeoman or other estates appeared between 1746 and 1790.   The total number of rated properties increased by very little :

Table 4

Land Tax Assessments ; Numbers and Ratings of Properties.   4s. in the £
Distribution of rated properties

Year	District	Under 1s.	1s.-10s.	10s.-£1	£1-£5	Over £5	Totals
1746	11 divisions of Plain Furness.[1]	167	343	44	8	2	564
1746	12 divisions of High Furness[2]	115	484	34	9	—	642
	1746 totals	282	827	78	17	2	1206
1790	11 divisions of Plain Furness, as above	254	329	54	18	2	657
1790	12 divisions of High Furness, as above	173	363	48	12	—	596
	1790 totals	427	692	102	30	2	1253

As need hardly be said, the same divisions of parishes[3] are used for both years, and the total assessment moneys for each division often remained unaltered between 1746 and 1790.   While the sums levied on individual properties seem exceedingly low by comparison with those often imposed in Midland counties, they are not unlike the assessment figures for a similar area like the county of Derbyshire, and are typical of North Lancashire.   The " acre equivalent " (amount of tax levied on the average per acre) was lower than the 9d. given by Mr. E. Davies as the equivalent for Derbyshire, and was approximately 4d. or even less.[4]   The 23 divisions of Furness accounted for in the above table cover more than nine-tenths of Furness proper, and to that extent give a fair idea of the changes in landholding over 44 years ; and it will now be in place to discuss some of the influences which caused the rather larger estates to appear.

---

[1]The township of Ulverston(e) is omitted, in order to give as true a picture of rural developments as possible.   Figs. from *Land Tax Assessments, N. Lonsdale (Holker MSS.)* and lists with the Clerk of the Peace, Lancs. R.O.
[2]*Ibid.*
[3]Hawcoat, Stainton, Dalton township, Upper and Lower Aldingham, Dendron with Gleaston, Leece, Bardsea, Much Urswick, Little Urswick and Broughton (Plain Furness), and Lowick, Torver, Blawith, Nibthwaite, East and West Colton (counted as one division), Hawkshead, Claife, Satterthwaite, Monk Coniston with Skelwith, Church Coniston, Seathwaite and Dunnerdale (High Furness).   [4]Davies, E., *The Small Landowner,* 1780-1832, *Ec. H. R.,* I, 1927, i, Table VII.   This authority of course took the entire acreages of counties into view.   The Furness figure is deduced from the known sizes of holdings at Newbarns, Salthouse and Hawcoat.

To take High Furness first : the demand for charcoal for the iron furnaces naturally caused the woodlands to increase in value, but the tenants of local manors originally had no right to the timber growing on customary estates.[1] In or about the year 1731, however; the customaryholders of Broughton, Seathwaite and Dunnerdale entered into a dispute with the lord of those manors, and an agreement was entered into between the parties that the several tenants should purchase the right of the wood growing on their estates, part of the purchase money to be applied to " pious and charitable " uses.[2] Hence these yeomen became woodowners. The fashion quickly spread, and in 1750 a commentator in *Aris's Birmingham Gazette*,[3] writing of North Lancashire and Cumbrian wood conservation, stated that " some Lords have sold the Woods growing, or that shall thereafter grow, upon the Customary Tenements within their Manors, to the owners of such Tenements, which encourages the Tenant to take the same care of improving their Woods as if it were on Freehold Land . . . " Land was actually turned from the plough " tho' Arable Ground is scarce, nothing like sufficient to supply them with Bread ".[4] A comparatively high proportion of the more substantial yeomanry of High Furness were, by 1748, owners of coppice woods and sellers of charcoal. In that year 52, and then a further 148, local woodowners signed the Penny Bridge Wood Articles (a statement that the signatories would undertake to sell charcoal only to the new ironworks at Penny Bridge)[5], and these persons were described by counsel in an ensuing legal examination as " nine-tenths of the woodowners in the country ".[6] Thomas West, writing about 1772, remarked that " the demands for coal, wood and timber for the mines are such, that land is daily setting off and enclosing for the purpose . . . the flocks of sheep thereby being greatly diminished ".[7] Pennant, after his visit to the district in the same year, observed of the woods that " . . . the owners cut them down in equal portions, in the rotation of fifteen years, and raise regular revenues out of them ; and often superior to the rent of their land, for freeholders of £15 or £25 *per annum* are known to make constantly £60 from their woods. The furnaces for these last sixty years have brought a great deal of wealth into this country ".[8] A reporter for the *Gentleman's Magazine* in 1803, one Statisticus, writing of the woodland district of Colton, remarked significantly that " the proprietors have ceased to breed sheep ",[9] thus appearing to confirm the correctness of West's forecast. The most mountainous hills were " private enclosures ", and being elevated too high for woodlands, had " become of little value, producing only ling, heath and savin ".[10]

[1]Cowper, H. S., *Hawkshead* (1898), 206-7. [2].*Public Charities*, 92, 97.
[3]21st Nov., 1750, quoted by Ashton, *Iron and Steel* etc., 16. [4]*Ibid.* [5]Copy in Barrow P.L. [6]*E.I.I.F.*, 152 sqq. The land tax lists for 1746 indicate that the owners were most numerous in the Crake Valley, Colton and Hawkshead, and were mainly persons in the 5s. to 10s. tax range. Myles Sandys of the Penny Bridge Furnace had lands in Satterthwaite. [7]*Antiquities*, 1774, xxxviii. [8]*Pennant*, 29. [9]*Gent. Mag.*, 1803, II, 1203. [10]*Ibid.*

But although the position of the sheep may have been threatened for a time, there were still 50,000 of these animals on the North Lancashire fells when Dickson made his survey of 1809-15.[1] The market for coarse wool must still have been considerable, and the local sheep afforded " mutton of a most excellent kind ". At Hawkshead there was then a fell sheep farm of 3000 acres[2] (suggesting that one of the local gentleman-woodowners was stocking his portions of the fell, or that some yeoman family had acquired an extraordinarily large area of common) and it is possible that the smaller yeomen felt the effects of privately arranged enclosures of the moorland common.[3] There was certainly disappearance of common family stock names from the parish registers and land tax lists of a moorland chapelry like Torver between 1760 and the end of the century, newcomers entering to occupy the holdings in a number of cases, and comparative engrossment of the still small holdings appearing in others.[4] This tendency was perceptible throughout the district. It did not as yet amount to the wholesale destruction of the statesman or yeoman, who was " far from extinct " in Dickson's day.[5] It may even have strengthened the position of the better-off members of this class.

The tree was as much a universal provider as the sheep—or the much-cited hog in the Chicago meat factory—and virtually everything about it was used to produce some article or means of employment. Birch and hazel, initially grown for charcoaling, gave

---

[1]*Op. Cit.*, 575-6.   [2]*Op. cit.*, 114 ; there were also several farms in the 100-300 acre range in the fells, but this is not remotely suggested by the land tax valuations. Common grazing rights were not taken into account.   [3]Cf. Cowper, *Hawkshead*, 207-8, where it is pointed out that much depended on the way in which the enclosures of fell were arranged. Moorland grazing rights were graduated in accordance with the sizes of flocks and the wintering capacity of farms. There are a few local instances of sale of or encroachment upon the commons during the 18th century ; e.g. Birk Knotts, Blawith, given in Brydson, *Two Lakeland Townships*, 186, Appx. VII (b) ; *Rec. Man. Muchland*, Torver Court Baron, 4th Oct., 1715 (tenants fined for encroachment on common—there must have been many such cases) ; and Stockdale, *Annals of Cartmel*, 197-8, 234-7, who gives copious documentary transcripts relating to encroachments on the Cartmel commons in 1757-8, 1775, and 1788.   [4]The 18th century population of Torver was between 150 and 200, and although a tiny example it is also a manageable one. Between 1690 and 1746 there was little change in the incidence of common names of inhabitants and land-holders assessed for church rates and land. In the latter year the average land tax assessment was 5s. on 41 rated properties with 37 separately distinguishable names (including 7 Atkinsons, 6 Parkes and 4 Wilsons). By 1790 there had been a considerable change ; there were 3 Parkes, 2 Atkinsons and 1 Wilson, and, as elsewhere in Furness, there was greater graduation in the sizes of holdings. Several persons then held comparatively large estates—a John Dixon (16s. 2½d.), a Parke (14s. 3d.) and an Atkinson (11s. 4½d.). A tanner, two gentlemen and two clergymen held parcels. The parish register shows that at least 36 outsiders had entered Torver between 1760 and 1792 ; but only 6 of these held land ; *Torver P.R.* 1599-1792 (*Lancs. P. R. Soc.*) and *B.T.* at Lancs R.O. for the remainder of the 18th century ; *Richmond Wills* ; *Land Tax Assessments*.   [5]*Op. cit.*, 90; but they were " somewhat on the decline ".

twigs for besoms and nuts for exportation.[1] The Backbarrow Company's large wood at Leighton near Arnside provided poles, hoops, boards, stangs, spars, helves and laths for Irish and other cargoes, as well as bark for tanners, while heavy timber was used in shipbuilding, house construction and hammer beams.[2] The woods produced props for the iron mines,[3] clog-wheel carts for carrying the iron ore, saddle-trees for the carriage of wool and charcoal, and hurdles for charcoal-burners and sheep-raisers. The charcoal itself was not only used in the local iron furnaces, but, at the end of the century, for the manufacture of gunpowder.[4] Coopery and " wood-mongering " became established as Ulverston trades,[5] and in 1807 alone that town exported 634,000 wood hoops and basket rods.[6] During the period of the Napoleonic Wars the demand for charcoal slackened considerably ; but the market for birch wood remained a lively one, and the latter was used for making parts of cart wheels and was " also very useful in the cotton manufacture ".[7] Fairly widespread local bobbin-making—in small water-powered factories—was the next development.

After the middle of the eighteenth century the supply of timber trees became exhausted,[8] and in spite of some systematic replanting,[9] the emphasis subsequently was on the large-scale cultivation of conifers so detested by Wordsworth. In Thomas West's *Guide to the Lakes*[10] occurs a mention of Scots fir plantations in High Furness (" a favourite tree with many people "), and it is evident from Gray's *Journal* of 1769[11] that this tree, together with the spruce, had found a home in the Lake District. Some thirty years later the demands of wartime gave an impetus to the planting of these comparative newcomers, and John Christian Curwen, the famous Cumberland agriculturalist, commenced the scientific cultivation of larch on Claife Heights by Windermere.[12] These trees, of course, belonged primarily to the larger estates, and Curwen's venture followed the Claife Enclosure Act of 1794.[13]

Changes were also taking place at the lowland end of the Furness peninsula. It has been indicated that agriculture there was backward, if not in a state of absolute stagnation, during the

[1]*Pennant*, 29-30. [2]*G.L.* (Backbarrow Co.), 1713-5, fols. 114 sqq., 129, 202, 218, 409, etc. ; *Gent. Mag.* and *Pennant, loc. cit.* [3]West, *Antiquities*, 1774, *loc. cit.* [4]*Gent. Mag., loc. cit.* (1803) ; savin, a species of juniper, was charcoaled for this purpose. There was a gunpowder works at Lowwood by 1799. [5]*Ulverston P.R.* (*cit.*). [6]Dickson, *op. cit.*, 639. [7]*Op. cit.*, 437, 441. [8]*Gent. Mag., loc. cit.* When oak timber was plentiful a small shipbuilding industry had been established " on the outlet of the River Crake " . . . " within seventy years " (of 1803) ; but timber was " exhausted " by that year. [9]*E.I.I.F.*, 83, 123, 125.
    [10]West, T., *Guide to the Lakes* (1780 ed.), Appx., 274. [11]*Op. Cit.*, 207, quoting the *Journal*. [12]Binns, J., *Agriculture of Lancs.* (1851), 41. [13]*Loc. cit.* ; for details of the Act, see p. 67 below. For a general survey of national conifer-planting, *vide* Clapham, *Econ. Hist. Mod. Brit.*, I, 11-13, which provides an essential background to the above comments.

first half of the eighteenth century.[1]   There is nothing to suggest that it did not remain comparatively backward during the second half, but by the time that the Board of Agriculture reporters Holt and Dickson made their comments on the district (in c.1793 and 1809 respectively), the Isle of Walney and the nearby neighbourhood of Plain Furness comprised one of the three main wheat-producing areas of Lancashire.[2]   The others were the Fylde and the lower Lune Valley.   William Close, the Furness antiquary and topographer, writing in 1809, stated that " the revival of the cultivation of wheat in Furness " had taken place within " the last seventy years ".[3]   Dr. Pococke, writing about 1754, referred to the exportation of corn from Ulverston,[4] and Pennant, less than twenty years later, mentioned that " Some wheat is raised in Low Furness, and on the Isle of Walney ", but showed more interest in the export of " much beans, which last are sent to Liverpool for the food of the poor enslaved *negroes* in the Guinea trade ".[5]

This remark is the first—and perhaps the only—direct hint that Furness agriculture was benefiting from the rise of colonial and other trade, of which this appalling traffic in human beings was a part.[6]   W. B. Kendall, meanwhile, has stated that " The rise in prices during the American War stimulated the Furness farmers ".[7]   There are signs that land at Bardsea rose in price steeply between 1748 and 1757,[8] and this increase may have been a general one throughout the district.   During the War of Independence the price of grain, nationally at least, tended to go down,[9] although it seems that experiments in wheat-growing took place in the Plain Furness hamlet of Salthouse ; generally the land was made to suffer crop after crop of oats until " completely exhausted and . . . left to grass over with its natural turf ".[10] After 1781 the yeomen of this hamlet began to adopt summer fallows, and ten years later they undertook the reclamation and division of coastal waste or moss.[11]   The township fields of a number of nearby hamlets, meanwhile, had been divided between their occupiers before the middle of the century,[12] and by about 1809 William Close was able to state that Plain Furness and Walney were " divided into large enclosures by verdant hedge-rows "[13] (we may question the largeness if not the enclosures), this in spite of the absence of any parliamentary enactment which might have speeded up the process.

[1]See pp. 11-12 above.   [2]Holt, J., *Agric. Lancs.* (1794), 25, and Dickson, *op. cit.*, 6, 19.   [3]*Memo. on land reclamation at Walney*, in *Itinerary (Close MSS.)*, and reproduced *in extenso* in Dickson, *op. cit.*, 523-40   [4]*Loc. cit.* [5]*Op. cit.*, 25-6.   [6]Barfoot and Wilkes reproduce Pennant's story in c.1790, perhaps misleadingly.   [7]*B.N.F.C.*, VI (NS), 1948, 33, and XIII, (1899), 62.   [8]*C. & W.* (NS), XX (1920), 165-6.   [9]See, e.g., Ashton, *The Eighteenth Century*, 239, Table I.   But there was a sharp rise in 1780-2.   [10]Kendall, *B.N.F.C.*, VI, *loc. cit.*   [11]*Loc. cit.*   [12]See p. 13 above and *B.N.F.C.*, V (NS), 1946, 26-8. [13]*Itinerary*, fols. 6, 19, 34, 190 ; *L. Tax Assessments*.   Walney was divided into 44 tenements in 1809, but only 23 persons on the Island paid land tax in 1790. There was engrossment of farms at Newbarns and on Old Barrow.

John Holt's reports of 1794 and 1795 commented upon the fertility of Plain Furness, but had little to say upon the subject of agricultural progress there. It is not until Dickson's report of *circa* 1809 (published in 1815) that a detailed picture emerges ; his survey, copious enough in local references, may be summed up in the statement that six or seven farmers (at least four of them tenants of the Cavendish or Braddyll families) were engaged in high or progressive farming soon after 1800.[1] Dickson's remarks, which were apt (like those of many contemporary agricultural writers) to concentrate almost exclusively on the improving few, must be regarded with much caution as giving a scarcely balanced picture of Furness or Lancashire agriculture. James Stockdale[2] and W. B. Kendall gave a somewhat bleak picture of local husbandry near the end of the eighteenth century, and Kendall stated that attempts by the Salthouse yeomen " to introduce clover and artificial grasses as a regular crop, or for laying down permanent pastures, failed at this period . . . turnips, sowed broadcast and never weeded, began to appear as regular field crops, but their cultivation was abandoned after 1815, to come in again . . . a quarter of a century later ".[3] The author of a contemporary article on Colton in the fells[4] supplies corroborative evidence regarding the use of turnips, and showed that this crop, with the cabbage, was being " raised in patches ", and that local cultivators had " begun with draining, and grubbing detached bushes and overspreading hedge-rows, both modes of improvement that immediately repay the expense . . . Lime of good quality is fetched from the adjoining parishes . . . " The cotton mills at Backbarrow and Penny Bridge had stimulated the planting of potatoes. Otherwise the variable quality of the soil in the small enclosures constituted " an hindrance to some sorts of crops ".

Wartime conditions of course provided a stimulus to wheat-growing, especially in parts of Plain Furness and Walney, and the Salthouse yeomen are stated to have made " large profits " from wheat before 1820.[5] In about 1809 William Close expressed the view that Walney was " as productive of wheat, oats and barley, as to deserve the appellation of the Granary of Furness "[6] ; Biggar (Walney) tenements changed hands at high prices in the wartime period,[7] and the improving farmers of the district certainly concentrated upon the crops mentioned by Close.[8] But Dickson makes clear that the mixed farm was still the rule.[9]

[1]The rents of the 22 Cavendish farms in Plain Furness showed an upward tendency in 1774-92 ; *Holker MSS., Accounts and Rentals.*
[2]E.g., Stockdale, *op. cit.*, 570-2. This author, although a chronicler of uneven value, spoke with some authority on local farming. [3]Kendall, *op. cit.*, 34. Kendall may be more reliable than Stockdale in his use of documentary evidence, as affecting the hamlet of Salthouse at least. [4]*Gent. Mag.*, LXIII, II (1803), 930. [5]Kendall, *loc. cit.* [6]*Itinerary*, fol. 6, and Dickson, *op. cit.*, 284-5. [7]Pearson, H. G., in *C. & W.* (NS), XI, 197. [8]Dickson, *op. cit.*, 232, 285, 292, 294-5, 303, 310. [9]*Op. cit.*, 408, 410, 419, 567-71.

The more ambitious or wealthy owners and tenants, several of whom received especial mention from Dickson,[1] may have set an example to others in the fields of more scientific crop rotation, new crops and better implements.[2] In 1805 a North Lonsdale Agricultural Society was founded at Ulverston,[3] but this society evoked little response, and equally little is heard of it thereafter.[4] Only a few could afford the heavy expense[5] of stocking a farm unit of good size, and the general increase in land values[6] made it difficult for the yeoman or small tenant to obtain a larger holding if he was not already established in a fertile estate and reaping the benefits therefrom. Although a few larger estates (by the standards of the locality) were appearing, the holdings or properties in the ten to twenty acre range were suffering a reduction in numbers,[7] and the " prosperity " of the wartime years was of course limited to comparatively small sections of the local population. Accordingly, few proprietors were able to make such improvements as were admired by Dickson, who revealed that " green crops have lately been introduced on the farms of Lord George Cavendish, and some other proprietors, but rarely to any considerable extent, though the soil and climate in most parts of the tract are admirably suited to this sort of cultivation ".[8] The turnip, as Kendall showed, had not yet found a secure home in the district.

There was, however, much reclamation of mossland and waste, and there was some parliamentary enclosure of waste and common during the war years and immediately afterwards. Several of the schemes propounded were so ambitious that they deserve a section to themselves.

LAND RECLAMATION AND ENCLOSURE

For over a century and a half, the great expanses of sandy waste in and near Morecambe Bay have exercised the imaginations of those who wished to see this barren ground transformed into good agricultural land. Several schemes for the reclamation of the sands were put forward after the middle of the eighteenth century. It was easily believed that if the sandflats and mosses near Lancaster and

---

[1]E.g. Thomas Ormedy (or Ormandy) of Gleaston Castle (a Cavendish tenant), Rowel of Holbeck near Roose (another Cavendish farm), Cranke of Urswick, Ashburner of Dalton, Dickinson and the brothers Yarker of Ulverston, Braddyll of Conishead and Rawlinson of Walney.   [2]*Op. cit.*, 282-4, 156-7, 161, 162-3, 174, 349-51, 357, 359, 361, 363, 384-5.   [3]*Itinerary* (misc. notes), fol. 214 ; Dickson, *op. cit.*, 650.   [4]*Itinerary* (misc. notes), fol. 213 ; on March 24th, 1807, " the third fair for the show of cattle . . . was held this day at Ulverston, (but) there was only a poor show of cattle ". This society was the forerunner of the later North Lonsdale Agricultural Society (1838). [5]Dickson, *op. cit.*, 146-54.   [6]*Op. cit.*, 120-1 ; cf. West, *Antiquities*, 1774, 16, which gives Ulverston pasture or meadow ground (*c.*1772) as worth £2 to £3 3s. an acre. By 1809 it had reached £7 an acre.   [7]See Table 4, p. 57 above (the 1s.-10s. range of taxees).   [8]*Op. cit.*, 231-2.

Cartmel (and in the Leven, Duddon and Kent estuaries) could be enclosed by embankments, then the alluvial deposits of the inflowing rivers would soon make the former into cultivable territory. A suitable embankment across the Bay would serve as a coach road—or, in nineteenth-century terms, as foundation for a railway—thereby considerably shortening the land approach to West Cumberland. The original aim of each of these schemes went far ahead of the actual achievement ; and the motives behind those of the eighteenth century were the same motives that gave rise to the numerous Enclosure Acts of the period, viz., to reclaim or enclose land for the purposes of improved husbandry and with the aim of enhancing farming profits. Coastal sands and mosses were tithe-free, and their reclamation would, it was felt, handsomely repay the investors in an embankment scheme.

The ironmaster John Wilkinson, whose local residence was at Castle Head near the shores of Morecambe Bay, was prominently associated with the earliest large-scale plan to enclose the Bay, although it would appear that the idea was not originally his own.[1] In and after 1778, however, Wilkinson directed his fertile mind to the work of land drainage and improvement at Castle Head,[2] and his enterprise and example were not without effect.

In 1786 it was announced that :

" A design is now under consideration to inclose and improve the sands, commonly called Lancaster and Milnthorpe sands. The plan proposed is in the first place to turn the course of those waters that fall into the sea from parts adjacent, viz., the River Ken (*sic*) and others of less note, which are to join the River Lune, near Lancaster . . . this addition will procure a benefit so considerable, that the most zealous support and assistance are expected from the town and neighbourhood, besides the concurrence and countenance of the proprietors and occupiers of lands contiguous to all other parts of the canal to be formed for this Purpose . . . The business is to be carried forward by a company formed from subscribers united and incorporated on this great and laudable occasion. When the subscription amounts to £15,000 they will, of course, proceed to embank and recover from the sea as much of the sands as can with probability of success be maintained and preserved; by which, among many other great advantages, the passage from Whitehaven to Lancaster will be much more secure and commodious."[3]

A Mr. Jenkinson was apparently the driving force, and according to John Holt, " a person was appointed to take the

[1]Holt, J., *Agric. Lancs.* (1794), 88 sqq. ; Dickson, *op. cit.*, 517 sqq.; Housman, J., *Guide to the Lakes* (2nd ed., 1802), 215-221. [2]Dickson, *op. cit.*, 471-3. Wilkinson earned himself unqualified praise from Sir John Sinclair for this work. [3]*Gent. Mag.*, 1786 Suppt., Vol. 56, II, 1140.

levels &c., which he did, and his plans are now in the possession of Mr. Jenkinson ", who in turn communicated his ideas to John Wilkinson. The latter envisaged an expenditure of £150,000 on the enclosure of 38,710 acres of sand and moss, he himself offering to advance £50,000 of this sum. But the project came to very little in the direct sense ; owners of fisheries objected, and certain lords of manors wished to claim all their foreshores without contributing to the expenses of reclamation.[1]

John Wilkinson meanwhile proceeded with his remarkable experiments in drainage and improvement at Castle Head.[2] It had already been suggested in the Morecambe Bay plan described above that about 1600 acres of the Ulverston sands might be reclaimed, and that the course of the River Leven could be diverted to the mouth of the proposed canal, where " it might be of service to the shipping by opening the channel ".[3] An Ulverston Enclosure Act of 1799 was a logical consequence of the Ulverston Canal Act of 1793, and the drainage of the Ulverston mosses, a necessary part of the canal works, aided the enclosure of 1109 acres of mossland and common near that town.[4] Meanwhile, James Stockdale, Lord Frederick Cavendish, Thomas M. Machell and George Bigland, with others, obtained an Act (1796) for the enclosure of a great extent of commons, waste ground and mossland in the parish of Cartmel, the moving spirits being two of the James Stockdales, respectively the father and grandfather of the author of the *Annals of Cartmel*.[5] Although, as has been shown, the idea of reclamation was not new,[6] this project must have gained impetus from the " war enclosure fever " following 1795.[7] The Enclosure Bill—a section of the Cartmel landholders petitioning against it—passed through Parliament in the spring of 1796, and the Enclosure Commissioners met for the first time on July 25 of that year.[8] They continued to carry out their work intermittently until the signature of the Enclosure Award on October 13th, 1809, this award accounting for 12,760 acres in all seven divisions of Cartmel, and marking the completion of the largest enclosure undertaking in the history of Lancashire.[9]

The effects of this enclosure, although worthy of an extended study, must be summarised briefly in these pages. Firstly, the petition against the Bill showed that there was a genuine opposition

[1]Holt, *Agric. Lancs.* (1795 ed.), 88 sqq. (*vide* also Dickson, *op. cit.*, 521 sqq. for the same). [2]I am greatly indebted to Dr. W. H. Chaloner for permission to see and use an MS. " The Agricultural Activities of John Wilkinson (1728-1808) Ironmaster ". [3]Holt, *op. cit.*, 91. [4]Depos. Act in Lancs. R.O. Award made in 1813.
[5]*Op. cit.*, 329. [6]*Loc. cit.* " Agitation " had been going on since 1768. [7]Described in Prothero, *English Farming Past and Present*, 440-1. [8]*House of Commons Journals* 9.2.1796 and *passim* to 26.4.1796 (R. Assent) ; and the rare *Cartmel Enclosure Commissioners' Minute Book*, Lancs. R.O. [9]*Vide* a *Handlist of Lancs. Enclosure Acts* (1946).

to the scheme, and the author of *Annals of Cartmel* felt obliged to state that " it was anything but beneficial to one part of the community—the small proprietors. . . . "[1] Secondly, the number of under-5s. land taxees in Cartmel was reduced by about 20 per cent. between 1796 and 1811 ;[2] and thirdly, those divisions of Cartmel which lost these small occupiers also—according to the Census details—lost population absolutely between 1801 and 1811.[3] It should be added that only four other parochial divisions in the whole of North Lonsdale showed a similar tendency during the same period. The former Cartmel commons fell into the hands of about 100 persons, but about ten received the lion's share, including representatives of industry and commerce. On the other hand, an effect of the enclosure was to bring new land into cultivation, and there was a marked increase in the " families engaged chiefly in agriculture " in Lower Holker between 1811 and 1821, and smaller increases elsewhere in the parish of Cartmel.[4] After the Census of 1821, however, there was no further noteworthy increase in the parish or its parts. The land tax lists indicate that during the period 1811-31 there was a reduction in the numbers of separately rated properties, but that in one division—Lower Holker again— there was an increase in the numbers of very small owner-occupiers.[5] By 1831 a very high proportion of the heads of Cartmel " families engaged chiefly in agriculture " were agricultural labourers.[6]

In 1808 William Close of Dalton-in-Furness, doubtless stimulated by the activities in Cartmel, put forward an ambitious scheme for the reclamation of 5760 acres of the Walney Channel.[7] Close, a remarkable and enterprising man by any standards,[8] apparently met with little response, although he succeeded in interesting R. W. Dickson in his project. The Walney sands belonged to the Duke of Buccleuch, an absentee owner, who was probably in a position to supply the necessary capital of £18,000. Close calculated that the Walney tenement-holders might themselves defray the cost of embanking the channel ; but had his exhortations to them been successful, the nature of local history would have been altered in form if not in content, for the small hamlet and port of Barrow lay by sands which Close wished to turn into wheatfields.

Although the Walney tenants were unwilling or unable to supply capital for such an enterprise, the yeomen of nearby Salt-house on the Furness mainland undertook land reclamation on their

---

[1]Stockdale, *op. cit.*, 326. [2]*Land Tax Assessments, cit.* [3]Upper Holker, Cartmel Fell, Lower Holker and Staveley. It should be added that according to the Cartmel Parish Registers, the local population was stationary or falling *before* 1796, but there is reason to believe that the later fall was more acute than elsewhere in the district.
[4]*Census of* 1811 and 1821 (*Abstracts* etc.), pp. 153-4 in each case. [5]*Land Tax Assessments*, Lancs. R.O. [6]*Census of* 1831, *Abstract*, etc., Vol. I, pp. 291-2. There were 461 agricultural families and 433 labourers in agriculture in the parish of Cartmel. [7]*Memorandum* in *Itinerary* (Close MSS.), repr. in Dickson, *op. cit.*, 524 sqq. [8]See pp. 118 sqq., below.

own account, and in 1814 they embanked and reclaimed Salthouse Marsh.[1] It is likely that numerous coastal farmers acted similarly. Meanwhile, an Enclosure Act for the commons, waste ground and mosses of Egton-with-Newland, near Ulverston, was obtained in 1802, the award being made in 1823.[2] Further reclamation works continued in the Cartmel district,[3] but in 1828 James Stockdale's embankments on Winder Moor were largely wrecked by the sea.[4]

The Parliamentary enclosures north of the sands were concerned with moorland common, waste and mossland, for the arable ground of Plain Furness had long been enclosed and divided. The earliest enactment was that of Claife (near Hawkskead), obtained in 1794, and resulting in a 1500-acre award of 1799 ; this affected Claife Heights and Commons, parts of which were purchased by John Christian Curwen for larch-planting purposes.[5] Then followed the Cartmel and Ulverston Acts (1796 and 1799 respectively), and the enclosure and drainage of commons, waste and mosses of Egton-with-Newland (Act of 1802, award of 1823).   In 1820 came two not very important enactments affecting Plain Furness parishes ; Little Urswick and Scales (award of 1822) had 89 acres of Skelding Moor enclosed, and in the same period, Pennington Moor, Swarthmoor and other waste land, to a total of 1163 statute acres, were enclosed and allotted by an award of 1827.   The moorland wastes of Kirkby Ireleth, Lindale and Marton were divided under the terms of an award of 1831 (Act of 1821).[6] In 1828 an Act for the enclosure of the commons, waste and mosses of Broughton-in-Furness was obtained, but the award was not finally signed until May 31st, 1847.   The latter enclosure was, next to that of Cartmel, the most extensive in the district, and related to 3226 statute acres in the award.[7]

Only four of these acts belonged to the war period proper, and only the Cartmel Act was of major importance in affecting the lives, work and destinies of numerous local persons.   There was some valuable work of land reclamation and drainage at the Ulverston[8] and Newland mosses, and for the rest, the walling and apportionment of the moors may have affected poorer users of the commons ; but if the Broughton award is any guide, the moorland commons were more or less equitably shared between several scores of local landholders or original claimants to common rights.[9]

[1]Kendall, *op. cit.*, 33-4. [2]Copy of Act depos. Lancs. R.O. ; the award was made under the terms of an amending Act. [3]Stockdale, *op. cit.*, 536. [4]*Op. cit.*, 537-8. [5]Binns, *op. cit.*, 40-1 ; award depos. Lancs. R.O. [6]Awards or copies of awards in Lancs. R.O. [7]*Broughton Enclosure Award* (transcript by courtesy of Professor G. P. Jones), 31.5.47. [8]*Minutes of the Ulverston Canal Co.* (MS. *Mins. U. C. Co.*), esp. 10.1.1800, 11.4.1801, 21.4.1801 and 30.6.1801, show that the Canal proprietors agreed with the Ulverston Enclosure Commissioners to improve the drainage of the Ulverston mosses. [9]*Broughton Enclosure Award*. About four-fifths of the Broughton allottees (1847) received under 20 acres of land.

The wartime agricultural boom undoubtedly stimulated local farming, increasing the area of land under cultivation, raising rents and wages, and generally affecting the local economy. In 1791, the 300-acre Cavendish farm at Gleaston Castle paid an annual rental of £120.[1] By 1809, 40s. to 60s. a customary acre was the normal rental in its immediate neighbourhood, while in the case of " several of the late enclosures on the north of the Lancaster Sands " the produce was " nearly doubled, and in some cases much more ".[2] New farms were established in the waste ; on Flan Hill at Ulverston the brothers John and Joseph Yarker succeeded in growing grain, turnips and artificial grasses on land of a most forbidding character, newly-enclosed lands in Cartmel afforded " full crops of wheat ", and the Backbarrow millowners (the employers of the unfortunate workhouse children) became improving farmers on reclaimed mossland.[3] Improvement reached up into the fells to the Hawkshead district, where Mr. B. Boddington had " a fine farm conducted under the improved method of tillage husbandry ".[4] At Ulverston there was " no great extent of land under the plough ", but grass-land near the town rented at £5 to £7 a customary acre—a figure probably unprecedented in the region—because, in Dickson's words, there was " here a great demand for milk in consequence of the numerous population ".[5]

The markets for produce, however, were not only local. As the Furness population grew, its consumption of food naturally increased, but there was a considerable exportable surplus. The heaviest emphasis of the local trade was on barley and oats rather than on wheat, the barley being sent to maltsters in Dalton and Ulverston. In 1807, 3551 quarters of malt and 794 quarters of barley were exported from Ulverston, while in 1806-9 inclusive this port sent 9291 quarters of malt and 4030 quarters of barley to the port of Preston alone, which appears to have had most of its supplies of these goods from the Furness district. Smaller quantities of malt and barley went to Poulton from the Furness port, and the former also received 2369 quarters of oats from Ulverston in the years 1806-8.[6] The existence of a modest but solid trade with such a seat of population as Preston is hardly surprising, and it is well known that food was poured into Lancashire from all over the north and west of England. But the process of food supply was not a smooth one, and country populations could go without in order that town dealers might live, as witness the following commentary :

" In speaking of the supply of grain in the Lancaster market, Mr. Bainbridge of Carnforth, a pretty large dealer in that article, as well as oatmeal and flour, observed that they had been supplied

[1]*Holker MSS.* (*Accounts and Rentals*).   [2]Dickson, *op. cit.*, 120-1, 198. [3].*Op. cit.*, 228-9, 280-1.   [4]*Op. cit.*, 281.   [5]*Op. cit.*, 121.   [6]Shipping returns of ports, repr. *op. cit.*, 634-5, 637.

with very little wheat from Liverpool, or any other place since the year 1790 ; and that for three years preceding the last, 1807, the district about them had grown more than was consumed by the population ; but that for the last two years they had had a good deal of wheat from Liverpool and Wales ; that at this time, 1808, there was not a sufficiency of wheat and oats, or of flour and oatmeal together, for the consumption of the numerous inhabitants of the district, notwithstanding it must be allowed that there was much oatmeal sent to the southern large towns as Blackburn &c., it being better made here than in other parts "[1]

Nevertheless, those who were in a position to sell cereals in quantity did well enough, and were enabled, according to William Close, to pay harvest wages which sometimes reached 7s. 6d. a day in about 1809—this on Plain Furness farms.[2]   Yet in this thriving arable district, day labourers' wages, although certainly much higher than they had been in Thomas West's day, were still only 1s. 6d. in winter.   The summer rate was 2s. 6d.   In the Ulverston district, in 1772, day labourers had received 1s. 2d. to 1s. 6d.[3]   On the other hand, the value of pasture land—in the same locality— had risen from £2 an acre in 1772 to between £5 and £7 in 1809, from which it may be deduced that wages had not risen in the pro- portion shown by land values.   Yet it was in Plain Furness and Cartmel that agricultural improvement was taking place.

Improvement in itself, however, seems to have had little direct effect on the course of wages.   During the next half century, Furness farm labourers' wages remained low by comparison with almost any other trade or occupation in the district ;   and whatever achievements the agriculture of this age may count to its credit, the marked and substantial betterment of the labourer's lot was not one of them.   Nevertheless, acute labour shortages within a given locality could influence the movements of agricultural wages in remarkable fashion.   It is well known, for instance, that labourers' wages near the main industrial towns of Lancashire were very high during the wartime period ;   according to Dickson, they rose as high as 3s. 6d. a day in summer time in 1808, and were not usually below 2s. 6d. in winter.   Yet in the Furness fells, about forty miles from any of the main industrial towns of the north-west, day labourers also received 3s. 6d. in summer and 2s. 6d. in winter, contrasted with 2s. 6d. and 1s. 6d. in Plain Furness.[4]   There should be no great mystery here, for it was possible for a Furness quarry- man to make 3s. to 5s. a day,[5] and there is some evidence that people were leaving the fell villages[6] and were thereby emptying

---

[1]*Op. cit.*, 604.   [2]*Op. cit.*, 303, and *Itinerary* etc., fol. 134, where Close stated that " great numbers " of hands were required for reaping, and that the labourers " come from all parts ".   [3]*Antiquities* 1774, 16, and *op. cit.*, 597. [4]*Op. cit.*, 592 sqq., 597-8.   [5]See p. 45 above.   [6]See p. 110 below.

given localities of their young and able-bodied workpeople. Yet the causes of population movement and the origins of " labour supply " in the Industrial Revolution inevitably appear complex when viewed at close quarters ; nor should it be supposed that apparently high money wages meant " prosperity ". As has been shown, local quarrymen had had a most determined bread-riot in 1800 ;[1] there was widespread pauperism in the district in 1803, and a tendency for poor expenditure to increase greatly during the war years ;[2] and the wages of the slate-quarrymen, while comparatively high by eighteenth-century standards, were not much higher in 1809 than they had been in 1792, when a man expert at riving had been able to make £50 to £60 a year.[3] According to Professor Silberling's calculations of the cost of living in these years, there was a steep rise in the prices of 15 articles of common consumption between 1790 (= 100) and 1813 (when the index figure had risen to 187, compared with an earlier peak of 174 in 1801).[4] A Furness mining labourer was paid 1s. 6d. in 1792 ;[5] and an average of 2s. (not counting harvest wages and perquisites) went to the agricultural day labourer of the same neighbourhood in 1808-9 ; from which it would appear that wages, even in an oatmeal-consuming district, lagged far behind prices, for according to the calculations of the same authority (Professor Silberling) the 1809 index figure was 175.

The man without capital, unable to obtain and stock a productive farm, was hardly in a position to profit from the agricultural boom conditions of these years. It is not surprising to find that at Dalton, a few years before 1805, the sons of farmers had " generally been bound apprentices to such mechanical employments as are indispensable in the country ".[6]

AGRICULTURAL DEVELOPMENTS TO THE YEAR 1850

An effect of eighteenth-century agrarian change had been to reduce the numbers of the small or middle-sized landholders of Furness—although not in any very sweeping fashion—and to increase the number of cottagers or smallholders in the villages.[7] Early in the following century Dickson observed that " In the portion of the county north of the Sands, there are great numbers of cottages, which have generally small gardens annexed to them, and in many situations the liberty of getting peats, an advantage that is supposed nearly to equal the rent, which is not more than two or three pounds. This is the case about Hawkshead . . . "[8] The

[1]See p. 45 above.   [2]See pp. 134 sqq., below.   [3]See p. 43 above.
[4]*Vide* Sir John Clapham's well-known treatment of the subject in *Econ. Hist. Modern Britain*, I, Appx. 601-2.   [5]*Backbarrow MSS.*   [6]*Antiquities,* 1805, William Close's Supplement, 342.   [7]See Table 4, p. 57 above.   [8]*Op. cit.*, 104-5.

70

tenants of the cottages, often paying a few pence in land tax for the " annexed " garden or smallholding, frequently eked out a living in the non-agricultural trades which have been described ; and about half of the persons rated for land tax must have been of this type. Even in 1831, when the assessment lists cease to be available, a great many twopenny or threepenny parcels appear in them. At the other end of the scale, there were still very few large properties or farms in 1831. There was undoubtedly some consolidation of property, and in eight rural divisions of Plain Furness the numbers of rated and exonerated land taxes fell from 376 to 275 between 1790 and 1831, while in eleven moorland or rural divisions of High Furness, the number of such taxes fell from 472 to 300 in the same period. Average assessments for divisions remained almost as low as they had been in 1746, nearly a century before, although a considerable number of properties—in fact, by far the great majority—had obtained exoneration under the Act of 1806.[1] As is shown below, owner-occupiers were very much in the minority by the third or fourth decades of the nineteenth century ; but owing to the peculiarities of the land tax lists available, it is not possible to find out what was happening to the former in the last few years of the previous century. It can be stated, however, that in the fell districts of Furness (or in eleven divisions thereof) the owner-occupiers, comprising nearly half of all land taxes, were reduced in much the same proportion between 1816 and 1831 as all other persons paying land tax.[2] Such further lists as have been examined suggest that in Plain Furness the reduction of both elements was less rapid than in the fells.

Wordsworth[3] painted a black picture of the destruction of the statesmen and of the consolidation of their estates by incoming gentry. The disappearance of the " yeomanry " was in fact a slow process during the nineteenth century, and had been going on slowly during the eighteenth also, if we may be permitted to generalise from the scanty evidence available. This does not mean, of course, that the local landholders did not face severe problems, or that there was little loss of people from the fell districts or turn-over in the occupation of property. In spite of a general tendency to vigorous natural increase of population, there was a considerable net loss by migration from the area before 1831, and especially in the ten years before that date.[4] It is clear that some of the fell

[1]46 *Geo. III, c.*133. The lists of " redeemed " properties continued to be made, in order that the assessments could be performed. [2]See my thesis, *cit.*, Table 5, p. 88. [3]*Guide to the Lakes* (1945 facsimile ed.), 80-1. Some of the notes for this work were compiled during the war years, when Wordsworth was conscious of the apparent threat to the position of the statesman. The *Guide* was published in 1835.

[4]For general nat. increase, *vide* the *Parish Register Abstracts* appended to the published and respective census enumeration reports (N. Lonsdale division).

parishes shared in this loss more or less heavily.[1] In the eleven fell divisions mentioned, there was a slight increase in the numbers of families " chiefly " employed in agriculture in 1811 (342), 1821 (352) and 1831 (360).

The word " yeoman ", which is capable of several applications, has so far been used rather tentatively. From now on, however, it can be used simply as the compilers of nineteenth-century directories employed the term—as signifying merely an owner-occupier. Both Parson and White's directory of 1829 and the land tax lists of 1831 agree on one point ; that owner-occupiers comprised no more than a one-third proportion of all individuals listed throughout Furness.[2] As we have seen, the tax lists for 1816 show that in comparison with the 1831 figures there was a fall in owner-occupiers between these years ; but the reduction applied to occupiers of all kinds. This development is of course quite consistent with the consolidation of property in fewer hands.

It would be a mistake, however, to concentrate solely upon those who are listed as farmers or cultivating occupiers. Dickson, as has been noted, referred to the large numbers of cottages with small gardens which were to be found north of the sands, and these, with their " annexed " gardens, entered into the land tax assessment lists. By using the 1831 Census data in combination with the latter and with the directory particulars of 1829, it is possible to determine with fair accuracy how many of these cottagers were in fact the owners of their own buildings and plots. The Census returns, giving totals of " occupiers " employing or not employing labour, agricultural labourers, " chiefly " agricultural families, and houses inhabited, empty and building, show that in ten sample divisions of High Furness, (a) the general total of " occupiers " listed by the census enumerators agreed closely with the grand total of " farmers " listed by Parson and White, that (b) almost exactly half of the people listed for land tax purposes were in fact farmers or cultivating owner-occupiers, and that (c) the remainder were for the most part cottagers paying very small sums for houses and gardens or houses and smallholdings. If we treat all of the remaining taxees as cottagers, then the owner-occupiers of this class were about as numerous as the owner-occupiers of farms. But this means that only about one-tenth of all house-dwellers in these areas were in fact the owners of their own habitations, or, if we exclude all farms from these calculations, perhaps one-sixth. The assistant

---

[1]If the baptisms and burials for Lowick and Blawith (1811-30) are combined, and compared with their respective census totals for 1811, 1821 and 1831, it appears that those townships lost upwards of 200 people in 20 years. [2]The Parson and White *Directory of Cumberland and Westmorland* (1829) includes the " yeomen " in its local lists of farmers.

overseer for Ulverston town and hamlet, William Brickell, [1] reported that many small houses and cottages in that locality were owned by " Manufacturers and Persons in easy circumstances "—this in 1834—and Dickson's assertion that Hawkshead district had numerous rented cottages is borne out by the sources quoted elsewhere in this paragraph.

Any calculations of this kind are in some measure vitiated by the difficulty of interpreting statements and figures of the time. [2] For instance, one would like to know more about the criteria actually followed by enumerators (as distinct from those laid down by John Rickman) in deciding whether a family was " chiefly " dependent upon agriculture or not. Many agricultural labourers entered in the census forms must in fact have worked in woodland employments, while others may have cultivated smallholdings and carted iron ore.

This being said, it seems fairly clear that the Furness agricultural population increased in 1811-21 and declined in lesser degree in the following decade, in the sense that the district lost a few agricultural families but gained in total population. If the census totals of labourers in agriculture mean anything for statistical purposes, then far more labourers were employed (as we might expect) on Plain Furness farms than on those of the fells ; but a proportion of three men to each farm, suggested by the 1831 Census, is hard to accept nevertheless. That might have been true of harvest time.

It is clear that there had been some consolidation of property ; but it is hard to determine the part played by the major landowners in this process. The greatest estate in 1831 was still held by the Cavendish family, and was taxed on territory in fourteen divisions of Furness and Cartmel, the assessment averaging 14 per cent. of the total rating in each. [3] In Plain Furness their estate still included the best and most fertile land in the peninsula, with 4483 acres in the parish of Dalton alone (1840). [4] Its entire area in Furness and Cartmel exceeded 10,000 acres, and was 12,681 acres in 1873 [5]—by far the greatest tract among the major estates of the area. The Dukes of Buccleuch, who had inherited the Lordship of the Liberty of Furness from the Montagu family, owned most of the ore-bearing territory of the locality. Other and smaller estates belonged to the heirs of J. C. G. Sawrey of

---

[1] *Rept. on the Administration and Practical Operation of the Poor Laws* (1834) *Answers to Town Queries*, Appx. B.2, Vol. I, Ques. 50-57, s.v. *Ulverston*. [2] In individual cases the compilers of directory lists and census enumerators must have had difficulty in deciding who was a farmer.

[3] Upper and Lower Aldingham, Dalton, Leece, Hawcoat, Stainton, Kirkby Ireleth and all seven divisions of Cartmel. [4] *Tithe Commutation Survey* of Dalton, q. *C. & W.* (NS), XLIII, 89. [5] *B. Her.* 4.3.1876.

Broughton-in-Furness,[1] Lord Muncaster (Lord of the Manor of Pennington), and in the fells, the Taylors of Finsthwaite and the Sandys and Rawlinson families, each owning extensive woods worth £500 or more a year.[2] The Gales of Bardsea had purchased the greater part of the town fields of that village in the previous century,[3] and it may well be that the more affluent landowners purchased numerous customary estates in enlarging their own.

These, however, were old-established landowning families. Of possible significance, as reflecting the trends of the time, is the story of Thomas Fresh, of an originally yeoman family of Newbarns in the parish of Dalton. His forebears were tenement-holders in the hamlet of Newbarns in the eighteenth century; but by 1821 Fresh was a large landowner with at least a dozen estates and properties all over Furness.[4] Newbarns provides another interesting case, that of Richard Robinson, an improving agriculturalist of local standing by 1845; his forebears, too, had been local tenement-holders who settled in the district less than a century before.[5] The man enterprising in farming and business, as is very evident, tended to prosper at the expense of the old-style customaryholding owner-occupier, whose destruction proceeded slowly but inexorably. In High Furness the statesmen were " not numerous " in 1850, although those who remained were " in easy circumstances ".[6] Perhaps the most authoritative account of the decline of the Cumbrian yeomanry was given by the agriculturalist William Blamire;[7] " their number ", he said, " is constantly diminishing; small estates are constantly being thrown on the market, and often bought by wealthier classes ", primarily large farmers or men who had made fortunes in trade. Their property was often encumbered, and many of them had got into debt in their attempts to improve their holdings.[8] There was much competition for small farms, with the result that rents remained high—a generalisation which may have applied to Furness a few years later, when the same competition was to be observed.[9]

---

[1]In 1799, J. C. G. Sawrey had 9 farms, an inn and a further 693 acres in the occupation of 25 persons; Park, *Some Ulverston Records*, 30, 79. [2]Binns, J., *Agric. Lancs.* (1851), 40-1. [3]C. & W. (NS), XX, 166. [4]By about 1821 Fresh held " the freehold estate of Stewnor Park, comprising 115 acres, three customary estates at Ireleth, two customary estates at Lindal, a tenement at Hawcoat, peat mosses at Ulverston High Moss on Kirkby Moor, and at Stone Dykes, near Roose, besides the turbary dales on Angerton Moss belonging to his several tenements. He also held parcels of land at Standing Lane, near Dalton, at Cross Gates, near Marton, and in the Manor of Bolton with Adgarley ". He owned a corn mill at Blawith and a half share in a Dalton quarry, and together with Col. T. R. G. Braddyll, was interested in West Cumberland and S. Wales coal and iron; Kelly, *Newbarns* (*op. cit.*), 29-31. [5]*Op. cit.*, 27, 29, 34. [6]Binns, *op. cit.*, 103. Directory lists (*Mannex*) of 1866 show a scattering of yeomen in most divisions of Furness. In Westmorland (1829) there were 899 statesmen, in 1849, 549, and in 1885, 439; Bainbridge, *C. & W.* (NS), XLIV, 91. [7]The architect of the 1836 Tithe Commutation Act; *D.N.B.* He was of course a Cumberland man, with special knowledge of the region. [8]*Sel. Cttee. on Agriculture*, 1833 (Parl. Papers, V), Q. 6697 sqq., esp. 6698, 6702. [9] Binns, *op. cit.*, 102.

At Dalton in 1833 there was " a good number of landowners ",[1] and there was little or no agricultural unemployment. The same applied to Hawkshead, where there were " seldom any able-bodied labourers out of employment ", although in that parish there were " not many " landowners.[2] At Church Coniston, where copper mines and slate quarries offered competition, there was a shortage of agricultural labour.[3] But at Hawkshead and Dalton alike it was reported that agricultural capital was " diminishing " or apparently so.[4]

Not until the early 'thirties did the main technical advances in farming begin to exert their effects locally, and a brief discussion of these effects is called for.

In 1813 William Cranke of Urswick introduced Teesdale cattle (shorthorns) into Furness ;[5] the earlier animals of common use were chiefly Galloway or Lancashire longhorns.[6] By the time of Dickson's report of 1809-15, as already indicated, the larger farmers and landlords had made some advances in crop rotation, use of fallows, land reclamation, the employment of improved ploughs and the occasional use of cultivators, drills and threshing machines. The next steps forward were in the departments of field drainage, general adoption of " green " crops (mangolds, turnips and potatoes in rotations) and further improvement of stock. John Christian Curwen, before his death in 1828, had introduced Southdown sheep into High Furness, but Leicesters were afterwards widely raised in the lowland parishes. The Earl of Burlington (Lord George Augustus Cavendish's heir to the Holker estates, and afterwards the 7th Duke of Devonshire) greatly improved the breeds of shorthorn cattle in his Plain Furness and Cartmel estates. Field drainage was much neglected until the eighteen hundred and thirties, but received powerful impetus after the formation of the North Lonsdale Agricultural Society in 1838, as did the use of green crops.[7] The larger farmers of the neighbourhood soon assimilated the techniques of the more advanced districts, and W. J. Garnett said emphatically that Furness in 1850 was " the redeeming feature in Lancashire farming ".[8]

The small statesmen, suggested Garnett,[9] were only then beginning to experiment with new techniques. But like many agricultural reporters, he concentrated his attention and lavished his

[1]*Report on Administration and Operation of the Poor Law, Rural Questionnaires* (1834), 271a.   [2]*Loc. cit.*, 273a.   [3]*Loc. cit.*, 270a.   [4]*Questionnaires, cit. Part III*, 271c, 273c.   [5]Garnett, W. J., *J.R.A.S.*, X (1849), 38.   [6]Dickson, *op. cit.*, 542, 567, 571 : Kendall, *op. cit.*, 33 ; Binns, *op. cit.*, 102, showing that Galloway cattle remained in use in 1850.
[7]Garnett, *op. cit.*, 36-44 ; Binns, *op. cit.*, 66-70, 105-6 ; Rothwell, *Agric. Lancs.* (1849), 6-7 ; *Jackson's Ulverston Almanacks* (in *W. B. Kendall Collection*, Barrow P.L.) for 1848, 1850, 1851, with reports of local farming competitions.
[8]*Op. cit.*, 35.   [9]*Op. cit.*, 36.

praises upon the major landlords and farmers, and his judgment is not to be accepted without question. The detailed conspectus of the agricultural history of the yeoman hamlet of Salthouse in Plain Furness tells something of the response of the yeoman or small farmer to fashions in agricultural improvement ; the following table is constructed from particulars recorded by the late W. B. Kendall, who obtained them from his farming forebears in Salthouse : [1]

Table 5

Improvements at Salthouse ,Plain Furness : four farms,
freehold, 80-100 acres

Year	Improvement
1791-9	Lime kilns built
c.1800	Use of winnowing machine
	,, ,, oaken clod-crusher
1814	Coastal land reclaimed
1802-27	Reconstruction of farm buildings in hamlet
1830	Use of horse-driven threshing machine
1830-40	Introduction of light iron plough
1836	,, ,, shorthorn cattle
1838	Use of chaff-cutter
1838-40	Improved varieties of clover and grass-seed
1840	Turnips used as field crop
1841	Turnip drills used
1842-48	Subsoil drainage with field tiles
1847	Mangold-wurzel grown
1850	Use of guano

The Salthouse yeomen, Kendalls, Kelletts and Brockbanks, had profited from the activities of " Saint Napoleon " and were enabled to survive and reinvest. Their tiny hamlet, however, was soon engulfed by the greedy spread of the new town of Barrow-in-Furness ; and the greatest and most profitable achievements of the locality were still those of the major tenants and proprietors ; the Patterson brothers in the Cavendish farm at Holbeck near Roose, almost certainly the best-equipped and most thriving establishment in southern Cumbria or North Lancashire, [2] and the Crankes of Urswick and Hindpool.

The surviving accounts of the Crankes' farm at Hawkfield, Urswick, give some insight into the activities of the more affluent type of occupier in the Furness coastal area ; Hawkfield Farm was of the mixed type, with sound breeds of sheep and cattle and a good produce of barley and oats, and was run by members of an astute

---

[1]Kendall, *Salthouse* (*op. cit*), 35-8. [2]Cf. Garnett, *op. cit.*, 37 sqq ; Binns, *op. cit.*, 106 sqq., and *passim* ; and Rothwell, *loc. cit.*

and gifted family. [1]   Between 1810 and 1825 its owners were carrying on a thriving business and rented out a second farm at Hindpool, which had a rental of £160 in 1821. [2]   Oats and barley were sent by canal and road to Liverpool, and it may be significant that the Crankes were among the Lancaster Canal Company's numerous shareholders. [3]   Such farmers were also aided by the Ulverston Canal and its commerce, which recovered life after the late 'twenties, and the construction of railways in the neighbourhood, commenced in the mid-forties, gave an added stimulus to agriculture. [4]   The story told by the Hawkfield accounts, up to 1825, is continued by the Whinfield Farm (near Dalton) accounts of William Penny [5] for the years 1841-50, wheat, barley and potatoes being the main crops here.   Throughout the first half of the nineteenth century, arable farming remained of prior importance in Plain Furness ; with the general emphasis on barley and oats, the former cereal being sent, as before, to maltsters in Dalton and Ulverston. [6]   The demand for grain benefited not only the major farmers and landowners, for, in 1849, one of the comparatively small farmers of the arable parish of Pennington " died worth £4500, the whole of which has been got in farming and principally by himself ". [7]   In parts of Plain Furness an extraordinarily large area of ground was under the plough in the years before the repeal of the Corn Laws.   The following particulars [8] will make the point clear :

Table 6

Land Utilisation in parts of Furness

1. *A High Furness parish*

Year	Parish	Total Acreage	Arable land	Meadow or pasture	Woodland, moors	Arable in 1905
1833	Church Coniston	10,720	619	836	305 wood 8960 comm.	—

2. *A pasture area*

1833	Ulverston t.s. and hamlet	1,770	350	1270	150 wood	—

3. *Arable parishes*

1833 and 1840	Dalton	15,594	11,796	3116	512 wood 170 comm.	3941
1840	Part of Dalton	9727	8332	399	996 wood	—
1846	Aldingham	4459	3257	1139	63 wood	1479
1839	Pennington	2758	1074	1684	—	507

[1] *Vide D.N.B.* (s.v. James Cranke), and Gaythorpe, H., *C. & W.* (NS), VI, **128** sqq.   The family produced two portrait painters in the eighteenth century ; and Stewards of the Liberty of Furness.   It seems that they owned very little land, but that they rented farm land from others ; the *Land Tax Assessments* give them very low ratings up to 1831.   [2] *Hawkfield Farm Accounts* (MS), Barrow P.L.   [3] *Ibid.*   [4] See p. 245 below.   [5] *Whinfield Farm Accts.* (MS), Barrow P.L.   [6] Garnett, 36.   [7] *The Diary of William Fleming . . . of Pennington, C. & W.* (NS), XLII, 1942, 136.

[8] From *Report on . . . the Poor Law ; Rural Questionnaires,* I, 270a, 271a, 277a. (1834) ;   *Tithe Commutation Returns* for Cumbrian pars., by Bainbridge, T. H., in *C. & W.,* XLIII (1943), 87.

The Dalton arable areas for 1833 and 1840 seem unbelievably large, but they are borne out by similar particulars from West Cumberland parishes[1] as well as by the total of arable land in the adjoining parish of Aldingham.

In spite of the concentration upon white crops, the land was no longer being driven to exhaustion. Green crops (but apparently not turnips) were being interposed into courses by the Salthouse yeomen from 1837 ;[2] summer fallows remained customary during the first half of the century, and, indeed, became obligatory " owing to a scarcity of hand labourers for the green crops ",[3] which had " increased four or five fold since the formation of the North Lonsdale Agricultural Society ",[4] this by 1850. In High Furness the soil and climate were better for dairying and for grazing young cattle than for grain ; but in the comparatively small patches of arable land, courses of turnips or potatoes now separated those of oats and barley, the former pair being manured from the farmyard.[5] Guano had reached both areas by 1850 ; Binns (whose report on Lancashire agriculture was published in 1851) mentions it in connection with High Furness, and the records of the Salthouse farms indicate that it had entered common use in Plain Furness by the former year. The agricultural revolution had wrought many changes in the district by mid-century, although its impact should not be exaggerated. Farm-buildings were still not of the best construction, holdings in Plain Furness (owing, perhaps, to the manner in which some of them had been consolidated) were ill-arranged, and land drainage in the fell valleys was as yet little understood.[6] High Furness farmers, as in earlier years, tended to neglect husbandry proper for woodland industries and the care of coppices ; there was still a considerable trade in hoops, basket rods and bobbins, the latter being sent away to Lancashire, Yorkshire, Scotland and Ireland. The basket rods went to St. Helens and Wigan and the hoops to Liverpool and Scotland.[7] The woodlands of Furness were still as important as its grain fields.

The social and economic effects of improved farming on the immediate region are not easy of analysis. Between 1801 and 1851, a slowly decreasing proportion of the Furness population was dependent on agriculture. In 1831, two-fifths of the adult male population was in some way connected with the land; but by 1861 the total male group in any way associated with farming had diminished to less than one-third.[8] Before this time, the great

---

[1]Bainbridge, loc. cit.   [2]M S. cropping notes of W. B. Kendall, by courtesy of Mr. J. L. Hobbs.   [3]Binns, op. cit., 104.   [4]Loc. cit.
[5]Binns, Op. cit., 101-2.   [6]Ibid,. and Rothwell, Agric. Lancs., 7-9.   [7]Binns, 40, 103.   [8]Census particulars. In 1831 the total agricultural section (occupiers of all kinds, and labourers) amounted to 2627 out of 5806 adult males; in 1861 the proportion was 3193 to 9488. Vide the Enumeration Abstracts of 1831 (Vol. I, 1833, 291-2), and the Occupation Tables for 1861 (Ulverston District).

extent of land under arable cultivation undoubtedly called for a larger labour force than the district could easily supply. At Dalton in 1833, women were employed in weeding green crops and corn, and on harvesting and haymaking in summer ; " They get cockles in winter ".[1] A woman might earn 40s. a year in this way.[2] But in spite of an undoubted shortage of agricultural workers, wages remained obstinately low between the end of the Napoleonic Wars and 1850. The student is often asked to admire the achievements of British farming, which supplied vast populations with food in these years ; but the historians who point this out too frequently forget that until the middle of the nineteenth century, the representative Briton was still not a townsman. The agricultural labourer, the chief figure of the countryside, was wretchedly paid, even though he may have benefited from slight reductions in the cost of living before 1850.[3] The north-country labourer was considerably better off than his southern counterpart, who often had to be content with little more than 8s. a week in 1850 ;[4] and certain it is that the North Lancashire land worker, assured of something like full employment and with his dignity unimpaired by an allowance system or by parish gangs, knew nothing of the wretchedness sometimes encountered in the south of England. Yet, when his wages are compared with those paid to industrial or railway labourers in the same region, it is difficult to understand why he did not change his occupation almost immediately. Again, demand for his services seems to have had little or no effect on the money wages paid by local farmers, save where there was acute competition from the local slate quarries. Accordingly, as has been shown, High Furness wages were higher than those paid in the lowland parishes with their much more advanced agriculture.

Agricultural wages are difficult and dangerous to put in statistical form. The labourer who took his meals at the farm was paid one wage, the man who did not was paid another, and the living-in farm servant yet another. All three might or might not obtain various perquisites, and annual or half-yearly wage payments in local farm accounts fluctuate oddly from year to year. The following wage figures, consisting of contemporary averages or estimates made by agricultural reporters and parish authorities, together with a few samples from farm account books,[5] are meant as general indicators only :

[1]*Rural Questionnaires, cit.* (1834), 271a.   [2]*Ibid.,*   [3]Caird, J., *English Agriculture in* 1850 *and* 1851, 518. It appears that the chief improvement in living costs took place after 1847.   Prof. Silberling (and, of course, the late Sir John Clapham) have argued a general improvement in the post-war period and in the 'forties.   Local price series from, e.g., farm account books, throw little light one way or the other.   [4]Caird, *op. cit.,* 510 sqq. (Letter LV) ; the Lancs. wage given was more than twice that of Wiltshire.   [5]See Table 7 below.   The other sources have been mentioned ; Dickson, Garnett, Binns, Rothwell and the Poor Law Commissioners' *Rural Questionnaire.*

Table 7.

Approximate Agricultural Wage-levels in Furness, 1809—50.

W. = winter. S. = summer. w.t. = with table.

Category	The wartime period, 1808-9.	Post-war, 1815-21.	1833	1843	1846	1850
Day labour						
Plain Furness	1/6 W. / 2/6 S.	(1818) 1/- w.t. (a) / (1819) 1/2 w.t. / (1821) 1/6 w.t.	2/- S.W. / 1/8 W. / 2/6 S.	1/- w.t. (x)	1/6 w.t. (x) (1849)	1/2 w.t. / 2/- W. / 2/3 S. / 2/2 S.W.
High „	2/6 W. / 3/6 S.	—				
Men servants						
P.F.	£20-25	£13-20	£26	£11—15 (x)	£16 (x)	£15—17
H.F.	£20		£20-26			£15—20
Women servants						
P.F.	£7		£7	£5—£5 . 10 (x)	£5 (x)	£4—5
H.F.	£4					£4—5
Harvest wages						
P.F.	5/6 day w.t.	(1815) 3/- w.t. (a) / (1822) 2/3 w.t.		2/- w.t. (x)	2/- w.t. (x)	3/- w.t.
Cottage Rents (mainly H.F.)	£2—3 p.a.	—	—	—	—	£2—£3 . 10

(a) Samples from the *Hawkfield Farm Accounts*.
(x) Samples from the *Whinfield Farm Accounts*.

According to generally accepted calculations,[1] agricultural money wages tended to fall—with few minor upward movements—between about 1814 and 1835, and climbed temporarily in 1835-9 and in 1846. The general outline of the post-war fall is visible here; and the Whinfield Farm records show the sudden wage jump of 1846. The accounts of this farm, too, show that the prices of

[1] Clapham, *op. cit.*, I, 126-9, esp. his table (after Bowley and Silberling), p. 128.

produce kept in step with wages in the 'forties : comparison with the earlier records of the Cranke farm at Hawkfield, Urswick, suggests that prices in the early 'forties were on a level with, or slightly below, those of the early 'twenties. [1]

Only a most detailed analysis of local retail as well as whole-sale prices, including those of all consumer goods, would enable us to develop any safe conclusions concerning changes in the labourer's standard of living. And, if this is true of one locality, it is a thousand times true of Britain as a whole ; a warning to students who accept too easily those arguments based on the Silberling indices.

In conclusion, it is interesting to note that in a number of areas little affected by parliamentary enclosure of any kind, Furness agriculture made considerable strides between 1750 and 1850. This is particularly true of the fertile district of Plain Furness, where " improvement " was by no means confined to the major land-owners and farmers. Coastal position and nearness to continually growing markets no doubt made a difference here ; but it should not be assumed that drastic major operations on the countryside were invariably necessary in order that a growing population might be fed.

[1]The position of the labourer may therefore have improved slightly. But a section of the Furness population was still on the oats-and-potato standard, and both went up in price sharply in 1846 (*Whinfield Farm Accts.*). There was misery in 1846 and 1851 ; see pp. 142, 241 below.

CHAPTER V

ROADS AND SHIPPING, 1760-1840

ROADS

In studying such a district as Furness, internal and external communications must be taken into account. It was easier, in the eighteenth century, to send a cargo of timber, corn or iron to south Lancashire, Cheshire or Welsh ports from Piel or Ulverston, than to move large consignments of goods over the sands to Lancaster, the administrative headquarters of Lonsdale.[1] Hence Lonsdale North of the Sands has customarily been called " remote ".

It is true that John Wesley, that indefatigable traveller, had a poor opinion of the oversands route into West Cumberland. The latter was, in his view, " ten measured miles shorter " than the approach *via* Kendal and Keswick ; " but there are five sands to pass, so far from each other, that it is scarce possible to pass them all in a day . . . I can advise no stranger to go this way ; he may go round by Kendal and Keswick often in less time, always with less expense, and far less trial of his patience ".[2] Wesley crossed the Millom Sands " without either guide or difficulty ", this in 1759. In the memorandum on the Jenkinson-Wilkinson scheme for embanking the Morecambe Bay sands, it was hoped that this plan would result in the formation of a post-road between Whitehaven and Lancaster, " by which not only the commercial towns, but all the intervening country would be much benefited ; whereas at present (*c.*1786) a person travelling between Lancaster and Ulverston, Ravenglass, Whitehaven &c. must either take a very circuitous route through a wild mountainous country, or wait a precarious dangerous passage over the sands. A reflection on the number of people who are anually lost in crossing these deceitful sands, touches the nerve of humanity. This dreadful circumstance would be remedied by banishing the tide . . .[3]." Since, however, no embankment took place as envisaged, light coaches were obliged to provide regular services over the sands between Ulverston and Lancaster,[4] and posts were carried over this route.[5]

---

[1]This route was used by local inhabitants until the opening of the Ulverston and Lancaster Railway in 1857 ; cf. *The Diary of William Fleming, cit.*, entry of 2nd Jan., 1852, where numerous Pennington people set off to the Lancaster sessions by gig or horseback.   [2]John Wesley, *Journal* (Everyman ed.), II, 448 (Sat., 12th May, 1759).   [3]Quot. Dickson, *op. cit.*, 522.
[4]*Cumberland Pacquet*, 11.9.1781 ; Coaching Bill of *c.*1800 in *Aldred Collection of Advertisements*, Barrow P.L.   [5]For gen. details, *vide* Melville, J., and Hobbs, J. L., in *C. & W.* (NS), XLVI, 77-107.

What of communications inland ? In 1714 the Backbarrow ironmasters sent pots and pans, using established packhorse routes, to Settle, Skipton, Swaledale and Askrigg in Wensleydale. [1] Kendal, a nearby centre of textile industries, [2] was fairly easily approached from Ulverston *via* Newby Bridge. This route was turnpiked by an Act of 1763, [3] the Kirkby Kendal—Kirkby Ireleth Turnpike Trust then controlling a road from Ireleth in Dalton parish *via* Lindal (missing the small town of Dalton), Rattan Row at Ulverston, Penny Bridge, Bouth and Newby Bridge, and running thence to Kendal. [4] It is a striking fact that the Rev. Edward Jackson, Vicar of Colton, was able to ride from his parish to Kendal one evening in February, 1775, after several days of heavy rain, [5] and the road was almost certainly a tolerably good one. Passing north-wards from the district, vehicles could run *via* Lindal, Kirkby Ireleth, Broughton and Duddon Bridge to Bootle in Cumberland; part of this road was improved in the eighteenth century, [6] but foot or horse travellers probably found it easier to pass over the Millom Sands from Ireleth Lane End (the route taken by Wesley in 1759), and the coach road, if such it can be called, was long and circuitous. It was however the only direct land approach to Whitehaven, and was not turnpiked. [7]

Furness and environs had a comparatively high density of by-roads and lanes by the middle of the century. [8] . A route ran from Ambleside through Skelwith Bridge *via* High Cross to Broughton, [9] and according to Pennant, there were " excellent roads" between Penny Bridge and Coniston, [10] while William Cockin, editor of West's *Guide to the Lakes* in c.1780, offered further testimony as to the good state of the High Furness roadways. [11]

Such comments owe not a little to purely subjective judgment, and the preamble of the Turnpike Act of 1763 (see above) stated that the Furness-Kendal road was " in a ruinous condition and, in several parts, narrow and incommodious ". [12] There can be no doubt that the Act effected some improvement, although, in spite

[1]*G.L.*, fol. 180 (*Backbarrow MSS*). [2]Young, Arthur, *Six Months' Tour Through the North of England*, III, 172. [3]Act of 3 *Geo. III, c.cxxxiii* (1763) ; not 1761, as in Cowper, *Hawkshead*, 239, and repeated by *V.C.H. Lancs.*, VIII, 383n. [4]*Act* contd. and enlarged by 24 *Geo. III, Sess.* 1, *cxxiii* (1784), and 39 *Geo. III, cxxiv* (1799) ; cf. also Fell, Wm., *Hist. and Antiquities of Furness* (1777 ; ed. Ayre, Ulverston, 1887) for ref. to Ulverston-Lindal road. The author was a schoolboy ! [5]*The Diary of Edward Jackson, C. & W.* (NS), XL, 1940, 4-5, esp. 7th Feb. Jackson was a Turnpike Commissioner. [6]*N. Lonsdale Magazine*, III, 10th Dec., 1899 ; Fell, Wm., *loc. cit.* [7]Infn. by courtesy of Mr. J. L. Hobbs. [8]*Brasier's Map of Furness, cit.* [9]Cf. Cowper, *op. cit.*, 240. [10]*Pennant*, 29. [11]*Guide, cit.*, 1780, Appx., 270. [12]Further details are in Mr. Hobbs's scholarly paper, " The turnpike roads of North Lonsdale ", *C. & W.*, LV, 1956, 250 sqq.

of the Rev. Edward Jackson's evening ride, that route remained desperately hilly ; the low-level road over Haverthwaite moss, for instance, was not then made, and there was a 700-foot climb over the shoulder of Gummer's How. Among the turnpike trustees were members of the Latham, Machell, Knott and Penny families, and it is significant that iron ore passing between Lindal and Conishead Bank was exempt from toll. [1] It is clear that the heaviest traffic flowed between the Plain Furness iron mines and the coast, and young William Fell, writing in 1777, remarked: " Pray do not be out of Humour with the road because it is a little red with the prodigious number of Iron Ore Carts which pass that way ". [2] A further Act obtained by the same Trust in 1799 imposed a toll of one halfpenny on ore carts moving to and fro between Lindal and Conishead, and this, of course, was still preferential treatment.

In 1818, following the formation of the Ulverston to Carnforth Turnpike Trust, [3] an improved inland route (opened in 1820) used and straightened existing lanes and passed *via* Greenodd, Wilson House, Levens Bridge and Beetham. Yet, although these roads were useful to business men and public carriers, the annual accounts of the trusts which ran them throw some light on the limited economic life of the neighbourhood. Between 1828 and 1846, when the trade of the Ulverston Canal grew more or less steadily, the annual income figures of the Kendal and Carnforth turnpike trusts showed little equivalent tendency to increase. [4] The reasons are not hard to find ; iron ore and slate, the produce of the neighbourhood, travelled little on the main roads described, and were of course carried by sea, first of all going down the Canal mentioned.

The Cartmel enclosure of 1796-1809 resulted in improvement of the roadways in that district ; and, due to the activities of the Ulverston Canal Company, some sort of road or road improvement may have been executed between the Kirkby slate quarries and Ulverston itself. [5] There was plenty of roadmaking material in the district generally, and pebbles from Walney were used in South Lancashire in about 1788. [6] But in spite of its dangers, the oversands route remained a fairly popular one, and is occasionally used even at the present day. [7]

---

[1]*Op. cit.*, 254. [2]*Loc. cit.* [3]Hobbs, *op. cit.*, 266 sqq. [4]The statements of accounts, *op. cit.*, 263-4, 284-5 ; the observations are mine. [5]Stockdale, *op. cit.*, 326, 339-40 ; *MS. Mins. of The Ulverston Canal Co.*, 13.6, 14.6. 1797, 10.11.1801, 10.11.1802. [6]*Itinerary*, fol. 14, and Dickson, *op. cit.*, 539. [7]A Trust under the Duchy of Lancaster still appoints guides (1955).

The development of the pre-1760 coastal shipping trade of the locality has already been sketched. The recognised harbour for the district was Piel of Fouldrey, which had been used as an anchorage for at least five centuries previously ; and until 1765 Piel was entered, in a statistical abstract of the Commissioners of Customs,[1] as the only customs office between Poulton and White-haven. In that year an office appeared at " Ulverstone ", both places then appearing in the returns. Both were creeks of the port of Lancaster, but only Piel had a harbour in the true sense.[2] Vessels were in the habit of calling at any place on the Furness shores where they could conveniently load goods and Wadhead (Bardsea), Baycliffe Below Gate, Conishead, Beanwell, Salthouse Pool Foot, Piel Harbour proper, Barrow, Pallace Nook, Ireleth Marsh, Kirkby Pool and Angerton Moss were all visited by ships during the century. Over the Duddon sands, Lady Hall Marsh and Borwick Rails, as well as a separate " Landing " for the Duddon ironworks, are other places mentioned.[3] Southwards over More-cambe Bay, Arnside and Milnthorpe receive some mention as minor ports during the period, the second of the two, an outlet and inlet point for Kendal goods, being the most important.[4] Greenodd on the Leven Estuary was used by the ironmasters of Furness, and may sometimes be mentioned under the name of Penny Bridge.[5]

Accordingly, any official entries for Furness creeks like Piel or Ulverston may be taken to mean almost any one of a score of landing places on or near Furness shores. Ulverston, a minor port of local consequence, was situated a mile from the sea, and its sea approaches were difficult. After 1796, when the Ulverston Canal was opened, the canal shipping was recorded separately, but other records[6] make it clear that vessels continued to use lesser landing places until well into the nineteenth century.

Mariners are particularly numerous in eighteenth-century local records, and in 1737 no fewer than 24 ships' captains were living on the west (Furness) side of Morecambe Bay, while the names of shipwrights, a roper and a sail-maker also occur. A ropery was then at work at Concle near Rampside, good pilots were reported

---

[1]*B.M. Addl. MSS.* 11255, *cit.* [2]For Piel, Jarvis, R. C., *C. & W.* (NS), XLVII, 152 sqq. [3]*Duddon Accts.* Furness landing places in *E.I.I.F.*, 313 ; I am indebted to the researches of Mr. J. L. Hobbs for confirmation. The writer in personal investigations, has found traces of iron ore at these points. [4]*C. & W.* (NS), XXXVI, 34 sqq. (The port of Milnthorpe.) [5]As in *Backbarrow MSS., G.L.*, var. refs. Pennant wrote of " Penny-Bridge or Crake-Ford " (*op. cit.*, 29) and saw a ship of 150 tons building there. The Crake may have been wider and deeper at its mouth in 1772 ; topographical signs suggest it, and as Pennant indicated, ships may have been built at Penny Bridge. [6]*Inspections of Ports* ; *Reports* ; H.M. Customs & Excise Library.

plentiful, and small vessels were evidently built in the neighbourhood of Piel, as well as at Arnside and later, Greenodd and Ulverston. [1] Nine Dalton mariners and a shipwright had their wills filed at the Lancaster probate court in 1748-92, while four Urswick mariners appear in the same sources of information, [2] and seven mariners occur at Broughton between 1755 and 1800. [3] Twenty-nine men of this calling were married at Ulverston parish church between 1755 and 1780, as well as six persons engaged in shipbuilding or associated trades like ropemaking, and a further 68 between 1781 and 1806. [4] Those engaged in seafaring pursuits were also numerous in the coastal hamlets and villages of Cartmel, [5] and an occasional sailor found his way into the wide world from the inland parishes of the neighbourhood. [6]

As has been shown, [7] the coastal vessels of Furness traded with Welsh and Severn ports ; and it is probable that in accordance with the fashion of the eighteenth century and later, they carried their cargoes to almost any district where there was a market for iron, slate and corn. In 1760, eleven ships from Ulverston, eight from Piel (averaging 30 tons each) and eighteen from Conishead Bank visited the port of Lancaster, which received in 1770 no fewer than 43 vessels from Ulverston. [8] Lancaster was then an entrepot redistributing goods coastwise. [9] It grew fairly rapidly during the second half of the eighteenth century, receiving some limited stimulus from the slave trade, and took in or redistributed cargoes from Staffordshire, Cheshire and Scotland. Linen is mentioned as having been brought in and re-exported from Ulverston. [10] The fluctuations in the volumes of trade of both Furness and Lancaster may be reflected in table 8 opposite. [11]

Furness shipping had reached its peak tonnage (2482 tons) in 1756, and thereafter slumped until 1766, when there was a recovery. During the wartime years, and probably afterwards, mariners left the Ulverston district and sought employment in Liverpool, and in 1772 Pennant noted that " the commerce of (Ulverston) in general declines ". Formerly, he said, there had been about 150 vessels " belonging to the place ", and " mostly let out to freight " ; but in 1772 there were " not above fifty " [12] It is clear from the customs returns that these were the twenty or thirty-tonners referred to elsewhere, [13] and the temporary decline in tonnages—amounting to

[1]Barnes, F., *Barrow . . . A History*, 90 ; Stout, *Autobiography*, 97 ; *G.L.* (*Backbarrow MSS.*), 220, (ship built at Leighton) ; *Pennant, loc. cit.* ; *E.I.I.F.*, 313. [2]*Richmond Wills, cit.* [3]Broughton-in-Furness P.R. (*Lancs. P.R .Soc.* Vol. 90) [4]*Ulverston P.R.* (Ed. Bardsley & Ayre). [5]*Richmond Wills.* [6]*Ibid.* [7]See p. 32 above. [8]Schofield, M. M., *Outlines for an Economic History of Lancaster* (Lancaster Hist. Assn.), 1946, IV, 24. [9]*Op. cit.*, 47.
[10]Schofield, *op. cit.*, 33 (the sentence should read " brought in from Ulverston and re-exported "). This trade was conducted by the brothers Abram and John Rawlinson, who were related to the Furness iron-smelting family of that name. [11]*Addl. MSS.* 11255. [12]*Pennant*, 25. [13]See note 8 above.

Table 8

Cf. Table 1, p. 32 above.

Shipping Based Upon Ports ; Tonnages

F = Shipping engaged in " foreign " trade

C = Shipping engaged in coastal trade

Entries Inward : Tonnages
B = British ships
F = Foreign ships.

	Piel and Ulverston		Lancaster			Ulverston		Lancaster	
	F.	C.	F.	C.		B.	F.	B.	F.
1765	329	730	2646	455					
1766	—	1767	3081	435					
1767	—	1651	3355	419					
1768	—	1651	3140	414					
1769	155	1216	3115	454					
1770	163	1138	2962	385					
1771	—	1200	2487	395					
1772	—	1200	2967	370					
1773	—	1240	2992	410		623	—	4015	80
1774	—	1280	3427	510		500	—	4939	—
1775	—	1340	3472	621		527	—	4602	—
1776	—	1500	3519	716		504	—	4553	120
1777	—	1620	3492	621		705	—	3777	—
1778	—	1620	3357	795		785	—	3549	—
1779	—	1963	3667	570		673	—	3436	500
1780	—	1963	3872	495		440	—	3200	100
1781	—	1863	3550	480		—	—	—	—
1782	—	1751	3125	410					

a slump in Ulverston and Lancaster for the years 1769-74—is shown in the statistics. [1]   In 1776-7 the Furness ironmasters were meeting strong competition from Swedish and Russian pig-iron, and furnace stocks are stated to have piled up in (or by) the year 1775. [2]   From that time onwards, however, the numbers or capacities of local vessels increased noticeably, in spite of a shortage of hands due to the work of the press-gangs, [3] and the complaints appearing in Furness ironmasters' epistles of the period must be regarded with caution.   As has been shown, the iron ore output of the district was increasing ; the local slate trade was certainly rising to some modest importance ; and the growth of the Lancashire populations engaged in manufacture was beginning to influence the general demand for agricultural produce.   Even by 1780, the home-based shipping tonnage had not reached the 1756 level, although, as can be seen reflected in the Ulverston marriage registers, the number of

[1]Even busy Whitehaven lost shipping after 1771 ; *ibid.*   [2]*E.I.I.F.*, 238, 310-11.   [3]*E.I.I.F.*, 327.   It is likely that there was a local shipping shortage, as Fell suggested.   Local tonnages did not keep pace with haematite output.

local sailors (or temporary settlers of that profession) became distinctly greater between 1781 and 1806 than at any time in the preceding thirty years ; and the haematite trade expanded markedly in the later period. [1]

A consequence of the increasing demand for haematite was the rise to local stature of the small port of Barrow, a hamlet of a few houses four miles from Dalton-in-Furness. The Backbarrow Company obtained a mine-floor (ore-dumping ground) there in 1776, and in 1780 the Newland Company purchased an estate at Barrowhead and built a quay there soon afterwards. On February 22nd, 1782, the first ship was loaded with ore at the new quay, and much ale was consumed in toasting what was, unknown to the men of the time, the birth of a great future port. [2] The advantages of Barrow harbour were already manifest, and the new quay reduced the cost of loading ore from 6s. 6d. for twenty tons to 1s. 4d. for the same amount, while the harbour itself was " safe " with " plenty of water ". [3] In 1790 the Newland Company found it advantageous to erect a better and longer jetty enabling 100 tons of ore a day to be loaded. Otherwise the infancy of Barrow was long protracted. A few labourers were housed there (in a number of cases in converted hen-roosts, as though in anticipation of the desperate housing shortage of mid-Victorian times), the hamlet had eleven dwelling houses in 1801 and a population of 65 in 1806, and it was described by William Close soon after the latter year as " one of the principal sea-ports of Furness, where great quantities of iron ore are laid up or shipped for exportation. It contains two good inns and is occasionally resorted to as a bathing place ". [4] But Close, a worthy and highly intelligent man, was also a local patriot, and his remarks are apt to be misleading : one might hardly suspect that he was describing a most unprepossessing and insanitary little hamlet, with cottages built roughly of unshaped pieces of sandstone, and cut off from civilisation by miry cart-tracks. It is evident that Barrow was hardly in a position to challenge Liverpool as a " sea-port ", and it remained unknown and—to the outside world—unimportant for another fifty years. Yet such are the surprises of history, that soon after the end of this half-century it was challenging Liverpool in earnest. In one respect, too, the eighteenth-century history of this tiny shipping point foreshadowed an important aspect of the development of the modern town ; in both cases its growth was influenced by the decisions of a single company which purchased land there and improved the harbourage.

[1]See Table 2, p. 35 above. [2]Barnes, *op. cit.*, 92 ; Kendall, W. B., *B.N.F.C.*, XVII, 1909, 189 sqq. (with notes by Harper Gaythorpe) ; *E.I.I.F.*, 323-4. [3]*Loc. cit.* [4]Places cited, and Close, *Itinerary*, fols. 20, 138. In his supplement to West's *Antiquities of Furness* (1805 ed.), p. 342, is further information regarding Dalton district. In p. 20, *op. cit.*, it is stated : " The country, from Hawcoat round the coast by Barrow to Rampside, is very unpleasant " . . .

Ulverston, lacking a good harbour, had merchants and gentry anxious to bring increased trade to their own doorsteps. The Ulverston Canal Company of 1791-3 was a result of their anxiety. The precise circumstances of the formation of this company have not been clearly stated, and the canal or elongated freshwater harbour which appeared soon after those years was a distinctly modest venture when compared with the mighty canal projects of the period. These circumstances may be reconstructed without straining at the facts. Firstly, the Newland Company, then (in 1790) the most influential charcoal iron company of the area, had clearly shown its intention of developing Barrow as a port; secondly, the haematite trade was generally on the increase, and several Liverpool merchants or gentry, probably interested in improving their lines of communication, invested in the new Canal Company; and thirdly, the "canal mania" atmosphere prevailed at the time, and the great Lancaster Canal scheme had already been broached by 1791. In July of that year "several Gentlemen" supported the Ulverston project "as an advantage to the town . . . and the Country adjacent", and then or soon afterwards William Burnthwaite junior, solicitor of Ulverston, undertook the initial survey, convened early meetings of the promoters, and arranged for the raising of subscriptions.[1]   According to a list of October 29th, 1792, 35 persons subscribed a total of £3,800, of which £1,200 came from Liverpool men.[2]   Meanwhile the Lancaster Canal Company planned to link the industrial areas of Wigan and Preston with the town of Kendal and environs,[3] and the Ulverston promoters were early in touch with that body. The Ulverston Canal Act was obtained on May 8th, 1793,[4] and in the October of that year John Rennie (engineer to the Lancaster canal) was brought over to Ulverston to make a survey and an estimate of costs.[5]   The Act contained provision for a possible communication between the Ulverston and Lancaster canals, while " coals, culm and cinders " carried between them were not to be liable to the duties imposed on seaborne traffic;[6] and it also empowered the Ulverston subscribers to raise £4000 in £50 shares. Rennie had estimated that the excavation of the canal would cost little more than £3000, and construction contracts were

[1]MSS. of William Burnthwaite, transcribed and quoted in Park, *Some Ulverston Records*, 17 sqq.   [2]*Loc. cit.* ; the Liverpool subscribers were Daniel Backhouse (8 shares), Henry Blundell (6), William and Samuel Pole (6), Peter Baker (2), and Thomas Clarke (2).   The remainder of the support was largely local and included Wilson Braddyll of Conishead (2), Thomas Sunderland, ore merchant and afterwards the company chairman (2), John Machell, probably of the Backbarrow Company (2), Robert Fell, Ulverston merchant and, later, banker (1), and Birch, Robinson and Walmsley of the Backbarrow cotton mills (with a total of 6 shares.)   The shares were £50 each.   [3]Priestley, J., *A Hist. Account of the Navigable Rivers, Canals and Railways etc.* (1831), 404 sqq. ; Curwen, J. F., in *C. & W*. (NS), XVII, esp. pp. 30-32.   [4]33 *Geo. III, c. cv* [5]*Ulverston Canal Co., MS. Disbursement Accounts* (Brit. Transport Commission archives), where £41 1s. is paid to " John Rennie, Engineer " between 6.10.1793 and 25.8.1794.   [6]Copy of Act., Barrow P.L.

signed on October 1st, 1793, with John Pinkerton of Brockhouse and John Murray of Lancaster. A further contract was made with the firm of Lancaster and Duckworth of Blackburn.[1]

These contracts provided for the completion of the canal on or before September 29th, 1794, but it was not until October 1796 that the works were completed. Pinkerton and Murray were in financial difficulties by the August of 1795, and their work was carried on by H. Baird ; while the disbursement records of the promoters suggest that a figure well in excess of £7000 was actually spent.[2] The excavation coincided with a general slump in trade, affecting ore and slate exports alike, and proved to be a greater task than at first envisaged ; the channel, only a mile long, passed through low-lying peat moss and marshland, and was designed to accommodate vessels of 350 tons burthen rather than the barges and narrow boats of the inland waterways. It was 65 feet wide between the banks and 15 feet deep, partaking of the character of an extended dock. Numerous peatmoss tenements had to be purchased, and a basin was constructed at the Ulverston end, dock gates allowing ships to enter the canal from the Leven Estuary. Sites for shipyards and warehouses were provided,[4] and the extensive wharfage space was correctly calculated to be an attraction to shipping and to local merchants. Nevertheless, this attempt to draw trade to Ulverston itself suffered from one serious drawback ; it did not overcome the caprices of the Leven Channel, which was apt to change course in troublesome fashion, and by 1803 the Channel had left the canal gates and had moved over to the Cartmel side of the estuary.[5]

Efforts were however made to control the channel, and shipping made regular use of the Canal during the wartime period ; but its trade evidently fell far short of expectations. In 1798, 94 vessels of a total tonnage of 4704 entered it, and in 1802-14 the yearly average is stated to have been 132 vessels of an annual average tonnage amounting to 6,600. The latter total included the following categories :

[1]*Disbursement Accounts of the Ulverston Canal Co.* (MS.), 1793-7 ; cf. also Park, *cit.*, 21-2. [2]*Passim.* [3]*Disbursement Accts., cit.* [4]The firm of Hart and Ashburner transferred an existing shipbuilding business to the Low Yard, land near the S. bank of the basin was offered at leasehold for slate and iron ore wharves, and a warehouse at Canal Foot was projected ; *Mins. of the Ulverston Canal Co.* (MS.), 18.3, 13.6.1797, 4.7, 20.7, 17.10.1798, 4.12.1799, 18.1.1800. [5]*Mins. U.C. Co.*, 10.11.1801, 1.8.1803 ; *Antiquities* 1805 (Close Supplement), 405, which stated that " the Leven is constantly changing its course . . . the navigation with larger vessels is impeded by banks of sand. This is the state at present . . . "

Timber	Coal	Slate	Iron Ore	Iron
566	1826	1888	316	123

This table compiled by William Salmon, may be incomplete or inaccurate, for in 1807 alone the registered tonnage of imports through the port of Ulverston totalled 18,018 tons, including 4763 chaldrons of coal and 8747 gallons of " spirituous liquors ", and the registered exports were 28,560 tons ; it is likely, however, that these figures included the trade of Barrow, Greenodd and other Furness shipping points. [2]   Hence the averages given above may show that the difficult approaches to the port of Ulverston, together with a depression in the ore trade which appears to have taken effect following 1804, [3] did seriously injure the Canal's prospects. It is certain that the remaining statistics of its trade (given below) should not be taken as a reliable index to the commerce of the district as a whole.   As has been shown, [4] local shipping was carrying on a regular trade in agricultural produce with other coastal districts of Lancashire, and the slate quarries were busy in about 1810.

Between 1814 and 1820 the directors of the Canal Company lost interest in its affairs, [5] although receipts from tolls comfortably exceeded ordinary expenses, and although improvements were made to the Canal works. [6]   In 1821 the Canal tolls were leased to William Town and T. B. Tolming, and no records of income or expenditure are available until 1828, when the company proprietors took it over once more.   The volume of trade (in terms of shipping tonnages) in 1820-4 was as follows : [7]

Table 9

Vessels entered and cleared outwards with cargoes at Customs House   Ulverston

Jan 5th-Jan. 5th	Inwards		Outwards	
	Vessels	Tons	Vessels	Tons
1820-21	443	24,977	605	34,585
1821-22	389	21,573	620	32,216
1822-23	386	21,603	539	29,125
1823-24	382	21,223	576	30,316

[1]Salmon, Wm., *History of the Ulverston Canal*, in *Jackson's Ulverston Almanack*, 1851.   [2]Dickson, *op. cit.*, 630.   [3]Cavendish, Lord E., *Barrow Times*, 27.7.1878, giving ore production figures from Buccleuch archives.   [4]See pp. 45, 68 above.   [5]*Mins. U.C. Co.*, 5.12.1814, 3.1., 25.1, 5.6, 19.6, 4.7, 12.7.1815 and *passim*.   In 1814-5, six meetings in seven months had to be adjourned on account of bad attendance, and, up to 1820, meetings were desultory.   [6]Figs. in Park, *op. cit.*, 24-5.   Receipts were £1,527. 12s. 7½d. (1815-20) and ord. expenses £866 1s. 2½d.   A new pier at Canal Foot cost £688 10s. 4d., and a new basin wall £341 12s. 7d.   [7]White, Wm., *Furness Folk and Facts*, 23.

By 1828, however, there was an improvement in trade, and although imports had fallen slightly below those of 1824, 695 vessels with cargoes totalling 37,431 tons left the Canal.[1]   Of the outwards goods, about 20,000 tons were iron ore and 10,000 tons were slate.[2] In June, 1828, the proprietors understandably concluded that " if the Canal was retained in the Hands of the Proprietors instead of being again let, it would produce much more than the usual rent obtained for it . . . they should keep it in their own hands until 4th June, 1829, for the purpose of ascertaining as to how far the belief as to the advantage of retaining it themselves over letting it, was correct . . . " (sic).[3]   Thereafter the business of the Canal grew with little intermission until 1846, when 600 coastal vessels discharged in the port and 344 (loaded) vessels left it, the total tonnage of all coastwise cargoes being 61,360.[4]   But the Canal Company did not declare its first dividend until 1835, when 5 per cent. was paid to shareholders[5]—the lack of any recorded payment for nearly forty years may have been a consequence of the heavy debts or losses incurred during the canal excavation and the early years of its history.[6]

In 1835, however, only a portion of the coasting trade of the immediate district passed through the Ulverston Canal—which in turn accommodated more vessels engaged in such trade than any of the smaller ports of the Lancashire seaboard—and if the tradesmen and gentry of that town had attempted to monopolise coastal commerce, they had failed perceptibly.   They met with competition from minor slate and ore-loading points like Kirkby Pool and Barrow, and the Leven approaches continued to offer difficulty. When the Furness Railway was opened in 1846, the fate of the Canal was sealed ; it is significant that the railway directors showed little or no interest in utilising the latter, and preferred to concentrate upon and improve the port of Barrow instead.   Although the Canal had some value as a public utility, it did not solve the transport problems of the local haematite and slate industries, and was at best a parochially inspired and limited venture.

The coastal trade of the Lancashire ports (excluding Liverpool) during the later years of the period was as follows :[7]

[1]Figs. to Jan., 1829 ; *op. cit.*, 25.   [2]*Parson and White* (Directory), *loc. cit.* [3]*Mins. U.C. Co.*, 4.6.1828.   [4]*Port Inspections* ; cf. also series of figures in White, *op. cit.*, 25-6.   [5]Park, *op. cit.*, 22, quoting *Burnthwaite MSS.*, etc. No dividend payment is recorded in the company minutes, which seem incomplete, until 5.1.1841.   [6]E.g., in 1801 the company was in debt, and decided to raise £370 on mortgage of tolls ;   *Mins. U.C. Co.*, 4.12.1801. Its business was not always efficiently conducted.
[7]*Port Inspections*.   The absence of shipping figures for a particular year does not signify an absence of trade ; merely that an entry is lacking in the above sources.   " Ireleth and Angerton " may be taken to mean Kirkby Pool, where slate was loaded from Kirkby-in-Furness quarries, and " Barrow & Walney " to mean primarily Barrow village with Piel Harbour.

Table 10

Vessels inward and outward : coastal trade only. (*Furness ports underlined*)

Ports or creeks	1834 In	1834 Out	1838 In	1838 Out	1839 In	1839 Out	1846 In	1846 Out	1847 In	1847 Out
Ulverston	343	322	466	563	419	449	600	344	571	341
Barrow & Walney	34	186	41	234	28	223	226	51[1]	263	50
Ireleth & Angerton	78	141	68	16	76	16	55	18	51	11
Lancaster	487	172	179	102	209	97	253	114	231	104
Glasson Dock	—	—	310	96	406	101	227	152	183	110
Poulton	—	—	9	2	13	—	—	—	—	—
Arnside Grange	74	72	52	63	67	69	94	75	80	75
Creek of Poulton	41	3	88	5	—	—	—	—	—	—
Lytham & Freckleton	343	295	270	166	—	—	—	—	—	—
Preston & Hesketh Bank	132	100	137	96	—	—	—	—	—	—

The above particulars clearly show Barrow's rise to comparative importance as a coastal shipping point. It was regularly and frequently used long before an important industrial town appeared near the site of the harbour, and the Furness Railway Company's decision to run a railway to it was therefore hardly surprising. The Newland Company, which habitually sent its iron ore through Barrow or Conishead Bank, apparently objected to the tolls charged by the Ulverston Canal proprietors in 1834,[2] and the latter refused to reduce their charges. The increase in outgoing vessels from Barrow (1838) may be noted. Meanwhile, the iron ore output of the Plain Furness mines increased fairly steadily, as output statistics for the Duke of Buccleuch's Dalton ore pits indicate :[3]

Table 11

Duke of Buccleuch's mines   Plain Furness

Average annual outputs by decades		Outputs in individual years	
Decade	Average annual tonnage		Tons
1811-20	4310	1810	7586
		1813	2914
1821-30	8086	1820	1584
		1825	7658
1831-40	13,341	1826	15,808
		1840	35,093
1841-50	45,884	1841	39,962
		1842	38,866

[1] " Rampside ", a locality facing Piel Harbour, was here entered.   [2] *Mins. U.C. Co.*, 6.5.34, 4.6.34.   [3] Cavendish, Lord E., *loc. cit.*

In 1840-3 the annual production of iron ore in Furness was about 75,000 tons, or almost double the quantity produced in the Buccleuch mines.[1] The destination of the haematite, as before, was primarily South Wales.[2] Great difficulty, however, was experienced in moving it in sufficient quantity from mine to ship, and in 1825 local merchants considered the possibility of an improved method of transport ; " considerable interest was taken in certain experiments and trials made on colliery tramways near Newcastle, in January of that year . . . It was thought that some form of horse rail or ' tram ' way might be utilised in Furness, but the suggestion was dropped "[3]

The port of Barrow was preferred by ore merchants by virtue of its sheltered position, and shipowners were prepared to give lower rates because of the relative safety of the Barrow Harbour and its approaches.[4] Although Ulverston was situated nearer to the iron mines of Lindal Moor, the lower freight charges at Barrow more than outweighed the higher costs of cartage to the newer port ; and the unwillingness of the Canal proprietors to accommodate the Newland Company has already been mentioned.[5] Accordingly the latter firm continued to use Barrow, and other merchants were beginning to show an interest in its harbour. In 1825 Thomas Fisher of Dalton, a substantial yeoman who had the leasehold of a number of ore pits there, began to ship haematite from Barrow in association with his brother Joseph Fisher ; and a nephew of the Fishers, Joseph Rawlinson, who was later to become one of the leading ore merchants of the district, engaged in the partnership of Town and Rawlinson which erected a second jetty at Barrow in 1833. The Fishers and Rawlinson purchased land in the village.[6] Six years later, Charles Storr Kennedy and partners,[7] known as the Ulverston Mining Company, caused a third jetty to be erected there. Kennedy and his sons Myles and Charles Burton Kennedy had a future of great prosperity before them.

These particulars, of limited importance in themselves, demonstrate that individual ore dealers fully appreciated the value of this small port some years before the Furness Railway Company decided to develop it, and the prior enterprise of the haematite merchants helps partly to explain the jealousy and distrust which later subsisted between the merchants on the one hand and the railway

[1]*Ibid.* [2]Detailed records of local shipping appear in Stephen Soulby's *Ulverston Advertiser*, first published in 1847. Many of the visiting vessels were from Welsh ports. [3]Melville, J., and Hobbs, J. L., *C. & W. Tract Series*, XIII, 1. [4]*MS. notes* by W. B. Kendall, by courtesy of Messrs. J. L. Hobbs and H. Kendall. [5]See p. 93 above. [6]*B.N.F.C.*, XVII (1909), 184 ; Fisher, J., *Popular History of Barrow*, 41 ; Richardson, *F.P. & P.*, II, 269 ; Casson, *A Few Furness Worthies*, 77-8. [7]*B.N.F.C.*, *loc. cit.*, and 183, 189 ; also mining lease in the Tytup Hall archives (Boughton Estates Ltd., by courtesy of Mr. H. A. Slater), of July 7th, 1838, for details of the partnership. See also p. 194 below.

directors on the other.[1]   In 1842, meanwhile, a fourth jetty was erected in the Barrow Harbour by H. W. Schneider and partners ; Schneider, a man who was to leave indelible marks on the economic history of the neighbourhood, commenced mining in Furness in 1839.[2]

The mere exportation of iron ore, however, could not produce a town or even a sizeable village at " Barrowhead ", and Ulverston remained, for another generation, the centre of commerce for the immediate region.   Until well into the eighteen hundred and fifties its canal remained busily occupied, and there can be no doubt that the latter, however parochially conceived, brought material benefits to the tradesmen of a place which hardly deserved to be a port at all judged in terms of nineteenth-century standards and geographical advantages alike.   Shipbuilding industries became well established in the vicinity of the canal, constructing vessels of up to 354 tons (600 tons burthen) in two yards, those of Hart and Ashburner (a firm established at Ulverston in the late eighteenth century), and Petty and Postlethwaite (1820).[3]   William White's painstaking enquiries into early Lloyd's shipping registers have shown that some 27 ships were launched from these yards between 1798 and 1829, nearly one vessel annually.[4]   Although it was not likely to absorb a large number of workers, local shipbuilding gave stimulus to a variety of associated trades ; ropes, sails and anchors were made in the locality, Petty and Postlethwaite became bankers and extensive timber dealers, iron and brassfounding became established in the town itself, and by 1828 a growing coastal trade supported eight coal dealers who had businesses there.[5]   This trade was associated with an increase in the number of shopkeepers (including wine and spirit merchants and keepers of inns and taverns) and the population of the township increased markedly during the first three decades of the nineteenth century ; and Ulverston gained from the exportation of woodland and agricultural products such as hoops and malt, iron ore, slate, gunpowder, cotton and linen goods and leather, while importing consumer goods to meet the needs of a growing local population.   On this old market town the economic life of the district was focussed.

Whatever wealth the district thought itself to possess, however, was still largely exported in the form of raw materials.   There was little or no important advance in local manufactures in the

---

[1]See pp. 182, 188, 211, 214 below.   [2]See pp. 173, 192 below. [3]*Mins. U.C. Co.*, 17.10.1798 ;   White, Wm., *op. cit.*, 32-3 ;   *Mins. U.C. Co.*, 4.11.1815, 23.12.1823.   [4]*Op. cit.*, 30-4, and 46-8.   [5]*Parson & White, loc. cit.*   The trades list given here may be compared with that given in the Barfoot and Wilkes *Directory* of 1794 (IV, 633, fragment held in Barrow P.L.).   The Ulverston population in 1801 was 2937, and in 1831, 4876.

period 1811-31,[1] although about a quarter of the population of 1831 was dependent on retail trade, and one-third on agriculture. Another—and the most important—type of wealth was leaving the peninsula, that represented by human beings. Although migrants, after making special arrangement, could move their families and chattels to other districts by coasting vessel, communications by land were still so arduous and inconvenient as to discourage the seeker after new employment in Lancashire industries. There were adequately organised coach and wagon services between the north and the central areas of the county,[2] but the poorer family was still obliged to travel by cart or foot across the sands. A somewhat more convenient mode of travel was established in 1835, when the steam packet *Windermere* commenced to ply between Ulverston Canal Foot and Liverpool *via* Blackpool;[3] the Canal Company nevertheless put obstacles in the way of this service.[4] A few years later the *Express* and *James Dennistoune* steamers began to sail between Bardsea and Fleetwood,[5] the Furness Railway taking over the latter service in 1847.

---

[1]*Census of* 1811, 1821, and 1831, *cit.*, s.v. Furness and Cartmel.   [2]Melville & Hobbs, *C. & W.*, XLVI (1947), esp. 85-9, 93-6.   [3]*Mins. U.C. Co.*, 4.9.1835 ; Melville & Hobbs, *op. cit.*, 97-8.   [4]*Mins. U.C. Co*, 3.11, 4.12.1835, 21.1, 18.4.1836.   The Canal proprietors attempted to charge the owners of the *Windermere* £10 *per annum* for each passenger " and his or her luggage so that such passenger luggage does not exceed 1 cwt."   No agreement was reached for five months, the Canal Company refusing to allow passengers to land at the Canal pier at one point in the argument.   [5]Melville & Hobbs, *op. cit.*, 98.

Sir,

Mr Romney most respectfully takes
the liberty to inclose a Bill of the
Pictures he has had the honour to
paint for Sir Gilbert Elliot, and begs
to know if Sir Gilbert now chooses
to have Lady Elliot and Mr Douglas's
Portraits sent to his house.

Pictures painted for Sir Gilbert Elliot
by —   Geo Romney

Lady Elliot, Portrait 39:⁰ — 18:18
Lady Morris's half length a copy 31:10
Sir Gilberts 39:⁰ — 18:18
Do for Sir James Morris — 18:18
Do for Mr Douglas — 18:18
                              £107 2

Holograph bill for some Romney portraits.   (for Romney, *see* p. 151)

At Conishead Bank, a typical 18th century Furness landing place—notice ore-loading in progress, and the oversands travellers in the distance (*see* pp. **82, 85**).

The end of the oversands route near Ulverston, showing the entrance to the Ulverston Canal (*see* p. 82 *and* ff.)

Dalton market place in the early nineteenth century, showing the obelisk, the cross (above which hung the May-pole) and the

Ulverston market place in the late eighteenth century ; a view down King Street. (*see* p. 121)

SHIPP'D, by the grace of God, in good order and well conditioned by Backbarrow Company in and upon the good Ship called the Mermaid whereof is master, under God for this present voyage, John Rush and now riding at anchor in the Ulverston Smith's Bank and by God's grace bound for Chepstow to say,

a Cargo of ___ Whitriggs Ore fifty eight tons or thereabouts

being mark'd and number'd as in the margin; and are to be delivered in like good order and well conditioned at the aforesaid port of Chepstow (the danger of the seas only excepted) unto Mr John Partridge of Monmouth Esqr

or to his assigns, he or they paying freight for the said goods according to the delivery of the Rate of seven shillings p Ton with primage and average accustomed. In witness whereof the master or purser of the said Ship hath affirmed to three bills of lading, all of this tenor and date the one or which bills being accomplished, the other two to stand void. And so GOD send the good Ship to her desired port in safety. AMEN. Dated in Ulverston 1st L. 1779

Per on Board John Rush

Bill of lading. 150 tons of Whitriggs iron ore sent per the vessel "*Mermaid*" by the Backbarrow Co. to Chepstow. (see p. 36 *and* ff.)

Greenodd as a Furness port. (*see* pp. **85, 237**).

Sir John Barrow's cottage at Dragley Beck, Ulverston. (*see* p. 123).

CHAPTER VI

THE POPULATION OF FURNESS, 1700-1831

The baptism, marriage and burial registers of Furness parishes indicate that the population of the district grew considerably during the second half of the eighteenth century. It is generally accepted that parish registers have their limitations as sources of reliable statistical information, and an element of incompleteness in their recordings can be taken for granted. Nevertheless, the entries of parish clerks and incumbents, in their various registers, agree in one essential matter ; that baptisms outpaced burials more and more during this crucial period. The general excess of the former over the latter was greatest in the parishes of Dalton and Ulverston, the first affected by ore-mining, and the demand for wheat and other cereals, and the second of these parishes by a development of commerce in the Cumbrian sub-region. The excess was apparently least in almost purely agricultural or woodland parishes like Aldingham and Colton, but was comparatively marked in Broughton-in-Furness, a small market centre with slate quarries and an iron furnace not far distant, and in Kirkby Ireleth, an adjoining moorland parish which contained a number of thriving slate quarries described elsewhere. [1]

In the following study, nine Furness parishes or chapelries receive detailed examination. They represent about 65 per cent. of the total area of Furness, and in 1801 their combined population amounted to 9706 souls out of 13,880 for the whole of the peninsula, or rather over two-thirds of its population. Five of these parishes embrace large areas of Plain Furness, which was the most populous part of the district in the eighteenth century and afterwards.

Needless to say, Furness was not alone in its apparently rapid multiplication of souls. The whole of Lonsdale Hundred (and, as will be far more obvious, the whole of Lancashire) participated in this increase. Yet these north-western districts are not to be lumped together, for Furness and Lonsdale experienced Cumbrian conditions, rather than those of industrial Lancashire; and it is fascinating to the local-historian-turned-demographer to find that the adjoining county of Westmorland increased in population by

[1]See pp. 42-6 above.

very little during the eighteenth century.[1]   Evidently, then, Furness and Lonsdale possessed their own special attractive forces or stimuli to increase, and present individual problems for our analysis. A statistical impression of baptisms and burials in these areas is rendered as follows :[2]

Table 12

	Furness			Lonsdale (35 registers including those of Furness)		
Years	No. of pars.	Average annual Bap.	Bur.	Years	Bap.	Bur.
1701-10	5	104	89	1700	439	410
1711-20	6	124	106	1710	394	367
1721-30	6	156	139	1720	495	403
1731-40	7	167	142	1730	496	456
1741-50	7	166	116	1740	543	391
1751-60	7	201	114	1750	539	390
1761-70	7	218	136	1760	715	369
1771-80	7	243	140	1770	690	394
1781-90	7	268	149	1780	815	472
1791-00	7	247	149	(ave.) 1781-90	835	499
				1791-00	940	540

The widening gap of post-1740—as between baptisms and burials—is fairly clearly seen here. As regards Furness, the gross excess of baptisms over burials shown by the seven[3] parishes amounts to 6463, and since the 1801 census population of the seven parishes amounted to 9268, a superficial estimate of population increase suggests a trebling during the century. Individual cases, however, show that the method of calculating population increase from simple excess of baptisms is an unsound one. By such standards, Dalton had risen from a minus quantity ; Aldingham almost certainly contained more than 200 souls in 1701 ; while the parochial records of Torver show that division to have been, by the standards of the vicinity, comparatively populous in the late seventeenth and early eighteenth centuries. It is far more likely

---

[1]According to the late Prof. E. C. K. Gonner, *Jnl. Royal Stat. Socy.*, LXXVI, (1913), 296.   The view is borne out by an examination of *Abstract of the Answers and Returns (Parish Register Abstract), Census* of 1811 (1812), giving county and hundred register totals collected by Rickman.   Some recent work of Professor G. P. Jones (made available by courtesy of the author), utilising Chancellor John Waugh's survey of the Deanery of Westmorland, leads to similar conclusions.   [2]The Lonsdale figures are from the *Parish Register Abstracts, cit.* See *infra* for local figures.   [3]The parishes or chapelries of Aldingham, Dalton, Kirkby Ireleth, Broughton, Torver, Colton and Ulverston.

that the centennial excess of baptisms, in particular cases, represents broadly the degree of migration from the parishes concerned. [1]

As will be seen, there were considerable individual differences between Furness parishes in respect of their demographic history. The large adjoining parish of Cartmel seems to have followed the moorland—or Westmorland—pattern in exhibiting a comparatively gentle rate of population growth until well into the second half of the eighteenth century, [2] and we must not rush to conclude that merely because a parish is situated on the seacoast it must tend to show a more rapid increase than its inland neighbours. Meanwhile, the calculation of the exact or probable size of a local population at any given time is, for a number of reasons, a difficult and dangerous procedure. There are many objections to the use of parish registers for this purpose, most of them well known ; e.g., dissenters often had their own burial grounds, and either had separate registration of burials or did not register in the local parish churches at all, or that parish clerks were occasionally careless and forgot to translate a birth into a baptism, or that non-dissenters sometimes evaded the registers for special reasons, or that taxes upon registration discouraged people from entering church for such a purpose. Sometimes a burial-ground was closed, and people of a given locality were interred elsewhere with corresponding alteration of the registers,

---

[1]The local demographic calculations in this chapter are based largely on the following sources : the *Bishop's Transcript* of the Aldingham parish registers, in the Lancs. R.O. ; the *B.T.* of the Dalton registers, supplemented by a detailed statistical abstract made by William Close in his notes to *Itinerary* (Copied by T. Alcock Beck), Manchester Reference Library ; *The Registers of . . . Torver near Coniston*, 1599-1792, supplemented by the *B.T.* for Torver, Lancs. R.O. ; Clark, J., and Dickinson, R., *The Registers of the Broughton-in-Furness Chapel . . .* 1634-1812 (Lancs. P.R. Soc. 1950) ; Dickinson, R., *The Registers of the Chapel of Lowick in the Parish of Ulverston*, 1718-1837 (Lancs. P.R. Soc., 1954) ; *The Registers of the Chapel of Blawith* (the same, 1954) ; Williams, A. A., and Burns, J. P., *The Registers of Colton Parish Church* (Kendal and London, 1891) ; Bardsley, C. W., and Ayre, L. R., *The Registers of Ulverston Parish Church* (Ulverston, 1886) ; and *The Registers of Kirkby Ireleth* (Lancs. P.R. Soc., 1912). Since the abstracted figures and calculations are based upon copies, albeit scholarly and reliable ones ; and since a small margin of error in totalling entries, and in transferring O.S. year entries to an N.S. year basis, must be allowed for, any statistics here given must be taken as indicative of general trends rather than as literally accurate in all cases. Other points may be noted as follows : (a) Dalton had parochial chapels at Walney, Ireleth, Rampside and Barrow, and registration of baptisms and burials was made at Walney after 1744 (cf. *C. & W.* (NS), XX, 102) ; (b) within the original bounds of Colton parish, Finsthwaite was made parochial in 1725, but contained less than a tenth of the Colton population in 1801 ; (c) the registers of Ulverston offered particular difficulty, and the entries for a number of moorland chapelries within the main parish (Lowick, Osmotherley, Blawith, Subberthwaite) had to be eliminated in order to give a picture of what was happening in the township of Ulverston, primarily before 1750.

[2]*B.T.* of the Cartmel registers, Lancs. R.O. The population altered little between 1670 and 1750, and may have increased by about a third (from *c*.3000 in, say, 1770 to 4007 in 1801) later in the eighteenth century.

or, as in the case of Ulverston, the inhabitants of a dependent (but separately registering) chapelry might betake themselves to the mother church for baptisms, marriages and funerals at different and inexplicable times.   In certain cases it is possible to test the effects of these movements or influences, and more often it is impossible to do so.   Under the terms of the Stamp Act of 1783, for instance, a stamp duty of threepence was levied upon every register entry of a burial, marriage or christening.   This duty was repealed in 1794, but there were not, in the aggregate, many more local entries in 1795 than in the previous year, and we have no proof that the unfavourable economic conditions of 1795 were not in fact responsible for the increased burials recorded in several parishes.   Regarding non-registration through negligence or evasion, it should be observed that it was almost certainly much more difficult to hide the news of a death than of a birth (which might well be most carefully concealed), and even in the scattered moorland settlements of southern Cumbria, public opinion and censorious talk alike must have helped in no little degree to smooth the way for the demographic investigator.   It is troublesome but not impossible to calculate the numbers of dissenters in a given place, and some exercises in this direction are set out below.

On the whole, it seemed justifiable to use the totals of register entries for decades to work out the probable populations of the most important Furness parishes at succeeding points between 1700 and 1801.[1]   The employment of a multiplier—a simple ratio, or combination of ratios, obtained by the division of average baptisms or burials for, say, 1791-1800 into the 1801 population, or of similar totals into the 1811 population—made such estimates feasible,[2] but has at least one serious drawback ; namely, that the births and deaths in 1801 do not bear the same relationships to the total local population of that year as, say, the births or deaths of 1750 to the total population of that point in time.   In other words, the " age-composition ", or distribution and size of age-groups in the population, changes over time, and the younger groups increase in size and relative importance as the population grows.   With this serious objection in mind, the following estimates were made.   At least one striking common feature emerged from these estimates, and from the close examination of the baptisms and burials which they entailed ; the decades 1751-60 and 1761-70 saw the largest relative increases for the century in the majority of the parishes investigated, and there can be little reasonable doubt that a general leap forward in local population growth took place in the space of the decades

---

[1]A table of probable populations is given in the writer's Ph.D. thesis in the University of London and Barrow-in-Furness Libraries, *The Economic and Social History of Furness*, 1711-1875, p. 120.   Although it may well be that, as guesswork, they are acceptable, they may lead the unwary reader into assuming that they are actual statements of population.   [2]The multiplier is then applied to earlier baptisms or burials.

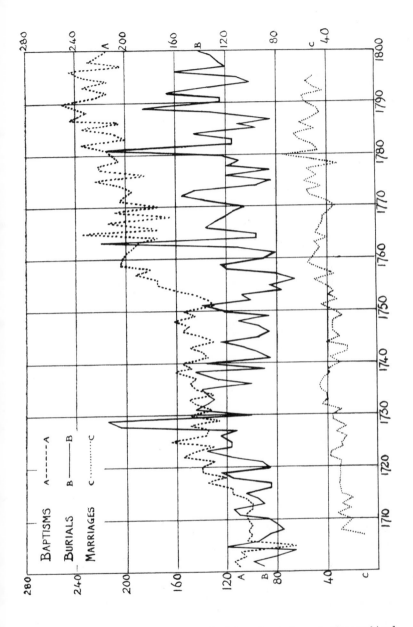

Fig. 5. Fluctuations in baptisms, burials and marriages in the combined parishes of Ulverston, Broughton, Dalton, Aldingham and Colton. (N.B. marriages, making much smaller totals, in fact rose in similar proportion to baptisms).

mentioned.   Numerous experts agree that the English population set out on a distinct climb following 1740, and to this extent, Furness was merely following the national trend ; on the other hand, the development has significance as far as local history is concerned, for in the first of these decades there was a known development in the industries of the area.[1]   It is the task of the regional historian to look for possible connections of this kind, rather than to cater for those who prefer to look at demographic problems semi-mystically.

The population of the moorland parishes or divisions tended to increase but slowly between 1700 and 1800.   This generalisation applies to Colton (and its adjacent parish of Finsthwaite[2]), and to Blawith, Lowick and Torver when allowance is made for the tendency of their inhabitants to register in Ulverston itself.   Father West's baptism figures for Hawkshead,[3] whether strictly accurate or not, give a similar impression of slow growth in the fells.   Nevertheless, the healthy ascendancy of baptisms over burials in a number of these parishes (following 1740 at least) indicates that they must have lost steadily by migration during the second half of the century. The comparatively rapid upward curve of the baptisms in the slate-quarrying parish of Kirkby Ireleth (very marked after 1770) indicates the direction and range of some of this migration ; that is, between four and seven miles over the fells to the westward. Broughton-in-Furness, as we have seen, also seems to have attracted people, and further evidence in this direction is discussed below.   The town of Ulverston grew very considerably during the eighteenth century, from an estimated 1168 in 1710 to 2937 in 1801 ; and the greater part of this increase took place between 1700 and 1760.   Ulverston's relatively slow growth thereafter is borne out by Thomas Pennant, who noted in 1772 that it had " about 3000 souls ",[4] which, as will be seen, is more than the 1801 figure.   During the second half of the century Ulverston appears to have experienced virtually the same movements as the parish of Dalton, where considerable immigration (probably of a coastwise nature) was seemingly balanced by emigration.[5]   The Plain Furness agricultural parishes of Aldingham and Urswick manifested the comparative sluggishness in growth of the moorland parishes.[6]   The population growth of Furness as a whole probably kept in step with the recognised estimates (for this period) of English trends.[7]   More than this one dare not say.

---

[1]See especially pp. 31-4 above, and pp. 57-8.   [2]For Finsthwaite, West, *Antiquities* (1774), 48 sqq.   [3]*Ibid.*

[4]*Pennant*, 29.   [5]Such emigration was taking place before the eighteenth century ;   the parish registers of Lancaster, Halton and Heysham give occasional evidence in this direction.   [6]Aldingham figs from *B.T.* ;   Urswick in *Antiquities, cit.*   [7]My totals for seven Furness parishes, obtained by adding together the individual estimates, compared with national growth (est. by Griffith, *Population Problems of the Age of Malthus*, 18) ;

	1750	1760	1770	1780	1790	1801
7 Furness parishes	6547	7310	8041	8723	9099	9318
England (000)	6252	6664	7123	7580	8216	9168

The marked local increase of 1751-70 was certainly not the only sharp step upwards during the century, and several baptism registers show an increase between 1711 and 1720 ; but the following two decades, locally as well as nationally, called a halt to rapid growth. In particular, the years 1728-9 produced disastrously high burial-rates in many parishes of the north-west, and during the 'twenties and 'thirties as a whole, every Furness register examined was able to show several years in which burials exceeded baptisms by a considerable margin. But the recovery of 1740-60 must have received some stimulus from the expansion of iron manufacture during those years, and from the growing trade in iron ore, wheat, barley, beans, slate and textiles. The precise form and nature of this stimulus is a matter for further exploration, and it is not suggested that the factors making for population increase are purely economic. But neither need they be detached from the social structure and from social processes. Other possible factors making for population growth are discussed elsewhere in this chapter.

In such a discussion, much depends on the adequacy of the registers as true recorders, or indicators, of births, deaths and marriages. The degree of carelessness attributable to parish clerks must remain an imponderable ; but religious dissent, almost certainly a cause of greater incompleteness, can be allowed for in a comparatively realistic estimate of nonconformity. The available registers of the Quaker burial grounds of Swarthmoor, Sunbrick and Colthouse[1] show the Quaker population of Furness never to have exceeded three hundred (i.e., Friends' burials never averaged more than five per annum in any one decade in the eighteenth century), and episcopal visitation reports probably exaggerated its extent. Yet, in the late seventeenth and early eighteenth centuries Quakerism had deep roots in the district, which provided George Fox with a wife and fellow-campaigner, combined in the person of Margaret Fell. Some Quakers, of course, used the parish churches if they were obliged to do so, and 19 " dissenters " were baptised at Colton between 1701 and 1706, out of 113 baptisms altogether.[2] This probably gives a fair indication of the proportion of dissent in the Colton area at that time, when Presbyterians, Baptists and Independents (as well as Quakers) were reported in the near vicinity. As for the Catholic element, four " Papists " were reported in Ulverston in 1717, and thirteen in 1767, while a Catholic mission was not established in Furness until 1779, and a chapel not until 1806. Likewise a Congregational church was opened in 1778, but no Wesleyan Methodist Chapel appeared in the Ulverston

---

[1] *Vide* (for transcripts) Harper Gaythorpe in *C. & W.* (NS), VI, 275 sqq. ; E. J. Satterthwaite, *Records of the Friends' Burial Ground at Colthouse* (1914), 53 sqq.   [2] But about 5 per cent. of the Colthouse burials were those of non-Quakers.

district before 1814 ;[1] Wesley himself passed through the peninsula in 1759, but did not stay or campaign locally.   Such developments must have affected the completeness of the parish registers comparatively little.   It has been suggested that an addition of 10 per cent.[2] to burial totals will suffice to translate them into deaths in a given area, but it is not unlikely that little more than five per cent. added to the Furness burial totals would produce figures from which reliable death rates could be calculated.   Ten per cent., however, can be accepted as on the safe side, and from the use of such a margin we can proceed (as below) to generalise about the health conditions of the district.   On the other hand, it may be that the baptisms failed to reflect births by a rather larger proportion, and of these recordings it can only be said that they kept fairly closely in step with the numbers of marriages recorded during the eighteenth century.   Unfortunately we have no idea where the incompleteness lay.

POPULATION CONSTANCY AND IMMIGRATION

Furness was emphatically not a closed community during these years, and it will be as well, before making any further estimates relating to population growth, to ask how much and how far Furness people habitually moved during their lifetimes, and how far away they originated if they were not local people in the first instance.   An analysis of the recurrence of surnames in the parish registers (or in other records like land tax lists) will give a rough idea of the " constancy " of local populations ;[3] likewise, a close examination of the places of origin of marriage partners will tell us a little of the movements of the people.   In making this examination, we must distinguish between two types of movement ; purely *localised* mobility, as between one parish and the next, and long-range movement.

The marriage registers of seven Furness parishes show that between one in five and one in six local girls found grooms outside their own parishes between 1731 and 1780, but that their husbands rarely originated more than fifteen miles away.   These records indicate that there was a slight tendency to increased movement *between* local parishes by the end of the eighteenth century, and an investigation of the recurrence and disappearance of surnames in certain parishes appears to support this view.   Professor G. P. Jones, analysing the surnames recorded in the Broughton-in-Furness registers, found a relative increase in new surnames entered there in the period 1751-75, and an equally marked disappearance of

---

[1]*V.C.H. Lancs.*, VIII, 356; for visitations &c., *op. cit.*, 285, 303, 318, 328, 338, 341, 342, 356, 360, 364, 369, 380, 385n., 386, 400, 406 ; *Antiquities*, 1774, 288 ; *Hist. Soc. L. & C.* (NS), XVIII, 220.   [2]Griffith, *op. cit.*, 35.   [3]E. J. Buckatzsch in *Population Studies*, v, 1951, esp. 65 ff.

names during the same years,[1] although the names themselves were
for the most part those of stocks well established in the area. Thus,
there was undoubtedly increased movement or turnover of people,
and the Broughton registers record the appearance of a few Scots
or Irish people after 1738. The indigenous population, however,
showed little tendency to wander far, as the following figures will
demonstrate :

Table 13

Distances of places of origin of marriage partners

Years	Parish	Total of marriage partners	Distance from parish			% of all partners from 10 + miles away
			10-15 miles	15-25 miles	25 + miles	
1701-12	Ulverston	200	6	5	1	6%
1754-9	,,	200	3	3	1	3½%
1791-5	,,	200	5	6	3	7%
1701-34	Broughton	200	10	4	4	9%
1755-75	,,	200	—	7	3	5%
1758-89	Lowick	92	—	1	4	4%
1813-37	,,	82	1	4	3	6½%

Although this table tells us something of the deeply-rooted
habits of Furness people, it is nevertheless apt to be misleading.
If, in dealing with the parish of Ulverston, we turn to surnames
recorded, rather over 1100 are entered into the registers there ;
but at least 485 of these appear for the first time between 1750 and
1812, a period covering about one-fifth of the total span of years
covered by those volumes (1545-1812). The striking general feature
of these new names is their distinctiveness from those of the local
family stocks, which nevertheless continued to appear with regularity ; well-established names of the region, like Atkinson, Benson,
Brockbank and Coward, may be contrasted with Abbott, Addington,
Anson or Anstey. About one-third of these new names were
entered in the registers only once, and a significant proportion of the
485 were those of birds of passage. Even more indicative of what
was taking place, however, are 72 Scots and Irish names which are
recorded during the same period (1750-1812), perhaps 30 of this
group being Irish (like Casteen, Looney, Quinn and Murphey).
Fifty of the surnames in this group were registered before 1800,
but only ten before 1780. Fourteen of the Scotsmen or Irishmen
are described as " mariner ",[2] and others were entered as blacksmith, furnaceman, ship carpenter and waller ; but only three were
husbandmen. Ulverston may have had a Celtic population of
possibly 150 persons by the year 1800. Meanwhile, there were

[1]Jones, *op. cit.*, 145.   [2]The Lorn (Newland Co.) and Goatfield (Duddon
Co.) furnaces were then operating in Scotland. Haematite was sent to both,
and iron and perhaps charcoal were brought back. This would help to
explain the presence of the local Scots contingent.

approximately as many new surnames in its registers between 1760 and 1800, as there were souls added to its population between the same dates—if, of course, the estimates adopted here bear any relation to the realities of the period. In other words, the town must have been a *pied à terre* for numerous migrants, many of whom had children baptised and then moved on. [1]

At Kirkby Ireleth, where the registers are not complete until 1728, and where the population grew steeply from 1760 onwards, some 363 surnames are entered between 1728 and 1812, and 156 new names appear during the period 1760-1812. Of these, 83 are names of known local or regional association, appearing more or less frequently in the registers of parishes in the area. About seven of the non-local names of post-1760 are Irish or Scots. The Kirkby slate quarries were flourishing by 1790, and then employed " all the labourers in the neighbourhood at high wages ". [2] The growth of population here was certainly connected with movement (towards the slate quarries on Kirkby Moor) from nearby parishes. Meanwhile, the entry of the names of non-local charcoal burners or " colliers " (Diamond, Doyel and MacEllen) at Broughton in 1738-40 was equally plainly connected with the establishment of the Duddon iron furnace to the north of the village in 1736. But the implied migration of local and non-local people seems to have affected the habits of the indigenous population comparatively little; nor does it follow that industrial development automatically led to any significantly intensified movement of people.

The account books of the Backbarrow Company are helpful here ; and it is clear that the expanded charcoal iron industry of post-1711 had no such easily marked effect as quarrying at Kirkby. Nearly all that company's employees, save a number of skilled furnacemen and forgemen, were persons of local or regional origin. Hence, the Backbarrow founder in 1714 was Christopher Burne or Burns, stated to be an Irishman, [3] and of the furnace fillers two were named respectively Cavenagh and Fitzpartridge (? Fitzpatrick) ; but another filler was named Holme (common enough locally) and the general labourers at the furnace bore names like Ormandy, Close, Townson and Turner, all of local association and occurrence. At Leighton in 1715 the furnace " keeper " was Richard Myres, one of his fillers was a Turner, and the general labourers there included two Stricklands (a characteristic Westmorland name), a Hird and a " Rushel " or Russell. It is chiefly in the case of the Backbarrow forgemen that there is real evidence of immigration. Men named Daw, Leonard and Rawlins were imported from the south-west by arrangement with Samuel Milner of Bewdley,

---

[1] Developments of this kind should warn fellow-students of regional demography against accepting certain types of conclusion vis-a-vis local fertility rates.
[2] See p. 43 above.   [3] *E.I.I.F.*, 287 sqq.

Thomas Sheels and Jacob Grout came from Staffordshire, and Robert Highly and William Cobb may also have come from that region. [1] John Lavinder, George Bevins and John Myers came from Ireland, but Richard and William Mayberry were smiths of local (probably Cartmel) origin. [2] In all, twenty finers and hammermen were employed by the Backbarrow Company between 1713 and 1715, of whom perhaps fifteen were importees. Not all of these workers found Furness congenial to them, and at least seven forgemen and furnacemen decamped within the two years mentioned. [3] But it was only in the refining department of their work that these ironmasters must have felt a real labour shortage ; other work, like general labouring, carpentry, carting and charcoal-burning, [4] was done by local persons. A few families, notably that of Bevins, became firmly established in the ironworking trades of the district, but there is certainly no evidence of any large-scale influx of workpeople.

Had the iron industry attracted any appreciable number of immigrants, the arrival of newcomers would have been shown in register and other entries of the immediate area. In the large parish of Colton, on the border of which lay the Backbarrow ironworks, [5] there is little evidence of any such tendency. [6] Even when waterpowered cotton mills were established on the Leven in about 1780, the baptism-rate of the parish of Colton showed little inclination to depart from the very gradual upward curve of previous decades, and a sharp climb in that rate was in fact noticeable only after 1800.

Nevertheless, a trickle of immigration affected even the most unassuming localities. The chapel registers of Lowick and Blawith, remarkable because they contain sets of entries giving three or fourgeneration pedigrees, [7] tell us something about the movements or origins of locally settled people during the course of the eighteenth century. It is possible to work out the descents of 108 individuals in those chapelries. Of these persons, some 10 per cent. had parents

---

[1] *Backbarrow MSS.* ; *G.L.*, fols. 319-21, and *Leighton Cost Account .Book* (1715-). Highly may have come from Bristol ; *G.L.*, fol. 250, where his wife is given money to go there. [2] *G.L.*, places *cit.*, and 327, 398 ; for the Mayberrys, *Ulverston P.R. cit.*, marriages, 14th Aug., 1654, " Nicholas Mayberrie of Cartmel, smith ". John Mayberrie was a witness. Abraham Darby I knew one of the " Maybery " family ; cf. letter reproduced by Dr. Chaloner, *loc. cit.* [3] *G.L.*, 398, which gives a list of losses on workmen, one of whom was brought to the assizes. [4] *G.L.*, 96, where 17 people with local surnames are supplying charcoal to Coniston forge in lots of two or three dozens at a time.
[5] The Backbarrow furnace and forge lay on the W. bank of the Leven, just within Colton parish. The apprentice-house of the cotton-mills was also within Colton. [6] A few ironworkers' names occur, however ; William Cobb d.1734 (Colton burials), Thomas Highly's name is mentioned 1723 (baptisms), and Richard Myers " founder of Low Wood " is entered in 1749 (burials). [7] Baptismal entries of this type appear at Lowick 1778-80, and in 1789-91 ; and at Blawith, 1778-80. Some similar burial entries occur. A few Furness and Lancs. parishes show examples.

or grandparents who had originated more than fifteen miles from the chapels concerned, and who included in their number individuals from distant places ; Portsmouth, Bolton, Blackburn and the Isle of Man. Several of the entries, while not reflecting immigration of this type, indicate a certain degree of movement in southern Lakeland—some Blawith people had forebears in Kendal, Crosthwaite, Bootle or Grasmere. A Blawith slate-quarryman had had a father in the last-mentioned place, while yet another quarryman of the same chapelry had evidently originated in Winster, Derbyshire.

Likewise the moorland chapelry of Torver, statistically a tiny sample but also suitable for close analysis on that account, experienced a marked turnover of population during the same century. Torver had never supported more than 200 people on its sheep pastures and stony lowlands near the foot of Coniston Water ; but some 277 surnames appear in the Torver chapel registers between 1599 and 1792, and, because certain families were firmly rooted in the local lands—notably Atkinsons, Parkes and Wilsons—there was unquestionably a considerable turnover of settlers, during that period but chiefly during the eighteenth century. In the second half of the latter there was a definite weakening of the old clans, whose names appear less frequently in the registers and land tax lists. Between 1760 and 1792, 28 married couples or families, or about 100 people altogether, entered the chapelry. Only six of their surnames appear in the land tax list for 1790 ; several were those of paupers, and a plainly Irish and very numerous family named Milligin produced one of the latter. From the parish of " Clanroughan " (Llanrhychwyn) in Caernarvonshire came John Tennant, miner,[1] who married in Torver in 1761, and who proceeded to raise a family in his Lakeland home. Other newcomers' names, like Slee, Spedding and Washington, suggest that their bearers came from other parts of Cumbria.

It should be emphasised that the total population of these moorland parishes did not grow rapidly, and that their rate of turnover, over the space of a generation or several generations, was not great ; the entry of one new family a year would make a noticeable impression on a list of names taken from the registers. It is almost certain that in the case of the coastal parish of Dalton-in-Furness, the rate of turnover or change was very much greater ; over the eighteenth century as a whole, Dalton's excess of baptisms over burials was of the order of more than 2000, and yet the 1801 population of the entire parish was only 1954. The rates of baptism and burial indicate that the total population of Dalton had increased

[1]Llanrhychwyn had an " abundance of pyrites, worked by a company from Liverpool ", and " extensive slate quarries " ; Lewis, S., *A Topographical Dictionary of Wales* (1833), Vol. 2.

only very gradually during the century ; and even the small market town of that name contained only 1052 inhabitants in 1801, compared with 612 in 1631.[1] William Close's separate enumeration of 1806 gave Dalton only 590 people (viz., the town as distinct from the parochial hamlets). While properly distrusting these figures, we can accept the very slow rate of growth ; and it is worth adding that iron-mining villages like Lindal and Martin were hardly populous at that time, and contained respectively 111 and 56 souls in 1806.[2]

What can account for the state of flux that is implied? The most convincing explanation is that the sea-carriage of iron ore and other goods from Furness was instrumental in causing some mariners to settle in Dalton parish, and equally responsible for the emigration of others. The late Mr. P. V. Kelly's account of the Dalton hamlet of Newbarns shows that tenements there were purchased by men from Caernarvon and Westmorland (both mariners) during the first half of the eighteenth century.[3] Shipbuilding and carting attracted others. These considerations, however, do not fully account for the relatively large numbers involved, and numerous travellers, crossing the sands from northward or coming over the hills from the east, may have found settlements in the locality. Meanwhile, emigration went on, and William Close's comment of 1805 that Dalton farmers' sons had been generally " bound apprentices to such mechanical employments as are indispensable in the country "[4] can be left to speak for itself.

It may be said by way of summary, then, that there was much short-distance movement within Furness during the eighteenth century, and some long-distance migration into the district from Wales, Ireland and Scotland. The numbers of persons involved in this long-distance immigration were never large, and there is no evidence that local industries led to the permanent settlement of many strangers from afar.

EMIGRATION FROM THE DISTRICT

It is not until the first decade of the nineteenth century that there is comparatively firm evidence of emigration from the district. The North Lonsdale census returns of 1801 and 1811 show that the population of that area increased absolutely by some 1178 persons between enumerations. The parish register abstracts[5] for 1801-10 give an excess of baptisms over burials amounting to 2588 souls ; and, since the baptismal registers are

---

[1]Barnes, *op. cit.*, 62 ; *Census of* 1801, *Abstract of Answers and Returns*, *Pt. I*, 165. The figures given in the last are probably worthless.   [2]*Itinerary*, 138.   [3]*B.N.F.C.*, V, (NS), 26-7.   [4]Close, *Supplement to Antiquities* (1805), 342.   [5]*Census of* 1811, *Parish Register Abstracts*, 73.

probably more incomplete than those for the burials, the total migration from the district (obtained by subtracting the census increase from the natural increase totals and making a small adjustment for any missing births) must have been of the order of 1500 persons. This would give an average loss of about eighty persons per parish in the ten years, or less than ten per cent of the local population in the same time. There is no reason to believe that the emigration rate ever exceeded this figure during the eighteenth century,[1] although Dalton, with its comparatively high " turnover " rate of about 2000 people in a century, must have maintained its ten per cent per decade fairly steadily.

Several Furness parishes lost proportionately more people than this during the decade 1801-10. The census enumeration totals (1801-11) for Kirkby Ireleth, Broughton and Colton, when compared with the total baptisms and burials recorded in each parish during approximately the same period,[2] show that a net loss of 15 to 17 per cent. of average total population had taken place at some time in the ten years. This is well above the average for the district, and it is interesting to note that each of these parishes contained industrial activity of some kind. The reader will not need to be reminded that industries, even at this period of economic development, were subject to the effects of depression in trade, and it is clear that the slate quarries of the district, including those in the Broughton and Kirkby localities, suffered following 1794 and in 1801, as did the iron ore mines of Dalton.[3] Pauperism was comparatively heavy in both Kirkby Ireleth and Broughton in 1802-3[4]—that is, by comparison with the rest of the area—and it is known that there was a stoppage of the Backbarrow cotton mills, on the boundary of Colton parish, in 1809 or 1810.[5]

We have already seen that the population of Kirkby Ireleth was partly built up by immigration in the late eighteenth century ; in the case of Colton, however, immigration and emigration seem to have been very marked within the same decade of 1801-10, when baptisms soared far above those for any decade in the previous century and reached the rate of 41.7 *per annum*, as against 18.9 for the burials. Yet the 1811 census total for the parish showed an increase of only 8 persons since 1801! Not only was there a strong tendency to natural increase in the parish ; there were numerous attractions in the vicinity for the migrating labourer. A gun-

---

[1]For an attempt to calculate net local losses by emigration during the 18th cent., see my thesis, *cit.*, Table 17, p. 135. [2]Using published registers, *cit.* [3]See pp. 35, 44-5 above. [4]*Parl. Papers, Sess.* 1803-04, Vol. XIII, *Abstract of Returns of . . . the Poor*, s.v. Lonsdale. Paupers of all kinds, including children, amounted to 179 in Broughton and 156 in Kirkby ; more than 15 per cent. of all persons in each case. [5]*Parl. Papers., Sel. Comm. Children in Manufactories*, 1816, III, 286.

powder works was established at Lowwood in 1799 ; it was said of Colton and district in 1803 that wood labourers' wages were " much advanced of late years, at least 50 per cent of their labour by the piece "[1] ; and, as has been seen,[2] the proprietors of the Backbarrow cotton mills had built a sizeable colony near their works, and the 1811 Census shows that there were numerous manufacturing families in Haverthwaite, Finsthwaite and Rusland. But migrants did not settle permanently in the locality, and it appears that the great disparity between baptisms and burials indicates the presence of a young and mobile population of work-people (who were, judging by their surnames, mostly from the immediate area) which moved out as well as flowed in.   People with large families and low living standards (in 1816, " very poor people and mostly Irish "[3]) sought employment for their children at the Backbarrow mills, probably to be pushed onwards when that employment ceased.

Such migrants do not seem to have gone to other Furness parishes to the north and west—even in Ulverston, population growth for the period 1801-10 was maintained largely by natural increase, allied perhaps to immigration which was nearly balanced by emigration—and the inference is that like the Backbarrow pauper children who were turned adrift to beg, they went across the sands towards Lancaster and the south.   In this way Furness supplied its quota of people to the economically advancing areas not many dozen miles away.

In the following decade, 1811-20, such emigration either ceased altogether or was masked by the return of soldiers and sailors to their homes in the district. The baptisms and burials recorded in the official abstracts indicate a natural increase of some 3620, and the censal increase was 3825.   Indeed, there are rather surprising signs that the migratory process was reversed, and it was stated by enumerators that Hawkshead and Kirkby Ireleth were receiving settlers from the " manufacturing districts "[4] (which could have included West Cumberland).   In the following decade, 1821-30, which included phases of acute agricultural depres-sion in the north-west and elsewhere, the emigratory process seems to have commenced once more ; the censal increase was 1421, but the natural increase at least 3512, suggesting that about 2000 people left the district in the ten years.   It is obviously unwise to read too

[1]*Gent. Mag.*, II (1803), 1201-2.   [2]See p. 51 above.
[3]*Sel. Comm., cit.*, John Moss's evidence, 184.   There were few Irish in Colton before then.   The registers give the surnames Daffady (1804) and Sophia Murphey of the poorhouse (1807).   [4]The Hawkshead statement was that local population increase was " ascribed to the depressed state of the manufacturing districts, causing the inhabitants to resort to agricultural parishes " ; *Census of* 1821, 154, notes (b) and (c).

much into these figures and statements, but there is at least a *prima facie* case for the closer investigation of those rural migratory movements which seem to have been connected with depression in or destruction of certain local industries. [1]

THE MECHANICS OF LOCAL POPULATION INCREASE

It is not difficult to demonstrate that the population of a given area has increased. The fact of increase, however, raises a great many more problems. Were people marrying younger and having more children after about 1740? Did the death-rate drop steeply, or the birth-rate rise? Although these problems offer a challenge which only the skilled historical demographer can meet in adequate fashion, it is most important not to confuse the technical and mathematical factors in the analysis of population increase with the *stimuli* to such increase, which may be environmental—the better food, housing and prospects offered in a particular area at a particular time. Generally speaking the local historian cannot be expected to involve himself in the technicalities of the subject, although he can sometimes throw light on probable stimuli to population growth and movement. The following comments, bearing upon probable birth, death and other rates, are made with some diffidence.

Firstly, it seems that there was no violent increase in the fertility of marriages during the eighteenth century, the ratio of baptisms to marriages remaining remarkably steady throughout most of that period. With the exception of the decade 1731-40, when the number of baptisms per marriage in seven Furness parishes fell to 3.71, the ratio did not sink lower than 4.07 (1711-20) and rise higher than 4.80 (in the following decade). Between 1751 and 1800 the decennial ratios fluctuated comparatively little, and were, in six Furness parishes combined, respectively 4.13, 4.34, 4.21, 4.39 and 4.17. [2] It is known that there was some population movement in and out of these parishes, and for this reason, in order to obtain as close a relationship as possible between marriages and the children born of those marriages, the figures for the latter in a given decade were divided into the baptisms for the same decade. [3] The resulting averages are to be regarded with great caution, although they do indicate a trend. They cannot take account of illegitimacy (even though the latter was not a serious factor locally), and they do not allow for probable under-registration of baptisms at different and non-uniform periods. Likewise, they are not to be confused with accurate fertility-rates.

[1]Further knowledge of this character might throw light on certain doctrinal controversies which continue at the time of writing. [2]Seven parishes were used for the decade 1751-60. They accounted for nearly two-thirds of the population of Furness in 1801, and the six parishes for more than 60 per cent. of it. [3]The usual method in such cases is to employ five or ten-year overlapping averages.

Unfortunately we know little about the average ages of Furness people at marriage until the late eighteenth and the commencement of the nineteenth century, when the figures for three parishes become available. There is little sign, then, that marriages in the Plain Furness parish of Aldingham—for the period 1790-95—were contracted noticeably early in life, for at 24 successive weddings the average age of the bridegrooms was 29 years (the oldest being 71 and the youngest 20), and of the brides, 27 years.[1] The median age of 14 Blawith bridegrooms (1803-13) was 27 years, and that of their brides, 23; and in 25 successive Lowick marriages (1802-12), the bridegrooms averaged 31 years of age, and the brides again 23. Other scattered entries giving ages at marriage occur in the Lowick registers (i.e., 1779 and 1790-1), and out of 46 sets of marriage particulars recorded in these Crake Valley chapelries, about six partners out of 92, including two known widows, appear to have re-married. It is not profitable to generalise from such comparatively small samples, although it does appear that in these rural localities the social habits affecting marriage ages had altered little in any direction which might tend to press those ages downwards; and what is known about the little-varying average size of the Furness family in previous decades also points to lack of such change.

Increasing numbers of baptisms and marriages, allied to falling burial-rates, combine to tell the same story of rapid population increase between 1740 and 1760. Before that period, burials tended to outstrip baptisms in numerous periods and parishes,[2] although this tendency was not so continuous or so great as to halt what was evidently still a limited increase of people in the district. The wastage of lives was particularly heavy in each of six sample parishes during the 'twenties; but more young people than in any previous decade came forward to get married during the 'thirties, as though anxious to make up for the losses sustained, and the gaps caused by death seem to have been more than replenished by 1750. Every parish showed a considerable fall in burials between 1730 and 1750, and the greatest overall increase in baptisms took place between 1740 and 1760. The widest divergence between the two, taking the first proportionately to the second, occurs about 1760; thereafter the gap remains open, but baptisms, burials and marriages proceed on what are roughly parallel lines, each showing a more or less steady increase until about 1790. In other words, there was a flattening of the upward curve of population increase after 1760.

It is more than likely that parishes like Ulverston, Broughton and Kirkby Ireleth (heavily represented in these calculations) are not fully representative of the district or region as a whole, in the

[1]Particulars in *B.T.*   [2]See Table 12, p. 98 above.

sense that they were subject to some localised migratory flux which brought in more young people than old ones ; this, indeed, must be a specialised problem affecting all parishes situated on trade routes or affected by industrial growth. But all the local parishes investigated seem to have been influenced by broadly similar social or demographic forces. The middle of the eighteenth century, it should be re-emphasized, was a period of marked local economic development. The items of evidence are manifold, and have been dealt with in previous chapters. The redistribution of lands in town fields by farmers anxious to make the best of their tenements ; the indications of growth in local shipping; the onset, after a phase of exhaustion, of a new period of intense cultivation of the local woodlands ; the increased production of potatoes, beans and wheat ; the development of iron ore mining and slate quarrying ; the erection of local furnaces in mid-century ; each of these factors coincides with or precedes what is palpably a growth of local population, affecting primarily agricultural or moorland parishes as well as those touched in some way by industry.

Since it appears unlikely that any permanent increase in the fertility of marriages was the cause of this increase, it remains to enquire into the probable parts played by rising birth-rates or falling death-rates. The calculation of movements in the latter must depend upon more or less accurate assessments of the size of local populations during the eighteenth century ; and since these estimates depend on what is mere arithmetical guesswork, the calculation of birth or death-rates is also of limited value. It was found, on employing one set of local population estimates, that the baptism-rates for seven Furness parishes combined rose from 24.7 in the thousand persons estimated living in 1731-40, to 29.2 in the thousand (1751-60), thereafter remaining fairly close to the latter figure until 1800 ; while the burial-rates fell from 21.0 in the thousand (1731-40) to a mere 16.5 in 1751-60, to fall slightly below this in the last three decades of the century. The latter, it need hardly be said, are not death-rates, and would need the addition of one or two burials or deaths in the thousand to make them into realistic estimates. It is worth adding that in 1841, the first occasion when a censal year coincided with civil registration, the death-rate in the Ulverston Registration District was 17.7 and the birth-rate 32 in the thousand souls living. The death-rate remained at about 18 throughout the eighteen hundred and forties.[1] Between 1774 and the mid-nineteenth century three authorities agreed that Furness was a particularly healthy district, and while we might expect that the local historians and patriots West and Close would affirm something of the sort, it is more to the purpose to find that the Registrar-General's office is in agreement with them.

[1] Published *Annual Reports of the Registrar-General.*

It seems likely, on the whole, that a more or less steadily depressed death-rate—from about 1740 at least—was the potent factor in local population increase. This, of course, agrees with the generally accepted view of eighteenth-century demographic history. If the local increase of people had been sustained by immigration in any important sense, unhealthy conditions would have killed off immigrants and their children just as the larger towns killed off their settlers.[1] There may have been, as we have seen, a sharp but temporary increase in birth-rates in the middle of the century, just as there were apparent sharp fluctuations in children born per marriage between 1731 and 1750 ; but these developments were evidently not decisive.

PUBLIC HEALTH AND SOCIAL CONDITIONS

Whatever may be said of the probable causes of rising birth-rates, there is no doubt that social conditions have a direct bearing on death-rates. Even if relatively more children are born year by year, a certain number of them will continue to be killed by filth or those diseases engendered by filth. But there is little doubt that conditions improved in Furness and the whole of Cumbria between the seventeenth and the end of the eighteenth century ; there was a disappearance of the bubonic plague, for instance, and local parish registers provide irrefutable evidence that such serious epidemics were far less frequently encountered in the eighteenth century as a whole. The latter, however, demands more attention. It is only too clear, when we examine an age which buried at least one-third of its children in infancy or youth, and very often many more than this, that the child or infant burial-rates are matters of some importance. The calculation of these rates must inevitably be a good deal rougher than that of all burials or baptisms ; for the ages of persons buried were entered in the registers only in the last two decades of the eighteenth century. The method used here relies upon the frequency of occurrence of the burials of " sons " and " daughters " (a scattering of whom, 5 per cent in one sample taken where ages were given, were unmarried adults), and the extraction of these entries, from all other entries in the largest Furness parishes, yielded some interesting and suggestive results.

It was found that throughout the eighteenth century the numbers of " sons " and " daughters " buried, decade by decade, made up a little-varying proportion of one-third of all burials in these parishes. After 1777 the burial ages in some registers became available, and when the actual child mortality (out of all persons buried) was compared with the rougher calculations for the earlier

[1] If the burial figures for boroughs given in Rickman's register abstracts mean anything at all, they are salutary.

decades, the results were most encouraging ; the more accurate calculations also showed, in the aggregate, a proportion rather less than one-third—up to 38.9 per cent. in populous Ulverston, but down to 25.0 per cent. in Colton (1791-1800). [1] We would expect a country or moorland district to be healthier than a town. As regards child mortality as a whole,) or what could be called, more accurately, juvenile mortality), the one-third proportion of the overall burial figure is of more than passing interest.

If, for instance, radical changes in the care of public health had taken place in the district at any point in the eighteenth century, then the burial-rates of infants and juveniles would have reacted accordingly, *ceteris paribus*. It is known, for instance, that small-pox and other contagious or infectious diseases were partiuclarly deadly in their effects on young children, who had little chance to build up resistance or immunity. But fortunately for these children, epidemics were either fairly infrequent or localised, and it is possible to chart their course and extent by examining the burial registers.

The first and second halves of the eighteenth century were examined separately with a view to isolating high-mortality years in Furness parishes. Two factors were distinguished once these years had been isolated ; the totals of all such yearly burials above the decennial averages, and the totals of " juvenile " burials above the averages of all such burials for each decade. [2] Such an investigation shows that local high-mortality years were slightly more frequent and rather worse in their effects in the second half of the eighteenth century than in the first half, and that proportionately more children suffered in the second half of the century!   This, again, would hardly square with any convenient theory of improvement in public health.   Against this, there is little doubt that child and adult death-rates were tending to fall or remain low, although it is also clear that they would have been even lower but for these epidemics and—what are equally important—years of privation and near-famine.

The first half of the century saw only one really serious period of high mortality, covering approximately the years 1728 and 1729. Juvenile mortality, as a proportion of all burials, was by no means the most outstanding factor in this period ; adults were the main sufferers, and it is known that famine conditions affected large areas of the north-west at the time. [3]   Thereafter, where heavy juvenile mortality did occur, it was centred mainly in the small towns of

[1]Owing to a desire to test the earlier figures against the more accurate ones, all burials of persons under 21 had to be extracted to obtain these figures. Under-5 mortality was obtained separately ; see my thesis, Table 20, p. 140.
   [2]*Vide* thesis, *cit.*, Tables 21, 22.   [3]Stout, *Autobiography*, 113 ; Tooke, *History of Prices*, I, 40-41.

Dalton and Ulverston. This is also true of the second half of the century. In 1758-9, some 126 children or young persons were buried in six parishes, the deaths of at least 95 of these sufferers appearing in the Dalton and Ulverston registers over the two years. There was also a heavy attack on the ranks of the young in 1763.

It is not until 1772 that register entries enable a prevailing disease to be identified, viz., smallpox. In this year the outbreak was confined to Dalton, Ulverston and Bardsea, and it took effect chiefly in the spring and summer months. In the disastrous year of 1781, high food prices and consequent privation were almost certainly responsible for the toll of deaths, although 18 Dalton children died of smallpox in that year, and the spread of disease, as in previous cases, may have had an economic basis. Burial-rates fell to normal in the two following years. The year 1789, perhaps the second in order of wretchedness recorded in the century, has left unmistakeable traces in the registers. The Ulverston sextons buried as many paupers in 1788-9 as they had interred in the fifteen previous years, and at Dalton the burial-rate rose to nearly double its average for the decade, evidently the consequence of a severe winter and high prices of provisions ; the deaths here were mainly among adults, and were confined largely to the towns.

The prevailing impression, on looking over the burial register statistics, amounts to this ; that deaths due to abnormal causes were on the whole very few in relation to the total population of the district (or of the parishes subjected to close investigation), and that child or juvenile mortality was certainly not high by early or mid-nineteenth century standards. On the other hand, there is nothing to show the beneficial effects—if, indeed, there were any in reality—of improved medical treatment of mothers, infants and the young generally. Yet treatment of a sort was commonly dispensed to the poor ; we have the testimony of Sir John Barrow, (b.1764) the son of a smallholder and tanner of Ulverston, that: " The medical gentleman—an honest Quaker[1]—who brought me into the world, inoculated me when very young for the smallpox, and gave me, no doubt, a dose or two for the measles . . .".[2] In 1775 the same surgeon had to ride out from Ulverston and treat the Rev. Edward Jackson of Colton, six miles away, the latter receiving purges and bleedings,[3] and it is hard to believe that the honest Dr. Fell, assisted as he was by Dr. Rowland Briggs, Dr. Ainslie and others in the neighbourhood, would have sufficient time and energy to spare for the adequate treatment of the majority of the local young, sick or poor. By the seventeen hundred and nineties—*on paper*—the district was comparatively well provided with surgeons ; three

[1]Dr. John Fell (1724-1803) of Ulverston. [2]Barrow, SirJ., *An Autobiographical Memoir* (1847), 488. In 1772 an Ulverston boy is recorded (in the burials) as dying from " inoculation ". [3]*Diary*, C. & W. (NS), XL, 9, 16-7.

in Dalton, two in Hawkshead, four in Ulverston, at least two in Broughton and a further three in Cartmel, giving a ratio per head (in Furness itself) of one medical practitioner to about 1180 persons. The ratio itself is quite impressive, until it is remembered that this was an age with poor roads, no motor vehicles and little rapid public transport. Hence it is not surprising to find that the eccentric Dr. Baldwin, Vicar of Aldingham, was dispensing medical aid to his parishioners shortly before 1800 ;[1] while at Ireleth in 1814 medical aid was furnished by the parsonage household to the district, an Ulverston physician having to travel six miles to deal with a case of more serious nature.[2] Moreover, this was still an age of the quack ; at Ulverston fairs in the late eighteenth century the travelling apothecary sold his " Balm of Gilead " or " Reverend John Wesley pills ".[3]

Not until the turn of the century did a local medical practitioner produce a visible effect upon public health. William Close (1775-1813), whose yeomen ancestors were of Dent, was the son of a Walney farmer ; apprenticed to a Burton-in-Kendal surgeon in 1790, he received a training at the Royal Infirmary and the University of Edinburgh in 1796-7, and began to practise at Dalton in the latter year. In 1798 Edward Jenner publicised vaccine inoculation, and in the following year Close introduced it into Furness. Taking up a temporary residence at Rampside, he inoculated the children of the local inhabitants at his own expense ; and a few years after this experiment, when vaccination had doubtless had time to overcome a little resistance, he made his analysis of the Dalton parish registers and claimed that the excess of baptisms over burials in that parish between 1799 and 1806 was " in part .....(due) to the exclusion of smallpox ".[4] It is a fact that Dalton child mortality was unusually low in those years, by the standards of the parish concerned and in spite of very high adult mortality in 1801. Having little in common with a Malthus, Close expressed joy at " a gratifying prospect of an unprecedented increase of population ".[5]

Writing in about 1803, Close recorded his own observations on the state of health in Dalton parish, remarking that the latter was " particularly healthy ". The air was good, and " scrofulous complaints " were " very uncommon ", while cases of phthisis were few.[6] In another passage he remarked that " the inhabitants of Furness are very healthy ", adding significantly that " medical advice is more necessary than formerly ".[7]

[1]Barrow, *op. cit.*, 135 ; for surgeons, *Barfoot & Wilkes* Directory, 1797-8, except Hawkshead (which 1794). [2]*Diary* of Margaret Ashburner, *C. & W.* (NS), XLIII, 1943, 57. [3]Bardsley, *Chronicles of Ulverston*, 7. Those who have read Wesley's *Primitive Physic* will see the point of the allusion. [4]*MS. notes* by Close, at the Manchester Reference Library. [5]*Ibid.* [6]Close's Supplement, *Antiquities*, 1805, 342-3. [7]*Op. Cit.*, 15 (Close's interpolation).

It is possible to test the veracity of these remarks, again by recourse to the burial registers. Close himself drew attention to the number of cases of longevity occurring in Aldingham in 1799-1801. An examination of the transcript registers for that parish, which are unusually detailed from 1789 to 1800, shows that 15 out of 42 persons died aged 70 years or more, and seven of them aged more than 80, but that 22 died under 50 years, including 11 children under 5. Throughout the larger parishes of the area, child mortality was very high by twentieth-century standards, although not emphatically not by those of the mid-nineteenth century. The Aldingham under-five mortality figure for 1791-1800, 25 per cent. of all burials (and 11.6 per cent. of all baptisms) was, it is clear, unusually high for a country parish in that locality ; even Ulverston did not aspire to more than 27.9 per cent. of all burials in the last decade of the eighteenth century. In Colton, between 1781 and 1810, under-five burials, by decades, did not average more than 15.9 per cent. of all interments. In Colton, Broughton, Ulverston and Dalton, the tendency during this period was unmistakeably a downward one as far as infant mortality was concerned, and the reduction seems to have taken place with or without Dr. Close's memorable introduction of vaccination. On the other hand, the " medical advice " to which that surgeon referred was probably beginning to bear fruit.

Equally striking is the longevity of many inhabitants. Sir John Barrow wrote of his mother Mary Barrow of Ulverston : " I can say that my mother never ailed anything while I was with her, nor to her last illness, which was that of old age, for she died in her ninetieth year ; and *her* mother had completed ninety at her death ".[1] The man who penned these words was 83 years old, and of Furness yeoman stock. Sir John and his forebears were representative of an important section of the Furness population, who somehow survived the supposed rigours of eighteenth-century life to complete long years of vigorous labour, sometimes achieving little but contentment, and sometimes eminence in the wider world, like Barrow himself. The following table will convey a fairly accurate impression of the numbers of people who lived to advanced age in three large and populous parishes.

Table 14

Distribution of burial ages

| Parish | Total burials where ages given | Percentages— | | |
		Died under 21	Died 21-70	Died over 70
Broughton, 1778-1810	612	32	35	33
Colton, 1778-1810	559	27	40	33
Ulverston, 1791-1800	538	37	35	28

[1]Barrow, *op. cit.*, 489.

Out of 46 old people who died at more than 70 years of age in Colton between 1781 and 1790, 27 were more than 80, and four were 90 or over ; and in the following decade, 30 out of 58 died at more than 80 years of age. It is important to add that a scattering of the octogenarians of the area were paupers, who survived to a great age in spite of poverty ; and the existence of unusually old people is not in itself an advertisement for the living standards of the locality.

Yet the fact is that average ages at death, in these rural districts, were markedly higher than in the industrial towns which were rapidly growing in South Lancashire and in the West Riding. This, of course, is what might be expected ; but it is nevertheless interesting to learn that in Preston the average age of all persons buried in 1783 was 31.6 years, of those buried in 1791, 28.6 years, in 1811, 19.9 years, and in 1821, 18.9 years. [1]   Numerous Furness people migrated in the direction of Preston ; but those who stayed behind enjoyed a much better chance of living to a ripe old age. At Broughton-in-Furness in 1781-90 the average age at burial was 34-5 years, rising to 47-8 years in the following decade, and falling by about two years in 1801-10 ; while at Colton it was 44-5 years in 1781-90 and went as high as 47-8 years in 1791-1800, standing at 44-5 years in Aldingham during the latter decade.   Even in Ulverston the average age at burial rose to 42-3 years in 1796-1800.   In rural Westmorland, the parishes of Barton, Brougham, Cliburn, Milburn and Crosby Garrett (in effect a random selection) enjoyed an average duration of life which was usually well in excess of forty years, [2] and at Shap (1780-99) " the median ages at death were about 52 for males and 57 for females . . . " [3]   In Ulverston the average burial age of persons who died at more than 21 years of age (in the period 1791-1800) was slightly over 60 ; in the other parishes mentioned the survival age was considerably higher.   Once a person had survived childish maladies and the occasional epidemic of smallpox or other serious disease, he could reasonably expect to live to advanced age.

The vital and other statistics given in these paragraphs cannot be entirely free from inaccuracy, but there is little doubt that the general impression conveyed by them is a truthful one.   It is sobering, as a matter of contrast, to examine the published reports of the Registrar-General for the middle decades of the nineteenth century, or the Reports of the General Board of Health.   It is scarcely relevant that many rural districts of England remained as healthy as Furness undoubtedly was ;   for the great shift from

---

[1]Calcns. from Preston Registers in *First Rept. of the Commrs . . . into the State of Large Towns*, Vol. I (1844), 176.   [2]Data by courtesy of Prof. G. P. Jones.   [3]Buckatzsch, E. J., unpublished *Notes on the Demography of a Westmorland Parish*, by courtesy of Professor Jones.

country to town was swelling from trickle to torrent between the end of the eighteenth century and the early years of Victoria's reign.

The tendency of population to increase cannot be altogether unconnected with the more solid expressions of a rising standard of life—better food, clothing and shelter.   Better housing is not the least of these desiderata, and the local historian will always do well to search for references to the construction or improvement of dwellings at different stages in history.   At a Pennington manor court in 1667, for instance, a tenant was ordered to make his house " tenantable with thatch " ; but even earlier than this, the inhabitants of the manor claimed a right to take slates for the repair of their tenements from the common and waste lands.[1]   It is thus probable that slate roofs were being constructed by the local peasantry ; the raw material, of course, lay near at hand.   Numerous strongly built farmhouses had appeared in the dales by the commencement of the eighteenth century ;[2] and during his visit to the district in 1772, Pennant commented favourably upon the character of the farmhouses in the Coniston Valley.[3]   Writing six or seven years later, Thomas West remarked that all Coniston houses were covered with blue slate, and that in the vicinity of Lowick, the cottages were similarly roofed.[4]   In 1772, Broughton had " the appearance of a new town ", some rebuilding of houses having taken place there in the middle of the century.[5]   Ulverston was " neat " and " excellently well paved " at about the same time, Dr. Close adding the epithet " clean " in 1805 and describing Dalton as " much improved of late, many of the worst houses having been pulled down and rebuilt in a plain neat manner and covered with slate ".[6]   In other words, thatch and crude house construction did in fact persist well into the eighteenth century, but mainly in places situated some distance from easily extracted building material.

There is some evidence that as slate was quarried in greater quantity, its use spread throughout Plain Furness ; hence, at Salthouse in 1760 " most of the buildings were in a ruinous condition ", but by about 1800 the farmhouses of that hamlet were rebuilt and roofed with slates, " the first to be used in the village ".   " One room on the ground floor of each house was boarded, another was flagged with free-stone, and the others with slate ".[7]   At nearby Newbarns all the clay biggins (clay and wattle hovels) had dis-

---

[1]Fell, Alfred, *A Furness Manor : Pennington*, 129, 160. [2]H. S. Cowper expressed a similar view at various places in his historical writings on Lakeland. [3]*Pennant, cit.*, 30. [4]West, *Guide (cit.)*, 46, 52. [5]*Antiquities,* 1774, 212 ; Jones, *op. cit.*, 140. [6]Pococke, *loc. cit.* ; West, *Guide,* 35 ; *Antiquities,* 1805, 342. [7]Kendall, *Salthouse (cit.)*, 37.

appeared by the middle of the eighteenth century. They had in fact been replaced intermittently by stone-built houses from 1683.[1] In parts of Plain Furness both limestone and red sandstone were available in quantity, and in Barrow village, Biggar and North Scale cobbles from the Walney shores were incorporated in dykes and cottage walling. By 1809 R. W. Dickson was able to affirm that stone and slated cottages were common in North Lancashire.[2]

Sound roofs and solid walls, allied to the good natural drainage of the district, may have had something to do with the infrequent occurrence of phthisis cases mentioned by Close. At Salthouse, however, inhabitants suffered badly from the ague in the eighteenth century,[3] and so did those who lived in low-lying parts of Cartmel. According to James Stockdale, the large-scale enclosures in that district (1796-1809) had the effect of eliminating this complaint.[4] A census enumerator of 1821, however, ascribed the population increase in Upper Holker, a part of Cartmel, not to the enclosure there but to " the prosperity of trade and the improvement of medical knowledge ".[5] Otherwise it is generally accepted that improved drainage had favourable consequences for public health, in the country as well as in the towns.

The 1801 and 1811 census returns throw a little—if only a little —light on housing conditions. The average ratio of persons to a house was just over five in both censal years—a common enough rural ratio throughout the nineteenth century. In both 1801 and 1811 the market towns or townlets of the district had a smaller number of persons per house—averaging 4.7 to 4.8 in each year— than the moorland or largely agricultural parishes.[6] It might be expected that the latter would hold more people in each dwelling, if only because the farmhouses had servants who lived in very frequently ; but the low ratio of the town houses is rather surprising, and is perhaps a commentary on the numerous tiny cottages which clustered in Ulverston, Dalton, Hawkshead or Broughton. Roughly one family in twenty shared a house. The number of persons per family (five) compares quite realistically with the baptism-marriage ratio of previous decades, if we make allowance for child mortality and for the older sons who migrated or the daughters who went away to service. Dr. Close, who conducted an unofficial but exceedingly interesting census of Plain Furness in 1806-7, found (not surprisingly) that the size of the average family varied considerably from parish to parish ; it was just over five in Dalton, 5.25 in Aldingham, but only 4.33 in Great and Little Urswick with

[1]Kelly, *Newbarns, cit.*, 34, 35.   [2]*Op. cit.*, 103-4.   [3]Kendall, *op. cit.*, 37. [4]Stockdale, *op. cit.*, 327-8.   [5]*Census of 1821, Abstract of Answers etc.*, p. 154, note (y).   [6]It should be remembered that 1801, and to a lesser extent 1811, were years of scarcity and privation. People may have been migrating.

Stainton and Adgarley.[1] One thing is quite certain ; whatever the lack of attention paid " to comfort, to ventilation, or the arrangement of bedrooms " (a complaint about Furness housing made more than forty years later)[2] there is little sign of the overcrowding that the urban England of the young Victoria was to know so well. Sir John Barrow's birthplace, in which that worthy's mother lived to ninety years of age, may still be seen at Dragley Beck just outside Ulverston ; squat, substantial and one-storeyed, it was built to protect its occupants from the Lakeland winds and rains, and we may take it as in every way typical. One can well imagine that more than five people would find life within it rather irksome ; but it was a durable home.

The erection of houses of this type must have been keeping pace with population increase long before the national census enumerations were instituted ; and the fact that housebuilding kept pace afterwards may or may not be a guarantee of improvement. Probably not, for much depends on the social class for which the houses were built. There was perhaps no drastic change in housing amenities until real industrialisation appeared in the district half a century later.

The subjects of diet and clothing, although fascinating and important, are generally ill-documented. In the mid-eighteenth century the common food throughout High Furness was " the thin oatcake ", but at Broughton in 1772, " tea, with itself " had " introduced wheaten bread ", and at Ulverston " tea and coffee (were) in general use " and oatmeal was " almost proscribed ".[3] But the latter remained a staple food of North Lancashire labourers for at least a century longer, [4] and was boiled with milk or water to produce " poddish " or was rolled unleavened and baked on a griddle-iron to make clap-bread. This is well known, and historians of the region are apt to write as though its labourers once lived on little else. The information collected by Sir Frederick Eden showed that the north-country labourer or artisan used quantities of milk with his porridge, and in one of Eden's specimen budgets a Kendal labourer is found sweetening his porridge with treacle, taking a little butter with his potatoes, and even aspiring to a few pounds of

[1]Close's figures for parish populations, in which he includes those for separate hamlets and settlements (see *Itinerary*, 136-7) may be compared with those in the official census returns by interpolating samples between parish totals for 1801 and 1811 :

	1801	1806-7	1811
Urswick	633	607	590
Dalton	1954	2072	2074
Pennington	273	252	271

[2]Binns, *op. cit.*, 103.
[3]*Antiquities*, 1774, 22, 212. [4]Dickson, *op. cit.*, 332 ; Garnett, W. J., *J.R.A.S.*, X (1849), 19.

meat annually.[1]   It is almost certain that the late seventeenth and early eighteenth-century Furness countryman had a more—not less—varied diet than this one. *The Account Book of Sarah Fell* (1673-8), although the record of a fortunately-placed household, refers to a wide variety of vegetables and fruits which were raised and sold in Plain Furness.   A bill of fare for Cartmel paupers (1735), a curious document, included meat " with broth and herbs " three times a week, and milk dishes four times, while water porridge appeared only once.[2]   In the hamlet of Salthouse, at the close of the eighteenth century, the inhabitants " lived principally on boiled salt beef . . . mutton was eaten at certain periods . . . Bacon, dried fish, cabbage, turnips, oatcakes and haver bread, porridge and other dishes made from oatmeal were also eaten . . . Fish was plentiful but seldom eaten fresh, being almost always dried before using, and the consumption of fish was comparatively small.   Geese were bred, or bought from drovers, fattened on stubbles, killed and salted down and then baked in pies ".[3]   The poorer people had their potatoes, which were grown in the district during the eighteenth century, and beans, which were also grown in Plain Furness.   Many tenements had their orchards, the husbandman or smallholder might have a few fowls, vegetables were obtainable, and newly-caught flukes could be obtained in coastal parishes.   But it is not until the early nineteenth century that we find a full and reliable list of fare consumed by a Furness family. Margaret Ashburner, the semi-lettered daughter of the curate of Ireleth, recorded details of the main dishes consumed by her family over 272 days in the years 1818-19.   Meat dishes of some kind occur roughly once in three days, fish less regularly but about once a week, potatoes or " scouse " once in six days and " poddish " or oatbread only sixteen times in all.   Greens, eggs and fruit receive little mention, but were certainly available, for the Ashburner family sold apples and eggs in Ulverston.   Salmon, flukes, crow pie and other delicacies occasionally appear, and " milk " was sometimes entered as a main dish, as was junket.[4]   Two points should here be made ; firstly, this curate's family was probably not superior in the social scale to the yeomen of the neighbourhood,[5] and secondly, the importance of milk in the countryman's diet should not be underestimated.   Even Sir Frederick Eden's Kendal weaver spent one-sixth of his annual income on milk, and his family consumed six gallons a week.[6]   So, apparently, did a rather poorer labourer's family of five persons.[7]

---

[1]Eden, Sir F. M., *The State of the Poor* (1797), 769, Vol. III ; *vide* also Vol. I, 496-510, 524-5, 542 ; III, 752-3.   [2]Stockdale, *op. cit.*, 172. [3]Kendall, *op. cit.*, 33 ; *vide* also Roeder, C., *Notes on Food and Drink in Lancashire*, L. & C., XX, 1902, 41 sqq.   A form of black-pudding, haggis or " hack-pudding " was consumed in Lonsdale.   [4]C. & W., (NS) XLIII, 55 sqq. [5]Wordsworth was at pains to point out the traditionally unassuming character of the clergy in the district.   [6]*Op. cit.*, III, 769.   [7]*Ibid.*

Without doubt the labourer's food was unvaried and mono-tonous, and in time of dearth, poor in quantity. Its quality is another matter, and it is still difficult to understand why so many persons of humble station survived to seventy or eighty years of age after lives of heavy labour and undoubted rigours. The general field of nutrition in history and in given regions obviously requires much more detailed examination, which might well throw light on at least one stimulant to population increase. [1]

It is perhaps impossible to show whether such a factor in living standards as that of clothing showed any great improvement in the eighteenth and early nineteenth centuries. We have West's state-ment of 1772-4 that imported clothes were supplanting home-made clothes in Ulverston, [2] but this did not put an end to local weaving ; more weavers appear in the Ulverston registers after 1790 than before that year. Cotton clothing—brought into this Furness port—and greater cleanliness, perhaps rather hazily reflected in a few register references to local soap-boilers, do of course have some bearing upon the health of the population. But it is perhaps more profitable to seek for evidence of a general rise in living standards, which may naturally have affected different social classes unequally, but which was nevertheless real in so far as it affected population growth. We can then turn to the parish registers for evidence of an increase in the number of retail traders in a small market town like Ulverston during the second half of the eighteenth century. Thirty-six members of the shopkeeper class appear in the Ulverston marriage registers between 1755 and 1780, and 45 in the years 1781-1806. There is nothing unexpected about this, and the town concerned was a retail trading and redistribution centre for a considerable area of south-west Cumbria. The number of cloggers, cordwainers and shoemakers bore a ratio of one to 150 of the local population by the end of the century (if the register entries are any sound guide), and for some reason these trades far outnumbered any others. [3] A more reliable enquiry reveals that Ulverston supported no fewer than thirteen clock and/or watchmakers between 1760 and 1800, although it is not clear exactly when they were in business ; it seems, however, that four to five were practising at any one time. [4] There were seven such tradesmen in the town in 1828 [5]. There were, in addition, at least three watch or clockmakers in Broughton in the period 1781-1800.

It is perhaps idle to attempt to trace any correlation between the number of tradesmen—even those who dealt in semi-luxury and luxury goods—and the general standard of living ; for if one social

---

[1] An eminent nutrition expert, the late Sir J. Drummond, has argued that the 18th century northcountryman was comparatively well nourished. [2] *Anti-quities*, 1774, 22. [3] The ratio was similar in 1828 ; *Parson & White*. [4] Infn. by courtesy of Mr. J. L. Hobbs. [5] *Parson & White*.

group or class[1] could afford to buy periwigs, clocks and watches, another was engaging the attention of the parish overseers and causing poor relief expenditure to increase in noteworthy fashion.[2] In outlining or hinting at the still more generalised social changes of this vital period, we are on somewhat safer ground.

In Chapter I it was calculated that in the early eighteenth century, about two-thirds of the Furness population was intimately connected with the land.[3] By the Census of 1811, 1701 Furness and Cartmel families were "employed chiefly in agriculture", and 2178 families were engaged in trades, handicrafts and manufactures, or were in none of these groups ; that is to say, the agricultural contingent had shrunk from two-thirds to less than half. As it stands, this calculation is not a very satisfactory one : but fortunately, the Ulverston marriage registers, copious in references to trades after 1753, support it admirably. These registers did not relate purely to the town of Ulverston, but also covered nearby townships and hamlets. They were analysed in two 26-year periods, 1755-80 and 1781-1806. There were 83 references to husbandmen and yeomen in the first period, and 110 such references in the second ; but there were 245 references to trades, industries and professions in the first and 419 in the second. The number of mariners increased from 29 to 68, that of weavers from 14 to 48, woodworkers from 13 to 25, and the professions or gentry from 19 to 47. As has been seen, the number of properties rated for land tax increased only slightly, and there was an actual reduction of medium-sized tenements in the second half of the eighteenth century.[4] References to labourers and paupers occur more and more frequently amid the parish register entries during the same period, especially at Kirkby Ireleth, Ulverston and Broughton. Hence, it would seem that a diversification of trades and industries was accompanied by a more obvious class stratification.

[1]There were "opulent tradesmen" in Ulverston in the 18th century according to the records of local taxation for the quindam or fifteenth ; Bardsley, *op. cit.*, 10.   [2]See pp. 136-7 below.   [3]See pp. 4-6 above.   [4]See p. 57 above.

CHAPTER VII

SOCIAL ORGANISATION : LOCAL GOVERNMENT, THE POOR LAW, SCHOOLS, AND OTHER INSTITUTIONS

1. LOCAL GOVERNMENT

The local government of the district altered little between Tudor times and the third decade of the nineteenth century. The formation of the Ulverston Board of Guardians in 1836 heralded the more rapid changes which were to follow. When the development of the Dalton ironfield was in full progress, the old systems of parish government were exposed and attacked as anachronistic ; but they were too deeply rooted to be transformed at once.

Before that eventful period the administration of Furness society was shared, as elsewhere, between parochial and manorial authorities. The typical parochial ruling body consisted of a closed vestry of twenty-four sidesmen, oligarchic and self-electing. Such bodies were common throughout the north and north-west of England,[1] although they seem to have adopted different forms in other parts of Lancashire.[2] They had, in the words of Sidney and Beatrice Webb, " no organic connection with the inhabitants at large, but—together with the Incumbent and the usual parish officers—acted in all respects in their name and on their behalf ".[3] Membership seems to have been based on the occupation of the land, here as elsewhere in the region.[4] Although the duties of the " Four and Twenties " were in the first instance church-centred— being concerned with the appointment and wages of clerks and sextons and the rotation of churchwardenships—they were, like the church itself, intimately bound up in many aspects of town and rural life. The Four and Twenties, from the sixteenth to the eighteenth centuries, became responsible for the administration of public endowments ; through their appointment of curate-school- masters and supervision of schools, public education came under their purview ; and they were responsible for the care of the poor. They took action against certain public abuses,[5] and by the imposition of church rates and cesses of all kinds, they reached into the pockets as well as the consciences of parishioners. Such bodies existed in Kirkby Ireleth,[6] Hawkshead,[7] Dalton, Ulverston and Cartmel. A revealing comment on the Dalton Four-and-Twenty

---

[1]Webb, *English Local Government* ; *the Parish and the County*, V, 174.
[2]In that area of Lancashire north of the Ribble their membership varied from eight to thirty ; cf. Tupling, G. H., *Trans. L. & C.*, LXII, 1950-1, 13.   [3]Webb, *op. cit.*, 173.   [4]*Op. cit.*, 244.   [5]As for instance in Cartmel, where the Twenty-four took ineffective action against encroachment on the commons there ; Stockdale, *op. cit.*, 198, 234-7.   [6]*Public Charities*, 88.   [7]Cowper, *op. cit.*, 112.

was made by Myles Sandys, jun., J.P., when reporting to the Poor Law Commission of 1834 : "They make parish affairs, I believe, a sort of ' close borough ' . . . Such vestries are very prevalent in this part of the country, and I consider them a great evil . . . It would be very difficult for the Annual Overseers to interfere with the 24, who are the oldest and richest farmers in the parish, and have established themselves as paramount ".[1] Vacancies caused by the deaths of Dalton sidesmen were filled by men chosen by the survivors,[2] and the Ulverston and Cartmel vestries were similarly oligarchic, the latter body including local gentry (Lowthers, Machells and Biglands) during the eighteenth century.[3]

The parishes of Dalton, Ulverston and Cartmel were, as has been shown, very large, and in each case there was some devolution of the vestry's authority. Dalton had four " bierleys " or divisions known as Dalton Proper, Above Town, Hawcoat and Yarlside,[4] and each of these, providing six sidesmen for the ruling vestry, was treated as a separate parish for the purposes of local and county cesses and for all the king's taxes. The divisions also maintained their own highways and appointed their own parish constables.[5] The parish of Ulverston was even larger than that of Dalton, and consisted of the Town and Hamlet of Ulverston, the four quarters of Osmotherley, Egton, Newland and Mansriggs, and the four chapelries of Lowick, Blawith, Torver and Church Coniston. Two churchwardens were appointed for Ulverston, one for the Hamlet and one for each of the four quarters ; while in the respective chapelries, a " chapel warden " was chosen by the joint consent of the vicar and the inhabitants.[6] The chapelry of Lowick had its own twelve sidesmen, the vestry here having a close relationship with that of the mother church in Ulverston,[7] and Church Coniston is mentioned as having had six sidesmen,[8] the multiples of six being a striking feature. The smaller but " independent " parishes of Aldingham[9] and Pennington[10] had twelve vestrymen in each case.

In the eighteenth and early nineteenth centuries, most of the Furness chapelries or divisions had their own overseers and managed their own poor, the parish of Colton having an overseer for each of five divisions.[11] In Dalton parish, however, the relief of the poor was centralised in the hands of the Four and Twenty,[12] and in Cartmel, which had an area of some 60 square miles embracing several parochial townships, all church and chapel wardens and

[1]Report on Admin. and Operation of the Poor Law (Rural Questionnaires), III, 1834, 271c. [2]Kelly, P. V., Dalton Church & Parish ,C. & W., XXIX (NS), 1929, 232. [3]Bardsley, op. cit., 17 ; Stockdale, op. cit., 196 sqq., for extensive references. [4]Kelly, op. cit., 231. [5]Loc. cit., and The Town's Book of Hawcoat (MS. copy), by courtesy of Mr. J. L. Hobbs. [6]Bardsley, loc. cit. [7]Bardsley, op. cit., 17 (note). [8]Public Charities, 110. [9]Humphris, Dendron (loc. cit.), 248. [10]Fell, A., Pennington (cit.), 277. [11]Public Charities, 41, 43. [12]Kelly, loc. cit.

overseers of the poor were appointed by the twenty-four vestrymen for the whole parish, an individual township like Lower Holker raising its own poor and constable rates during the eighteenth century.[1] After March 28th, 1692, the Cartmel vestry ceased to appoint surveyors of highways,[2] and the work of maintaining the roads was left to the separate townships. The administrative pattern then more closely resembled that of Dalton parish. In those parishes where administration was not complicated by the existence of subordinate tiers of local government, like Pennington, the appointment of officials followed the familiar plan—the parish, with its three or four hundred inhabitants, had its twelve sidesmen, two constables, two assessors, two overseers and two church-wardens.[3]

Furness, as distinct from Cartmel, was divided into eight large parishes with or without their respective chapelries or divisions. In the eighteenth and nineteenth centuries there were no fewer than sixteen manors or sub-manors in the peninsula proper, by no means always coterminous with parochial divisions ; although a part or whole, as at Torver and Pennington, might be so. Manorial administration was entangled with that of the vestries. Torver and Church Coniston appointed constables through manor courts, the Court Leet for the Manor of Ulverston appointing, by the early nineteenth century, constables for Blawith, Osmotherley, Mansriggs and the town of Ulverston.[4] The chapelry of Torver was also a bailiwick[5] of the manor of Muchland, which, at the period under review, included portions of the parishes of Aldingham and Urswick, and which was a Crown Manor.[6] Hence the latter extended into three separate parochial areas. The Manor of Plain Furness, held by the Dukes of Buccleuch, comprised the parish of Dalton (including the chapelry of Walney,[7] which was not a bierley) with the exception of Dalton township, but took in also the extra-parochial district of Angerton. in Kirkby Ireleth parish.[8] The Dukes of Buccleuch were Lords of the Liberty of Furness,[9] and in addition to the manor described, they held directly the bailiwick of Hawkshead, the manor of Egton-with-Newland and the manor of Ulverston, continuing to exact most customary rents and fines until the present century.[10] The other manors of the district were constitutionally held of the Lord of the Liberty, and remained in being throughout the period examined.

[1]Stockdale, *op. cit.*, 261, 309-10, 312. [2]*Op. cit.*, 162. [3]Fell, *op. cit.*, 277 (quoting the *Old Church Book of Pennington*, 1673-   ). [4]*Ulverston Almanack*, 1837, 31 (*list of officials*). [5]Term used advisedly by Mr. Edward Walker, a former deputy steward of several Furness manors ; his notes in *Rec. Man. Muchland, cit.* [6]cf. also Kelly, P. V., in *C. & W.*, XXIV, 1924, 264 sqq. [7]Gaythorpe, H., *C. & W.*, XX, 1920, 97 sqq. [8]Butler, Wilson, *op. cit.*, 325. [9]Descent, *Antiquities*, all eds. [10]Butler, *passim.*

There are signs that the local manorial administration was beginning to decay in the eighteenth century. At Pennington, for instance, the last Court Baron at which orders were made, and tenants presented for offences, was held in 1799. At about the same time prolonged negotiations between tenants and lord, regarding enfranchisement of customaryhold tenements in the manor, resulted in deadlock.[1] At Coniston in *circa* 1810 the lord had " still his boon days, and (was) strict in requiring his tenants to perform suit and service &c." There were signs, nevertheless, that the tenantry found such obligations irksome, and since the Flemings, lords of Coniston, no longer kept a good bull and boar for the use of inhabitants, the latter " occasionally avail(ed) themselves of the circumstances, in order wholly to avoid such services ".[2] In 1849 the agricultural reporter William Rothwell commented with apparent surprise that in parts of High Furness the lord claimed " two of the most valuable articles on the farm " when the tenant died, or' that such articles, in other instances, were claimed at the lord's death. Heriots were not commuted at Pennington until about 1850.[3].

In spite of these signs of decay, the manorial courts were administratively important for two reasons. As long as customary tenure remained common in the district, they carried on a considerable volume of business relating to the descent or alienation of property, and the courts held at Dalton Castle, Hawkshead, Brough, ton and Ulverston were local events of some consequence. Secondly, the courts were responsible for the appointment of a variety of township and hamlet officials, whose work was either independent of or complementary to that of the parish officers, and was concerned primarily with the regulation of common fields, dales and dykes.

As has been shown,[4] Furness had numerous township fields in the eighteenth century. A distinction has to be drawn between those township fields with arable strips and dales, common peat-mosses with turbary dales, and the moorland common used for grazing purposes and for the harvesting of bracken. In addition, as at Broughton, manorial tenants might enjoy common hayfields. Common land of whatever type was supervised by chosen officials who ascertained that manorial tenants did not override court agreements, whether on the coastal mosses of Ulverston township, the mosses of Angerton, or the bracken-dales of Osmotherley moor or Birkrigg. (It should be added that as far as can be ascertained, dales of any kind were treated as part and parcel of a customaryhold property, were sold as such, and were not exchanged'

---

[1]Fell, *op. cit.*, 113-4, 117-23.   [2]Dickson, 93.   [3]Fell, 114 ; Rothwell, 9.
[4]See pp. 11-13 above.

year by year.) A Pennington manor court of 1665 ordered that " all that hath any ground in Carley Templands and Wilbinhawe shall meet at Templands Gappe upon the first of April to appoint a keeper for the said fields upon pain of every one that neglects sixpence ".[1] Constables, assessors, hedge lookers and moor lookers were sworn at this court.[2] Four years later, every tenement was ordered to pay 12d. " towards the hiring of two sufficient men to keep the Common ".[3]

A number of hamlets in Plain Furness—Biggar on Walney Island, Newbarns, Salthouse and Hawcoat [4]—which were originally granges of Furness Abbey with their adjoining township fields, continued to appoint their local officials until almost within living memory, and were known as " gravewicks ". The head man of the hamlet was known as the grave, and each person to occupy this office was appointed in rotation from a list known as the grave-round, in which the holders of tenements were taken in order. The grave was assisted by one or more pain-lookers. The meaning of this latter term becomes clearer when it is added that a local sixteenth-century court roll refers to a " pain " as a bye-law with a penalty attached to it.[5] The tenants of Biggar appointed two herds to supervise the common pasture, one of whom had the right of whittlegait and the other a cottage and a small piece of ground at a low rental.[6] At Broughton bye-law men or " barleymen " watched over common fields, the term meadow-looker occurring elsewhere in the same manor.[7] Nomenclature varied with the tasks of the officials concerned ; Osmotherley had its bracken-lookers, Torver its hedge-lookers, Pennington its moor-lookers, Ulverston its hedge-, hog-, and moss-lookers, and Coniston its common-lookers and pinfold-lookers.[8] But the manorial courts, which were nominally responsible for the appointment of these officials, were certainly not always held at regular intervals, and it was alleged in 1733 that the Pennington court had been " neglected to be held for the space of from seven to twenty years and more ".[9] Accordingly it appears that the system of appointment by rota was carried on without formal swearing-in at the court.

The local courts continued to exercise their jurisdiction through-out the nineteenth century, although, if the Pennington and Torver court rolls are any sound guide, the numbers of presentments slackened noticeably in the eighteenth century. The enclosures of

[1]Fell, *op. cit.*, 159. [2]*Ibid.* [3]*Op. cit.*, 160. [4]Kelly, P. V., *C. & W.* (NS), XXIV, 1924, 268 ; Pearson, H. G., *C. & W.*, (NS), XI, 1911, 189 ; *The Town's Book of Biggar* (MS), Barrow P.L. ; *The Town's Book of Hawcoat, cit.* ; Kendall, W. B., *op. cit.*, 31. [5]Fell, *op. cit.*, (*transcript of Pennington court rolls*) 149-51. [6]Pearson, H. G., in *C. & W.* (NS), XI, 188, and *B.N.F.C.*, XI, 75. [7]Butler, Wilson, in *C. & W.* (NS), XXIX, 298. [8]*Ulverston Almanack, cit.* ; *Rec. Man. Muchland* ; Fell, *op. cit.*, 159 ; *V. C. H. Lancs*, VIII, 367. [9] Fell, *op. cit.*, 139.

commons and waste, commencing at Claife in 1794, did not put a stop to the appointment of manorial officials ; and it was not until the eruption of the industrial stronghold of Barrow-in-Furness in the midst of this anachronistic order that the old world and the new came visibly into conflict.   The greedy spread of the new town absorbed the Dalton gravewicks one by one, the Biggar tenants fighting hard but unsuccessfully to guard their ancient common pasture of Biggar Bank against transformation into a public recreation ground. [1]   Barrow's rulers, the Furness Railway Company and its representatives, were soon at loggerheads with the Dalton Four and Twenty, and the Ulverston vestry-and-manor regime was dismissed, by an Inspector of the General Board of Health, in the following words : " There is no local government, other than is provided by the general Acts of the country ". [2]   The vestry slumbered for several years afterwards, and several hundred people died needlessly from those diseases engendered by filth.   Industry brought the need for better roads, sewers had to be laid, water had to be provided, newly-appearing streets had to be lit ; and the establishment of a large industrial working-class in the district provided the foundation for modern local government.

2. PAUPERISM AND THE NEW POOR LAW

We have seen that the social and economic changes in eighteenth-century Furness undoubtedly brought a widening of the range of employments available to local people.   It is very likely that this widening was itself a direct cause of population growth ; but as the population increased, pauperism increased also.   It is perhaps idle to debate whether local poverty—or pauperism—was worse in Furness than in other similar parts of England and Wales ; in fact, it seems to have approximated very closely, at different stages, to the average for England· and Wales, in terms of both numbers of paupers and expenditure.   For the eighteenth century as a whole, however, we have little sound guidance as to the total number of paupers in the district at any one time, and can judge degrees of poverty only by the numbers of paupers buried and the sums of money spent on relief of the poor by individual parishes and townships.

Interestingly enough, a return for the year 1636 has been printed. [3]   It appears that Furness and Cartmel had then 464

---

[1]For a full account, vide Marshall, J. D., in North-Western Evening Mail, 9.9, 16.9, 23.9.1949.   [2]Reports to the General Board of Health : Ulverstone (1853 published 1855), by Robt. Rawlinson, p. 11.   [3]S.P.Dom : Chas. I, CCCXXX, 99, Returns made by Justices, 1.7.1636 to 31.12.1636.

paupers altogether, 176 being relieved by boarding-out with local inhabitants, and 288 by means of pensions. The baptism and burial rates of a number of Furness parishes suggest that the local population of *circa* 1636 was considerably smaller than in the mid-eighteenth century, and that, indeed, it could have been smaller than in late Tudor times. It is impossible to avoid mere guess-work in putting the Furness and Cartmel population for that year at some six to seven thousand souls ; but this estimate cannot be very far from the mark, in which case the proportion of paupers (presumed adults only) was about 15 per cent.

For a number of reasons set out below, it seems that between the early and middle eighteenth century, local pauperism was no very serious problem. Such sources as have been readily available— some overseers' or parochial records, official overseers' returns to the government, and references to pauper burials or baptisms—all provide particles of evidence which combine to point towards that conclusion. The burial entries of Colton, Ulverston, Broughton and Kirkby Ireleth record many more pauper burials after the middle of the eighteenth century than during the previous decades, although the same sources also make clear that 1731-40 was a period of increased pauperism—a tendency which agrees with other known developments of that decade.[1] The later increase of such entries is most noticeable after about 1770, the decade with the greatest number of pauper entries being 1781-90, when the latter amounted to 12.6 per cent of all burials in five parishes investigated.[2] It may well be, of course, that clerks and incumbents were careless in indicating accurately the status of deceased persons, and it seems probable that they were more likely to refer to a pauper when registration was taxed (as in 1783-94) than at other times ; although it should be said that there are quite as many references to paupers in the Broughton registers during the ten years before 1783 as during the subsequent decade.

Fortunately other and perhaps more convincing evidence is available. There can be little doubt that pauperism increased considerably in the last three decades of the eighteenth century, as the following particulars will make clear. On the other hand, the *numbers* of paupers in Furness scarcely increased at all between 1803 and 1813, and the total number for the district had not greatly swollen in 1834 :

[1]E.g., a relatively low baptism rate and a still high burial rate. [2]The four parishes mentioned above, with the addition of Torver. Torver had numerous pauper burials throughout the century.

Table 15

General trends in expenditure on the Furness poor [1]

Total expenditure (t.e.) or total of poor assessments (p.a.)	(1) 14 fell townships or pars.	(2) 5 Plain Furness pars.	(3) 7 divs. of (ex. Cartmel Ulverston)	Totals	Est. nat. aggreg. amt. of poor rate	Movement of Silberling price indices (1790)	100
	(£)	(£)	(£)	(£)	(£ mill.)		
1776* (t.e.)	551	336	253	1140	1.52		
1783 (p.a.)	933	499	427	1859		(1783)	93
1784 (p.a.)	1076	565	528	2169	2.00	(1784)	90
1785 (p.a.)	1026	541	497	2064		(1785)	85
1803* (t.e.)	2340	1230	1269	4839	4.07	(1803)	140
1813* (t.e.)	3252	1554	2045	6851	6.65	(1813)	187
1814* (t.e.)	3283	1548	2165	6996		(1814)	176
1815* (t.e.)	2822	1586	2114	6522		(1815)	150
1834-6						(1834)	102
(ave. t.e.)	3526	2537	2276	8339	6.31	(1836)	111

* Year ending Easter of year given

It will be seen that between 1784 and 1813 the local poor moneys (expended or assessed) [2] kept almost exactly in step with the national aggregate figures given by Mr. and Mrs. Webb. [3] Before 1785 the increase was relatively greater. But in order to obtain illumination, it is necessary to take sample information from parochial records.

At least one considerable township in the Furness neighbourhood, Lower Holker in Cartmel Parish, provides what may well be a representative case history. The population of Lower Holker was 1039 in 1801 and (following the Cartmel enclosure) 931 in 1811 ; we must assume that the mid-eighteenth-century figure was six to seven hundred. In 1720, 11 names of " poor housekeepers " and apprentices are mentioned in the Flookborough Chapel (Lower Holker) records. In 1723, five " Poore Pentioners " appear ; in 1746, eight paupers, and in 1759, eleven once more. [4] In 1802-3 the total number of paupers in the division was 59 (38 adults of all types and 21 children), and in 1813 the number of adult paupers was 41. [5]

James Stockdale, when compiling his *Annals of Cartmel*, collected together a series of five-yearly expenditure figures for the same division in the eighteenth century, distinguishing both the

[1] Figures from *Parliamentary Papers, First Series, Vol. IX (Provisions, Poor)*, 1774-1802, 297 ; Thomas Gilbert's reports of 1777 and 1787, with abstracts of returns by the overseers of the poor are given in this source ; and *Parl. Papers, Sess. 1803-4, Vol. XIII, Abstract of Returns*; *Parl. Papers Abstract of Returns pursuant to Act 55 Geo. III*, 1818 ; *Appx. to 2nd Annual Report of Poor Law Commissioners* (1836), p. 530. [2] Some scattered returns for actual expenditure in 1783-5 (ten Furness townships in all) show that moneys assessed were nearly always fully expended. [3] *Vide English Poor Law History*, Pt. II (1929), Appx. II, 1037 ; before 1803, conjectural. [4] Stockdale, *op. cit.*, 260 sqq., 276-7, 280, 309-10 (transcripts of parish records). [5] Parliamentary returns, *cit.*

poor and the constable expenditure. Moneys spent on the poor did not approach £50 annually until well after the middle of the century ; in 1767, 1782 and 1792 the division spent more than double that amount, and in 1797, five times. In 1817 more than £400 was being expended.[1] Stockdale's figures show two particularly sharp " jumps ", one in the mid-sixties, and one in or near 1782 ; otherwise the burden seems to have grown much as the general expenditure for Cartmel indicates. The very low level of the figures for the first half of the century is worthy of note, and the subsequent increase of pauperism, or at least spending on the poor, seems to have outstripped by far any conceivable population increase in this township. The same appears to have happened at Pennington in Plain Furness, which had 12 persons receiving relief in 1764, 14 in 1765, but 25 in 1803, 32 in 1812 and (for some reason) 20 in 1813.[2] Expenditure on the Pennington paupers increased four or five times, from £31 in 1776 to £139 in 1813.

The marked increase of the general poor expenditure of the district between 1803 and 1813 was very largely the result of price inflation. In 1803 the total number of permanent adult paupers in Furness and Cartmel (excluding Ulverston only) was 644 ; in 1813-15 the average number of persons in the same category was 663. The totals of all adult paupers, including those occasionally relieved, were respectively 1105 and 1194. Figures relating to adults only, however, are useless if it is desired to express pauperism as a percentage of population. Large numbers of children were affected, and the returns for 1802-3 give full details of all paupers, including children, and are therefore especially valuable. Outside the town of Ulverston, then, in 1803, there were 1581 paupers of all kinds in Furness and Cartmel, in townships and parishes with a total population of 14,650 at the 1801 Census. The percentage of pauperism was therefore 10.8. Of the grand total given (1581), 456 were children under 14 years, and these were members of families receiving relief " out of the house ". Parish register references (and other sources) for earlier decades show that local paupers of the mid-eighteenth century were often elderly people, and were probably widows of husbandmen (or of other unfortunate individuals) left without support. Towards the end of the century, however, references to child paupers (e.g. in the Colton register) grow more and more numerous, and it is obvious that whole families are finding some sort of refuge in the Colton and Ulverston poorhouses. (Relief in the poorhouse was not widely practised in this district.) It also becomes clearer that what we are seeing is unemployment and poverty on a comparatively large scale, and is not merely an index to age, helplessness and infirmity.

---

[1]Stockdale, *op. cit.*, 309-10 ; Parl. returns. [2]Fell, *Pennington*, 279 (giving extracts from *The Church Book of Pennington*) and parliamentary returns, *cit.*

It will be as well, before introducing any overtones into the story, to examine what was happening in other parts of the region. Cumberland poor rates had been low in the closing decades of the eighteenth century,[1] and in 1802-3 the poor expenditure per head of population was 5s. in that county and 6s. 10d. in Northumberland.[2] The *per capita* figure for Lancashire, at the same period, has been estimated at 4s. 10d.[3] By contrast, the figure for Furness and Cartmel was 6s. 11d. in 1803 and 8s. 4d. in 1813. The large land-occupying population north of the sands, however, ensured that the poor rate of Lancashire's northernmost district was kept down to a mere 1s. 8½d. In the Manchester and Bolton divisions it was 7s. 8d. and 6s. 9½d. respectively in 1802-3.[4] The manufacturers, as John Holt remarked,[5] " encourage(d) settlers " who were then apt to suffer all the miseries of seasonal or technological unemployment, but the former paid for the privilege in heavy poor rates. The landless poor of Lonsdale's submerged tenth had, if they were able-bodied, every stimulus to move into the industrial districts and to join the labour armies there.

On the organisation of local poor relief : Speenhamland, and all that it implied, were almost unknown in this part of England, and the allowance system was little practised. It was reported at a somewhat later date that parish allowances were " never done " in the major Plain Furness parish of Dalton, and Hawkshead had likewise never employed the system.[6] The same applied to most of the parishes of adjoining Cumberland. [7] Throughout the eighteenth century and the Napoleonic Wars the emphasis was on out-relief, and the establishment of the Ulverston Board of Guardians did little to change this state of affairs. Some light is shed on the administration of this side of local government by details from the overseers' accounts of Lower Holker, which in 1737-8 had four or five persons in a workhouse in the township, these inmates being engaged in working up " junk " and spinning. But one woman was boarded out, and in 1711, 1720 and 1723 there is reference to poor housekeepers and pensioners ; and in 1759, out of 11 persons receiving relief, three had their house rents paid for them.[8] At Pennington the poor received small doles or pensions out of the parish poor stock (modestly swollen by charities and gifts) and out of the rates; and in addition schooling, books and clothing were

[1]Bailey, J., and Culley, G., *General View of the Agriculture of Cumberland*, 262. [2]Estimates in Griffith, *op. cit.*, 153. [3]*Loc. cit.* It should be added that the average for six southern counties was 14s. 10d. [4]Table in Dickson, *op. cit.*, 135. [5]Holt, *Gen. View . . . Agric. Lancs.* (1795 ed.), 210, 213. [6]*Appx. to 1st Report from the Commissioners of the Poor Laws* (1837), 271d, 273d. Ques. 40. [7]*1st Report of Poor Law Commissioners* (1834), pp. 239 sqq. Out of 42 Cumberland parishes, 31 gave no allowances of any kind in normal circumstances. [8]Stockdale, *op. cit.*, 260, 276-7, 270-1, 280.

given out. [1] In April, 1812, however, it was stated that " The poor of the Parish of Pennington are solely supported by assessments on the proprietors or their farmers in proportion to the property and as circumstances require. The following are at present upon the Poor's Roll of this Parish and receive from one shilling to three shillings and sixpence pr week, and occasionally more if sickness or infirmities require it . . . " [2]

The children of the poor were apprenticed by a rota system. In 1770 the Cartmel Four and Twenty is found deciding that " no poor children shall be put out as parish apprentices till they be full eight years of age ; and that such apprentices are to be fixed upon some particular estate during the term allowed by law ; and that the best estate shall take the first apprentice, and that estate which is next to it in value shall take the next apprentice, and so on in order through the whole of every township respectively . . . " [3] In Pennington, the allotment of apprentices was performed by means of a ballot ; " . . . no Estate in the Parish is freed from the next balloting, only such as has had apprentices before, which can be sufficiently made proof of . . . " (1815). [4]

In 1802-3, only £479 was spent on the relief of poor persons inside the local workhouses or poorhouses, as against £5100 on out-relief, and accordingly the workhouse accommodation of the district was not large. Cartmel had one or more workhouses by 1736, Dalton had one in the same year, [5] and Ulverston obtained Neville Hall for its poorhouse in 1753. [6] By 1776 the Dalton institution was large enough for 20 people, and further houses had appeared at Colton (with room for 18) [7] and Broughton-in-Furness. By 1803 Aldingham, Hawkshead and Kirkby Ireleth were keeping a few of their poor in special houses, and in 1813 Egton-with-Newland and Urswick were doing the same, although in that year only 125 out of 634 adult paupers in Furness and Cartmel were in poorhouses or workhouses. In 1822 a new poorhouse appeared at Flookburgh, [8] some time before 1834 one appeared at Allithwaite, [9] and in 1832 even Pennington had acquired a poorhouse and let out the management of it to a contractor. [10] In other words, the assembling of poor persons in a central parish institution was becoming slowly more popular, although there is no obvious sign of economy-mindedness until the eighteen hundred and twenties.

[1]Fell, 278-9.   [2]Op. cit., 280.   [3]Stockdale, op. cit., 233 ; vide also Deed of Apprenticeship of a poor child, Margaret Dixon age 8 of Dalton (MS.), Barrow P.L. MSS. z.180.   [4]Fell, op. cit., 281.   [5]Dalton P.R.(B.T.) ; the Workhouse and Parish Relief Accounts (in the custody of the Vicar of Dalton) begin in 1735.   [6]Bardsley, op. cit., 17 ; Park, cit., 69.   [7]Abstract for year.   [8]Stockdale, op. cit., 312.   [9]Op. cit., 198.   [10]Fell, op. cit., 282.

From 1820 to 1822, districts all over the north-west were sending petitions to Parliament to complain of the distressed state of agriculture.[1] Farming ratepayers reacted accordingly; and several instances of their behaviour are forthcoming. At Pennington in 1822 a vestry meeting was held to " take into consideration the propriety of reducing the pensions of the paupers ", and in 1824 the same vestry " resolved that no more than 3 Guineas per an. shall be advanced to any individual pauper for House Rent ".[2] In 1821-2, Lower Holker township acquired a Select Vestry under the terms of the Sturges Bourne Act of 1819, and set about the provisioning and furnishing of its poorhouse;[3] and Select Vestries also appeared at Hawkshead and Ulverston, the ratepayers afterwards declaring themselves " content " with their services.[4] In 1827, ratepayers in the Cartmel township attempted to prevent farm hirings by the full year, on the ground that such hirings could lead to settlement in the division by farm servants;[5] and Dalton farmers similarly took to hiring by the half year " in order that their servants might not gain settlements ".[6] There are signs that Furness parishes were taking more interest in the Law of Settlement at—or before—the commencement of the nineteenth century; by 1803, much more was being spent on constables' and legal expenses than in 1783-5 or 1776, and in 1813-5, very much more.[7] It is most dangerous to assume that this law was a dead letter simply because it was ignored in the manufacturing centres; although difficult to apply, it was frequently invoked.

Not all the Furness parishes were forced to increase their spending on the poor during the lean years of the 'twenties, and perhaps a third of them successfully avoided any such extra burden. In 1834-6 seven out of twenty-eight Furness parishes and divisions were spending less on poor relief than they had done in 1813-5, and all seven were moorland townships. At Dalton the poor's expenditure of 1831 was double that of 1821, local ratepayers had attempted to prevent settlement in that parish, and it was claimed that agricultural capital was diminishing due to " the Rates being considerably increased ". Dalton (according to the Poor Law Commissioners' returns of 1834) had two-thirds of its area under arable cultivation, and out of its population of 2697, 745 are stated to have been agricultural labourers.[8] This was by far the most fertile and agriculturally developed parish in Furness, with several large farms belonging to the Earl of Burlington. It evidently suffered badly from the slump in corn prices in the 'twenties.

[1]*Parl. Papers*, 1822, *Vol. V.* [2]Fell, *op. cit.*, 281. [3]Stockdale, 310-12. [4]*Appx. to* 1*st Rept. from the Commissioners of the Poor Laws* (1837), 273d, and Part III, 237c. [5]Stockdale, 313. [6]*Appx. to* 1*st Rept.*, *cit.*, 271d, Ques. 38. [7]*Abstracts, cited.* Expenses on journeys are referred to. [8]Figs. from 1834 *Report, cit.*, 271a, and *Appx. to* 1*st Report*, 1837, 271d.

The details of expenditure on poor relief[1] in the Poor Law Commissioners' returns of 1834 reveal that several of the main Furness parishes—in selected years at least—were spending little more on the poor than the average *per capita* for the whole of industrial Lancashire; in 1821, 4s. 1d. in Dalton, 9s. 5d. for the town of Ulverston, 5s. 10d. in Hawkshead and 10s. 1d. in Coniston, as against an average of approximately 7s. for the county. There was a marked differential in favour of the county only in 1831 and 1834-6. The difference was not due to industrialisation purely; Cumberland appears to have spent quite as little on its poor as the County Palatine, and there was no great flow of migrating folk out of Cumberland before 1831[2]. But in the case of Furness there seems to have been a gentle and constant trickle out of the district in the 'twenties and 'thirties, with the result that at Hawkshead in 1834 there was " seldom any able-bodied labourer out of employment ", and at Dalton " In general none in summer " and in winter, none.[3] In 1836 there were 1582 paupers in the whole of Furness and Cartmel—about 6 per cent. of a population of some 25,000, a proportion below the known or estimated averages for England and Wales at that period.[4] Some of the localised demand for employment was being met at Church Coniston, where numerous persons were working in the slate quarries or copper mines (and where there was a shortage of agricultural labourers), in new slate quarries at Satterthwaite, and in bobbin mills in the same locality.[5] Pauperism was therefore no great problem in Furness, and some southern districts were committed to two, three or four times the local expenditure on their own poor. On the other hand, there was harsh poverty in the area.

So much for generalities; what of the actual administration of the poor law on the eve of the establishment of the Boards of Guardians and the new workhouse system? Fortunately a fairly full account of the state of affairs in the town of Ulverston has been recorded.[6] We learn that the Ulverston Select Vestry—working through two overseers with an assistant, all usually tradesmen—was making real attempts to " distinguish between the idle and industrious ", by excluding from the local workhouse (at Nevile Hall) those who showed signs of wanting to go there. The same vestry, however, was nevertheless operating a scheme of relief in aid of wages—perhaps one of the very few in the north-west—which

---

[1]Details obtained from *Abstract* of 1818; 1834 *Report*, Part I, 270a, 271a, 273a, 277a; Appx. to 2nd *Report of the P.L. Commissioners*, 1836, 530; 3rd *Rept. of the Poor Law Commrs.*, 134; Griffith, *op. cit.*, 153. [2]Griffith, (*op. cit.* 161-2) expresses the view that Cumberland suffered little loss of people at this period; the parish register abstracts and census returns combined suggest as much. [3]1834 *Report, cit.* [4]*Vide* Webb, *op. cit.*, 1040, for some figures. [5]1834 *Report, cit.*, 270a, Ques. 7-12. [6]1834 *Rept., Answers to Town Queries*, Appx. B.2, Vols. I & II, esp. Vol. I, Ques. 7-27, Vol. II, Ques. 30-59.

provided for assistance to a man who earned less than 10s. a week and who had at the same time a wife, and children under ten years of age. It appears, from statistics given by the Ulverston assistant overseer, that local weavers and labourers were living perilously near to the level at which relief was granted ; a weaver's annual income was estimated at £22 2s. and a labourer's at £20 16s., although the labours of wife and children might add 4s. a week to these sums. Such earnings, it was stated, would allow the family to subsist on oatmeal, milk and potatoes, but there would be no margin left for savings. It says much for the rootedness of the country poor, and their corresponding lack of response to the attractions of the new industrial towns, that they stayed in their homes in spite of such conditions. One-quarter only of the Ulverston labouring poor were in fact non-parishioners, and one-third of this residue were Irish.

William Brickell, the assistant overseer, stated that there was general objection to entering the workhouse, the population of which had averaged 45 inmates over three years, and which was confined largely to the aged, infirm and children under ten years. The elderly folk were treated with some little humanity—" aged females " were allowed 6d. a week for tea—and men and wives were allowed to live together. The able-bodied were employed at street-cleaning and stone-breaking, thereby providing the road surveyors with 300 free cartloads of stones *per annum*. It appears that the situation had altered little since 1813-5, when roughly the same number of persons had been in the workhouse at Neville Hall, and when fewer than 200 persons were receiving relief of any kind " out of the house " ; certainly the *per capita* expenditure had changed little. [1] According to Brickell, the number of able-bodied men in receipt of relief had tended to increase, but there is no evidence of widespread demoralisation by the system of relief in aid of wages, which had certainly not been allowed to get out of hand by 1834, and which seems to have been motivated by a judiciously controlled kindliness on the part of the local vestry. The latter, of course, did not face the appalling problems which beset parish authorities in the south of England.

The Poor Law Amendment Act of 1834 resulted in the establishment of a local union of parishes. Many unions were formed during the summer of 1836, and the Ulverston Union began its existence as from August 26th of that year. [2] It comprised all the parishes and townships of Lonsdale North of the Sands, 21 of these electing a single Guardian, and the large parishes of Colton, Dalton, Hawkshead, Broughton-in-Furness and Aldingham, two Guardians

---

[1] *Abstract of* 1818, *cit.* [2] *MS. Minutes* of the Ulverston Guardians, Lancs. R.O. It was the eighth largest union in England and Wales in respect of territory—162,197 acres ; *13th Rept. of the P.L. Commrs.*, No. 11, 264.

each. Ulverston was entitled to four, the allotment in all these cases being made on the basis of population. The controlling Board, as was laid down by the exact requirements of Somerset House, was equipped with regulation instructions, minute and account books, a Treasurer, an Auditor and a Clerk ; and its permanent chairman was William, Earl of Burlington and later Seventh Duke of Devonshire. The latter was a convinced utilitarian and Liberal.

A body of this character could not conquer the supposed evil of large-scale out-relief at a stroke, and like a great number of similar unions throughout the country, it never attempted to do so. The main principles guiding the new system were twofold—that an able-bodied man could receive relief only in the workhouse, cut off from any ancillary sources of income, and that the state of workhouse inmates was to be made less desirable than that of any independent worker outside the walls of that institution—the famous principle of " less eligibility ". In their pristine state these ideas seemed most attractive to the utilitarians of the time, who were anxious to prevent waste, maladministration, and the evil effects of the confusion of wages and poor relief. In fact, many north-country districts, like Furness itself, had no need of such drastic reform ; and it is not surprising that in more industrialised areas the new Poor Law met with violent resistance.

The Ulverston Board of Guardians, upon its inception, found itself in possession of three already existing workhouses in Ulverston, Dalton and Colton, and on November 3rd, 1836, three committees of the Board were formed to supervise these.[1] The (theoretical) inadequacy of this workhouse accommodation may be gauged from the fact that at Christmas, 1836, only 270 paupers out of 1582 in the whole Union were being relieved " indoors " (i.e. in the workhouse) ; and the figures for the following Christmas were respectively 242 and 1575.[2] The local Guardians, at any rate, felt that they could not carry out what was demanded of them, and they petitioned for an amendment to the new Poor Law.[3] But the hand of parsimony was soon apparent ; a central Union workhouse would have to be built, and a mere £524 was spent on 1312 outdoor paupers in the first quarter of the Board's existence. It should be borne in mind that the average annual expenditure in 1834-6 (most of it on out-relief) was £10,089 for Furness and Cartmel.

The new workhouse, designed ultimately to accommodate 350 paupers and costing £5,800, was built in the Gill, Ulverston in 1838.[4] It is certain that this institution was never used as

---

[1] *Mins. Ulv. Gdns.* for date.   [2] Rept. from *Select Cttee., cit.,* 1837-8.
[3] The same, *Appx. to Part I,* list of petitions received. Details wanting. Many places petitioned for total repeal.   [4] *Appx. to 3rd Annl. Rept. of P.L. Commrs.,* 124, and *Appx. to 13th Rept.,* B, 11, 256.

originally intended, and it is pleasant to record that for reasons little connected with any administrative reforms of the Guardians, it was never filled to capacity. The 'forties saw a considerable local fall in expenditure on the poor—£6,912 was the lowest figure reached, in 1846. [1]

The population of the Union was 26,752 in 1841 and 30,442 in 1851. In the first of these years some 5s. 10d. was being spent on poor relief per head of population, as compared with 6s. 0½d. in England and Wales. In March, 1850, some 1045 persons were on out-relief in the Union, and 198 in the Ulverston workhouse. [2] Judging by the returns published in the *Ulverston Advertiser* for the years that followed, this is a fairly representative statement, and the total numbers did not depart far from those given.

So much for the purely statistical side. The Guardians were not responsible for the slow but steady reduction in pauperism, and they cannot be held fully responsible for the decrease in expenditure. This point is worth stressing, if only because the story of poor relief in this remote district of North Lancashire probably mirrors that of many rural districts of England. The haematite trade made important advances in the 'thirties and 'forties, [3] local agriculture made advances during the same period, [4] and the Furness Railway was under construction in 1845-6. From that time onwards the district suffered from a shortage of able-bodied labourers, and its pauperism represented the hard core of sickness, helpless age, instability and general misfortune in the lives of the workpeople. For the very poor, the change to the new Poor Law meant more hardship and degradation. We are not here concerned with the " Bastille ", for the great majority of the local people never saw the inside of one ; but the personal relationships of the village gave way to the parsimony of a centralised board, and although " less eligibility " proved to be an unworkable principle, the farmers who fought ruthlessly to keep down the rates under the old system did not have their attitudes changed ay the new. Probably the union administration was more efficient, bnd the surviving minute-books of the Guardians suggest that all expenditure was scrutinised minutely.

The members of the Board, gentry, farmers and tradesmen, seem to have carried on their business in humdrum fashion. If they intended to keep the rates down, they were successful ; [5] and if they disliked the iron hand of the " Three Bashaws of Somerset House ", they were not alone. The Earl of Burlington, still a young and comparatively inexperienced chairman, recorded a series of

---

[1]P.L. Commrs. *Annual Reports.*   [2]*Ulverston Advertiser*, 7.3.1850.   [3]See pp. 92-4 above.   [4]See pp. 75-8 above.   [5]During the first twenty years of the Union's existence, the rates were kept as low as one shilling in the pound, rising occasionally to 1s. 6d.

stormy meetings in the spring of 1842, when the Poor Law Commissioners refused to countenance a proposed reduction in the salaries of the Ulverston Union's medical officers.[1] The medical and relieving officers of the Union had large areas to supervise, and as later events were to show, fully earned whatever payment they received. In 1842, however, the members of the Board had not foreseen the unprecedentedly rapid growth of population which was to take place within the Union district. In 1815, the total value of real property within the latter, for rating purposes, was £80,624 ; in 1841, it was £127,124, and in 1854, still only £127,996. Thereafter it nearly doubled in twenty years.[2]

As in many other unions, the emphasis on out-relief remained. Ulverston, indeed, was one of the few unions in the country to apply an Outdoor Labour Test Order by 1847, to the effect that " If any able-bodied male pauper shall apply to be set to work by the parish, one-half at least of the relief which may be afforded to him or his family shall be in kind ".[3] In other words, even the able-bodied were not automatically directed into the workhouse, nor were they inevitably relieved in kind only.   The physical and social problems of administering the Poor Law in a district of this character were manifold and complex enough to defy any theorist. There was no room for the various classes of poor in any one local institution, and the Guardians would never have countenanced the building of further premises for the aged, for the infirm, and for children.   But the ugly shadow of the building in the Gill remained. The writer has been able to discover very little about this institution ; the Guardians' records show that local tradesmen undoubtedly benefited from its demands in some small degree, while a Board of Health report of 1855 refers to its stinking privies.[4]

3. EDUCATION

Eighteenth-century life in a district of this character was apt to be rough and simple, but it would be a mistake to suppose that it was unredeemed by a measure of education and even, among numerous individuals, intellectual accomplishment.   In the late seventeenth century, Furness numbered many dissenters among its people ; heterodox religious views were held by an active minority of the yeomanry and tradespeople, whose independence of mind bespeaks not merely perversity, but something of a far higher order—the ability to judge, discuss and criticise, and to forge conviction with argument.   That the majority of the poorer landholders existed in a fog of superstition and unlettered ignorance

---

[1]*MS. Minutes (Mins. Ulv. Gdns.)*, 10.2, 10.3, 24.3.1842 ; *MS. Diary* of the Earl of Burlington, 14.4.1842.   [2]*Abstract* of Returns, 1818 ; Tyson, J., *Abstract of Accounts, Dalton Local Board* (1887), table of rateable values in the Union ; 14th Rept. of the P.L. Commissioners, Appx. C, No. 3, p. 171.   [3]Cf. Webb, *op. cit.*, Appx., 339, 342.   [4]Report for *Ulverston(e), cit.*, 14.

cannot be doubted, and some long-established practices, like that of driving beasts through a need-fire in times of cattle-plague,[1] and examples of illiteracy on the part of churchwardens and sidesmen,[2] show that Furness did not differ fundamentally from many other areas of rural England.

But it is clear that during the seventeenth and eighteenth centuries a marked desire for education, even of the simplest, existed. For the most part the initiative in founding schools came from individual benefactors, whose actions did not take place without reference to prevailing attitudes of mind. Thus Thomas Boulton, by a codicil annexed to his will dated November 14th, 1622, reciting that the parishioners of Dalton intended to erect a free-school house in or near Dalton, bequeathed to the Four and Twenty of that parish the sum of £220, to be used to purchase land on which to erect the school building. Two centuries later the school was still in existence, catering for between 80 and 130 scholars. In 1729 the Boulton bequest was used by the sidesmen to purchase a farm on Walney Island, and the investment proved such a sound one that during the Napoleonic wheat boom a rent of £137 *per annum* was obtained from the tenant of the farm, one of 24 acres with rights of common. This sum was devoted to providing the schoolmaster with a salary of £100 a year, £35 going to his assistant.[3] In this way agricultural profits were turned to good account.[4] By the end of the eighteenth century some provision for education, however slender, was to be found in the most sparsely populated chapelries of the district, thanks to benefactors who frequently laid down in their wills that the interest accruing from a legacy was to be devoted to the cost of maintaining a schoolmaster, a school, or both. Often the master was an incumbent or curate, performing his tasks on a part-time basis, although he was not invariably a clergyman. It should be emphasized that little enough is known about the smaller schools of the district, and even the word " school " is used advisedly as connoting the means whereby a teacher came into contact with pupils—whether in a building provided for the purpose, or in a church vestry. At least one of the Furness establishments, founded by the redoubtable Archbishop Edwin Sandys in the reign of Elizabeth I, attained fame because it gave Wordsworth and a succession of lesser but distinguished men their education ; namely, Hawkshead Grammar School. Urswick also obtained a charter for its Grammar School in that period, and Cartmel Grammar School appeared in the same century ; Ireleth Free School and Dalton Free School were early Stuart foundations. Ulverston's Town Bank Grammar School was not founded until 1736.

[1]Example of 1749 given in Kendall, *Salthouse* (*loc. cit.*), 33. This practice was common throughout Cumbria. [2]More than half of the churchwardens of Aldingham, between 1710 and 1750, were illiterate and made marks ; *Aldingham P.R.(B.T.)*, the documents comprising this being of course made out in the parish. [3]*Public Charities*, 55-6. [4]*Loc. cit.* The Schoolmaster of Dalton Free School, evidently a man of principle, returned £2 of the £137 to the Walney farmer.

This completes the list of educational establishments which were in any way noteworthy. As is clear from the Charity Commissioners' Report of 1820, only a very small proportion of the juvenile population of Furness attended them ; and Hawkshead, perhaps one of the best schools of its type in the region, catered partially for the sons of outsiders. It is more to the point to enquire what means of tuition were available to the sons of the yeoman or tradesman in some village at a distance from the main schools. It should be borne in mind, in examining a list of all the establishments or arrangements for tuition that have so far been traced, that the total yearly income from all educational legacies in Furness and Cartmel amounted to about £600 by 1815,[1] but that a number of schools were not wholly dependant on such income, their masters accepting fees or quarterage.

Table 16

Educational establishments in Furness and Cartmel, sixteenth to eighteenth centuries[2]

School	When founded, early mention, or date of bequest	Remarks (All schools in existence in 1820, unless otherwise stated)
Hawkshead G.S.	1585	For details, *vide* Cowper, *Hawkshead*
Urswick G.S.	1586	Date of charter. Endowed by rent charge on Norfolk farm
Cartmel G.S.	1598	First mention given by Stockdale, *Annals of Cartmel*, 37
Ireleth Free Sch.	1612	Small chapel schl. Giles Brownrigge's charity.
Dalton Free Sch.	1622	See p. 144 above.
Dendron	1644	Legacy founding chapel and sch.
Walney	1662	Provision for tuition by curate
Colton	1662	Adam Sandys bequest. Schoolhouse built
Pennington	1675	Mention in *Acct. Book of Sarah Fell*. Children taught in church, 1736.
Swarthmoor Friends' Sch.	1680 *circa*	*Vide* Gaythorpe, *C. & W.* (NS), VI. Schoolmaster prb. 1700-1776.
Upper Holker	1685	Geo. Bigland's charity. Small sch. at Browedge
Seathwaite	1717	Poss. a church sch. in 1650. No. sch. in 1820
Lowick	1717	Definite agreemt. for curate to teach, 1757.
Finsthwaite	1724	Schoolrm. built by parishioners
East Broughton	1731	Chapel sch. ; curate taught
Ulverston G.S.	1736	Woodburn's charity. A small sch. previously. Controlled by vestry

[1]Estimate based upon poor relief *Abstract* of 1818, with additional data from *Public Charities*. [2]Matter from *Public Charities* ; *V.C.H. Lancs.*, VIII, 338, 347, 357, 358, 363, 364, 380, 387, 391, 406, 463, 470 ; Fell, *Pennington*, 63 ; additional infn. by courtesy of Mr. J. L. Hobbs.

Rusland	1745	Schoolrm. existed at date. Use lapsed later
Sawrey	1766	Schoolrm. then erected
Kirkby Ireleth	1769	Saml. Wilson's bequest.
Osmotherley	1770	House built and land purchased at date
Blawith	1772-7	Lancasters' charities. V. small sch. built afterwards
Torver	1777	Fleming's charity. V. small sch. later built
Subberthwaite	1778	School erected
Bardsea	1781	Braddyll's charity. Sch. already erected
Broughton-in-Furness	1784	Small grammar sch. Edward Taylor's bequest, £100

The dissenters of the district, of whom the Quakers were the most numerous body, probably formed small schools other than the establishment at Swarthmoor. Some Friends appear to have sent their children out of Furness to be educated,[1] and the others may have been content with purely local arrangements. Some dissenters, if their means permitted, would be able to send their sons to Caled Rotheram's academy at Kendal, where the ironmaster John Wilkinson received an aducation.

The local education pattern conforms to the national one of a host of small charity schools (generally declining somewhat in popularity after the reign of the first two Georges),[2] performing a restricted but most important function. The local schools, controlled by vestries and trustees, were in all cases church-based, and clergymen performed most of the instruction. The initiative in founding them, however, came generally from lay parishioners and not from clergymen. The " inhabitants " (a term often signifying merely the vestry) took the decision to build a schoolroom in a few cases, anticipating, as at Dalton, Sawrey and Bardsea, a charitable bequest which would enable them to pay a schoolmaster or buy land.

How far did this type of education reach out to the rural masses? In a few cases, as at Blawith and Sawrey, it was expressly laid down that a number of poor children should be educated, while none of the schools made any stated distinction as to the types of children that were to be accepted, save in one important sense—where scholars were to be " appointed " by trustees. This, of course, could be a serious matter where the trustees were members of a parish clique. By 1820, the picture becomes a much clearer one ; it is apparent that then, and probably much earlier, fees in themselves were no great barrier against the family of modest means, that few people were obliged to pay more than a nominal charge for

[1]Gaythorpe, *C. & W.* (NS), VI, 272. [2]Adamson, J. W., *Short Hist. Education*, 201-2.

146

elementary instruction, and that social and other conditions ordained that more than half the children in Furness received little or no formal schooling.

In the case of the parish of Cartmel, it is only too clear that educational opportunity was restricted to those whose fathers could, firstly, pay fees and maintenance, and secondly, dispense with any income to be gained from their sons' labour. Regarding Cartmel Grammar School, we are told in 1820 that " not many children of the poor . . . go to this school ", and that " the instruction here begins where their education usually ends ".[1] Mr. Knipe curate of East Broughton in the same parish, had given up teaching in the schoolhouse there, and taught in a house of his own : " He has 16 boarders in his house, and about the same number of day scholars ; but his terms are too high for poor children ".[2] In both of these examples, however, and likewise at Hawkshead Grammar School, there was educational aspiration ; at Cartmel and Hawkshead schools the instruction was far more than elementary, and in the latter establishment it aimed at the Universities. Yet both Cartmel and Hawkshead were nominally open to the poor, and were constituted as free schools.[3] Like many " public " schools of the present day, they had moved far.

In the smaller villages and townships, a measure of elementary education was provided on a democratic enough basis. The township of Finsthwaite, with its school dating from 1724, had 30 scholars in 1820—nearly as many pupils as Cartmel Grammar School, which had rather over 40. For twopence a week the children of Finsthwaite could learn reading, writing and accounts,[4] although the Finsthwaite and Haverthwaite districts, owing to the influence of the Backbarrow cotton mills, were comparatively populous at that period, and it is by no means clear how many children of the 7-13 age group remained to be catered for. Similar small schools in Osmotherley and Sawrey appear to have given elementary instruction to at least half the local children in that group.[5] Dalton Free School, in 1820, took up to 180 scholars, the comparatively affluent master there giving some tuition in classics, arithmetic and mathematics, but leaving a body of pupils to be instructed by his assistant " on Dr. Bell's system ".[6] The education here was wholly free, and the title of the school was not a misnomer. By 1820 it was open to all the children of " parishioners ", though under the terms of the original charity those not of the town of Dalton were to pay an entrance fee of 12d.[7]

---

[1] *Public Charities*, 7. [2] *Public Charities*, 28. [3] Both did in fact accept children of the poorer sections. At Cartmel in 1712, low rates of quarterage were paid for Latin and English tuition, but poor children had fees paid out of the poor stock of their township. By 1820 a quarterage of 7s. 6d. was paid for instruction in writing ; *Pub. Char.*, 6. [4] *Pub. Char.*, 46. [5] *Pub. Char.*, 85, 120. [6] *Pub. Char.*, 56. [7] *Pub. Char.*, 55.

147

Where so little is known of the quality of the education offered by local schools, [1] an estimate of quantity will have limited enough value. Nevertheless such an estimate is worth making, if only because it may serve as a rough indication of the number of children who were receiving no formal instruction at all :

Table 17

Estimate of educational provision in Furness parishes or townships where average number of scholars attending school is stated [2]

School	Number of scholars	Remarks	Potential scholars as 1/9 of 1821 Census popn. of div.
Dalton F. Sch.	80 (ave.)	As given	
Ireleth F.S.	10 ,,	Reading, accounts, Latin	272 (Dalton par.)
Barrow	10 (est.)	Not given in Report	
Urswick G.S.	40	Elem., Latin, Greek	87 (Urswick par.)
Ulverston G.S.	100	80 b., 20 g., 10 boys learning Latin or Greek	479 (Ulv. t.s.)
Academies in the town of Ulverston	200	There were 15 " academies " [3] in the town in 1828. This is a broad estimate	
Bardsea	20	Elementary, 3 R's	(In Urswick par.)
Hawkshead G.S.	20	40 in all. Half were the children of outsiders	132 (H'head w. Monk Coniston)
Sawrey	25	Elementary	50 (Claife)
Finsthwaite	30	Elementary and Latin	30
Osmotherley	29	N.s. but certainly elem.	20
Totals	555		1079

Roughly one-half of the 7-13 age group in Furness and Cartmel is accounted for here if we assume that the former group is approximately equal to one-ninth of the Census population at any one time. In parishes or divisions where the numbers of scholars are not stated, Dendron, Broughton-in-Furness, Blawith, Lowick, Colton and Torver, each had some form of educational foundation, varying from a charitable provision for the education of a few poor children to a more or less thriving chapel school, as at Dendron in Aldingham parish. Here " all the children " (perhaps 30 of school age) in Leece, Gleaston and Dendron could receive something of an education in the basic skills of writing and arithmetic, together with some Latin and Greek ; [4] but few chapelries were as well provided as this one, and it is clear that more than half of the children of Furness were dependent on what occasional or inefficiently taught smatterings they could pick up, or were forced to remain unlettered.

[1] A number of exercise books of this period are preserved at the Barrow Public Library. They show great diligence and care, but generalisations cannot be based upon them. [2] Details from *Pub. Char.*, 56, 59, 71, 85, 101, 105, 120, 125, etc. [3] *Parson & White.* [4] *Pub. Charities*, 2 ; Humphris, *Dendron, cit.*, 249.

148

This proportion seems to have been a common one throughout the country in about 1820.[1]

The types of education offered, in the local examples given, might have been encountered anywhere in the district or region during the eighteenth century, even though the introduction of Bell's system at Dalton was a sign of change.

Schools and society were undoubtedly successful in instilling a modicum of literacy. Of over 150 men married at Lowick and Blawith between 1750 and 1830, five out of six could at least sign their names in the marriage registers, although one in three of the women could not do so. The Registrar-General's abstracts (following 1839) of those who made crosses in marriage registers show that Cumberland and Westmorland were—as far as it is safe to trust these figures—much more literate than was common among the English counties. Developments like those described in this chapter played a part in the achievement of such standards.

The new factory industry at Backbarrow made its slight contribution ; the cotton firm of Birch, Robinson and Walmsley, no doubt feeling a sense of obligation to those whom they exploited, provided their parish apprentices with tuition by the curate and schoolmaster of Finsthwaite. These unfortunates—140 of them altogether in 1805—were employed in the Backbarrow mill for 14 hours a day, but were allowed two hours on Sunday evenings for what their local supervisors later called study of " the Bible, New Testament, or Spelling Book, according to their ability ".[2] In the year mentioned two of the Brighton Guardians of the Poor visited Backbarrow to investigate the condition of apprentices who had been sent from that town, and having found little which they regarded as demanding criticism—the 14-hour day did not excite their disapproval—the visitors remarked that " respecting (the children's) education, it is more limited than we had reason to expect, as the clergyman that has charge of them attends for only two hours each Sunday evening ; consequently their improvement cannot be much, as there are 140 children ; nor has any one of ours been instructed to write ".[3] Some ten years later it was stated that the Sabbath was strictly observed by the children, that the latter went to Finsthwaite Chapel in the mornings of that day, and that they received instruction in the afternoons.[4] So much for Peel's Act of 1802,[5] which laid down that a part of the working day of factory apprentices was to be given up to instruction in reading, writing and arithmetic.

[1] Brougham's calculations of 1820, quoted in Adamson, *op. cit.*, 261.
[2] *Rept. on Children in Manufactories*, 1816, *cit.*, 210.   [3] *MS. Minutes of the Incorporated Guardians, Brighton, Sussex*, June 3, 18, 1805, quoted by Webb, *Eng. Poor Law History*, Pt. I, 202.   [4] *Rept. of 1816*, etc., *loc. cit.*   [5] 42 *Geo. III*, c.73 ; it applied to the first four years of apprenticeship.

The Backbarrow children had their Sunday school, and no account of educational development at this period would be complete without some reference to the Sunday school movement of the late eighteenth century, and especially to the Ulverston Town Bank Sunday School. This was founded at a meeting on October 16th, 1787, for reasons set out as follows :

" Whereas the establishment of Sunday Schools seems to us a measure well calculated for the instruction and improvement of those poor children who, by poverty and inattention of their parents, are deprived of every other method of education . . . (resolved to) carry out a similar scheme for the parish of Ulverston . . . ".[1] It was laid down that masters and mistresses should open school at seven o'clock in summer and eight in winter, and that children were to be taught reading until the time of divine service. The privileged pupils were then marched to church, whence they returned to be employed in any religious instructions until 6 p.m. in summer or 4 p.m. in winter. About 1836 it was thought desirable to teach the Sunday scholars in the Ulverston National School.[2]

The culture of a community is not confined to the four walls of a schoolroom. Ulverston had a book-binding establishment, or at least a capable book-binder, in Richard ffell of Ulverston in 1673 ;[3] Houghton introduced printing into the town in 1791, and Ashburner printed a Bible and other works there in and after 1798. Houghton's widow married John Soulby, and one of their sons, Stephen Soulby, published the first newspaper in Furness, *Soulby's Ulverston Advertiser and General Intelligencer*, which ran from 1847 to 1914.[4] In 1828 Ulverston had three booksellers (each of whom seems to have operated a lending library), two " good libraries, one clerical and the other general ", a small theatre, two news-rooms, and even a small museum of " birds, quadrupeds &c."[5] The theatre mentioned was in existence in 1775, when there was a local performance of *She Stoops to Conquer* ; it was a converted barn belonging to the White Hart Hotel.[6]

The detailed story of the local National School movement, while well worthy of attention, is not given here ; the educational problems of the district were far from solved between 1820 and 1860, and in the Barrow district at least, they became seriously worsened in the 'seventies.

[1]Some account in Barber, *Furness and Cartmel Notes*, 321-5.   [2]*Loc. cit.* [3]*Vide* Fell, *op. cit.*, 277.   [4]Barnes, *Barrow & District . . . a History*, 118. [5]*Parson & White.*   [6]*The Diary of Edward Jackson, cit.*, 5.1.1775, and note by Mr. T. E. Casson, p. 2.

This topic, which follows naturally from that of education, has more to do with social history than social organisation as such. The early careers and memoirs of outstanding men of the locality can sometimes tell us a little of the true nature of eighteenth-century society in this part of England.

George Romney and William Wordsworth are the best-known names. Each spent early and impressionable years in the district. Both the painter and the poet received a measure of education in Furness schools, Romney at Dendron Chapel School and Wordsworth at Hawkshead Grammar School. Romney was born at Beckside, Dalton-in-Furness, on 15th December, 1734. He was not apparently of the humblest stock, and his father, a joiner or cabinet-maker named Rumley or Rumney, was of a trading and farming family with professional or middle-class connections, and was himself a man of considerable ingenuity who constructed pumps for use in the local iron mines.[1] The young George was sent as a boarder to Dendron School, £1 *per annum* being paid for his tuition and 3d. a day for his board and lodging. His father removed him in 1745, when he was ten years old, and allowed the boy to assist him on an estate at Cocken, in Dalton parish, where John Rumley combined agriculture and cabinet-making. During this apprenticeship George developed a talent as carver and gilder, constructing violins and flutes. In this local environment the young Romney spent his most impressionable years ; when twenty-one years of age he became apprenticed to a travelling portrait painter named Steel, supposedly during a visit of the latter to Dalton, and accompanied him to Kendal.[2] The rest of his career has been dealt with by numerous authorities.

Wordsworth, by contrast, was not originally of the district, but was born in Cockermouth in 1770 of a professional family, his father being an attorney-at-law and land agent to the famous coalowner Sir James Lowther. It is significant that John Wordsworth chose Hawkshead Grammar School as suitable for his son ; and as is well known, the future poet spent nine years there (1778-87). It is beyond question that the school made a deep and abiding impression on him. His reactions are recorded in verse written at the time or soon afterwards, and Wordsworth's own references to his school life provide important evidence as to the

---

[1] *C. & W.* (NS), XXVI, 358, 363 and *passim*. The mention (*op. cit.*, 363) of John Rumley's engineering activities is slightly substantiated by *Duddon MSS.*, Bar Iron Accounts for 1750, fol. 41, where " John Rumley of Dalton " received a small quantity of bar iron. [2] Humphris, *Dendron, cit.*, 250, and Kendall, *Cocken, B.N.F.C.*, XII, 51 ; also *D.N.B.*, which deals sketchily with this period.

quality of the education provided at Hawkshead for (in 1820) two guineas' entrance fee and one to three guineas cockpenny or Shrovetide offering. His favourite master, the Rev. William Taylor, emerges in idealised form as the *Matthew* of his verses, and he greatly appreciated the freedom as well as the encouragement that he received there.[1] The poet's testimony as to his schooling supplements well the factual observations of the Charity Commissioners of 1820 regarding Hawkshead School.

In this district, with its yeomen, shepherds and small tradesmen, his early democratic sympathies were nurtured. He wrote in *The Prelude* that :

> " It was my fortune scarcely to have seen
> Through the whole tenor of my school-day time,
> The face of one, who, whether boy or man,
> Was vested with attention or respect
> Through claims of wealth or blood . . . "[2]

He retained his affection for the immediate district for long afterwards, frequently visiting Furness Abbey, and spending a holiday at Rampside, then known as a small bathing resort.[3] He lived long enough to denounce the desecration of the Furness Abbey grounds by the local railway company,[4] and he showed feeling over the gradual disappearance of the yeoman class of the Lakeland fells.[5] Charged with sentiment as the poet's attitude may have been, that attitude nevertheless provides an apt commentary on the period. The bucolic life of the fells was idealised by Wordsworth, but in this period of social and economic change, something was lost.

It is a sharp descent from Wordsworth to the lesser men of the area. The Crankes of Urswick, mentioned hitherto in these pages as enterprising farmers,[6] produced two notable if not first-class portrait painters during the eighteenth century,[7] and at this point outstanding local contributions to the arts may be said to end. But local schools or society produced several men eminent in other spheres. This was a period of great social mobility ; it was possible for a young man without great weight of influence or undue stupidity to fight his way to economic and sometimes administrative power, and the growing order of society recognised certain talents increasingly as it distributed its rewards more and more unequally. Unfortunately, little is known of the men who left fell villages and

---

[1]Regrettably little is known of Furness schoolmasters of this period. An early Dendron master, George Barker, was described variously as a " man of sober life and honest conversation ", and " a meer Orbilius, and an indiscreet, passionate, cuffing churl ". It can be seen which is the pupil's account. Humphris, *loc. cit.* [2]*The Prelude*, IX, 218-222. [3]Barnes, *op. cit.*, 93. [4]*At Furness Abbey*, June 21st, 1845. [5]*Guide to the Lakes, cit.*, 80-1. [6]See pp. 75-7, above. [7]*C. & W.* (NS), VI, 128 sqq. ; *D.N.B.*, sv.. James Cranke.

prospered in the industrial towns, or in the ways of commercial enterprise. Occasionally a local document gives an inkling, and in 1734 the Broughton-in-Furness parish register mentions [1] " Jonathan Jackson, mercht. of the Spanish Town in the Island of Jamaica and grandson of Matthew Jackson, Harthwayte Bank, hus (bandman)". Somewhat later, one John Bolton or Boulton (1756-1837), the son of an Ulverston apothecary (and later known as Colonel Bolton, or " Rub-a-dub, Fire Away! "), did indeed rise to affluence as a West India merchant and a dominant personality in Liverpool commerce and politics. [2] He attended the Ulverston Town Bank Grammar School, but it is not clear how this helped him to control the Tory electoral machine in the Lancashire port and to mobilise support for Pitt and Canning, or to distribute bribes with effect. [3] Bolton refused a peerage and killed an opponent in a duel, and was unquestionably one of the most colourful personalities the locality has produced ; but his contributions to history, although spectacular, have no solidity about them. A later adventurer of some interest was John Brogden (1798-1867), who was born at Marton or Martin near Dalton-in-Furness, of a farming family, and who received " an ordinary village school education ". He became a contractor, maker, director, owner and worker of railways, a coalowner and ironmaster in South Wales, and an investor in many fields. Most of his life was spent in the Manchester district ; but half a century after his birth, Brogden returned to his home territory with his sons to promote and administer the Ulverston(e) and Lancaster Railway. [4]

Brogden was certainly not the only man of local origins who made good in the industrial field, and the case of Thomas Fresh— whose career in fact ended in disaster—has already received mention. [5] Generally speaking, however, the men who left more or less humble homes to triumph in the industrial struggle for survival —or at least, gain a modest affluence— have not left memoirs or autobiographies. As the exhumation of north-country business records proceeds, more will become known about them. Meanwhile, it is not altogether inappropriate that the men whose achievements did not rest largely upon mere sharpness of wit or desire for gain, but whose claims to remembrance were based upon something finer, are also those whose biographical data have been preserved in greater or lesser detail.

No local history would be complete without reference to Sir John Barrow, Bart., (1764-1848) who did indeed originate in a humble cottage at Dragley Beck, Ulverston. Like John Bolton

[1]Broughton *Burials*. [2]Casson, *A Few Furness Worthies*, 13-20 ; he is also noticed in Picton, Sir J., *Memorials of Liverpool*. [3]He was not the first Furness policitian to engage in such activity, and was certainly not the last. [4]Casson, *op. cit.*, 66-8, and below, pp. 204, 214, 215-8. [5]See p. 74 above.

the merchant, he received some education at the Town Bank Grammar School, and what is more important, some encouragement. He went to Liverpool in early life, worked in an iron foundry, went on a whaling expedition, studied languages, and after service as an usher in a Greenwich school, obtained a post in Lord Macartney's Embassy to China. Ultimately he became a permanent Secretary to the Admiralty and one of the founders of the Royal Geographical Society. [1] This triumphant progress was not achieved without the exertion of influence and a measure of good fortune ; but Barrow was a gifted geographer and linguist. He was also an able civil servant. [2]

Furness produced several physicians of note. Sir Isaac Pennington, M.D. (1745-1817), was of Longmire in Colton, and became Regius Professor of Physic at Cambridge ; he left his fortune to St. John's College with the recommendation that part of it was to be used to found exhibitions " to be given by preference to natives of Hawkshead and Colton ". [3] The work of William Close has been described. [4] Isaac Swainson, M.D. (1746-1812), of a Hawkshead family, was an able physician and botanist. [5]

Furness and Cartmel are associated with at least two outstanding mathematicians ; Joshua King of Lowick (1797-1857), a miller's son who became Lucasian Professor of Mathematics from 1839 to 1849 and President of Queen's College, Cambridge, from 1832 to 1857 ; and William Gibson (1720-91), a self-taught genius from the Appleby district who spent most of his life in Cartmel, and who amused himself with advanced algebraic problems while at work on his farm. Although Gibson himself has become a figure of legend, his extraordinary brilliance is a fact—Sir John Barrow gave independent testimony to his skill [6]—and this former labourer was in great demand as an enclosure commissioner. Another John Bolton (1791-1872), born in a cottage so humble that the rent was only fifteen shillings *per annum*, became a learned and original geologist and a friend of Sedgwick. [7] Born in Urswick, Bolton attended the Grammar School there until he was obliged to move to Ulverston at the age of nine ; and labouring " hard from morning to night in a weaving shop for eighteenpence a week ", he managed to educate himself further. After some years as a weaver he became a land surveyor, and, like Gibson, ultimately served as an enclosure commissioner. [8] But his passion was geology, and he was induced

---

[1] *Vide* his *An Autobiographical Memoir* (1847). [2] He was a relative of the mother of Charles Dickens, and seems to have been the original of Mrs. Micawber's wealthy relation ; *vide* Pope-Hennessy, Una, *Charles Dickens*, 1-3. [3] *V.C.H. Lancs.*, VIII, 384. [4] See p. 118 above. [5] Cowper, *Hawkshead*, 406. [6] See Barrow's *Autobiographical Memoir*, 10. [7] His *Geological Fragments* (1869) gives autobiographical matter, especially the Introduction (iv, vii) and p. 123. [8] For Kirkby Ireleth (Award of 1867).

by Sedgwick and others to publish *Geological Fragments*, fascinating as a local study, in 1869.

Among the ecclesiastical figures of the area, Edmund Law, D.D. (1703-87), Bishop of Carlisle from 1768 to his death, was a Cartmel man and was educated at the Grammar School there. Any local churchman must be in some measure overshadowed by the towering figure of Archbishop Sandys, who was Hawkshead-born, and who of course belonged to another age ; yet many local men, wishing to become " priests ", became ordained and aspired to real scholarship. Each of the local grammar schools produced prominent or famous men, and it should be remembered that they never catered for more than a few dozen pupils at a time. Gifted individuals appear in almost any society, and a few examples do not in themselves constitute evidence of high educational or cultural standards. Such persons, however, do not flourish without some original stimulus in impressionable or formative years. The agricultural reporter William Dickinson, writing of Cumberland in 1852, commented on the number of outstanding men of the small farming and statesman class of that county who had gone into business and trade in London, Liverpool and Manchester.[1] Furness undoubtedly provided its due quota ; and the success of many of these migrants is explained by the educational advance, the local culture and the atmosphere of opportunity and social mobility which have been described or implied in these pages.

Of the established local gentry little need be said in this section. One man who might have taken a prominent part in northern industry, but who by an accident of circumstances did not, was Colonel Thomas Richard Gale Braddyll (1776-1862), of Conishead Priory, for many years chairman of the Ulverston Canal Company, and the inheritor of a great family fortune. Braddyll possessed iron and coal-bearing estates in Cumberland and County Durham, and in 1838 he was a major shareholder in the South Hetton Coal Company (Col. Braddyll and partners) which in that year commenced " one of the most formidable and costly winnings ever accomplished " at Murton near Dalton-le-Dale. The cost of sinking two deep shafts at Murton was estimated at £250,000,[2] and whatever may have been the ultimate gain of colliery proprietors there, Braddyll was ruined.[3] He was forced to sell his Conishead estate,[4] after having spent £140,000 on the rebuilding of his Gothic mansion there between 1821 and 1836. By a quirk of fortune, Conishead Priory was later occupied briefly by H. W. Schneider, a man who invested in heavy industry quite as largely as its original owner, but whose career was one of great material success.

---

[1]*J.R.A.S.*, XIII, 220.   [2]For description, *vide* Galloway, R. L., *Annals of Coalmining*, 2nd Series, 14-16.   [3]Bardsley, *op. cit.*, 96.   [4]Park, *op. cit.*, records of sale of the Conishead estate.

The industrialists of mid-Victorian local history demand separate treatment. They subsisted in a world and environment that had undergone deep-seated change, and several of the most prominent of them were non-local in origin or rose to wealth with the development of Furness heavy industries. This world, instead of giving forth a Romney or a Wordsworth, produced thousands of tons of iron and steel. The emphasis was no longer on success in the arts, sciences and commerce of the larger world, but on revolutionary economic change within the district itself.

5. SOCIAL INSTITUTIONS

(i) *Banks*

There was no formally established bank in Furness during the eighteenth century. The local iron firms of that period, however, acted as bankers for the neighbourhood. In 1772-5 the firm of William Latham and Son, of the Duddon ironworks, was accepting loans at rates of interest varying from 4 to 10 per cent., and in 1783 the Newland Company, with a share capital of only £9410, had accepted deposited moneys from carters, boatmen and sailors to a value probably much greater, the total loan capital held by the company amounting to £24,750.[1] The almost legendary incumbent of Seathwaite, the Rev. Robert (" Wonderful ") Walker,[2] immortalised and perhaps sentimentalised by Wordsworth, invested £300 in the Newland Company for a number of years, and the Corporation of Kendal made a loan of £800 to the latter by 1782, the rate of interest charged being 4½ per cent.[3]

By the last decade of the eighteenth century the country banks of Maude, Wilson and Co. and John Wakefield and Sons were established in Kendal, and the monetary difficulties of the iron firms decreased as notes came into circulation more readily.[4] The Backbarrow Company was dealing with the first-named bank in 1795.[5] In 1803 there was still no reputable bank in Furness, and the proceeds of the sale of the Cartmel commons, following the Enclosure Act in that parish, were deposited with Worswick and Co. of Lancaster.[6] The Fell family of Ulverston stepped into the breach at about this time. The commercial career of the Fells had commenced with Andrew of that surname, " mercer " of Ulverston in the late seventeenth century ; they became linen, cotton and check manufacturers as well as bleachers and sailmakers, and seem to have developed a small banking business by the end of the eighteenth century.[7] The chief representative of the family at

---

[1]*E.I.I.F.*, 333-4 ; *Duddon MSS.* DDX/192/4, fols. 35-8. The Backbarrow Co. performed a similar function ; *Backbarrow MSS*, 1795 ledger. [2]*E.I.I.F., loc. cit.* Walker (1709-1802) belongs properly to a list of notable men of the district. [3]*Loc. cit.* [4]*E.I.I.F.*, 335. [5]*Backbarrow MSS.*, ledger cited. [6]Stockdale, *op. cit.*, 347. quoting Mins. of the Cartmel Enclosure Commissioners. [7]Park, *op. cit.*, 49.

this time was Robert Fell (d. 1832), who went into partnership with Miles Theodore Burton to form the firm of Fell, Burton and Co., which acted as banker to the Ulverston Canal Co. Both Robert Fell and Miles Burton were directors of the latter until about 1819.[1] They acquired a further partner, John Pearson, by 1810, and the firm was afterwards styled Fell, Son and Pearson, flax and tow spinners as well as bankers. In 1828 their premises were on Duke Street, Ulverston, and they are recorded as having drawn on Masterman, Peters and Co.[2].

It was but a short step from local manufacture and commerce to banking, and the firm of Petty and Postlethwaite, shipbuilders and timber dealers, also became bankers for the locality after about 1820, drawing likewise on Masterman, Peters and Co. in 1828.[3] The firm of Fell survived the country banking crises of the period, as did that last-mentioned. Other banks of the region were less fortunate, Worswick and Co. of Lancaster failing in 1822, and Dilworth and Co. of the same place in 1826.[4] The apparent soundness of these small Ulverston firms was probably due to their position as offshoots of well-established businesses.

Neither of the Ulverston banks developed into a larger organisation, Wakefield, Crewdson and Co. and the Lancaster Banking Co. afterwards taking their places in the locality. After about 1860 the last-named company became dominant in north-west Lancashire. The Fell family of Ulverston nevertheless remained largely interested in local industries, wielding a powerful influence on Furness affairs through the agency of John Fell (1826-1910), a descendant of the Robert Fell alluded to. The former became an unofficial political representative of the Cavendish family in Furness and an important investor in Barrow heavy industries, as well as a leading member of the Barrow-in-Furness town council.[5]

Not much can be said about those aspects of economic history associated with money and banking. There are some interesting comments affecting the immediate region in the Report of the 1833 Select Committee on Agriculture, in which the famous farmer William Blamire asserted that " canals and railways in Cumberland . . . have brought into circulation a great deal of money ",[6] and that Scottish pound notes were still widely used south of the border, even though their use in England was illegal at that time. Cumberland prices, he suggested, were probably higher than they need have been, and his notion that there could have been such a phenomenon as local inflation is an ingenious one.

---

[1]*Mins. Ulv. Canal Co.*, 1796-1819, *passim*. [2]*Parson & White* (p. 729). [3]White, *op. cit.*, 33 ; *Parson & White.* [4]*V.C.H. Lancs.*, VIII, 20. [5]For information on this family I am indebted to Sir Matthew H. G. Fell, K.C.V.O. [6]*Sel. Cttee., cit.*, Ques. 6633 and *passim*.

(ii) *Friendly Societies*

Ulverston had its " Friendly Society " as early as 1779.[1] This was followed by an Amicable Friendly Society, established in 1792,[2] and Hawkshead likewise formed an Amicable Friendly Society in April 14th of the same year.[3] The seventeen hundred and nineties, marked by the enactment of Rose's Act of 1793,[4] which gave encouragement to voluntary societies for the mutual relief of sickness, old age and infirmity, saw an increase in the number of societies in Cumberland.[5] Hawkshead's Female Union Society, claimed to be the oldest friendly organisation for women in England, was formed on August 6th, 1798.[6] It may well be that these bodies struck root because growing pauperism affected the sense of security of the townsman and countryman alike. The movement to mutual self-help was of course much more evident in the towns, and Kendal, with its handicrafts and manufactures, had no fewer than twenty societies—some of which were trade clubs—when Sir Frederick Eden was collecting information in the 'nineties.[7] In 1801, according to Eden's estimate, more than one in fifteen persons in England and Wales was a member of such a society or club, and another estimate of 1815 put the porportion at about one in eleven.[8] In the same year Furness and Cartmel had 1291 members out of a population of about 20,000, and was lagging behind the average proportion. Ulverston had then 659 members in perhaps three clubs, and Dalton 275 ; there were only 280 members throughout the whole of the Furness fells.[9] The *Westmorland Gazette* of June 9th, 1827, wrote that " Ulverston has been noted for these clubs, having at one period three strong ones, the third having been established 28 years, and is still healthy ".[10] The original Ulverston Friendly Society of 1779 was still fairly substantial in 1836, with a membership of 142, but it was beginning to decline.[11] The movement experienced a renaissance in the 'fifties and 'sixties of the nineteenth century, e.g., in November 1864, no fewer than 16 friendly societies had accounts in the Ulverston Savings Bank.[12]

This last institution deserves a brief note ; it was founded on May 21st, 1816, thereby anticipating George Rose's Savings Bank Act of 1817.[13] By 1828 it had deposits amounting to £30,000, roughly two pounds for every man, woman and child in Furness.[14] There can be no doubt that the friendly societies, in spite of their Whitsuntide celebrations and their conviviality, played a large part in encouraging this thrift. The bank had £82,000 in deposits in 1864.

---

[1]*Aldred Collection of Broadsheets* ; see also White, *op. cit.*, 88. [2]*Kendal Mercury*, 4.5.1826, quoted Casson, *op. cit.*, 93. [3]Cowper, *op. cit.*, 529. [4]33 Geo. III, c.54. [5]Bailey and Culley, *op. cit.*, 262. [6]Cowper, *op. cit.*, 529-47, for list of rules dated 1808. [7]*Vide* the comments of Clapham, *Econ. Hist. Modern Brit.*, I, 296. [8]*Op. cit.*, 211, 297. [9]*Abstract* of Poor Returns, 1818, *cit.* [10]Quoted White, *op. cit.*, 104. [11]Infn. by courtesy of Mr. J. L. Hobbs. [12]*Mannex*, 395. [13]57 Geo. III, c.130. [14]*Parson & White.*

CHAPTER VIII

FURNESS SOCIETY BEFORE THE RAILWAY AGE

CLERGY AND PEOPLE

The relationships between clergymen and their parishioners tell us something about a society at a given period. It is true, likewise, that in certain individuals the virtues and failings of a given society are precipitated. This is particularly true of clergymen. In the eighteenth century, as Dr. Plumb has written, " they were not quite gentlemen " ; near to the land, they often farmed their glebe and were close to the people of the countryside while yet engaging in intellectual pursuits and hunting or mingling with the local gentry. They were suspended between two social classes, the peasantry and the squirearchy.

This was noticeably so in Lakeland, where the clergy were often drawn from the ranks of the yeomanry and peasantry. Many yeomen of the north-west had an overriding ambition where talented sons were concerned—for those sons " to acquire Latin and Greek enough to pass the ordeal of examination for the church, a priest, as they proudly said ".[1] The result of this preference was, as is hardly surprising, a frequently close kinship between the clergyman and his flock. Moreover, the latter might take a keen and active interest, deeply protestant and puritan in origin, in the election of their own curate, incumbent or chapel reader. Bishop Gastrell's visitation report of 1717 remarked contemptuously of the chapelry of Lowick that " The inhabitants, and especially those called the Twelve, and the feoffees of the chapel, pretend a right to choose a curate ".[2] The inhabitants of Lowick went on pretending, and each of their curates during the eighteenth century bore a local or regional name—Sawrey, Watterson, Moor, Forrest, Borrowdale and Hartley. At adjacent Blawith the roll of curates includes the names of Jackson, Atkinson, Hartley, Hodgson and Ashburner, each with associations of the same character. Of Urswick in Plain Furness, where eighteenth-century incumbents were successively named Inman, Swainson, Holme, Addison and Ashburner (each surname having the strongest possible connection with the neighbourhood) it was stated that in 1788 the patrons of the living were " the inhabitants ", although ,no doubt, those with a greater share in the tithes had a correspondingly stronger voice in the elections.[3]

---

[1]*Gent. Mag., cit.*, 1202 ; *C. & W.* (NS), LV, 1956, 198.   [2]*V.C.H. Lancs.*, VIII, 362, n.12.   [3]*V.C.H., Lancs.* VIII, 337.

Taking these cases together, there is little doubt as to cause and effect. These were not rich livings, and the curates or chapel readers of a Torver, a Blawith or a Lowick were plain and simple men, often lacking any university degree and sharing the poverty of their parishioners. Rather over 60 persons raised between them £5 1s. 1d. yearly for " the priest wages " at Torver in 1690. [1] It was there that Robert " Wonderful " Walker served his apprenticeship to a saintly frugality in 1734. A curate in such a place, of course, could not live on his " wages "—he had to labour on his own parcels of land or rent some from others, and to engage in the sheap-rearing and spinning which were the mainstays of his flock. But before Walker, of whom so much has been written, can be held up as even partly typical, he and his fellow-clergy must be examined more closely.

Many—perhaps most—of the eighteenth-century local clergy had roots in the area, irrespective of their social origins. In the nineteenth century the situation altered, and as the lists of incumbents' names testify, the majority were then " offcomes ". Before this transformation took place, local men seem to have taken local livings, including those of gentle family. The Rev. John Sunderland of Ulverston and Pennington, at least two members of the Sandys family and Dr. Roger Baldwin of Aldingham were of the Furness gentry. Several presentees of the better livings were also pluralists—like Dr. Baldwin, they would leave much or all of their work to a curate or curates—and at least one (Dr. Baldwin again) was a learned eccentric. The pattern then becomes more like the traditionally accepted one for the eighteenth-century clergy. Fortunately we are in a position to see a little way into the mind and heart of one of these ministers, the Rev. Edward Jackson, Vicar of Colton from 1762 to 1789, and pluralist Vicar of Ulverston for the three years following 1786. Jackson's diary [2] consists largely of laconic entries, but it was consistently kept, and, by careful analysis of his recurring observations it is possible to learn much about his tastes and movements.

Edward Jackson was a man of wide interests, most of which had little connection with his duties as a minister. He was an enthusiastic botanist, sportsman and lover of the company of the local gentry. A bachelor, he was neither rich nor dissipated, but an *homme moyen sensuel* fairly typical of his age if not of his district. This, it should be remembered, was the age of Tillotson's popular sermon on the text " His commandments are not grievous", [3] which succeeded in reconciling worldly and heavenly virtues, and

[1]See misc. documents in published Torver *Registers, cit.*, 89 sqq.   [2]Transcribed by Mr. T. E. Casson, *C. & W.*, (NS) XL, 1 sqq.   [3]It is not surprising to find that three volumes of " Tilletson " were catalogued at Blawith chapel in 1773.

there is no doubt that by such standards Jackson aspired to a place in heaven.   The entries in his diary need only a little stirring in the imagination to give the reader a vision of a Jane Austen world. There are trips, occupying one-quarter of his considerable leisure time, to the Pennys' residence or to the Machells (the ironmaking squires) at Hollow Oak ; there are hunting and shooting expeditions ; and there are visits to his book and gambling club at Backbarrow, on at least one occasion graced by a call from Lord George Cavendish.   Yet his living was not an unusually remunerative one.   His total income, made up of a small salary obtained *via* a collecting brief from the several extensive divisions of his parish, of rentals from various persons, and the results of a little trading in books and furniture, amounted to not much more than £100 yearly. This, it is true, was six times a labourer's income, and his year's board amounted to a mere £2 14s. 3d. (he lived in lodgings with a " Dame ").   The cheapness of living enabled Jackson to spend spacious and golden days in a manner that leaves no doubt that those members of the community who were not shackled by the direst poverty—the small freeholders or yeomen with a steady income from their woods, for instance—could also live lives containing simple delights as well as rigours.

One would like to think that he was a source of spiritual strength ; but certain items in his diary point in another direction. Early in the January of 1775 he makes several references to the preparation of sermons, but thereafter, generally speaking, such references lapse.   By October 21st he had run out of material, and noted that he was " busy vamping a sermon in the evg. "   Yet he also records praying with a dying parishioner, Mary Addison, and settling a dispute between two of his flock.   Generally, however, the joys of the parlour and the countryside were paramount.   His " botanising ", his fishing, his shooting, his rides with local hare hunts, his trips to Ulverston to dine with the justices or the Commissioners of Land Tax, or to see plays there—these take pride of place in his mind and affections.

Jackson was probably better, and certainly no worse, than hundreds of contemporary clergymen ; he was latitudinarian enough to associate with the Jesuit priest Father West, was a man of some learning, and may have compared well with a previous Vicar of Ulverston, Edmund Atkinson, who remained in that living from 1714 to 1765 and collected no fewer than four wives during the half-century of his ministry.   Atkinson, with the assistance of a local constable, attempted to arrest George Whitefield when the latter was fighting down " some small resistance " on the part of Satan at Ulverston in June, 1750.   Through the doubtless prejudiced eyes of the great Methodist, the Vicar of Ulverston " looked more like a butcher than a minister ". " I never saw a poor creature sent off in such disgrace ", recorded Whitefield[1] with satisfaction.

This was not the first time that Ulverston had felt the impact of a dynamic campaigner. George Fox had made an onslaught there a century before, and his followers, sober and cohesive, were still going about their business in the district. But Methodism—although it did not strike deep roots in Furness until widespread industrialisation arrived—was on the rise, whereas Quakerism had long passed its period of truly fiery inner light and was hardening into tradition. The Quaker emphasis on the individual had appealed to local yeomen and tradesmen. As has been seen already, the Quaker population of the district did not exceed three hundred persons at any time in the eighteenth century,[2] and the records of burials at Sunbrick, Swarthmoor and Colthouse indicate either greater longevity on the part of the Friends or a falling off in numbers during the course of that century. An Ulverston Congregational Church, meanwhile, was opened in 1778, and the first small Catholic Chapel was opened there in 1806. The Wesleyan Methodists, as has been noted, did not open their chapel in the same town until 1814.[3]

The reaction against the eighteenth-century established church and clergy took manifold forms, and the glorification of the simple, industrious Robert Walker, curate of Seathwaite, was merely one expression of the general trend. It is no denigration of Walker, who was certainly a saintly enough figure by the standards of his day, to place him against his historical background. One has only to compare Walker's way of life with that of Edward Jackson to see the stark contrast ; giving instruction to Seathwaite children in the chapel there during the entire week, Walker (curate from 1736 to his death in 1802) worked on his smallholding, acted as scrivenor for his neighbours, laboured constantly on his spinning wheel, gave hospitality to visitors, and travelled many miles carrying yarn or wool to market. All this has been said innumerable times. Craig Gibson, however, pointed out a century ago that Walker was " carrying with him into the Church the stern habits of frugality, industry, temperance and self-denial in which he was reared, and which doubtless he had seen practised in his father's family from his earliest childhood ", and went on to say of Wordsworth, Walker's most prominent panegyrist, that " One really might suppose that the late Poet Laureate . . . (was) struck with admiring astonishment on discovering such an assemblage of homely working-day virtues in a clergyman ".[4]

[1]*The Life and Times of Whitefield*, quoted in Nightingale, *Lancs. Non conformity*, ii, 255. [2]See p. 103 above. There was also a small Quaker burial ground at Low Kiln Bank, Ulpha. [3]*V.C.H. Lancs.*, VIII, 356 ; Barnes, *Barrow . . . A History*, 78. [4]Gibson, A. Craig, *The Old Man* (c.1850), 83.

What, then, of the people themselves, who must have possessed some of the virtues which Robert Walker had absorbed so completely? The Jesuit priest Thomas West thought highly of the inhabitants of Furness, and his well-known eulogy of them, which first appeared in his *Antiquities of Furness* in 1774, will stand repetition yet once more :

" Universal civility and good manners are the characteristic of Furness, and distinguish it from those parts of the kingdom where an unfortunate curiosity degenerates into the rudeness and barbarism so flagrant and offensive amongst those of the lowest stations. At Church and market their appearance is decent, and sobriety is a general virtue. Quarrels and affrays are seldom heard of at fairs and public meetings. The modesty of the female sex and sobriety of the men prevent irregularities before marriage and secure conjugal love and affection through life. The women are handsome, the men in general robust. As the air of Furness is salubrious, so the inhabitants live to a good old age."

This characterisation has been regarded as intolerably condescending, but it should not be set aside merely as one of the *curiosa* of regional history. It is worthy of analysis.

The statements regarding " civility " and decent behaviour, made by a man who had travelled fairly widely, are nevertheless liable to have been based on the most subjective of standards. The most that can be said is that the Rev. S. Stebbing Shaw, who visited Furness a few years later, confessed himself struck by " the simplicity of northern manners, where every native that passes by salutes you with a good morrow ".[1] Such descriptions contrast strikingly with those of (say) colliery communities in England and Scotland at the same period.[2] Coalminers, however, followed a dirty, dangerous and sometimes brutalising labour, and were often bound by legal as well as economic bonds. The yeomen, small tradesmen and labourers of North Lancashire and Cumbria must also have lived hard lives in many respects, but the status and environment of such persons was very different. Good manners and lack of " unfortunate curiosity " were the characteristics of people who lived secure and ordered lives without too much or too little contact with the outside world ; of people who were not knowingly exploited by any obvious or visible agency, who accepted their earthly lot with calm if not complete resignation, and who therefore showed neither hatred nor contempt for any well-fed visitor who might appear in their midst. Numerous Furness people had opportunities (or were forced) to travel abroad by sea,

---

[1] *A Tour to the West of England in* 1788 ; author anon., but as above.
[2] *Vide* Ashton and Sykes, *The Coal Industry of the Eighteenth Century,* 150.

and in the second half of the eighteenth century the region had many visitors from afar. [1]

Security—certainly an ambiguous word—was enjoyed by many of the people. The customaryholder or copyholder, with his little holding, might struggle to live satisfactorily, but his status carried certain advantages ; he could not easily be evicted, and his fines remained certain. [2] In the moorland hamlets the ties of marriage and intermarriage ensured that he was surrounded by his kinsfolk. It was the slow breaking up of the ramifying family group, due partly to competition for holdings, partly to the destruction of certain handicrafts, and partly to indebtedness and encumbrances, which sent recruits to industry and commerce ; but this process took time, and the close-knit communities of the Furness hills and lowlands accepted naturally the notion that a man was to some extent his brother's keeper. Pauperism was no very great threat during much of the eighteenth century, and if a villager or parishioner became crippled, sick or prematurely aged and poverty-stricken, there was often a local charity to save him from starvation. It was only at the end of the eighteenth century that the poor became an obvious burden ; local occupations and trades, meanwhile, had grown and diversified considerably, although the parish registers also suggest that the sons of some husbandmen and yeomen had become general labourers or even paupers. In the middle decades of the eighteenth century, when the charcoal iron industry was flourishing, the people of Furness must have known near-full employment, and markedly improving living standards if not prosperity. West remarked that they were " decent " in appearance, and that they were beginning to eat wheaten bread and to drink tea and coffee.

A local writer [3] has observed that " A limited number of the gentry were in the Commission of the Peace for the County, but there is little to indicate much demand for their frequent services ". More recently, a study of the history of a group of Furness inns during the eighteenth century has shown few cases of ill-conduct serious enough to result in appearances at Quarter Sessions. [4] Inns, however, became remarkably numerous in Ulverston during the nineteenth century, while bread and other rioting, as has been seen, took place in the district during the Napoleonic Wars.

[1]West's *Guide to the Lakes* was written for the visiting "Quality". [2]*Vide* Collingwood, W. G., *Lake District History* (1928 ed.), 135-6, for some comments in support of the above. [3]John Fell in *C. & W.* (OS), XI, 381. [4]Infn. by courtesy of Mr. J. L. Hobbs. Ulverston had an " Association for the Prosecution of Fellons " (*sic*) between *c*.1810 and *c*.1840 (*Minute Book* in Barrow P.L.), but these bodies were common in the absence of an effective police force. In the 1830's there were complaints of noisy Sunday hiring fairs at Dalton.

Much has been written of the sexual promiscuity of village life in Georgian England. Here, it will be noticed, the notion—as affecting Furness—is flatly contradicted by West. It must be added that the latter's view carries considerable authority, for he anticipated the present writer by two hundred years in investigating the parish registers of the area ; and he must have noticed what is indeed the case—that baptisms of illegitimate children, although distinguished in the registers, are remarkable by their infrequency. Between 1761 and 1790, baptisms of illegitimate children in Broughton, although on the increase, never rose above 4 per cent of all baptisms ; at Colton, between 1751 and 1790, the total of such baptisms never rose above 2 per cent ; and even Ulverston recorded a similarly tiny percentage. It may well be that the entries of such baptisms were not always consistently made, but the trend is clear enough. There was an increase in such entries towards the end of the century, when some demoralisation was appearing. Out of 15 couples who married at Blawith between 1803 and 1812, four had to get married hastily, and three of these imprudent couples married younger than was customary in the district. But other samplings of marriage and baptism dates show that such moral defections were rare during previous decades, and that West was speaking the literal truth.

It is worth noticing that West referred to the good health and longevity of Furness people. The subject of local public health has been discussed at length, and little more need be said here, save to add that the parish registers, once more, substantiate West's remarks. It can be said that the worthy priest's account of the people of the neighbourhood, at first glance the utterance of a fervent local patriot, does not drift beyond hailing distance from the reality.

If we allow for the narrowness and limitation of outlook of a peasant community, it appears that the eighteenth century clergy might have been superior to their parishioners in the way of learning, but that they were superior to their flocks in few other respects.

RELAXATIONS

Almost the whole of this history has been taken up with work and workaday matters. But the eighteenth-century countryman did not labour all the time ; if a domestic worker and responsible for the choice of his own working hours, he was noted for his love of holidays. Even the Rev. Robert Walker took Saturday afternoons off to read the newspapers. The more popular and less intellectual types of amusement were twofold ; individual and organised. In a country district without heavily enclosed and guarded estates, with open fell, stream and river, there was scope for the man who wished to shoot or fish. The Rev. Edward Jackson did so at very moderate cost. There was also organised hunting of hare and fox—the local " Mayor Hunts ", at which a leader or Mayor was elected at each meeting—and in the years before the hills or commons were enclosed by hedges or drystone walls there was ample scope for equestrian excursions. Certainly the local gentry, made affluent by the demand for charcoal and iron, indulged themselves in fox-hunting and in the accompanying celebrations. Family papers have been found to refer to the Ulverston Mayor Hunt in 1745 and 1746, while a letter in one collection remarks of the local hunt : [1]

" At one of 'em w'ch was the finest to be sure, all the gentm. had the pleasure to get heartily drunk and many of them returned satisfied indeed with their diversion."

Jackson's diary refers also to hunts organised from Bouth and Penny Bridge (1775), while the Dalton Rout, " an annual festival in which the gentlemen of the district partook of the sports of the field during the day, and joined the ladies in the ballroom at night ", was discontinued in 1789. [2] The sports themselves, however, were not exclusively the preserve of the gentry, and in 1843 a local chronicler remarked that " With all classes hunting is still a favourite pastime . . . though not now so warmly supported as formerly ". [3] Lakeland hunting has long had a democratic tradition, and as the fells were enclosed a foot-follower and experienced fell-walker could go where horses could not.

Traditional athletics and sports took place on the bed of the channel between Barrow village and Barrow Island in the first half of the eighteenth century—the events included climbing the greasy pole, wrestling, horse-racing and trotting [4]—but the most obsessive local sport, filling the space in the popular imagination which is now occupied by football, was cockfighting. It was an activity in which an entire population could directly or indirectly participate or obtain vicarious pleasure. According to one authority [5] thousands of cocks must have been slaughtered annually within a ten miles radius of Ulverston, and the fields were dotted with cock walks (specially erected huts and pens on small plots of ground rented from farmers), where the birds received attention and delicacies denied to child or mistress, and a training such as is given only to boxing champions. " Cockings " or cockfighting mains took place at hiring fairs held at Bouth, Dalton or Broughton, and might last three or four days and involve the destruction of a score of birds. The passion of the eighteenth century for a wager was in-

---

[1]Quoted John Fell ,*op. cit.*, 382.   [2]Jopling, *Sketch of Furness and Cartmel*, (1843), 14.   [3]*Op. Cit.*, 13.   [4]Barnes, 134.   [5]*Vide* the illuminating account by Francis Nicholson in *V.C.H. Cumberland*, II, 475-9.

dulged to the uttermost, and, since the gentry followed and encouraged the sport vigorously, large sums of money changed hands. But the humbler countrymen put money on their birds, and the husbandmen of Walney celebrated the sport :

" . . . Two dozen lads from Biggar came
         To Tummerel Hill to see the game ;
         They brought along with them that day
         A black to match the bonnie grey.

     . . . Now the black cock he has lost their brass
         And the Biggar lads did swear and curse
         And wish they'd never come that day
         To Tummerel Hill to see the play."

The " play " was carefully regulated, the clergy frequently officiating as high priests at the Shrovetide and other gatherings. Inter-regional mains were arranged, the gentlemen of Ulverston meeting the gentlemen of Chester on an auspicious occasion, and one Furness enthusiast had a cockpit constructed in his drawing-room. Indeed, there are signs that the mains were sometimes kept exclusive ; the admission fee to the cockpit might be deliberately raised " in order that the receipts might realise something towards the expenses and keep out the ' rough ' element ".[1] There was much that was brutal in these fights, and a well-trained cock could strike with savage force—one, at Ulverston, drove its steel spur through a thick plank at the side of the pit. Particularly well-attended meetings were held at Arradfoot near Ulverston, the mains being held here and at Ulverston in conjunction with horse-racing. The organisers of the Arradfoot gathering, presumably local gentry, went further and organised a ' stag main ' for a number of years. Cockfighting, which reached peak popularity about 1820, was evidently not bloody enough for them.

More innocuous was the amateur wrestling which became increasingly popular during the first half of the nineteenth century, and which drew great crowds to the Flan at Ulverston. It does not seem to have been well organised in southern Lakeland until the great Ambleside sports meeting of 1809. The establishment of railway communication rapidly improved its following—until professionalism began to poison the sport—and in the contest between William Jackson and Richard Atkinson for the championship of all England (held at the Flan), fought on October 8th, 1851, great numbers of persons travelled to Ulverston from London, Liverpool and Manchester, while the newly opened Whitehaven and Furness Junction Railway brought others. By the middle of the century,

[1]*Op. cit.*, **477.**

Whitsuntide wrestling meetings were being held at Ulverston, Barrow, Arradfoot and Flookburgh. [1]

Hound trailing, which of all these pursuits is the most popular at the present day, was beginning to feature in local sport programmes before 1850 ; it was in progress in West Cumberland by 1839. [2] It does not belong specifically to the pre-railway age, however, and a generation was soon to settle in the district which knew nothing of the bucolic pastimes of Georgian Furness.

Male writers almost invariably frame their comments on the assumption that a population is composed entirely of males. What of the womenfolk? Such scanty evidence as is available suggests that they lived lives narrow in the extreme. If " Wonderful " Walker slaved for a pittance, then his wife toiled with as little relaxation and less intellectual life. The more comfortably placed yeomanry and professional people might arrange diversions for wives and daughters, and in the late eighteenth century a girl might be provided with a dancing master at 15s. for ten weeks' tuition. The diary of Margaret Ashburner suggests an existence confined largely to meals, kitchen and other domestic labours, with a wonderful diversion in the form of the Dalton assembly, when the Ashburner girls were enabled to spend the night at Dalton, or of occasional balls at the same town, or of tea-drinking expeditions to neighbour Postlethwaite's. But these young women were the daughters of a poor curate ; how fared the Janes, Jennets, Hannahs and Susannahs who made up the womenfolk of the husbandmen and and labourers, one can only guess. They and their children could, and often did, spend lives as hard as anything that can be imagined in the present century ; but it is doubtful whether they were worse off than a Victorian mother with a large family in the kitchen of a terrace house. The transformation from cottage to terrace row was soon to take place.

[1] V.C.H. Cumberland, II, 487-8.   [2] Op. cit., 459.

Sir James Ramsden as King Midas.

Barrow's rulers as part of the title of Richardson's satirical paper, *Barrow Vulcan.*

PART TWO

VICTORIAN YEARS; TRANSPORT, TOWNS AND METAL.

Within an hundred years more has been accomplished in facilitating and expediting intercommunication than was effected from the creation of the world to the middle of the last century.

Dr. Dionysius Lardner,
Railway Economy (1850).

An Opposition Cartoon.

CHAPTER IX

THE GENESIS OF THE FURNESS RAILWAY

THE GENERAL BACKGROUND

When seen against the general background of national and even regional railway history, the Furness Railway, as originally conceived, was a most modest venture, and was little more than a length of mineral track. When its affairs are brought into closer focus, two factors must be borne in mind ; the momentous spread of the rail network towards the Scottish border, and the ultimate local and regional importance of the F.R. as a hitherto tiny company which— after setbacks—flourished steadily and escaped absorption by the giants of the period, becoming at once the virtual creator of a new industrial town and the arterial system of a major ironfield.

A railway line through Furness was already projected in 1836, as an extension of a proposed line along the north-west coast and as a consequence of the promotion of the Maryport and Carlisle Railway. [1] This new line was to be called " The Grand Caledonian Junction Railway ". In the August of the following year, local inhabitants were persuaded of the seriousness of the scheme, for George Stephenson appeared in the district and made an ocular survey of the Morecambe Bay coastline and sands, afterwards making a similar examination of the coastline up to Whitehaven. [2] Among the recommendations in a report given by Stephenson was one advocating the wholesale reclamation of land in Morecambe Bay. As has been seen, this was not a new idea, and John Wilkinson had been moved by a like vision. [3] In the following December (1837), a public meeting of the inhabitants of Ulverston and neighbourhood met at the National Schools in that town and approved the plan for a railway passing through Furness, meetings of townsfolk in Appleby and Penrith being (not surprisingly) in favour of an inland route into Cumbria. [4] A local committee of ore merchants, tradesmen and gentry was formed to support a petition urging the adoption of the coastal route, and to request the Earl of Burlington to present it.

As the nation-wide enthusiasm for railway schemes temporarily waned, the plan for a route along the coast of Furness and Cumberland was abandoned and never revived in its original form. Meanwhile, the " Grand Caledonian Junction Railway " project remained alive for at least another year, and its sponsors, the Whitehaven Provisional Committee, instructed John Hague to prepare a further

---

[1]Simmons, J., *The Maryport and Carlisle Railway* (1947), 1.   [2]Melville, J., and Hobbs, J. L., *Early Railway History in Furness* (1951), C. & W. Tract *Series*, XIII, 2.   [3]See pp. 64-5 above.   [4]Melville & Hobbs, *op. cit.*, 4-5.

plan for constructing a railway line across Morecambe Bay. Hague, an engineer who had reclaimed parts of the Lincolnshire foreshore, succumbed even more completely than Wilkinson or Stephenson to the notion of the recovery of tracts of sandy waste in the Bay. He envisaged a £400,000 embankment which was to be instrumental in reclaiming 46,300 acres of land. The cost of the whole operation was estimated at some £543,000—nearly three times that of the scheme proposed by John Wilkinson.[1] Hague's plan was subjected to careful and justifiable criticism, and even the prospect of over one million pounds' worth of new land (to be sold, at £23 an acre, to defray the cost of the railway) did not bring forth the necessary support. Otherwise the imaginative drive of his project can only command admiration; nearly half a century elapsed before the Midland Railway completed the majestic undertaking of the Settle and Carlisle line, at enormous expense and inconvenience, but even at the present day Morecambe Bay remains a barrier to quick railway and other transport. Its vast acres lie relatively useless.[2]

The net result of the reclamation plans lay, in purely local terms, in stimulus to discussion and other very minor activities, just as, more than a generation earlier, John Wilkinson's project led to considerable discussion and, it would seem, to the Cartmel and Ulverston enclosures.[3] Railway development, meanwhile, was establishing its outposts in the region. By the end of 1840 the Preston and Lancaster Railway, the Preston and Wyre Railway, and the Maryport to Aspatria section of the Maryport and Carlisle line were alike completed. During the planning and laying out of the first-mentioned line there was much examination of further alternative routes through Cumbria towards Scotland, and it was felt at the time that a West Cumberland coastal route passing through Furness was too costly.[4] Thus the path followed by future railway building was marked out; lines along the north-west coast were constructed in piecemeal fashion by purely local enterprises.[5]

During these years, however, the Cumberland and Furness ironfields had not reached their mid-Victorian stature, and there was as yet no obvious guarantee of traffic heavy enough to justify great expenditure on a through coastal line; moreover, there seemed little likelihood that persons who were not local landowners, and who therefore did not stand to gain from land reclamation, would be induced to invest in such an enterprise. Secondly, proposals to accommodate passenger traffic between the mainland of Lancashire

---

[1]Cf. *Civil Engineer and Architect's Journal*, I, 1837-8, 409-17, and *op. cit.*, 6-10. [2]The reclamation and route-shortening schemes have been discussed on numerous occasions during the past century, and were revived by a committee during the recent war. [3]See p. 65 above. [4]*Brit. Parl. Papers*, XLV, 1840; Melville & Hobbs, *op. cit.*, 8-11. [5]Pollard, S., *C. & W.*, LII, (1953), 160-1 and *passim*.

and the Furness peninsula were already being made. In 1838 the Preston and Wyre Railway Company, which had been engaged in the development of the port of Fleetwood,[1] proposed to run a steamer service from that new port to Rampside, near Piel, and thereby to link up with Stephenson's projected line by means of an economical railway to Ireleth on the west coast of Furness. A service between Liverpool, Blackpool and Ulverston Canal Foot already existed.[2] Probably because similar traffic appeared likely to expand in the near future, the banker John Abel Smith, of the firm of Smith, Payne and Smith,[3] took it upon himself to purchase Roa Island, near Piel; and in the parliamentary session 1840-1 he " promoted a Bill to form a Harbour Company with wide powers, amounting almost to ownership of the navigable waters for miles around ".[4] During the early months of 1842, when the Bill was still under examination, the Ulverston Canal Company reacted vigorously and demanded the insertion of a clause protecting their own harbour ;[5] but since the Bill interfered with the ancient rights of Piel Harbour to be regarded as a Harbour of Refuge, it was withdrawn in any case. Smith, however, did not abandon his speculative interest in the neighbourhood, and by coincidence he too succeeded in stimulating a certain interest on the part of local men of influence.

By 1840 iron-mining in Plain Furness had made advances both in output and technique.[6] In 1839 H. W. Schneider had entered the district as a young though apparently experienced speculator and dealer in metalliferous ores, and according to his own accounts he was unimpressed by the methods of haematite-raising which then prevailed.[7] He commenced a series of costly searches, joined with other merchants in causing new jetties to be erected at Barrow, and, in his own words, " in the years 1840 and 1841 an effort was made to get a tramway from the mines to the port of Barrow ".[8] As has been indicated, the idea of a local railway or tramway had been scouted previously,[9] and this second attempt met with little initial success. Lacking capital or determination or both, the iron ore masters deputed Schneider to request the assistance of the Duke of Buccleuch, who was asked to make a loan of £40,000.

[1]Lancs. & Yorks Rly. Co., *An Historical Account of the Port of Fleetwood* (1877). [2]See p. 96 above. [3]For a few biog. details, Easton, H. T., *The History of a Banking House* (1903), 26-8. By 1845, John Abel Smith's subscription to the Preston & Wyre Rly. Co. was 27% of the total subscribed ; *Ec. H. R.*, Dec. 1955, 204, n.2. [4]Melville & Hobbs, 14. [5]*Mins. Ulv. Canal Co.*, 4.1.1842, 10.1, 14.1, 20.1, 26.1, 3.2, 10.2, 4.3.1842. [6]See p. 93, Table 11, above ; also refs. in *Mining Journal*, X, 163. [7]In 1839 horse-gins were in use, and there were " no pumps in the whole district, and, in fact, water, being reached, put a stop to further operations " ; Schneider in *Trans. C. & W. Assn. for the Advancement of Lit. and Science*, X, 1884-5, 105 ; cf. Leach, *Barrow, Its Rise and Progress* (1872), Appx. 26. [8]Schneider, *Trans. cit.* [9]See p. 94 above.

It appears that the latter asked for a guarantee of interest on this sum, and " so little was the spirit of the times " that the guarantee was not made and the Duke accordingly refused his assistance. [1] Action, however, did not cease at this point, although the next stage in the birth of the Furness Railway is somewhat obscure. The main sources of information are, first, Schneider's own versions of the story, made after a considerable interval of time, and, secondly, such scattered items of information as may be obtained from an important primary source like the private diary of the Earl of Burlington, and from manuscripts left by the late W. B. Kendall. [2]

Schneider, then, stated that " the origin of the Furness Railway Company was due to pure chance ". [3] Both the Duke of Buccleuch and the Earl of Burlington had taken some interest in the earlier scheme for a north-west coastal railway, and were of course acquainted with the nature of the respective schemes for local land reclamation. It so happened that Buccleuch had employed the distinguished engineer James Walker [4] to draft plans for an expensive harbour at Granton on the Firth of Forth, [5] and in 1841 Burlington requested Walker to examine the Duddon Estuary " and various railway plans ". [6] Burlington's interest in the Duddon Estuary sprang from his ownership of the slate quarries at Kirkby-in-Furness, and from the possibility of improving or reclaiming land in that neighbourhood ; it may also be noted that the shipping trade of " Ireleth and Angerton ", the slate-loading points near the quarries, had slumped badly as between 1834 and 1838-9, [7] and the progress of the quarries, as shown in Burlington's diary, was a matter of great concern to him. [8] If Schneider's account can be believed, coincidence then followed coincidence ; the former was " a personal friend of Mr. James Walker . . . and especially drew his attention to the advisability of the formation of a railway from the mines to Barrow ". [9] What appears to the general historian as the inexorable logic of the railway age could, of course, appear to the promoters of the time as a series of more or less happy accidents.

After submitting an initial report, in which he suggested that the Earl of Lonsdale, the Earl of Burlington and the Duke of Buccleuch might alike be affected by possible roads, railways or

[1] Account by Schneider reptd. in *Ulverston Advertiser*, 27.8.1857, and the foregoing reference, *cit.*
[2] Ably used and summarised by Messrs. Melville & Hobbs, *passim.*
[3] *Transactions, cit.*   [4] For a brief biog. of Walker, *vide Proc. Inst. C. E.*, Vol. 22, 630. He was President of the Institute of Civil Engineers from 1834 to 1845 continuously, and was a worthy peer of Stephenson and Telford. [5] Memoir *cit.* ; also *D.N.B.*, *sub nomine Montagu-Douglas-Scott* (5th Duke of Buccleuch, etc.).   [6] Melville & Hobbs, 14 ; at least one of the plans was drawn up on behalf of the ore merchants by the engineer Job Bintley of Kendal. [7] See Table 10, p. 93.   [8] *MS. Diary* of Burlington, 10.2, 15.2, (" I am almost in despair about the quarries . . ."), 2.3, 6.4, 22.7, 9.9, 12.9, 26.10.1842. [9] *Trans. cit.*

land reclamation, Walker went over the district again in July, 1842, and submitted a detailed report in the September,[1] this time to the three interested parties.[2] He suggested that the east side of the Duddon Estuary might be provided with an embankment, and that 4000 acres of land could be reclaimed at an estimated cost of £50,000. With some alteration in the initial plan a railway from the slate quarries might be laid along the embankment, and for £1000 a mile a good tramway could be laid along the latter.[3] This rail or tram track was to run to Barrow. Further enclosure of coastal waste and sands in the Barrow district was suggested. Burlington, whose private observations on business affairs are revealing from this year onwards, remarked concerning the report that " it appears sensible and recommends less than had been expected ".[4] It is significant that Walker considered Barrow to be the most suitable shipping place for slates and ore (as opposed to Kirkby Pool Foot or Ulverston Canal Foot), and " while the time might come when Roa Island and Piel Harbour would offer inducements to go there, that was not so at present ".[5]

Meanwhile, the lessees of the local ore mines had not been inactive ; prompted, perhaps, by H. W. Schneider, they had engaged the Kendal engineer Job Bintley to survey alternative routes for a tramway from the Dalton iron mines to Barrow. Horse traction was to be employed—there is no mention of the use of steam power at this stage—and it is also noteworthy that Walker commented favourably on the prospect of such an ore tramway. " . . . It is to be wondered at," he remarked in his report, " that one should not have been made ere this. It would carry down the other produce of the district and bring up coals and other supplies of consumption ; so like a good turnpike road, it would benefit all who have property within its influence, and therefore especially the Duke of Buccleuch and Lord Burlington and their tenants."[6] Such commonsense conclusions appear almost painfully obvious to the historian, and so they must have seemed to Walker when he was making his recommendations. The latter did however succeed in " selling " the ore merchants' project to Burlington and Buccleuch, although not in the form suggested by Bintley. Walker and his partner Alfred Burges drew up a further report[7] which was supplied to the two lords on June 1st, 1843, and which detailed a plan for a railway connecting Rampside (near Barrow) with Kirkby-in-Furness, with a branch to Barrow, and for an iron-ore track to

[1]*MS.* summarised by Melville & Hobbs, *op. cit.*, 14-16.   [2]The Earl of Burlington's land adjoined that of Lord Lonsdale in the Duddon Estuary. [3]*Loc. cit.*   [4]*MS. Diary*, 20.8.1842.   It appears that Burlington saw the report in the August.   [5]Melville & Hobbs, *loc. cit.*   [6]*Loc. cit.* [7]*Report on the Furness Railway to the Solicitors of the Duke of Buccleuch and the Earl of Burlington, by Walker and Burges*, 1st June, 1843, quoted Melville & Hobbs, 17-18.

the Dalton mines. The total length of track envisaged was eighteen and three-quarter miles, and the estimated cost, £100,000. It has been stated that Bintley's plan for an ore line from Millwood, near Furness Abbey, to the iron mines, was the subject of " considerable local opposition ".[1] Yet, as is shown below, the final scheme of Walker and Burges also met with much opposition,[2] and later developments indicate that the ore merchants were now either hostile or neutral in their attitude to a new railway, primarily, perhaps, because they feared that those to whom they paid rents, wayleaves and royalties[3] might exact unreasonable tolls for the transport of haematite to Barrow. This port, too, had been developed by the merchants in the first place.[4]

Thus, in a fashion slow and halting, the ground was prepared. Little remained of the grandiose schemes which had originated in the visions of John Wilkinson and which had been elaborated, in terms of railway transport, by George Stephenson and John Hague. The idea of land reclamation faded into the background once more ; and the possibility that Furness might become an important link in a through north-western railway route was still vigorously but unavailingly acted upon by John Abel Smith, whose nuisance value was shown to be considerable. The anti-climax was complete. Out of a mountain of imaginative labour emerged a very small mouse.

THE CONSTRUCTION OF THE RAILWAY

The prospectus of the Furness Railway[5] was published soon after Walker and Burges had outlined their plans. It estimated the future income of the new line to be divided as follows : £7,500 *per annum* from the carriage of iron ore to the quantity of 100,000 tons (both estimates turned out to be entirely reasonable), the toll charged to be 1s. 6d. a ton ; £1,125 from the transport of 15,000 tons of slate, at the same rate of toll ; £1,875 from 25,000 tons of coals and general traffic ; and £2000 from the carriage of 20,000 passengers. The total gross revenue was to amount to £12,500 *per annum*. This statement added nothing new to the obvious economic arguments in favour of a railway, and it made reference to the possibility that the new line might become " part of any main line of Railway which might hereafter be continued to the North from Fleetwood . . and at once place this District . . upon

---

[1]Melville & Hobbs, 17. [2]See p. 177 below. [3]Buccleuch, as Lord of the Manor of Plain Furness, received most of the iron ore royalties, amounting customarily to 1s. 6d. a ton ; for charges, *Backbarrow MSS.* and Fell, *E.I.I.F.*, 34-6, 37, 48-9, 62. Lord Muncaster and Lord Burlington likewise received royalties ; e.g. *Mills v. Muncaster* papers, Barrow P.L. [4]See p. 94 above. [5]Copies in *MSS.* of W. B. Kendall and at Barrow Library ; the prospectus is quoted in full in Melville & Hobbs, *op. cit.*, 18-21.

the highway to all parts of England ". It also envisaged an extension of the railway to Ulverston, and took into account the possible use of steam traction.

In making the observation quoted in the foregoing paragraph, the projectors were probably casting a wary eye upon John Abel Smith, who had obtained an Act, on June 27th, 1843,[1] to build a pier on Piel Island and to construct a railway embankment between Piel and Rampside. This work was not completed for several years. There is no evidence, however, that the promoters of the railway to Barrow were greatly concerned by the activities of Smith at this stage, for while the harbour at Piel offered few of the physical difficulties to shipping that were encountered in the Barrow Channel, the embankment planned by Smith was needed to bring the rail wagons to a deep-water quay. Barrow foreshore, already surveyed by Walker, was more conveniently situated for the Kirkby slate traffic and was provided with ore jetties, and Burlington's diary— he examined the envisaged wharfage space at Barrow in the autumn of 1842[2]—suggests that the siting of the railway terminus there was conditionally agreed upon from the first.

No explicit reference has been made to the F.R. promoters themselves, beyond showing the obvious connection of Burlington with the proposed line. The evidence of his diary, again, suggests that he may have had very little real interest in the project, making two references to it in 1842 as against nine to his slate quarries ;[3] that is to say, he was interested in it only to the extent that he wanted the latter to prosper. It is clear that a driving influence was now the enthusiasm of Benjamin Currey, who was the probable author of the railway's prospectus, a legal adviser to the Cavendish family, and Clerk of the House of Lords. Currey already saw very clearly the possible advantages to the Cavendish estates that might arise from the construction of a line. After the projectors had applied to Parliament for powers and deposited plans for the railway, both actions taking place in November, 1843,[4] a revealing entry appears in Burlington's diary. Edward Coward, the manager of his Kirkby slate quarries, was " very much against the railway, and indeed so is everyone in this neighbourhood, but Currey is confident they are mistaken ".[5] The latter, indeed, was so enthusiastic that when the subscription contract,[6] was signed on January 25th, 1844, he let his name go forward with a subscription of £15,000, equivalent amounts being entered only against the names of the Earl of Burlington and the Duke of Buccleuch. The other subscriptions are no less revealing; one iron ore firm was represented, the former Newland Company (through the sub-

---

[1]6 & 7 *Vict.*, c.42; copy at Ulverston U.D.C. offices. [2]*MS. Diary*, 10.9.1842. [3]See p. 174 above, n.8 [4]More precisely, notices of application were posted in the November; Melville & Hobbs, 21. [5]Entry of 19.12.1843. [6]An initial and a supplementary list are given in *op. cit.*, 21-3.

scribers Benson Harrison, Montagu Ainslie and Richard Roper, with £1000 between them), and nearly all the other personalities listed were legal or business connections of the two noblemen. Of the ten names on the earliest contract list, those of Burlington, Currey, J. I. Nicholl (a connection of the Duke of Buccleuch), H. H. Oddie, R. W. Lumley and F. J. Howard are most frequently met with on the board of directors for a number of years. These, it may be said, were the original promoters of the Furness Railway, together with the Duke of Buccleuch—who did not become a director for over twenty years, and who rarely attended meetings even when a member of the board—C. R. Freeling and William Pott.

The list shows that of the £56,500 originally entered as subscribed, £55,500 came from London addresses, with those of Burlington and Buccleuch included. It may reasonably be supposed—and supposition, unfortunately, is all that is possible —that Benjamin Currey had rounded up most of the support, for Burlington had certainly not let any solicitations worry his mind,[1] and Buccleuch was a passive party throughout. A further campaign gained a little more aristocratic support in the persons of Lord Brooke (£1100) and the Marchioness of Ailesbury (£3500). More significant, in the light of future history, was the adherence of one Joseph Paxton of Chatsworth, who subscribed £1000 ; while John Robinson McClean, who became the chief engineer to the railway and a distinguished figure in the world of civil engineering generally, was prevailed upon to enter a similar amount. Harrison, Ainslie and Co., the former Newland partnership, were represented on the second list and not the first, on which local capital and industry had no place at all ; and James Walker had faith in his railway plan to the extent of £5000.

The Furness Railway Bill received the Royal Assent on May 23rd, 1844,[2] the authorised capital being £100,000, of which £75,000 was to be raised in shares and the remainder obtained by loan. The shares were then already taken. No obstacle was encountered during the parliamentary examination of the Bill, and the line appeared in every way a sound and reasonable proposition. Alfred Burges, acting for the projectors, had no difficulty in making a case.

On July 17th, 1844,[3] the directors held their first meeting under the chairmanship of Benjamin Currey. This and subsequent

[1]No such references appear in his diary at this stage.   [2]7 *Vict. c.22* ; the terms of reference for this and later enactments are in the useful handlist of Melville & Hobbs, Appx., p. 66 sqq.   [3]*MS. Minutes of the Furness Railway Directors (Dir. Mins. (F.R.))*, for date.

meetings during the autumn dealt mainly with the normal business necessitated in the preparation of ground and tracks ; valuing of land, further surveying, specifications of tenders for the construction of the line, and arrangements for the purchase of rails and chairs.[1] Three directors only conducted this business ; Currey, Lumley and Nicholl. It was known, meanwhile, that a railway from Whitehaven to Furness was projected,[2] and the Furness Railway engineers McClean and Wright expected that this northerly line might link with the still unbuilt F.R. near Dalton-in-Furness.[3] The coastal route concept came once more into the foreground.

The items so far set out may serve to indicate who the promoters or instigators of the line really were. The *minutiae* of its affairs, while doubtless of some interest to the specialist student of railway history, are of limited value in this context except in so far as they relate to the main stages of economic history in the area, and to the history of Barrow itself. A reference in the directors' minutes of November 13th, 1844, mentioned that that port was to be equipped with a landing stage with lines of rails running on to it, in order to make Barrow a suitable place for the accommodation of the ore merchants who would use the railway ; and a " cut " was to be made to " improve the navigation of the (Barrow) channel ". At the other end of the proposed track to the mines, the line was to stop short one mile from Lindal, at or near Crooklands limekiln, and from that point cheap tramlines were to be made to the mines.

On February 12th, the firm of John and William Tredwell was successful in tendering for the construction of the track at a cost of £47,789, the latter to be completed by September 30th, 1845. The work of building it was commenced when the great " railway mania " was already in progress, prices were rising, and a considerable proportion of the labour required had to be brought or attracted from outside. The pay schedules[5] show that relatively high wages had to be paid by the contractors. Masons were offered 5s. a day, and carpenters, bricklayers and smiths 4s. 6d. By the early March of 1845 the Earl of Burlington was obliged to give his quarrymen large increases in wages " no doubt . . . mainly owing to the Furness Railway which is in progress, and at which high wages can be earned ".[6] The figures of expenditure in the Ulverston Union[7] suggest that this work may have led to a slight decrease in pauperism in the district, which however suffered from a chronic

<hr>

[1]*MS. Minutes*, 17.7, 24.7, 7.8, 7.9, 13.11, 16.11, 27.11.1844. The rails and chairs were obtained from Staffordshire and Midland firms, including Bagnall & Sons of West Bromwich. [2]Melville & Hobbs, 38. George Stephenson had surveyed a possible line for the Earl of Lonsdale in 1844. [3]*Dir. Mins. (F.R.)*, 7.8.1844. [4]*Minutes* for date. [5]Given in Melville & Hobbs, 24, from *Kendall MSS*. [6]Quoted from Burlington's *MS. Diary*, 6.3.45. [7]See p. 141-2 above.

shortage of labourers before and after the railway period.[1]
Labourers received 3s. a day of ten hours, a noticeably higher
payment than that made to farm workers in the immediate vicinity.
At the same period, day labourers at Whinfield Farm near Dalton
were receiving 1s. 1d. to 1s. 2d. a day, after staying at 1s. in 1841-4
inclusive ; but their wage had risen to the dizzy height of 1s. 6d.
by the spring of 1846.[2]   By November 1st, 1845, a special meeting
of the directors became necessary, the increased costs of labour and
iron for rails making it necessary to raise additional capital.[3]

Otherwise there were few serious obstacles in the way of the
builders ; and an examination of the present line of railway—the
original F.R. route—between Salthouse, Roose, Furness Abbey and
Dalton, as shown in the ordnance survey maps for the district,
makes clear that at no point did it have to climb more than 100 feet
above sea level, and that the local topography distinctly favoured
a gentle approach to the iron mines.   There were no deep cuttings,
few bridges and no viaducts, and it is evident that James Walker
had planned well and used the lie of the land with skill.   The
directors' minutes refer to no serious trouble with landowners.
The stretch of line from Kirkby slate quarries, running as it did along
the level Duddon shores, was to prove little more difficult of realisation.

By the June of 1845, however, the railway promoters met with
opposition of a somewhat different kind.   The ore line had then
reached the grounds of Furness Abbey, which belonged to the
Earl of Burlington, and on the 21st the Tredwells' labourers were
observed spending their dinner break amid the ruins of the Abbey.
The observer in this instance was Wordsworth, who thundered into
a sonnet at seeing one of his favourite scenes desecrated not by the
workmen but by the proprietors' action in driving a railway track
within a few yards of the Abbey buildings.   Wrote the poet :

> " Well have yon Railway Labourers to THIS ground
> Withdrawn for noontide rest.   They sit, they walk
> Among the Ruins, but no idle talk
> Is heard. . . .
> Profane Despoilers, stand ye not reproved
> While thus these simple-hearted men are moved ? "

Posterity may be grateful that Walker's eye for a good level,
and the determination of a noble lord to do what he liked with his
own, did not result in something even more serious.

By the August, **Burlington** was able to comment that " the line

---

[1]See pp. 78-80, 142 above.   [2]*Whinfield Farm Accounts* (*MS.*).   [3]Melville
& Hobbs, 25, and also *Dir. Mins.* (*F.R.*), 16.7, and 23.7.45, when the raising
of additional loan capital was discussed.

has made much progress, and in some parts is nearly finished ". [1]
Meanwhile, the mania for railway investment had taken a firm hold
upon his confederates, and the atmosphere was full of new schemes.
The prospectus of the Whitehaven and Furness Junction Railway
had already been issued, and even before acts for that line were
obtained (on July 21st, and August 3rd, 1846), [2] its promoters
suggested an extension southwards from the expected Furness
Railway terminus at Ulverston, to meet another proposed line from
Leeds and Skipton ; while the Lancaster and Carlisle Railway
Company was envisaging a line to Ulverston *via* Greenodd. [3] It is
hardly surprising that Burlington found occasion to observe, on
May 21st, that " I went . . . to Currey's this morning, where I
met many railway people. There are schemes without end for
lines in the neighbourhood of Holker and all anxious to gain my
support, but at present I have kept clear of all ". [4] In the September, when looking at the railway, he found " Currey and his
sons and Paxton also looking at the line ". [5] The latter, too, was
developing into a railway enthusiast. Whatever lobbying and
discussion may have taken place resulted in a final decision to
extend the Furness Railway to Broughton-in-Furness and to
Ulverston. A subscription contract was signed on December 23rd,
1845, with the inclusion of two notable names on the list of supporters ; John Brogden, whose Furness origins and status as a
railway builder have already received mention, [6] and John Barraclough Fell of Spark Bridge, who later became a well-known railway
speculator. [7] A Furness Railway Extension Act was obtained on
July 27th, 1846, [8] with a view to making links to the two towns
mentioned ; and it is clear that the F.R. directors welcomed the
prospect of a through route from Yorkshire into Cumberland. [9]
This concept, however, was still well in advance of realisation.
The Furness line was not even opened until the June, and the
links with Lancaster and Cumberland were still at the paper stage.

A further preoccupation of the F.R. promoters is worthy of
brief mention. They did not ignore the possibility of attracting
tourist traffic into Furness and thence into the Lake District,

[1]*MS. Diary*, 12.8.1845.   [2]Cf. Handlist of Messrs. Melville & Hobbs, *cit.*
[3]*Dir. Mins.* (*F.R.*), 21.5.1845.   [4]*MS. Diary* for the same date.   [5]*MS.
Diary*, 3.9.1845.   [6]See p. 153 above.
    [7]J. B. Fell later became an associate of Thomas Brassey and was a member
of the partnership of Fell and Jopling which associated with the great railway
builder in the work on the Central Italian Railway in 1854 ; *vide* the reference
in handlist of contracts, Helps, Sir A., *Life and Labours of Mr. Brassey*, 161 sqq.
He was interested in local tourist transport, and afterwards specialised in the
construction of alpine and military railways. For refs. to him, *vide* White,
Furness Folk and Facts, 18, 41, 42, 103-4.   [8]Melville & Hobbs, handlist *cit.*
[9]*Dir. Mins.* (*F.R.*), 21.5.45 ; " Resolved that this Company will give every
support to the Scheme proposed by the Whitehaven and Furness Junction
Railway Co. . . . and our best allies being those who will carry our produce to
the East, and not the Lancaster and Carlisle . . . "

although there is no explicit reference to tourists in their original prospectus. In 1845 there was as yet no direct approach by rail into the Lakes, but it was then well understood that steamer services could be run between Fleetwood and Piel, and this, of course, was John Abel Smith's presumption. As early as May, 1845, the erection or purchase of inns at Kirkby and Furness Abbey was considered by the F.R. directors, [1] and in February, 1846, a definite agreement was made (by them) with John Abel Smith and Mr. Laidlay of Fleetwood to co-ordinate train and steamboat services, the latter to be run by Smith himself. [2] It is evident, however, that the F.R. directors had little hope of gaining much income from purely local passenger traffic, and their first order for rolling stock, made in December, 1845, contains these suggestive items : four railway carriages with first and second class compartments, but no third class. [3]

In the same month the highly important question of iron ore carriage tolls came before the F.R. board. In anticipation of the completion of the Barrow-Dalton section by the following March, the latter fixed the toll over that line at 1s. 6d. an imperial ton of ore carried in the company's wagons. [4] The ore merchants, still lukewarm in their attitude to the railway, objected. [5] But on March 25th, when it was known that the opening of the line would be delayed, the tolls were nevertheless fixed. Secondly, the company was faced with a difficult problem in the accommodation of its employees and labourers, [6] and on January 16th, 1846, its directors decided upon the erection of a small colony of cottages at Salthouse, near Barrow village. Ten small cottages were to be built " as cheaply as could be ", the price was not to exceed £100 each, and a further four were to be built at £210 each. Other dwellings were to be erected at Salthouse Junction and Little Mill, and, more important, an engine shed and smith's shop were to be constructed at Barrow for £1000. [7] In other words that village had been chosen not only as an ore port but as the railway headquarters. There is little that is extraordinary in the decision, for the Newland Company had understood the uses of this unprepossessing little waterside settlement more than half a century previously, [8] and there was no other obvious choice.

At the end of the same month of January, one James Ramsden

---

[1] *Dir. Mins.*, *ibid.*, and 16.7.45.　[2] *Mins.* 27.2.46.　[3] *Mins.* 1.12.45. [4] *Dir. Mins.* (*F.R.*), 30.12.45.　[5] *Dir. Mins.* (*F.R.*), 16.1.46.　[6] Fisher, J., *Popular History of Barrow* (1891, an early and now scarce study), 83-4, gives a grim if entertaining picture of the overcrowding in Barrow village at this time ; even the F.R. engineer F. C. Stileman was living in what was little more than a converted henroost.　[7] *Dir. Mins.* for date. The building proposals seem to have originated from one of the Curreys.　[8] See p. 88.

was appointed Locomotive Superintendent.[1] This new official, twenty-three years of age, was the son of a civil engineer, Mr. W. Ramsden of Liverpool. He had been apprenticed to the famous locomotive engineer, Edward Bury, of the firm of Bury, Curtis and Kennedy. Bury had been chief of the engineering department of the London and Birmingham Railway, and the young Ramsden had acquired experience of the latter's Wolverton works (later absorbed into the London and North Western). Bury was a pioneer of the four-wheeled bar-framed locomotive type which bears his name, the standard engine of the London and Birmingham and the Midland Counties railways in the early 'forties; [2] and the F.R. board, now entirely converted to the idea of steam traction, ordered two of these locomotives from the Bury works in the July of 1845, and Ramsden is said to have accompanied these engines on their sea trip to Barrow, entering the district in March, 1846. As yet no General Superintendent of the line had been appointed, but the duties of the post fell upon him from the start, and at least one amusing anecdote illustrates his position as maid of all work to the company. It is doubtful whether Ramsden then realised that he was to become a General Manager. Thus began a career which, had it reached fruition somewhat earlier, would certainly have engrossed the attention of a Samuel Smiles.[3]

Wagons as well as locomotives had to be brought by sea from Fleetwood, the latter being of the standard 0—4—0 " Bury " type with haycock firebox. When looking at the sole remaining specimen (the famous *Coppernob*), until 1941 preserved in a case at Barrow station and now at the Horwich railway works, it is not difficult to see that only a few years of engineering practice separated these engines from the " Rocket " and " Locomotion ". The Buries were efficient, however, and were to see many years of service on the Furness line; and engines of their type were exported to the United States " with the result that the bar frames became a standard American feature ".[4] The rolling stock ordered by the directors consisted of sixty ore wagons and ten slate trucks, and with this equipment, four locomotives and the railway carriages described, the Dalton-Barrow section of the line was opened on June 3rd, 1846, an official opening of the Furness Railway following on August 12th.[5]

[1] *Dir. Mins.* (*F.R.*), 29.1.46.   [2] For background refs., *vide* Ellis, C. Hamilton, *British Railway History* (1954), 60, 134.

[3] For general memoir, *Proc. Inst. Civ. Eng.*, CXXIX (1896-7), 385 sqq. An anecdote (p. 385) ,would have appealed to Smiles: " Mr. Ramsden observed one Sunday that the engine was running fast, and making signals for the train to stop he found that the driver was intoxicated . . . (as a result) he worked the traffic himself ".   [4] Ellis, *op. cit.*, 135; for tech. descripn. of the locomotives, Gradon, W. McG., *Hist. Furness Railway* (1946), 46-8.   [5] *Dir. Mins.* (*F.R.*), 1.12.45, 25.2.46; *Kendal Mercury*, 6.6.46, 22.8.46; *MS. Diary*, 20.10.46; Melville & Hobbs, 26. There was no special ceremony other than a dinner.

A major impediment to the development of Furness iron mining was thus removed, and the physical problem of the transport of thousands of tons of haematite was at last overcome.

THE EARL OF BURLINGTON—A BIOGRAPHICAL NOTE

The frequent references to Burlington in the foregoing text will show that he was closely associated with the Furness Railway's origins.   Still more was his life interwoven into the ensuing history of the Furness district, if only because he was in some wise connected with every major decision affecting its course between 1842 and 1887. Nevertheless this statement must be carefully qualified, for if the Furness Railway was one of the very minor results of the great railway mania, and the later rise of the local ironfield a result of the boom in Bessemer steelmaking, so it was a coincidence that the business interests of the Cavendish family (and of this member of it in particular) became increasingly involved in local industrial development.

The Cavendish family's ownership of slate quarries[1] and agricultural estates[2] in Furness and Cartmel was primarily responsible for whatever interest they showed in the district before the promotion of the railway.   As is well known, they owned vast estates in England and Ireland, and the Dukes of Devonshire and their close relatives disposed of six country seats or other main residences— Chatsworth, Hardwick, Holker Hall, Compton Place at Eastbourne, Lismore Castle and Chiswick.   William Cavendish (1808-91), the Earl of Burlington here noticed, was a grandson of Lord George Augustus Cavendish, and a son of the fourth Duke of Devonshire. Born in London, he attained distinction at Trinity College, Cambridge, in 1829, becoming a Senior Wrangler and obtaining a first class in the classical tripos.   In 1834 he acceded to the revived Earldom of Burlington when already a Member of Parliament for his university, and in the same year, when still only twenty-six years of age, he became Chancellor of the University of London.   It was then more easily remembered that he was a descendant, on his mother's side, of the great scientist Robert Boyle, and, perhaps somewhat less relevantly, that his great-grandfather was first cousin to Henry Cavendish.[3] Burlington's keen intelligence was reflected in comparatively advanced liberal opinions, and his championship of Reform—unpopular enough at Cambridge—lost

---

[1]See pp. 43-6 above.   [2]See p. 73 above.   [3]For biog. material, *D.N.B.*, XXII, Suppt., s.v. *Cavendish* ; *Proc. Royal Soc.*, 1892, LI, xxxviii-xli ; *Proc. Inst. C.E.*, CVII, 393-8 ; Gibbs, Vicary, *Complete Peerage*, 350. He was styled Lord Cavendish until 1834.   Much is added to these biographies in following pages, but no attempt is here made to write his life.   Such a task, although a major one, has (quite unaccountably) never been attempted.

him his seat there, but he was returned to Parliament at Malton, Yorkshire, in 1831.

Next in the line of succession to the Dukedom of Devonshire (he became the seventh Duke in 1858), Burlington was, then, already playing an active part in ruling-class politics, albeit of an advanced kind. Later he was to show an equally keen interest in industry and agriculture. By 1836 he was in fairly regular residence at Holker Hall, the former seat of his grandfather, Lord G. A. Cavendish, and his political utilitarianism may have led him to accept the office of chairman of the Ulverston Board of Guardians in that year.[1] His attendances at the meetings of this body were not at first frequent.[2] Happily married to the former Lady Blanche Howard, and with a family of three sons and one daughter,[3] he spent much of the years 1838 and 1839 touring in Italy and Germany.[4] In 1840, however, he experienced a tragic turn in his fortunes ; on April 27th his wife died (possibly from the effects of a series of closely-spaced confinements), and as is only too evident from his intimate diary entries for many years following, it was long before he recovered from the shock.

H. W. Schneider afterwards commented, as we have seen, that the origins of the Furness Railway were due to " pure chance ".[5] This remark carries more significance than it may appear to contain. Burlington, morose and in a state of deep religious introspection, retired to Holker Hall, obtaining some solace now in the pursuit of estate management, the development of his slate quarries, and the administration of the Poor Law. He was immersed in these local activities by 1842.[6] The Duke of Buccleuch,[7] the only other aristocrat with important Furness interests, had, like the Cavendishes, great estates elsewhere and regarded the locality distantly through the reports of bailiffs and stewards. It is possible that Burlington's new interest in the area was decisive in winning the support of Buccleuch for a railway, although it should be emphasised that the former was no railway enthusiast at this time ; his own assent to the idea of slate and ore lines, however, caused his astute and able family solicitors, the Curreys, to bring their energies to bear on the project. They were naturally mindful of any advantages to the Cavendish estates and fortunes which would be reaped thereby, and were, perhaps, not unmindful of advantages to themselves.

---

[1]See p. 141 above.   [2]MS. Minutes (Ulv. Gdns. Mins.), of the Ulverston Guardians, passim.   [3]His eldest son was of course the Marquess of Hartington of the Gladstonian era, and the later 8th Duke.   [4]MS. Diary of Burlington, Book I, 1838-9, which begins the almost unbroken series of volumes in the Chatsworth House archives.   [5]See p. 174 above.   [6]MS. Diary, passim.
[7]The 5th Duke of Buccleuch & Queensberry (1806-1884) ; D.N.B.

Here speculation must end, with the reflection that sooner or later experienced men of business like H. W. Schneider, the Harrisons and Ainslies or John Abel Smith would in any case have caused some type of railway to be opened in the neighbourhood. Burlington's own connections and standing made possible the mustering of financial support for this rather puny railway scheme of 1842-6, and opened the way for investment by a group of lesser but influential men. The favourable economic circumstances of the time called forth and reacted upon personalities, whose careers, unbeknown to themselves, were already being shaped. The persistence and astuteness of men like Schneider and James Ramsden, strongly tinctured with ambition and self-interest, were soon to show much prescience, and to that extent the individual also played his part in the shaping of regional history ; but it is very doubtful how far Burlington's considerable intelligence, but sober and literal imagination, penetrated into the future.

CHAPTER X

RAILWAY AND IRONFIELD, 1846-61 (1)

EFFECTS AND FORTUNES OF THE F.R., 1846-50

The effect of the new railway system on the iron ore and other trades of the district was both marked and immediate. In February, 1850, James Ramsden stated that 470,000 tons of minerals had been carried over the F.R. since the line opened, together with 78,000 passengers.[1] Well over 100,000 tons of haematite and slate passed over the railway in the years 1847 and 1849, and in 1848, a year of trade recession, the latter cannot have carried much less than this tonnage. Statistically, the trade of Barrow harbour in 1848-9 is shown as follows :[2]

Year	Vessels entering	Ballast discharged	Total cargo	of which iron ore—
1848	1413	10,180 t.	120,000 t.	100,000 t.
1849	1911	23,280 t.	160,000 t.	150,000 t.*

*Includes supplies (coal, timber &c.) for the mines.

The total number of vessels with cargoes using " Barrow and Walney " in 1839 had been 289 inwards (with merchandise, coals &c.) and 223 outwards.[3] By 1849 the total iron ore output of the Plain Furness mines was at least treble the 1840-3 average of 75,000 tons. Ulverston was still sending away quantities of the local ores, but its exportation and shipping were decreasing, and Barrow had already outstripped it by 1850. The effect of the railway upon the older port is reflected in the following figures.

Table 18

Ulverston Canal Traffic, 1839-49[4]

Year	No. of vessels	Tonnage	Year	No. of vessels	Tonnage
1839	640	41,600	1845	912	59,280
1840	560	36,400	1846	944	61,360
1841	656	42,640	1847	688	44,720
1842	528	34,320	1848	368	23,928
1843	544	35,360	1849	388 (to	25,220
1844	688	47,720		June)	

Such a quantitative summary can tell little of the underlying

---

[1] *Ulverston Advertiser*, 7.2.1850. [2] Half-yearly F.R. report in *Ulv. Adv.*, 28.2.1850. [3] *Port Inspections, cited.* [4] From a longer series (1828-49) given by White, *Furness Folk*, etc., 25-6. In several instances the numbers of vessels have been checked against those given in *Port Inspections*, and the figures tally only in 1846. It is clear that White's list is from some local return, and its accuracy cannot be vouched for. It reflects quite credible tendencies.

story. It would, for instance, be hard to believe that the Furness Railway directors had experienced several months of acute concern and even panic during 1848, when it appeared that their line was in a sorry state of unprofitableness and mismanagement ; but this was nevertheless so. Only grudgingly did Ulverston observers concede that " Barrow is becoming an important seaport ",[1] but proprietors in that town were understandably jealous, and were soon to become thoroughly aware that the owners of the railway had little interest in their fortunes.

The F.R. began its working career in promising enough fashion. In February, 1847, at the end of the first half-year's progress, it was able to declare a dividend of four per cent.,[2] the income from the carriage of minerals and merchandise ($£4,639$) falling near the figure envisaged in the company's prospectus. Already in the previous September Burlington had noted that the railway seemed " to do well in its short time ", but there was then " no convenience for shipping slate ". The ore transport was " well managed ", and there was a steamer service running between Piel and Fleetwood. Many visitors used this service to make excursions to Furness Abbey, but, noticed Burlington with relief, " after the train returns to Piel the mob vanishes ".[3] Barrow, too, was being rapidly prepared for a greater volume of ore traffic, and the pier there needed extension almost as soon as the Barrow-Crooklands line was opened in the June of 1846, the F.R. board having agreed to buy out the ore merchants' landing slips and stages.[4] The merchants meanwhile renewed their grumblings over the 1s. 6d. ore toll exacted by the railway proprietors, the latter nevertheless getting their way.[5]

During the winter of 1846-7 it was still confidently expected that the Whitehaven and Furness line would soon realise its plans for an extension southward from Ulverston. In the November Burlington reported a meeting with Robert Stephenson, who seemed " disposed to adopt the plan of his father in most respects, and to cross the (Leven) estuary from the Ulverstone side to the Old Park on piles, diverting the river ".[6] Burlington did not like this plan and hoped that the Admiralty would " force them to a more circuitous line by Greenodd ".[7] There had also been opposition to the proposed line on the part of Ulverston inhabitants,[8] and in the following January the Earl noted that " nothing seems to be doing

[1]*Ulv. Adv.*, 5.4.1849.   [2]*Herapath's Railway Journal*, Mar., 1847, for Co. meeting of 27.2.1847.   [3]*MS. Diary*, 9.9.1846 ; *Dir. Mins.*, 19.8.46 ; the steamer was hired by the F.R. for two months, the Company paying half the cost of it, and J. B. Fell and partners, with the Preston and Wigan Railway Co., the remainder. Others now shared Wordsworth's pleasures.   [4]*Dir. Mins.* (*F.R.*), 25.2, 22.7.1846.   [5]*Dir. Mins.* (*F.R.*), 22.4.46, 27.2.47. The directors claimed that they based their charge on the rates hitherto paid for the cartage of ore.   [6]*MS. Diary*, 12.11.46.   [7]*Ibid.*   [8]*Kendal Mercury*, 27.6.1846.

respecting the line by this place ".[1]   In the same month the F.R. directors examined tenders for the Broughton extension, and in the February that of Fell and Jopling, for £7200, was accepted after some negotiation.[2]   The same partners soon afterwards undertook to operate a steamer service between Barrow and Liverpool, and to provide a steamer and omnibus service from Dalton, Ulverston and Broughton to Windermere and Coniston. John Barraclough Fell, who had clearly foreseen manifold opportunities for profitable enterprise, also offered to contract for the construction of an extended line from Dalton-in-Furness to Lindal, thus taking the system a stage nearer the ore mines and Ulverston.[3]

Thus far local railway affairs appeared to be going well, and the appearance was maintained in the July of 1847.[4]   The line from Dalton to Rampside was now doubled, space having been left on the trackways by the foresight of engineers and directors, and a four per cent. dividend was again declared in the August.[5] But in the same summer John Abel Smith, who plainly hoped to trap and outmanoeuvre the F.R., attempted to impose upon the latter the payment of harbour dues at Barrow, and refused to make his Piel pier available to the railway company.[6]   The directors sharply refused to pay the dues demanded by Smith, sought an injunction against him, and eight months later made arrangements to take the Fleetwood steamer service out of Smith's hands.   Almost immediately, too, the latter's obstructiveness led to the use of Barrow harbour for passenger landings as well as mineral loading, sailings commencing on June 1st, 1847.[7]   But at this time the limitations of Barrow were becoming obvious to the directors; sailings were dependent on tides, and the co-ordination of rail and steamer timetables became a serious problem to officials and passengers.[8]   This co-ordination was to be a problem for many decades to come.[9] Smith therefore occupied a strong bargaining position—he controlled the traditional deep-water anchorage of Plain Furness—and his nuisance-potential was still considerable.   The attempt to obtain an injunction against Smith having failed, the Railway Company was still obliged to use Piel, and in May, 1848, the directors decided to obtain a clause in any further Furness Railway Act to empower them to lay out up to £25,000 on a steamer of their own.   Hitherto they had proposed to leave the operation of the Fleetwood-Piel and the Fleetwood-Barrow services in the hands of Smith, Fell and

[1]MS. Diary, 29.1.47.   [2]Dir. Mins. (F.R.), 23.1, 13.2, 24.2.47.   [3]Dir. Mins. (F.R.), 2.6.47, 19.1, 16.2, 19.4.48.   [4]MS. Diary, 15.7.47.   [5]Melville & Hobbs, 33.   [6]Dir. Mins. (F.R.), 13.5.47, 16.2.48.   See also p. 177 above ; it will be remembered that Smith owned Roa Island, where the " Piel Pier " was built, and had previously claimed harbour rights over the nearby waters. [7]Melville & Hobbs, 29.   [8]Ibid.   [9]Vide Proc. Inst. C.E. Suppt. (1903), CLIV, 132, for the relative advantages of passenger ports.

Jopling and the Lancashire and Yorkshire Railway Company. [1] Fortunately for the F.R., the passenger traffic over this route was not large enough to affect the railway's fortunes seriously, and the result of Smith's hard dealing was to increase the determination of the directors, or an influential individual like J. R. McClean, the company's engineer, to develop Barrow as a port. [2]

At the half-yearly meeting of February 29th, 1848, it was reported that the " depression in the money market " had affected the Company's affairs, and the ordinary dividend had to be reduced to two per cent. [3] As need hardly be said, the F.R. was not a costly line by contemporary standards. Its promotion amounted to a potentially profitable experiment by a small and wealthy group of individuals. The directors, however, had been spending fairly heavily within the limits of the project ; the Kirkby-Broughton extension was completed but was not yet paying its way, debenture stock to the value of £25,000 had been issued, a £6000 loan had been obtained from the Duke of Buccleuch, and a mortgage debenture of £7,300 from the firm of Randall, Hatfield and Wilmer. The Company now had to ask for a temporary bank loan to repay the latter, and by the April Burlington was seriously concerned. Benjamin Currey had died suddenly while performing his duties at the House of Lords, and was never to see the achievements of the line he had been so anxious to promote. In the same month Burlington was appointed a director in the latter's place and was immediately elected F.R. chairman ; whereupon he found the company in a " deplorable state " and was obliged to seek Joseph Paxton's advice. In the late summer Paxton, together with a number of George Hudson's officials, attempted to diagnose the ills of the ailing organisation, in which they found " great fault, both with the original expenditure and with the mode of management ". General retrenchment followed ; staff dismissals, abandonment of new works, wage reductions, and an increase of mineral tolls. By the February of 1849, when the line had " done badly this half year ", Burlington was even ready to lease the line to another party or parties on the recommendation of J. R. McClean and another person. The directors, fortunately for themselves, rejected the idea. [4] They had had their taste of the psychological effects of a tightening of the money market, and Burlington became even more sober in his

[1] *Dir. Mins.*, 13.5.47, 19.1, 16.2, 4.5.48. The steamer *Windermere* was bought by the Company and renamed *Helvellyn*. [2] *MS. Diary*, 13.9.48 ; McClean had stated that " Piel must be abandoned and Barrow improved ". [3] Rept. quoted in Melville & Hobbs, 33.
[4] For the fundamentals of the story, *Dir. Mins.* (*F.R.*), 24.11.45, 25.2, 22.4, 20.5.46 (mortgage loans), 22.8, 4.11.46 (calls on shareholders), 19.4, 19.6. 48 (crisis meetings), 11.10, 21.11.48 (retrenchment), and half-yearly meeting (reptd. *Herapath*) of 29.8.48 ; and *MS. Diary*, 14.3.48, 19.4, 20.4, 11.9, 12.10.48. For the offer by McClean, *MS. Diary*, 19.2.49, *Dir. Mins.* (*F.R.*), 27.2.49.

appraisals than before. But the work of physical transformation nevertheless went on ; human labour saw to that, in spite of the idiosyncracies of a system of laissez-faire and the amateurishness of the capitalists concerned. By the spring of 1849 the panic was over ; the line was again " doing well ",[1] even though the half-yearly meeting of the February had shown a loss on working. By the August, the sun shone. Receipts for the half-year exceeded expenditure by £3,500, work on the main line towards Lindal had been re-started, and the Whitehaven to Ravenglass railway was opened on July 19th[2] (a coach service from Ravenglass to the F.R. terminus at Broughton connecting the two railways). But eight years were to elapse before the mainland of Lancashire and the ironfields of western Cumbria were directly joined by rail.

Each new scheme or development produced another which fed on it. Now that there was to be a line between Whitehaven and Furness, Burlington saw a new importance in the plan for connecting Dalton and Ulverston, and John Barraclough Fell, whose men were once more at work on the short line from Crooklands (Dalton) to Lindal, proposed to contract for the building of a line from Broughton-in-Furness—the meeting point with the Whitehaven rail-and-coach service—to the copper and slate of Coniston.[3] This idea, too, did not reach fruition for a number of years. Burlington was at first typically dubious ; " I fear it will not go on for want of funds ".[4] But it was worthy of notice ; the F.R. directors had now learned solid sense, and for the time being no longer flirted with the notion of opening up Lakeland to tourist traffic. They had already decided, very wisely, that minerals and goods traffic should be " primarily considered ".[5]

THE TRADE IN IRON ORE

The directors'-eye view of local history, examples of which are given above, is a revealing although somewhat limited one. It would be misleading to imply, even inadvertently, that Burlington and his confederates were the only persons whose activities were shaping the substance of local affairs. The Furness Railway so far owed its rather limited success not to the percipience of the men who (after powerful promptings) had decided to build it, but very largely to the superior quality of the Dalton haematite ore. This quality, as before, was fully recognised by ironmasters in South Wales and Staffordshire, and the dealers of the district had no difficulty in finding markets. In letting railway lines and wagons take the place of clog-wheel carts, the men who built the railway

[1]*MS. Diary*, 12.4, 26.4, 27.6, 13.7.49.   [2]Summaries of repts. of half-yearly meetings, Melville & Hobbs, 35-6.   [3]*MS. Diary*, 31.8.49, 5.11, 8.11.49. [4]*MS. Diary*, 8.11.49.   [5]*Dir. Mins.* (*F.R.*), 21.11.48.

had smashed a bottleneck, and the riches of the district began to flow out almost immediately.   It was the iron ore merchants of the neighbourhood who arranged for the raising and sale of the haematite, even if they did not decide rail tolls ; and it was their men, local labourers and migrant Cornishmen, who made the wealth available, with or without the blessings of advanced mining technique.

Of the Plain Furness ore merchants of the time, none, perhaps, knew all this better than Henry William Schneider.   As has been noticed, he had entered the district in 1839, and had played some part in the agitation for a local railway.[1]   His subsequent role is so important that he merits a brief biographical account even at this stage, although it is unfortunate that comparatively little is known of his early life, the substance being contained in a memoir[2] (composed either by himself or a close friend) published nearly half a century after the events now described.   He was the only real or notable newcomer into the ranks of the haematite merchants of the 'forties, and, although anglicised, was descended from an ancient Swiss family of the Canton of Berne, a member of which settled in England in the middle of the eighteenth century.   This Schneider founded a merchant's business in London, which was carried on by the second and third generations of the English branch of the family, and which came to devote itself to dealing in metalliferous ores, particularly of the precious metals.   In 1835 this firm was known as the Mexican and South American Company, and was based at 10 New Broad Street Mews, London.   H. W. Schneider, who acted in association with one John Schneider, was at this time the secretary of the company,[3] which was then or some time afterwards " extensively concerned in Mexican affairs ", and which " for many years acted as financial agents of the Mexican government, under which it held large contracts for the coinage of silver ".[4] In 1835 we find the promising young man of business arranging for shipments of wagons and other merchandise to Tampico from London, Cornwall and Swansea.[5]   Unlike most of the other ore merchants of the locality, he plainly had wide and cosmopolitan connections, and was an experienced and comparatively affluent dealer when he entered the district.

The exact circumstances of his arrival in Furness are not entirely clear.   According to the memoir quoted, he was engaged on

---

[1]See p. 173 above.   [2]*Proc. Inst. C.E.* (1888), XCII, 40 6 sqq.
    [3]*MS. letters of the Mexican & S. American Co. to Hayle Foundry, Cornwall,* dated June-Sept., 1835, for the use of which I am indebted to Mr. T. H. Harris of Camborne, and to Miss M. E. Coate, who put me on touch with him. [4]Memoir, *cit.*   [5]*MS. letters, cit.*   According to the memoir, the firm had " a considerable establishment at Guanajuata ",. where it coined gold and silver Tampico would be the port used.

a trip to the Lake District in 1839 when he was introduced to Mr. Jopling, who managed the Kirkby slate quarries for the Earl of Burlington, and who showed him the haematite mines at Park near Askam.[1] According to his own account,[2] he made a special journey from Liverpool in the same year " at eight o'clock in the morning, and did not arrive at the Sun Inn (Ulverston) till ten o'clock at night, and then I was informed that I had a further distance to go to the iron mines . . . When I reached the mines I found the ore was raised by means of a few miserable horse-gins ".

In early 1840 he obtained a lease of ore-bearing territory on the land of the Earl of Burlington, and together with his father he took into partnership James Farrell and James Davis and formed the Furness Company, which erected a jetty at Barrow in 1842.[3] Meanwhile, convinced that rich deposits awaited discovery, he engaged competent geologists and arranged for the sinking of a shaft at Haggs Springs Hill, in the royalty of the Duke of Buccleuch.[4] The result was discouragement, and so the partnership played for safety by purchasing an already productive mine at Whitriggs from Thomas Fisher and P. Butler for the sum of £3,500, this site being occupied by them in 1843.[5] To quote Schneider again, " . . . my first operations were most discouraging, but extending my research by taking property from other owners, I established my mines sufficiently encouraging to enable me to persevere ".[6] Seven years were to elapse before the first signs of a resounding discovery were to be manifested.

Other ore merchants, chiefly local men, were also extending their operations. In 1839 there were three main firms in the district ; Harrison, Ainslie & Co., working mines on Lindal Moor, the Ulverston Mining Co. at Lindal Cote (operated by the brothers Kennedy), and that of Thomas Fisher at Butts Beck and Whitriggs[7]. In 1843 the number of merchants or firms had increased to five ; a pit at Stainton, in the royalty of the Earl of Burlington, was being worked, and the firm of Town and Rawlinson was established at Butts Beck, while Schneider's partnership, the Furness Company, was then at Whitriggs. In 1849, three years after the opening of the Furness Railway, the haematite output of the district had greatly increased beyond that of 1843 :

[1]Memoir, cit.   [2]Speech reptd. in Appx. to Leach, op. cit., p. 26.
[3]Gaythorpe, H., Notes on Barrow Village in B.N.F.C. XVII, 1909.   [4]Fisher, Pop. Hist of Barrow (cit.), 67-9.
[5]Fisher, loc. cit.   [6]Paper in Trans. Inst. Mech. Eng. (1887), 377.
[7]Kendall, J. D., Hist. of Mining in Cumberland & N. Lancs., N. of E. Inst. of M. & M.E., XXXIV, 93.

Table 19

Iron ore firms, pits and output in Furness, 1849 [1]

Firm	No. of pits	Output, 1849, tons
Harrison, Ainslie & Co., Lindal Moor	3	55,000
Town & Rawlinson, Crossgates	3	42,000
Ulverston Mining Co., Lindal Cote	4	29,000
Schneider, Davis & Co., Mouzell	3	25,000
Charles Kennedy, Haulm	1	12,000
Geo. Huddleston, Stainton	2	12,000
Geo. Ashburner, Elliscales	1	7,000
Totals	17	182,000
West Cumberland : 5 firms ,,	13	100,000 (approx.)

Just as the main *dramatis personae* of the railway company had commenced their activities in the locality, so the major iron ore masters of the vital succeeding twenty years were now established in business with one or two noteworthy exceptions—the Brogden family and Robert Hannay, H. W. Schneider's later partner. [2] Harrison, Ainslie and Co., a firm whose business origins went back to the foundation of the Newland Company nearly a century before, [3] were the chief lessees of iron mines in the north-west of England at this time, were the only iron ore merchants of the neighbourhood who had shown any willingness to invest in the Furness Railway, [4] and were still engaged in the charcoal-smelting of haematite pig-iron at Bunawe or Bonaw in Argyllshire, Warsash in Hampshire, Newland and Backbarrow. Some quantities of pig were brought from Bunawe to Ulverston, and thence shipped to Liverpool and sent by dealers to Brest and Harfleur for the manufacture of cutlery, while in 1829 it was stated that Furness bar iron was sent to Sheffield to be converted into steel. [5] The specialised nature of the markets and the high quality of the local iron enabled charcoal smelting to remain alive. [6] This firm, whose principals after about 1840 were Benson Harrison, Montague Ainslie and Thomas Roper (the latter an astute and hard-dealing general manager) turned its activities increasingly to the shipment of ore, and is one of the few examples of—for lack of less clumsy phraseology—local capital accumulation and continued reinvestment in local industry.

The Ulverston Mining Company consisted of Charles Storr Kennedy [7] (the son of an Ulverston customs supervisor, he had

[1]*Loc. cit.* [2]See pp. 204-5 below. [3]See p. 29 above. [4]See p. 177 above. [5]White, *Furness Folk* etc., 79 ; *Parson & White*, 721. [6]The Shah of Persia, anxious to obtain information on the improved smelting of iron, is stated to have applied to Thomas Roper through an intermediary in 1839 and on a later occasion : *vide* Richardson, *Furness Past & Present*, II, 184-5. [7]For Kennedy and his sons, *vide* Casson, *op. cit.*, 78-81.

married the daughter of the banker Myles Burton), George Huddleston, surgeon of Ulverston, James Park, Richard Smith and Thomas Petty of Preston, manufacturer, [1] the latter being the only non-local partner. Kennedy and Huddleston were also in occupation of mines at Haulm, and Stainton (see Table 19). This firm obtained a lease of mining territory at Lindal Cote in 1838, at a payment of a regular rent of £37 10s., with royalty arranged on a sliding scale. [2] In 1839, they were using the services of a high-pressure steam engine, and were the only local firm to use such equipment. [3] In 1842 Robert Town, of Water Park, Colton, and Joseph Rawlinson, of Dalton-in-Furness, obtained a twenty-one year lease of mining ground in the royalty of the Duke of Buccleuch, viz., at Tytup ; [4] the Joseph Rawlinson of this partnership also became a prominent ore merchant, and was a relative of the Fishers of Dalton, [5] shipowners and merchants, who in turn played a notable part in the opening up of the ironfield and the early history of Barrow. All of the local ore masters, in fact, seem to have had professional or mercantile connections, and disposed of sufficient capital and experience to take advantage of the rapid growth of their trade.

The great bulk of the local haematite was raised from land in the royalty of Buccleuch, to the north and north-east of the town of Dalton. The Furness ironmasters of more than a century previously had obtained their ore from this land, but had not dreamed of the mineral riches that lay underfoot ; or certainly not of their physical quantity, for the economic demands of a later age turned that which lay untouched into wealth. The merchants of 1846, however, were generally working on or near sites which had long been productive, and many of which receive mention in the early eighteenth century. [6] As the exploitation of the haematite deposits became intensified, so the latter were apt to peter out or disappear without warning, forcing the lessees to engage in new and sometimes expensive searches. The ore merchants, who formed an influential group which could offer opposition to the Furness Railway Company when the occasion seemed to warrant it, had their own worries and preoccupations.

Allusion has already been made to the earliest disagreements between railway directors and merchants. [7] During the crisis period of 1848, tolls for the carriage of haematite were raised to 2s. a ton, and in the December of that year, when it was expected that the trade would make some recovery, the merchants waited upon the directors with a proposal to stop all horse-cartage of ore to Barrow

---

[1]*MS. draft lease* of 7.7.1838. Buccleuch archives, Tytup Hall, Dalton. H. W. Schneider married an Augusta Smith of Urswick in 1842, the daughter of this Richard Smith. [2]*Loc. cit.*
[3]Richardson, *op. cit.*, II, 186. [4]*Lease of* 22.3.1842, Buccleuch archives. The royalty, as in the case of the Ulverston Mining Co., was 1s. 6d. a ton, and the ground rent £37 10s. [5]Casson, *op. cit.*, 77. [6]For examples, pp. 23, f.n. 4, and 35, above. [7]Pp. 182, 188 above.

if the F.R. would agree to lower its freights to 1s. 9d. a ton, claiming by way of justification that Whitehaven ore merchants could sell their produce at 13s. a ton when they themselves received only 11s.[1] The directors refused, but promised that they would reduce the rates to those firms which agreed to use the new F.R. extension to Lindal-in-Furness, in return for a guarantee of traffic on the part of the merchants.[2] The latter were contentious. One of the Kennedy's complained that he had made sidings and paid five per cent. on rails supplied by the railway company. Eventually he received a toll reduction of one penny a ton. Schneider's partnership, and that of Town and Rawlinson, had not yet constructed tramlines from their pits to the railhead at Crooklands, evidently feeling that the railway directorate should assist them. This assistance was duly given, the company exercising its powers of compulsory land purchase.[3] Tramways were not in fact constructed by the middle of 1849, and in the April of that year the ore merchants were obliged to raise the cartage rate (paid by them to private carters and local farmers) from 1s. to 1s. 3d. a ton in order to attract a large enough number of vehicles to keep the F.R. wagons fully loaded at the Crooklands railhead.[4]

Nevertheless, many of the traditional difficulties of the trade were now overcome. When roads were so bad as to prevent cartage for several months of the year, mining firms had been obliged to make sizeable dumps of ore (on " mine floors ") at their numerous loading points on the neighbouring coasts. Now, provided that frost and flooding did not render the extraction of haematite impossible, transport could be kept going most of the time, and in the December of 1849 vessels were introducing a new feature into the history of Barrow by entering its harbour at night.[5] Between 600 and 700 tons of ore could be sent down the railway in a single day and it was stated that a similar number of horses would have been required to do this work.[6] The highway between Dalton and Barrow was becoming grassgrown for lack of use.[7]

Although Barrow was now visited by at least three times as many ships as entered Ulverston (that is, in 1849),[8] the larger port was by no means abandoned in the eyes of the ore merchants Huddleston and Kennedy, who had interests in the Ulverston Canal Company, and who were opposed to the F.R. and Whitehaven and Furness Railway plans to make a through route *via* that town. Quite rightly, they feared that the Canal would be rendered redundant.[9] The merchants generally continued to use it for some years afterwards.[10]

[1]*Dir. Mins.*, 12.12.48. This was the price paid for local haematite in 1772. [2]*Ibid.* [3]*Ibid.* [4]*Ulverston Advertiser*, 5.4.1849. [5]*Ulv. Adv.*, 20.12.1849. [6]*Ulv. Adv.*, 16.8.1849. [7]*Ibid.* [8]*Vide* shipping lists published in the *Ulverston Advertiser* at this time, and p. 187 above. [9]*Mins. Ulverston Canal Co.*, 4.12, 30.12.1845 and *passim.* [10]See p. 211 below.

Only much more extensive research than has been possible here would establish the identity of the major iron firms which were using Furness haematite at this period. The bulk of the local trade, however, was still with South Wales, and the most frequent destinations of vessels (or places of origin reported in newspaper shipping lists[1]) were Ellesmere Port, Llanelly, Newport, Porthcawl, Barry, Port Talbot, Swansea, Cardiff, Runcorn, Liverpool and Glasgow. In late October, 1848, twenty-four of these craft entered Barrow Harbour in six days, and during one week in the following March, four of them loaded 760 tons of ore between them;[2] while on April 1st, 1849, there were no fewer than 70 vessels in the same harbour.[3] It is little wonder that the *Ulverston Advertiser* conceded that " Barrow is becoming an important seaport ".[4] The shipping record was doubtless puny enough compared with that of Liverpool or a Glasgow, but nothing like it had ever been seen in the history of the locality, and the provision of a few miles of railway track,[5] a handful of small locomotives and several dozen wagons was already instrumental in transforming it. Similar changes were taking place in other parts of the British Isles, if not quite so suddenly ; and it must often strike the investigator as tragic that the advance of human health and happiness did not, in this period, keep pace with technological progress.

BARROW HARBOUR AND VILLAGE

It was in the above circumstances that Barrow Harbour acquired its Commissioners by a special enactment of June 30th, 1848. The harbour was vested in this body, which was authorised to borrow £5000 from the Furness Railway Company. The chairman of the latter was always to be a Commissioner,[6] and at this time and for many years afterwards the railway directors were faced by the constant need for improvement of the harbour facilities. Barrow was still a creek of the Port of Lancaster, and remained so until 1872. Nevertheless, the Barrow Harbour Commissioners, who at first met only infrequently, considered the wisdom of applying to make Barrow an independent port as early as August, 1849,[7] although nothing more is heard of the idea for some time afterwards. In spite of the marked growth of local trade and the directors' obvious determination to develop the still tiny village and port to the utmost, all but the smallest vessels were prevented from entering

---

[1]*Ulv. Adv., passim.* [2]*Ulv. Adv.,* 1.11.48, 29.3.49. [3]*Ulv. Adv.,* 5.4.49. [4]*Ibid.* [5]Viz., the short line which connected Barrow and the iron mines. This was the key section for many years to come.
[6]*Barrow Harbour Improvement Act.,* 11 & 12 *Vict., c.*35, 12.6.48 ; *Mins. Barr. Harb. Commissioners* (*MS.*), 13.12.48 ; *Ulv. Adv.,* 14.12.48. The members were C. D. Archibald, William Gale, Montague Ainslie, Thomas Ainsworth, Stephen Eddy, Robert Wheatley Lumley, T. Y. P. Michaelson and a nominee of John Abel Smith. Burlington was chairman. [7]*Mins. Harb. Commrs.,* mtg. of 31. 8.49.

the harbour at periods of neap tide.   The latter had to be provided
with elementary equipment like buoys, lifeboats and a Harbour
Master.[1]   Many years were to elapse before craft of any size could
enter Piel Bar and find safe anchorage between the Island of Old
Barrow and the mainland ; at low tide, indeed, it was possible to
cross from Barrow and Hindpool shores to Walney Island by means
of stepping stones, but when waters were rising a strong and sometimes torrential and destructive current rushed through Barrow
Channel.   This current, with its powerful scour, was afterwards
turned to good account.[2]   The chief advantage of this otherwise
unprepossessing place was its sheltered nature ; possibly, too, the
traditional leaning of the ore merchants to it, together with John
Abel Smith's obstructive tactics at Piel, influence the choice of the
directors, who lengthened the railway pier at Barrow in 1849 and
provided more berths for shipping.   These last were used in conjunction with tippler wagons and small cranes.[3]

In the village itself there were small but noticeable changes.
In 1843 its population had been 150, in 1846 some 325 persons ; and
in 1850 it had 661 inhabitants, including 180 seamen.   The mere
business of ore shipment, even at the rate of two or three thousand
tons a week, did not create anything more than a feverishly active
harbour.   At the time, and during the succeeding ten years, there
was no great influx of immigrants into Barrow as such, for there were
few other industries to absorb them.   Even the maintenance and
working of the still diminutive Furness Railway did not call for the
employment of many workpeople.

The railway directors, fully aware that the services of a large
labour force would ultimately be needed, planned well ahead.   A
row of cottages, erected at what are now Nos. 1-10 Salthouse Road,
Barrow, were completed in 1847 at their behest.[4]   These stood
about a quarter of a mile from the old village, which had only 30
houses in 1845.   In 1848 James Ramsden, Thomas Roper, Thomas
Fisher and R. Brocklebank formed the Barrow Building Society,[5]
this as a private speculation rather than a railway-inspired venture,
and in the following April (1849) it was reported that " the Railway
Company have it in contemplation to build half a dozen cottages
to the end of those already erected by them ; and the Building
Society also intend shortly to commence operations.   House
accommodation has long been wanted, as at present the labourers
either live at a distance, or two or more families are obliged to crowd
in a small house ".[6]   Ramsden, who was already coming to the
fore[7] in his chosen but still modest sphere, had been engaged in

[1]*Mins*. of same, 13.12.48.   [2]It was useful in preventing silting ; see also
Close, in Dickson, *op. cit.*, 524.   [3] *Dir. Mins.* (*F.R.*), 27.2.49 ; *Ulv. Adv.*, 13.3,
19.4.49.   [4]See also p. 182 above.   [5]*Ulv. Adv.*, 12.9.50.   [6]*Ulv. Adv.*, 19.4.49.
[7]In November, 1846, he became (cont.)

designing a school, library and reading room for the small railway colony at Salthouse, and on New Year's Day, 1849, he laid the first stone of this building.[1] The directors and engineers of the line subscribed towards the cost of the institution, but the former decided to use the accumulated fines of company servants to equip the library,[2] thereby foreshadowing one aspect of the future "welfare state" in making the underprivileged pay for certain privileges. Local "inhabitants", however, met to consider the uses of the library and reading room (afterwards restricted to F.R. employees) ; Ramsden appointed a schoolmaster, Ralph Hordley,[3] who spent the remainder of a long life in Barrow ; and the building, community centre as well as educational establishment, was opened in the September. A small neo-Gothic edifice (still, in 1957, standing in School Street, Barrow), it was given the title of the Barrow Mechanics' Institute. In January, 1851, its library had 250 books and its school an average attendance of 63.[4]

Ramsden, even at this stage, was something of a visionary. At a meeting held to celebrate the opening of the school, he said, speaking of education, that ". . . in the rising generation it is to be hoped that a higher standard will be adopted . . . there is an actual loss in the way of health and strength if young children are bound to labour before they are 13 or 14 years of age". He urged, too, not without emotion, that women should receive the benefits of education,[5] and addressing the young, held up before them the example of Sir John Barrow, the Ulverston tanner's son who had become a prominent geographer and Secretary to the Admiralty, and who had died, greatly honoured in his native town, but two years previously.[6] In view of the present-day tendency to regard Victorian worthies in kindly fashion, we must not forget to test aspiration against performance. Ramsden, by all accounts, had not come from the poorest of homes, and very few of the men who later dominated the history of the locality arose from humble cottages. John Barrow, in spite of disadvantages of birth and background, received generous encouragement and even educational opportunities[7] of a type which were to be denied to thousands of children in James Ramsden's Barrow. This, however, is to pre-

assistant engineer to the F.R. as well as Locomotive Superintendent ; and in May, 1850, he became Secretary to the Company ; *Dir. Mins.* (*F.R.*), 4.11.46, 13.2.47, 3.10.49 (gratuity for profits of the company), 12.12.48 (confirmed as Manager of the line), 10.5.50 (temporary Secretary).   [1]*Ulv. Adv.*, 4.1.49.   [2]*Dir. Mins.*, 17.4.49.   [3]Brought over as a very young man from Christ Church Training School, Liverpool. He compiled useful historical notes on the early village in his old age.
   [4]*Ulv. Adv.*, 28.11.50, 23.1.51. In the November the Ulverston Philharmonic Society gave a concert at the Institute, performing choruses from the *Messiah.*   [5]*Ulv. Adv.*, 7.2.50.   [6]*Vide* p. 153 above. The well-known monument on Hoad Hill was erected to Barrow's honour in 1850.   [7]*Vide* his *An Autobiographical Memoir* (1847), esp. pp. 5-11.

judge later developments, and the enthusiasm, ability and ambition of the F.R. Secretary are very apparent. He seems to have missed few opportunities to advance his own career, and was a most competent administrator from the beginning of his fateful stay in the district.

Events were now moving more rapidly. In early 1849, the company's carriage shed was moved from Rampside to Barrow. [1] It was decided to lead water from " near Rampside " to the new colony, and to attend to other sanitary requirements there. [2] The Building Society commenced the erection of houses near the Barrow foreshore in the winter of 1849-50, the first row being known as Burlington Terrace, [3] and a second row of railway cottages was built at Salthouse at the same time. These Salthouse cottages were spaced and arranged in such a way as to suggest that they were planed as the nucleus of a larger colony, a space for a main roadway being left between them. Before many years had passed, however, James Ramsden, whose main interest was in the laying out and development of this small colony, was aspiring to the planning of an urban unit far too large to merit such a title. It seems that he had had some experience of railway colonisation at Wolverton in Bucks, where his former master Edward Bury had worked for the London and Birmingham Railway. [4] Barrow's early development was not particularly tidy, and was hindered by the shortage of building land. Thomas Roper, a member of the Barrow Building Society, complained in 1850 that " the land of Barrow is in few hands, and these hands have a most tenacious grip . . . until Lord Burlington agreed to sell a small slice to the Building Society, it could not obtain an inch of land at any reasonable price on which to lay a foundation ". [5] The " town " had " not increased as it ought to have done ". [6] The railway company and its collaborators owned little land in the immediate neighbourhood as yet, and even the Duke of Buccleuch, one of its major shareholders and owner of the foreshore, was unco-operative. [7] A tract of territory to the west of the village belonged, fortunately for the company, to the Earl of Burlington, and here much development later took place. For the rest, the ground in and about the village and colony was divided between six estates, [8] the owners or trustees of which were astute enough to see that their land was growing greatly in value. The

[1]*Dir. Mins.* (*F.R.*), 12.12.48, 27.2.49.   [2]*Dir. Mins.* (*F.R.*), 27.2.49. [3]*Ulv. Adv.*, 14.2.50.   [4]*Ulv. Adv.*, 7.2.50.   A description of Wolverton is contained in Head, Sir F. B., *Stokers and Pokers* (1861 ed.), 82, where it would seem that there are superficial similarities to early Barrow.   [5]*Ibid.*   [6]*Ibid.* [7] " . . . if the shore is of such value to the Railway Company, it must also be of value and importance to myself . . . I certainly shall not accept less than that which I have received for the shore already sold to the Railway Company " ; Buccleuch to R. W. Lumley, letter in *Kendall MSS.*, dated 18.2.50, by courtesy of Mr. H. Kendall.   [8]*Tithe Commutation Map of Dalton* (*Hawcoat District*), 1841, with additional details by courtesy of Mr. J. Melville.

F.R., meanwhile, did not obtain a considerable estate of its own until 1854, and the Building Society, which proposed to build cottages for speculative purposes, [1] had achieved little by the autumn of 1850. Thomas Fisher, one of its promoters, commenced the erection of the Barrow Harbour Hotel in that year. [2]

Although a number of significant events were to take place in the colony and village during the next ten years, Barrow remained of little account as a social entity until the mid-'sixties, for reasons which will be clear ; namely, that the transport of ore and the maintenance of a small railway system did not call for the services of a considerable labour force. [3] The development of the iron ore mines near Dalton did however lead to the immigration of work-people, and more is said about this below. [4] It is possible that the town of Barrow would have grown somewhat more rapidly had the Furness Railway and others been able to push ahead with an effective building programme, thereby attracting small trades and industries to a more obviously flourishing settlement. This, however, is mere speculation. The town did not rise to importance until heavy industries were established there, and the appearance of these industries came only after another chapter in the history of the local ironfield had been completed.

[1]Details and prospectus in *Ulv. Adv.* 12.9.50.   [2]*Ulv. Adv.*, 14.2.50.   [3]As a matter of statistical interest, a population return for 1850, compiled by James Ramsden, gives the following figure for Barrow and environs :

Hindpool and Patent Slip	21
Barrow	252
Old Barrow Island	40
F.R. Co.'s cottages	117
Salthouse and Junction	51
Avge. seamen in port during the year	180
Total	661

Adult males : 175. Adult Females : 111. Children : 195. The population of Barrow in 1806 was 65 and that of Salthouse, 20. At the Census of 1851 the total for the above places was 690, with 52 men and 16 women lodgers. [4]See Chapter XII below.

CHAPTER XI

RAILWAY AND IRONFIELD (II)

By the commencement of the year 1850, H. W. Schneider and his local mining partners had made no significant haematite discoveries, although Schneider had then been prospecting for ten years. The latter afterwards remarked that " nothing was so uncertain and deceptive as the ore deposits. The most encouraging ventures have ended in disappointment, and the most discouraging trials have ended in supreme success ".[1] According to his own testimony he had expended " between £25,000 and £30,000 " on his searches before he " received one penny back ".[2] Indeed, a local anecdote has it that his financial resources were exhausted at this time, and he is credited with the jocular remark that " I haven't five pounds to buy a dinner with ".[3] Victorian eulogists, however, following the pattern of Samuel Smiles, tend often to exaggerate the self-sacrifice and determination of their subjects. It will be noted that Schneider was wealthy enough to spend a comparatively large sum with little or no return, and some recently discovered particulars show that his Furness investments were in fact mere side-speculations.

His business activities had already extended as far as Mexico, and the headquarters of his family firm was still in the City of London. Investment in Australia now enters into the picture. The directors of the South Australian Company wished to engage in copper-smelting in that state, and with this end in mind they established relations with H. W. Schneider of New Broad Street Mews, City of London, thereby forming the Patent Copper Company in 1849. By the middle of 1850 works were established at the Burra Copper Mine, and a year later the Company recorded a turnover of £180,000.[4] Schneider's comparative poverty can therefore be discounted. By the end of 1851 he was a director of the English and Australian Copper Company, which was formed to take over the concerns of the Patent Copper Company's works at Koaringa (Burra) and the Spilty Copper Works at Llanelly, Carmarthenshire. The new company had a capital of £350,000 in £5 shares, of which Sir William Foster of the City of Norwich, (a later political backer of Schneider) had 20,000 and Schneider himself had 15,000.[5] The

---

[1] *Proc. Inst. Mech. Eng.* (1880), 372.   [2] *Sel. Cttee. Rating of Mines, Brit. Parl. Papers,* 1857, Sess. 2, *XI,* 122 sqq.   [3] Quoted in Fisher, *Popular History of Barrow, cit.*   [4] Details by courtesy of Mr. D. H. Pike, of the University of Adelaide, South Australia.

[5] *Deed of Settlement, Eng. and Australian Copper Co.,* dated 13.12.1851. The works at Burra and Llanelly were purchased for £306,108, and the company had branches at Adelaide and Swansea. Schneider does not seem to have visited Australia.

company's places of business were at 10, New Broad Street Mews and 17 Gracechurch Street, London, both addresses being used by Schneider in other transactions.[1] The English and Australian Copper Company does not appear to have made any very substantial profits until about 1860.[2]

These particulars are relevant to the following narrative. They suggest that only the veriest freak of circumstance caused this very astute and busy financier to remain interested in Furness haematite-mining. The "freak of circumstance" was the discovery of the Park haematite deposit near what is now the small industrial colony of Askam-in-Furness; and the events leading to its successful exploitation can be traced. Secondly, the resounding success of the Patent Copper Company in 1850-51 may have caused Schneider to pursue his Furness ventures with redoubled zeal, although it should be added that particulars of a few years later (1856-7) show that Australia and South Wales were by no means his only fields of operation.[3] Lastly, it is a measure of the profitability of the local mining of haematite in the 'fifties that the cosmopolitan Schneider settled in Furness and concentrated much of his capital and energy upon the development of the district. It is only fair to add, nevertheless, that the Lakeland background would appeal even to a busy financier, and that Schneider had married a Furness woman. Sentiment, as well as business, doubtless played a part.

About 1840 he had taken a lease at Park near the Duddon shore, in the royalty of the Earl of Burlington, and there carried out some of the unsuccessful searches mentioned. In 1850 a site near Slater's farm, originally abandoned on account of his having met with no co-operation from mining neighbours, was again selected for trial; and it has been stated[4] that he was on the point of abandoning the quest once more, but that his miners offered to work for a week without pay. On October 29th, the *Ulverston Advertiser* reported that Schneider and Co. had discovered ore at Park, and two days later[5] the Earl of Burlington noted that Schneider and Davis had "found ore on my farm at Parkhead, and are going to put up a small engine". The local historian Joseph Fisher claimed that one of his forebears, Schneider's agent Thomas Fisher, found the deposit and received the offer of a renewal of the lease from Burlington.[6] In this way the second greatest haematite ore deposit in British history[7] was discovered; what was later to be revealed as a continuous mass of ore measuring 200 by 300 yards, and containing between eight and nine million tons of best quality haematite.

<hr/>

[1]See, e.g., p. 205 below, note 6.   [2]I have to thank Mr. Pike for generously supplied data.   [3]See p. 209 below.   [4]Memoir, *cit.*   [5]*MS. Diary*, 1.11.50.   [6]*Pop. Hist. of Barrow* (*cit.*), 116.   [7]The largest was that at Hodbarrow, near Millom, for which see p. 223 below.

For several years the vastness of this mineral wealth was barely suspected,[1] for experience had taught the prospectors to be forewarned against the sudden disappearance of apparently rich sops or pockets ; but in 1852 the Park Mine was showing considerable promise,[2] and Burlington had a good prospect of substantial royalties therefrom—how substantial, he was doubtless unable to guess. Schneider himself was content to remain clear of embroilment in local railway affairs—indeed, he must have regarded such concerns as slightly beneath his notice—and having ensured that the mining was carried on as efficiently as possible,[3] was preoccupied chiefly with the sale of the ore in South Wales and elsewhere.

Schneider was not the only financially well-endowed ore merchant to commence important local operations at this time. John Brogden senior had become a shareholder in the Furness Railway Company in 1846,[4] and was therefore watching local events between that year and 1850.[5] In the following year Brogden and his sons John junior, Alexander and Henry promoted the Ulverston and Lancaster Railway Company. Meanwhile the family had taken ore-mining territory at Stainton, in the royalty of Burlington, and were developing the mines there by the December of 1850, installing winding engines and pumping machinery.[6] In the April of the following year, Burlington saw and admired their new pumping engine of fifty horsepower, which was capable of raising water fifty feet.[7] Throughout the early years of the decade, the companies at work in the ironfield were engaged in building tramways from the mines to the main F.R. railway lines at Lindal and elsewhere, until the fields around Dalton were covered by an ever-growing network.[8]

THE FURTHER DEVELOPMENT OF THE IRONFIELD

The result of this expenditure and activity is shown in ore production figures. In 1849, seven companies working 17 pits between them were raising 182,000 tons of haematite, but in 1855, eight companies working 19 pits were raising 336,829 tons.[9] Thus the total output had almost doubled in six years ; a period, be it noted, when Bessemer had not yet invented his steelmaking process, and when, therefore, an extraordinary stimulant to the production

[1]For a detailed account, vide F.P. & P., II, 187. It produced eight and a half million tons in 34 years. [2]MS, Diary, 12.11.1852 ; " . . . the mine is doing well ". [3]E.g., Ulv. Adv., 29.2.49, where Schneider & Co., are importing boilers for pumping engines. [4]See p. 181 above. [5]For light on the activities of the Brogden family, Proc. Inst. C.E., XV, 1856, 94.
[6]Ulv. Advertiser, 5.12.50 ; Diary of Edward Wadham (MS ; hereafter given as Wadham Diary), by courtesy of H. A. Slater and Boughton Estates Ltd., 24.7.51. Wadham was the mineral agent to the Duke of Buccleuch. [7]MS. Diary, 26.4.51. [8]Wadham Diary, 7.4.53, 10.1, 13.2.54, 12.10.54, 10.5.55 and passim. [9]Mineral Stats. U.K. (Ed. Hunt, 1854).

of haematite had not appeared.

In August, 1853, the Park mine was producing up to 60,000 tons of ore *per annum*, and Schneider was looking forward to an output of 100,000 tons.[1] Thereafter it contributed a considerable proportion of the output of the whole ironfield, by 1856 producing about 120,000 tons[2] out of 464,853.[3] By that time Schneider had taken into partnership one Robert Hannay of Kirkcudbright, a landed gentlemen with a background rather different from that of the Mexican and Australian ore dealer. Hannay had inherited an entailed estate, and went into business " to provide for his younger children ".[4] His connection with the iron trade commenced in 1846, after some earlier experience with a firm of Turkey merchants.[5] The partnership took effect on January 1st, 1853 (Schneider having relinquished his connection with James Davis), and soon afterwards the two capitalists set about a considerable extension of their operations, taking an important lease of mining ground at Lindal, in the royalty of the Duke of Buccleuch, in March, 1854. This lease embraced nearly 211 acres altogether and was to run for 21 years at a yearly rent of £450. The indenture allowed for the extraction of a minimum quantity of 7,200 tons of haematite yearly, and bound the partners to convey by the Furness Railway only. The ore pits were to be worked in a proper manner, with " proper levels, air gates and drawing gates according to the best and most approved method of working and winning mines of that nature ", and shafts were not be be allowed to fall into ruin.[6]

Other ore merchants were no less active. Joseph Rawlinson of Dalton made extensive searches to the north-east of that town after September, 1854, and took a 21-year lease at Tytup and Butts End in February, 1855 ; while in March, 1857, a lease of several hundred acres at Lindal Cote and Crossgates was taken by John and Alexander Brogden together with a son of C. S. Kennedy, Henry Kennedy of Brighton.[7] It is clear, from the leases and take-notes then granted by the Duke of Buccleuch and his agent,[8] that every available portion of ore-bearing territory was being surveyed in

---

[1]*MS. Diary*, 29.8.53.   [2]A computation from royalty figs in *Sel. Cttee. Rating of Mines*, etc., 1857.   [3]*Min. Stats., U.K.*   [4]Letter in *Ulv. Adv.*, 5.7.60. [5]Memoir of Hannay in *Proc. Inst. C.E.*, XL, 261.   He was b. 1807, d. 1874. [6]*Deed of lease*, 25.3.54 (by courtesy of H. A. Slater and Boughton Estates Ltd.). " The Duke of Buccleuch . . . with Henry William Schneider of No. 17, Gracechurch St., in the City of London, merchant, and Robert Hannay of Rusko in the Parish of Amooth in the Stewartry of Kirkcudbright, merchant . . ."   The terms of this contract are fairly typical.   [7]*Take-note* of 1.9.54, and *leases* of 8.2.55 and 2.3.57, Boughton Estates Ltd.   A further search license or take-note granted to Joseph Rawlinson, 6.11.56, giving the right to search in the S. of the manor of Dalton, included a workman's compensation clause.   [8]E.g. 22.5.55, (Harrison, Ainslie & Co.) 1.11.56 (Schneider & Hannay), 11.11.58 ,(Denney Bros), 3.1.59 (Schneider & Hannay, Newton).

these years. No further newcomers appear to have entered the district in the 'fifties, the main companies in 1855 being the following : [1]

Harrison, Ainslie & Co.	Lindal Moor, Whitriggs, Gillbrow
Schneider, Hannay & Co.	Park, Mousell, Whitriggs, Old Hills, Newton.
C. S. Kenndy	Roanhead
J. Rawlinson	Crossgates, Carr Kettle, Rickett Hills
H. Kennedy & Co.	Lindal Cote, Eure Pits
Brogden & Co.	Stainton, Adgarley, Bolton Heads
J. & G. Fell	Stainton
G. B. Ashburner	Elliscales

The iron ore output of Furness, as of other districts, is dealt with authoritatively in the published mineral statistics for Great Britain (edited by R. Hunt and made available for 1854 and succeeding years). The following short series, abstracted from those sources, will show accurately the magnitude of local output compared with that of West Cumberland, while other data included in the same volumes show how the produce was distributed :

Table 20

Furness Haematite Production [2]

Year	No. of Pits	Total output (tons)	Shipped at Barrow (tons)	Sent via Ulverston Canal	Cumberland output
1854	15	364,685	332,673	18,512	245,251
1855	21	336,829	313,797	19,181	200,788
1856	22	464,853	445,013	16,290	259,167

Of the ore shipped at Barrow in the boom year of 1856, about 200,000 tons went to South Wales and the remainder to Staffordshire, the West Riding and Cleveland. Virtually all of the haematite shipped went initially down the Furness Railway's line from the Dalton ore mines, and as has been seen, a condition of the Duke of Buccleuch's leases was that merchants used the F.R. for the transport of their produce. It will be noted, too, that the Furness ore production far outstripped that of Cumberland at this period [3]. Neither ironfield was as yet smelting any considerable quantity of its own ore, some 20,000 tons of pig iron being produced (1854) in the two districts together, while in 1855, only 2350 tons of haematite were consumed by the charcoal furnaces of Harrison, Ainslie and

---

[1]*Mins. Stats. U.K.*   [2]From *Mins. Stats. U.K.* s.v. *Lancashire* (1854 Vol., p. 58, 1856 Vol., pp. 57-8) and *Cumberland.*   [3]The Cumberland pits then producing (in the Whitehaven district) were at Bigrigg, Cleator, Todholes, Crowgarth, Eskett, Woodend, Birks, Agnes, Yeathouse, Parkside and Highouse. Ten companies were at work, as against eight in Furness (1855).

Co. in Furness itself.   In 1856, 1424 tons of bar iron were sent *via* the Ulverston Canal to Liverpool, Fleetwood and Glasgow, and this seems to have been the total produce of the locality ; larger bar iron exports might have been encountered in the local charcoal iron industry of the previous century.   Until 1857, all of the exported Furness haematite was seaborne.

Comparatively great as these outputs were (Table 20), they were soon to be much increased.   Of the mining itself, it may be noted that the ore raised in Furness was obtained from only about 100 acres of ground[1] (iron mining being necessarily more extensive in its surface effects than coal mining), and that in 1854 only 546 miners were employed in North Lancashire iron mines. [2]   These workers were shared by eight companies, showing that individual enterprises were not in themselves large.   Some valuable economic data relating to the mines were vouchsafed by witnesses before a Parliamentary Committee of 1857.   The major mining firm of the locality, then, was still that of Harrison, Ainslie and Co., with pits in the royalty of Lord Muncaster at Pennington and the Duke of Buccleuch at Whitriggs and Lindal Moor.   The firm raised more than 100,000 tons annually at Pennington, upon which quantity Lord Muncaster received more than £6000 in royalties, the rate being 1s. 3d. a ton ; and in addition, the Duke of Buccleuch received between £2000 and £3000 from the same firm.   Further royalty payments were made to the Earl of Derby (Lord of the Manor of Bolton with Adgarley), the Earl of Burlington and Mr. Mackinnon, M.P., the total output of the company's mines being about 200,000 tons. [3] The average value, or sale price at the mine, of the ore raised had been 11s. a ton for several years past, [4] giving the total produce of the firm a then value of some £110,000 *per annum*, and the total produce of Furness a value of about £250,000 in 1856.

Fortunately a statement[5] covering the years 1857-64 gives details of the profits of this company, Harrison, Ainslie & Co., and from the figures given it can be calculated that for each ton of ore raised or sold in 1857, worth 11s., 12 per cent. or about 1s. 4d. went to profits, a very similar proportion to royalties, and the remainder to other charges and costs, including railway tolls at the rate of 2s. a ton. [6]   It may however be noticed that payments to railway and royalty owner were often made to the same person, the Earl of Burlington or the Duke of Buccleuch, each being a possessor of mineral rights and a railway shareholder.   Of the remaining costs, that of mining labour does not seem to have been excessively large ;

---

[1]*Sel. Cttee. Rating of Mines,* Thos. Roper's evidence, p. 132.   [2]*Min. Stats. U.K.*   [3]*Sel. Cttee, cit.,* 131-2.   [4]*Sel. Cttee,* Schneider's evidence, p. 122.   [5]Given in Park, *Some Ulverston Records,* 55-6.   [6]*Dir. Mins. (F.R.),* 9.5.56.

an able-bodied miner received about 20s. a week in 1857,[1] and according to the statistics for 1854, each man employed in iron-mining as such was producing an average of 10.5 tons weekly. At this rate the cost of wages per ton of ore raised was about 2s., the further 4s. of the tonnage-price of haematite going on amortisation of gear, interest charges, wayleaves and construction of tramways,[2] searches, wharfage charges and administrative and legal expenses. The firm of Harrison, Ainslie & Co., a long-established partnership, received between seventy and eighty per cent. of its profits from mining, but owned four charcoal furnaces, nine schooners, three sloops, an ore yard at Greenodd, a water mill at Newland and cottages at Lindal, Barrow and Backbarrow. As has been seen, the company's mines raised about 200,000 tons in 1857 and realised a profit of rather over ten per cent. of the sale price of the ore—a proportion, be it added, which would have been considerably greater but for royalty charges. The profits (presumed net) of the company are given as follows :

Table 21

Profits of a Furness haematite firm, 1857-61.[3]
The fluctuations of the output of the company's mines are not known ; the annual output of all Furness iron mines (thousands of tons) is in column 1

Year	(1) 000 t.	Mines £	Furnaces £	Ships £	Other property £	Total £
1857	592	24,342	4,637	697	431	30,089
1858	438	19,596	1,677	495	437	22,205
1859	445	22,500	2,770	155	553	25,978
1860	521	21,144	3,338	336	406	25,224
1861	519	14,027	3,973	167	487	18,654

Some measure of the extent of the output of the Park Mine may be obtained from Schneider's statement, made in 1857, that " I shall pay to Lord Burlington upwards of £8000 this year ",[4] a figure confirmed by Burlington's representative, William Currey, who mentioned that £7000 had been the largest sum paid before 1857, and that the royalty paid on Park ores was 1s. 3d. a ton.[5] Schneider's profits therefrom are not stated, but we may assume that they were not proportionately smaller than the royalty paid by him.

[1]An average figure given by Thomas Roper (*loc. cit*),. who also stated that " we have a mining labouring population of 1,400 ". This, however, must refer to dependents as well as direct employees. [2]*Vide Sel. Cttee*, Schneider's and Roper's evidence. The Furness ore firms had spent, before 1857, £35,000 on light railways and tramways. It is difficult to understand the size of this figure (for only 22 miles of light track), and it can only be concluded that heavy wayleave and other territorial charges were the cause of it. [3]From Park, *loc. cit.* [4]*Sel. Cttee*, Schneider's evidence. [5]Currey's evidence, *loc. cit.*, 115 sqq.

It is unfortunate that more is not known about the comparative profitability of haematite mining, in so far as it may have appealed to an investor like Schneider. The statistics relating to the industry are of limited value in themselves, but somewhat fuller examples might throw a little light on the motives of this speculator, who, before many years had passed, was concentrating almost all his energies on the development of local industry. Yet Schneider's own account of his business activities in and immediately before the year 1857 demonstrates that he had numerous interests in English and Welsh industries as well as in South Australia ; he had, for instance, spent " about £100,000 " on the equipment and working of a tin mine, the Wheal Vor, near Helston, Cornwall, which employed 1,200 workers and was making a return of about £6000 " in some months ".[1] He had also commenced the exploitation of coalmines on the borders of Carmarthenshire and Glamorganshire in the summer of 1856, and had expended some £20,000 on them.[2] He had become chairman of the English and Australian Copper Company in 1854 ; but neither the Wheal Vor nor the Burra enterprise seems to have borne much fruit,[3] and henceforward the solid and steady prospects of Furness haematite engrossed much of his attention, which was turned within two years to the smelting of the local produce. It seems idle to speculate whence his capital originated ; in Australia in 1850, in Mexico at an earlier date, from the Park discovery, or from some investments so far untraced.

THE FURNESS RAILWAY AND THE ORE TRADE

Although the Furness Railway had made possible a great development of the local haematite trade, it was now the latter which sustained the railway company and its promoters, as the following details will show :

Table 22

| Year | Furness Railway | | | Furness Ore Output | | | |
	Revenue £000	Expenditure £000	Profit(x) £000	Total 000 t.	Carried by F.R. 000 t.	Passengers. 000	Ord. dividends
1851 (6 mths)	11.3	5.6	5.7	—	—	—	3%
1852	24.1	11.6	12.5	—	—	—	3%
1853	31.3	13.2	18.1	c.250	226	96	4%
1854	44.8	—	—	365	333	145	6%
1855	44.3	21.8	22.5	337	306	169(y)	6%
1856	58.7	24.4	34.3	465	445	184	8%

(x)Gross profit including debenture interest.
(y)The receipts from passenger traffic in this year (1855) were only £5583, most of the passenger-journeys being very short.

[1]*Sel. Cttee.*, Schneider's evidence ; the " balance of outlay over return has amounted to £100,000 ". [2]*Loc. cit.* He had also spent £3,500 on mining trials on Exmoor in 1856. [3]*Vide Railway Record*, 9.1.1858, where the East Wheal Vor tin mine, Helston, was paying 3½ per cent. in January, 1858. In the view of Mr. D. H. Pike, the English and Australian Copper Co. made no substantial profits until 1860, when new copper discoveries at Moonta overshadowed those at Burra.

The year 1856 represented a high peak of prosperity for the period ; by 1858 a temporary depression had set in, and the dividend fell to 6 per cent. The latter was not restored to 8 per cent. until the second half-year of 1860. Nevertheless, the Furness was one of the most successful local lines of this period, and its record may be compared with a selection of others ; the comparison shows the rapid progress of the Furness Railway as against five other lines in " remote or poor regions ". It should be added that this rapid development of traffic was, at a somewhat later stage, common to nearly all the mineral lines of the north-west coastal region.

Table 23 [1]

Value of Annual Traffic per mile, Six Lines in Remote or Poor Regions

Railway	1852	1856	1859
	£	£	£
Caledonian	1300	1746	1975
Cork & Brandon	266	327	418
Dundee & Arbroath	788	948	993
Exeter & Crediton	511	780	849
FURNESS	634	1270	1273
Glasgow & S.W.	638	963	1058
Average of six lines	690	1006	1094
Comparative			
London & N. Western	2394	2638	2265

Of these lines, the Furness was perhaps the most dependent on mineral traffic, and none of the others made such a great stride between 1852 and 1856, although the five remaining lines were relatively better off after the recession of 1858. Local passenger traffic was of little importance, and the numbers of passengers given in F.R. statistical returns are misleading, [2] while traffic in general merchandise did not exceed 44,000 tons yearly between 1853 and 1856 ; and even the slate carried does not seem to have amounted to more than 11,000 tons *per annum* at this period. Yet puny as the railway still appeared, the lusty sapling was taking the form of the small tree and was putting out new branches during this decade.

---

[1]Data from *The Economist*, 8.12.1860.   [2]The short journeys which were enforced upon local travellers at this period have the effect of exaggerating the importance of the figures for numbers of passengers carried. It seems, indeed, that the F.R.'s passenger services were uneconomic and were subsidised by the ore and other traffic. Between June, 1855, and November, 1856, a check was taken on the traffic passing through the Lindal tunnel. During this period of 17 months, 7494 passenger trains carrying 112,050 passengers travelled between Dalton and Lindal, or about 15 passengers per train. In the same period, only 2107 goods trains carrying 204,566 tons of minerals passed through the tunnel. Figs. from Stileman, F. C., in *Proc. Inst. C.E.*, XIX, 229.

It was already far too promising a proposition to be sold without careful thought and stern conditions.

Such stern conditions as the directors thought fit to impose fell, not without protest, upon the ore merchants of the district. Before April, 1849, the merchants had paid carters 1s. a ton to transport their ore to Barrow,[1] but in the February of that year the railway company was insisting on 1s. 6d. for a similar service, and in the same month of 1851 H. W. Schneider was paying 2s. for the transport of ore by rail between Park Mine and Barrow. Schneider, not surprisingly, asked for a reduction. In May, 1851, the Brogdens' Stainton ore, carried between Dalton and Barrow, was charged 1s. 6d. a ton, but in May, 1856, the toll over the same route was 2s. (but 1s. 6d. from Dalton to Ulverston). In August, 1857, the Dalton-Barrow charge was still 2s. On this last occasion a deputation of ore merchants gave an estimate of how much the company was making from this traffic; in 1856 the F.R. had carried 425,000 tons of haematite at 2s. a ton, receiving £42,500 for this service, or, as the merchants claimed, the excessive figure of threepence-halfpenny a ton-mile compared with a halfpenny, three-farthings or seven-eighths of a penny charged by other lines. The Whitehaven merchants (who were then using the Whitehaven Junction Railway) had, it appeared, saved 1s. on each ton by sending their ore by railway.[2] Whatever the truth of this statement, it was estimated in 1854 that out of every £20,000 in traffic receipts the F.R. took £18,500 from the carriage of minerals and merchandise.[3] It will be understood that these proportions showed fairly well the F.R. emphasis, although the rapidly growing income of the line was certainly not achieved by carrying the ore at a merely nominal charge; and as the mines lessees of the neighbourhood were doubtless well aware, as much as one-third of the sale price of a ton of ore went into the pockets or bank accounts of those who chanced to be royalty owners and railway shareholders simultaneously. Where the Furness ironmasters of the eighteenth century had held the whip hand over the woodowners, the railway directors now had a virtual monopoly over local transport, and were to develop a degree of control over the economic affairs of the district which, if not unparalleled, was remarkable in the extreme.

The merchants in general co-operated. As the profits of at least one ore firm may demonstrate,[4] they did not lose heavily by such co-operation; and on the whole, they were a positive force in railway affairs during these years. The Brogdens took the initiative in causing a line to be built between Ulverston and Carnforth,[5] thereby bringing Furness into rail communication with

[1]See p. 196 above. [2]*Dir. Mins.* (*F. R.*), 27.2, 29.11.49; 12.2, 25.5.51; 9.5.56, 27.8.57. [3]*Herapath's Rly. Journal*, 26.8.54. [4]See Table 21 above. [5]See p. 213 below.

Lancashire, Yorkshire and the Midlands.   This section of railway was opened in 1857.   In 1852, H. W. Schneider proposed to the F.R. directors that he obtain screw steamers for use in shipping ore from Barrow to South Wales.   The first of these steamers did not begin to ply until March, 1854,[1] but by that year the Brogden brothers had taken the lease of the Tondu ironworks and 6000 acres of the Ogmore coalfield,[2] indicating that Schneider and the Brogdens were utilising extensive business contacts and were in fact instrumental in disposing of much of the local haematite.   In lesser matters, the ore merchants as a whole offered help to the F.R. directors, and in February, 1853, they decided to provide free the services of a steam tug, to run between Barrow and Piel for an experimental period of one month " to encourage vessels to come to the said port of Barrow ".[3]

In 1857-9 Schneider, Hannay and the Brogdens, although dependent on the vital collaboration of the railway company, were nevertheless responsible for some major developments in local history.   These are dealt with at length below.

LOCAL RAILWAY POLITICS IN THE 'FIFTIES

The steady upward sweep of the Furness Railway's fortunes, as shown in a statistical table, can tell little of what was happening at the boardroom level during these years.   The year 1848 had seemed a disastrous one to the directors,[4] who, with one or two significant exceptions, showed much caution and little initiative for several years afterwards.   The next important development was not of their making, and was the opening of the Whitehaven and Furness Junction Railway's[5] extension to Broughton on October 29th, 1850.[6]   As the final work on this extension was being carried out, the Lancaster and Carlisle line turned " their attention to a line from Lancaster to Ulverston, principally with a view of bringing ore in that direction", and the Earl of Burlington[7] thought that " It would probably be useful rather than otherwise to us, and at any rate we must not discourage it ".   The Whitehaven and Furness

---

[1]*Dir. Mins.* (*F.R.*), 24.12.52, 4.6.53, 21.6.53, 9.4.54 ; *Wadham Diary*, 31.2.54.   Schneider stated that he was anxious to conclude a contract with a S. Wales firm to send the latter 120,000 tons of ore *per annum*, and in addition to making the steamer proposal he required the F.R. to supply him with 200 wagons.   This was not done.   The steamers (*vide* Melville & Hobbs, 42) were not a success.   [2]Acct. quoted in *F. P. & P.*, II, 236-9 ; *vide* also *Proc. Inst. C.E.*, XV, 94, memoir of John Brogden junior, where his participation in the Glamorganshire Iron and Coal Works is mentioned.   Schneider, as shown, had been connected with the Spilty Copper Works at Llanelly (see p. 202 above).   [3]*Report of Iron Trade Meeting of Furness Merchants*, 21.11.53, Barrow P.L.   [4]See p.190 above.   [5]The correct title of the line.   Although the directors of it referred to " The Whitehaven and Ravenglass Railway ", this title merely described, for convenience, the first section built.   (See also p. 191 above.)   [6]*MS. Diary*, 29.8, 28.10, 30.10, 31.10.50.   [7]*MS. Diary*, 11.5.50.

Railway directors, however, were already making " unreasonable " demands[1] in respect of traffic and other arrangements, and the pressure from north and south-east led to intensified activity on the part of J. R. McClean, James Ramsden and the Brogdens. The latter family in particular wished to promote a line between the town of Ulverston and the Lancaster and Carlisle Railway at Carnforth, thereby anticipating any move from other companies. The F.R. was now, slowly and with some difficulty,[2] pushing out its own extension towards Lindal and in the direction of Ulverston, and the time seemed ripe for the major step beyond Ulverston and over the Cartmel sands. This step, however, was not taken by the F.R. as such ; the deeply indented, rocky Morecambe Bay coastline must have seemed a formidable barrier to men, who, like Burlington himself, rode frequently across the treacherous sands.

Burlington, still very conscious of his lack of experience in business matters, was sceptical when McClean and the Brogdens solicited this new idea, but afterwards came round to their point of view with some misgiving.[3] It was soon made clear that the Brogdens were to take most of the responsibility for the Carnforth line, which would involve two long viaducts over the Kent and Leven estuaries and a great deal of excavation and levelling. In May, 1851 the Ulverston and Lancaster Railway Bill went before a Commons Committee,[4] and received the Royal Assent on July 24th, 1851.[5] Meanwhile, there was underlying but marked suspicion of the Brogden group on the part of Burlington and other F.R. directors ;[6] and to the former, J. R. McClean and Sir Joseph Paxton (of Crystal Palace fame) now adhered. The Scots engineer and John Brogden senior were in fact anxious to take a lease of the F.R. line, and an agreement was actually signed by Burlington and Brogden. But the F.R. directors refused to ratify it, showing that a majority of the board possessed at least a spark of the astuteness of the Manchester railway promoter and his sons.[7] In this way an incalculably valuable prize was very nearly lost to the Earl of Burlington and the Cavendish family. On the other hand, it is unlikely that any change in the balance of power, represented by such an amalgama-

---

[1]*MS. Diary*, 30.5.50; this was Ramsden's view. [2]The contractor for the Lindal extension, Wheatcroft, was in financial difficulties ; McClean recommended that he be " propped up ". *MS. Diary*, 10.5, 11.5, 16.5, 30.5, 25.6, 17.7.50. [3]Burlington had been, if anything, in favour of a line from Ulverston to Bowness-on-Windermere, to link with the Kendal and Windermere line, and objected to the " cutting up " of his land near Holker Hall. Perhaps he had been influenced by Wordsworth's sonnet on Furness Abbey. *MS. Diary*, 30.10, 14.11.50, 5.5.51 & *passim*. [4]*MS. Diary*, 13.5, 15.5.51. [5]14 & 15 *Vict., c.cii.* [6]*MS. Diary*, 15.5.51, 26.5, 28.5.51. [7]In November, 1851, Brogden offered to take a lease of the F.R. line at 3 per cent. for 3 years and 4½ per cent. in perpetuity ; *MS. Diary*, 13.11, 14.11.51, 10.12.51 and 21.12.51, when the F.R. agreed to take half the shares in the U. & L. line " for our protection ".

tion of interests, would have made an important difference to the course of local history.

The Ulverston and Lancaster Railway Company held its first meeting on August 8th 1851, and for a considerable time its directors (John Brogden senior, his sons John junior, Alexander and Henry, James Garstang and Joseph Paxton)[1] were concerned with preparatory matters. Work on the line was not in full progress until September, 1853.[2]

The F.R. board, relieved of the responsibility for this troublesome undertaking, had its own especial preoccupations. Even so small an extension as that from Dalton to Lindal, a distance of about a mile, was not ready for use until May, 1851, the cost of the tunnel and line being much more than anticipated.[3] This extension had been made easier by the co-operation of two of the main mining companies, Harrison, Ainslie & Co. and Kennedy Bros., each of which had taken £5000 of preference shares issued by the F.R. " in return for concessions ".[4] Meanwhile, the directors still had to contend with John Abel Smith, who remained in possession of Piel Pier until 1853. In June, 1851, they had given the construction contract for a further rail extension towards Ulverston to George Boulton of Leeds, John Barraclough Fell having applied unsuccessfully. Fell, disgruntled at the rejection, went into alliance with Smith, and the pair sought to win the support of Lords Derby and Muncaster and the ore merchants for a new railway line from Piel to the Lindal mines. The resultant Furness and Piel Harbour Railway Bill was bitterly opposed by the F.R. and abandoned in 1852 ; but not before the merchants, who had not received all the concessions they wished for, had shown signs of swinging *en masse* towards Smith and Fell. In December, 1852, Piel Pier was severely damaged by a storm, and Smith afterwards agreed to sell it to the F.R.—together with Roa Island and the embankment to the mainland—for £15,000.[5] The banker, having lost his local powers of nuisance-creation, disappeared from the scene, as did J. B. Fell, and Piel Pier was afterwards regularly used by the steamer services of the Furness Railway Company. After the pier had been purchased from Smith, the Earl of Burlington observed that " there seems some question whether the introduction of screw steamers may not render Piel of more importance to us than we had imagined " ;[6] but

[1](Sir) Joseph Paxton became a director on November 15th. [2]*MS. Minutes of the Ulverstone and Lancaster Railway* (*Dir. Mins. U. & L.*), 8.8.51 to 30.7.53 *passim*. [3]*MS. Diary*, 9.4.51 ; Melville & Hobbs, 41. [4]*Dir. Mins.* (*F.R.*), 29.11.49 ; *Ulv. Adv.*, 6.1.50.
[5]The outline of the story is in *Dir. Mins.* (*F.R.*), 14.10.51, 11.5, 5.6.52, 17.2, 11.4, 3.5.53 ; and *MS. Diary*, 22.7, 30.8.51, 26.2, 1.5, 7.5, 11.5, 13.5, 14.5, 2.7, 29.12, 31.12.53. According to Burlington's entry of 11.3.1852, several iron merchants had " practically engaged themselves in Mr. Smith's favour ". For some useful and reliable details regarding Smith and the pier, *vide* Melville & Hobbs, 31-2. [6]*MS. Diary*, 31.3.53.

there never was any question of abandoning Barrow as a port.

In the period 1850-3 the Barrow Harbour Commissioners were not markedly active, spending a few hundred pounds on deepening the Barrow Channel and borrowing a total of £1300 from the F.R. at 5 per cent. In June, 1853, a report on the state and possibilities of the harbour was made by J. R. McClean, who proposed to the Commissioners that the centre of the Barrow Channel be excavated to a depth of three feet, making a depth of 18 feet at mean tide. Then, it was hoped, vessels of large draught would not become grounded. This Plan was adopted by the Commissioners, but the deepening was not effected straight away because of the local labour shortage, the amount of shipping in the Channel, and because, by 1854, a suitable contractor could not be found.[1] James Ramsden, who was the driving force behind the improvement scheme, suggested a practical arrangement for working vessels through Walney Channel to Hindpool, leaving the Barrow Harbour free for two or three hours a day so that excavations could take place there ; the contractor T. C. Hunter, who " rose " with the new town of Barrow and helped to build the later docks, organised the work ; mud from the dredging was deposited in such a way as to make an extension of the F.R. wharves ; and by 1857 the Barrow Channel was deep enough to allow 500-ton vessels to take cargo at neap tides.[2] The F.R. made loans[3] to the Harbour Commissioners, and its directors remained determined to develop Barrow as a port, if only because sea communications were going to be of the utmost importance to it in the foreseeable future.

The F.R. extension to Ulverston, which had encountered numerous obstacles, was not open for traffic until April, 1854.[4] In 1853 the work was retarded by bad weather, and Boulton, the contractor, was reported to be " scamping " the work, while in October, 1851, a local farmer's diary had noted that " The Railway is progressing very slowly the contractors not being willing to pay so high a price for the land ".[5] In 1853, too, a shortage of labourers was holding up the Barrow Harbour improvement scheme,[6] and there is reason to believe that a similar problem beset almost any contractor in the locality at this period. Meanwhile, the Brogdens' line from Ulverston to Carnforth was also proving an onerous undertaking. After the F.R. engineers McClean and Stileman had

---

[1]*Mins. B. Harb. Commissioners*, 31.8.49, 28.8.50, 27.8.51, 30.8.52, 21.6.53, 10.8.54. [2]The same, 10.8.55, 27.8.56, 27.8.57. [3]Of £2750 at 4 per cent. (1853), and £9000 (1855). [4]April 4th was " a Galla (*sic*) day for the Navies on the occasion of the opening of the Ulverston line for Traffick, two waggons of coals ran through from Whitehaven to U'ston station " ; *The Diary of William Fleming of Rowe Head, Pennington, C. & W.* (NS), XLII, 1942, 144. [5]*The Diary of William Fleming*, 139. [6]J. R. McClean's report to the Barrow Harbour Commissioners, *Minutes B. Harb. Commrs.*, 21.6.53.

made the original surveys, the Brogdens appointed James Brunlees as their engineer, this primarily because he was believed to be expert in the bridging and embankment of marshy or coastal land. In 1850 he had been at work on the Londonderry and Coleraine Railway, and had been obliged to build an embankment over Rosse's Bay on the River Foyle, surmounting great difficulties. Like McClean, he later became famous as a civil engineer, and his work for the Brogdens, on the engineering of the Leven and Kent viaducts, earned him praise from men of the stature of Locke and Hawkshaw.[1] It seems, however, that some of this praise should have been reserved for Messrs. W. & J. Galloway of Manchester (the noted boiler-making firm), who undertook the bridging of the estuary of the Leven, and who experienced a troublesome time both with Brunlees and with the Brogdens in 1856-7.[2] Brunlees and the Galloways together made civil engineering history by introducing " a novel form of pile as better adapted to the situation (of shifting sands) than the ordinary screw-pile ", driving the former down into the sand by means of jets of water. These engineers soon afterwards made use of a similar technique in erecting Southport Pier.[3] The Brogdens, meanwhile, had some arrangement for supplying the Galloways with iron fitments from their Tondu iron-works,[4] but this economical arrangement did not prevent the former from sinking into serious financial difficulties early in 1856.[5] In 1855 Brunlees referred to " the high price of labour during the last season " (viz. ,1854)[6], but this alone cannot have been responsible for the problems of the Brogdens, whose business interests were not of course confined to the north-west. The F.R. directors did not show any great sympathy until the December of 1856, when they had reason for a change of attitude.

In the October, Burlington recorded that " I am afraid we shall have a troublesome business settlement . . . with the Brogdens—the Coniston line[7] seems likely to go on, and a line is projected from Barnard Castle to Tebay, which is likely to be very useful to us, and which therefore we shall further as much as we can ".[8] This line, provided that the railway to Carnforth was complete, would have the effect of making a direct communication between the Furness iron-mines and the smelting districts of the East Coast. A few days after Burlington received the news, a group of Westmorland gentry and East Coast railway promoters

[1]Memoir in *Proc. Inst. C.E.*, CXI, 367-71 ; cf. also *Proc. Inst. C.E.*, XIV and XVII (Kent and Leven viaducts), and also *Proceedings* of the same, 1888-9, IV, 401, memoir of F. C. Stileman, where it appears that after 1853 McClean and Stileman expanded their operations considerably.   [2]*MS. letters*, W. & J. Galloway to Messrs. Brogden, 1856-8, and details from *John Galloway's diary of work on the Leven Viaduct* (24.3 to 9.9.1856) by courtesy of Dr. W. H. Chaloner ; *vide* also Dr. Chaloner's paper on *John Galloway*, etc., *L. & C.*, LXIV, 1954, 112-13.   [3]*Mannex* (1866), 250, and Chaloner, *loc. cit.*   [4]*MS. letters*, W. & J. Galloway to U. & L. Rly. Directors, 23.8.56, 28.11.57.   [5]*Dir. Mins.* (*U. & L.*), 5.2.56, and meetings foll., when Alexander Brogden is trying to arrange debentures without success.   [6]*Proc. Inst. C.E.*, XIV, 239.   [7]See p. 191 above.   [8]*MS. Diary*, 29.10.56.

met at Kirkby Stephen with the aim of connecting " the coal and ironstone on the East with the ports and manufactures of the West ".[1] John Wakefield, of Wakefield, Crewdson and Co., the Kendal bankers, was in the chair ; on his right hand, as Vice-Chairman, was Henry Pease and the full might of the Stockton and Darlington ; and a long list of provisional directors of the proposed line included H. W. Schneider and Robert Hannay (representing Furness interests), one of the Quaker Croppers, and John Vaughan of Middlesbrough.[2] This meeting was held on November 18th, and on December 11th the Furness Railway directors, not having met meanwhile, resolved that " it may be desirable that the Company should assist in promoting the completion of the Ulverstone and Lancaster Railway by an advance of money for that purpose ".[3] Fifty thousand pounds were required, and Burlington was asked to provide half the money, acting as joint guarantor with the Duke of Buccleuch.[4]

Thereafter the Brogdens were rescued from their plight.[5] The Ulverston and Lancaster Railway was opened within nine months (on August 10th, 1857, single-line and for goods traffic), and " numerous " trains were passing over the Leven viaduct before Messrs. Galloway considered it ready for other than careful use.[6] There was, as events were later to show, no need for such desperate hurry or for any wilful danger to the lives of the public that might have been occasioned. The Barnard Castle-Tebay line, known as the South Durham and Lancashire Union Railway, was not opened until July, 1861, and its completion was one of the notable engineering feats of the century, for it passed over difficult moorland terrain at the highest altitude reached by any English railway.[7] Mean-

[1] *Promoters' Records and Minutes, South Durham and Lancs. Union Rly.* (MS.), 18.11.56. [2] The same, and meeting of 9.12.56. [3] *Dir. Mins.* (*F.R.*), 11.12.56. [4] Burlington and Buccleuch were to hold equally a total of £150,000 of U. & L. Railway shares as security, and were to be indemnified by the Furness Railway Co. ; *ibid.* [5] Not immediately, however ; the Galloways, after a terse but fairly lengthy correspondence with the Brogdens, were still demanding outstanding payments in January, 1858, " or we shall at once place the matter in the hands of our Solicitor ". *MS. letter* to Alexander Brogden, 21.1.58. [6] *MS. letter*, W. & J. Galloway to James Brunlees, 4.9.57 ; " We presume that we are not considered as responsible for any damages that may occur to the Viaduct from want of the Rid about the Piles . . . many of the piles have very little sand to sustain them—The trains are numerous and pass over without slackening speed ". Passengers were carried on the line from the 16th August.
[7] Nock, O. S., *The Railways of Britain Past and Present*, 18-19. Exact details relating to its construction are in the various *MS Minutes* of the *S.D. & L.U. Rly.*, examined by the writer at the British Transport Commission archives at York. Bouch's famous Belah viaduct was the most celebrated engineering feat in connection with the line. There was F.R. support for the latter, Schneider and Pease soliciting subscriptions of £5000 from Buccleuch and Burlington ; *S.D. & L.U. Report of Directors*, 5.8.57 and *Finance Committee Minutes*, 6.10.57, 28.10.57. Gen. details of the line are in Tomlinson, W. W., *Hist. of the North-Eastern Railway*, 561, 568, and are given there correctly.

while the Brogdens,[1] still heavily in debt, were sadly mistaken if they imagined that the opening of the Ulverston and Lancaster line would immediately open floodgates to new traffic, for in the November of 1857 there was again " stringency " in the iron trade, and during the next nine months traffic over the track did not " come up to expectations ".[2] The Ulverston and Lancaster directors approached the Furness board for a new loan in the same month, and an offer of £100,000 was made only on condition that the line was sold to the F.R. at par for four per cent. preference stock—undoubtedly a well calculated slight for the Brogden family. This offer was declined without hesitation by Alexander Brogden, who had succeeded his ageing father as the dominant force in U. & L. policy-making.[3] Thereafter the U. & L. slowly began to justify its existence, and the two companies worked in uneasy partnership for five years, the F.R. running its own rolling stock over the Brogdens' track.

Nevertheless, the construction of the new line was a considerable achievement. It completed the last link in a railway route between West Cumberland and the Lancashire mainland, and although this final link was a poor and circuitous substitute for the Morecambe Bay embankments envisaged by Wilkinson, Stephenson and Hague, it was to play a most important part in the economic development of Furness and West Cumbria. Furness people welcomed its completion, and had good reason to do so, for it brought them the obvious and undiluted benefits of the transport revolution. No longer was it necessary to waste hours travelling along the turnpike *via* Levens Bridge, or risk disaster on the Leven, Kent and Lancaster sands in order to reach the county town. The town of Ulverston, which acquired its Brogden Street, at first gained little industrial or economic advantage from the railway, which struck the final blow at the utility of the Ulverston Canal.

The Furness Railway system had now, but for one minor episode—the promotion of a track between Broughton and Coniston —completed the first phase of its expansion. Burlington was able to declare in August, 1857, that " so far as the Furness Railway was concerned, they had no reason to complain ; it had been as profitable a concern as any in the country ".[4] By the August of 1858, however, the F.R. dividend fell to seven per cent., and then to six per cent. in the following February, a result of depression in the iron trade. Economies were made by the board of directors,[5]

---

[1] John Brogden jun. died in 1855.   [2] *MS. Diary*, 19.11.57, 20.7.58.   [3] *MS. Diary*, 17.11.57, and *Dir. Mins.* (*F.R.*) for the same date.   [4] Speech in *Ulv. Adv.*, 27.8.57. report of the dinner to celebrate the opening of the U. & L. line, at which, *inter alia*, Henry Pease and the Earl of Lonsdale were present. [5] Judgment based on *MS. Diary*.

but there was no atmosphere of panic ; this was no 1848 repeated. In 1858 the F.R. carried 133,000 tons of ore less than it had carried in 1857, which remained the peak year until 1862. The company had now (1856) £599,933 authorised capital, and £464,420 issued.[1] After slight wavering the dividend climbed up to eight per cent. in the second half-year of 1860,[2] thence moving on to further evidence of solid gain on the part of its promoters and shareholders.

The Coniston line requires brief mention in an economic history of the district. The idea of a mineral track from Broughton-in-Furness to the Coniston copper mines and slate quarries, originally suggested by John Barraclough Fell in 1849,[3] was again broached in the boom year of 1856. An Act was obtained on August 10th, 1857, and the Coniston Railway Company was formed by a group of F.R. directors, nominally as a separate enterprise. The contractors for the line, Messrs. Child and Pickle of Bradford, were soon in difficulties, adding to the growing list of F.R. contractors who encountered trouble at some stage in their operations. Although the excavation of the Lakeland terrain proved to be " easier than expected ", Child and Pickle were bankrupt in August, 1858, and the work was finished by local contractors under the supervision of F.R. staff. This small line, eight miles 67 chains long, and a familiar and useful object to many Lakeland visitors of the present day, was opened on June 18th, 1859, having taken eighteen months to construct. The Furness Railway took £10,000 in shares, guaranteeing two and a half per cent. to Lady le Fleming, Lady of the Manor of Coniston, and her lessees who were working the copper mines there.[4] It was early realised, however, that some of the prosperity of the track would depend upon tourist traffic, and the present modest but solidly built station at Coniston was finished at the end of 1859. The Furness Railway directors and officials working through the Coniston Railway Company arranged excursions for visitors, and were responsible for the launching of the " Steam Gondola " on Coniston Water in October, 1859.[5]

This minor railway extension was a small enough mouse to emerge from such a mountain of profitable investment. Much of the real wealth of Furness, however, was being sent away from the southern tip of the district by sea and rail, and this was the only case in which its hinterland benefited directly from the industrial and economic changes of the 'fifties.

[1]Rept. in *Herapath's Rly. Journal*, Aug., 1856. [2]*General Meeting Book* (*F.R.*) ; 31.8.58 (7%) ; 25.2.59 (6%) ; 10.8.59 (7%) ; 16.2.60 (6%) ; 8.8.60 (7%) ; 19.2.61 (8%). [3]See p. 191 above.
[4]*Dir. Mins. of the Coniston Railway Company* (*MS.*), 27.8.57 and sqq. ; *MS Diary*, 28.8.57, 23.3.58, 26.8.58 ; *Dir. Mins.* (*F.R.*), 9.2, 27.2.57 ; and Melville & Hobbs, 49-50, where there is a brief but reliable account. The copper mines of Messrs. J. & W. Barratt, which were considerable, are dealt with at pp. 222-3 below. [5]Melville & Hobbs, *loc. cit.*

From the end of 1856 onwards, H. W. Schneider and his partner Robert Hannay began to take some part in regional railway politics, and as has been indicated, they were associated with the formation of the South Durham and Lancashire Union Railway. In late 1857, Schneider and Henry Pease prevailed upon Burlington and Buccleuch to subscribe to this railway project,[1] Burlington already having shown interest in the idea.[2] A group of Westmorland investors in the S.D. & L.U., however, supported a scheme for a line from Appleby *via* the Eden Valley to Clifton, which would have tapped the haematite supplies of the Whitehaven district, and which would have brought the West Cumberland ore trade into competition with that of Furness. On April 9th, 1858, Schneider attended a meeting of the S.D. & L.U. promoters as a representative of Buccleuch and Burlington (who had then become the seventh Duke of Devonshire), and objected strongly to the Eden Valley plan. Furness, he said, " could supply all the haematite wanted on the east side of the island, and . . . it therefore seemed to him that this company should not go out of its way to encourage a line which would take from them the dues for several miles, especially as the return traffic to that district in the shape of coal etc. could not be anything considerable. The inducement to himself and to other Furness shareholders in subscribing had been the prospect of the ironstone traffic . . . "[3] Henry Pease, in the chair, was non-committal ; " the Stockton and Darlington directors of course saw that their interest lay in getting traffic from all sides ". Schneider retorted that " had both lines been launched at the same time, the Furness proprietors would not have subscribed a farthing to either . . . he therefore gave notice that such a proposition (viz., the Eden Valley line) would meet with most determined opposition ". The meeting nevertheless passed a resolution in favour of the Eden Valley Bill, and the opposition retired beaten. On May 21st an Act for the Eden Valley line was obtained (21 *Vict.*, C.14), and the latter was opened in 1862.

This development did not diminish the ultimate usefulness of the S.D. & L.U. link (opened in 1861) to Furness industry. Instead of Furness haematite going to Durham and Cleveland in large quantities, as had been envisaged, Durham coke was sent over the moors to North Lancashire. Schneider and his colleagues must have thought of this possibility almost immediately, and it was not long before a local iron-smelting project was on the way towards realisation. He himself stated that " In the early part of 1858 our plans

---

[1]See p. 217 above, f.n. 7.   [2]See pp. 216-7 above.   [3]*Railway Record*, 1.5.1858 ; *Mins. of the S.D., & L.U.*, Extraordinary General Meeting, 9.4.1858, which shows that Roper, Schneider, Hannay and Edward Wadham were there to make up the Furness lobby ; cf. Tomlinson, *op. cit.*, 568, for a general but accurate reference.

were matured ",[1] but it was not until the December that the Furness Railway directors asked him " to take a large plot of ground at Barrow on which to build a furnace ".[2] Neither Schneider nor Hannay was an experienced ironmaster, and so they sought to avail themselves of the most expert technical advice that could be obtained. They were fortunate in obtaining the services of Josiah Timmis Smith,[3] of Windmill Hill, Dudley, who was engaged as their consultant engineer. Smith was a widely experienced technologist, with a special knowledge of continental smelting practice and fuel economy, having spent some time at Le Creusot by way of interval in a long and impressive apprenticeship at Dundyvan, Chesterfield, Stanton and in Staffordshire. He had studied under Samuel Black-well, " the most scientific ironmaster of the period ".[4] At that time, as Mr. D. L. Burn has shown, the scientific ironworks manager was a rare enough phenomenon,[5] and Schneider and Hannay left nothing to chance. Smith supervised the erection of the Hindpool furnaces, which began in January, 1859, and by the October two of them were ready for use. Meanwhile, Smith agreed to become manager of the new works.

Three furnaces were erected, but provision was made for a fourth. They were open-topped and relatively small, 43 feet in height, and were liberally provided with up-to-date technical devices, including high-power blast equipment, as well as inclined-plane loaders. They were situated about a mile from the Furness Railway's wharf at Barrow village, on level ground with adequate space for slag-tipping and the construction of additional works and railway lines, 5,600 yards of which were laid along the Barrow water-front and around the furnaces. Three and a half million common bricks and firebricks were used in building them, thereby giving a stimulus to the local brick-making industry.[6] The land itself was supplied " at a reasonable rent "[7] by the Furness Railway Company.

The first and second furnaces were blown in on October 17th, and the formal opening of the works took place on the following day amid scenes of great enthusiasm.[8] A special train was run from Ulverston to Barrow (still, from the point of view of Ulverston tradesmen and men of affairs, a place at the extremity of civilised parts), and Ramsden, Schneider and Alexander Brogden made the

[1]*Proc. Inst. Mech. E.*, 1880, 372.   [2]*MS. Diary*, 7.12.58.   [3]Smith was b. 1823, and d. 1906. Like most of his colleagues at Barrow, he had enjoyed initial advantages in his career, and was the son of an ironmaster of Duckmanton, near Chesterfield. Memoirs in *Jnl. of the Iron and Steel Institute* (*J.I.S.I.*), 1906, I, 269 ; *Proc. Inst. C.E.*, CLXVIII (1906-7), II, 356. [4]*J.I.S.I., loc. cit.*   [5]For a characterisation of this period in ironmaking, *vide* Burn, D. L., *Economic History of Steelmaking*, 1-10.
[6]*Ulverston Advertiser*, 20.10.59, for details. For the brickmaking firms, see p. 286. The firm of Woodhouse built the furnaces.   [7]*Loc. cit.* ; see also p. 221 above, f.n. 2.   [8]*Loc. cit.*

inevitable speeches, Ramsden going out of his way to deny—correctly—that the two ironworks partners had been assisted by the Duke of Devonshire.[1] J. T. Smith claimed that he had tried to make the new ironworks " one of the best works out ".[2] It had been a long journey through local history since the water-blast furnace had been built at Backbarrow nearly one hundred and fifty years before, and the effect of these modern furnaces was to be far more revolutionary, for they were to cause an important industrial town to spring into being. But just as William Rawlinson had received skilled advice from Abraham Darby I,[3] so Schneider and Hannay were guided by a later practitioner of the ironmaster's art, an inheritor of the accumulated technical knowledge of the industrial revolution.

It has been stated, incorrectly, that the Backbarrow furnace was the first of its type in the north of England ;[4] and similarly, the Hindpool furnaces were not the earliest to be established in the north-west at this period. The Whitehaven Haematite Iron Co. was founded in 1841, and in 1854 two West Cumberland iron furnaces were in blast ; by 1857 the Seaton and Harrington works, belonging respectively to Messrs. Smith and C. H. Plevins, had appeared ; and in 1858, four furnaces were built at Kirklees Hall near Haigh, Lancashire.[5] It is very noticeable that rapid progress in north-western iron smelting belongs to two distinct periods, the first half of the eighteenth century and the fifth to the seventh decades of the nineteenth.

An important phase in local history was now complete. The ground was clear for a rapid industrial and urban development which has few parallels in mid-Victorian history ; perhaps only the Middlesbrough district and parts of South Wales provide comparable instances.

Furness copper-mining, to which allusion has been made,[6] calls for brief treatment in this chapter, for reasons which will be made clear. After about 1830 John Barratt revived the Coniston mines and placed the local copper trade on a firm footing. By 1834 the industry was thriving, and in the words of W. G. Colling-

---

[1]Viz., the 7th Duke, previously the Earl of Burlington referred to in the foregoing text. [2]*Loc. cit.* It seems that he had succeeded; see p. 249-51 below. [3]See pp. 24-6 above. [4]A statement for which Alfred Fell was responsible. I have been informed, by several authorities at different times, that this was not so, but have been unable to pursue the matter independently.

[5]Wood, O., *Development of the Coal, Iron and Shipbuilding Industries of West Cumberland*, 1750-1914 (Ph.D. thesis in the University of London), 273. The present study should be read as complementary to this work in a number of respects. See also (for the Haigh furnaces), Folkard, H. T., *History of Wigan*, 35. [6]See pp. 47-9 above.

wood, " a new era of prosperity began". [1]In 1849 the firm employed 400 men—almost certainly more than any single haematite firm in Furness at that time—and extracted 250 tons of ore monthly. [2] Alexander Craig Gibson, the Lakeland antiquary, who was the medical officer to this company for a number of years, has left a detailed account of its operations, [3] from which it appears that the mining had penetrated to a depth of 190 fathoms in the hillside above the village of Coniston, that a " little town " of sheds, offices, workshops and waterwheels was established at the Ghyll, that as many as thirteen waterwheels were in operation at one time, and that the processes of washing, picking, crushing, jigging and " buddling " were performed at these works. " For several years," said Gibson, " nearly all the underground work has been done by bargain, a party of men undertaking to excavate a given number of fathoms in a certain locality, and in an assigned direction, at so much per fathom; the result of their labours being brought out by waggons along the levels, or horizontal workings, and by kibbles . . . up the shafts ". [4] In 1865 the output was again given as about 250 tons per month. [5]

The Furness Railway caused its Coniston line to be made in order to gain the traffic from these mines, [6] and also, of course, to transport slate and tourists. The slate trade was much as it had been for fifty years, and the quantity of slates and flags sent from the mountain district served by the line averaged about 2000 tons per month in 1865. [7]

The founders of the Coniston Mining Company, John Barratt, who had come from Cornwall, and William Barratt, his nephew, were associated with a much more notable venture. In 1855 they joined with Dr. R. T. Bywater of Coniston, W. S. Caine, James Barratt, John Bewley and the Ulverston solicitor Thomas Woodburne, to search for iron ore at Hodbarrow near Millom. In 1856 their boring operations reached " about 80 feet of solid haematite ", and eventually revealed a deposit of ore which was the largest in England—taking pride of place even over the Schneider discovery at Park—and the biggest in the world until the opening up of the Lake Superior deposits. [8] An account of this mine belongs properly to the history of West Cumberland industries, adequately dealt with elsewhere, [9] but it is mentioned here because the mining and smelting of the Millom neighbourhood naturally came to exert some

[1]See p. 139 above. [2]Collingwood, W. G., *The Book of Coniston* (1897), 82. [3]Gibson, A. Craig, *The Old Man* etc. (originally compiled 1844-50, 3rd ed., *c*.1865), pp. 111-16.
[4]Gibson, *op. cit.*, 111. [5]*Mannex* (1866), 399. [6]Local slate traffic had previously passed down the traditional route through the Crake Valley *via* Greenodd, where J. B. Fell, who suggested the construction of a Coniston railway, had a wharf in 1852 ; *vide* White, *Furness Folk*, etc., 41, for details of the wharves at Greenodd. [7]*Mannex, loc. cit.*, and 417. The slate output at Kirkby was then 6000 tons *per annum*, and 300 labourers worked there. [8]Wood, *op. cit.*, 246 sqq. ; *Proc. Inst. C. E.*, CLXV (1905-6), II, 156 sqq. [9]Wood, *passim*.

influence over local trade, industry and railway politics.

INDIVIDUALS IN LOCAL HISTORY

The role of the individual in any given historical study is entirely a matter of emphasis or selection on the part of the historian. On the other hand, personalities inevitably stand out in any local history that is worth writing. But it is possible to fill this part of the canvas with too heavy a limning in of detail, a most dangerous process in view of the lack of intimate biographical data concerning several of the main characters in the story. Hence only those individual actions, characteristics or aspirations which had, or may have had, some important effect upon the course of local history are given due emphasis here. From time to time some biographical assessments are attempted in the course of the narrative, but their purpose is simply that of enabling the reader to examine local trends and influences as fully as possible.

H. W. Schneider and James Ramsden await exhaustive biographical studies, and it is therefore somewhat difficult to see them as individuals in the fullest sense. Much more is known about the Earl of Burlington (seventh Duke of Devonshire), for his intimate diary, examined by the writer and others, covers the greater part of his life. The temptation here is to give too heavy an emphasis to the part played by Burlington in local industrial development,[1] if only because his diary is such an important source of information relating to Furness industrial concerns and his rôle in them. The sections with relevance to local affairs, however, comprise but a fraction of the full story of his life. Ultimately, the ruler of vast estates, he regarded the Furness Railway and ironfield as a means of securing the Cavendish family fortunes, and his conversion to a genuine interest in matters of commerce and industry occupied many years. We have seen that he very nearly lost control of the F.R. in 1851,[2] when he had reached the maturity and discretion of early middle age, and, conscious of his lack of business experience, he lamented the lack of a " practical " man on the F.R. board of directors.[3] He soon afterwards taught himself, or was taught, to interpret the company account books,[4] and he invariably supervised the affairs of the railway conscientiously. But, as is hardly surprising, he was dependent on others for advice and guidance, and from this dependence James Ramsden, and occasionally one " Macleane " (sic),[5] derived much power over local events. Burlington, however, was too shrewd to be merely a figurehead, and

---

[1]See the admirable article by Dr. S. Pollard in Ec. H.R., Dec., 1955, dealing with the Duke of Devonshire and Barrow. Its emphasis, however, might lead to mistaken impressions. [2]See p. 213 [3]MS. Diary, 19.2.52. [4]MS. Diary, 14.4.52, 3.2.53. [5]Passim.

The first Furness Railway cottages at Salthouse, Barrow. (*see* pp. 182, 198, 243).

An early community centre. The Barrow Mechanics Institute and School (*see* p. 199).

Travelling by the oversands route in the pre-railway era.

Urswick—a typical Furness village.

The Leven viaduct soon after its opening in 1857.   John Galloway of
Manchester is in the centre foreground.   (see p. 216 and ff.   By courtesy of
Dr. W. H. Chaloner).

A survival—the Dalton Court Leet assembles c. 1900. (*see* p. 130)

Hindpool as a residential area—Job Bintley's pipe-dream. (*see* pp. 228-232).

By way of compensation—Abbots Wood, Sir James Ramsden's mansion overlooking Furness Abbey (*see* p. 226).

Cavendo Tutus — the 7th Duke of Devonshire. (*see* pp. 224-5, 279).

Henry William Schneider. (*see* p. 225).

The planner—Sir James Ramsden. (*see* pp. 352-3).

The technician—J. T. Smith. (*see* pp. 221, 343).

A result of Ramsden's planning—Abbey Road, Barrow-in-Furness.

A result of Smith's planning—close-up of Barrow ironworks, 1874,

The gentleman amateur — Robert Hannay. *(see* p. 205).

The bustling businessman — Alexander Brogden. *(see* p. 218).

The newspaper editor — Joseph Richardson. *(see* pp. 296-7, 323-4, 415).

Family representative — Lord Frederick Cavendish. *(see* p. 396).

very soon he had new motives for potentially profitable investment. On January 18th, 1858, he became the seventh Duke of Devonshire on the death of his cousin at Chatsworth, and was dismayed to find that his predecessor had left the Chatsworth estates heavily encumbered.[1] Thereafter he became more and more immersed in Furness industries, at the same time encouraging the development of the resorts of Buxton and Eastbourne, which lay on his estates. Fully aware of the power of applied science in agriculture[2] and in industry, he did not hesitate to use his knowledge and influence as an improving landlord ; although there must be comparatively few in the latter category who encouraged the growth of towns on their territory.

The new Duke of Devonshire was a man of strict rectitude and was, in spite of his ability to master the details of industrial and scientific projects, apt to be literal-minded, humourless and retiring. Intellectually, he was outstanding in his social class. H. W. Schneider, whose life is less well-documented, was more representative of his. As will have been made clear, he belonged to an upper stratum of the industrial middle class, and was in many ways a typical member of it—efficient, self-confident, ambitious, an astute investor and a thrustful and occasionally unscrupulous politician. By way of contrast with the modest and profoundly religious Duke, Schneider was apt to be flamboyant, indiscreet[3] and given to advertising his religious interests and principles from the political platform. Schneider did not finally settle in Furness until the early 'sixties, when his local responsibilities were rapidly growing. In 1857 he stood as a Liberal in the Norwich parliamentary election, being supported by Sir William Foster of the English and Australian Copper Company,[4] and was elected as one of the Members for that City—only to be unseated two years later on a charge of corruption.[5] Thereafter he took an increasingly active part in North Lancashire politics.

Unless further biographical material is discovered or made available, James Ramsden will remain something of an enigma, a mere shadowy figure guiding local railway affairs and industrial development from a position very close to a ducal chairman's elbow. It is known that he was above all a diligent and effective administrator, combining the posts of Secretary and Manager of the Railway Company, Secretary of the Harbour Commissioners, and Secretary of the Coniston Railway. He was Barrow's *de facto* mayor long before that town reached borough status, and the planning of this

---

[1]*MS. Diary*, 26.1.58. [2]For his agricultural improvements while at Holker Hall, *vide* Binns, *Agric. Lancs.* (1851), 66, 70, 91, 105, 108-9. [3]For a good example, see p. 308 below. [4]See p. 202 above ; inf. by courtesy of the City Librarian, Norwich. [5]*Rept. of Committees on Elections*, 1859, Sess. 2, IV (Norwich election).

remarkable place was done very largely on his responsibility. Unlike Schneider, he was never indiscreet, and was ultimately given a knighthood ; but like Schneider, he was full of energy and self-confidence. The seventh Duke of Devonshire, at this period and later, made distant and usually impersonal references to both men in his diary, but never a cordial one over nearly thirty years. The F.R. directors [1] fully appreciated Ramsden's usefulness, and decided in 1857 to provide him with a house worthy of his positions ; as though compensating for the desecration of the Furness Abbey grounds, they caused the neo-Gothic mansion of Abbots Wood to be built on the hill overlooking the Abbey. [2]

It is not necessary to take refuge in the over-simplifications of historical determinism to suggest that the needs of the times would, in any case, have called forth men like this. James Ramsden's interest in town planning was certainly a striking, if not a singular, trait, but for the most part it extended to superficialities. Individual characteristics and actions determined the final form of events ; otherwise the behaviour and background of the industrial coloniser tended to conform to a pattern. [3]

[1] The directors during the 'fifties included J. I. and F. l. Nicholl, James Walker, Stephen Eddy, Alexander Boyle and F. J. Howard.   Most of these represented the family interests of Buccleuch or Devonshire.   [2] At a cost " not exceeding £2000 ", and with a rent of 2 per cent. of moneys expended ;   *Dir. Mins.* (*F.R.*), 27.2.57·; *MS. Diary*, 5.8.57.   [3] The town of Middlesbrough had its Bolckow and its Vaughan as well as its individual peculiarities ; Edward Watkin seems to have been something of a Ramsden *vis-a-vis* Great Grimsby ; and no doubt examples could be multiplied indefinitely.

CHAPTER XII

POPULATION AND SOCIAL CHANGE, 1841-61

ANTICIPATION OF POPULATION GROWTH

During the intercensal period 1851-61 the population of the parish of Dalton-in-Furness approximately doubled, moving from 4592 to 9022. The reason will already be apparent ; iron ore miners, building workers and transport labourers were entering the district and settling in that parish. Nowhere else in Furness was a similar increase recorded, and in several parishes and townships of Furness and Cartmel, as will be shown, there was an absolute loss of population. The village of Barrow, within Dalton parish, did not grow as fast as the township of Dalton, and by 1859 the village itself could count only about 900 souls,[1] an increase of roughly 300 over the 1851 figure.[2] The reasons for this slow growth have been outlined ; an initial hindrance to a more rapid increase was the difficulty of obtaining land for housing and industrial development,[3] while the operation and maintenance of ore jetties and railway establishments did not call for a very large labour force. In 1859 the Hindpool furnaces of Schneider and Hannay commenced working, and the growth of Barrow proceeded in earnest after that date.

It is a noteworthy fact that James Ramsden, and through him the directors of the Furness Railway Company, anticipated this future inrush of people by several years. There is no mysterious prescience or intuition about their actions in this respect, for the flourishing state of the ironfield in the 'fifties gave them every cause to believe that sooner or later heavy industries, and the masses of human beings required to work in them, would appear in the Dalton neighbourhood.

Until 1853, however, the F.R. had little land in Barrow. In the February of that year its directors decided to approach the Duke of Buccleuch with a view to purchasing 1000 yards of the Barrow foreshore facing Old Barrow Island.[4] Trade improved notably during the year,[5] and in the December, James Ramsden advised " large expenditure " on the docks there.[6] The directors then caused more railway cottages to be built at Back Rabbit Hill,[7] the surface of the

---

[1]H. W. Schneider's estimate before committee of enquiry, *Proc. . . . Division of Barrow-in-Furness and Dalton* etc. (pamphlet), 1871, Barrow P.L.
[2]See p. 201 above, f.n. 3.   [3]See p. 200 above.
[4]*Dir. Mins. (F.R.)*, 17.2.53.   [5]*MS. Diary*, 3.2., 17.3., 21.7, 6.10.53.
[6]*Dir. Mins. (F.R.)*, 1.12.53.   [7]*Dir. Mins. (F.R.)*, 16.12.53, 23.2.54 ; *Tithe Commutation Map for Dalton, Hawcoat Div.*, field nos. 143, 144. The land ran N.E. of what is now the E. end of the Strand, and on it Albert St., and part of Church and School streets are now sited.

road from Salthouse Gate to Barrow was raised, and new railway lines were laid into the village. A little more land was becoming obtainable, but there was still scarcely room for the building of a colony. To the north-west of Barrow village lay a number of fields belonging to the Earl of Burlington, but this territory stretched inland,[1] and the directors were still anxious to obtain " additional frontage especially in connection with the proposed alteration and improvements in Barrow Harbour ".[2] Southwards of Burlington's property, and adjoining the shore of the Walney Channel, lay the Hindpool Estate of 160 acres, owned by the Crankes of Urswick and Ulverston. John Cranke, solicitor of Ulverston, had been a Furness Railway shareholder ;[3] and this fact may be of some relevance, for the Railway Company was given an opportunity to buy the estate, and on it a great ironworks and steelworks, together with the important suburb of Hindpool, were afterwards erected.

It should be emphasised that Ramsden and the Directors were not the only persons who foresaw that a town would appear on this land. In August, 1854, particulars of the proposed sale of the estate were published together with a plan showing portions " laid out in lots, suitable building sites in streets and detached villas, including a site for a church, and ornamental pleasure grounds . . . " The auctioneer, Richard Crewdson of Ulverston, was in fact offering a future town or suburb for sale.[4] A plan attached to the prospectus[5] suggested a possible town layout, to cover about twenty acres, at the southern end of the estate adjoining Barrow village. This included a " Furness Abbey Road "[6] and a non-rectangular arrangement of streets and avenues not at all like the close gridiron of later reality and fashion. The would-be planner, Job Bintley of Kendal,[7] was evidently thinking in terms of a superior residential suburb. With a remarkable lack of realism he had sited his residential area near the Barrow foreshore.

The sale was due to take place at the Sun Inn, Ulverston, on August 9th ; and on the previous day an F.R. directors' meeting recorded that " the expenditure of the purchasing of the Hindpool Estate was considered . . . the Secretary was instructed to

---

[1]*T.C. Map*, field nos. 729-45. [2]*Dir. Mins.* (*F.R.*), 10.8.54. [3]See orig. lists of subscribers, Melville & Hobbs, *op. cit.*, 22-3. John Cranke died before the estate was sold. The Hindpool farm was owned by the Crankes of Hawkfield, Urswick, leading progressive farmers, for whom see pp. 75-7 above. [4]*MS. notes* by P. V. Kelly, *Particulars of the Sale of Hindpool Estate*, Barrow P.L. [5]Attached to *Particulars of Sale* etc. [6]Almost in the position of Barrow's fine approach avenue, Abbey Road. [7]Bintley's presence in the district is explained by the fact that he was engineer to the Ulverston Waterworks Co. Although he is associated with abortive schemes (see also pp. 175-6 above), Bintley or his son afterwards designed the architecture in Barrow's " show " thoroughfare, the Strand. The latter is now undergoing demolition.

negotiate for the purchase and agree for it if the property can be obtained for £7000 ".[1]   On August 17th the *Ulverston Advertiser* announced that this purchase was completed, the F.R. having obtained the 160 acres for the sum stated, " together " (according to the original prospectus) " with a Joiner's shop, dwelling house and several cottages, also a Pew in Dalton Parish Church ".[2]   As it ultimately appeared, the F.R. had made an excellent bargain, for twenty years later land on that territory was selling for up to £5 a yard.

Other local landowners now deemed that the time was ripe for selling.   On November 3rd the Barrowhead Estate, belonging to the Trustees of the late Mrs. Town, and consisting of 70 acres of fields and closes to the immediate north-east and north-west of Barrow village, was made available by auction.   There was " spirited bidding ", and certain building lots went under the hammer at 9½d. to 2s. a yard—[3]a considerably higher figure than that paid by the F.R. for its 160 acres.   Greengate Close and Greengate Meadow, in close proximity to the village, were sold at the extortionate price of 13s. 4d. a yard, and Skelding Meadow and Moor Close, adjoining the Burlington Estate, for an average of 10s. a yard.   The two latter fields, together with Long Reins (13s. 4d. a yard), appear to have come into the possession of Harrison, Ainslie and Co., and through this firm's manager Thomas Roper into the hands of the Barrow Building Society, thus making land available for further building activities by that body.[4]   This is the commencement of a long chapter of land speculation in the history of Barrow.   Henceforward the Railway Company, assisted by the future Duke of Devonshire's ownership of another large portion of neighbouring land, was generally able to buy or provide space cheaply when, as a result of its own operations, lesser elements almost invariably had to pay a heavy price for it.

Some three weeks later, on November 23rd, Ramsden " submitted a plan " to the F.R. directors " for laying out part of the Hindpool Estate with the view of providing timber yards and other accommodation, and partly with reference to the disposal of land for building . . .   It was resolved that the plan be approved and that the General Manager be authorised to lay out a sum not exceeding £3000 in the construction of the necessary roads and approaches, sewerage and other purposes ".   The initial wording of this minute provides a useful pointer as to the approximate date of the plan's preparation, for it would seem that Ramsden had caused it to be

---

[1]*Dir. Mins. loc. cit.*   [2]The Hindpool farm equipment was also purchased ; *MS. notes of valuation* etc., 22.9.1854, *Kendall MSS.*   [3]*Ulv. Adv.*, 9.11.54. [4]Postlethwaite, J., *Particulars of the Valuable Estate called Barrowhead,* etc., Barrow P.L. ;   *T. C. Map.*, field nos. 121, 133, 74, 75, 85, 86 ;   *Ulv. Adv., loc. cit.*, and var. refs. in Fisher, *Pop. Hist. of Barrow* (*cit*).

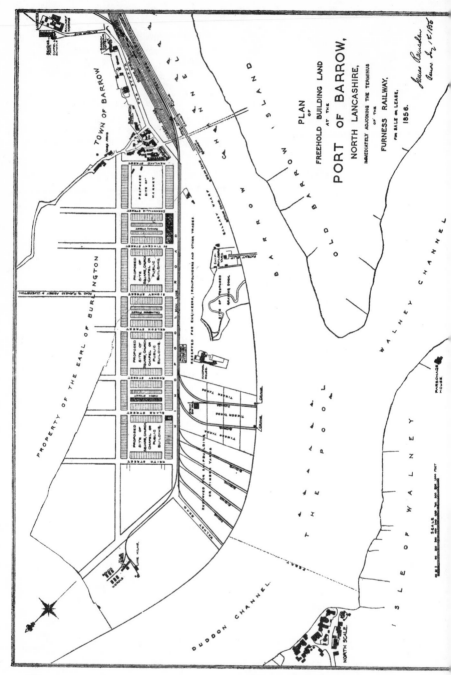

Fig. 6.   Plan of Barrow in 1856 with Ramsden's proposed development.

230

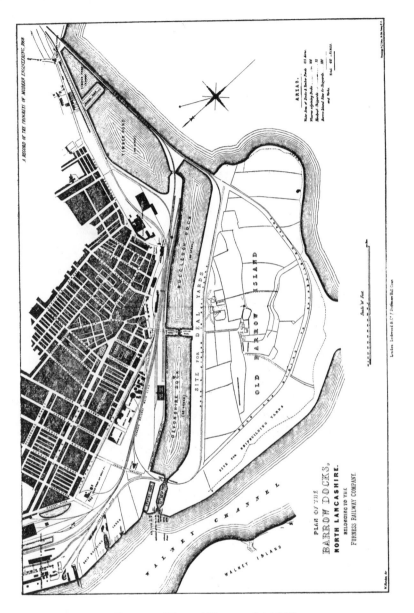

Fig. 7.　Plan of Barrow in 1866.

231

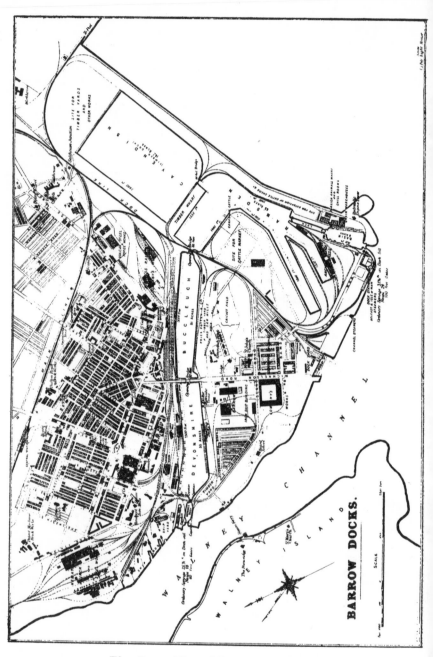

Fig. 8.   Plan of Barrow in 1885.

prepared between the August and the November; and hence it is likely that Barrow's town centre was conceived in those months.

For this is what the Ramsden plan signified. Little over a year later a mounted version of it was made available to encourage industrialists and others to take sites on the Hindpool Estate.[1] He had improved considerably on the Bintley plan by allowing for industrial development on the Barrow waterfront (then purchased from the Duke of Buccleuch) to a depth of 1000 feet or so, and by providing the proposed industrial estate with a railway line. To the north of this land was a further large site for timber yards, well provided with branch lines, and the whole of the Hindpool-Barrow waterfront was translated into about 1700 yards of wharves, docks and shipbuilding space. The remainder of the map showed an arrangement of building plots and roadways. Here the shape of things to come was already unpromising. Free use of the T-square produced a rectangular street arrangement broken by open spaces for " Square, Church, Chapel or Public Building ", and this part of the plan was in effect a blue-print for the bye-law planning of the 'seventies. The main roadways, however, were to be 50 or 60 feet wide, and the side-roads 40 to 50 feet; and it was afterwards shown that as far as the main streets of Barrow were concerned, this was a promise made in earnest. The use of space was liberal, and yet there was no provision for a park or green space, while it is clear that even gardens did not occupy Ramsden's mind. Here, however, there is no mystery, for his aim was to encourage builders to build and industrialists to invest. Even the broad, straight thoroughfares, down which it was easy to lay sewers and gas-mains, were to some extent a concession to mere outward appearance, for they were to show to advantage any impressive facades, frontages and public buildings. The nature of the world behind them was, as too often happened, a different matter. This map dictated the development of the north-western and central portions of Barrow-in-Furness, and its outlines can be clearly distinguished in the layout of the modern town ; in the main axes of Duke Street, Abbey Road and Hindpool Road, in the arrangement of streets in part of Hindpool. and in the disposition of dockside industries and railway lines. Its gridiron shape naturally affected later streets and road plans as the latter were surveyed outwards, and James Ramsden must be acknowledged, if not praised without qualification, as the planner of modern Barrow. His broad vistas anticipated the age of the motor vehicle, and his neat rectangles the 1875 Public Health Act.[2]

[1] *Plan of Freehold Building Land at the Port of Barrow . . . for Sale or Lease*, Jan. 1st., 1856, with facsimile signature of James Ramsden, Barrow P.L. For a discussion of this plan, *vide* Pollard, S., paper, *Town Planning in the 19th Century*, etc., *L. & C.*, LXIII, 1952-3, 93-4. [2] It is just possible that the well-informed Ramsden was influenced by the activities of Baron Haussmann in Paris. These had commenced two or three years before.

Ramsden's plan at first evoked little response, and only a few minor industries established themselves in Barrow between 1856 and 1859.[1] Until the latter date there were only "six cottages and three shops" on the whole of the Hindpool Estate. Elsewhere in the vicinity of Barrow, the first iron foundry was built on Salthouse Marsh in 1856 by William Gradwell for Thomas Beveridge, who had entered the district to superintend the erection of pumping and winding engines for Schneider and Davis. This foundry, like an undertaking started by James Davis at Ulverston,[2] specialised in the production of mining gear; shafts, pipes and pumping engines.[3] But it is certain that Barrow would have remained a small and unremarkable place for many years, had not investment of a more ambitious type given a fresh impetus to the influx of workpeople, and thence to building, importation of raw materials, constructional engineering of all types, and to the distributive trades.

Within twenty-five years, more people were to be packed within two square miles of Barrow territory than in two hundred and forty square miles of Furness and Cartmel. Such was social change as the Railway Age gave way to Free Trade and Steel.

THE POPULATION OF N. LONSDALE TO 1861

The population growth of Barrow and District cannot satisfactorily be seen in isolation, if only because the industrial changes which took place there naturally led to the movement of people in Furness and Cartmel. What later became an inrush of immigrants from all over the British Isles was at first foreshadowed by migration from moorland and agricultural townships in Furness and southwest Cumbria. Such localised movements of people were to be observed throughout the three decades following 1841, as numerous country folk sought to better themselves in the rapidly growing industrial districts of Barrow and Dalton.

[1]There were a few before that period. The builder James Wearing was employed to build the railway cottages at Salthouse, " and for that purpose he imported the first cargo of timber ever shipped into Barrow "—a somewhat dubious statement; Richardson, *F.P. & P.*, II, 245. William Gradwell, from farming stock at Lowick in the Furness Fells, came into the Barrow district in 1845, commenced business as a builder at Roose, built the first F.R. pier at Barrow, and became the timber wholesaler for the district, importing Baltic softwood for the iron mines. In 1855 he established sawmills and joinery works at Hindpool, and commenced business as a brickmaker; memoir in *Barrow News*, 9.9.1882, details in Richardson, *op. cit.*, 245-7, and his advertisements in *Ulverston Advertiser* in the 'fifties. William Ashburner, formerly of Ulverston, came to Barrow in 1847 and established a small ship-repairing yard at Hindpool. His brother Richard joined him at Hindpool towards the end of 1850, and a few small sailing vessels were launched from the Ashburner yard between 1852 and 1859 ; Richardson, *op. cit.*, 245-6, White, *Furness Folk* etc., '35, and infn. by courtesy of Mr. J. L. Hobbs.   [2]Davis, after parting company with Schneider, had a foundry, before long a failure, at Canal Side, Ulverston.   [3]Richardson, *loc. cit.*, supported by *Wadham Diary*, var. refs:

In the early decades of the nineteenth century, as has been shown, people were tending to leave Furness for other districts (almost certainly to the southwards). This emigratory tendency was particularly marked in the decade before 1811 and that before 1831. There was no absolute loss of population, however, and when the rural districts of Cumberland and Westmorland were losing people most heavily (in the decade 1831-41), Furness showed a recovery—perhaps because of the revival of the trade in iron ore (although this is not borne out by the census returns for Dalton and Pennington) and more probably because of a new demand for woodland products and slate. At any rate, the outward movement of people was largely halted, although there was still a considerable drain from parts of Plain Furness and the parish of Cartmel, where agricultural " improvement " was most marked.

In 1841-51, when the civil registration figures are available for use, the natural increase of the district, as shown by the excess of registered births over deaths, exceeded the censal increase by some 300 souls, and—in all probability, before 1846—there was evidently movement out of the district on a somewhat smaller scale than hitherto. In the following decade the reverse seems to have been the case, and there was slight net immigration. The fluctuations and trends of the half-century are shown below :

Table 24

(a)

Decennial rates of population growth in Furness and Cartmel, 1801-61, as compared with those of rural districts of Cumberland, Westmorland and Lancashire, including small towns of less than 2000 inhabitants

Area	Population						
	1801	1811	1821	1831	1841	1851	1861
Furness & Cartmel	17,887	19,065	22,890	24,311	26,747	30,556	35,738
Ulverston township	2,937	3,378	4,315	4,876	5,352	6,742	7,414
						Barrow	3,135
Furness & Cartmel less Ulverston, and Barrow	14,950	15,687	18,575	19,435	21,395	23,814	25,189
Percentage increase	—	4.93	18.41	4.83	10.09	11.31	5.77
Percent. incr., groups of parishes in Furness district :							
5 fell parishes and townships [1]	—	6.76	23.45	7.12	17.67	1.81	3.92
6 similar parishes and townships [2]	—	4.08	12.54	4.85	11.50	0.93	10.0
Cartmel parish	—	1.72	24.98	2.48	2.60	5.80	2.04
2 arable, non-industrial parishes in Plain Furness [3]	—	1.58	20.30	5.75	1.95	11.45	13.45
2 Plain Furness ore-mining parishes [4]	—	5.30	12.50	20.30	7.96	42.9	93.9
Rural districts of [5]							
Westmorland	—	13.23	10.21	6.21	3.39	3.39	5.01
Cumberland	—	12.69	13.41	6.45	3.76	6.02	3.86
Lancashire	—	20.44	20.20	13.29	12.50	12.67	20.46

(Notes Overleaf)

235

Births and deaths in the Ulverston(e) Registration District, 1841-60 [6]

	Births	Deaths	Excess		Births	Deaths	Excess
1841	867	473	394	1851	1024	603	421
1842	869	445	424	1852	1074	685	389
1843	854	438	416	1853	1098	767	331
1844	843	478	365	1854	1142	685	457
1845	868	431	437	1855	1174	602	572
1846	926	524	402	1856	1248	595	653
1847	930	587	343	1857	1200	623	577
1848	914	539	375	1858	1262	671	591
1849	1005	567	438	1859	1271	734	537
1850	1094	538	556	1860	1319	679	640

	Total	4150			Total	5168

Intercensal incr., 1841-51 3809   *Intercensal incr.*, 1851-61 5182

N.B.—The registration and Census districts coincided.

The registration figures in section (b) of the above table show that Furness population increase began in earnest from the year 1846, when the local railway was opened ; and that the natural increase rate accelerated most markedly when the ironfield was being developed rapidly, between 1851 and 1856. [7]   The almost exact coincidence of the censal and natural increases for the second decade shown would seem to suggest that there was little or no emigration or immigration to disturb the local balance; but, as will be seen, migration from adjoining districts cannot be ruled out. The percentages in section (a) of Table 24 show the sharp fall in the rates of growth of the moorland townships, and the great increase in the Dalton district. These falling percentages, culminating in several cases in absolute loss of population, cannot be taken to mean that the natural increase of the fell hamlets and villages was itself failing. The births and deaths for registration sub-districts are available from 1848 onwards, and it is evident that the rural localities were as fertile in their production of people as ever.   It is most instructive to examine these particulars in some detail.

It is not difficult to guess what was happening, and the local historian can almost be forgiven for saving himself a great deal of work by making a common-sense generalisation based on guess-work. Unfortunately, serious historians like to be sure ; and although—in the absence of publicly available MS. particulars for the Census of 1861—it is not possible to provide perfect mathe-

---

[1]Dunnerdale & Seathwaite, Broughton-in-Furness, Kirkby Ireleth, Church Coniston and Torver.   [2]Hawkshead with Monk Coniston & Skelwith, Claife, Satterthwaite, Colton and Blawith.   [3]Urswick and Aldingham.   [4]Dalton and Pennington.   [5]Percentages for rural districts from Price Williams, *Jnl. of the Royal Statistical Soc.*, XLIII (1880), tables in Appx. A, p. 476 and ff.

[6]Figures from the 5*th* to the 23*rd Annual Reports of the Registrar-General* ; from 1848 onwards the particulars for the Ulverstone Registration District are given at pp. 36 and 72 in each volume.   [7]Compare Table 20 (p. 206) and Table 22 (p. 209) with that above.

matical proof, data approximating to such proof are available in the registration figures for local sub-districts (1851-60) and in the enumerators' comments of 1861. It will be worth while, then, to examine these districts one by one.

The registration sub-district of Hawkshead included Church Coniston, Claife, Hawkshead with Monk Coniston and Skelwith, Satterthwaite and Torver. The population of these divisions was, as before, dependent on sheep-farming, quarrying, copper-mining, bobbin-manufacture and other woodland industries. In 1851 their combined population was 3763, and in 1861 it had fallen to 3599. But the births in the Hawkshead district for 1851-60 were nearly double the number of deaths, and the excess of registered births over deaths was 517. To this figure we may add an absolute intercensal loss of 164 souls, making an estimated net loss by emigration of 681 souls. In fact, there was an increase of population in Church Coniston Chapelry, owing to the continued expansion or success of copper-mining there,[1] and this division did not suffer serious loss of people until the following decade. For the remainder, the census enumerators' notes are helpful in explaining the migration which was taking place ; the loss at Hawkshead with Monk Coniston and Skelwith was " due to removal of agricultural labourers to manufacturing districts ", and the decrease of population in Satterthwaite was due to the " uncertainty " of the bobbin mills and the effect of the introduction of new machinery on that manufacture.[2]

The sub-district of Colton embraced townships and divisions not unlike those of Hawkshead. Blawith and Lowick, in the Crake Valley, were statistically insignificant, Colton was dependent upon wood conservation and wood hoop and basket making, there was bobbin-making at Nibthwaite in the same parish,[3] and Egton-with-Newland included the formerly flourishing minor port of Greenodd. The excess of births over deaths for this decade, in the sub-district, amounted to 449 souls. But there was again an absolute loss of population (182), giving a possible net loss by emigration of about 631. The Census enumerators' notes are helpful in this case ; the loss of population in Colton Parish was the result of " the discontinuance of flax and bobbin mills ".[4] The opening of the Coniston Railway, meanwhile, must have injured the slate and copper trade of Greenodd and the Crake Valley, but this would not take effect until 1859.

The natural increase in Cartmel parish and sub-district amounted to 630 souls over the same period ; but the 1861 Census showed an absolute loss of 105 (due to a drain of people from the

[1]*Census of* 1861, *Population Tables, Numbers and Distribution*, p. 582 (notes). [2]*Ibid.* [3]The *Mannex* directory (1866), 436-8, is helpful here. [4]*Ibid.*

237

townships of Upper and Lower Holker), and the probable loss by emigration may have been nearer the 735 that is suggested. The population of Cartmel, however, had fluctuated greatly over the decades covered by the Census records (see Table 24), and in spite of the considerable agricultural improvement that had taken place there,[1] it had in all probability lost more people over fifty years— that is, since the period of large-scale enclosure in Cartmel—than any other division of North Lonsdale. In 1851 Jonathan Binns reported that the land there was much improved by drainage and the green crop system.[2] There were farms of up to 250 acres in extent, and the tenants of the Earl of Burlington were " bound to cultivate in a husbandlike manner " ; iron ploughs, harrows and implements had been introduced by Burlington, although the smaller farmers could not afford them, and James Stockdale had experimented in the provision of allotments for labourers.[3] A few cornmills and maltkilns represented the main industrial activity of several of the Cartmel divisions,[4] but Upper Holker, which lost people heavily, had its Lowwood Gunpowder Works. An enumerator's note of 1861 is explicit regarding the loss of population of Lower Holker, the most populous and agriculturally improved division in the district: " The decrease . . . is attributed to the removal of many of the labouring classes to the iron ore districts ".[5]

A check on the birth and death figures for the Ulverston sub-district reveals that the growth of that town and its environs (Mansriggs, Osmotherley and Pennington) was due very largely to natural increase : an intercensal increase of 1161 may be compared with a natural increase of 1175 (1851-60). Pennington, with its iron ore pits, may have had its immigrants from further afield, and H. W. Schneider, speaking of the pits of the Dalton district, observed in 1857 that " All our surplus labour has been drawn from other parts of the same district ".[6] The Dalton area alone completely reverses the demographic tendencies that have so far been demonstrated ; its registered average annual births (1851-60) nearly doubled in the decade while its deaths increased by only about one-third annually, its excess of births over deaths amounted to 1954 for the ten years, and yet the intercensal gain of population for Dalton sub-district was 4701—in other words the apparent net immigration figure was about 2747. The total estimated net emigration figures for the divisions of Hawkshead, West Broughton, Colton and Cartmel amount to 2746 (another remarkable coincidence of figures), thereby suggesting that population movements in the neighbourhood were almost entirely localised in the decade, and that H. W. Schneider was stating the literal truth. But we must nevertheless be cautious ; of the registration districts adjoining Furness and Cartmel, or

[1]See pp. 65-6 above. [2]Binns, *op. cit.*, 106-9. [3]*Ibid.* [4]*Mannex* (1866), 440 ff. [5]*Loc. cit.* [6]Reptd. in *Ulv. Adv.*, 2.7.57.

238

situated a short distance away, Lancaster, Bootle (Cumberland), Westmorland (West Ward) and Garstang were losing people heavily in the years 1851-60.[1] The following table[2] indicates that some of them came to Furness :

Table 25

Birthplaces of the inhabitants, Ulverston(e) District, 1861
Total population : 35,738

Males		Females		Total	Where born	Per cent
Under 20	Over 20	Under 20	Over 20			
8793	9488	8316	9141			
of which :						
7672	6739	7379	6578	28,368	Lancashire	79.4
254	704	255	854	2,067	Cumberland	5.8
325	798	224	696	2,043	Westmorland	5.8
70	242	49	175	536	Ireland	1.5
95	197	75	164	531	Yorkshire	1.5
53	139	62	115	369	Scotland	1.0
36	61	55	45	197	Staffordshire	0.6
20	69	13	44	146	Cornwall	0.4
268	539	204	470	1,481	All other counties (44 in all)	4.0
						100.0

Those of Lancashire origin must, on the strength of the evidence already given, have been Furness people for the most part; although it is possible that the opening of the Ulverston and Lancaster Railway (1857) quickened the trickle from other parts of the County Palatine.[3] The still very small proportion of immigrants from nearby Cumberland and Westmorland, however, leaves no doubt as to the very restricted nature of the migration under review.

The development of local industry and transport has already been surveyed at some length. By 1861 the balance of local occupations had been completely shifted by comparison with that of earlier decades. In the mid-eighteenth century, as has been argued above, about two-thirds of the Furness population had some direct interest in husbandry and the land. In 1831 the proportion of such persons was well under one-half, and in 1861 it was less than one-third. The local Industrial Revolution, still in its first stage, was taking effect very obviously by the last-mentioned year, although, of course, the national movement of the same name had operated indirectly on the district for many decades. A few general impressions of the nature of the change can be obtained from a comparison of the 1831 and 1861 census particulars. Such a comparison must be far from

[1] *Vide* the 23*rd Annual Rept. of the Reg.-General*, 212, 234. [2] *Census of* 1861, *Pop. ,Nos. and Distn.*, 661. [3] More precise particulars would, of course, be vouchsafed by the 1841 and 1851 census documents at the *P.R.O.*, but it is doubtful whether they would greatly modify these remarks.

239

wholly satisfactory, if only because the 1831 particulars adopt less minute and accurate classifications than those of the 1861 Census.

Between those dates the population of Furness increased by almost exactly one-third, but the number of persons locally employed in agriculture increased by little over 10 per cent. (It is interesting to find that the number increased at all.) Agricultural labourers and farm servants gained by only a few dozens, and the class which was most augmented in numbers *appears* (if the census categories do not mislead) to have been that of the various retail traders. The Furness Railway, which brought new trade to the doorsteps of the latter, itself employed only 55 full-time " servants " in 1861, and in the same year the iron-miners, upon whose shoulders a great part of the local economy rested, were 1038 strong—making less than one-ninth of the adult male population. This figure may not include labourers employed about the mines, nor may it allow for those who still made a living carting ore from pit to railhead or port ; but it is not wholly misleading, for the earliest mineral returns of 1854 gave the number of miners for that year as half the 1861 total. Numerous railway labourers had come into the district and probably settled, and, as always happens when town-building develops, the building trades were beginning to increase. For the rest, the new economic developments were leading to a noticeable swelling of distributive and non-productive trades—a tendency which may or may not indicate a higher standard of living. Probably it does, if it is also remembered that beershops and sanded sugar do not necessarily stand for an improvement in the quality of life. It is noteworthy, meanwhile, that the number of women domestic servants was reduced slightly between 1831 and 1861— fewer women, perhaps, were being forced to " go into service ", even though there were few alternative employments outside the home and the farm. A few score worked in the Ulverston cotton mills, and 344 women in the registration district were milliners or dressmakers in 1861. Nearly half of all the womenfolk over 21 were " wives ".

FURTHER ASPECTS OF SOCIAL CHANGE

We have seen that local villagers were on the move ; and it will now be in place to ask why. Part of the evidence has already been supplied ; the failure or destruction of local woodland industries (particularly the bobbin mills) coincided with a keen demand for labour at iron mines which were only several hours' cart journey from the remotest hamlet in the Furness Fells. Agriculture now offered a barren future to hundreds of people in the fell parishes ; even the sons of farmers, who by training and background were most likely to follow their fathers' calling, were engaged in a desperate struggle to find a small farm of their own.

" There is great competition for small farms," wrote Jonathan Binns in 1851, " among farmers' sons who aspire to the renting of a little land, in order to avoid the conditions of farm servants or labourers. It is supposed that if these young men had the advantage of education and capital, they would frequently migrate to the manufacturing districts to become tradesmen."[1] This remark related specifically to High Furness. In 1849, however, it was stated that in Plain Furness that " The minerals . . . joined to the rich produce of the farms, are a combination rarely met with, and the consequence is that labour always bears a comparatively high price, much higher than the rate of wages in a purely agricultural district ".[2] It can be satisfactorily shown that railway labourers' and servants' wages were indeed markedly higher than those of the farm labourer ; otherwise this statement is a misleading one, for on Binns's own showing (as well as that of at least one farm account book for the locality), High and Plain Furness farm labourers' wages in 1850 or 1851 were approximately the same, namely 2s. to 2s. 3d. a day.[3] It was not that wages, even in High Furness, were markedly low—they were princely by comparison with those of labourers in southern counties of England—but rather that the labourer faced the prospect of complete unemployment if he did not move. Hitherto the bobbin mills or slate quarries had saved him from this fate ; now, undoubtedly attracted by the talk of higher wages in the iron ore mines, he felt obliged to seek one of the new cottages in the Dalton district (herded out of the way, it was complained, in airless corners[4]), to put his wordly belongings on a carrier's wagon, and to commence a new life in the damp and dirty ore pits. The element of compulsion, unfashionable though it may be to stress it, is given much weight here ; the notion that country people reacted solely to the prospect of higher wages may be taken, needless to say, to over-simplify grossly the facts of human behaviour.

Money wages in themselves cannot tell us very much, and the unqualified quotation of a few examples might be harmfully misleading. In 1846, labourers on the Furness Railway received 18s. to 21s. a week. This, however, was during a period of rapidly rising commodity prices (demonstrated very plainly in the account books of the Whinfield Farm, near Dalton), and even the Whinfield wages were increased in 1846. The F.R. and Whinfield wages were reduced in 1848 and 1847 respectively. By 1850, according to F.R. paysheets, a railway labourer (platelayer) received 15s. a week, a porter 16s. and an ore weigher 17s.[5] The agricultural labourer in nearby farms, according to Binns, had " 2s. in winter

---

[1]Binns, *op. cit.*, 102.   [2]*Ulv. Adv.*, 29.11.49.   [3]Binns, *op. cit.*, 103, 105 ; see also Table 8, p. 80 above. Day labour at the Whinfield Farm was paid 1s. 2d. a day with table (*Whinfield Farm Accts.*) in 1850, and the Pattersons' model farm at Roose was paying men 7s. a week with table (Garnett, W. J., in *J.R.A.S.*, X, 1849, p. 49).   [4]*Ulv. Adv., loc. cit.*   [5]*F.R. pay schedules*, transcr. by Melville & Hobbs, *op. cit.*, 39-40.

and 2s. 3d. in summer ; the labourer has also the advantage of the employment of cutting peat for fuel, at 3s. per day, often taking two of his children, who have, for spreading the peats, 10d. to 1s. per day each ; he has also harvest wages and mowing wages ;—all these, with economy and good management, ought to make the labourer comfortable ". [1] This somewhat complacent statement is sharply qualified by a remark in a Furness farmer's private diary for the year 1851 : " Potatoes this Year are about 3 parts destroyed by the Blight which has for so many years been so great a misfortune to the Poorer Classes who depended greatly upon them for food they are now sixpence to 7 pence per stone ". [2] There is no doubt, however, that the demand for railway labour could have the effect of forcing up agricultural wages. Until 1853 Cartmel labourers were receiving 15s. a week, but during the construction of the railway line between Ulverston and Carnforth (1853-7) their wages rose to 16s. and then to 17s., falling back to 15s. after the line was completed. [3] This may explain why farmworkers in the Holker district, having had a taste of higher wages, then travelled down the newly completed line to Dalton, where iron ore miners were paid 20s. a week in 1857. [4] But in general, a great many influences could stimulate the movement of people ; high prices and semi-starvation, desire to be near relatives and friends who had already moved, personal frustrations of many kinds, bad housing (Binns wrote of High Furness that " Most of the cottages are very old, and in the building of new ones too little attention has been paid to comfort, to ventilation, or the arrangement of bedrooms "), and, behind all else, the simple fact that the countryside lacked jobs.

The displacement of population had some interesting minor consequences. In the villages and fell townships outside Ulverston and Dalton only 211 new houses were built (throughout Furness and Cartmel) in the period 1851-61, as against 790 in Dalton parish and 155 in Ulverston. In 1851, 226 houses, or 6.3 per cent of the total number for the district outside the latter towns, were left uninhabited, as against 2.3 per cent. in Dalton and Ulverston together. In 1861, nearly 9 per cent of the houses in the non-industrial parishes were uninhabited, as against 6.3 per cent. in Ulverston (which had started to lose people to the new town of Barrow) and 4 per cent. in Dalton. By 1851 the pressure of persons per household had reached the highly uncomfortable figure of 6.04 in Dalton parish (which still included numerous non-industrial hamlets), as compared with 5.38 for Furness and Cartmel, 5.8 for Lancashire, 5.3 for Cumberland and 5.2 for Westmorland. [5] In 1861 the Dalton pressure fell slightly, to 5.85, and that in Ulverston

---

[1]Binns, *op. cit.*, 105. [2] *The Diary of William Fleming of Rowe Head, Pennington, cit.*, 139. [3]Article on *Agricultural Wages, Cartmel and Lower Holker Almanack*, 1914. [4]See p. 237 above ; see also p. 208. [5]Comparative figs. in *Census of* 1851, Vol. I, xcv.

remained well below this figure, being only 5.03 in 1851. Ulverston, nevertheless, was by far the most unhealthy place in the entire district (more is said about this below), and although Dalton had its " airless corners ", the results do not appear in the mortality figures of the time, if only because Dalton had a predominantly young population. The obvious overcrowding should not be ignored on that account ; in 1850, according to a return of James Ramsden,[1] 117 people were crammed into twenty cottages belonging to the Furness Railway at Salthouse, and the resulting pressure, 5.85 per house, is not appreciated until these structures, still standing and inhabited, are examined.[2] They are solidly built of stone, but cramped in the extreme ; and they were in every way typical of the new local housing of the period. The ore miners' terraces of Dalton were similar, and were equally overloaded. The tendency to overcrowding, evident then and in the succeeding two decades, makes it very doubtful whether the incoming labourers had made a good bargain in exchanging their slated cottages in the fells for betterbuilt but still very cramped houses in an iron-mining village.

Furness was still a healthy district by the standards of the time. Those standards, however, are worthy of brief comment. The mortality-rate of Furness and Cartmel did not exceed 18 in the thousand persons living during the period 1841-50, and the district shared, with the Fylde, the second lowest death-rate in Lancashire. In the following decade it dropped to fourth place out of 26 Lancashire registration districts, with 20 in the thousand. This latter figure would have been much lower but for the evil influence of the town of Ulverston, which had an average deathrate of 26 in the thousand in the years 1845-51 inclusive.[3] Hawkshead, by contrast, dropped in some years to about 14, and the fell districts were usually recording under 20 deaths in the thousand. The mortality-rates of late eighteenth-century and early nineteenth-century Furness have already been examined, and allowing for imponderables and inaccuracies in the earlier calculations,[4] it would seem, superficially, that the health of the district had undergone few startling changes. Yet, on examination of the ages at which local people died in the period 1851-60, we find that no fewer than 32.1 per cent. of all individuals buried in the quinquennium 1851-5 were children under 5 years (the figure being 33.09 per cent. in the following quinquennium), and that at the other end of the age-scale, fewer than 24 per cent. of the Furness men and women who died in that decade, 6644 in all, attained the age of 65. This contrasts strikingly with figures (in a previous table [5]) abstracted from eighteenth-century parish registers. William Close, some fifty years before, had stated

---

[1]See p. 201 above, fn. 3.   [2]The houses are at Nos. 1-20, Salthouse Road, Barrow-in-Furness.   [3]*Health of Towns Report etc. for Ulverstone* (1855), in *Reports of the General Board of Health*, 1850-7.   [4]See, for instance, fig. 5, p. 101 above.   [5]See Table 14, p. 119. The calculations for the 'fifties are based on *Reports of the Registrar-General* (16*th* to 23*rd* Rept.), pp. 114-15.

that cases of phthisis were few ;[1] but out of 3302 registered deaths for the period 1856-60, 445, or 13 per cent. of those occurring in the district, were caused by phthisis or consumption, and a further ten per cent. by respiratory diseases. Typhus, diarrhoea and whooping cough were the next most prevalent diseases, but each of these accounted for less than 5 per cent. of all deaths.[2] It is on the whole, hardly realistic to compare estimated death-rates for the late eighteenth century with those of mid-Victorian days ; not because the former are necessarily wildly inaccurate, but because fifty years of population-growth had radically changed the age-composition of the local populace. It is very evident, from the death-ages alone, that there were proportionately many more old people in the Furness of 1795 than in the Furness of 1855 ; but it should also be borne in mind that the superficially low death-rates of the new industrial areas might in fact conceal an evil state of affairs. Of the males in the Ulverston Registration District in the year 1861, nearly 70 per cent. were under the age of 40, and of the females, 75.2 per cent.[3] By 1871 both quantities exceeded 80 per cent. in the Dalton sub-district (Dalton and Barrow-in-Furness), and they may well have done so in the Dalton of the 'fifties. All in all, it cannot be accepted that " things were getting better ".

Ulverston, which may have had more than its share of old people who were approaching their death-beds, and which attracted the attention of the General Board of Health, was almost certainly as insanitary as it had ever been in the eighteenth century. An Inspector of the Board, Robert Rawlinson, found (1854) that " an air of cleanliness " imparted to Ulverston's houses by their plastered or limewashed appearance was " not confirmed by a more close inspection ". Housing was crowded together, windows were far too small, flagged floors collected damp from adjacent land, privies, cesspools and middens were in close proximity to cottages " and even beneath sleeping rooms ", pumps were situated near to these centres of infection, and there was " no general system of sewers and drains capable of removing the sewage of the district ".[4] Ulverston, however, was being isolated and, ultimately, depopulated by the activities of the Furness Railway Company. The local tradesmen, gentry and landowners were not prepared to take a genuine interest in its local government, and were evidently glad to take advantage of the Inspector's recommendation that " no further proceedings be taken " (the consequence of a challenge regarding the accuracy of the Ulverston mortality figures). The question of a local board for the town was left in abeyance.[5] It was not until many more individuals, particularly the very young, had met untimely deaths in Ulverston,

---

[1]See p. 118 above.   [2]*19th* to *23rd Rept. R. Genl.*, pp. 157, 169. [3]*Census of* 1861, Vol. II, population tables.   [4]*Health of Towns Rept.*, *Ulverstone, cit.*   [5]*Loc. cit.* The Board of Health was, of course, ineffective.

Dalton and Barrow that outstanding problems of sanitation were satisfactorily solved.

The district had its public utilities and amenities, however. Ulverston had had a gasworks since 1834, managed in the 'fifties and 'sixties by J. K. Hodgson, a commercial agent to the Earl of Crawford and Balcarres. Wigan coal was imported from the latter's collieries, and in 1854 the gas was sold at 6s. 8d. per 1000 cubic feet.[1] In 1851, Edward Wadham (agent to the Duke of Buccleuch) was negotiating with James Ramsden about the possibility of establishing a gasworks at Dalton.[2] The latter duly appeared in 1853, £700 having been raised by the ratepayers of the town from the sale of land to the Furness Railway Company, and spent on installing the works.[3] The Ulverston Waterworks Company commenced operations in 1853.[4] The reason for the appearance of such enterprises is not far to seek ; the provision of gas and water could be made into a more or less profitable activity, while adequate sewering and roadmaking seemed likely to throw expense upon the owners of property and brought little monetary advantage to anyone except (occasionally), contractors. Accordingly gas and water-pipes might be laid, but not sewers—a state of affairs typical of the age. *Laissez-faire* too easily degenerated into *laissez-mourir*.

The majority of the Furness inhabitants, however, were not yet townspeople, and the casual visitor would still have classified the district as an agricultural one. It is generally acknowledged that railways and railway-building gave a stimulus to agriculture in many localities, and the establishment of regular steamer services from Piel and Barrow to Fleetwood, Preston, Blackpool and Lytham, largely a result of the activities of the Furness Railway Company, enabled cattle, pigs and malt from Furness farms to reach Preston and Manchester markets cheaply and with despatch.[5] Local agriculture had progressed considerably before the advent of the railway,[6] and the larger farmers were well able to take advantage of these new opportunities. Many of the smaller farmers of the neighbourhood, however, had opposed the building of the railway[7] with some reason, for its opening meant that they lost the income derived from the hire of carts to the ore merchants. The building of mines tramways in the early 'fifties deprived them of any remaining income from this quarter, and Stephen Eddy, a mineral agent to the Cavendish family, reported in 1857 that the

[1]*Health of Towns Rept., cit.* ; *Mannex*, 1866. 395.   [2]*Wadham Diary*, 3.9.1851.   [3]Tyson, *Dalton Abstract*, etc., 31.   [4]*Health of Towns Rept., cit.* ; *Diary of William Fleming, cit.*, 141.   *Proc. Barrow Corpn. Bill*, 1873, 1-4.   [5]Joseph Fisher's evidence, *Sel. Cttee Rating of Mines, cit.*, 287.   In 1857 produce was sent to Liverpool and Preston at 1s. 6d. to 2s. a quarter.   [6]See pp. 75-8 above.   [7]*Vide* p. 177 above.

installation of the tramways had led to the lowering of certain rentals in the iron-mining area.[1] These unfortunate effects were localised, and the general tendency of rents was upwards ; 15-32s. an acre in Plain Furness in 1848-9, and 25s. to £2 an acre in the same district in 1857.[2] In consequence the owners of the most fertile estates, including the Duke of Devonshire, undoubtedly benefited.

According to H. W. Schneider and others, the existence of the mining industry also stimulated agriculture, a claim which is entirely credible. The ore miners, however, not only consumed the produce of the local farms, but were lent to farmers for harvesting and other purposes " to save the necessity " (as Thomas Roper put it) " of bringing men from Ireland ".[3] In other words, Dalton's several hundred iron miners were not only producing considerable quantities of haematite but were enabling agriculture to prosper at the same time. The iron ore merchants, for their part, showed some concern for the welfare of these useful beings. Said Schneider : " . . . we have established a club into which each man pays 18s. a year, who obtains a certain amount of wages. If he does not receive the wages, we pay it for him. Whenever they are sick we allow them 10s. a week, and pay for medical attendance. When accidents happen, we maintain them, and we provide for their wives and families . . . "[4] Harrison, Ainslie and Co. operated a similar scheme, but, said Thomas Roper, " It is quite true that the the miner pays three-fourths of the expense of maintaining himself during sickness, and the club has always a balance on hand. The miner takes care of himself under our advice ".[5] As has been shown, friendly societies were not new in the neighbourhood,[6] and the subsequent record of the Dalton ore miners in the field of consumers' co-operation[7] suggests that they were well able to look after their own welfare ; nor, in Schneider's pits at least, was there any adequate provision for the removal and treatment of men injured when at work,[8] and it was only after a lapse of several years that his much-advertised benefit club began to function.[9]

The ore miners were a semi-skilled group scattered in comparatively small detachments over a variety of work-sites. Unlike the coalminers, they had no tradition of trade union organisation or vigorous struggle, and it was not surprising, therefore, that three decades passed before a durable, if locally originated, miners' union appeared in Furness.[10] But they were self-reliant, thrifty and occasionally militant, and were, as events showed, able to form

[1]*Sel. Cttee, cit.*, 135. [2]*Garnett, op. cit.*, 36, and Schneider's evidence (*Sel. Cttee*), as reptd. in *Ulv. Adv.*, 2.7.1857. [3]*Sel. Cttee*, 131. [4]*Loc. cit.* [5]*Loc. cit.* [6]See p. 158 above. [7]See p. 310 below. [8]See pp. 308-9 below. [9]Schneider was still talking about his sick club and " the course his firm mean to take " in 1861 ; *vide* Devonshire's acid reference in *MS. Diary*, 21.3.61. [10]See pp. 307-8 below.

temporary organisations when such action seemed called for. The erstwhile country labourers who composed the bulk of the mining force began, if only slowly, to understand the significance of combination.

It was among the skilled artisans that local trade unionism first appeared, the engineers and building workers taking a lead in this respect. One of the New Model unions established its first outpost in the locality in February, 1857, when a branch of the Amalgamated Society of Engineers (with twelve members, millwrights and fitters in the F.R. workshop) was formed in Barrow.[1] A respectable and sober organisation,[2] it had little influence on local affairs for many years afterwards ; but its formation was a sign of the times, and it was not long before trade union activity of a much more militant character appeared. Particularly was this so in the case of the Barrow building trades after 1862.[3]

Before that date the annals of working-class life are thin in content. An illustration of working conditions in Ulverston occurs in 1860 ; in the spring of that year a strike took place against excessively long hours in the building trade, and it appears that men had been working from 6 a.m. to 6 p.m., and were working a full day on Saturdays (the Saturday half-day was not then general) making a week in excess of 60 hours.[4] The participants demanded a wage increase as well as a reduction in hours, and the outcome of the strike is not known. Such an isolated example is not in itself evidence that local conditions were worse than was customary at the period ; and bad conditions alone do not produce trade unionism. Like certain types of plant, it must have a soil of suitable composition, and an excellent seed-bed was already being laid in the neighbourhood. Men who had already learned to bargain over their labour, migrants from other districts, were soon to be brought into close association with others who were quickly to learn what their more experienced workmates had to teach. The successes of the capitalist were often enough in evidence ; the workman responded by setting a higher price upon his own services.

In what other respects were the lives of Furness people changing? Little has been said on the subject of education in this early Victorian period. Perhaps, fortunately, there is no need to undertake another detailed review of it. We have the illiteracy figures, and they tell their own story. If any value may be attached to the rough calculation on pages 148 to 149 of the foregoing text, about one half of the Furness children of 1820 did not attend schools.

[1] I have to thank the Amalgamated Engineering Union, London, for permission to view the MS. of First Quarterly Report, Barrow No. 1 Branch, A.S.E.   [2] See p. 313 below.   [3] P. 314 below.   [4] *Ulv. Adv.*, 24. 5.60.

Over a generation later, in the decennial period 1851-60, 1483 (31.6 per cent.) out of 4688 persons married in the Ulverston Registration district were obliged to sign the marriage register with marks. About one-third of the women, as against one-quarter of the men, manifested this fairly sure sign of illiteracy.[1] The development of the National School movement may have made some headway in the inculcation of basic skills, but it is certain that—in face of a growing population—the progress made was limited in the extreme, and may have been (locally speaking) actually less than in the second half of the eighteenth century. Manufacturers and industrialists were beginning to feel the need of a literate class of mechanics and labourers, but were, as yet, nowhere near the point of decisive action.

[1]14th to the 23rd Annual Reports of the Registrar-General, pp. 20-1.

CHAPTER XIII

IRON, STEEL AND RAILWAY PROGRESS, 1861-70

THE HINDPOOL IRONWORKS

The Hindpool ironworks of Schneider and Hannay were constructed upon an ambitious plan ; their original cost is not known, but after five furnaces had been added to the original three, the whole undertaking, including the Park Mine, was sold to the Barrow Haematite Steel Company for £500,000.[1] The cost of erecting the earliest furnaces and allied works cannot have been less than £100,000. They had been designed to produce 800 tons a week, and in twenty-eight days of January, 1860, the output of the three furnaces amounted to " no less than 3,491 tons of the superior haematite iron ",[2] and was therefore exceeding expectations. Early in that year the proprietors were already erecting a fourth furnace, and were aiming at 5,280 tons of pig a month.[3]

They were more than successful. In the winter of 1862-3, M. Samson Jordan, a French metallurgist of some standing, visited the district and was able to report that :

" Six furnaces are at present in blast, producing about 2500 tons of pig metal a week—or an average of upwards of sixty tons per furnace in twenty-four hours, a production hitherto unparalleled in the metallurgy of iron . . . "[4]

The Durham-North Lancashire (S.D. & L.U.) railway link was opened in 1862, making a direct route for supplies of coke from the north-east to the Barrow furnaces. But the economical use of coke and waste gases was forced upon the Hindpool manager, J. T. Smith, by the geographical position of the works. Durham coke—from the works of J. Pease and Co.—cost 9s. a ton at the kiln, but 18s. a ton at the Barrow end of the railway link after being transported about 130 miles.[5] The Durham ironmasters paid only 10s. a ton for their locally produced coke, but the Furness haematite ore was far richer than the ores of Cleveland, averaging about sixty per cent. iron content against the latter's thirty. One local advantage counterbalanced the other, and iron prices in Barrow and the East Coast moved in close harmony and were of similar magnitude.[6]

---

[1]See p. 252 below. [2]*Ulv. Adv.*, 14.2.60. [3]*Loc. cit.* The works were " quite equal, if not superior, to anything in the kingdom ". [4]*Colliery Guardian*, 23.5.63, translating an article by Jordan in *La Revue Universelle*. [5]*Loc. cit.* [6]*Colliery Guardian*, 30.5.63.

249

The average cost statistics (1862) for a ton of Hindpool haematite pig may be compared with the cost statistics of the Backbarrow charcoal furnace for the year 1747 : [1]

Table 26

						Backbarrow, 1747	Hindpool, 1862
Cost of	wages	per ton of iron produced				4s. 6d.	6s. 0d.
,,	fuel	,,	,,	,,		50s. 6d.	17s. 4d.
,,	ore	,,	,,	,,		24s. 0d.	18s. 10d.
,,	limestone	,,	,,	,,		4d.	9d.
,,	sundries	,,	,,	,,		5s. 11d.	5s. 1d.
		Total cost per ton				85s. 3d.	48s. 0d.

The quantity of haematite used per ton of pig iron made had hardly altered in a century and a half ; 1.64 tons of haematite at Backbarrow in 1715, [2] with a cold blast, and 1.7 tons in 1862. Above all the statistics show, as nothing else could, the impact of the coke-smelting and railway revolutions. It was cheaper to produce, and then to bring a ton of coke 130 miles by rail, than it had been to burn and transport a few dozen sacks of charcoal in the Furness woodlands, [3] and when considerable changes in general price-levels are taken into account, the difference is even more striking. Wage-costs, proportionately higher, had not altered in the same degree, and the productivity of the ironworker had increased greatly, [4] although a comparatively large labour force is accounted for in the Hindpool statistics.

It was noted, in 1863, that the haematite pig of Hindpool " appears to have special aptitudes for the making of steel—particularly by the Bessemer process—for which purpose the greater portion of it goes to Yorkshire and Sheffield ". [5] By this time both Henry Bessemer and John Brown [6] had established successful converter plants in the Yorkshire town, and the Barrow works seems to have traded very largely with these firms. Haematite, of course, was non-phosphoric, and was ideally suited for the Bessemer process. It was typical of the growing complexity of the British economy that fuel won by the Durham coalminer was going to Furness to make iron, and that the iron then found its way to the steelmills of the West Riding. But the small town of Barrow,

[1]*Ibid.*, and *E.I.I.F.*, 236. [2]*G.L.*, fol. 364. [3]*Ibid.* One and five-sixths dozens of charcoal per ton of iron were used in 1715, at 27s. 6d. a dozen. [4]A complement of 7 to 8 men, at one furnace produced twenty tons a week in the early 18th century ; about 140 men, at six furnaces, produced 2,500 tons in 1862. [5]*Colliery Guardian, loc. cit.* [6]Bessemer, Sir H., *Autobiography* (1905), 176-7, 180, 187. Haematite ore, said Bessemer (pp. 178-9) was indispensable for his purposes ; but Workington pig was " contaminated with phosphorus ". Accordingly Barrow was his main supplier. John Brown was an early licensee, and in April, 1863, Devonshire visited Brown's Bessemer plant at Sheffield ; *MS. Diary*, 9.4.63.

where the Hindpool works lay, was still only a link in the chain of production. The Age of Steel, however, was on the way.

In 1862-3, 120,000 tons of pig-iron were sent away from the district,[1] but over 400,000 tons of haematite ore were exported through Barrow or sent away by rail, the total ore raised in the district (1863) amounting to 626,121 tons.[2] Furness was still a supplier of raw material to more developed areas. The bulk of the ore sent inland *via* the Ulverston and Lancaster Railway—and part of that sent by ship from Barrow—went to Staffordshire, and in 1862, 60,000 tons of haematite were sent to Yorkshire.[3] Much smaller quantities now found their uses in the South Wales markets, and only 27,907 tons of ore went to the North-East coast in 1863, and a mere trickle to Scotland. Meanwhile, almost the entire local produce of 1863 was carried over the tracks of the Furness Railway,[4] and when the figure of some 600,000 tons of ore is added to an estimated 250,000 tons of coal, coke and pig, the striking prosperity of this line, with only 50 miles of route to maintain, is easily explained. The output of the Park Mine, about 200,000 tons in 1862-3,[5] contributed one-third of the ore raised in Furness ; and since this great source of steel and iron-making material was owned by Schneider and Hannay and was paying substantial royalties to Devonshire, the tendency of wealth to accumulate in the hands of the original investors in the ironfield, and its transport system, was enhanced further. The fortunes and policies of the Furness Railway are dealth with below ;[6] but it is emphasised here that its rapidly unfolding prospects, and the atmosphere of uninterrupted gain, led to a series of closely-spaced and important investments on the part of the railway directors and to further enterprise on the part of the ironmasters.

The possibility of establishing a steelworks at Hindpool was discussed before the end of 1863, originally between Ramsden and Devonshire ; and soon afterwards, in January, 1864, " the arrangements (were) nearly completed " with Schneider and Hannay, who agreed to take shares of the value of £40,000 out of a capital of £120,000. Devonshire was to take shares of £10,000, and " others connected more or less with the district or railway (had) the remainder ".[7] By the following March, work on the new steel shops had already begun, and the latter were expected to be ready by the end of the year ; but " owing to the scarcity of labourers " (a familiar-sounding complaint!) the undertaking made " less progress than we expected ".[8] In August, however, there was a

---

[1]*B. Her.*, 14.3.63 (rept. of evidence for the Barrow Harbour Bill). [2]*Min. Stats U.K.* [3]*B. Her., loc. cit.*, and *Min. Stats, U.K.* [4]Ramsden's ev., *B. Her., loc. cit.* [5]*B. Her.*, 14.3.65. [6]See pp. 258. [7]*MS. Diary*, 29.12.63, 15.1.64. [8]*MS. Diary*, 14.3, 9.8, 21.9.64.

recovery, the work proceeded more rapidly, and the establishment of one of the greatest steelworks of the nineteenth century was on the way to realisation. In May, 1864, experiments with a small Bessemer plant, conducted under the supervision of J. T. Smith, brought promising results, and the Bessemer shop was completed in April, 1865.[1] Operations were at first confined to the making of ingots, rolling machinery being installed and ready for use in the September of the same year.[2] The success of J. T. Smith's steel-making experiments caused the directors of the Barrow Haematite Steel Company[3] to decide upon the purchase of Schneider and Hannay's ironworks and mines in their entirety, and, significantly, Devonshire noted in the August that " the original objects of the Co. are much enlarged ".[4] The successes of John Brown and Mark Firth in Sheffield were evidently a powerful stimulant.[5]

In the following winter the Steel Company directors decided, by special resolution, to increase their capital from £150,000 to one million pounds, and to buy the Schneider and Hannay works for a total of £500,000. This latter sum measured the economic develop- ment of a few years ; from the time of an accidental ore discovery at Park in 1850, and the progress of a works which had commenced production with three furnaces in 1859. The composition of the Steel Company board can best be examined after the railway history of the locality has received further discussion ; it was, however, a Furness Railway-Cavendish organism, with Lord Frederick Cavendish, H. W. Schneider and James Ramsden as its first members (1865). Devonshire, Hannay, William Currey and F. I. Nicholl joined it in the November of 1865.[6] In 1865 there were 25 ordinary shareholders, and the bulk of the shares (10,000 at £100 each) were held by Schneider, Hannay, Devonshire (together with his family, agents and friends), Ramsden, Thomas Brassey (who was executing a dock contract in Barrow) and H. S. Thomp- son of the North-Eastern Railway. Numerous minor shareholders were added to the list in March, 1866.[7]

In 1864, John Brown's undertaking at Sheffield had been turned into a limited liability company with a capital of one million,[8] and the Haematite Company became, financially, the second largest firm of its type in Britain. Its primary aim was rail production, combining the Bessemer process with rail-rolling on a large scale ; in this respect it was one of the pioneering enterprises. A theoretical function of the capitalist is that of risk-bearer, and there arises the question of where and how the new works was going

[1]B. Her., 22.4, 27.5.65.   [2]MS. Diary, 15.9, 27.9.1865.   [3]List and particulars in Barr. Haem. Steel Co. file, 1126C, at the Registry of Joint-Stock Companies, Bush Ho., London.   [4]MS. Diary, 10.8.65.   [5]On this topic, vide Grant, Sir A., The Story of John Brown's (1950), 19-22.   [6]Co. file, loc. cit.; special resolution of 15.11.65.   [7]Loc. cit.   [8]Grant, op. cit., 22.

to dispose of its steel rails. The wrought-iron rail, only one-quarter as durable, was still widely used in the permanent ways of Britain and the Continent ; but the likelihood that any real sense of risk bore heavily upon the minds of the Haematite Company board and shareholders can be disposed of fairly simply. The Seventh Duke of Devonshire was not a man who gambled with his own money or with that of other people ; Thomas Brassey, whose knowledge of the railway schemes and rail markets of Europe and the New World was probably unequalled, held shares in the company to the value of £44,000 ; and the directors were in touch, through their shareholders H. S. Thompson, W. E. Hutchinson and James Allport, with the guiding influences of the Midland and North-Eastern Railways. It is evident that the Barrow group were not merely awaiting the arrival of a new fashion ; they were going to play their part in creating one.

The new works, even by rapidly rising contemporary standards, were immense, consisting of two sheds 750 by 250 feet and containing converters, regenerative furnaces, rail, bar and tyre mills. The converters were to be charged direct from the adjoining Hindpool blast furnaces to avoid re-smelting, and according to an account of 1866, the cost of the metal in the former did not " exceed 50s. a ton "[1]—that is, little more than the cost of the pig at the blast furnace. The rolling mills were designed by J. T. Smith, whose technical acumen was mastering steelmaking just as it embraced fuel economy[2] and furnace design. Indeed, it may be no exag-geration to suggest that the whole vast edifice rested upon the shoulders of Smith and his skilled workmen. Of the Haematite Company directors, only Schneider and Hannay were directly versed in the ways of the iron trade; otherwise the gulf between technician and capital-supplier was complete, and the remainder of the board were railway or ducal representatives.[3] But just as the F.R. directors had found their " practical man " in James Ramsden, so the steelworks owners had theirs in J. T. Smith.

The steel company, however, did not experience the painful birthpangs of the Furness Railway. Adjoining its works were the richest ore mines in England, at Park and Hodbarrow, limestone quarries at nearby Stainton, adequate supplies of sand and water, and growing dock space in the new port of Barrow. Near its sheds

[1]For description of the works, vide Engineering, 11.5.1866, 15.2.1867. [2]On Oct. 21st, 1861, Smith had taken out a patent for " an improvement or improvements in collecting the inflammable gases evolved from a blast furnace " ; Ulv. Adv., 10.4.62. His method, a forerunner of the modern cap-and-cone system of furnace feeding, was to build brick arches over the furnace top, and to collect the gases by an outlet pipe at their crown. The open inter-stices in the brickwork were blocked by charge material. [3]The Duke of Buccleuch, himself a shareholder, was represented on the board by F. I. Nicholl.

was an already developed and lavishly equipped ironworks, the railway system of the locality was controlled by its own directors, and in the absence of local coal measures, supplies of coke from Durham were assured. The whole was a triumph of self-levitation, but, saving the magnitude of the new industry itself, there was little that was spectacular about the enterprise in the adventurous sense. Rather it appeared to follow an inexorable logic ; the men of 1711, bringing their charcoal twenty and thirty miles over moorland tracks and settling their skilled ironworkers in a remote and inhospitable part of England, were the true risk-bearers and adventurers.

By the end of 1867, the company's profits were nearly £140,000, or about 30 per cent. of capital expenditure.[1] The profit, noted Devonshire, came chiefly from the company mines and furnaces. In 1868, a year of relative depression, Devonshire discovered that the undertaking had again " done very well ",[2] on this occasion by virtue of the unfailing richness of the Park Mine. In 1869 its directors experienced worrying moments ; home railway-building was slack, and the Bessemer royalty, hitherto confined to a few, was approaching expiration.[3] These were but teething pains ; the world of heavy industry was soon to wonder at the company's progress, even though the Gilchrist-Thomas discovery was later to destroy its privileged position. Its markets already extended to the New World ; between 1867 and 1869 an estimated 15,000 tons of rails were sent from Barrow to the U.S.A., of which 10,000 tons were exported in the latter year.[4] In the winter of 1869-70 the local rail output reached 1100 tons a week,[5] the firm was the largest employer of labour in North Lancashire and Cumberland, and orders could " scarcely be filled as fast as they are received ".[6]

THE EXPANSION OF LOCAL IRONMAKING

The Hindpool successes did not fail to attract would-be emulators. As early as 1864 it occurred to outside capitalists that the southern tip of the haematite area might provide a suitable site for iron furnaces, and accordingly the firm of Walduck and Company, of Manchester, made arrangements to erect blast furnaces near the

---

[1]*MS. Diary*, 31.12.1867.   [2]*MS. Diary*, 15.2.1868 ; the company was however manufacturing for stock ; and 10.8.1868, when rail orders were coming in steadily.   [3]*MS. Diary* 13.2.1869, when profits were less than in 1867, and 12.3.1869, when, in spite of the approaching end of the Bessemer royalty, the company was again doing well.

[4]*B. Times*, 20.11.69. The *New York Tribune* was here quoted as stating that : " The first Barrow rails in this country were put down three years ago on . . . the Hudson River Railroad depot at Thirtieth Street, and as yet they show scarcely a sign of wear ". The New York Central line was also using them. [5]*Ibid.*   [6]*Ibid.* The Haematite Co. was also in competition with the Ebbw Vale Co. for the Fermoy and Lismore tender ; *MS. Diary*, 8.12.69.

railway junction at Carnforth.[1] The initial arrangements for a Furness Railway-Midland Railway link between Carnforth and Wennington, making a direct approach to the Leeds and Sheffield route, had then been completed.[2] The new firm, known as the Carnforth Haematite Iron Co., Ltd., had four furnaces in course of construction during 1865. These were well equipped with powerful blast engines, had a potential output of 2000 tons a week, and required a labour force of 300.[3] " Ere long," claimed a current trades directory, " Carnforth may become a second Barrow ".[4] The works obtained its haematite from Furness and Cumberland, and did in fact stimulate the growth of the small town of Carnforth, giving added traffic to the F.R. at the same time.

In 1864-5, meanwhile, the firm of Wakefield, Mackinnon and Co. arranged for the erection of furnaces at Askam-in-Furness, to the north of the Park Mine. In the latter year the ground was being cleared, and work on the furnaces was in progress.[5] Almost simultaneously the iron ore firm of Kennedy Bros. discovered a rich new ore deposit nearby.[6] Smelting did not commence until August, 1867, and the aim of the new firm, afterwards known as the Furness Iron and Steel Co., was to make iron into steel on the site. This project was soon abandoned, but Middlesbrough capital and technical acumen were imported to complete and develop yet another lavishly equipped if rather small works.[7] The chosen site, Askam, was on the level shore of the Duddon within a few hundred yards of haematite and within throwing distance of the Furness Railway. The site for a new industrial colony was laid out, and in a few years the townlet of Askam appeared as a satellite of Barrow itself ; one of Barrow's leading building contractors, James Carruthers, was busy there in 1866, and the extension of the works stimulated engineering in the " older " town.[8] The iron company acquired mines which had been worked by Kennedy Bros. and Joseph Rawlinson, leasing them from the landowner and company partner W. A. Mackinnon.[9]

On the west side of the Duddon estuary, similar developments were taking place at Hodbarrow, near Millom. The Hodbarrow Mine has already received mention ;[10] and in 1865 an open space suitable for slag-tipping, about half a mile from the mine, was used

[1]B. Her., 11.6.64. [2]See p. 262. [3]Engineering, 11.5.66 ; Mannex, 565. [4]Mannex, loc. cit. [5]B. Her., 1.4, 12.8.65. [6]B. Her., 1.4.65. [7]The Works consisted of two blast furnaces only, heavily equipped with re-heating apparatus. The erection engineer was C. E. Clarke, of Gilkes, Wilson & Co., Middlesbrough. In 1869 William Crossley, formerly of Cochrane's, Middlesbrough, became resident engineer and managing director ; F.P. & P., II, 166 ; The Engineer, 28.7.71. [8]B. Her., 14.7.66 ; F.P. & P., II, 167. [9]B. Her., loc. cit. [10]See p. 223 above. Over 117,000 t. of ore were raised from it in 1865 ; Edward Wadham was interested in this mine (Wadham Diary, 19.12.63, 19.2.64, 22.4.64) and Thomas Woodburne of Ulverston was one of its directors.

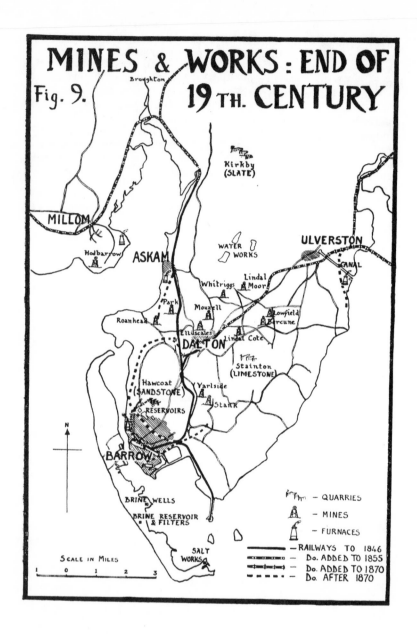

MINES & WORKS: END OF 19TH. CENTURY

Fig. 9.

Broughton

Kirkby (SLATE)

MILLOM

Hodbarrow

ASKAM

WATER WORKS

ULVERSTON

CANAL

Whitriggs

Lindal Moor

Park

Mouzell

Roanhead

Ellascales

Lowfield

Bercune

Lindal Cote

DALTON

Stainton (LIMESTONE)

Hawcoat (SANDSTONE)

Yarlside

Stank

RESERVOIRS

N

BARROW

BRINE WELLS

BRINE RESERVOIR & FILTERS

SALT WORKS

— QUARRIES

— MINES

— FURNACES

—— RAILWAYS TO 1846

— Do. ADDED TO 1855

— Do. ADDED TO 1870

— Do. AFTER 1870

SCALE IN MILES

1   0   1   2   3

256

as the site of another ironworks. The chief projector of this works was Thomas Massicks, formerly of Whitehaven, and the new smelting company became known as the Cumberland Iron Mining and Smelting Co.[1] It remained independent of the already existing Hodbarrow Mining Co.,[2] and its furnaces commenced working in 1866. Nearby, at Holborn Hill, a further workman's settlement appeared during the next few years.

As can be seen, the period 1863-6 was a turning point in the history of the local ironfield. The district was ceasing to be an exporter of raw haematite, and was beginning to smelt its ores on a large scale. In 1863, about one-third of the Furness haematite output went into local furnaces ; in 1865, nearly one-half ; and in 1868, more than five-eighths. Ore output moved steadily but never violently upwards ; from 520,829 tons in 1860 to 784,507 tons in 1869. The race with West Cumberland, in which Furness had enjoyed such a marked advantage in 1857, was now being lost, although the contest remained a close and fluctuating one. West Cumberland reached the million ton mark in 1870.[3]

IRON MINING IN THE 'SIXTIES

Local iron mining altered little in character during these vital years. The industry remained in the hands of a small and well entrenched group of lessees, mainly members of family firms. The Haematite Steel Company became the major mine-owner by virtue of its purchase of the Park Mine ; and Harrison, Ainslie and Co. now had powerful competitors in the Kennedy brothers, whose discovery and exploitation of a great new ore bed at Roanhead, near Askam, now assured their prosperity.[4] The Brogdens, Joseph Rawlinson and G. B. Ashburner continued to work mines as before.

It is significant that the number of exploited ore pits did not increase in these years ; there were 21 in 1855, 20 in 1863, and 20 again in 1866.[5] Only one " outside " group, the Ireleth Mining Company[6] (an undertaking connected with the Askam ironworks) joined the ranks of the established firms in the 'sixties, and it was difficult, if not impossible, for the small man to enter the field. Searching for the ore was costly, and the overhead expenses of the existing firms were heavy ; while the prices paid for the ore, averaging about 10s. a ton at the pit, altered little during the decade. The ore firms concentrated their activities in already proven and productive deposits ; and as the depth of mining increased, so technical

---

[1]Wood, thesis cited, 274. [2]See p. 255 fn. 10. Wadham's advice was asked on smelting at Hodbarrow ; *Wadham Diary*, 3.8.65, 13.9.65, 5.12.65.
[3]*Min. Stats. U.K.* [4]Myles Kennedy, of this firm, was able to boast of a fortune of £276,000 at the end of his career ; cf. Fisher, *Pop. Hist. Barrow*, 124.
[5]*Min. Stats. U.K.* [6]According to *Wadham Diary*, 25.8.64, there were two Ireleth Mining companies, one being apparently a concern of the Brogdens. For a reference to the other, *vide F.P. & P.*, II, 164.

changes were forced upon them—the adoption of more powerful winding and pumping gear, and sinking and boring equipment. But a writer in *The Engineer*[1] in 1871 suggested that the mining technique employed at the Lindal Moor pits was still rather primitive at that time, and it is clear that the local industry as a whole had not yet fully emerged from the era of the jackroll and the horse gin. [2] Much still depended on the hard physical labour of the ore-miner, whose numbers greatly increased during the period. [3]   The main improvements seem to have been in transport of the ore, [4] and as tramways were continually extended, light locomotives were used to draw wagons from the mines to the F.R. sidings.

The royalties paid to landlords, which according to later arguments had a depressive effect upon wages and profits, [5] altered little at this stage, and varied from 1s. 3d. to 2s. a ton. [6]   It was stated in July, 1871, that the total royalties paid in the Dalton district amounted to between £40,000 and £50,000 *per annum*, [7] a figure which implies that the lower of the two rates given was nearest to the average.   The Dukes of Buccleuch and Devonshire were, of course, still the main recipients of these payments.   The mining proprietors were themselves accused of profiteering ; [8] but, lucrative as the trade then was, the railway and ducal group were concentrating larger sums in their banking accounts and reserve funds than were the mining firms, and were able to re-invest these in local industries.

Much timber was used in the iron mines, and the importation of props from the Baltic became a major activity of the port of Barrow. As the timber was required for other purposes—building and railway sleepers—so the new port became a storage and redistribution centre.

RAILWAY DEVELOPMENT IN THE 'SIXTIES

Prosperous as the Furness Railway had been during the 'fifties, it was even more so during the next ten years.   This prosperity-phenomenon, however, was common to the mineral lines of the north-west coast, all of which gained notably from the Bessemer

---

[1]*The Engineer*, 28.7.71.   [2]Kendall, J. D., *Proc. N. of E. Inst. of M. & M.E.*, 1885-6, 99.   [3]In 1873, it was stated that 3222 persons were employed about the Lancashire haematite mines ; Kendall, *op. cit.*, 98.   [4]*Wadham Diary*, 26.2, 24.5.61, 8.3.62, 10.1.63, 29.3.64. 24.5.64, 2.12.64.   [5]Chiefly on wages ; cf. Wm. Kellett's ev., *R. Comm. Mining Royalties* (1*st Report*), 1890, Ques. 3233.   [6]*R. Comm.* (2*nd Rept*)., *Appx. XLVI*, for local examples. [7]*The Engineer, loc. cit.*   [8]*B. Her.*, 29.8.1863 ; according to William Presow of the Ulverston Guardians, the proprietors were " shovelling money by spadefulls into their pockets ", and were fortunate to escape poor rates.

boom and the growing market for non-phosphoric ore. The record
of these lines is best illustrated by a table of average yearly dividends. It should be borne in mind that the average dividend of all
British railway companies was only 4 per cent. in 1863-66 :

Table 27

North-Western Lines : Average Yearly Dividend, Per Cent. , Ord. Cap.

Line	1858	1859	1860	1861	1862	1863	1864	1863-6(ave.)	1870-3
Furness	6½	6½	7½	8	8	8½	10	9½	9½
Whitehaven & F. Junc.	1¼	2½	3½	3⅛	2¾	5¼	5¾	9½	8(1)
Whitehaven Junc.	4½	7	8	5½	7	8½	10	11¼	10(2)
Whitehaven, Cleator & Egremont	7	8	10	10	10	13½	12	9	11½
Maryport & Carlisle	4½	5¾	6¾	7	6½	8½	9	9½	12¼

(1) Paid by the F.R.   (2) Paid by the L. & N.W.R.

Each of these companies worked small systems, and each
owed its profitability to the carriage of ore and fuel.   By 1863 the
Furness company had purchased the Coniston and Ulverston and
Lancaster lines ; it was expending large sums on the doubling of
tracks, rolling stock and general improvement of its system, so much
so that while its total capital expenditure for 1846-60 amounted to
£584,018,[1] the figure had risen to £1,185,941 by March, 1863 ;[2]
and yet it was able to pay dividends between four and six per cent.
higher than the average paid by all British companies.   On the
other hand, as a " lightweight " among railway lines, it had few of
the burdensome commitments which arose from the provision of
amenities for a large number of passengers, or from the obligation
to cater for a mass of varied merchandise.   A more intimate record
of its progress is contained in the following particulars,[3] which of
course can give no indication of the sums paid to shareholders, but
which do serve to indicate the increasing profitability of the line,
not reflected commensurately in the rise of the company dividends.
It will be seen that the net receipts of the line bear only a broad
relation to the increase of the Furness ore output ; understandably,
for the establishment of local furnaces gave the F.R. an increasing
traffic in the carriage of coal, coke and pig, and Cumberland as well
as Furness ores were carried inland down the Ulverston and
Lancaster line (viz. to Carnforth) towards the West Riding and
Midlands.

[1]Herapath's Rly. Journal, Aug., 1860.   [2]B. Her., 7.3.1863.   [1] Abstracted
from the published Board of Trade Railway Returns.

Table 28

F.R. Receipts and Expenditure, 1860-70 (£000)

Year	Receipts from all sources	Total working expenditure	Net receipts	Average ord. div. (%)	Furness ore output (000 t.)
1860	71.7	31.8	39.9	7½	521
1861	76.5	35.0	41.5	8	519
1862	131.0	57.6	73.4	8	559
1863	154.6	74.1	80.5	8½	658
1864	177.4	?	?	10	691
1865	176.2	101.5	74.7	10	607
1866	236.6	114.8	121.8	10	686
1867	279.1	139.6	139.5	9	667
1868	272.1	121.3	150.8	8	768
1869	287.5	123.4	164.1	6½	785
1870	334.9	136.0	198.9	8½	872

The fall of the dividend in 1867 is explained partly by a slight falling off in the iron trade, but largely by the extreme sensitivity of the company (which was heavily indebted and was making great investments) to this recession.[1]   Its total capital in December, 1866, was as follows:[2]

	Authorised	Issued
Ordinary capital	£2,284,500	£880,462
Preference ,,		£832,500
Debenture	£715,766	£481,323
	£3,000,266	£2,194,285

The story which accompanies this statistical record is an eventful one.   It has been outlined several times,[3] and since the railway history of the north-west coast is now a well-explored subject,[4] the reader may be spared a very detailed account of the month-by-month activities of the Furness Railway board and its antagonists or collaborators.   It is plain that the successes of the F.R. were not due to any especial qualities or astuteness on the part of its directors, who enjoyed much the same fortunes and opportunities as other men of that time, class, and region.   A review of their deeds is valuable only in so far as it throws light on the motives of men who, by a series of acts of investment, brought into being a major industrial town.

[1] James Ramsden (reptd. in *B. Times*, 8.5.69) said " no doubt the interest on that capital which is not immediately remunerative reduced our dividend.   Our capital is little short of three million ".   [2] *Brit. Parly. Papers*. (1867), LXII, 516.
[3] E.g., Pollard, S., and Marshall, J. D., *The Furness Railway and the Growth of Barrow, Jnl. of Transport History*, Vol. I, No. 2 (Nov. 1953), 109-126 ; Gradon, W. Mc.G, *The Furness Railway : Its Rise and Development* (1946) ; Melville & Hobbs, *op. cit.*, 51 sqq.   [4] Pollard, S., *North-West Coast Railway Politics*, C. & W. (NS), LII, 1953, 160 sqq.

From the standpoint of general railway politics, the Furness Railway was distinguished by one salient characteristic ; it remained an independent line, and was not absorbed by any larger company. Since it was never in any real danger of such absorption in the 'sixties, the " political" manoeuvrings of the locality have much of the merely parochial and insignificant about them. A recent study[1] has shown that although Furness and West Cumberland provided a possible railway route to Scotland, and although two great rival companies—the Midland, and London and North Western—came to exert considerable influence in the region, no far-reaching or successful attempt to amalgamate the north-western coastal lines, in the interests of a "through route", was made in these years. Accordingly the Furness (which might very well have com-manded a sale price formidable even in the eyes of one of the major companies) was left to exploit and develop its own district in com-parative peace, and was able to bargain and collaborate with the Midland Railway almost as an equal. Its geographical position reduced its vulnerability, and it was obliged to make only one defensive foray outside its chosen territory.[2] As a consequence, capital which might easily have been devoted to the expansion of the company's system, in other circumstances and in an earlier stage of national railway history,[3] was invested in local port installations and industries. The Barrow Haematite Steel Company, which helped to girdle the world with steel rails, was one result of this policy ; the phenomenal enlargement of the town of Barrow was another.

The Furness district was becoming steadily more industrialised during the 'sixties, and the local ironfield was rising to importance ; but the F.R. directors, who were naturally concerned with their traffic first and foremost, were fully aware that their territory lacked any industrial hinterland. Their main hope in attracting traffic, therefore, lay seawards. If the port facilities of Barrow could be rendered steadily more attractive, and if larger companies could be encouraged to send goods and passengers in the Furness direction, the F.R. problems, it was hoped, would be largely solved. If Barrow, stage by stage and as part of a policy of planning, could be made into an industrial stronghold as well, manufactures and commerce would stimulate each other, and an ever greater variety of trade and industry would be attracted to the neighbourhood. In this way the former ore-shipping hamlet might very well become a minor Sheffield and Liverpool combined. These considerations, which

---

[1] *Loc. cit.* [2] Viz., the purchase by the F.R. of the Whitehaven and Furness Junction Railway in 1865.
[3] *Vide*, for instance, the well-known story of the Midland Railway, which started as a small line in the Nottinghamshire coalfield ; Stretton, C. E., *History of the Midland Railway* (1901). An even better example is that of the North-Eastern Railway (Tomlinson, *passim*) which had functions in Durham and Cleve-land not unlike those of the F.R. in Furness ; but it did in fact expand rapidly, and it invested in docks rather than industries when " exterior " investment is considered.

seem intemperate and visionary at first glance, undoubtedly lay in the minds of a group of sober and by no means foolhardy men ; and they throw much light on the atmosphere and state of mind to which groups of influential capitalists, in this industrial " Golden Age ", were accustomed.

The idea of the ambitious enlargement of Barrow harbour originated as early as 1861—from suggestions put forward by J. R. MacClean,[1] who, without doubt, had his own professional engineering prospects and fees to consider. Devonshire remarked (characteristically) that " this is a serious question requiring much consideration ".[2] An F.R. petition for powers to construct docks was considered but postponed for a year,[3] and in August, 1862, the matter was again raised on the F.R. board.[4] Ramsden was asked to approach the directors of the Midland Railway, who, it was thought, might be interested in such a project. The Midland system had thrown out a tentacle as far as Lancaster by its use of the " Little " North-Western line between Skipton and that town. This connection enabled the Midland to reach the Lancashire coast and to utilise the unsatisfactory steamer landing at Poulton (Morecambe).[5] Otherwise its way to the north was blocked by the L. & N.W., over whose Lancaster and Carlisle section[6] it had to forward its Scotland-bound traffic. The M.R. still had no direct link with Furness territory, but its line down the Lune Valley from Clapham to Lancaster Castle station ran not many miles from Carnforth junction, at the terminus of the Ulverston and Lancaster line, which had been taken over by the F.R. in the winter of 1861-2.[7] (Wennington, a village on the M.R.—" Little " North-Western line some ten miles N.E. of Lancaster, was the point chosen for a connection with Carnforth and with the F.R. system.)

In September, 1862, the Midland triumvirate Beale, Hutchinson and Allport visited Furness to discuss with the local directors " the prospect of connecting themselves with our proposed docks by a line from Carnforth to Wennington ".[8] The Furness company

---

[1]*MS. Diary*, 7.8.61. [2]*Ibid.* [3]*MS. Diary*, 15.10.61. [4]*MS. Diary*, 20.8.62.
[5]Stretton, *op. cit.*, 147-8; Williams, *The Midland Railway*, 209. [6]The line of the Lancaster & Carlisle company was taken by the L. & N.W. in 1859 on a 900-years' lease. For a full acct., Stretton, *loc. cit.* [7]A detailed account of the last few " independent " years of the Ulverston & Lancaster line is omitted as having little value. Briefly, the line began to pay its way in 1859-60 ; there were rumours that the Brogdens might sell out to the L. & N.W. ; Currey and Ramsden began to press for its purchase by the F.R. ; and on October 15th, 1861, Alexander Brogden proposed a lease of the line to the F.R. A draft agreement was accepted in the December, the U. & L. shareholders having 5 per cent. preference stock passed over to them in payment for the line. The Ulverston Canal, purchased previously by the Brogdens, was bought by the F.R. for £22,000 at the same time : *Dir. Mins. (U. & L.)*, 23.2.59, 31.8.59 and *passim* to 21.1.62 ; *Dir. Mins. (F.R.)* ; *MS. Diary*. [8]*MS. Diary*, 26.9.62.

was required to find half the necessary capital, and the Midland would then agree " to transfer all their Irish traffic from Morecambe to Barrow ".[1] This proposal acted as a profound stimulus to the F.R. directors, and a few days later, on September 30th, Devonshire and Ramsden went to Liverpool and Birkenhead to " get a better notion of the works we contemplate at Barrow ".[2] On the 9th of the following month the F.R. board decided to obtain powers to build these docks.[3] Hence, just as Devonshire later clarified his " notion " of a steelworks in Sheffield, so the great dock installations of the Mersey provided the Furness projectors with a pattern.

The Furness men soon experienced difficulty in dealing with the hardened negotiators of the Midland. The former submitted a memorandum in which, briefly, it was proposed that, firstly, the capital of £120,000 for the Carnforth-Wennington line was to be held in equal shares ; that the two companies were to exchange running powers between Leeds and Bradford, and Barrow, Piel and Coniston ;[4] that the Midland were not to construct any new lines west of the Lancaster and Carlisle Railway ; that the M.R. was to work the Carnforth-Wennington ; and that the whole traffic between the Midland system and the Lake District and Ireland was to be carried over the Furness line.[5] The third item was the cause of contention ; the Midland had given notice of a Bill for a line which was to run from Milnthorpe to Arnside (provisionally known as the " Kendal and Ulverston "), and the F.R. board was determined to oppose this project,[6] by which the Midland intended to use a short length of the Ulverston and Lancaster (F.R.) line to reach Kendal along the Kent valley. The self-assurance of this proposal not only annoyed Devonshire and his colleagues, but stung them into positive action ; for a few weeks later (during the winter of 1862-3) they were considering an F.R. extension along the west bank of the Leven Estuary, connecting Plumpton, near Ulverston, with the small port of Greenodd—but also a step towards the tourist region of Windermere.[7] This line was not built until 1867-9 ; meanwhile, this slight conflict had no lasting effect, and Ramsden considered the Midland move of little importance.[8]

The London and North-Western Company also had to be reckoned with. It controlled the length of line between the Stockton and Darlington (formerly S.D. & L.U., later N.E.R.) junction

---

[1]Ibid.   [2]MS. Diary, 30.9.62.   [3]Dir. Mins. (F.R.), 9.10.62.   [4]The Coniston Railway was amalgamated with the F.R. when the negotiations to lease the U. & L. were in progress ; the Duke of Devonshire, by way of payment, was to accept two-thirds of the F.R. dividend on his Coniston line shares ; Dir. Mins. (F.R.) ,13.11.61.   [5]Dir. Mins. (F.R.), 9.10.62 and Dir. Mins. (Midland Rly.), for an original draft (afterwards altered by McClean and Currey), 1.10.62, Memo. 6211.   [6]MS. Diary, 18.12.62.   [7]Dir. Mins. (F.R.), 25.2, 5.8.63.   [8]MS, Diary, 24.12.62.

at Tebay, and Carnforth junction, down which coke passed from Durham to Furness ; and in addition, Hindpool pig-iron, *en route* for Sheffield, had to travel a further six miles of L. & N.W. line from Carnforth to Lancaster. This company was watching the F.R.-Midland negotiations with some interest, for the proposed Carnforth-Wennington line would swing Midland traffic directly across its main artery to the north, and would certainly rob the L. & N.W. of Furness traffic.

The Carnforth-Wennington scheme came before a Commons Committee in March, 1863, while a Barrow Harbour Bill was submitted simultaneously by the F.R. The former Bill was opposed originally by seven petitioners, but ultimately by the L. & N.W.R. alone, and the second by Lord Lonsdale, the Cumberland iron and railway potentate, and the Commissioners of the Port of Lancaster.[1] The aims of the Furness, as stated by Devonshire in his evidence,[2] were simple enough. In the case of the F.R.-Midland Bill, the company's aims were to open up better communications with the " districts of Yorkshire ", and to send away pig-iron by the quickest route. Ramsden[3] maintained that it was essential to bring Yorkshire coal into Furness, and Schneider[4] urged that it was a great inconvenience to send his pig-iron over the L. & N.W. Carnforth-Lancaster section, because the double junction encountered *en route* caused delay. The Furness group argued hard and carefully—Schneider, who was not and had never been a shareholder in the F.R.,[5] was now an effective sharpshooter in the latter's interest—but they did not meet with entire success. Counsel for the L. & N.W., Mr. Hope Scott, who seemed unperturbed that the Midland was taking no part in the argument, made a show of shadow-boxing. At the crucial moment there was a whispered conference (as observantly reported by a pressman),[6] and the ramparts were pierced, the L. & N.W. having secured equal running powers over the Carnforth-Wennington line. " This ", noted Devonshire, " we gladly acceded to " ;[7] for it was already obvious that the Furness would need an ally in opposing the Midland's Kendal-Arnside (or Kendal and Ulverston) Bill, which was also before the Committee. This assistance was readily given, and the Midland was out-manoeuvred—the Kendal and Ulverston Bill was withdrawn.[8]

The Barrow Harbour Bill fared better, and was " settled after a slight tussle with Lord Lonsdale ",[9] who opposed the extension

[1]Rept. of Ev. in *B. Her.*, 14.3.63. [2]*Ibid.* [3]*Ibid.* [4]*Ibid.* [5]*Ibid.* [6]*B. Her.*, *loc. cit.* [7]*MS. Diary*, 12.3.63 ; *Vide* also 11.3.63, where he was impressed by the L. & N.W.'s " vigorous opposition ". [8]*MS. Diary*, 13.3.63 ; " We had united with the (L. & N.W.) to oppose it, and were not parties to the arrangement, with which we are by no means satisfied. However, it did not appear that we could interfere." [9]*MS. Diary*, 12.3.63.

of the jurisdiction of Barrow Harbour into the Duddon estuary because his thriving ore port of Borwick Rails would thereby be affected. A non-interference arrangement was duly made ; but the Cumberland magnate, as was later shown, was by no means disposed of. The Commissioners of the Port of Lancaster objected to the Harbour Bill because Piel was within *their* jurisdiction, and because they would lose tolls from vessels passing up to that anchorage. Their objection was overruled ; Devonshire pointed out that Piel was officially a harbour of refuge, whereas Barrow was a commercial port, and the harbour of the latter was " at present dry at low water ". " If the docks are not constructed by the Railway Company ", he added, " there is not much chance of any other parties constructing them ".[1]

The Barrow Harbour Bill[2] and the Furness and Midland Railway Bill[3] received the Royal Assent on June 22nd, 1863. The Midland, as is hardly surprising, lost interest in the Carnforth-Wennington project and in the following February showed signs of abandoning it ;[4] but the strong representations of the F.R. members of the Joint Midland-Furness Committee kept them to their course.[5] By that time, however, work on the Barrow docks had commenced, and the F.R. directors, who thereby showed that they were in earnest, had a powerful bargaining counter.

The Barrow Harbour Act carried borrowing powers of £137,000, and was therefore the expression of a far-reaching scheme. The Duke of Devonshire and several of his railway colleagues thought in terms of extensive dredging and deepening operations to make the Barrow Channel navigable at low tide, but J. R. McClean and Ramsden, always well to the fore in pressing for new expenditure had more ambitious ideas. The former wanted an extensive stone dock-wall in the harbour, and Ramsden wished for a definite fulfilment of his plan of nine years earlier, with a network of railway lines along the dock side.[6] In September, 1863, nine firms of contractors[7] submitted tenders for the dock contract, the two largest being those of Messrs. Lee, and Brassey and Field. The proposed works were to be as ambitious as Ramsden could desire. The Barrow Channel, about 300 yards across at its widest point, was to be walled up and converted into two great dock basins. The suitability of the Channel for conversion meant that the construction of the docks could be executed comparatively cheaply, and Brassey's firm proposed to carry out this part of the work for £82,427 ; but his was not the lowest tender, and the estimates

---

[1]*B. Her.*, *loc. cit.* [2]26 & 27 *Vic.*, *c.*lxxxix. [3]26 & 27 *Vict.*, *c.*lxxxii. [4]*MS. Diary*, 9.9.63, 18.2.64. [5]*Dir. Mins. Jt. Ctee.* (MS.), and *MS. Diary*, 18.2.64. [6]*Dir. Mins.* (*F.R.*), 8.9.63, *MS. Diary*, 9.9.63. [7]Messrs. Boulton, Brassey, Lee, Lawton, Sharp, Waring, McCormac, Allen and Ritson.

varied so greatly—that of Messrs. Waring, for the entire contract, involving the construction of an embankment, wharves and bridges, amounted to nearly £200,000—that accordingly the F.R. Directors sought refuge in the reputations of Brassey and Lee respectively, offering them the option of reducing their tenders from some £137,000 to £132,000.[1] This Brassey agreed to do, and his firm secured the contract ;[2] but the great railway-builder, in undercutting his rivals, exposed himself to ultimate loss.

The docks were not completed for nearly four years, and a shortage of workers, together with recurrent labour troubles, set Brassey and Field many problems. Nevertheless, several thousand labourers were obtained and the population of the still small town of Barrow increased rapidly. In October, 1864, the firm of Benton and Woodiwiss secured a contract for the construction of the Carnforth-Wennington line, and this work was in progress during the years 1865 to 1867.[3]

By the summer of 1865 about £400,000[4] had been spent on the Barrow docks and shipping accommodation (i.e., since the Barrow Harbour Commissioners and Furness Railway had first started improving them), and the F.R. directors were acutely sensitive to any threat, real or potential, to their Barrow traffic. In the autumn of 1864 there commenced an unedifying conflict with the Whitehaven and Furness Junction Railway Company, which was then enjoying the benefits of an increasing ore traffic from Cumberland into Furness.[5] But the circuitous route *via* Foxfield, along both sides of the Duddon Estuary, still seemed costly and uneconomic, and yet another sand-crossing proposal was initiated —this time in the form of a viaduct scheme—by the Wh. & F.J.R.[6] The immediate stimulus to (and occasion for) this proposal lay in the greatly expanding output of the Hodbarrow mine—some 600 vessels visited the adjacent port of Borwick Rails in 1864[7]—and while the F.R. board certainly did not welcome it, they offered co-operation.[8] As was afterwards argued,[9] a shortened coastal route was likely to benefit them. Lord Lonsdale, the royalty owner at Hodbarrow,

---

[1]*Loc. cit. (Dir. Mins.)* ; Messrs. Sharp offered to do the work for £77,800, and Messrs. Lee and Lawton for slightly larger sums. [2]*Dir. Mins.*, 20.10. 63. [3]*Dir. Mins. Jt. Cttee*, 28.10.64, 17.2.65, 13.6, 26.10.65, 10.4, 22.10.66, 8.2.67, 11.8.68. [4]Ramsden's evidence before H. of C. Cttee., *B. Her.*, 18.3.63. [5]" An important outlet southward for the Cleator ore had been created " ; Pollard, *op. cit.*, 172. See also the Company's dividends, p. 259 above. [6]In July, 1845, the Wh. & F.J.R. had obtained parliamentary powers to make a railway " to a point of junction with the Furness Railway in the parish of Dalton " and to extend their line to Ulverston(e). [7]Hodbarrow output was 32,521 t. in 1863, 78,993 in 1864 and 117,329 in 1865 ; *Min. Stats. U.K.* ; for shipping, *B. Her., loc. cit.* [8]*MS. Diary*, 28.10.64, and *Dir. Mins. (F.R.)*, for date. [9]H. of C., Rept. of Cttee, *B. Her.*, 11.3, 18.3.65.

was the dominant influence in Wh. & F.J.R. circles, and he no doubt preferred to send away local ores on a line in which he was the main shareholder. Accordingly, the matter was much complicated when the Wh. & F.J.R. threatened, on October 31st, to build a line to Lindal on the Furness peninsula.[1] Opinion in the then languishing town of Ulverston, which regarded itself as abandoned by the major capitalists of the district, was thereby much excited,[2] for the proposed line would run in the Ulverston direction and cut out Barrow entirely. The F.R. directors, distinctly alarmed, took the extreme measure of promoting a rival bill for a Duddon crossing,[3] in order to put themselves in a position to divert southbound traffic towards Barrow where necessary. The envisaged F.R. crossing, which Devonshire thought to " effect the object much more satisfactorily ", was further to the west and pointed more nearly towards Barrow.[4] The rival bills were examined before a Parliamentary Committee in March, 1865, and to the surprise of the F.R. directors, although not to Devonshire's great alarm, the F.R. Duddon Crossing Bill was rejected in favour of that promoted by the Whitehaven and Furness Junction.[5]

As has been suggestively indicated,[6] this rather parochial contest gains interest by virtue of a possible—though far from certain—connection with the activities of the two great companies, the M.R. and L. & N.W. In the winter of 1864-5 the Midland had negotiated with the L. & N.W. for joint control of the Lancaster and Carlisle line, only to meet with a rebuff ; consequently it was obliged to prepare a survey of the afterwards famous Settle-Carlisle route from the August of 1865.[7] Contemporary journalists were apt to assume that one or other of the great companies would rapidly achieve the amalgamation of the north-west coastal lines in order to make a through route to Scotland ;[8] but recent researches[9] have shown that the minutes of the railway boards concerned lend little support to the theory of any deep-laid plot on the part of the Midland board or its rivals, or to the assumption that Lord Lonsdale's challenge to the F.R. was a stage in a manoeuvre aimed at the formation of a through route to the north. Lord Lonsdale, who wielded considerable influence in north-western railway and industrial circles, was quite capable of bringing pressure to bear upon the F.R. for his own ends, and his actions are explicable in terms of more restricted aims ; if the F.R. could not be forced to

---

[1]For a fuller account, *vide* Pollard, *op. cit.*, 173.   [2]*B. Her.*, 10.12.64 ; *Ulverston Mirror* and *Ulv. Adv.*, 2.12, 17.12.64 and *passim*.   There was a ferocious combat between the press of the two towns.   The *Ulverston Mirror* even urged Lord Lonsdale to build a branch line from Kirkby to Ulverston ; it was replied that this would have necessitated a tunnel five miles long!   [3]*Dir. Mins. F.R.*, 20.12.64.   [4]*MS. Diary*, 20.12.64 ; for plan of crossings, *B. Her.* map supplement (B.M. file, Colindale), 28.3.65, and Melville & Hobbs, *op. cit.*, 52.   [5]*MS. Diary*, 18.3.65 ; *B. Her.*, 11.3, 18.3.65.   [6]Melville & Hobbs, 53-7.   [7]Pollard, *op. cit.*, 169.   [8]E.g. *Railway News*, 4.3.65 ; *Railway Times*, 15.7.65 ; *Carlisle Journal*, 2.6, 9.6.65 ; *B. Her.*, 17.6.65.   [9]Pollard, *passim*.

purchase the Wh. & F.J.R. at a good price, the latter would still run profitably. [1]

The former was in fact obliged to make a defensive purchase of the Wh. & F.J.R. at the inflated price of 8 per cent. [2] Since, however, the purchase was regarded with the express approval of the L. & N.W. [3] it was thought by journalists—as mentioned above —that amalgamation of the coastal systems was likely. A few weeks later, in July, 1865, the L. & N.W. acquired both the Cockermouth and Workington, and Whitehaven Junction railways, gaining part control of the Cockermouth, Keswick and Penrith line and attempting to buy or lease the Whitehaven, Cleator and Egremont at the same time. [4] The Furness, on the other hand, was willy-nilly forced to extend its interests as far as Whitehaven, to take over thirty miles of distinctly poor track, and with it the obligation (embodied in the Wh. & F.J.R's successful Duddon Crossing Bill) to construct a viaduct over the Duddon estuary. This was the only occasion in the F.R's history in which it was seriously out-manoeuvred or threatened, and henceforward its directors were accountable to themselves only for all major developments in the Furness peninsula.

The L. & N.W. meanwhile set about the strengthening of its southernmost prong into the haematite region by making an arrangement with the F.R. to construct a joint line between Arnside and Hincaster, on the Lancaster and Carlisle section, [5] but building in this case was not commenced until 1871. The larger company agreed not to make any new line to the west of the Lancaster and Carlisle route, [6] and had, indeed, every reason to be magnanimous, for it was now able to reap the benefits of the traffic of two rapidly advancing ironfields and was able to leave the Furness to its own devices without inconvenience. The F.R. directors, during these years, had never shown signs of wishing to sell their line, and they may never have been asked to do so.

The continued independence of the F.R. was—as becomes unquestionably clear at a later stage in the narrative—a factor of the utmost importance, for the personalities of the F.R. board showed an intensive and growing interest in the exploitation and indus-trialisation of the locality ; more interest, certainly, than might have been expected from a group of individuals based on Euston or Derby. The local line was, and remained, a ducal appanage in

---

[1]Cf. Pollard, op. cit., 172, which gives a reasonable interpretation ; it is likely, however, that directors' minutes alone will not tell all the story.   [2]7 per cent. at first ; Dir. Mins.(F.R.) 2.5, 13.6, 20.6.65. 8 per cent. was agreed in the June.   [3]MS. Diary. 9.5, 18.5.65 ; the L. & N.W., noted Devonshire, appeared " to be disposed to act favourably towards us ". [4]Carlisle Journal, loc. cit. ; Pollard, op. cit., 176.   [5]Dir. Mins. (F.R.), 2.5.65 ; the " Furness and Yorkshire Union ".   [6]Dir. Mins. (F.R.), 2.5.65.

considerable measure ; and Devonshire evidently had sound reasons for wishing to retain control of it. The heavy commitments of the company in Barrow docks, meanwhile, would have served to discourage any would-be purchaser.

The remaining years of the decade saw continued heavy investment on the part of the F.R., and towards the end of the period, some retrenchment. In October, 1865, the company applied for an Act to build a line from Greenodd on the Leven[1] to Newby Bridge at the foot of Lake Windermere, in order to develop local tourist traffic, and made initial arrangements to promote another bill jointly with the Whitehaven, Cleator and Egremont line for the construction of a track from Cleator to Sellafield on the Wh. & F.J.R. route,[2] with the aim of increasing the flow of haematite southwards along the F.R.'s newly-acquired line. The company re-laid sections of its track with Haematite Company steel rails in 1866, £115,000 was earmarked for the Newby Bridge contract together with dock warehouses, a steamer, carriage shops, and short lines at Barrow and elsewhere ; £100,000 was to be raised for short extensions at Stainton and Ulverston ; £75,000 was to be spent on a Duddon crossing ; and large new additions to rolling stock were being made. New locomotives (including " Sharpie " tender goods engines) were needed to cope with the heavier traffic on the Lindal bank, and train loads were becoming too heavy for the existing stock.[3] About £100,000 was being spent on the Carnforth-Wennington connection,[4] and, as has been seen, £132,000 on the Barrow dock basins. Thus the immediate commitments of the company were demanding a total expenditure of the order of £500,000. In 1865-7, the total receipts of the line amounted to some £692,000, and total expenditure on all working to £355,000.[5] Thus, although the revenue of the line was a considerable one (the total net receipts of the F.R. for the period 1860-7 were about £600,000), it seems, in the absence of rather more comprehensive financial particulars, that the rapidly multiplying projects of these years had to be financed partially (and perhaps even largely) by the issue of debenture stock. By August, 1867, debentures to the value of £494,000 had been issued to members of the public, at interest rates averaging 4½ per cent. There had been nearly a fivefold increase in the issue of this type of stock since 1856.[6] On the other hand, the F.R. had issued £880,462 of ordinary shares by

---

[1]*Dir. Mins.* (*F.R.*), 26.10.65.   [2]*Loc. cit.*   [3]Gradon, *op. cit.*, 50-2.
[4]*Dir. Mins.* (*F.R.*), 23.3.65, 26.10.65, 3.8, 22.10, 15.11.66 ; *Joint Cttee. Mins., cit.* ; *Herapath's Rly. Journal*, gen. mtg. rpt. of 8.9.1866.   [5]Cf. Table 28, p. 260 above.   [6]The debenture stock of the F.R. was issued in the following proportions :

	3½%	4%	4¼%	4½%	4¾ or 5%	(£000)
Aug. 1856	4	25	—	57	17	
Aug. 1867	—	2	136	246	110	

Cf. the published B. of Trade *Railway Returns*.

December, 1866, on which it was paying 10 per cent. to the fortunate shareholders.[1] During the year 1866, therefore, about three-quarters of the company's net receipts were going into the bank balances of these parties, but the F.R. could borrow at about half the interest rates the latter were receiving, and use such comparatively cheap money to finance its new projects. Equanimity reigned in the boardroom ; " After charging everything we possibly could to revenue," observed Devonshire in August, 1866, " we have a dividend of 10 per cent. and increase our balance by about £1000."[2] In the following February it was decided to proceed with the building of the Duddon viaduct, because the Whitehaven traffic was increasing and the price of iron was low.[3] In April, 1866, when the prosperity of the railway reached a peak, and several new furnaces were in blast locally, it was stated that 140,000 tons of Hodbarrow haematite *per annum* were being put on board ship at the Borwick Rails pier, and it was hoped that this would soon be carried over the new viaduct.[4] In March, 1867, as has been indicated, the Haematite Steel Co. was able to divide at the rate of 30 per cent. " A few objections to the accounts were made, but all the shareholders were well pleased ".[5]

The Carnforth-Wennington line was opened on June 6th, 1867, and the Barrow docks, after numerous delays and difficulties encountered in their construction, were opened in the August. A trade recession was then under way, and railway traffic was falling off " due to the depression in the iron trade ". In the same month the F.R. directors reluctantly declared an 8 per cent. dividend and decided to defer all work in progress, and, if possible, to commence no new undertakings.[6] The making of the line from Plumpton (Ulverston) to Newby Bridge—the Greenodd-Newby Bridge line mentioned earlier[7]—was temporarily checked, and in the November, work on the Duddon viaduct was suspended, with the result that sections of ironwork rested uselessly on the shore of that estuary for long afterwards.[8] Yet furnaces continued to smoke, few (if any) local industrialists were ruined, and in 1866-7 the Furness ore output fell by less than 20,000 tons or barely over 2 per cent. It was revealed in the August of the same year that over £300,000 of F.R. capital expenditure was still unproductive.[9] Work on the Newby Bridge extension[10] nevertheless proceeded, and in May, 1868, the directors faced the fact that their total liabilities amounted to £674,396,[11] roughly equivalent to three years' net receipts from the

[1]See p. 260. [2]*Ms. Diary*, 3.8.66.
[3]*MS. Diary*, 9.2.67 ; *Dir. Mins.* (*F.R.*), 9.2.67, when a tender of £29,736 was accepted. [4]*MS. Diary*, 13.4.66 ; a branch line from Holborn Hill station was being laid to the proposed viaduct. [5]*MS. Diary*, 6.3.67. [6]*MS. Diary*, 8.8.67. [7]See p. 269 above. [8]*MS. Diary* and *Dir. Mins.* (*F.R.*), 7.11.67 ; Melville & Hobbs, *op. cit.*, 59-60. [9]*Herapath's Rly. Journal*, Aug., 1867 ; debenture rates then approached 5 per cent. [10]This in fact ran to Lakeside, Windermere. [11]*Dir. Mins.* (*F.R.*), 13.5.68, for full table of estimates.

whole of the Furness Railway system. They were therefore sensitive to the slightest tremor or negative fluctuation in the otherwise steady upward sweep of the traffic returns, and, likewise, any tightening of the money market caused them to catch their breath and seek retrenchment.

In 1868, then, there was a fall in the company's receipts of less than three per cent. ; and by virtue of an even greater fall in working expenditure, the net income of the line was larger than in any previous recorded year. But in the same year Devonshire was " rather disappointed " with the traffic receipts, and was obviously uneasy. Owing to the high prices at which the Furness-Midland Joint Committee had had to buy land, the cost of the Carnforth-Wennington line (originally a mere £10,000 had been earmarked for land purchase, but £50,000 were now required) was much greater than expected.[1] At the half-yearly general meeting of February, 1869, the dividend on ordinary shares was reduced to six per cent., a figure which carried auguries of ruination to men who were devoting hundreds of thousands of pounds to those projects which might assure them 10 or 15 per cent. in perpetuity.[2]

In May, 1869, the directors submitted a bill for the abandonment of the Duddon viaduct scheme, and their representatives argued that the shorter route over the Duddon sands would be uneconomic and would involve the company in a loss of some £6000 a year, equivalent to the F.R.'s own income from the carriage of 150,000 tons of ore transported annually between Whitehaven and Carnforth;[3] A Committee of the House of Lords was by no means convinced of the disinterestedness of this argument, and in passing the bill imposed—as something of a moral judgment —the " onerous condition " that the F.R. should charge tolls commensurate with the direct distance of three miles across the estuary, instead of the coastal distance of six and a half miles *via* Foxfield.[4] The railway company, however, were not the only sufferers. The Furness Iron and Steel Company claimed that it had spent £80,000 on its works in anticipation of the completion of the crossing,[5] while the estimated cost of the viaduct was only £75,000.

The viaduct was never constructed—Barrow, and the Barrow docks, were the main preoccupations of the railway board at this time and for many years afterwards—and as a result the region was to be burdened with a railway line that was too circuitous, and docks that were never used to their full capacity. A generation ago it was customary to condemn almost without thought the achievements

---

[1]*MS. Diary*, 10.8, 11.8.68. [2]Rptd. in *B. Times*, 27.2.69 ; " a large proportion of the heavy outlay during the last few years was rendered necessary by the rapid development of the iron trade of the district ". [3]J. R. McClean's *Memo.* in *Dir. Mins.* (*F.R.*), 27.10.68 ; *B. Times*, 8.5.69 ; *MS. Diary*, 7.5, 10.5.69. [4]*B. Times, loc. cit.* [5]*Loc. cit.*

271

of the Victorian industrialist or projector ; today, in mid-twentieth century, students are being encouraged to react (if anywhere at all) in the opposite direction, and an appreciation of Victorian works might well be tempered by much-needed research into the social wastefulness and squandering of material resources implicit in many of the activities of the men of that age. [1]

In 1869 the F.R. postponed the scheme to build its " Furness and Lancaster and Carlisle Union " Railway, this the grandiloquent and altered title of the short line from Arnside to Hincaster.   Some opposition from the Durham coke interests of Pease and Co. (who had to pay tolls over the longer route *via* Carnforth) was expected and diplomatically overcome, and final abandonment was attempted by the F.R.,[2] with the result that a time extension was obtained.   But, as the line had been promoted at the behest of the London and North Western Railway, such a powerful influence had to be placated, and the line was shortly afterwards built.   In June, 1869, the Newby Bridge line was duly opened, and the Cleator extension was ready for use two months later.[3]   By the December practically all outstanding matters between the Midland and the F.R. (as affecting the Carnforth-Wennington) were satisfactorily settled ; whereupon the Midland Railway, when traffic was running as originally envisaged between its north-west Yorkshire route and the Barrow docks, promptly lost all interest in the Furness outside the sphere of established formalities. [4]

The Furness Railway's system was now virtually completed. From the year 1860 it had grown comparatively rapidly.   With 22 miles, 38 chains of line in that year, it had (by the acquisitions of the Coniston, U. & L. and Wh. & F.J.R., and numerous minor extensions, but excluding that at Cleator), increased its route-mileage to 109 miles, 28 chains by 1870.   Hence it was still a comparatively tiny organisation in purely physical terms.   Even by 1883, when the economic and industrial wealth of the district had grown remarkably, it controlled just over 129 miles of route.

PORT AND PASSENGERS

The F.R. board hoped for much from the Barrow docks.   Nor were they alone ; long before the basins were completed, the *Barrow Herald*[5] had stated that the London and North Western company had secured wharves there " in anticipation of Barrow

---

[1]E.g., small towns with two stations, as compared with larger towns with one only ; two lines doing the work of one ; unnecessarily circuitous routes ; the economic starvation of one district as against over-investment in another.   [2]*Dir. Mins.* (*F.R.*), 9.8, 8.12.69, 11.2.70 ; *Herapath's Rly. Jnl.*, Feb., 1870. Relations with the L. & N.W.R. were uneasy ; *B. Her.*, 7.5.70, *B. Times*, 5.1.72.   [3]*B. Times*, 5.6.69, *MS. Diary*, 9.8.69.   [4]*Dir. Mins. Jt. Cttee* and *MS. Diary*, 9.12.69.   The Committee held only one meeting between 1872 and 1882.   [5]*B. Her.*, 11.3.65.

becoming the best port between the Mersey and the Clyde ". This confidence, although misplaced, was understandable. The dock works were huge, and the basins were 68 acres in extent ; large enough to make something of a challenge to Liverpool, but only a fraction of the size of the Barrow docks which appeared within a few years.[1] The earliest basins, named the Buccleuch and Cavendish docks respectively, were formed from the existing Barrow Channel without undue engineering difficulty ; straightforward excavation and deepening, the construction of coffer dams, and the building of over two thousand yards of dock wall and wharfage were the main tasks accomplished. The work was heavy, nevertheless ; Brassey and Field used a labour force of about 2000 men during the three and a half years which were taken to complete their contract. The stone for the dock facings was obtained from the Hawcoat sandstone quarries, to which the F.R. made a short railway line.[2]

It is clear that such a vast undertaking could not have been justified by whatever steamer traffic the Midland Railway might draw or direct to Barrow. The capturing of this traffic, indeed, was a preliminary only ; the docks were made on a grandiose scale in anticipation of the appearance of new industries on the Hindpool Estate, and of a corresponding growth and increasing variety of the trade of the port itself. And, should this scheme prove difficult of realisation, Ramsden and his colleagues had further plans. The establishment of ship repairing, and possibly shipbuilding, was discussed some time before the opening of the docks (although the F.R. directors apparently had no intention, at that stage, of investing in such an industry themselves), and land was made ready for this purpose on Barrow Island, which had been purchased by the F.R. in 1863.[3] The Island was ideally suited for this industry, and it is not without interest that the " Site for Shipbuilding Yards " chosen in 1867, where Barrow Island sloped down to the east side of the Walney Channel, has been used for the launching of vessels until the present day.[4] Geographical advantages, however, were not enough to encourage outside investors to establish a shipyard at this upstart port, so far from the traditional centres of the industry, and the F.R.-Steelworks capitalists eventually had to undertake such work on their own initiative. The entire east frontage of the Barrow Island was laid out for timber yards, and the importation, stacking and distribution of timber

[1]For comparisons with other docks, *vide* Vernon-Harcourt, L. F., *Harbours and Docks*, I, (1885) 554, 632, and *passim*. For a plan of the docks in 1867, *Engineering*, 20.9.67. [2]Melville & Hobbs, *op. cit.*, 62. [3]*Dir. Mins.* (F.R.), 20.10.63. The land was purchased from T. Y. P. Michaelson and remained (for the most part) unused for a further seven years. A small shipbuilding industry (see p. 234 above, note 1) already existed at Hindpool. [4]Map in *Engineering*, *loc. cit.*

did in fact soon become a major local industry. A timber pond of 35 acres was made out of Salthouse Pool.[1]

After numerous delays and difficulties,[2] the Barrow docks were opened on September 19th, 1867. The opening ceremony[3] was attended by W. E. Gladstone, and may best be described by Devonshire himself, who entertained his fellow-Liberal at Holker : " Many more attended than we expected, mainly no doubt in consequence of Gladstone having agreed to attend. After an inspection of the docks, furnaces and steelworks, we had a large dinner of 1200 in the carriage shed. I was obliged to preside and had a good deal of speaking which I did very indifferently. Gladstone proposed the town and trade of Barrow and of course spoke well . . . "[4] Gladstone, for his part, remarked that " some day Barrow will become a Liverpool. Let it become a Liverpool if it will and can, the old Liverpool will be none the worse, but better for it ".[5]

The dock opening coincided with the incorporation of the borough of Barrow-in-Furness, then a town of 14,000 to 16,000 inhabitants, and as the excited crowds cheered, a great bonfire lit up the sky, and the more privileged guests and visitors banqueted or wondered at the iron furnaces and the vast steelworks, one man in particular might well have regarded the proceedings with mixed feelings. This man was Thomas Brassey, who had lost heavily on the dock contract.[6] The extent of his loss may have been comparatively small when the vastness of his other enterprises[7] is taken into account, but it is known that the great railway contractor was in extreme financial difficulties at this period. He nevertheless received what can only be described as a substantial consolation prize in the form of holdings to the value of £44,000 in Barrow Haematite Steel,[8] thereby joining a privileged and fortunate group of shareholders. The Furness Railway's directors had every reason to thank him for docks executed cheaply and well, although it may be doubted whether Brassey, an ageing and soon afterwards dying man, was able to respond with enthusiasm.

No great influx of shipping followed the completion of the dock basins, although numerous iron ore vessels and timber ships used them. A customs official even reported in 1869 that " the trade

[1]*Loc. cit.* ; also report of McClean and Stileman, *Herapath's Rly. Journal* (F.R. gen. mtg.), 15.6.67, for an account of the dock-building progress. [2]*MS. Diary*, 25.7.66, 3.8.66 (" Brassey the contractor was there and assured us that the works would now proceed fast ") 7.9.66, 26.12.66 (" progress . . . much less than we hoped for "), 19.1.67. [3]*B. Her.*, 21.9.67 ; *Illustrated Times,* 28.9.67. [4]*MS. Diary*, 19.9.67 ; also 20.9, 21.9, 22-4.9.67.
[5]*B. Her., loc. cit. Punch*, 5.10.67, in characteristic vein, said, " Barrow, we are told, is to be a second Liverpool, Birmingham, Sheffield, Dudley and Cardiff, all rolled into one ". [6]Helps, Sir A., *Life and Labours of Mr. Brassey* (1872 ed.), 147. Brassey lost £44,000 on the Barrow dock and Runcorn Bridge contracts together, by 1866. [7]*Passim.* [8]Company file, *cit.*

of this place (Barrow), which at one time promised to be very
extensive, is gradually dwindling away. The number of foreign
vessels with cargoes was : in 1866, 65 ; 1867, 45 ; 1868, 30 ; and
the Foreign trade outwards from which, it is alleged, so much was
anticipated, is now simply ' nil ' ".[1] This was certainly not an
adequate record, for according to a local petition of 1869, 3262
vessels entered and left the port of Barrow during the year 1868,
200,000 tons of pig iron and iron ore were exported, 80,000 tons
of general goods imported and exported, and 23,000 head of
livestock imported.[2] Even by 1873, when the trade in timber and
general merchandise had advanced considerably, as well as the
export of steel rails, the total number of vessels entering and clearing
was 3845 (of an average of 179 tons each), as against eight times
that number, with more than twice the average tonnage, at
Liverpool.[3]

The ironworks, steelworks and dock investments did however
have the effect of attracting other industries to Barrow during
the 'sixties, as the following list will make clear :

Table 29
Barrow's Industrial Basis in 1867.[4]
H.E. : On Hindpool Estate (F.R. land)

Firm	Date of establishment	Nature of manufacture etc.
Furness Railway	1846	Engine works, wagon works, fitting shops
Wm. Ashburner	1847	Small shipbuilding yard (H.E.)
Wm. Gradwell	1855	General contractor and builder (H.E.)
T. Beveridge	1856	Castings for mining industry (Salthouse).
Messrs. Stuart	1858	Hemp and wire ropes (mines) (H.E.)
A. J. Woodhouse	1858	Brick manuf. (furnaces, building) (H.E.)
Hindpool Furnaces	1859	(H.E.)
Kennedy & Eastwood	1863	Cranes & dock fittings, gen. eng. (H.E.)
Waddington & Longbottom	1863	Millwrights
Andrew Waddington	1863	Building and general joinery
Haematite Steel Co.	1864-5	(H.E.)
Westray & Forster	1866	Engineering, ironworks machinery (H.E.)
Messrs. Woodall	1867	Bridge & girder works (H.E.)
B. Townson	1867	Cabinet & upholstery factory (H.E.)

Of these firms, only the Hindpool ironworks and steelworks
appears to have employed more than 200 men. William Gradwell
had been importing timber from about the year 1857,[5] and by 1867
he had a large timber store at Hindpool, used for meeting the

[1] *Bulky PB/64*, H.M. Customs & Excise Library, London, by courtesy
of Mr. R. C. Jarvis.
[2] Petition from Barrow Corporation to the Lord Chancellor for an extension
of Admiralty Jurisdiction to the Ulverston County Court District ; *B. Times*,
8.5.1869. [3] Vernon-Harcourt, *op. cit.*, Appx. VII, 643. [4] The sources in
this case are : *B. Times*, 1.12.67, 27.7.67, 2.11.67 (articles on local firms) ;
F.P. & P., II, 267 sqq. ; Leach, *Barrow, Its Rise & Progress* (1872), 74 sqq.
[5] At this date or earlier, advtmt. in *Ulv. Adv.*, 6.8.1857. He was importing oak,
pine and elm logs from the Baltic and Quebec.

requirements of the local building trade as well as those of the iron mines,[1] and replenished by cargoes from the Baltic and Canada. The mines had long used large quantities of home and foreign softwood props, and the expansion of building activity in rapidly growing Barrow gave new life to the timber trade. "The Railway and Dock Companies", it was reported in late 1867, " are desirous of encouraging the importation of timber with a view to making the district a depot for all kinds of timber for distribution in the various towns along the route of the Midland and London and North Western Railways ".[2] In July, 1867, the F.R. Board placed an order for 9½ miles of railway sleepers with the firm of Price, Potter, Walker and Co. of Grimsby and Gloucester,[3] thereby drawing the attention of that important firm to Barrow. One of its partners, Richard Potter,[4] afterwards stated that the firm decided to establish timber yards at Barrow because the land set aside by the F.R. was very cheap (" twenty acres of ground for a small sum ") and because there was " easy access to and from the consuming districts of Lancashire and Yorkshire, particularly for the Canadian trade ".[5] This firm occupied a yard on Barrow Island in early 1869, with noticeable results ; 12,000 tons of timber were locally imported in that year, and 18,000 tons in 1870.[6] Baltic and Canadian softwoods soon afterwards accounted for a great part of Barrow's imports.

Nevertheless, this was the only redistributive trade of any consequence which was drawn to Barrow docks in these years. The railway company caused large warehouses to be built on the town side of the docks,[7] and evidently hoped for a considerable import of grain and bonded goods. The degree of its success is discussed below.

The subject of local steamer and passenger traffic requires brief mention. The carriage of passengers was far less profitable than the transport of minerals, and the former did not become a major preoccupation of F.R. directors for over a generation.[8] According to one statement,[9] out of £132,000 of Furness Railway receipts in the year 1868, only £22,000 came from the fares of passengers. As the population of the district increased, however, and more people used the Cumberland coastal route, the passenger-

---

[1]*B. Times*, 1.12.67. [2]*Ibid.* [3]*Dir. Mins.*, 11.7.67.; it seems arguable that the F.R. was deliberately putting out widely dispersed orders to draw the attention of such firms ; Gradwell could have obtained the sleepers, and indeed had a plant for preparing them. [4]The father of Beatrice Webb ; *vide My Apprenticeship* (Pelican Ed., 1938), I, 19-21. [5]Ev. before Ctee. on Barrow Corporation Bill, 1st May, 1873, Ques. 272-6, and 20th June, Ques. 114. [6]Leach, *Op. cit.*, 97. [7]*Dir. Mins.*, 23.3.65, 25.4.66, 3.8.66 ; *Herapath's Rly. Jnl.*, *loc. cit.* [8]Alfred Aslett in *Railway Magazine*, Aug., 1898, esp. pp. 126-32. [9]*B. Times*, 8.5.69.

income of the line rose accordingly ; from less than a fifth of all receipts in 1869 to more than a quarter in 1876.[1] The tourist traffic to the Lake District, and *via* Piel Pier or Barrow to and from Ireland and the Isle of Man, also accounted for some of this increase. But although the F.R. did in fact attempt to cater for tourists—it had, indeed, been making such attempts since the opening of its system—the services offered were not such as to excite admiration, and a doubtless jaundiced and partisan comment, in the columns of a Durham newspaper,[2] claimed that the local line was " decidedly behind the age, and even behind the North Eastern Co. in accommodation. Their second class carriages are hardly equal to London and North Western or Great Northern thirds, while the numbers of trains running daily are reduced to such a minimum as to leave ample time for reflection and meditation after the dispatch of business at any town on their route ".[3] The London and North Western, however, was refusing to synchronise its own services with those of the F.R. in 1871, apparently with a view to keeping travellers on its Lancaster and Carlisle route rather than encouraging them to use the coastal system.[4] The same company, likewise, had in early 1868 made overtures to the Midland regarding a possible abandonment of the Settle and Carlisle section and a renewed joint working of the Lancaster and Carlisle and Kendal to Windermere routes. This proposed arrangement (which did not of course materialise, for the famous and costly Settle to Carlisle line was soon afterwards in use) threatened to deprive the F.R. of the traffic along its then building Newby Bridge branch, and Devonshire's sharp letter to the Midland directors brought only an evasive reply from W. E. Hutchinson.[5] The F.R. board, desperate to justify their great expenditure by the attraction of every kind of traffic, were left to solve their problems as best they could.

They had hoped for much from the transference of the Midland Railway's steamer services (Belfast-Morecambe) to Piel. A fleet of iron paddle steamers, jointly owned by the Midland, the F.R. and Messrs. James Little and Co. of Glasgow, began regular services between Piel, Belfast and the Isle of Man in 1867.[6] Devonshire noted in 1869, however, that the "Irish steamers have not paid ".[7] Later in the year this traffic improved.[8] But the problem of using the Barrow docks to their full capacity still remained. The F.R. attempts to fill them, not merely with small timber and pig-iron vessels, but with ocean liners, are given separate treatment below.

---

[1] *Board of Trade Returns.*   [2] *Northern Echo* (Darlington), quoted *B. Times,* 22.1.70.   [3] An examination of the F.R. timetables in 1865 shows that eight trains ran daily from Barrow to Carnforth, taking 1hr. 20 mins. to 1 hr. 50 mins. (summer timetable).   In the " revolution " of the 'nineties the no. of trains was increased to 15.   [4] *B. Times,* 5.1.71.   [5] *Div. Mins. (F.R.),* 4.2.68. [6] Melville and Hobbs, *op. cit.,* 51, which contains much valuable material, from local sources, not available in the official F.R. minutes.   [7] *MS. Diary,* 12.2, 9.8.69.   [8] *MS. Diary,* 9.8.69.

The members of the F.R. board were for the most part remote from the industrial population whose lives were being transformed in these eventful years. Devonshire still took a dutiful interest in the affairs of the Ulverston Guardians, and continued to act as their chairman.[1] The one man who was deeply concerned with the progress and problems of the new Barrow, James Ramsden, became —significant title!—" resident director " in February, 1866.[2] Few railway boards can have had a more diligent or ambitious general manager than Ramsden. Devonshire, interestingly enough, showed little enthusiasm for the latter's elevation to the board, and noted that " I have not been able to see the advantage so decidedly . . . at all events, I can see no harm likely to result from it ".[3] Until Ramsden's appointment, the Furness Railway directors had had no direct representative on any of the local vestries, and on February 9th, 1867—only a few months before Barrow-in-Furness became a municipal borough—he was empowered by his fellow-directors to represent the Company " at any parish meetings at which the Company may be interested ". Yet the F.R.-Steelworks group (including, of course, Schneider and Hannay, neither of whom were officially concerned in the affairs of the railway) had been, and remained, responsible for every major development in Barrow, Dalton, and indeed the entire district.

There was little change in the balance of interests on the board during these years. Ramsden's appointment had been made possible by the resignations of Rickards and Boyle, who found that certain decisions were being taken without their knowledge. Until that time the directorate consisted of associates of the two dukes, Devonshire and Buccleuch, and it was proposed that the other vacancy be filled by H. S. Thompson, chairman of the North-Eastern Railway, over whose lines the vital fuel for local furnaces passed ; but Ramsden considered the choice an impolitic one, fearing that the suspicion of the mighty powers on the F.R. flanks, the Midland and the L. & N.W., might all too easily be incurred. Devonshire, however, was " anxious that we should have a Director unconnected either with myself or the Duke of Buccleuch ",[4] and Thompson duly took his place. Technical and administrative— as well as diplomatic—matters were nevertheless entrusted regularly to Ramsden, and less often but fairly frequently to the engineering partners McClean and Stileman. It was the pressure of these three which brought about one costly investment or experiment after another. J. R. McClean (d.1873), President of the Institute of Civil Engineers in 1863,[5] was an eminent engineer with many achievements to his credit by this time, and he was succeeded as F.R. engineer-in chief by his colleague F. C. Stileman (1824-89) in

[1]*Mins. Ulv. Gdns.* and *MS. Diary, passim.*   [2]*Dir. Mins.*, 8.2, 14.2.66
[3]*MS. Diary*, 8.2.66.   [4]*MS. Diary*, 14.2.66.   [5]Obit., *B. Her.*, 19.7.73.

1868.[1]   As we have seen, it was McClean (or, as Devonshire would have it, " Macleane ") who pressed for improvements in the Barrow Harbour, and, ultimately, for the vast dock scheme of 1863-7.   This man was no wild visionary, and his portrait[2] is that of a calm and canny North Briton who could see both sides of a problem and argue for either of them with equal force, conviction and clarity.   Just as the F.R. directors depended heavily upon Ramsden in matters administrative, so McClean and Stileman, through their advisory rôles, were able to exert considerable influence in the F.R. boardroom.   Their reports told the directors how they ought to spend their money, and usually the directors did as they were told.   These engineering partners were of course men of standing and wide experience, and had been consulting engineers to the Dover Harbour scheme and the Surrey Commercial Docks, as well as to the Lemberg and Czernovitz Railway.   Their sons Frank Stileman (1851-1912) and Frank McClean (1837-1904) carried on their work as advisers to the F.R.[3]

It fell to the lot of the company chairman, Devonshire, to interpolate a word or two of caution and an occasional searching question into any counsels dominated by General Manager and engineers.   This caution is evident enough in his diary—an occasional note of distaste[4] (or at best, lack of enthusiasm) in response to a further instalment of spending advocated by Ramsden, or a sign of doubt and determination not to be taken in,[5] tell us something about the man ; but it is clear, too, that he was heavily if not completely dependent upon Ramsden, McClean and Stileman for advice bearing on railway progress and policy.[6]   This is not to suggest that the Furness Railway filled his thoughts day and night during these years, or that the men named above were any more to the Duke than very useful agents—beings like the able Cavendish agents at Holker (Drewry), Buxton (Wilmot), or Eastbourne (Simpson).[7]   Devonshire visited each of these fairly frequently, and he had as little and as much direct responsibility for the growth and development of Eastbourne or Buxton as for the growth of Barrow ; he listened, encouraged, made money available, and allowed extremely capable underlings to get on with their work. On the positive side, he was a good enough judge of men to be able to appoint and keep these assistants, and his personal influence

[1]Obit., *Proc. Inst. C.E.*, 1888-9, IV, 401.   [2]Portrait at the Institute of Civil Engineers, Great George St., London.   [3]*Proc. Inst. C.E.*, 1911-12, III, 347 ; 1904-5, II, 391.   [4]E.g., *MS. Diary*, 27.12.61 ; " I fear Ramsden will soon want some additions to the workshops &c."   [5]E.g., his reaction (*MS. Diary*, 7.8.61) to McClean's dock proposal ; " . . . this is a serious question requiring much consideration ".   [6]E.g., *MS. Diary*, 1.1.62, 6.2, 20.8, 30.9, 24.12.62, 12.2.63, 13.5.63, 10.8.64.   [7]It may be added that McClean was the engineer responsible for the gas supplies and sewage system of Eastbourne ; cf. *MS. Diary*, 4.9.67.

and great social standing carried some weight in negotiations with more powerful railway companies than the F.R. He was very much more than a figurehead, and his attitude to Furness affairs was that of a well-informed and observant " improving " landlord. This Senior Wrangler and owner of great estates, anxious to put the Cavendish fortunes on a sound basis, was becoming more and more involved in Furness industries and speculations.

Not much need be said about the other Duke, Buccleuch. He rarely attended F.R. meetings, but lent capital and a name to local companies. The F.R. shareholders contributed to local deliberations almost as little ; " We had our half-yearly Furness meeting today," wrote Devonshire in 1862, " It passed off quietly, and as usual very few shareholders attended." [1] In the May of the following year " Only one shareholder excluding the directors was present, and of course no opposition was made ". [2]

[1]*MS. Diary*, 28.2.62. [2]*MS. Diary*, 12.5.63.

CHAPTER XIV

SOCIAL ORGANISATION AND URBAN GROWTH ; BARROW AND DISTRICT IN THE 'SIXTIES

BARROW AND THE RAILWAY INFLUENCE

The published Census statements of 1861 do not treat Barrow as a separate entity.   The energetic Ramsden, however, had caused the church of St. George to be erected on Rabbit Hill, Barrow village, in 1859-60,[1] and accordingly a district chapelry was created. The latter embraced Barrow, Old Barrow Island, Salthouse, Hindpool, and the surrounding fields as far as the boundaries of Rampside to the east, Longreins to the north, and the borders of Cocken hamlet to the north-west.[2]   The assignment of this ecclesiastical district was confirmed by an Order in Council made on October 11th, 1861,[3] and was anticipated by the local enumerators, who produced the following locally published Census figures in the September of that year ;[4]

1861	Houses occupied	Houses unoccupied	Houses bldg.	Total houses	Population Males	Females	Total
Proposed Dist. of St. George, Barrow	514	7	59	580	1691	1444	3135

These figures were included in the totals for the parish of Dalton-in-Furness, which were :

1861	1566	56	65	1687	4821	4201	9022

The village of Barrow and environs, which had had but 690 inhabitants in 1850, now accounted for rather more than one-third of the greatly increased Dalton population total.

According to H. W. Schneider, who was undoubtedly well-informed on the subject, Barrow's population increased from 800 to 3135—viz., in little over two years—" entirely by the erection of the (Hindpool) furnaces ",[5] the new ironworks having been partly staffed with workmen from Staffordshire.[6]   Hence Barrow was not a railway colony properly so-called ; but it was railway-inspired and railway-dominated, as has been indicated already.

[1]Built by subscriptions of the F.R. board, the two Dukes and the ore merchants ; cf. Gaythorpe, H., *Church Congress Guide to Barrow* (1906), 73. [2]Tyson, *Abstract of Accounts* . . . *Dalton* (1887), 146, gives a full perambulation.   [3]*Ibid.*   [4]*Ulv. Adv. Supplement*, 12.9.61 in *Miscell. Papers*, Barrow P.L.   [5]Schneider's ev., *Proceedings, Barrow-in-F. Corporation Bill*, 1871, Ques. 292.   [6]J. T. Smith's ev., *Notes, Proc. Div. of Dalton etc.* (1871), 73 (pamph. in Barrow P.L.).

From 1847 onwards, the Furness Railway directors had delegated much of the responsibility for the supervision of affairs in their Salthouse and Hindpool possessions to James Ramsden, as the company's resident administrator. It is likely, therefore, that many of the F.R. actions here described were in fact taken on his own initiative, for none of the directors of the 'fifties and early 'sixties had a personal interest in Barrow. The Salthouse railway colony early had a piped water supply,[1] five or six years before the town of Ulverston ceased to rely on wells and pumps for its water,[2] and the erection of the Hindpool furnaces entailed the provision of reservoirs,[3] at first constructed for the use of the iron works. In October, 1861, the F.R. board decided to make a waterworks at Ireleth, to be paid for out of moneys obtained from the rent or sale of the Hindpool ironworks land to Schneider and Hannay.[4] Afterwards, the F.R. took the main responsibility for supplying water to the public of Barrow, acting through a nominally separate organisation, the Barrow Gas and Water Company.[5] Meanwhile, a small gasworks was commenced at Hindpool in 1862 under the sponsorship of John Storey and a number of local businessmen.[6]

The Railway continued to make some provision for local education between 1849 and 1861, authorising the expenditure of £600 on Barrow school and reading room in 1858, and £365 on the enlargement of the school in 1861.[7] In the following year a number of rather more noteworthy steps were taken by the company ; it set in motion the planning and building of a " Market House and Public Room ",[8] a passenger station and enlarged railway works in the town.

Ramsden was careful to see that his plan of 1854 was followed in all its main outlines, and even by 1863, the result was impressive to a visitor from nearby Ulverston :[9]

" It is some years since we had an opportunity of going through Barrow. Since we last saw it, the town has increased greatly in population, and its improvements are many. The Strand will form a fine order of buildings when completed . . . Hindpool, Salthouse, Hindpool Road, Dalton Road, remind us of the spacious streets of Manchester and Preston . . . As to the roads—ah; well . . . fearfully and wonderfully constructed and obstructed ; building

[1]Ramsden's ev., *Proc. Bill* . . . . 1873, Ques. 56-63. [2]See p. 244 above. [3]In 1855 there was an F.R. scheme, not acted upon, to make a reservoir at Furness Abbey. [4]*Dir. Mins. (F.R.)*, 15.10.61. [5]Formed in August, 1863 ; *Dir. Mins. (F.R.)*, 5.8.63. I am indebted to Dr. S. Pollard for further particulars. [6]Leach, *op. cit.*, 122. Storey was one of the highway surveyors in Hawcoat Division in 1862-3 ; *B. Her.*, 11.4.63.
[7]*Dir. Mins. (F.R.)*, 24.2.58, 15.10.61. [8]*Dir. Mins.*, 28.2.62 ; £1500 was earmarked for this purpose. The Town Hall which resulted was built in 1864-5. [9]*Ulv. Adv.*, 28.5.63. (Letter from an Ulverston Wesleyan.)

debris and the like scattered about to impede the pedestrian at almost every step . . . ''

The new town bore every sign of railway influence. In 1862-3 the F.R. built and opened its railway station at St. George's Hill (described by the Ulverston visitor quoted as " light, airy and spacious ") and Ramsden supervised the layout of the grandilo- quently named Strand, a thoroughfare connecting the station and the F.R. works with the main axis of Hindpool Road, fronting the proposed docks. The shops, offices and Royal Hotel in the Strand were designed " in the station style of architecture " by Bintley of Kendal.[1] That this had the desired effect on visitors is shown above.

But within the framework of Ramsden's spacious thoroughfares, the rest of the town, increasing rapidly in population, was left to grow of its own accord ; not, it is true, out of conformity with Ramsden's rectangles, and also with a fairly liberal use of space, but nevertheless in a somewhat piecemeal fashion. The Ramsden- Furness Railway control had effect chiefly in the Hindpool Estate and in Salthouse, and even there concerned itself very largely with appearances. The ambiguity of this control is expressed in an incident of 1861 ; in that year the Duke of Devonshire, who owned sixteen fields and closes adjoining the Hindpool Estate,[2] sold a parcel of property near Barrow village to one Tyson for £2,102. In 1864 Devonshire noted that this land had " suffered the usual annoy- ances in the neighbourhood of large works, fences being broken down and fields trespassed upon ".[3] Ramsden then proposed that " he should take the land, set it out for building, and meanwhile make what he can ot it ".[4] Tyson, however, was enabled to retain the land and to sell it to the unfortunate Barrow Corporation (in 1885) for the sum of £13,713,[5] or between six and seven times its original purchase price. The F.R., however, was not a modern local government body planning a housing estate, and on the whole it lacked the spirit of the founders of New Lanark and Saltaire. The hard-pressed Ramsden, weighed down by a mass of railway cares, preferred to deal with local social and administrative problems as they arose. The latter multiplied at an alarming rate. That they were never dealt with before much harm had been done, is a criticism of an age and a form of society rather than a judgment upon particular individuals. *Laissez-faire* had brought about almost everything that the influential men of the neighbourhood recognised as progressive, and it was hardly surprising that the development of

---

[1]*B. Her.*, 17.1.63 ; The architect (perhaps the Joseph Bintley jun. mentioned in the contemporary advertisements) may have been connected with the Bintley who drew up an early Barrow town plan in 1854. See p. 228 above. [2]*Tithe Commutation Map* (1841), field nos. 730-745 inclusive. Some of this land was exchanged for F.R. Hindpool land. [3]*MS. Diary*, 3.2.64. [4]*Ibid.* [5]Gaythorpe, *B.N.F.C.*, XVII (1909), notes on early Barrow, 189.

Barrow should be left to a free enterprise restricted only by the grip of the larger man of business on the smaller.

In July, 1864, the population of Barrow reached an estimated 8176.[1] That is to say, it had nearly trebled in three years. But in 1863-4 the still empty parts of the Hindpool Estate were relatively little developed for housing purposes, and only one street (Anson Street) was shown in a plan of 1864 as having completed rows of houses on both sides, while three or four other Hindpool streets were half built-up.[2] Perhaps 200 houses, accommodating about 1200 people, were to be found here. Barrow's centre of gravity (in terms of population) appeared beyond the confines of railway land, in the Dalton Road—Church Street areas not far from the original F.R. colony.[3] The prospect of rapid town growth inevitably attracted the professional speculator, whether builder, lawyer or tradesman. A number of builders bought and sold land as part of their normal business, and at least one of them, William Gradwell, worked closely with Ramsden and the F.R. in the important early stages of town development. In 1862 William Clayton of Blackburn joined Gradwell in purchasing Barrowhead property (formerly part of the Paxton estate in the village of Barrow), and in 1860 William Foulis, a local shopkeeper, began a similar career as successful speculator;[4] these men were in a position to profit phenomenally when Barrow's population increase exceeded any sane forecast in the early 'seventies. Even in the mid-'sixties, building plots in the Strand could be bought at 10s. a yard and immediately sold for 25s.[5] The building of Barrow docks naturally stimulated land dealing and sent prices soaring.

The policy of the Railway Company was that of selling the leaseholds of its own land for building purposes. Both land and houses were then offered for sale by Gradwell and others, and were guaranteed to pay " a very high rate of interest ".[6] In 1863 a second Barrow Building Society was formed, to pay interest at the rate of 33 per cent. during the following three years, over £16,000 having been paid into this small and rather select society in that time.[7] Two years later, in 1865, the Furness and South Cumberland Permanent Benefit Building Society was founded. This was

---

[1]*Mins. Ulv. Gdns.*, 21.7.64. [2]Furness Railway, *Gas and Water Plans and Sections*, Barrow P.L. ; apparently parts of what are now St. Vincent, Duncan and Sidney streets. [3]Ground belonging to one of the former landowners in Barrow village, Paxton of Dalton, was used for building sandstone houses and shops—hence Paxton Terrace in the modern town. William Fisher of Dalton acquired 86 acres of Barrowhead land for the insignificant sum of £147 17s. 11d. (in 1861), and on it Mount Pleasant, Church St., and Ramsden St. were built ; Deed, *Buccleuch to Fisher*, 7.3.61, *Deeds and Conveyances, Barrow Corpn. Act.*, 1871. [4]Deeds (*loc. cit*), 24.1.62, 28.6.62, 29.7.62. [5]*Ulv. Adv.*, 2.6.64. [6]E.g., *B. Her.*, advtmt., 12.12.63. [7]*B. Her.*, 7.7.66.

originally controlled by a committee which included William Gradwell, William Park and Benjamin Fish (representing the building trade of Barrow), Myles Gregg (a brickmaker), and Benjamin Townson. This second society does not seem to have been as lucrative as its forerunner, paying only 7 per cent. on its £10 shares in 1866-7.[1] These organisations were not, in practice, calculated to help the artisan to purchase his own dwelling ; they served the purpose of canalising savings and small investments into cottage or terrace property, and were useful to established builders on that account.

Working in conformity with the Ramsden plan, Gradwell laid out and sold off a further large area near Barrow village in 1865. Land at Barrowhead and Salthouse, and in the Hindpool Estate, was already in process of development. A sketch-plan of the late W. B. Kendall,[2] shows that not only the great " show " thoroughfares of Barrow—Duke Street, Abbey Road and the now (1957) decayed Strand—but also the shape of the major part of the Victorian town as finally built, were surveyed, marked out, or otherwise mapped by the mid-'sixties, when the population was still one-quarter of the 1875 figure. The main roads of the Hind-pool Estate were used as base-lines for the planning of one great housing grid ; the old-established lane of Greengate was used as the base-line for a second. A small asymmetrical wedge, made up of roadways near the old Dalton road (then called " Dalton Street ") lay between these grids, this small area having developed fanwise from the site of the original Barrow village. In this way a great modern town received its shape, determining the routes later taken by shoppers and motor omnibuses, and influenced not only by Ramsden's master-plan but also by accidents of ownership and the positions of ancient tracks. It is not to be regretted that the latter played their part, and that the plan of the town did not consist of unrelieved rectangles.

The plan of 1865 and a published plan of 1867[3] show that the Duke of Devonshire's land, adjoining the Hindpool Estate, was also laid out for building if not actually occupied. This section of his estates stretched into what soon became the housing area of Hindpool, and during the 'sixties it lay in reserve, until such time as the population of Barrow should rise to a point nearer the 40,000 expected by Ramsden.[4] The Hindpool Estate was also provided with a water-main, and by 1866, with sewers and drainage.[5]

---

[1]Details of first meeting in *B. Her.*, 14.10.65 ; it was originally entitled a " Temperance Building Society " and working men were invited to invest in it. It did business at Hodbarrow, Millom and Ulverston—hence its modern title. It planned to borrow at 5 to 7 per cent. Cf. also its first *Annual Report and Prospectus* (5.2.67), Barrow P.L. [2]*Kendall MSS.*, letters etc. to F.R. Co., *Plan of Freehold Land at Barrow*, 1865, *sold by Wm. Gradwell to various parties*, Barrow P.L. [3]*Engineering, loc. cit.* [4]*B. Her.*, 13.10.66. [5]*Ibid.*; *F.R. Plans & Sections.*

House-building became Barrow's second largest industry in these years. By 1865 there were 22 firms of bricklayers and builders in the town, with 7 firms of brickmakers, 9 of painters, plumbers and glaziers, and 8 of stonemasons.[1] The firms of Forshaw, Gradwell, Gregg, Holliday, Myerscough, Rawcliffe and Woodhouse were making bricks ; the builders Forshaw and Gradwell were also timber dealers; and Gradwell and Woodhouse carried on a business in limeburning. William Gradwell had the most extensive business; a builder from Roose Cote, he had built ore miners' cottages in the 'fifties,[2] executed pier and other work for the Furness Railway, and now had a large joinery works in the Hindpool Estate, mass-producing doors and window-frames. His was a highly integrated concern.[3] Several brickworks (including those of Gradwell) sought to meet local demand by using the glacial clays of the immediate district, and the firm of Woodhouse, Son and Andrews was manufacturing 25,000 bricks daily by late 1867.[4] General house-building, traditionally a conservative trade, was stimulated into the use of an organisation and technique which, five or six years before, would have been unbelievable. Barrow, with its streets unmade or roughly filled in with furnace slag, looked more and more like a vast builder's yard.[5] Between 1861 and 1868 the number of houses in Barrow increased from 521 to 2,950.[6] The building workers of the district had contrived to erect an average of 400 houses a year in this still little-known town.

Not much can be said on the subject of the houses themselves. Various specimens remain. The earliest, erected before the establishment of large-scale brickmaking in the town, were made of sandstone from Hawcoat, and are to be found in the vicinity of Paxton Terrace. They are unpretentious buildings, and the earliest terrace rows consisted of comparatively small cottages. The standards of workmanship to be found in them have varied greatly ; some have been found to have no adequate foundations, and others to have the invisible parts of walling made up with rubbish,[7] but a great many of the houses of this period have remained tenanted until recent years. The house-building boom of the 'sixties greatly enhanced the price of land, and probably, too, the prices of materials. In 1865 terrace houses in Keith Street, Hindpool, were offered for sale at £175, and could not find a purchaser ; but a similar house in Newland Street was bought for £152.[8] The average price of

[1]*Mannex* (1866), trades list, 377-82. [2]*Wadham Diary*, 28.11.51. " Colliers' houses " are alluded to here, but the meaning seems clear. [3]*B. Times*, 1.12.67, when Gradwell owned two brickworks, a timber yard and a sawmill. [4]*B. Times*, 2.11.67. [5]Cf. *Engineering*, 15.2.67.

[6]1867-8 fig., *Treasurers' Accounts*, Barrow Corporation. The population was then estimated at 16,000, and the figures are credible. [7]I am greatly indebted to Mr. G. W. Warbrick, Building Inspector, Barrow Corporation, for views based on much close examination of this type of property. [8]*B. Her.*, 9.9.65.

working-class property, to the speculator or investor, lay perhaps between the two figures. In the same year, however, a number of better-type dwelling houses were offered for sale at £550 each.[1] Rents had to be kept high to give the investor his ten per cent. return, and in 1866 it was stated by the editor of the *Barrow Times*[2] that " scarcely anything is to be got under 5s. or 6s. a week ". The result was overcrowding ; families shared houses where they could.[3]

At this stage Barrow had no " residential area ", nor was there much sign of one. Houses of a more comfortable type were being built at Storey Square, on slightly higher ground than in other parts of Barrow, and these were provided with very small front gardens. As houses were built along the northern portion of Dalton Road,[4] these, too, were given small front plots or gardens.[5] In the Hindpool Estate proper, workers had allotments which were soon to be engulfed by the building activity of the 'seventies and 'eighties, and space was left for a cricket ground at the foot of Abbey Road ; otherwise, gardens or green spaces were absent from the new town. Greenery was sacrificed to the wide streets and carriage-ways, which are probably unique among British towns of similar size even in the present century.[6]

Barrow's rate of growth slackened after the completion of the docks in 1867,[7] only to increase enormously three years later. By that time the town had a council and corporation, and the eventful years 1870-5 are given separate treatment below. The town of Dalton, too, was growing rapidly in the 'sixties, and its population was stated to have increased by 3000 in the years 1861-4.[8] It was a more unprepossessing place than Barrow,[9] and its new ore miners' houses, built by James Garden and the ore merchant Joseph Rawlinson,[10] still hugged the "airless corners" of the 'fifties. The standard of housing here was beyond question worse than that of the neighbouring town, and the terrace rows of decidedly cramped cottages were built of the local limestone; Barrow, it would seem, had no bricks to spare, or the builders considered it hardly worth their while to bring such materials between three and four miles down the railway line. Miners' settlements were growing at Lindal and Marton, and the houses here were of the Dalton type.[11] Ulvers-

[1]*Loc. cit.* [2]*B. Times*, 18.8.66. [3]*Ibid.* [4]The name was " Dalton Street " until about 1866. [5]*Early town map of Barrow* (undated, but *c.*1872) in the Borough Engineer's Dept., Barrow. [6]Abbey Road was 80 feet wide, and Duke Street about the same width. Most of the back streets anticipated the 36 feet of the " bye-law " age. Narrow alleys almost invariably ran between the back yards, however, and calculations of population density are apt to be misleading. [7]*Borough Treasurers' Reports.* [8]*Ulv. Gdns. Mins.*, 14.7.64. [9]*Ibid.* [10]Rawlinson was a limeburner and brick manufacturer ; both are in *Mannex* (1866), 373-4. [11]It is true that Harrison, Ainslie & Co. provided schools at Lindal ; but there is no warrant for stating that it was a " model village " (Pollard, *L. & C.*, LXIII, 114, n. 104).

ton had virtually ceased to grow in population, and was paying the penalty for its lack of a local board.

During this period of breakneck urbanisation, unprecedented in the history of the region, Barrow lacked any form of effective local government (save the *de facto* government of the railway company) for seven years of the decade, and Dalton and Ulverston for the whole of this time. A discussion of the means by which local citizens ordered their affairs is therefore demanded.

LOCAL GOVERNMENT AND MISGOVERNMENT

In 1864, when the new Furness steel town and port had over 8000 inhabitants, it was discovered by its recently-founded newspaper, the *Barrow Herald*,[1] that it lacked any " legally constituted authority having power to make even a simple bye-law for sanitary improvement ".[2] It lacked baths, washouses, a suitable poor relief system, a hospital and even an adequate supply of medical practitioners ; a service for disposal of filth and nightsoil, firefighting equipment, a local magistracy, a burial place, an adequate postal system, and even numbering of houses.[3] This last inconvenience may explain the tendency of local settlers to crowd at the railway station,[4] no doubt wishing to prevent letters from their relatives from disappearing for ever, and in the absence of any mail, hoping for news by word of mouth. Until the summer of 1863 the Barrow population obtained its water-supplies from " cisterns, wells and rain-water tubs ",[5] but the railway company laid distribution pipes through the Hindpool Estate in the August, when a town service reservoir was almost completed.[6] This water system, however, owed its origins to the needs of the Hindpool ironworks, and it may be doubted—without impugning any humanitarian motives of Ramsden and his colleagues—whether it would have been provided as promptly in the absence of industrial demands.

Water, whether from sky or tap, had to be led away, and the draining and sewering of the town remained bad for another ten years. In the absence of a sanitary authority, the Ulverston Board of Guardians (which by this time included several influential representatives of Barrow industry, among them Ramsden and Schneider) appointed a " Removal of Nuisances Committee for the Parish of Dalton " in 1864. This body took a census of the Barrow

---

[1]First pub. 10.1.1863 by Jas. Waddington jun., Barrow ; weekly ; 1½d. Editor, Geo. Carruthers (1831-79). [2]*B. Her.*, 10.9.64. [3]*B. Her.*, 7.2.63, 28.2.63, 23.7.64, 18.6.64, 9.1.64. [4]*B. Her.*, 25.4.63 ; it was a heartfelt complaint that mail, for part of this period, was not carried by train from Barrow. [5]*B. Her.*, 18.4.63. [6]*Dir. Mins.* (*F.R.*), 5.8.63. A water main between Ireleth and Hindpool (*Loc. cit.* ; shown in *F.R. Plans and Sections*, 1863-4) was already in use.

population in the same year (putting the figure at 8176), and was accordingly able to calculate its mortality-rate with some exactitude. An enquiry was made as to the sanitary state of Dalton parish, and the findings of the Committee were made public in the July.[1] The Dalton death rate was put at the hardly abnormal figure of 20.92 per thousand living, based on returns for six months " at an exceptionally high rate of mortality ". It was stated that the town of Dalton had a higher mortality-rate than Barrow, and that the iron-mining villages were badly sewered and insanitary.[2] At Barrow " a large amount of drainage works " had been carried out, but some districts required draining at once. The non-railway area of the town (including John Street, Dalton Road and Paxton Terrace) was marked by " a serious public nuisance ". Open privies were still the rule, but where a " sufficient supply of water " could be obtained, it was hoped that soil pans would be substituted.

Public comment in Barrow was less dispassionate. Local sanitary reformers found the *Barrow Herald*, a conscientiously Liberal newspaper with a good news service and genuinely free correspondence columns, an excellent vehicle for the propagation of their views, and the *Herald* itself set the tone by declaring that " our industrial armies are cut down by the camp diseases which are generated by . . . inadequate house accommodation, and by want of sanitary arrangements which are never carried out in the neighbourhood of new works ".[3] A correspondent of September 2nd, 1865, was more explicit, and claimed in a vigorous letter that animal excrement blew around the town as dust " into everybody's face ", or clung to the clothes of walkers in wet weather ; that there was a " pestilential breeding hole " in Salthouse Marsh ; that offal was deposited in back premises in Salthouse Road ; that there was a pool of standing water in Rawlinson Street ; that houses in Newland Street were badly ventilated ; and related, in general, a story of bad paving and filthy ashpits. The writer referred to an outbreak of typhus two or three years previously, and hinted at the " difficulty of dealing with persons of avaricious propensities . . . and when these are combined with a degree of petty wealth and interest, the difficulty will become increased ".[4] The basis of

---

[1] *Mins. Ulv. Gdns.*, 14.7.64 ; *B. Her.*, 16.7.64.   [2] At Lindal and Marton. The colonies were administered by Harrison, Ainslie & Co. and the Duke of Buccleuch. The former had provided a school at Lindal, 1854, and enlarged it in 1860 ; *Mannex*, 1866, 330. That, evidently, is one side of the story. [3] *B. Her.*, 13.8.64. This is a quotation from one of the Registrar-General's reports.
   [4] *B. Her.*, 2.9.65. The typhus outbreak was probably in 1862, when there was a sharp increase in registered deaths in Dalton and Ulverston. Newspaper letters of complaint are at *B. Her.*, 18.8.64 (open cellar holes and lack of a public washhouse), 23.7.64 (a bitter catalogue), 3.9.64, 20.5.65, 2.9.65, 1.9.66. Other letters were facetious in drift, complaining of Barrow's " Kingdom of Mud ", e.g. *B. Her.*, 5.11.64 ; " I have sent some of my artists into John St. to put up a shooting box, as it promises to be a good place for ducks during the winter months ".

Barrow's sanitary problem was perhaps illustrated by H. W. Schneider, who said in 1866 that " the whole of the Hindpool Estate was well drained and on a good system . . . in other parts of the town there was . . . much jealousy, and . . . great difficulty to get the owners of property to make drains to run into the main drain ".[1]

Even a passing acquaintance with reports by the Inspectors of the General Board of Health in the early 'fifties suggests that these were not exceptionally bad sanitary conditions for the period. They were bad enough, however, and they were combined with a great many serious and petty inconveniences, particularly affecting artisans, labourers and the very poor.

The Ulverston Guardians, the only legally constituted local government body of any standing in Furness, had a resident medical officer in Dalton, Dr. Hall. He had been appointed when Barrow contained a mere handful of inhabitants and when Dalton itself was little more than a village. By 1862 his division of the Union had become far too populous for any one medical officer to supervise, but in that year he was blamed for the death (through non-attention) of a Barrow man named Wilcock. In defending himself against criticism by the Barrow members of the Board, Hall pointed out that " When medicine cannot conveniently be sent for to my surgery by my patients at Barrow I am in the constant habit of sending it (by) train or post ".[2] In this sentence he revealed the degree of attention which sick paupers in the Barrow neighbourhood might hope to receive. In 1864 the inadequacy of medical provision for the Barrow poor was made the subject of a complaint to the Poor Law Board, as was the question of relief for the destitute in the same district. The Relieving Officer for Dalton, George Simpson, resided at Little Urswick, six and a half miles from Barrow by road, and was utterly incapable of dealing with urgent cases in the new town. H. W. Schneider, in 1862 and in 1864, led a vigorous campaign which had the object of making Dalton into a separate Poor Law district,[3] but even the energetic ironmaster was able to do little against the inertia of the tradesmen, farmers, small gentry and minor men of business who comprised the Guardians for Ulverston and the outlying parishes. A further seven years had to pass before the efforts of Schneider, Ramsden and John Fell led to an enquiry and final Poor Law autonomy for the Barrow district. Here, it will be seen, Barrow's *de facto* rulers showed both responsibility and initiative ; but the new town was indeed their responsibility in every sense, if only because it was the result of their plans and business

---

[1]*B. Her.*, 13.10.66 (enquiry into the proposed incorporation of Barrow. [2]*MS. letter* of Edward Hall to the Guardians, 9.12.62. *Vide* also *Mins. Ulv. Gdns.*, 16.10.62, 23.10.62. [3]*Mins. Ulv. Gdns.*, 25.9.62, 23.10.62, 21.7.64, 18.8.64.

activities. Their energy and organising ability, as will now be apparent, were extraordinary, but they were not always as sensitive to social problems as this. It should also be added that Barrow and Dalton had a high level of employment and low pauperism figures throughout this period, usually about 1.5 per cent. of population as against Ulverston's 3 or 4, and 2 to 3 per cent. for the whole Union.[1] Furthermore, it was claimed by James Stockdale[2] that Barrow was seriously under-assessed for county rate purposes, and although the bustling men of Barrow had a hearty contempt for Ulverston's diehards, expressed at one notable period in acrimonious meetings of the board,[3] there was also dislike and jealousy of the F.R. group on the part of Ulverston members,[4] some of which may have had its origins in the Whitehaven and Furness Junction Railway incident of 1865.[5] Accordingly, Schneider's championship of ill-used vagrants,[6] while no doubt earnest enough, is not to be taken at its face value.

When a neglected pauper fell sick and died in Barrow, or when an able-bodied worker died of cholera or was crushed by a railway wagon, the disposal of his body offered a further problem, for Barrow had no burial ground. In 1861 the Dalton churchyard became overcrowded, and a parochial vestry, acting under the provisions of the Burial Board Act,[7] formed a burial board for Dalton parish and laid out a new cemetery—again at Dalton. This brought Barrow ratepayers into conflict with Dalton vestrymen, and ensured that Barrow corpses had to be carried three miles to their last resting-place. Much animosity was occasioned, flaring into the open in 1866, when at an election for assistant overseer and cemetery registrar for the parish, a trainload of Barrow inhabitants descended on a Dalton vestry meeting and caused uproar.[8] The Barrow partisans were not however successful in getting their nominee elected.

The oligarchic Four and Twenty of Dalton[9] still remained in being, as did that of Ulverston, and until 1867 this self-elected and

---

[1]Statements of pauperism published in the local press, weekly; typical figures for the middle of the decade (*Ulverston Mirror*, 3.6.65) are 258 paupers in Dalton parish (population, more than 20,000, giving little over 1 per cent.), 335 in Ulverston, and 1134 in the Union, out of about 45,000 souls. It might be added that Schneider's first campaign for the separation of Dalton coincided with an increase of pauperism in the Union—the new paupers, thought Devonshire, were " persons sent in from manufacturing districts ". *MS. Diary*, 11.9.62.
[2]Reptd. *Ulverston Mirror*, 3.6.65 ; the real value of Barrow and Dalton for county rate purposes, as made out by the then Guardians' assessment committee, was £59,000, but the rates were paid on an assessment of £19,000.
[3]Even the restrained Devonshire referred to the " asperity " of a meeting at which the Dalton-Barrow group demanded additional relief ; *MS. Diary*, 13.10.70.   [4]*MS. Diary*, 27.12.69.   [5]See p. 267 above.   [6]*Mins. Ulv. Gdns.*, 23.10.62.   [7]15 & 16 *Vict.*, c.85.   [8]For the full sequence of events, *B. Her.*, 5.5.66, 9.6.66, 26.6.66, 7.7.66.   [9]See p. 127 above.

then totally redundant body was Barrow's nominal ruler. It was of little account, however, and scarcely entered into contemporary discussions. Special vestry meetings at St. George's Church (in Barrow), and at Dalton parish church were convened for purposes of highway administration and the provision of gas and lighting. The Hawcoat division of Dalton parish was enabled, following long-established practice,[1] to appoint its road surveyors, who now (1864) had 35 miles of highway to supervise within this single division. A separate surveyor had to be appointed for the district of St. George's (Barrow) in 1864, at a salary of £4 *per annum*, two more such officials supervising the roads in the remainder of Haw-coat division, one for Hawcoat and the other for Walney.[2] Desultory meetings of ratepayers met to examine lamp inspectors' accounts, and by early 1864, 53 public lamps had been erected in Barrow.[3] Dalton and Ulverston already had public lighting at this time.[4]

Barrow's gas company was now a thriving venture, and it was revealed, in November, 1864, that it had been paying 15 to 20 per cent. to its fortunate shareholders, J. T. Smith remarking that the consumers " had paid more for their gas than was intended ". A meeting of interested persons was called in this month, and gave its approval to the sale of the company to the newly formed Furness Gas and Water Company, at £150 a share.[5] This was an F.R. venture,[6] and the gasworks were on the Hindpool Estate ; with a capital of £40,000 the new company proposed to restrict its dividends to the 10 per cent. that the Furness Railway board and shareholders considered a reasonable return on capital invested. Its directors were members of the F.R. board.

Other matters, not so susceptible to profitable enterprise, had to be dealt with by more disinterested inhabitants. The lack of any suitable means of extinguishing fires was the subject of warnings by the *Barrow Herald* ; and in January, 1863, on the occasion of a destructive farm fire at Rampside, it was necessary to bring a horse-drawn fire engine from Ulverston over a distance of six miles.[7] In 1864-5, desultory agitation continued, and in January, 1865, 37 inhabitants headed by the publisher of the *Herald*, signed a petition to the church-wardens of St. George's, Barrow—who were, as now seems hardly surprising, James Ramsden and William Gradwell—demanding the provision of a fire engine.[8] A meeting was called on January 25th, and the engine, a cart with a hand-lever

---

[1]Kelly, *C. & W.*, XXIX (NS), 232. [2]*B. Her.*, 11.4.63, 2.4.64, 16.4.64.
[3]*B. Her.*, 23.1.64. [4]See p. 245 above. [5]*B. Her.*, 12.11.64, 25.2.65.
[6]*Company file*, Registry of J.S. Cos. ; *Dir. Mins.* (*F.R.*), 17.2.65. It received parliamentary approval in the October of 1864. I am indebted to Dr. S. Pollard for details of this company. [7]*B. Her.*, 17.1, 24.1.63.
[8]*B. Her.*, 31.12.64, 14.1.65, 21.1, 28.1.65 ; a vestry could take advantage of the 43rd Section of the Lighting and Watching Act to maintain a fire engine.

pump, duly arrived at some time in 1866. It was stated at the meeting that " although up to that time there had been no occasion for a fire brigade, it was impossible to say how long that good fortune might continue ", and it was, indeed, a matter of good fortune that the town of two thousand houses was not consumed by a conflagration. The cost of the engine was defrayed, happily enough, by utilising " the remainder of the fund from the 10th of March celebration in honour of the marriage of the Prince of Wales ".[1]

It was becoming clearer every month that both Barrow and Ulverston needed a local government board. Ramsden himself was aware of the problem, and in October, 1864, he told an Ulverston meeting that he had " serious intentions " of " promoting " the 1858 Local Government Act at Barrow.[2] There was, however, a delay of three inconvenient and insanitary years before the F.R. General Manager's deliberations had final effect,[3] and it is evident that his declared " intention " was less the result of his interest in sanitary reform, than the result of a public criticism of the state of affairs in the Dalton district and in Ulverston—a majestic pronouncement from the Registrar-General's office, couched in the following terms :

" It is a singular circumstance that the mortality often augments with the increased prosperity of a district, and this is curiously illustrated by Ulverston (Registration District) . . . Ulverston, in the ten years 1841-50, was one of the healthiest districts in England ; the mortality rate did not exceed 18 in 1000. A change took place, and in the ten years 1851-60 the mortality rose to 20 in 1000. The deaths in the last quarter were considered above the average of previous years, caused, says one of the registrars, ' in part by the increase of the population and in part by the prevalence of scarlatina and measles'. He adds ' but there is no distress ; work is plentiful, wages good and provisions cheap . . . '

" The population of many of the townships and parishes of the Ulverston district, at the feet of its fells, is stationary, and in some instances has declined . . . The mortality of the district of Ulverston, exclusive of Dalton, in the last two quarters, was at the rate of 26 and 23 in 1000; while that of Dalton was at the rate of 42 and 31 ; and it is in this sub-district that the spectacle is presented of ' work plentiful, wages good, provisions cheap ' and ' the

---

[1]For details, Leach, *op. cit.*, 123-4. [2]*B. Her.*, 15.10.64. For this Act, *vide* Redlich & Hirst, *English Local Government*, 139-43, 148-9. It was to be read as part of the Public Health Act of 1848. [3]This delay was in part the result of a lack of strongly organised independent opinion locally.

prevalence of destructive epidemics '. This coincidence is reproduced over and over again . . . " [1]

Ulverston, at this time, provided an object lesson in the effects
of procrastination and neglect. In the first quarter of 1865 its
death rate rose to 36.93, [2] although more than ten years had elapsed
since the question of a local board for the town had been discussed. [3] The town already had a Highway Board, [4] and in the
previous September a committee of the Guardians met a committee of this Board to examine the sanitary state of Ulverston.
It was found that scarlatina had attacked one in 40 of the population during July and August, 1864, and in the October an agitation
for the adoption of the 1858 Local Government Act commenced in
earnest. [5] At a town meeting, attended by several leading Barrow
representatives, it was pointed out that Poulton (Morecambe)
already had a local board, [6] although the latter was still a smaller
place than Ulverston or Barrow. A conflict between the supporters
of the Highway Board and the enthusiasts for a properly constituted
sanitary authority then resulted in deadlock. The vigorous and
public-spirited editor of the *Ulverston Mirror*, Joseph Alexis
Bernard, [7] regarded the Highway Board supporters as " the
advocates of dirt ", and assailed, as did the *Barrow Herald,* a temporary shift or compromise between the Ulverston parties by which
the " dirt " faction agreed to withdraw from the argument if the
death rate exceeded 27 in the thousand (about 220 persons) for six
months, on condition that the " local board " party agreed to the
then Highway Board becoming the Ulverston Board of Health. [8]
Editor Bernard wrote bitterly on the subject. " They demand ,"
he said, " a sacrifice of some forty persons in the half year." [9]

Estimates of death rates, although buttressed by official
registrar's figures and an occasional unofficial census (as in Dalton),
are apt to be somewhat inaccurate. Those for birth rates are also
open to criticism. The Dalton and Barrow Registrar of Births and

---

[1]In the *27th Annual Rept. of the Reg. General (Abstract for* 1864), 1 (50).
[2]*Ulverston Mirror*, 15.4.65 ; H. W. Schneider's figure.   [3]See pp. 243-4 above.
[4]*Mins. Ulv. Gdns.*, 1.9.64 ; this was apparently a body formed in pursuance of
the Highways Act of 1862 (25 *& 26 Vict., c.*61). The Lancashire Record Office
held (1955) no documents relating to it.   [5]*Mins. Ulv. Gdns.*, 25.8.64, 1.9.64,
13.10.64.   [6]*B. Her.*, 15.10.64. It could have been added that many small
towns were busily engaged in obtaining " local boards " in order to resist the
1862 Highways Act ; for this tendency, *vide* the writings of Mr. and Mrs. Webb,
and Clapham, *Econ. Hist. Mod. Brit.*, II, 205-6.   [7]For biog. details, *vide*
Casson, *A Few Furness Worthies*, 83-7. The *Mirror* was established in opposition to the *Ulverston Advertiser* on 14.4.1860. Bernard (d.1880) fought for the
right of the press to be admitted to Guardians' meetings ; the earliest editions
(*B.M. Newspaper Library*) show Casson's account of this episode to be correct.
The *Mirror* fought numerous battles on behalf of worthy causes, and attacked
John Stanyan Bigg (*D.N.B.*) of the *Advertiser*. [8]*Ulverston Mirror*, 2.9.65 ;
B. Her., 2.9.65. [9]*Ulv. Mirror, loc. cit.*

Deaths, George Simpson (who was also the Relieving Officer) lived at Little Urswick, [1] several miles from Barrow. In April, 1866, the *Barrow Herald* complained in the strongest terms that bereaved persons were obliged to make this long journey on foot in order to register a death, and pointed to some cases of shocking misery. In the event of a birth, Simpson could visit the parents' home. [2] As has recently been pointed out, however, birth registration in the mid-nineteenth century tended to be defective [3] in any case, and might miss as many as 18 births per 1000 in 1861-70. Although some estimates of local rates are attempted here, therefore, it is not assumed that they do more than show tendencies very broadly, or that they are much more accurate than the eighteenth century rates in an earlier chapter ; the Victorian registration was more complete than that in the Georgian parishes, but the population of Dalton parish fluctuated considerably in the 'sixties.

Estimating the growth of Dalton's population (including that of Barrow) proportionately to the increase in births between 1861 and 1871, the death-rate for that parish was 20.7 in 1861, 27.0 in 1862, and 21.1 in 1863. Thereafter, as young people flooded into the district and the registered births rose to nearly three times the 1861 figure, the estimated death-rate—after drawing the attention of Dr. Farr's men by rising to *circa* 24 in the thousand in 1864—seems to have fallen to typically rural levels in the late 'sixties, moving around 17 for several years of the decade. Those for the Furness Fell districts—Colton, Hawkshead, Broughton, with the inclusion of Cartmel—were more uniform and easier to calculate, and showed a mean death-rate for the decade of 18 to 19 ; while Ulverston's, also easier to calculate by virtue of its nearly static population and steady annual birth and death totals, were shockingly high, reaching 34.3 in 1864 (a bad year locally) and 28.8 in 1866. The mean rate was well up in the middle twenties.

It is evident enough that newly-established industrialisation was not solely, or even mainly, responsible for these figures, which are considerably worse than anything that can be computed for the same area during most of the eighteenth century. But—*pace* the enthusiasts for the meliorist view—the shifting of people caused by industry and industrial growth has to bear a share of the blame. Ulverston kept the older people of the area, and a proportion of the very poor and shiftless, while new communications probably meant easier transit for the microbe and the virus. Similar phenomena account for the surprisingly high death-rates in a number of fell areas. The unexceptional rates in Dalton (and perhaps infant Barrow) mask a high child mortality rate, common enough in the

---

[1]*Mannex*, 1866, 390. [2]*B. Her.*, 28.4.66. [3]Glass D. V., in *Population Studies*, V, 1951-2, 70-71.

industrial north but certainly no improvement over the record of Georgian Furness.

The Registrar-General's particulars of " causes of death " in Ulverston Registration District (that is, the whole of Furness) show that measles, scarlatina and typhus outbreaks occurred in 1864, and the Dalton figures reflect the increased mortality which followed. An analysis of these causes of the period 1856-70 shows that next to the pulmonary and respiratory diseases, scarlatina or scarlet fever occurred most frequently in the district, if those deaths caused by it are any guide ; and the enquiry also shows that the zymotic diseases (measles, whooping cough, diphtheria, typhus and so on) became suddenly more serious when overcrowding was worsened by a great influx of people into the Dalton district in 1864. This development, of course, attracted the attention of the Registrar-General's office, and led to the publication of the strictures already quoted. [1]

In the quinquennium 1861-5 there was a marked and serious increase in local deaths caused by " diseases of the respiratory organs " ; 15 per cent. of all deaths, against 10.4 per cent in the previous quinquennium. This increase may have been caused by conditions of work in the expanding iron-mining industry. Child mortality, nearly always heavy in this period and age, also worsened noticeably, moving from 33.1 per cent. (1856-60) to 36.1 per cent. of all deaths (1861-65). [2] Hence, when we talk of the deficiencies of local government, and of serious shortcomings in the public health of the neighbourhood, this is not idle phrasing. Furness Railway capital and enterprise may have brought higher wages, but the industrialisation which followed from both helped to bring death to many. Yet, even so, Furness was still not an unhealthy district compared with many other parts of Lancashire—the civil registration abstracts show it plainly.

Eleven hundred inhabitant householders signed a petition for the incorporation of Barrow-in-Furness during the summer of 1866 ; a counter-petition was signed by 24 persons only, representing property of the total value of £1202. [3] The will, therefore, existed. It is not known who initiated the collection of signatures, but railway company and steelworks were soon afterwards shown to be in full support, and James Ramsden's influence was undoubtedly at work. The period of delay was at an end ; and its duration perplexed at least one person, for Joseph Richardson, the editor of the newly established *Barrow Times*, declared: " Middlesbrough

---

[1]See p. 293. [2]The relevant figures are in the 19*th Report of the Registrar-General*, p. 157 (Deaths from Several Causes) and pp. 114-15 (Deaths at Different Ages) and the *Reports* for the years following. [3]*B. Her.*, 13.10.66 and Leach, *op. cit.*, 19-20.

has for twelve years enjoyed a local government . . . We really
think that Barrow might have had local government more than
three years since, if its people had sought for it." [1]

In consequence of the petition, an enquiry was held before
Capt. Donnelly, R.E., Commissioner of the Privy Council, on
October 12th, 1866. Ramsden, Schneider, and the Duke of
Devonshire's agent William Currey prepared their cases carefully,
and were not only able to point to the rapid growth of Barrow and
its manufactures, but were also able to ask for what must have
seemed (in view of the physical extent of the town, then less than a
square mile all told) an extraordinarily large borough district of
7570 acres, or 8.2 square miles excluding sands. [2] Ramsden
produced a plan showing the street layout for an estimated population of 40,000. [3] It was shown that building operations had already
reached Newbarns and Hawcoat, villages respectively one and a
half and two miles from the site of the old hamlet of Barrow, and
Ramsden urged that Piel Harbour, which was to be extended for
the accommodation of more shipping, should be included within
the proposed town boundary. The area within the latter embraced
roughly one-third of the parish of Dalton (17,961 acres) ; the Duke
of Devonshire would then have 2900 acres within the borough, and
Ramsden's mansion at Abbots Wood was to be included within its
confines. [4]

H. W. Schneider stated that he had signed the petition at the
will of the Steel Company. [5] Counsel for the petitioners urged that
" Her Majesty would be pleased to appoint the Duke of Devonshire
to nominate the first officers of the town ", because this would avoid
a five months' delay in the election of councillors by the normal
method. The appointment of councillors was opposed by John
Poole, acting for the counter-petitioners ; Poole, himself attorney
and land agent, [6] somewhat artlessly argued that the nominated
council might be " a clog on the prosperity of the town . . . this
might apply particularly to the solicitors who had so large an
interest in the building and in its prosperity ". [7] Nevertheless,
he was able to represent the interests of democracy after his fashion,

---

[1]*B. Times*, 27.1.66. Richardson was a Cleveland man ; biog. in pamph.,
undated but *c.* 1890, *Joseph Richardson*, viewed by courtesy of Mr. J. L. Hobbs
and Richardson's grandson, Mr. S. B. Gaythorpe.   More is said about him
below. [2]*B. Her.*, 13.10.66 (full report of enquiry). [3]For the precise boundary,
vide Tyson, *Abstract of Accounts, Dalton etc.*, 24.   It did not include Walney
Island, but reached Millwood in the N.E., the Roanhead-Dalton road in the
N.W., and the Concle-Rampside highway in the E.   [4]Ramsden's ev., rept.
of enquiry, *loc. cit.*   [5]*Loc. cit.*   [6]Poole, as was later shown, was one of the
most energetic land agents in the town, and was afterwards a persistent opponent
of the town council.   [7]It seems hard on Poole to assume that he regarded
drains as a clog on prosperity.

and he "objected on principle against the appointment being placed in the hands of any single individual, no matter who that individual might be", earning some applause for this statement.[1]

The need for a corporation was brought out plainly enough at the enquiry. The leading petitioners had in their minds the cholera scare which was widespread in the summer of 1866, and in Barrow, as in other towns, renewed interest was taken in the prevention of this disease.[2] Comparatively vigorous measures by the Nuisance Committee of the Guardians had, in Schneider's words "failed to do what they had set out to do . . ." The system of drainage in the town was chaotic, due to "the parsimony of some and the jealousy of others".[3] The more parsimonious property owners were soothed by the assurance that the appointment of a Town Clerk would involve a burden of only about £150 on the rates, and the charter of incorporation, if granted, "would not create any change beyond the town's affairs being placed under the control of a municipal body instead of the vestry and the Board of Guardians".[4] As far as the next few years were concerned, the words were more prophetic than the speaker knew.

As was made clear in the discussion, the 1858 Local Government Act would have to be adopted in any case ; but by obtaining a large and separate borough district, the dominant Barrow elements would be able to administer their own territory unimpeded by jealousy and obstructiveness in Dalton and Ulverston.[5] The timing of the incorporation however, should not escape mention. The town's charter was received on June 13th, 1867, some nine months after the initial enquiry, and the first meeting of the Barrow-in-Furness Town Council was held on July 15th. The Devonshire Dock was completed in the August and formally opened on September 19th. The dock contract had taken roughly three years to complete, and nearly three years passed before Ramsden's expressed desire for adequate local government received some satisfaction. Devonshire and Gladstone, guests of honour at the dock-opening ceremony, were appropriately welcomed by Barrow's first Mayor, James Ramsden. It is not clear whether all the inhabitants of the town appreciated the happiness of this coincidence.

[1]Devonshire makes no reference to the appointment of councillors in his *MS. Diary* ; it is evident that he was pressed to do so, and had little interest in the matter. [2]The Nuisance Committee of the Guardians acted fairly energetically in the August and September. 57 notices to enter premises were served in Barrow, and 16 filth cases were brought before the bench on Sept 3rd.; *B. Her.*, 18.8, 8.9, 13.10.66. [3]Schneider's ev. at enquiry; *loc. cit.* [4]Counsel's ev., *loc. cit.* [5]The next major move of the Barrow group was to obtain separate Poor Law jurisdiction for Barrow (1871).

The new Council,[1] as declared in the charter, consisted of a
Mayor, four Aldermen and twelve Councillors. Ramsden ranked
as an alderman, and his three colleagues represented haematite ;
Myles Kennedy, H. W. Schneider and Robert Hannay. The
councillors were as follows :

Edward Wadham [2]	*Mineral agent*	Jas. Fisher [8]	*Shipping agent*
J. T. Smith [3]	*Steelworks manager*	Jno. Hunt [9]	*Publican, Ship Inn*
W. J. A. Baldwin [4]	*Dalton landowner*	Wm. Gradwell [10]	*Builder, contractor*
Jos. Rawlinson [5]	*Ore merchant*	J. Westray [11]	*Ironfounder*
J. K. Hodgson [6]	*Coal agent*	Wm. Ashburner [12]	*Shipbuilder*
W. Boulton [7]	*Farmer*	Jos. Allison [13]	*Surgeon*

The new members of the council were by no means inexperienced in
matters of local government. Several of them were, or had been,
Guardians, highway surveyors or churchwardens ; and the choice
of individuals, whether in fact Ramsden's or not, appears to have
been reasonably sound from the administrative viewpoint. Ten
of the members, however, were (excluding Ramsden) in some way
or other connected with railway company, steelworks, or the
haematite trade ; a state of affairs which was probably inevitable
in the circumstances, but which necessarily affected the conduct of
local government in some degree. It made them extremely ready to
listen to Ramsden's advice in the discussion of all major topics, and,
generally, to concur with his wishes. There were no concealed or
overt political divisions, and one member only is known to have had
doggedly Conservative views ;[14] Schneider, Ramsden and their
business associates from the Duke of Devonshire downwards were
avowed Liberals, and in later years, when polling results provided
direct evidence, the overwhelming weight of opinion in the town
lay also in that quarter. Political divisions were to have no real
meaning in any case ; there was only one " party ", and it was
ruled from railway offices and steelworks.

Although the town had a small Town Hall, the Council held a
series of early meetings in the Board Room of the Furness Railway's

[1] *Charter of Incorporation, Barrow-in-Furness*, and *Minutes of the Council*
(MS.), from July 15th, 1867, by courtesy of the Town Clerk. [2] Wadham
(1828-1913) was mineral agent to the Duke of Buccleuch, and his business and
private diary (by courtesy of Mr. H. A. Slater and Boughton Estates Ltd.) is
occasionally referred to in these pages. [3] Smith receives frequent reference
in these pages. [4] Biog. notes in Kelly, *Newbarns, B.N.F.C.* (NS), V, 32.
[5] Biog. in Casson, *op. cit.*, 76 sqq. [6] *Mannex* (1866), 407. [7] *Op. cit.*, 376 ;
he is given as a farmer of Park House. In 1865 (*Ulv. Gdns. Mins.*) he was a
Guardian for Dalton. [8] Biog. notes, Fisher, J., *Popular Hist. of Barrow*,
158 ; *F.P. & P.*, II, 269-70. [9] *Mannex* (1866), 380. [10] Frequent references to him are made in the text. He was not to remain the lone builder for
many years. [11] I am indebted for information on Westray to Messrs. J. B.
Westray, Leadenhall St., London ; details of his firm in Leach, *op. cit*, 74-5.
[12] Notes in White, *Furness Folk etc.*, 35-7. [13] The town's public-spirited
elder surgeon ; frequent references are made to him in the text. See also
F.P. & P., II, 241. [14] Edward Wadham, on the evidence of his diary.
His employer, the Duke of Buccleuch, was also Conservative in persuasion.

offices at St. George's Square,[1] and this arrangement, presumably, was more convenient for an excessively busy Mayor. It certainly provided an appropriate atmosphere for the commencement.

The 1858 Local Government Act was adopted on August 20th, 1867, and the adoption was confirmed in the November. This was the sole important business of the Council during that year, and its very modest activities were otherwise concerned largely with the preparation for the dock-opening ceremony.[2] Not until the beginning of 1868 did the governance of the town commence in any significant fashion. The Council had, however, appointed its officials.[3] W. T. Manclarke, a solicitor of Barrow and Broughton, was the Town Clerk, and Robert Wallas, manager of the local branch of the Lancaster Banking Co., was the " Trustee " or Treasurer. Manclarke became Secretary of the Local Board of Health at £100 *per annum*, and William Harrison, resident engineer to the Furness Railway, became Borough Surveyor at £5 *per annum*. Meanwhile, an *ad hoc* committee was formed to appoint a collector and to ascertain his duties.[4]

It had been stated by counsel at the incorporation enquiry that there were 8000 ratepayers in the town, and " the amount of assessment was upwards of £40,000 ".[5] But it is clear that the new body did not expect a high rate product, and so it set about the task of ensuring other sources of income. In October, 1867, negotiations were commenced for the purchase of the Furness (Railway's) Gas and Water Company installations.[6] When the transfer of this undertaking took place a year later, the corporation acquired a fruitful source of income. The private company paid 10 per cent. to its shareholders in 1867.[7] Its purchase was financed by means of a loan from the Rock Assurance Company ; the Town Hall, Market Hall and Police offices, owned by the Furness Railway, were also transferred to the corporation ; and the Market Hall was to be maintained not out of the rates, but by means of gas and waterworks profits, while the 5 per cent. interest on the Rock Assurance loan of £10,000 was to be paid off by Market Hall and other rentals at £745 *per annum*.[8] The Market Hall and Town Hall were sold by the F.R. at a price approximating to original cost, for £15,000.[9] Ramsden presented all this, correctly, as a neat financial arrangement.[10] Private enterprise was transmuted into public enterprise—

[1]*B.T.C. Mins.*, 5.8, 20.8, 2.9, 7.10, 4.11, 2.12.67, 6.1, 3.2.68. Eight of the eleven earliest meetings were held at the F.R. offices. The Town Hall was then in use, and was afterwards used regularly.
[2]" The course to be adopted " was decided on Sept. 2nd, and robes of office and maces were acquired for the auspicious occasion. [3]For list, *vide* also Leach, *op. cit.*, 21. [4]*B.T.C. Mins.*, 20.8, 2.9, 10.9, 4.11, 9.11.67. [5]*Loc. cit.* [6]*B.T.C. Mins.*, 7.10, 2.12.67. [7]*B. Times*, 12.10.67. [8]*B.T.C. Mins.*, 24.8.68 ; *B. Times*, 29.8.68. [9]*Dir. Mins. (F.R.)*, 13.5.68. [10]*B. Times*, 29.8.68.

albeit with little real philanthropy on the part of the railway company—and the Mayor's skill as an administrator becomes apparent.

The sale of the Town Hall to the corporation was bitterly criticised by a group led by John Poole.[1] This group, calling itself the Ratepayers' Protective Association, was the only organised opposition to the dominant elements and was composed, according to the *Barrow Times*, of ambitious persons who were out of favour with the major industrial interests or who had private axes to grind.[2] Poole did however make the point that the F.R. valued the Town Hall and Market Hall land at 1s. 3d. a yard (in fairness to the F.R., a comparatively low price), when it had been worth 2d. a yard a few years previously.[3] The point was hardly valid, unless Poole expected the Railway Company to take a philanthropic, as apart from a business, interest in Barrow.

The 1858 Local Government Act gave the corporation a wide range of powers, particularly as affecting the control of nuisances or bad drainage.[4] But its adoption was a mere formality, giving the Council the status of a local board. A definitive Barrow Corporation Act was still required, and was obtained in the summer of 1868.[5] It embodied the conventional provisions of 1858, and its major purpose was to enable the corporation to acquire the Gas and Water Company, the Market, Town Hall and other buildings, and to enable it to purchase and hold baths, wash-houses, public libraries, schools and museums.[6] All streets, sewers and drains were to be vested in the corporation, which was to that extent no longer a body which merely enforced private improvements. It could purchase land without having recourse to the Land Clauses Consolidation Act, make its own bye-laws and enforce police regulations, and operate a variety of controls over markets, fairs, slaughterhouses, registration of common lodging houses, weighing machines, parks and public clocks.[7] Of more interest is the power to enforce a minimum width of ten yards in new streets, and that stipulating four hundred cubic feet of space for every lodger in dwelling-houses.[8] The use of cellars as dwellings was expressly forbidden;[9] so much for good intentions. Clause XVIII of the Act laid down that the corporation's land purchase powers were to take effect in three years; an arrangement which undoubtedly cost the ratepayers dearly, for by 1870-1 land prices had rocketed.

[1]*B. Times* 20.6.68, 29.8.68.   [2]Joseph Richardson in *B. Times*, 7.11.68, 10.4.69 and *passim*. He called the Association the " Cabal " ; they were builders and land agents who disliked paying rates.   [3]*B. Times*, 29.8.68. [4]Redlich and Hirst, *loc. cit.*   [5]31 & 32 *Vict. c.*civ. (July 1st, 1868).   [6]Preamble to the Act, and Clauses IX, X.   [7]*Ibid.*, Secns. 54, 57, 59, 62-4, 66, 72, 76-7 ; Clses. VII-IX, XII,XIV, XVIII.   [8]Secns. 88, 121. This provision was a pioneering one ;   *The Engineer*, 5.6.68, commented on it with interest. [9]Secn. 121.

Owners of railway and agricultural land were to pay only one-fourth of the borough rate, the corporation could rate owners instead of occupiers only when the rateable value of property was less than £9, and the compulsory recovery of street improvement and other expenses from owners was not to exceed 5 per cent. *per annum.*[1] In consequence, the financial foundations of the corporation were somewhat slight when measured against the concentrated wealth of the industries within its boundaries. Section 27 of the Act, by laying down the provision that the gas rate was not to exceed 6s. per 1000 cubic feet, offered modest protection to the consumer. (The maximum rate—considered a high one by the *Barrow Times*[2]— was charged in 1868-9, and 5s. for the following ten years.)

Besides obtaining the powers detailed, the corporation became a Burial Board under the Act,[3] and thus completed the first stage of its battle with Dalton.

It will be seen that the founders and rulers of Barrow (notably James Ramsden) had sound enough intentions, and although far too little research has been devoted to the subject, it would seem that this was one of a number of local Acts of Parliament which foreshadowed some of the more enlightened and socially important provisions of the 1875 Public Health Act. To see these progressive enactments, inhibited as they were by an acute awareness of the rights of private property, purely as manifestations of that ill-defined phenomenon known as " the Victorian conscience ", is to run the risk of confusing or distorting history.[4] In this particular (and therefore only partially representative) case a group of eminently practical men, obliged to pick their way to council meetings through pools of filthy water, were simply reacting sensibly to obvious defects in social life. Ramsden, an industrial manager and organiser *par excellence*, had had eight years in which to learn something of the problems of a rapidly growing community, and was able to apply his managing and organising technique to the affairs of local government ; and his was an almost complete autocracy within his chosen sphere. On the other hand, the corporation had to be run like a business mechanism, in terms of profit and loss. The latter, it is true, are not always tangibles— has not the man of business learned the importance of good will in his dealings with customers, and the value of industrial welfare *vis-a-vis* his workmen?—and the Furness Railway manager and his associates had some reason to believe that a reasonably well-run Barrow represented a good investment ; an investment which could

---

[1]Clses. XV-XVIII. [2]*B. Times*, 7.12.67, where it was stated that 4s. to 5s. was charged in other towns. [3]Clause XI. [4]It should not be forgotten that Dickens made Mr. Gradgrind an avid reader of Blue Books.

be measured in terms of their time if not in terms of the railway and steelworks shareholders' money.[1]

That the enlightened clauses and sections of the 1868 Corporation Act remained ineffective for many years, is only partly a reflection of Ramsden's limitations, but a very clear reflection of the limitations of the society in which he was carrying out his experiments. Within two years, an unparalleled boom in haematite, iron and steel led to a further and breakneck expansion in local industries, and the overburdened general manager of this company town, caught up in the desperate pursuit of some opportunities and the making of others, was faced by local social problems which multiplied faster than before.

The years 1868 and 1869, when business was somewhat dull in the district as a whole, afforded a breathing space. Large numbers of workers left the town as the docks were completed, houses lay empty, and the rateable value of the borough declined.[2] The *Barrow Times* of May 8th, 1868, commenting on the depressed state of the locality, lamented that " the rate will never be collected ", and a remark by J. T. Smith reveals that property was not adequately rated at all.[3] This need not surprise the investigator ; the temporary check to industrial development gave the council its own reasons for doing little with any drive and resolution, and no doubt it would have been utopian to expect the senior members of that body to put into effect the necessary preparations for the population of 40,000 foreseen by James Ramsden. The Corporation's *Treasurer's Reports* show that the rate product was actually lower in the boom period of 1871-2 than in the comparatively depressed one of 1868-9 ; that in the four accounting years commencing in 1868, a total of £10,523 was spent on sewers, sanitation and highways as against £15,778 on public buildings ; and that it was possible to keep the borough rate at 1s. 10d. or less because the newly-acquired gas and water department began to play a more important part in the council's financial calculations than did any income to be extorted from unwilling ratepayers. The gas and water income exceeded that from the rates by 1870-1 ; not surprisingly, for the town had many more water consumers than ratepayers (3520 of the former in 3311 houses in 1870),[4] and there were in addition 1302 gas consumers in 1871, from which it follows that the generality of the population were paying their full share of the cost of local government by providing the gas and water department

<hr>

[1]This paragraph is offered as a working hypothesis only. The visionary element in Ramsden's makeup is not overlooked, but the historian is forced to judge in terms of deeds, not aspirations.   In any case, we know too little of the real motives of philanthropy, in given cases or in general.
    [2]*B. Times*, 10.8.67, 29.8.68, 6.3.69.   [3]Cf. his remarks reptd. in *B. Times*, 8.1.70.   [4]Evidence before *Committee on* 1873 *Barrow Corporation Act* (*published rept.*), p. 3.

with a large profit.　On the other hand, the larger property owners could not consider themselves overburdened with rates, railway property paying only one quarter of the borough rate.　The Poor Rate was 1s. 8d. in 1869, falling to 1s. 4d. in 1870, and did not rise above the former figure for half a century.

On February 17th, 1868, the Council formed itself into three main committees—Highways and Health, Finance, and Gas and Water.　Of these the first was the most important to the general public, if the last-named was the committee which counted most with the Council and Treasurer, and its initial report revealed a sad state of affairs in the borough.　The worst sanitary shortcomings were almost literally under the noses of the councillors.　There was privy filth in the ashpits in Cornwallis Street, a few yards from the Town Hall ; a large number of houses in the Hindpool Estate (St. Vincent, Duncan, Sidney and Keith Streets) lacked drainage ; open privies were " universal " ; not one street between Dalton Road and Duke Street was properly formed ; sewers behind Preston and Rawcliffe streets were inefficient, and drainage was flowing over open land. [1]　There were a few signs of progress; the Steel Company, which had a number of houses in Hindpool, [2] was equipping the latter with " superior drainage ", and the shipbuilder and councillor William Ashburner, who owned 40 houses [3] in the same district, had " begun to use the closet pans ".　William Gradwell and other owners had completed a number of private streets and desired them to be passed over to the corporation as public highways. [4]　In May, 1868, William Harrison, the Borough Surveyor, reported that all public roads were in " good repair " but that numerous private streets were " almost impassable ". [5]　Sewage carters were depositing filth in Abbey road " too near the buildings ", and it was shown soon afterwards that the dumping ground belonged to the Furness Railway. [6]　In the June, Harrison retired, and his place was taken by Peter Black, a conscientious official whose tenure of office was also short.　In early 1869 the *Barrow Times* reported that the " Nuisance Inspector " (presumably the Surveyor) was " not functioning ". [7]　Black nevertheless drew attention to the deplorable state of the ashpits in the town. [8]　This last was chiefly due to the absence of any regular system of scavenging, and an adequate organisation for the removal of nightsoil was not developed until 1872.

[1] *B.T.C. Health Committee Mins.*, 20.3.68.　　[2] Fifteen houses, according to the *Borough Rate Books* (MS.).　[3] *Ibid.*　[4] Ctte. Rept., *cit.*　[5] *Health Committee Mins.*, 1.5.68.　[6] *Ibid.*, and 13.6.68.　[7] *B. Times*, 2.1.69.　[8] *Health Committee Mins.*, 3.7.68.

Although the corporation did not at first qualify for sizeable loans from dukes, railway or steelworks,[1] it was a useful provider of business and modest income for the builders of the town, who kept their men at work on the metalling and completion of streets during the relatively quiet year of 1869. Between February, 1869 and August, 1870, fifteen streets and thoroughfares were adopted as public highways. Seven of these were in Hindpool,[2] and were evidently paid for, in part or whole, by the F.R. A little light is thrown on the aloofness of the railway company by an incident of January, 1869, when the corporation had to pay for a sewer which crossed F.R. territory between the Strand and the docks.[3] Ramsden laid down the law in this matter. On the other hand, the large companies which had fathered the corporation were not obstructive in paying for street improvements, and the existence of that body provided them with a useful means of divesting themselves of irksome responsibilities. Legally enforced private improvements were a far greater burden on the small property owner, actively championed by the Ratepayers' Protective Association.[4]

This body, contemptuously dubbed " the Cabal " by Joseph Richardson of the *Barrow Times*, forced Gradwell and Westray to resign from the Council in April, 1869, by writing a letter of complaint to the Home Secretary ; Gradwell had supplied the corporation with limestone and Westray had provided it with iron pipes. Both were closely associated with the dominant powers, and the Council was outmanoeuvred, but it refused to think ill of them. Hotly defended by Joseph Richardson, the two councillors were back in its ranks by the July.[5] " Men of thorough business habits," as Richardson called them, could be relied upon to work diligently enough at the very limited tasks the new governing body considered necessary.

No apology is offered, or should be needed, for this rather pedestrian description of a pedestrian local council in its early days. Modern local government, recognisable only in veriest form and convention, had appeared in the Furness which not many years

---

[1]The Duke of Devonshire soon afterwards (i.e. in the early 'seventies) made a large loan to the corporation ; but the *Treasurer's Reports* are not explicit as to the details. [2]*B.T.C. Mins. (Gen. Mtg.)*, 1.2, 6.2, 11.9, 9.11.69 ; 7.2, 1.8.70 ; *B. Times*, 6.8.69. The Hindpool Streets were not paved at all before improvement and adoption. [3]*B.T.C. Mins. (Gen. Mtg.)*, 4.1.69. [4]Poole and Fish, its leaders, defaulted on private improvement accounts ; *B .Times*, 10.7.69. For the attitude of others, *Wadham Diary*, 1.3.69.

[5]*B. Times*, 10.4, 10.7.69. Richardson, although a man of fire and courage, and a frequent and sometimes savage attacker of Ramsden's group in later years, was still favourably disposed to the latter in 1869. We need not search for an economic motive in the actions of every man, but it is fair to add that he executed printing contracts for the corporation in the late 'sixties (as at other times), and no doubt hoped for more business.

before had known only Four and Twenties, manor courts and parish meetings. Eight or nine years before the incorporation of Barrow, there was not even a sizeable town to govern. The graves and painlookers of the agricultural hamlets in the district were still appointed, and in some cases the duties of these officials were carried out ; especially was this so in the hamlet of Biggar on Walney Island. But the yeoman settlement of Salthouse, referred to elsewhere in these pages,[1] had 123 houses on its land in 1871, as against 6 in 1851,[2] and Newbarns and Hawcoat, only yesterday quiet hamlets in a remote district, were already touched by the tide of bricks and mortar. They were being reached by less material but no less significant influences ; the Town's Book of Biggar, recording the administrative affairs of that hamlet, contains the following pregnant entry for the year 1863 : " *Pd. herd for overtime, 2s.*"[3] Events were moving fast, and were soon to move too fast for the men who governed Barrow.

---

[1] *Vide* esp. p. 76 above.   [2] Kendall, *Salthouse, B.N.F.C.,* VI (NS), 38.
[3] Cf. Pearson, H. G., *C. & W.* (NS), XI, 194.

CHAPTER XV

WORKMEN AND TOWNSMEN IN THE 'SIXTIES

We have seen something of the economic and business organisation of the Furness ironfield during these years, and have been able to examine, albeit briefly, the local government of the neighbourhood. Thus far the story has been one of industrialists, guardians and councillors. What of the generality of the population, the unskilled labourers from nearby villages and the skilled workers from farther afield?

Haematite was the foundation of the local economy, and the labour of the ore-miner produced the life-blood of its prosperity. The metaphor has more than one application ; the damp, greasy ore stained everything it touched, leaving reddish trails on roads and lanes, dripping from carts and railway wagons. The countryside around Dalton was transformed by spoil heaps and by the gashes and scars left by tramway cuttings and embankments. Everywhere among the limestone walls and cottages of Dalton were the red marks of its staple industry.

The lives and work of the ore miners may be described in the following fashion ; they worked in dirty, sometimes dangerous and highly unpleasant conditions for what was sometimes a fairly high money wage. The first authoritative miner's view of his fellows' conditions was not published until nearly a generation after the period now described, but there can be no doubt that much of what this writer says applies also to the 'sixties. Firstly, then, there was a great disparity of wages for the same work in different haematite mines. Secondly, the work was dangerous and many men were disabled, their widows sometimes ending in the workhouse. Thirdly, the work tended to be irregular ; shallow pits were easily flooded with water, and the deeper mines had inadequate pumping apparatus, with the result that the miner was plunged into periods of unemployment in winter. [1] These conditions not surprisingly gave rise to attempts to form trade union organisations : and according to the statement mentioned, [2] the Dalton and District United Workmen's Association (or miners' union) of 1888 was formed only after two previous unsuccessful attempts to establish similar bodies in the district. There is reason to believe that the latter took place in 1862-3 and 1872.

---

[1] *Prospectus of the Dalton and District United Workmen's Association* (1892) in the S. & B. Webb Trade Union Collection, British Library of Political and Economic Science, London School of Economics. The Association was founded on Dec. 22nd, 1888. [2] *Ibid.*

Indeed, something is known of one of these sallies on the part of the miners. In the spring of 1863, a number of the workmen at the pits of Harrison, Ainslie and Co. are stated to have enrolled their names with the organisers of " the miners' union recently established in this district ", and this firm thereafter appealed to the Ulverston Guardians to make the men—who were apparently on strike—ineligible for poor relief. It was alleged that " these men had left work when they had an opportunity of making good wages ". The Guardians decided that they could do nothing " unless the men became recipients of relief ".[1] Although little more is heard of this combination, it would seem that the haematite miners, like workers in Barrow industries, were responding to the " prosperous " conditions of the time[2] by seeking to make their own lot a better one.

The introduction of more efficient surface haulage and winding gear undoubtedly speeded up the miner's work. H. W. Schneider, who was human enough to throw out an occasional indiscretion, and who could speak his mind freely in an age when the master was strong and the workman comparatively weak, announced jestingly (not long after the above incident) that " my men in the mines do a very large amount of work for their wages, and some of them get 27s. a week. I get 27s. worth of labour out of them (*laughter*)".[3] But not all his listeners laughed ; ratepaying farmers as well as political radicals disliked the industrial regime that disfigured their countryside, and Richard Presow, a farmer-guardian, hurled back the accusation that the mining proprietors were " shovelling money by spadefulls into their pockets, and as they made many cripples the mines ought to be rated in proportion to the burthen they inflicted ".[4] Accidents to haematite miners appear fairly frequently in the local press of this period,[5] and Schneider and his colleagues had their critics. A letter in the *Ulverston Mirror* alleged that men injured at the Park Mine were not provided with an ambulance chair and were likely to be carried home in a cart. Citing a particularly tragic case, the writer went on : " It struck me at the time what an amount of expense and ingenuity were lavished in producing machinery to raise the ore at less cost ; but the poor wealth producer, engaged in his hazardous calling, cannot have a decent conveyance to carry him home."[6] Whether these quotations, embodying sharply defined and perhaps revealing viewpoints,

---

[1]Reptd. *Ulv. Adv.*, 2.4.63.   [2]See quotation from *Reg.-General's Rept.*, p. 293 above.   [3]*B. Her.*, 29.8.63.   [4]*Ibid*. This revealing exchange took place at a meeting of the North Lonsdale Agricultural Society. The iron mines were of course exempt from poor rates. Presow, a yeoman farmer of Upper Aldingham, was a particularly outspoken member of the Board of Guardians.

[5]Deaths from " violence " increased very slightly in the district in these years ; from 4.3% of all deaths in 1856-60 to 4.4% in the next quinquennium, and then to 4.7% in 1866-70 ; *Reg. Genl.'s Repts., cit.*   [6]*Ulverston Mirror*, 4.3.65.

give a fair picture of the miner's conditions or not, they hint at the social attitudes which led to combination on his part. It appears that according to Schneider's testimony, a very hard-working miner could earn more than a skilled artisan ; yet conditions in the pits were such that men remained discontented.

Schneider himself had referred to " widows and families of people killed in (his firm's) service ",[1] and had considered the organisation of a benefit club at his mines.[2] But the miners sought their own means of countering the effects of sickness, injury or bereavement, and the friendly society movement in Dalton and Ulverston grew rapidly in the 'sixties, to such an extent that the former town had five lodges in 1865 with a total of over £5000 in accumulated deposits, and no fewer than 16 friendly societies had accounts in the Ulverston Savings Bank.[3] In this respect both towns were stronger than Barrow, although the societies were growing appreciably in the new town and had a powerful membership by 1870. Not only did Oddfellows and Foresters find ready support in the mining community ; the co-operative movement prospered in Dalton far more noticeably than in the other Furness towns. The Dalton-in-Furness Co-operative Society was not the first of its kind to be established hereabouts ; the Barrow " co-op ", founded in 1860, has that distinction,[4] but it was followed very closely by the Dalton, and Ulverston and Swarthmoor societies respectively, both founded in 1861.[5]

These local societies, the workman's answer to overcharging by shopkeepers and to the uncertain quality of the goods sold by the latter, still await their historians. Discussion of them is demanded in a social history, but is introduced here with the additional purpose of throwing a little light on the conditions in which co-operation flourished. Dalton was a small town and a homogeneous community of ore miners ; and at least one " tommy shop " is known to have existed there,[6] pointing to the practice of paying wages in the form of truck, viz. by means of tickets, checks or vouchers which were exchanged, often for very inferior goods, by a shopkeeper who was an associate or underling of an employer. The gross abuses implicit in this system of payment have been dealt with by historians, and will be fairly obvious. The progress of the co-operative movement was a sign that the worker was breaking away from this type of

---

[1]Cf. pp. 246-7 above. [2]*Ibid.* [3]*Ulverston Mirror* 17.6.65 ; *Mannex* (1866), referring to the previous year (figs. for Nov., 1864), p. 395. [4]Inf. by courtesy of the Barrow Co-operative Society and Mr. B.Wyld.

[5]For the Dalton society, see above. A few particulars concerning the Ulverston society are in White, Wm., *op. cit.*, 89-90. The first premises were in a private lobbied house in Market St. Swarthmoor, it may be noted, was then an ore miners' settlement. [6]Infn. by courtesy of Mr. J. Goodman Edwards of Dalton-in-Furness. The shopkeeper concerned, one Uren, is listed in the 1866 *Mannex* directory.

exploitation, while its success gave him an added stimulus to do so. The local ore miners, as is indicated by friendly society statistics, were thrifty ; but the progress of their co-operative society[1] leaves no doubt as to their " enlightened self-interest " :

Table 30.

Statistics of the Dalton Co-operative Society, 1861-70
To the nearest £

	Cash recd. for goods	Net profit	Members' dividend	Non- members' dividend	Educa- tion Fund
1861	1668	76	54	15	—
1862	5547	262	204	7	—
1863	4956	424	352	11	—
1864	6528	624	507	13	—
1865	8087	753	664	7	—
1866	9253	799	723	10	25
1867	10,091	903	806	8	23
1868	12,194	1292	1159	7	32
1869	19,551	2061	1878	10	52
1870	21,898	2573	2351	7	64

During the period covered by the table the Dalton membership grew from about 200 to 1112—that is, it succeeded in covering a very large section of the mining community in the town.

The society in Barrow, by contrast, had much more laboured beginnings. It opened its first shop at Church Street, in 1860, one of the founders of the society being an auditor of the earliest A.S.E. trade union branch in that town, John W. Webster.[2] By 1864 it was £600 in debt, and the average weekly takings at its shop were only £30. The construction of the docks brought in a large influx of population, and by October, 1865, it was out of serious debt. But it had only 399 members after twelve years of existence,[3] although a separate Hindpool Co-operative Society was founded in April, 1870, and had 108 members soon afterwards. But in 1873 the Dalton society had 1787 members, or about three times as many as could be counted in both of the Barrow organisations.[4] An explanation for this disparity of growth may be sought in the fact that the Barrow population was shifting and fluctuating, and very far from homogeneous ; that is to say, it was not settled near or dependent upon one specialised industry which tended to bring

---

[1]Given in *B. Her.*, 26.11.70. [2]*A.S.E. Quarterly Repts.* ; inf. of the Co-operative Society. [3]1860-72. [4]For annual and quarterly reports of local co-operative societies, *B. Her.*, 14.1, 14.10, 31.12.65, 17.12.66, 26.11.70, 10.12.70, 30.7.70, 8.10.70, 1.5, 25.11.71, 4.5.72, 13.4.72 ; *B. Times*, 27.11.69, 14.1.71, 4.2.71, 7.1.71 and *passim*. The Dalton 1873 figure is from *B. Her.*, 21.2.74.

men and women together in the common interest, but consisted of a number of social groups divided not only by type of employment but by regional and national origins—Scots, Welsh, Irish or Midlander. It may be significant that the ironworkers of Hindpool formed their own co-operative society.

One further factor may have retarded the development of co-operation in the new steel town. During its periods of abnormally rapid growth (1860-6 and 1869-75) shopkeepers of all types swarmed and proliferated there, transforming cottages into grocery and general stores, and any co-operative venture must have encountered the most desperate competition. Dalton again provides a contrast ; it was and remained a small town, and if the 1866 Mannex trades directory is any guide, it had fewer than two dozen grocers' and general shops in the period under discussion.

The progress of co-operation in this miners' stronghold suggests, also, a rising standard of life on the part of the inhabitants themselves. This, however, is a difficult and dangerous question, for the population of Dalton, like that of Barrow, was increasing, if in less violent fashion. In 1864 it was stated by a local registrar that " work is plentiful, wages good and provisions cheap. Labourers are earning 3s. 6d. a day ; artisans 4s. 3d. and upwards ".[1] It is clear that the 27s. a week wage payments advertised by Schneider were certainly not the rule, although the 21s. a week indicated here represented some advance on the local labourer's wage of the late 'forties and 'fifties.[2] But the whole question of real and money wages is too complex to be dealt with satisfactorily in a purely localised study, and sources of information are generally too scanty to allow of firm conclusions. The available matter can, however, be put together as suggestively as seems reasonable.

SOCIAL CONDITIONS AND THE TRADE UNIONS

Barrow was a turbulent place in the 'sixties and early 'seventies. The causes were many, and some at least are fairly obvious. There was great competition for building and other labour ; skilled and unskilled workers from other parts of the county and from all over England were thrown together in unpleasant conditions ; and according to numerous contemporary comments, prices and housing rents were high. In 1863 an Ulverstonian claimed that commodities in Barrow were 10 per cent. dearer than in Ulverston ;[3] in 1866, housing rents in the new town averaged 5s. to 6s. a week ;[4] and in late 1867 it was stated that wages were perhaps 2s. more than in Preston, but that rents were 3s. higher. The spokesman esti-

[1]Quoted in 27th Report of the Registrar-General, cit.   [2]See especially p. 241 above.   [3]News item in B. Her., 10.1.63.   [4]B. Times, 18.8.66.

mated that out of a labourer's wage of one pound, 5s. went on rent. [1] A member of a carpenters' trade union branch put the average Barrow rent at 5s. 6d. in the December of the same year, and said that everything was " dear in proportion ". [2] It should be noted that these observations were made by men who had experience of prices in other towns, and the former speaker thought that big land-owners were behind the high rents in Barrow. Not surprisingly, trade unionists entering the town sought to adjust wages to a level which afforded them the standard of living they had known else-where.

Unfortunately, we have no satisfactory lists of commodity prices in Barrow at this period, if only because those market prices relating to the town itself were not regularly published until 1869. Ulverston market prices were printed weekly in the *Ulverston Adver-tiser* and other local newspapers, and an analysis of some specimens of the former indicates that they behaved very much like retail prices elsewhere during the 'sixties. The published market lists for 1869 (for Ulverston and Barrow) show that the new town was indeed " dearer " than the old metropolis of Furness. [3] We may therefore conclude that the trade unionists' testimony, while unquestionably partisan, was nevertheless founded upon fact. The differences in the cost of living within so small an area of England go far to explain why Barrow rapidly developed a reputation as a place of unrest and strife. While it is certain that skilled workers in many parts of England had more and varied foodstuffs on their tables than in previous decades, [4] this very taste of a better life would make the migrant artisan demand more when he entered a new town. The labourer who was obliged to pay 5s. a week in rent and maintain a typically large Victorian family cannot have had much opportunity of entering into the realms of luxury.

Wages and prices alone, even when analysed satisfactorily, cannot tell us all that ought to be known about the life of the worker. His working conditions and hours, the intensity of his labour, the regularity of his employment, and his comparative freedom of move-

---

[1]*B. Times*, 10.8.67. [2]*B. Times*, 7.12.67. [3]Specimen prices may be set out as follows :

Median prices at Ulverston market in the 'sixties				*Barrow*
Layton & Crowther,				*market,*
retail price index	1859	1865	1866	1869	1869
(1850 = 100)	107	107	114	113	
Butter, lb.	1s. 1d.	1s. 1d.	1s. 3d.	1s. 3d.	1s. 5d.
Beef, lb.	6¾d.	7½d.	8d.	7¾d.	8¼d.
Potatoes, stone	6d.	4½d.	7d.	6¾d.	7½d.

These prices were of course subject to much seasonal variation, and the upper and lower limits of any one day were also published in the weekly lists. The means within these limits were used to find the annual averages. [4]For a lucid discussion, based upon the findings of Mr. G. H. Wood, *vide* Cole and Postgate, *The Common People*, 350-1.

ment must all enter into a discussion of this subject. Here again, the types of data uncovered in local historical research rarely provide complete illumination. It may however be useful to trace the actions of particular bodies of workers in a given general situation. This " general situation " has been broadly described in foregoing pages, and was one of extremely rapid building and industrial expansion, high profits, high rents, and—it may fairly be concluded—comparatively high prices with a tendency to climb.

We have seen that Ulverston building workers, in 1860, were working what may have been a 60-hour week.[1] Barrow had its small A.S.E. branch from 1857 onwards, and the membership of this body fluctuated considerably ; it commenced with 12 members, dropped to 8 in 1859, reached 14 in September 1860, had 23 by 1864, 40 by the July of 1866, and 62 by December, 1867.[2] In January, 1868, it was reported in the local press that the branch had experienced no strikes—viz., in its own immediate field—during the eleven years of its existence, but that " one or two " employers had then reduced wages.[3] The friendly society aspect of its work is very plain, and by that time this small twig upon the tree of a great " New Model " union had acquired a balance of some £250 in favour of its 62 members. The latter were doubtless highly respectable men, and—perhaps because they consciously belonged to the aristocracy of labour—they were far from militant. They were also unrepresentative, save in the sense that the branch included typical Barrow immigrants—men from Lancaster, Harecastle, Todmorden, Hull, Leeds, Birkenhead, Salford, Bury, Dudley, and Halifax received " tramp " relief in 1867.[4]

The local building workers organised themselves far more energetically. In January, 1862, there appeared a lodge of the Operative Carpenters' and Joiners' General Union,[5] nationally a loosely-run body which was reorganised and centralised in the following year. The " General Union " (Secretary, Robert Last), was a rival of the better-known Amalgamated Society of Carpenters and Joiners, Applegarth's union, and was strong chiefly in the north.[6] By the end of 1863 a branch of the Operative Stonemasons' Society had appeared,[7] and in 1864 there was mention of " union bricklayers " as well ;[8] and in 1866 a local branch of the Manchester Operative Housepainters' Alliance[9] was in existence.

[1]See p. 247 above. [2]*A.S.E.* (published) *Monthly and Quarterly Repts.*, 1851-60, and years ff. [3]*B. Times*, 4.1.68. [4]*A.S.E. Repts.*, 1867.
[5]*G.U.Op.C. & J. Repts.*, June, 1866 (viewed by courtesy of the A.S.W., Manchester). [6]Higgenbottam, S., *Our Society's History* (*A.S.W.*, 1939), 34. [7]Inf. courtesy of *A.U.B.T.W.* [8]*B. Her.*, 25.6.64 ; these men were probably members of the *Manchester Unity of Bricklayers*, for whom *vide* Postgate, R. W., *The Builders' History*, 222-5. [9]*R.C. Trade Unions*, 1867-8, *B.P.P. XXXII*, 1st Report, p. 81.

In 1864 no more than 175 trade unionists[1] can be accounted for with certainty out of a working population of perhaps 2000 men. Thereafter the number increased rapidly, until in 1866 the " General Union " of carpenters alone had 275 members in Barrow ; and the effect of even a relatively small leaven was far-reaching.

We now learn something of the wage-levels of the carpenters. In March, 1864, the General Union lodge asked headquarters for permission to withdraw their labour for a 2s. advance and in order to gain weekly pays.[2]   The carpenters' wage was then 24s., and may be compared with the Manchester figure of 30s. for a $55\frac{1}{2}$ hour week (1864) and the London rate of 33s. for a $56\frac{1}{2}$ hour week (1864).[3] It should be added that the custom of the Barrow building contractors was to pay wages monthly instead of weekly, an arrangement which no doubt saved clerical labour but which showed little consideration for the convenience of the workman.   This threat of strike action was only a straw in the wind, and an explosive situation was forming elsewhere in the town.

It became manifest in the April.   Brassey's dock construction contract had commenced four months earlier, and his firm imported Irish labour into the town.   A rumour—probably well enough founded—spread that the Irishmen were to be used for undercutting wages, and a riot immediately followed.   It was set in motion by the men working under T. C. Hunter, one of Brassey's local sub-contractors, and these workers made common cause with others working not in the docks, but at the construction site of the new steelworks in Hindpool.   On Tuesday, April 19th, a corps of vigilantes scoured the town for Irishmen, and numbers of these nationals left the town on the following day, a body of about 250 men engaging in the pursuit.   There were sharp conflicts with the police, who were few in numbers and badly worsted, and 130 special constables were enrolled on the Wednesday night.   But having disposed of the Irishmen, the demonstrators ceased to interest themselves in national prejudices, and on the Wednesday midday they marched to the building workshops of Gradwell and A. J. Woodhouse and called for strike action there ; following this move, a similar call was made at Schneider and Hannay's ironworks, and rioting in Hindpool streets ensued.[4]

Gradwell's joiners, among whom may have been numbered the General Union men, left work in a body on the 21st.   This union's demand for 2s. advance and weekly pays duly appeared in the *Barrow Herald* of April 23rd, together with a reply from the building employers which attacked the G.U. secretary as a drunkard " and

[1]*A.S.E. Repts., cit.* ; *B. Her.*, 3.12, 10.12.64.   [2]*G.U. . . . Repts.*, Mar., 1864.   [3]Higgenbottam, *op. cit.*, 70.   [4] Lengthy rept. in *B. Her.*, 23.4.64.

renowned schoolmaster in this town ".[1] But the secretary had performed his tuition well, and the 2s. demand was conceded.

The atmosphere of discontent remained, and in the June, bricklayers were alleged to be holding up work on the F.R.'s new Public Hall and Market House by further strike action.[2] But antagonisms did not arise only from directly economic causes. The law of Master and Servant, the very title of which throws considerable light on certain prevailing social concepts, was brought to bear in the following month by A. J. Woodhouse on one of his brickmakers. It was stated that this man, married with six children, had broken his contract of employment and neglected his work. Woodhouse insisted before an uneasy bench that the law be rigorously applied, and the defendant was committed to prison for two months.[3] It can only be said that the union " schoolmaster " lived in conditions of considerable hazard, and, whether addicted to drink or not, had to display much singleness of purpose.

Social antagonisms could run deep; but so, apparently, could liberal sympathies. The General Union lodge, even after the town had been plunged into riot, was by no means regarded on all sides as a cabal of dangerous conspirators. In the December it held an enlivening anniversary dinner, reporting to its members that it was in a " prosperous condition ", and that it had more than doubled its membership over the previous year ; and the lodge was addressed, *inter alia*, by the editor of the *Barrow Herald*, George Carruthers. [4] The latter proclaimed himself a trade unionist, if of a modest and moderate kind. The significance of his action should not be overlooked. Carruthers, as his writings plainly show, was the mildest of radicals, but he was glad to have allies, and knew well that the ultimate control of the town's affairs was in the hands of persons far too few in number for the advancement of its social health. He also catered deliberately for a readership which included trade unionists. [5] But, like his later fellow-editor, Joseph Richardson, he was a courageous man and was not frightened of writing or speaking his mind. The town's journalists, backed by the trade union movement and a few public-spirited individuals, afterwards played an important part in keeping local democracy alive.

Trade union activity followed more peaceful paths during the winter of 1864-5, when outdoor constructional work on docks and houses was necessarily slowed down. In March, 1865, open unrest once more appeared, when the stonemasons struck successfully for

[1]*Loc. cit.*   [2]*B. Her.*, 25.6.64.   [3]*B. Her.*, 9.7.64.   [4]*B. Her.*, 10.12.64.
[5]The *Herald* then had a weekly circulation of about 1500, and was read throughout Furness ; as has been seen, trade unionists used it to express their piont of view through published letters and continued to do so afterwards (i.e. in the years following 1863-5).

the Saturday half-holiday. The General Union lodge achieved a similar objective, shortening the working week by two hours. [1] Such a gain provided the worker with a little of the extra leisure indispensable to a civilised existence, but it also had an immediately practical advantage ; it enabled single men who shared lodgings to do their shopping at week-ends before the greengrocers' and other stores were sold out. The arrival of spring, too, meant a longer working day in normal circumstances.

Unrest was not confined to the building trades, for it spread to the quarry labourers at Hawcoat (whence Brassey obtained his stone for the dock walls) and these workers struck, in the July, for 2d. a day increase. The journeymen boot and shoemakers in the town then combined successfully to demand higher rates from their employers. [2] Towards the end of August the dock stonemasons struck against the dismissal of a comrade by an overlooker, and it may be significant that a number of men involved in this dispute did not merely stay idle, but demonstrated their feelings by leaving the town to seek work in Manchester. [3] Meanwhile, the *Ulverston Mirror*, doubtless making a sideways glance at Barrow's turbulence, remarked that strikes in Ulverston were " less frequent than in many places . . . there are no large bodies of workmen in one particular branch." [4]

The winter of 1865-6, again, was marked by little strike activity ; but in one unhappy instance the Master and Servant law bore its particularly evil fruit. The semi-secretive type of combination, specialising in guerilla warfare, was already dominant locally, and in late October a bricklayer, William Blackburn, was accidentally killed or murdered near his home for working among non-union men. The " rattening " incidents at Sheffield were still fresh in the public mind, and Carruthers of the *Barrow Herald* was quick to draw a parallel. The affair evoked vigorous discussion for a few weeks, and it was claimed that Blackburn had been killed in a drunken scuffle by stonemasons, not bricklayers, from which it would appear that one of Barrow's fifty or so beerhouses had a share of the responsibility. Members of the respectable or " model " unions pleaded their case in the *Herald* columns with great skill and not a little embarrassment, [5] and the tense and searching debates which took place before the 1867 Royal Commission on Trade Unions were here foreshadowed at the local level.

The guerilla warfare went on. In the December, one of the building employers bitterly described the tactics of some joiners he had dismissed for refusing to work with non-union plasterers ; the

---

[1]*Ulv. Mirror*, 4.3.65.   [2]*B. Her.*, 8.7.65.   [3]*B. Her.*, 2.9.65.   [4]*Ulv. Mirror*, 8.4.65.   [5]For the full incident, *B. Her.*, 4.11, 11.11, 18.11.65.

joiners, he averred, had retaliated by arranging for the withdrawal of all their fellow-craftsmen from another of this employer's building sites in School Street.[1]   The employers then went into combination themselves ; in April, 1866, Alfred Mault of the Master General Builders' Association visited Barrow and evidently had little difficulty in arranging for the formation of a local branch, with William Gradwell as chairman and Jabez Forshaw as secretary.   The result was a counter-attack—an attempt to smash, once and for all, the General Union lodge which was the headquarters of the militants. The lodge, which struck soon afterwards for an increase to 30s., found itself facing a lockout instead ; and by the June, Robert Last, general secretary of the union, was appealing for financial assistance " to prevent one of the strongest and hitherto most liberal branches of our institution being crippled by the influence of our old enemy, the Master Builders' Association ".[2]   The Barrow lodge, said Last, had 275 eligible members of whom 108 were out on strike.[3]   The outcome of this particular dispute is not recorded.   All that is known is that the local joiners did in fact achieve an advance to 30s., and that branches of the General Union were formed at Ulverston and the new townlet of Askam.[4]   The local building employers did not succeed in destroying trade unionism within their own field, but the trade recession of 1866-7 weakened the local lodges ; the published reports of several of the unions show a falling membership from that time until about 1870.

Alfred Mault, of the Master Builders' Association, was supplied with information from Barrow, and in the following year, when presenting a case before the 1867 Royal Commission on Trade Unions, he was able to describe the tactics of the Barrow stonemasons.[5]   In November, 1866, the latter threatened to strike after learning of an arrangement to import ready-worked stone from Liverpool ; the masons concerned were then at work on the construction of St. Mary's Roman Catholic Church in Duke Street, Hindpool.   " A general meeting of masons in the town " was called, and it was agreed that the importation of worked stone was " a direct violation of their local code of rules ".[6]   In the outcome, it was agreed that the masons at work on the church should be paid for the time taken to work the stone at Liverpool ; and the employers, Grindrod and Hargreaves, " had to promise not to introduce any worked or dressed stone into Barrow again ".[7]

[1]B. Her., 16.12.65.   [2]B. Her., 21.4.66 ; G.U.Rept., June, 1866.   It will be noticed that there is no reference here to the unity or co-partnership of " capital " and " labour ".   [3]G.U. Rept., cit.   [4]B. Her., 8.12.66, 7.12.67. Last was a guest of honour at a dinner held by the Barrow G.U. lodge in December, 1866.   [5]R.C.T. Unions (1st Rept.), Ques. 3015 ff., p. 129.   [6]Loc. cit. ; letter of 26.11.66 given in Mault's evidence.   [7]Loc. cit.

In the following month, December, the dock stonemasons struck against excessive hours in the midst of a rush to complete the dock contract. [1]   Three hundred labourers, apparently following the lead of the craftsmen, left the work site at the same time with the demand that the working day be reduced by half an hour. [2]

This bare record of industrial strife in building and constructional schemes may give the impression that it was almost impossible to get any work done at all.   Such an impression would bear little relation to the truth.   But, before discussing the efforts of local workmen, it will be appropriate to quote the views of a leading spokesman of the possessing class of the district.   Thomas Roper was a principal of the firm of Harrison, Ainslie and Co., which, some years before, [3] had attempted to make would-be trade unionists ineligible for poor relief.   In 1867 he made a speech appraising the economic progress of the district, in which he drew attention to the then well-known achievements and designs of the iron and steelworks owners : [4]

" . . . a Directorate, whose commanding influence and business enterprise must soon place them at the very head of the Iron Trade of the World, unless success is checked, and the whole trade of the country paralysed by the baneful effects of trade unions, which have already driven a vast amount of trade out of the country ; and unless our workmen come to their senses, and refuse to obey the leading of selfish demagogues, will more and more enrich our continental neighbours, and impoverish us."

It will be enough to say that this was a common attitude then, and that similar views have been reaffirmed, with many variations, up to the present day.   It seems, however, that he had overlooked the achievements of a Barrow labour force which can never have exceeded four thousand men between 1860 and 1867.   During those years a town had been created ; nearly three thousand houses and dwellings had been built, together with a great steelworks, several smaller industrial concerns, a Market Hall, a Public Hall, a passenger station, warehouses, several churches and chapels, a bank, a theatre, several schools, at least 170 shops and over 50 beerhouses. [5]   By February, 1867, nearly 6000 feet of wharf wall had been constructed, together with 1,100 feet of sea wall, this work providing the essentials of a vast and impressive dock basin. [6]   Brassey, it is true, lost money in causing this dock scheme to be carried into effect ; but landlords

[1]B. Her., 15.12.66.   [2]Loc. cit. ; cf. also MS. Diary, 26.12.66, 19.1.67, where Devonshire made clear that a delay of some months in the dock work was " owing to the weather ".   [3]See p. 308 above.
[4]Roper, Thos., A Short History or Sketch of Barrow, 1867 ; pamph., Sept. 16th, 1867, Barrow P.L.   [5]Data from Mannex (1866), list of trades and establishments, and numerous local sources, many of which are cited in these pages. [6]B. Her., 28.2.67.

had prospered, local building societies had flourished, the furnishing of gas and water had proved to be a profitable business, the steelworks had achieved its 30 per cent. return and the railway company its 10 per cent. Pockets had been filled ; but what is far more important, something solid and durable had been created, in what must surely be a record time, out of the labours of British workmen skilled and unskilled. Somewhat similar urban growth and industrial achievement were to be encountered in many other parts of Britain ; in Middlesbrough, Birkenhead, Crewe, Grimsby, the West Riding and industrial Midlands, and in many parts of South Wales. In this particular case it is only too evident that the workman was not enabled to enjoy a very few of the rewards of economic progress without—in certain significant examples—a vigorous struggle on his part. His Saturday half-holiday, his weekly pay-days, his rates of pay and his working hours generally, were obtained or adjusted by action on his part, even though boom conditions and a comparative shortage of labourers undoubtedly assisted him in his endeavours.

The attitude of the local employers towards their " labour " depended very largely on circumstances. The Furness Railway Company disposed of the services of a minority of the workpeople of Barrow, and even by 1871 there were only 402 railway employees in the borough out of a total of 6170 males over twenty years of age. The company had always, through the efforts of Ramsden, shown an attitude of responsibility for the moral and social welfare of its employees—who were, although few in number, vastly important to the success of its operations—and these workers were given dinners, excursions and the use of a library and reading room.[1] Even so, trade unionism invaded the citadel of the F.R. on February 2nd, 1866, when a branch of the Locomotive Steam Enginemen and Firemen's Friendly Society was formed with 35 members.[2] Some five months later a similar spirit was in evidence at the Hindpool ironworks, for an approach was made to the Executive Council of the Friendly Society of Ironfounders, who resolved that " A branch be opened at Barrow-in-Furness, North Lancashire ".[3] Here commenced a long chapter of struggle, for J. T. Smith, like Thomas Roper and the building employers, was no lover of trade unionism.[4] In the same month of June a branch of the Amalgamated Society of Carpenters and Joiners appeared in the town ;[5] but it was hardly an effective rival of the General Union lodge at first, and was closed down in 1869.[6]

---

[1]*B. Her.*, 5.12.63, 29.10.64, 11.2.65, 24.6.65. [2]*Barrow Pilot*, 16.1.75. [3]*Executive Council Minutes, F. Soc. Iron Founders*, 20.6.66. The membership, composed of craftsman moulders, was 28 in 1868 and 113 in 1878. [4]Smith resisted the unions in the steelworks bitterly in the mid-'seventies. [5]*A.S.C. & J. Repts.*, 1866. [6]*Repts.* of the union, 1869, when the branch membership fell to 6.

The General Union lodge fared scarcely better. In January, 1868, its secretary reported that " . . . we are not without hope that before many months elapse we shall see our union thriving and busy, with the new and commodious dock warehouses just completed . . . Several new public works are projected . . . but the Railway Company, who take the lead in all public matters (and through the influence of whose directors and managers we have obtained the Act of Incorporation for the town) are like most public bodies, holding a tight rein on their finances . . . "[1] By the August, however, the membership of this formerly thriving organisation had fallen from 141 (August, 1867) to 39. It is well enough known that trade union activity has fluctuated with the ebb and flow of trade ; but it should also be pointed out that the trade unionist was subjected to far greater inconvenience in a slump of this character than the member of the much smaller possessing class, for the former had to tramp elsewhere for his livelihood. The latter, if he lived locally, was in no serious danger of bankruptcy, unless his ineptitudes ordained that he deserved such a fate. The fortunes of a host of human beings, meanwhile, were dependent on the investments and decisions of a few. The records of several of the local union branches show that their members were either forced to discontinue their subscriptions or were departing from the town between the summer of 1867 and early months of 1870. Even the Barrow branch of the A.S.E. lost a few members in this period, and did not begin to increase its balance until January, 1870.[2]

FURTHER LIGHT ON SOCIAL CONDITIONS

The majority of the local people were not trade unionists, and it may therefore be felt that the small (and not always militant) bodies so far described cannot be taken as representative of the many. Such an objection misses the point. Trade unionism appears in response to certain social conditions, and even a slight acquaintance with mid-Victorian social history—that is, with the period of the New Model unions—will show that the respectable and steady craft unionists of the period were not always as docile as is sometimes suggested in textbooks.[3] And if the workman's general conditions improved in certain respects, trade unionism continued to develop also ; and industrial unions, in their varying stages, naturally tell us something of their environments.

[1]*G.U. Reports*, 1868, Monthly Trade Rept., Jan., 1868.   [2]*A.S.E. Repts.*
[3]Middlesbrough, a town with a history not unlike that of Barrow, experienced vigorous wage struggles in the period 1858-66 ; *vide* Martin, W. S., (thesis for the M.A. degree of Manchester University), *Economic and Social Development of Middlesbrough*, 1830-1888, pp. 44-6, 47-8.

The human element ; inside Barrow Jute Works, 1874 (*see* p. 387).

The human element ; at the theatre, Barrow, 1874 (*see* p. 329).

The Barrow Flax and Jute Works in the 'eighties. (*see* p. 349).

The seat of power—the Furness Railway Company offices at Barrow.
(*see* pp. 299-300)

The original F.R. station at St. George's Square, Barrow. (*see* p. 283).

" In the station style of architecture." The former Royal Hotel, Strand, Barrow.
(*see* p. 283).

More " station style "—part of the former Town Hall, Market and Police
Offices, Lawson St.   (*see* pp. 282, 300).

Free Trade and Steel—Haematite Company furnaces, 1874.

Model housing, 1884 style ; flats at Old Barrow. (*see* p. 413)

Barrow's first steam tram, 1884.

The Buccleuch Dock, Barrow. The buildings in the foreground stand over the approximate site of the former village of Barrow.

The liner "*City of Rome.*" (*see* p. 389).

"Free trade in food," cattle sheds and shipping in the Barrow docks, mid-'eighties. (*see* pp. 390-91).

A study of town life in these years will naturally seek to throw a little light on the daily living conditions of the many. We have seen that the immigrant workman might encounter lack of sanitation and an absence of the simplest amenities. Barrow, for instance, had only four practising doctors in 1866 ;[1] these worthy men had to cater for a population of 16,000, and had a far greater task before them than the Furness surgeons of the late eighteenth century,[2] even though the medical men of that age had to ride considerable distances to visit their patients. Yet the death-rate, and the incidence of illness, in an industrial town was usually higher or more marked than in the nearby rural areas. Barrow had 2,950 dwelling houses in 1867-8, and in 1866, when the population of the town was more numerous than in 1868 (the corporation estimate of that year was 14,000),[3] the number of houses may have been about 2,500. It can therefore be concluded that the pressure of persons per house was in excess of six in the earlier year. In the early 'seventies, when the Census particulars make a more exact estimate possible, the record was worse.[4] Even in 1866-7 we are left in no doubt that shocking overcrowding existed. In the *Barrow Times* of August 18th, 1866, Joseph Richardson[5] wrote :

" . . . something might be done towards providing a labouring man with a house at a moderate rent. Now scarcely anything is to be got under 5s. or 6s. a week, and is it likely that a man with a family, whose daily provision costs nearly double what it did three years ago, can afford to pay this sum ? What is the result ? Why, that two or three families often herd together in a single house of four rooms . . . In a street between Duke Street and Hindpool Road the state of things is truly awful. Some of the dwellings, which are very small, are inhabited by 20 persons. A family of six are living, or rather existing, in the same room . . . *Even at the present price of labour, a very decent cottage house may be built for a returnable 8 per cent., to let at 3s. 6d. or 4s. a week.*"

Richardson then pointed to Saltaire as a place which provided comparatively good housing at reasonable rents.[6] But unfortunately for its inhabitants, Barrow was not a Saltaire ; and whatever may be said of Titus Salt and his achievements, it seems likely that very few towns or industrial colonies could boast of a similar concern for working-class residents.

Barrow living conditions, then, were uncomfortable. We have no evidence that the overcrowding led to severe epidemics in the

---

[1]*Mannex* (1866), 382. [2]See pp. 117-8 above. [3]*Treasurers' Reports* ; the figure is based on rated properties. [4]Cf. also Dr. Pollard's calculations, *L. & C.*, LXIII, 109 ; the figure was 6.7 in 1871, rising to 7.32 by 1874. [5]Richardson, who came from the Middlesbrough district, wrote under the pseudonym of *Erimus*, the motto of the Cleveland town. [6]*Ibid.*

'sixties, and it is fortunate indeed that none occurred, for the town lacked any hospital until August 12th, 1866, and it had no adequate hospital accommodation for many years subsequently. The story of the establishment of the North Lonsdale Hospital is itself illustrative of the social attitudes of the age. Barrow's rulers, although many charges can be laid against them, were certainly not untypical of the representatives of their class or type in other towns and industrial districts, and they were devout if sometimes demonstrative adherents of the established church. More is said on this subject elsewhere.[1] Nor is it suggested that they were unusually insensitive or inhuman, for they recognised the need for a hospital. Their main preoccupations, however, were elsewhere. Railway and industrial organisation or expansion absorbed most of their energies, and town planning for effect, with some noteworthy provision of public buildings and churches, emerged as a by-product. Meanwhile, the underlying activities of daily labour went on, and it was singularly unfortunate that Barrow's main industries—iron and steel, and railway maintenance and transport—were alike dangerous to life and limb.

From 1864 onwards, ghastly accidents are reported in the local press. Two deaths by accident occurred at the Hindpool works in the autumn of that year, and in the case of one of them a labourer, " dreadfully injured " and subsequently deceased, had to be taken to Lancaster, thirty miles away, to receive hospital treatment. In October, 1864, a report of an accident to a dock worker revealed that no stretchers were supplied at any of the works in the neighbourhood.[2] The year 1865 brought the following bloody harvest ; these were major mishaps only, reported in the *Barrow Herald* with much horrifying and sordid detail :

Nature of accident	Place	Date of rept. in B. Herald
Man thrown from furnace platform	Hindpool	11.2.65
Man run over by wagon ; serious injury	,,	18.2.65
Man's thigh broken at steelworks	,,	,,
Crushing on steelworks railway line	,,	22.4.65
Man burnt to death in furnace	,,	29.4.65
Thigh smashed at Hawcoat quarry (no stretcher)	Hawcoat	27.5.65
Compound fracture at ironworks	Hindpool	12.8.65
Man crushed by wagon buffers	Gradwell's	12.8.65
Fatal crushing at waterworks	F.R. waterworks	16.9.65
Crushing at railway works	F.R. workshops	30.9.65

This list is not necessarily complete. The student who is dispassionate as well as compassionate will note that the number of persons injured over twelve months, according to this table, is

---

[1]See pp. 330-2 below. [2]*B. Her.*, 13.8, 1.10, 8.10, 22.10.64.

statistically insignificant, for between three and four thousand men were working locally. This, however, was a mere beginning, for 75 accident cases were admitted to Barrow's (later) hospital in 1870, and 155 in 1871.[1] The Census particulars of males employed in the main works indicate that the accident rate was about 1 in 25 in the latter year, although these sufferers were at least fortunate in that they had a hospital to receive their shattered bodies.

To return to the subject of this institution : in October, 1865, the *Barrow Herald* contained two eloquent editorials on the lack of a hospital, and pointed out that a canvass had been made " a few years ago " with the aim of raising money for a hospital by a levy on wages. The editor, George Carruthers, asked why " the employers of much labour " had not raised money by such means, and estimated that over £3000 a year could be thus obtained. This sum, he thought, would more than adequately finance a hospital of fifty beds ; and there was, prudently enough, no suggestion that the employers should contribute largely.[2]

On November 15th, a special resolution of the Barrow Haematite Steel Company[3] moved that the undertaking contribute £4000 for a new church at Hindpool " for the Company's workers ", and £500 for educational purposes and hospitals. The priorities in the minds of the directors will be noted. Almost immediately afterwards a popular campaign, aided by the *Herald* editorials and reports, was set in motion. The exact identity of its initiators is unknown, but the Rev. T. S. Barrett, Vicar of the parish church of St. George, was prominently associated with it, and a series of penny readings raised money for the hospital during the early months of 1866.[4] In the March the *Herald* noted that the support for the Readings Committee was largely working-class, and advocated an approach to the " leading tradesmen and gentry ".[5] By this time the campaign was receiving additional support from Joseph Richardson in the *Barrow Times*, and from the town's senior doctor, Joseph Allison. Allison had particular reason to appreciate the horrors engendered by the lack of a hospital, and at one of the readings he described graphically the plight of an injured man " in a working man's house, where some six or eight people live in one or two rooms, and besides a man with a broken leg or arm ".[6]

The Barrow Cottage Hospital was opened in the August,[7] not a moment too soon, and with five beds instead of fifty. Two cottages

---

[1]Rept. of N. Lonsdale Hospital in *B. Her.*, 12.8.71. Meanwhile, a letter in the *Barrow Times* of 9.1.69 remarked that " it is your unfortunate duty to have *almost weekly* (the present writer's italics) to record accidents of a most serious or other nature, at the Iron and Steel Works ". The press reports of course continued to confirm this statement.
[2]*B. Her.*, 21.10.65.   [3]*Co. file*, Reg.J/S. Cos.   [4]*B. Her.*, 20.1, 10.2, 24.2, 10.3, 24.3, 21.4.66.   [5]*B. Her.*, 10.3.66.   [6]*B. Her.*, 10.2.66.   [7]On August 12th ; the premises were in School St. *B. Times*, 18.8.66.

were laid together to make the building, and according to his own account,[1] Joseph Richardson of the *Barrow Times* had promised to obtain nurses from the cottage hospital at Middlesbrough.

The Rev. T. S. Barrett continued to administer its affairs, and within a year or two of its foundation the hospital had 18 beds. In 1869, however, the number of beds was reduced from 18 to 14, and it was alleged that the management of Barrett and a number of lady helpers was extravagant. Workers in the town continued to contribute towards its upkeep, and between June, 1868 and June, 1869, £125 was obtained through their subscriptions, rather over £400 coming from other sources during the same period.[2] By this time the ruling group had become interested in the affairs of the hospital, and Devonshire himself was seriously alarmed at the " ultra high church views " of Barrett, which were believed to have led to indiscriminate charity on the latter's part.[3] It is also true, however, that the belated interest and interference of Ramsden and Devonshire annoyed Barrett and Richardson. A biographical account of Richardson—written either by himself or a close friend —referred scathingly to persons who " ought to have had the enterprise and charity to found (the hospital) themselves ",[4] and Richardson stated elsewhere that " it was taken out of Mr. Barrett's keeping through Mr. Ramsden's influence ".[5] But very little was done to provide accommodation suited to the high accident-rate in the town ; in 1870 the hospital had 16 beds, and in 1871, when the number of accident cases had increased from 75 to 155, the number of beds remained at 16. In 1875, when the population of Barrow had risen to 37,000, it had 25 beds, and was managed by a committee consisting of the chief industrial and other personalities.[6]

It should not be necessary to justify this extended account of a comparatively small episode in the growth of a large town, even though the hospital that was founded, later taking the name of the North Lonsdale Hospital, became an important institution in the region. Nothing could more clearly show the limitations not merely of a group of industrialists, but of a social system. It was not that Devonshire and his colleagues were consciously inhuman, or even that they lacked a sense of duty ; the system of which they were a part was itself dehumanised. The Duke, who on the evidence of his intimate recordings showed genuine solicitude for his retainers at Chatsworth and Holker, was separated from his steelworkers by

[1]Richardson, *Farewell Address to the Ratepayers of Barrow* (pamph., 1886), Barrow P.L. The author exaggerated his own part in the campaign for the hospital, although he did support it during 1866. [2]*B. Times*, 31.7, 9.10.69. [3]*MS. Diary*, 19.2.68, 6.10.69 ; Devonshire was a devout anglican. [4]*Joseph Richardson, cit.*, 14. [5]*Farewell Address, cit.* [6]*B. Her.*, 12.8.71 ; *B. Times*, 22.1.70 ; Leach, *op. cit.*, 115-16 ; *F.P. & P.*, II, 313.

the great gulf between one social class and another.[1]   A deeply
religious man, he was willing to donate large sums towards the
erection of churches and chapels in Barrow ; and so, indeed, were
Ramsden and Schneider ; but the men who were later to cause
several millions of pounds to be spent on local industrial undertakings, and who, in the middle and late 'sixties, were fully conscious
of the vastness of their plans, yet had to leave the essential matter
of a hospital to the initiative of a radical newspaper editor and a
clergyman.   The latter's neo-Catholic deviations were of more
interest to the Duke than the miserable inadequacy of the two converted cottages, and naturally enough, after Devonshire and his
directorial colleagues had been prevailed upon to take responsibility for the hospital, its maintenance was left in part to public
subscription.   We hear much of the Victorian conscience, and the
historian sweeping through the wide spaces of the nineteenth century
can produce many examples of increased social awareness on the
part of ruling groups, both local and national ; but it is sometimes
more instructive to view its workings at close quarters, and to see,
occasionally, the sluggishness of its reactions to the most appalling
wastage of human life and health.   Yet it should be emphasised
that this is not a diatribe against individuals.   Of the Liberal
aristocracy of the mid-nineteenth century, there were few more
intellectually able and upright members than the 7th Duke of
Devonshire.   But the social and industrial relationships of the
period ordained that he was to show far less personal concern for
his steelworkers than for his tenant farmers (whose rents he refused
to raise during thriving days for agriculture[2]) and for his personal
servants.   Barrow, too, was a collective responsibility ;   and the
men who surrounded him in the control of its industries and welfare
were unfortunately of lesser stature than the Duke.   The hospital
episode, meanwhile, was a warning.

BEERHOUSES, TEMPERANCE AND CHURCHES

Barrow's rapid growth did not escape the notice of contemporary journalists, and the opening of the great docks in 1867 drew
widespread comment.   The town gained notoriety for a number of
reasons ;   the ambitions of its industrialists, the turbulence of its
people, their alleged insobriety, and—by no means least in importance—the connection of H. W. Schneider with the new

[1]The late Beatrice Webb (*My Apprenticeship*, I, 60), well characterises the
outlook of her father, an enlightened Liberal capitalist, as giving " a queer
psycho-mechanical twist to my conception of the labouring classes . . . I never
visualised labour as separate men and women of different sorts and kinds ".
Richard Potter became, after 1869, a close associate of Ramsden and Devonshire.
As has been shown, part of the Potter family's income came from the Barrow
timber yards ;   see also *My Apprenticeship*, I, 19.   The popular Pelican
edition is referred to.   [2]*Vide* his obituary in *Proc. Royal Society*, 1892, LI,
xxxviii and ff.

borough. Mr. Punch, in producing a typically facetious but also biting commentary on the dock-opening ceremony, alluded to Schneider's large-scale corruption of parliamentary electors at Lancaster in 1865,[1] and used the occasion to deliver the following admonition :[2]

" Suppose M. Schneider were to set himself in real earnest to wipe out the recollection of Lancaster by the redemption of Barrow ? What if he were to prove himself the ditto of M. SCHNEIDER of Le Creusot, not in name only but in deed, and to make Barrow-in-Furness the Creusot of England, in morals, manners, civilisation, education, domestic comfort and culture, as well as in industry, energy and money-making ? Here is a work worthy of the noblest ambition, the most determined energy, the highest intelligence, and certain of the richest reward—a reward not to be gauged by dividends, it is true, but beyond the measure of millions. Let there be two SCHNEIDERS known in the world for their noble conception and perfect discharge of the duties of a great captain of industry, and let one of them be an Englishman."

How far did Schneider and his colleagues take this to heart ? It may be no accident that they showed more interest in the hospital a year or two later ; the 1868 Barrow Corporation Act was drafted within a few weeks of the delivery of this diatribe ; the Barrow Council commenced its career ; and a sizeable Workman's Club and Institute appeared in the town with the assistance of the upbraided ironmaster. Mere order of chronology does not constitute evidence, although it may well be that *Punch*'s very occasionally radical conscience had its victories. Subsequent events indicate that the anonymous sermoniser was expecting far too much, if only because the hearts of Barrow's rulers remained in new industrial projects rather than in social welfare as an end in itself.

Mr. Punch had referred to the " hard-drinking " of Barrow's workers. It is not surprising to find that beerhouses proliferated, for iron and steelworkers are traditionally and understandably thirsty. By their ownership of the Hindpool Estate—for many years a major part of the new town—the ruling group had it in their power to control the establishment of public houses and drinking-dens. A sincere desire to let trade and enterprise take their course, or sheer lack of interest, ensured that this power was never effectively used.

There were attempts to use it. In 1866, 51 beerhouses and 16 hotels or larger public houses were listed in the Mannex directory,

---

[1]For the details of this corrupt election, see Marshall, J. D., in *L. & C.*, LXIII, 117 and ff. [2]*Punch*, 5.10.67, p. 135. The denunciation was lengthier and more scarifying than this excerpt would suggest.

but of these, only 8 beerhouses and 2 hotels were to be found in the Hindpool Estate,[1] and a conveyance of this time contained the provision that " no public house should be erected " on a plot of ground in Nelson Street ; but some years later the stipulation was waived, and—in the perhaps unfair and biting words of a local solicitor— " the great care for public morality was sold by the Duke of Devonshire and the Furness Railway Company for the sum of £34 19s., when James Thompson bought it to build a public house upon it ".[2]

Such sanctions were in any case negative in spirit, for the beerhouse or " pub " was a centre of social life for the workman. Not only did he occasionally get drunk there, but his trade union lodges and friendly societies—if not avowedly teetotal—met there also. Many writers have exclaimed in wonderment at the density of beerhouses in mid-Victorian England ; heavy drinking, however, was not confined to industrial populations. Barrow, in 1866, had one place of refreshment to about 240 inhabitants ; Ulverston in 1854 had one to 129 inhabitants, Plymouth had one to 152 in the same year, and Middleton, near Manchester, had one to 137.[3] Barrow soon afterwards bid fair to make up its leeway in this respect, and the number of drinking establishments does not give a reliable indication of the amount of liquor consumed. There was plenty of drunkenness in the town, and offenders were duly haled before a bench which consisted of Ramsden, Schneider, Alexander Brogden, John Fell and Robert Hannay,[4] other notabilities being added to the magistracy from time to time.

The local temperance movement was vigorous from the very early days of Barrow's history. In 1862 supporters of this cause erected the first public hall to be opened in the town—the Temperance Hall in Greengate ;[5] while in 1865 an estimated 2000 people gathered at a mass temperance demonstration.[6] The various total abstinence friendly societies were moderately well patronised, although not enough to raise them into positions of much influence. This movement, worthy within its limitations and springing quite as much out of the consciences of workpeople and tradesmen as out of the consciences of employers, was fundamentally negative, and did little to provide the social conditions in which the worker could find more varied leisure-time activities. Chapel communities, of which

[1]*Mannex* (1866).   [2]*Proc. of Enquiry*, 1873 (*Barrow Corporation Act*), *relating to prices of land in Barrow, July*, 1873, pamph. in Barrow P.L., Wm. Relph's evidence, p. 89.   The F.R.-Steelworks group later tried (*c.*1871) to restrict public house building on Barrow Island, but their efforts were again strangely ineffective.
   [3]*Health of Towns Report; Ulverstone* (1855), 13-14.   [4]Local press, *passim* ; Schneider was deprived of his magistracy in consequence of the Lancaster election case ; *vide B. Times*, 6.11.69 *et al.*   [5]Leach, *op. cit.*, 116.
   [6]*B. Her.*, 2.7.65.

more is said below, did play some part in giving meaning to the social life and intercourse of many people, and bodies of this kind also provided elementary education.

The *Punch* sermon was foreshadowed by another from a different quarter, less scarifying but equally to the point. This one, surprisingly enough, appeared in the pages of the Mannex trades directory of 1866,[1] and was, like the invective of Mr. Punch, aimed at the rulers of Barrow. It expresses a contemporary viewpoint so well that it is worth quoting at length :

" Many social wants will, however, inevitably remain, for a time, unprovided for, wherever a new town springs up ; but a place of meeting, such as a Workman's Hall, where social intercourse may be held, and by which people are so much benefited, both intellectually and morally, ought to be established as soon as possible ; and, as workingmen have not the leisure, and in many cases lack the means, it is evidently the duty of employers to assist in providing what may be required in this respect. And, if it be the duty of the wealthy portion of the community to provide rational amusement for the operative classes, *a fortiori* is it their duty to see that decent and becoming places of worship and proper schools be erected. Although much still remains to be done, it is satisfactory to find that much has been done towards providing accommodation for religious worship for a large portion of the residents of this new colony."

This much more tactful approach was likely to strike a responsive chord in Barrow's chieftains. Like the preacher-employee of P. Mannex and Co., they gave priority to churches, but were soon afterwards to take some interest in the provision of a Workman's Club and Institute. Their reaction was, as might be expected, somewhat sluggish, and the opening of a small workingman's club in Cornwallis Street (December, 1866), following the publication of the Mannex directory, was almost shamefaced ; at least, it was not widely advertised.[2] H. W. Schneider, however, entered into correspondence with the Registrar of Friendly Societies, Tidd Pratt, concerning the rules to be adopted for the conduct of a larger institution, and it was estimated that about 8000 people might be induced to support it with a 3d. a week subscription. The new Institute was to supply games, drinks and cheap meals. It was not opened until August 7th, 1871 ; one of the " architectural ornaments " of the town, and in appearance not unlike the Institute at Saltaire, it cost £3,450. Schneider and Ramsden contributed towards this sum.

---

[1] *Mannex* (1866), 333-4. (s.v. *Barrow-in-Furness*). [2] Viz., in the local press. For a stray reference, *B. Her.*, 23.7.70.

By 1872, however, the degree of support for the Institute turned out to be disappointing, a maximum of 600 workers joining it—this in spite of the offer of such amenities as a library, a billiard room, lecture rooms and a refreshment bar. It is not easy to see the main reason for its lack of success ; Schneider, having given largely, took a close interest in its management, and was accused of interference in the affairs of the Institute.[1] It may also be noted that the earnest working-class students who attended the Institute's classes in chemistry, French and drawing—perhaps Barrow's earliest experiments in adult education—would also include a type of person who would be most disposed to insist on the right of the members to run their own club business without paternal control. Otherwise, this institution faced the strongest possible competition from the cosy warmth of several score places of refreshment. The latter lined the back streets ; the Institute was designed as part of the façade of Abbey Road.

Working-class housing of the period was erected on the assumption that a hip-bath, or at worst a souse under a cold tap, was good enough for the hygienic requirements of the many. In 1953, 7720 houses in the borough lacked bathrooms,[2] almost all of them dwellings erected in the Victorian age. The munificence of James Ramsden provided the inhabitants of the town with a swimming-bath—not a washhouse—as early as 1871,[3] and this building, adjoining the Club and Institute, made a further adornment of Abbey Road.

Needs of a different kind were satisfied at the Theatre Royal, Albert Street, built in 1864,[4] and once it was opened, the inhabitants of the new colony were no longer obliged to trek to Ulverston for cultural purposes. From the commencement the Theatre Royal aimed fairly high, and in 1865-7 performances of *Faust*, *Hamlet*, and *Il Trovatore* took place there, Miss Emma Stanley, " The Great Artiste, Pianist, Harpist, Guitarist, Vocalist and Delineator " providing lighter relief with her celebrated entertainment " The Seven Ages of Woman ".[5] The town did not acquire a music hall until about 1866, when the Alexandra Music Hall in Forshaw Street was fitted up and opened.[6] On New Year's Day, 1872, the Alhambra Palace, a music hall seating nearly 2000 people,[7] was

---

[1] *B. Her.*, 23.7, 13.8, 30.7.70, 4.5.72 ; Leach, *op. cit.*, 119-20 ; *F.P. & P.*, II, 285 ; the Saltaire Institute may still be seen, but *vide* also Stewart, *Prospect of Cities* (1952), 162. The Barrow Institute averaged a membership of 500 up to 1880. [2] *Basic Survey Schedule*, Barrow Corporation, 1952-3, by courtesy of the Town Planning Officer, Mr. C. R. Whitehead. [3] *B. Her.*, 13.8.70, 22.7.71 ; Leach, *op. cit.*, 121. [4] *B. Her.*, 8.10.64, where the new theatre was commenced " immediately behind the Royal Hotel " ; Leach, *op. cit.*, 127, erroneously gives the date as 1862. [5] *B. Her.*, 4.2.65 (where *Hamlet* was spoiled by a noisy audience), 24.3.66, *B. Times* 6.7.67 ; also handbill, Barrow P.L., reprod. in Barnes, *Barrow*, 135. The theatre was " under the distinguished patronage of James Ramsden Esq." [6] Leach, *op. cit.*, 127. [7] *Loc. cit.*

opened in Cavendish Street. Here the town's workpeople were able to find their Saturday night relaxation, and the appearance of these establishments softens an otherwise exceedingly bleak picture; for during the first two decades of the town's existence there were few healthy amusements for the inhabitants at large. The absence of a public park was a serious shortcoming, although the more enterprising used Walney Island for walking and sports, and the Furness Abbey grounds lay not far away. But the country rambler ran the risk of trespass, working hours were long, and the labour by which the majority made a living was heavy and fatiguing. There was still no Saturday half-holiday for many, and at this time it was customary for ironworkers to work in two twelve-hour shifts daily, with a break every second week from 5 a.m. on Sunday to 5 a.m. on Monday.[1] Sunday was therefore a day of rest, in the literal sense, for many hundreds. For others, the Sabbath was to be taken seriously in the conventional manner.

The proprietors of Hindpool ironworks, knowing that many employees were required for Sunday shift work, and considering, evidently, that church accommodation was lacking in the town, caused work to stop there every morning between 11 and 12 a.m. in order that divine service might be held in one of the shops.[2] This practice led to the origination of a sardonic story, popular in local folk-lore. On the occasion of a shop foreman reading *Exodus*, XXIII, 12, an unknown interruptor called out " On the seventh day . . . *thou shalt do a double shift* ! "[3] This was an age when strict Sabbatarians had opposed Sunday excursion trains,[4] and the significance of the story lies not in its truth (which cannot be proven) but in its popularity. The marksman was something of a Robin Hood, and in spite of the offer of a reward to any person who would betray his identity, he was not captured.[5]

The religious convictions of the dominant group, however, are not in doubt. Schneider, Ramsden and the Duke of Devonshire were enthusiastic and active churchmen, and they were always ready to assist church and chapel communities by providing land in the town. Barrow had its parish church of St. George several years before any other public building of note appeared there. H. W. Schneider boasted that £120,000 was spent on churches, hospitals, parsonages and schoolhouses in the Furness district between 1857 and 1872,[6] and it is known that this ironmaster and Robert Hannay gave at least £80,000 for the use and building of such institutions or to various charities during their respective lifetimes. The

[1]*B. Her.*, 24.6.65.   [2]*B. Her.*, 22.4.65.   It is not known how long this practice continued.   [3]Quoted in Gaythorpe, *Church Congress Guide to Barrow* (1905), 75n.   Harper Gaythorpe, F.S.A. (Scot) was a tireless collector of local anecdotes as well as a skilful antiquarian.   The writer has heard the above story related independently.   [4]Pimlott, J. A. R., *The Englishman's Holiday* (1947), 163.   [5]Gaythorpe, *loc. cit.*   [6]Leach, *op. cit.*, *Appx.*, 27.

churches, as is only too evident, received the greater part of this large sum, and " hospitals " but an insignificant fraction of it.[1] The predilections of the reader will put this contribution into seemly proportion ; it will be enough to say that we are concerned to balance as carefully as possible, the pathology of an age against its achievements. Most of the church-building took place in Barrow, and the chief personages there were the reverse of sectarian, perhaps enforcedly. Their colony was overwhelmingly nonconformist or Catholic, and nearly all of the spontaneously flourishing groups of the 'sixties fell into these classes.

A Baptist congregation was meeting on Walney Island in 1853 ;[2] the Independents had a small chapel in Hindpool in 1857, enlarged in 1863 ; and the Wesleyans established a place of worship in Hindpool Road in 1862.[3] A Welsh chapel, designed to meet the needs of seamen from the ore boats, was opened in May, 1863,[4] the Baptists and Primitive Methodists soon followed by opening chapels in 1865, and in the following year the foundation stone of the Hindpool Roman Catholic Church (St. Mary of Furness) was laid.[5] The Baptist and Congregationalist buildings were designed to accommodate 600 and 500 people respectively, and there were 1300 Catholics in Barrow in 1865-6.[6] The strong nonconformist element has a clear connection with the traditional leanings of the old-established iron districts, Staffordshire particularly, from which the skilled workers of the town were migrating, and the Catholic element was strengthened by immigrants from Ireland and central Lancashire. In 1872 the Wesleyan flock numbered about 700 ; the Presbyterians, with a chapel in School Street, were already planning to build a new one ; there were two Primitive Methodist chapels with accommodation for between 850 and 1000 ; the Welsh Presbyterians had a smaller chapel which seated about 300 ; and the Baptists, Particular Baptists and Bible Christians were flourishing. The Congregationalists were then much in evidence, and through their minister, the Rev. W. H. Fothergill, were beginning to exert some influence on town affairs.[7] Needless to say, these bodies were self-supporting and self-administered, but the Presbyterians were aided by a gift of land from Ramsden, the Baptists by a similar gift from Devonshire (1873), and the Congregationalists by an earlier gift from the duke (1857).[8] Ramsden

---

[1]Barrow's hospital has been dealt with ; Ulverston had a workhouse infirmary from 1863 and a cottage hospital in 1873. Barrow also had a wooden smallpox hospital in 1871. [2]Gaythorpe, *op. cit.*, 52, who deals with earlier activities by religious groups. [3]*F.P. & P.*, II, 305 ; *Mannex*, 334. [4]*B. Her.*, 28.2.63. [5]Gaythorpe, *op. cit.*, 54 ; *F.P. & P.*, II, 301-2. [6]*Mannex, loc. cit.* [7]Leach, *op. cit.*, 104-6 ; *B. Her.*, 3.2.72 ; *F.P. & P.*, II, 303 sqq. ; these are all contemporary sources. The Rev. Fothergill was a member of the Barrow School Board after its foundation. [8]*F.P. & P.*, II, 303, 307, 309.

and Devonshire—on behalf of the Furness Railway Company—combined to provide ground for the Hindpool Catholic Church in 1863.[1]

The established church, to which Devonshire, Ramsden and Schneider adhered, did not remain out of the picture for long. St. James's Church in Hindpool was " built and partly endowed by the chief proprietors of the neighbourhood " in 1867-9, and opened in the latter year, and St. Paul's church in Newbarns was completed in 1871.[2] Thereafter Ramsden decided that vigorous action was called for, and " conceived the idea of appealing to the noblemen and gentlemen connected with Barrow, with a view of raising a fund to build and endow four new temporary churches in the town. This appeal was liberally responded to ; £24,000 was required, and His Grace the Duke of Devonshire . . . gave practical effect to the scheme by placing £12,000 to the credit of the fund "[3] the Duke of Buccleuch, Lord Frederick Cavendish, Schneider and Ramsden also subscribing large sums. In consequence, four churches, dedicated to Matthew, Mark, Luke and John, were opened on one day, September 26th, 1878.[4] In the few years that had elapsed, however, the population of Barrow had increased enormously, and the events of this fateful period must be examined separately. It can be said that during the first two decades of Barrow's growth the " dissenters " made most of the running, and most truly represented the religious leanings of its people. Where they built places of worship on their own initiative, these were nonconformist or Catholic.

It was fortunate indeed that church and chapel organisations provided a modicum of schooling. In 1861-70 more than a quarter of 6490 persons married in Furness were illiterate—1756 men and women in all, or 27.1 per cent. ; the women, as before, signed the register with marks more frequently than the men.[5] The position had improved, however, when compared with that of the previous decade,[6] although it is impossible to ascertain exactly what caused it to do so. Perhaps the incomers from afar were better-educated, or perhaps the local schools were doing their work more efficiently during the 'fifties. The educational provision of the mid-'sixties is far from impressive. In 1865, St. George's church school at Barrow provided some sort of accommodation for " about 220 children "[7] and the Barrow Baptist schools for 130 ; in addition, the Primitive Methodists and Wesleyans each had a school in the new town. The

[1]*Op. cit.*, 301 ; the references to individuals are perhaps misleading. Ramsden administered the Hindpool Estate. [2]Leach, 99-102. [3]*F.P. & P.*, II, 297-8. [4]*Ibid.* [5]*24th* to the 33*rd Report of the Registrar-General*, pp. 20-1 *passim.* See also the comments on the identification of illiteracy by this method, 31*st Report*, xxxviii. [6]See p. 247 above. [7]*Mannex*, 334.

National School at Dalton (enlarged in 1862) was attended, in 1865, by " upwards of 500 pupils ", and there were smaller National Schools at Newbarns and on Walney, while the iron-mining village of Lindal had a school for 180 children.[1] Barrow itself had a total of thirteen schools of different types and denominations, if eight private academies and a " nautical academy " are included. Fifteen schoolteachers appear in the Barrow directory relating to 1865-6, and their work must have been heavy in the extreme ; at the St. George's church school on Salthouse Road only two teachers were responsible for the 220 children.[2] According to the 1871 Census there were only twelve schoolmasters in the town, but there were 8964 persons under twenty years.[3] Temporarily at least, the educational position in this busy and crowded part of the Furness peninsula was hardly better than it had been in the district as a whole in the early years of the century.[4]

In the rest of Furness, there were improvements which go a little of the way towards explaining the slight though welcome reduction of illiteracy. Ulverston had large National Schools, founded in 1834 and enlarged in 1860 and 1862, with a total of 420 scholars of both sexes. In addition, the town had an infant school with room for 200 children (the number attending). The endowed grammar school at Town Bank was still in existence, with 70 to 80 pupils, and there were Catholic, Wesleyan and commercial schools, as well as seven private " academies " in the old town. There was a National School at Coniston with 110 pupils, and another at Penny Bridge (founded in 1837). Lowick had a small government-aided school, established in 1856. Kirkby Ireleth had an endowed school which was enlarged in 1853, and Broughton-in-Furness had a smaller institution of the same type which was rebuilt in 1865. Satterthwaite and Rusland had their National School in the early 'fifties (with 80 children), and Cartmel National School (195 boys and girls) was erected in 1861, while nearby Grange also obtained such a school in 1864 ; and the Duke of Devonshire had paid for the erection of a fairly capacious school for the children of his tenants and servants at Holker.[5] The population of Cartmel was 5108 in 1861, and about 500 of its children were attending the main schools there a few years afterwards ;[6] it would seem, therefore, that far fewer children were escaping school in the country districts of Furness and Cartmel than had escaped it in previous decades.

Barrow, on the other hand, was very largely unprepared for the great inrush of immigrants and their children which would soon

---

[1]*Mannex*, 329-31. [2]*Mannex*, 337, s.v. *Academies*. [3]1871 *Census*, Vol. III, Ages and Occupations of the People, 440. [4]See pp. 145-8 above. [5]Details of Furness schools in *Mannex* (1866), 394, 398, 400-2, 406, 418, 421, 429, 431-2, 436-7, and Cartmel, 442-8. [6]*Ibid.*

cause its new School Board to struggle desperately against the current. This topic, however, calls for separate treatment.

The politics of the workman, where they were expressed at all, were those of his employer. The borough of Barrow had no separate parliamentary representation until 1885, and during the 'sixties Furness and Cartmel were included in the constituency of North-West Lancashire. From 1857 to 1868 the member for the division was the Marquess of Hartington (eldest son of the 7th Duke of Devonshire) and, needless to say, the Marquess was vigorously supported in his political campaigns by the dominant Barrow and Furness faction of Schneider, Brogden, Ramsden and John Fell, the latter acting as his unofficial agent in Furness. The group had its direct or non-aristocratic parliamentary representative in H. W. Schneider, who was M.P. for Lancaster in 1865 ; the Lancaster election of that year, however, developed into a more than usually lavish battle of bribes, and Schneider was unseated for his conduct during it. The Hindpool ironworks staff, under the direction of Schneider and J. T. Smith, imported parcels of sovereigns into the county town in an attempt to out-bribe the Conservative candidate, Edward Lawrence, who was a supporter of the Earl of Derby and a representative of Liverpool shipping interests. Schneider's activities came too late in the history of electioneering to be excused even by wealthy parliamentarians, and Schneider—and through him the Barrow group—achieved an unwelcome notoriety. Schneider himself showed little shame, perhaps because he knew that others had sinned and escaped where he had suffered.[1] Ejected from Parliament, and deprived of his local magistracy, he seemed content to remain an over-size fish in a small pool, and was an active Barrow council member for the major part of two decades.

The dominant group adhered largely to the Liberal side, following the Cavendish family in this respect. Schneider's partner, Hannay, unsuccessfully contested Kirkcudbright (1868) in the same interest, to which J. R. McClean, Alexander Brogden and other local notabilities adhered. The Marquess of Hartington's Barrow election committee of 1868 comprised nearly every prominent individual in local industry and affairs, and included Ramsden, J. T. Smith, the builders Gradwell, Forshaw, Townson and Wood-house, and other well-known persons like the ore merchant G. B. Ashburner, Joseph Allison, Joseph Richardson, W. T. Manclarke, William Relph and Robert Loxham, together with some 90 other leading burgesses. Schneider, in what passed for disgrace, was not officially on this committee, but he nevertheless insisted on speaking in Hartington's campaign.[2] The Marquess afterwards lost his seat

[1]Marshall, *passim.*   [2]*B. Times*, 19.9, 3.10, 4.8.1868.

to the Hon. Frederick Stanley, and so strong was local partisanship that Joseph Richardson—far from questioning Schneider's activities —alleged that Stanley and Col. Wilson Patten had not defeated Hartington without a suspicion of bribery. [1]

Of the major Furness capitalists, only the Duke of Buccleuch and his agent Edward Wadham are known to have been avowed Conservatives. But their precept or influence carried little weight, for until the August of 1873 there was not even an attempt to form a Conservative party organisation in Barrow itself. [2] A Barrow Liberal Association was in existence in the late 'sixties, [3] but in 1873 a local Conservative alleged that " a committee meeting had not been called since its formation ". [4] Such an unhealthy state of affairs was bound to bring repercussions, and before many years had passed the dominant group—whether avowedly Liberal or not, and irrespective of their party political affiliations—were bitterly assailed in the local press.

If there was no real clash of opinion in the parliamentary field, there was little more at the level of municipal politics. The Barrow Ratepayers' Association was attacked as a mere junta of self-interested malcontents—builders and their agents who were outdone in the general jockeying for favour or position—and its representatives received little support when members of the nominated council had to face re-election. [5] The local franchise, in any case, was still exceedingly narrow. The Burgess Roll of 1867-9 listed 374 voters; that of 1868, 878 voters, and that of 1871, 1,957. [6] Even in the latter year only about one-fifth of the adult male population was represented. Voting was of course open, and in October, 1869, the *Barrow Times* [7] published a letter demanding the ballot and insisting that employers' pressure was brought to bear at the polls. The workman, whatever his politics, was often voiceless ; he expressed his feelings in good-natured ribaldry at election times, or concentrated upon trade union organisation.

---

[1]*B. Times*, 29.11.68.   [2]*B. Her.*, 9.8.73.   [3]*B. Times*, 9.1.69 ; Benjamin Townson was the president.   [4]*B. Her.* (letter), *loc. cit.*   [5]*B. Times*, 7.11.68, 6.11.69.   [6]*Burgess Rolls* for years, Barrow P.L.   [7]*B. Times*, 16.10.69, 6.11.69.

CHAPTER XVI

THE OVERCROWDED YEARS (I): CAPITAL, LABOUR AND INDUSTRIAL DEVELOPMENT, 1870-3

CAPITAL

More happened, economically and industrially speaking, in the short period 1870-3 than in any other comparable period in the history of Furness. The choice of years is in fact arbitrary, for 1869 was a year of recovery in certain industries and returning optimism in others.

It is necessary to describe the background. National iron ore output moved from 11.51 million tons in 1869 to 14.37 (1870) and then to 16.33 (1871).[1] In the same years the local haematite output, climbing less steeply, reached 7.74, 8.72 and 9.31 hundred thousands of tons,[2] and haematite prices rose in unprecedented fashion; the ore at the Haematite Steel Company's Stank mine, near Roose, was 13s. 6d. a ton in 1871 and 25s. in 1872.[3] Cumberland iron ore prices behaved in a similar manner.[4] A driving force behind this violent boom, the precursor of long years of local depression, lay in the great increase of British exports of rail and pig iron. There was a particularly heavy demand for iron and steel rails in the U.S., which received 52 per cent. of the total British rail export in 1870-2.[5] In the latter year the Haematite Company was supplying rails to the Grand Trunk Railway of Canada and the U.S., and by mid-1873 its rail output was of the order of 3000 tons a week, or at least 150,000 tons annually. Best Furness haematite ore, which the Steel Company sold in quantity as a major mineowner in the ironfield, reached the hitherto unknown level of 30s. to 35s. a ton,[6] when it had rarely moved far from 10s. a ton during previous decades.

In such circumstances, it is hardly surprising that the great establishment at Hindpool rapidly became greater still, and that it was, according to Devonshire, very prosperous in 1870-1.[7] The extreme success of the steelworks is the key to a great deal that happened in the Barrow district during these years. An expansion of the iron industry in general was one of the striking features of the early 'seventies, and the Steel Company itself responded, like

---

[1]*Min. Stats. U.K.*; *vide* also *Brit. Parl. Papers*, 1890-1, LXXVIII (ore output figs.). [2]*Min. Stats. U.K.* [3]*MSS.* of Edward Wadham, Buccleuch archives, Tytup Hall, Dalton. [4]*V.C.H. Cumberland*, II, 390. [5]Cf. Burnham and Hoskins, *Iron and Steel in Great Britain*, 1870-1930, 33-4. [6] *Vide Iron* (the contemporary trade journal), reports from iron districts, s.v. Lancashire, 1.2, 15.3, 5.4, 12.4.73. [7]*MS. Diary*, 11.3,70 and also 12.2.70; " We have the usual dividend and bonus . . ." These occasional references are of the utmost importance, for the company meetings were not publicly reported at this period.

hundreds of other firms, to the favourable conditions of the time ; but the Steel Company directors soon began to look outside their own immediate field of operations, with fateful results for many thousands of human beings.

The Furness Railway Company, intimately connected with the steelworks, naturally benefited from the expansion of local iron and steelmaking. It had started its career as an ore-carrying line ; the Hindpool furnaces gave it a growing traffic in coke and coal, and the steelworks at Hindpool, and the furnaces at Askam, Carnforth and Millom, provided the railway system with a newer and greater tidal wave of traffic in these raw materials. But although this traffic and these industries were fundamental to the fortunes of the Railway Company, the growing population of the Barrow district meant also that it carried more passengers and merchandise, while the efforts of the railway directors to equip the Barrow docks as lavishly as possible—and, before long, to establish steamship lines with Canada and the East—brought more trade in timber and other goods through that port. These developments can best, perhaps, be examined in tabular form : [1]

Table 31

(a)

Furness Railway Receipts and Expenditure etc., 1869-76

Year	Total expendr. £(000)	Total receipts (£000)	Net receipts (£000)	Total income minerals (£000)	Total income, (x) other (£000)	Divi- dend (%)	Total stock & share cap. (£ mill.)
1869	123.4	287.6	164.2	192.2	36.2	6½	2.219
1870	136.0	334.9	198.9	227.3	42.0	8½	2.382
1871	158.8	368.0	209.2	240.9	58.9	10	2.446
1872	182.2	412.9	226.7	254.5	80.2	10	2.687
1873	240.6	472.6	231.9	280.8	98.2	9½	2.888
1874	219.7	461.1	241.4	255.6	108.3	6¾	3.470
1875	220.8	466.3	245.5	267.8	84.1	6½	3.493
1876	211.7	464.1	252.4	268.7	74.2	6¼	3.780

(x) Income from the carriage of merchandise and livestock. Income from passengers may be calculated broadly by subtracting this figure plus mineral income from the total receipts. There were, of course, other minor heads of income, but these are not shown in the official returns.

(b)

F.R. traffic deriving from iron and steel industries [2]

Year	Minerals carried over F.R. (mill. t.)	Furness iron ore output (000 t.)	No. of local furnaces in blast	Furness ; estimated annual output Pig (000 t.)	Steel (000 t.)
1871	2.975	931	18	250	130
1872	3.144	909	26	—	156
1873	3.518	926	23	—	—
1874	3.286	914	21	286	182
1875	3.417	834	—	—	—
1876	3.578	908	—	—	—

[1]The figures in section (a) of the table are taken from the published Board of Trade *Railway Returns*.   [2]Figs. from *J.I.S.I.* and *Iron*.

F.R. traffic deriving from non-basic industries, the growth of local
population, and traffic through the port of Barrow

Year	General merchandise carried	Number of passengers	Population [1] of Barrow	Value of imports [2] through Barrow
	(000 t.)	(000)	(est.)	(£000)
1871	302.4	1,146	18,911	—
1872	364.9	1,378	20,000	—
1873	418.2	1,693	28,000	732
1874	432.0	1,697	35,000	622
1875	400.1	1,661	35,000	257
1876	408.4	1,636	37,000	367

Furness had 16 iron furnaces in blast in 1869 ; and over the mountain barrier in Cumberland there were 17 furnaces in blast in 1869 and no fewer than 34 by 1871. [3]   Since north-western haematite pig was sent to Sheffield in quantity, [4] great quantities of it passed over the F.R. system *en route* from West Cumberland.

James Ramsden and his colleagues were exploring the possibility of extending Barrow's industrial base anew in the early months of 1868, and, as could have been expected, the rapid economic developments of these years only stimulated their plans until, as the trade journal *Iron* put it, " No sooner is one manufacturing industry (in Barrow district) successfully launched and put in operation than others, which have been projected for some time, and plans for which have been fully matured, are commenced ". [5] It may be of value to trace out the story in some detail.   As early as May, 1868, Joseph Richardson of the *Barrow Times* was purveying a rumour " about building flax mills ", [6] and it is therefore clear that Ramsden and his immediate entourage in Barrow itself had discussed this project with a discretion merely formal.   In 1869 the Suez Canal was opened, and this event seems to have had some effect upon Barrow plans.   At a stroke it became cheaper and easier to import jute from Calcutta, and accordingly, arrangements for the launching of a jute works were " nearly completed " [7] in the December of that year.   The establishment of such a works had a two-fold advantage ; a yet unemployed and unexploited section of the local population, the womenfolk, could be utilised at wage rates lower than those usually paid to males, and additional dock traffic might be stimulated.   A limited company, the Barrow Flax and Jute Co., was duly formed, and work was commenced on the mill buildings in the May of 1870. [8]   Ramsden was the Secretary

---

[1] *Treasurers' Repts.* [2] *B.P.P.* ; *Tde. & Navigation of the U.K.* [3] Wood, thesis *cit.*, 275-6, for Cumberland figs. [4] Also the output went, in some cases, to Cammell's and Krupps ; *vide* account of Askam works in *Engineer*, 28.7.71. [5] *Iron*, 12.4.73. [6] *B. Times*, 8.5.68. [7] *MS. Diary*, 27.12.69. [8] *MS. Dairy*, 11.2.70 ; Leach, *op. cit.*, 26.

of the new company, and the directors included Lord F. C. Cavendish, Schneider, William Currey and John Fell.   The establishment of a large and well-equipped flour mill was planned at the same time by the same persons, and so was an artificial manure plant.[1]   A new iron-making firm, to be styled " The Furness Abbey Iron Co.", was also under consideration,[2] and this too, seems to have been prompted by the Furness Railway group or pressure-supplying syndicate behind the local scenes.[3]

Company formation was not entirely the prerogative of these individuals,[4] and a steel implement company, a cattle dealing company and a deep sea fishing company were also formed or projected by leading Barrow citizens during the summer of 1869. The same year was also marked by a public-spirited effort on the part of Joseph Richardson (of the *Barrow Times*) to secure adequate exploration of the coal measures which he was sure must eventually be found in proximity to the limestones of Furness.   Unfortunately, the full carboniferous system of strata exhibited in the coal-mining area of Cumberland did not exist in Furness, and expensive borings by the Haematite Steel Company eventually revealed not coal, but a large new deposit of iron ore at Stank, near Roose.[5]

The most important local venture of all, the Barrow Shipbuilding Company, was also conceived during the late months of 1869. Joseph Richardson, a useful if not fully reliable source of information relating to this period, unreservedly gave James Ramsden the credit (or the responsibility) for the idea of introducing large-scale shipbuilding into Barrow.[6]   It has been shown that something of the sort was planned in the mid-'sixties,[7] and in February, 1870, Devonshire noted that arrangements for such a scheme were " fairly started ", and the jute works, shipbuilding works and steam flour mill were discussed simultaneously during or immediately after a Furness Railway directors' meeting on the 11th of that month.[8] In the March, Ramsden took the Duke of Devonshire for a walk on Barrow Island, explaining his (Ramsden's) idea " as to the site of the shipbuilding yard, and also as to that of a better class of houses which seem to be much required ".[9]   The industrial projector, as

[1]*MS. Diary*, 11.2.70 ; *Co. files*, by ctsy. of the Registrar of Joint-Stock Cos.; *vide* also Pollard, *L. & C.* LXIII. *cit.* (" Town Planning in the 19th Cent."), 162, Tab. I.   [2]*B. Times*, 11.12.69.   [3]This concept is correctly used by Dr. Pollard in his paper, *cit.*   [4]See *B. Times*, 19.6, 17.7, 7.8, 23.10.69, and 24.12.70.   The promoters of the implement company were Thomas Roper, Edward Wadham and John Westray of the firm of Westray and Forster. Little or nothing was heard of it later.   The fisheries scheme also came to nothing.   [5]*B. Times*, 2.1, 23.1, 30.1, 27.2, 6.3, 13.3, 20.3, 15.5, 5.6.1869 ; *J.I.S.I.*, 1874, Vol. I, 301 ; *F.P. & P.*, II, 189-90.   [6]*F.P. & P.*, II, 281. [7]See p. 273 above.   [8]*MS. Diary*, 11.2.70.   [9]*MS. Diary*, 22.3.70.

sometimes happened, was obliged to assume the rôle of town-builder. Only Messrs. Price, Potter and Walker had as yet been prevailed upon to take premises on Barrow Island, and the western side of the latter lay unused. Whether this was a result of deliberate planning over the years cannot satisfactorily be shown.

" Throughout the year 1870 " wrote Francis Leach, " there was a decided activity in every department of industry in Barrow, and a consequent increase in general prosperity." Work on the Jute Works and the Steam Corn Mill began on May 4th and 16th respectively, and two large firms, S. J. Claye and Cook & Swinnerton, purchased land in the town.[1] The first of these was to make wagons for the F.R., and the second planned to manufacture wire from the rail-ends accumulated at the steelworks. Constructional work on the new shipbuilding enterprise was at first slow to get under way, and any sluggishness in the preparation of the new industrial installations was caused by the local shortage of housing accommodation.[2] By the August the inauguration of a line of transatlantic steamers, using Barrow as a base, was under discussion,[3] and during the same summer an attempt was made to establish a large new iron company in the Ulverston district. This project may have had its origins, partially at least, in the Furness Iron and Steel Company of Askam-in-Furness, and it was reported that Talbot, a former Askam manager, was " working hard to prevent the scheme ending in failure ".[4] The new iron firm is mentioned at this stage in order to avoid any suggestion that the Furness Railway group controlled all enterprises in the locality. But it is true that project after project was now discussed in the Furness Railway boardroom at St. George's Square, Barrow. The railway station entrance, with its swarms of immigrants and relatives of immigrants, lay in the Square, and every time a carriage passed by with James Ramsden or Devonshire as the occupant, it was likely that some decision had been taken which vitally affected the onlookers.

Where did the Furness Railway's functions end, and those of the railway-fostered companies begin? The former were becoming more and more ambiguous up to the year 1870, and it need not

[1]MS. Diary, 28.1.71 ; B. Her., 26.11.70 ; Leach, op. cit., 26.28.
[2]MS. Diary, 27.9.70, when the Jute Works construction was slowed down " owing to the difficulty of getting bricklayers ", and 4.1.71, where Ramsden told the Duke that a thousand new cottages would, if built, be occupied at once.
[3]MS. Diary, 9.8.70, where Duncan (Clyde shipbuilder) and James Little were stated to support such an idea, which interested the F.R. board.   [4]The capital of the new company (ultimately the North Lonsdale Iron Company) was to be £100,000, part of which was to be supplied by the mining firms of Brogden and Kennedy ; the Ainslies and Kennedys ultimately helped to capitalise it. For refs., B. Her., 16.7, 7.9, 24.9.70 ; Dir. Mins. (F.R.), 9.8.70 ; and for the company as finally established, Co. file 7730, Bush House, London.

be a matter for surprise that railway companies of this age were prone to exceed their terms of reference as approved by Parliament. Devonshire was conscious of the problem, and expressed himself plainly before a parliamentary committee in 1869 :[1]

" We have purchased lands not authorised by Act of Parliament, as I believe every other railway company in the country has done the same. We had found considerable inconvenience in providing accommodation for persons employed on the railway . . . A farm of 200 acres coming into the market, we bought it, and on it a large portion of our railway works now stand."

This was disarming. In practice more perplexing complications could ensue. In February, 1869, the F.R. auditors drew attention to irregularities in the railway accounts ; " considering the intimate relations which subsist between (the Haematite Steel Co.) and the Furness Railway Co., it seems to us desirable that the respective liabilities of each should be clearly defined, and that the monies of one should not be advanced for the purpose of the other ".[2] The auditors found that company land in Hindpool had " not been acquired under any parliamentary power ", and Ramsden, in a sharp letter of reply, admitted that " the company exceeded its powers in purchasing it . . . but the point does not appear to the Directors to come within the province of the auditors ".[3] Successive Acts,[4] however, extended the company's legally owned lands, and matters like this do not seem to have arisen later. It was hardly of great moment whether the Furness Railway, the Haematite Steel Company or the Duke of Devonshire held large tracts of Barrow and Furness territory, for the ultimate control emanated from the same personalities in each case. In July, 1870, the F.R. was making arrangements to sell land to the newly-formed Flax and Jute Co., work on the buildings having commenced two months previously. It was suggested that the latter company " pay a rent calculated at 1s. a yard for the first 5 years, 2s. a yard for the second 5 years, and at the expiration of the second 5 years the Company to purchase at 4s. a yard. The Co. is however to have the option of purchasing at 3s. a yard at the expiration of the first five years ".[5] The site of the Jute Works lay on the Hindpool Estate, on a large rectangle of land to the S.E. of the Haematite Steel Company's works, and laid out on a plot originally reserved—according to Ramsden's 1854 plan—as a " site of square, church, chapel or proposed public building ".[6] The rent of the land, when measured against " free " rental levels

[1]*B. Times*, 8.5.69.   [2]The auditors claimed the right of responsible comment under Clause 30 of 30 & 31 *Vict.*, *c.*127. It seems that there were other irregularities in the accounts ;   *Dir. Mins. (F.R.)*, 12.2.69.   [3]*Ibid.* [4]E.g., 32 & 33 *Vict.*, *c.cliv* (9th Aug., 1869) " for the construction of works and the acquisition of lands ", and 39 & 40 *Vict.*, *c.xlvii* (June 27th, 1876). [5]*Dir. Mins. (F.R.)*, 6.7.70.   [6]For other details of this plan, see pp. 229-33 above.

in other parts of the town, was merely nominal.   In such circumstances any offshoot company of the F.R. clearly enjoyed a great
advantage.

By 1871 the paid-up capital of the railway-associated industries
was divided as follows : [1]

Barrow Shipbuilding Co.	£17,400
Flax and Jute Co.	£57,400
Haematite Steel Co.	£700,000
Barrow Steam Corn Mill	£7,506
Barrow Rolling Mills Co.	£5,850
Barrow Patent Linseed Co.	£645
	£788,801

The steelworks was still by far the best advertisement for
Barrow prospects.   In 1871 the works as a whole consisted of 16
blast furnaces and three steelmaking sheds over 700 feet long, and
was equipped with 18 Bessemer smelting cauldrons, three rail mills,
a plate mill, a merchant mill and a tyre mill.   The productive
capacity at Hindpool was, by the standards of the time, enormous ;
according to the iron trade journalist Samuel Griffiths[2] it was
(1871) :

250,000 tons of	pig iron at £9	per ton ;	£2,250,000
104,000 ,,	steel rails ,, £20	,,	£2,080,000
600,000 ,,	haematite ,, 33s. 6d.	,,	£1,005,000

But, as Griffiths indicated, about 130,000 tons of the pig iron
were used for conversion into Bessemer steel and sold as rails, plates,
tyre parts and forgings.   He gave weekly steel production as about
2000 tons a week, a figure confirmed elsewhere by what may be a
more reliable source.[3]   The greater part of the local ore, too, was
utilised on the spot and not sold as raw material ; and hence
Griffiths's statistics, on which he based the claim that Barrow left
Krupps and the Le Creusot works far behind, are of little value as
they stand.   But the firm was enabled to advertise proudly under
the heading " Capital One Million ",[4] and its called-up capital did
in fact reach that level in 1874.[5]

In the former year (1871) the Duke of Devonshire
increased his holding of shares to the value of £175,000, H.W.
Schneider having the largest with £200,000.   Robert Hannay,
Schneider's partner of former days, had £83,000 invested in the
works, but had transferred his attention to the ill-fated Blochairn

---

[1]Calncs. by courtesy of Dr. S. Pollard, from the company files.   [2]In his
Guide to the Iron Trade of Great Britain (1872), 30, 40-41.   [3]*J.I.S.I.* 1871,
Vol. II, 139-41.   [4]Griffiths, *op. cit.*, xviii.   [5]*Co. file*, Bush Ho.

works in Glasgow.[1]   There were still only 25 shareholders altogether, and of these, six were members of the Cavendish family
(with total holdings of £272,000), and four were members of the
Currey family, legal agents to the former.   Furness Railway
interests were represented by Ramsden, who had £33,500 of shares
at Hindpool, and who was now on the way to becoming very
wealthy, Devonshire himself, F. I. Nicholl, William Currey, J. R.
McClean, the latter's son Frank McClean and F. C. Stileman,
while the North-Eastern Railway influence was personified by
H. S. Thompson and H. Meysey-Thompson (later Lord Knares-
borough).[2]   The systems of both railway companies carried a great
traffic in coke from the east (coal was brought from Barnsley and
Wigan[3]), and Griffiths claimed that the iron and steelworks at
Hindpool consumed 450,000 tons of coal and coke *per annum*.[4]

Not a little of the success of the steelworks, in the purely
technical sense, was due to the personal skill and knowledge of
J. T. Smith.   As one expert observer put it, " all would have been
in vain if they had not got a good manager . . . and in Barrow they
had Mr. Josiah Smith ".[5]   It is very much to be doubted whether
the other members of the steelworks board were well versed in the
technicalities of the industry—the chairman Devonshire, at any
rate, evidently did not feel himself equal to addressing the Iron and
Steel Institute (as its first President) without background help,[6]
and even Schneider was primarily a merchant and a financier.
Smith was perhaps one of Schneider's best investments.   The company was constantly extending its works under the direction of the
former, and, leaving its practical affairs in his hands, Ramsden,
Devonshire and their other colleagues were able to turn their attention to other matters.

The result was that the authorised capital and the scale of
operations of the Shipbuilding Company and the Jute Works soon
afterwards increased considerably, in consequence of a thorough-
going attempt to repeat the successful *coup* represented by the
Steelworks.

The first provisional meeting of the Barrow Shipbuilding
Company was held at Ramsden's private house, Abbotswood, on
January 28th, 1871, with James Little, Duncan the Clydebank
shipbuilder, Devonshire, Ramsden and Robertson (the new manager)

[1] *Vide* Griffiths, *op. cit.*, 280 ; Casson, *A Few Furness Worthies*, 75-6 ;
Wadham Diary, 30.9.74, 31.10.74.   Hannay's death in 1874 was, it seems,
hastened by the failure of these works.   [2] *Co. file, cit.*   [3] E.g. *R. Comm. Coal,
1871*, B.P.P. XVIII, Rept. of Cttee. E., 156 ; *Iron*, 15.2.73. [4] Griffiths, *op. cit.*,
33 ;   *MS. Diary*, 24.6.72.   [5] R. Fothergill, M.P., in *J.I.S.I.*, 1874, I, xiii.
[6] *MS. Diary*, 6.3.69, where the Duke notes that Lowthian Bell, the famous East
Coast ironmaster, is to give him material for an address.

present. It was agreed that the initial outlay was to be some £92,000, and on February 18th the new company was registered with an authorised capital of £100,000 in 4000 shares of £25.[1] At the same time an independent company was formed to " trade with Barrow, India, China &c. by way of the Canal ", to be known as the Eastern Steamship Co., and with a total authorised capital of £500,000 in 500 shares of £1000 each. Devonshire himself was listed as holding £25,000 of shares in this venture, but (nominally at least) it was not controlled by the F.R. group and was managed by R. and J. Carlyle of 69, Lombard Street, London, while two Liverpool merchants, Cox and Greenshields, held £20,000 and £10,000 of shares in it respectively.[2] The two ventures—shipowning and shipbuilding—were nevertheless intimately connected, and in the March it was agreed that the Shipbuilding Co. was to build four steamers for the Eastern Steamship Co. at a cost of £60,000.[3] In this particular case it does appear that outside speculators had supposed that Barrow might become a second Dundee, importing great quantities of jute from Calcutta, and that the Barrow investors were more than happy to let capital flow in from outside. Meanwhile, the proposed capital of the new Barrow Rolling Mills Co. (purely an F.R. speculation) looked no less impressive on paper, being £100,000 in four thousand £25 shares, members of the Cavendish family holding £12,500 worth.[4]

By means of such arrangements, which had the effect of a powerful propaganda offensive, the Barrow group was able to announce its intentions to the world. In the May and June even more ambitious plans were under discussion, relating to the promotion of a steamship line between Canada, Liverpool and Barrow. One of the prime movers here was Richard Potter, of Price, Potter and Walker, the timber importers, and he proposed the formation of a company with a capital of £600,000 to trade with Canada. It was hoped that James Little, Henderson of the Anchor Line and the Furness-Midland Railway Joint Committee would provide £100,000 each towards this venture, which—for obvious reasons— was not to compete with the existing Liverpool-Canada trade. Ramsden saw a further opportunity of improving the prospects of local shipbuilding, and was evidently in league with Potter, who for his part suspected the motives of Henderson. The latter controlled what would have been a powerful competing steamship line (the Anchor), and, possibly for this reason, the discussion remained indeterminate for a few months.[5] By the August, however, it was found that the most important line in the Canada trade, the Allen Co., was proposing to " sell up ", and it is remarkable evidence

[1]*MS. Diary*, 28.1.71 ; *B. Times*, 4.3.71, q. *Investors' Guardian*. [2]*B. Times*, 4.3.71, q. *Liverpool Journal of Commerce*. [3]*MS. Diary*, 11.3.71. [4]*B. Times, loc. cit.* Cf. also Dr. Pollard's account of these developments in *Ec.H.R.*, VIII, 2 Dec., 1955, 214 sqq. [5]*MS. Diary*, 23.5, 15.6, 12.7, 5.8.71.

of the sanguine attitude then prevailing in Barrow counsels that
Potter proposed the purchase of this line if it could be bought for
one and a quarter million pounds " or less ".[1] Allens were willing
to sell at one and a half million ; there was anxious negotiation
during the November and the early weeks of December, and by the
12th of that mongh the line was to be purchased for £1,350,000
including stores, Devonshire being responsible for finding half the
capital and Henderson the other half. In fact the negotiations
nevertheless foundered, and by January 2nd, 1872, the grandiose
scheme was abandoned.[2] It was symptomatic of an almost
desperate attempt to ensure the prosperity of the syndicate's
industries through the general prosperity and status of the port
itself. Had the plan assumed concrete form, and attained initial
success, it would still have represented the sober Duke of Devonshire's most enormous gamble, although it must remain open to
doubt whether he saw it as such. Any misgivings seem to have
been silenced by Ramsden, in whom the Duke now reposed—if only
for a time—immense confidence.[3] The former had discovered a
powerful ally in Potter, a man of like stamp, who was chairman of
the Grand Trunk Railway of Canada as well as Barrow's chief
timber importer.[4] On the other hand, H. S. Thompson of the
North-Eastern Railway and the Haematite Co., whose opinions
were no less weighty, already had misgivings concerning the " high
spending " at Barrow, and opposed an attempt by Ramsden to
unite the different F.R.-Barrow companies in the early months of
1872. Thompson was willing to support the amalgamation of the
Rolling Mills Co. with the steelworks (thereby showing the business
sense that might have been expected from him), and H. W.
Schneider, who was constantly working in the background, wished
to unite the Shipbuilding Co. and the steelworks. Devonshire
presciently admitted to himself that " the reasons against seem to
be very strong ",[5] and events were to show that both Devonshire
and Thompson were fully justified in their caution.

The most important industries of the neighbourhood were now
connected financially, if not administratively, with the Furness
Railway boardroom. New firms which had no such connection were
inevitably dependent upon that board's support and favour. In the
late months of 1870, for instance, it was reported that S. J. Claye, of
the Manor House Works, Long Eaton, Derbys., had bought seven

---

[1]*MS. Diary*, 5.8, 12.9.71 ; regarding Allens, the Duke doubted " the
earnestness of their intentions ". [2]*MS. Diary*, 23.10, 10.11, 18.11, 12.12.71,
2.1.72. [3]*MS. Diary*, 2.1.72 ; " Ramsden is as confident as ever with respect
to the future of Barrow and expects some other plan for having first class
steamers connected with the port will soon be in operation." Regular services
to Canada commenced in March, 1872. [4]See pp. 276, 325 above. [5]*MS.
Diary*, 21.3, 10.5.72, for entries far more revealing than was usual.

acres of land at Salthouse[1] with a view to establishing a £10,000 works for the building of wagons, now increasingly demanded by the F.R.[2] These works were not completed until 1873,[3] and although the enterprise was a comparatively small one at first,[4] it fitted well into the general plans of the railway group ; wagon-making contracts were bait to attract a new industry into the town itself, and F.R. capital was left free for uses that were potentially more profitable than the mere extension of the railway's own carriage and wagon shops. The F.R. may have found the arrangement more advantageous than did Claye himself, for in 1872 " the iron work required for the wagons (had) been brought from the works at Long Eaton ".[5] Claye's shops adjoined the F.R. locomotive sheds at Salthouse, and soon grew considerably, accommodating, a few years later, 50 to 100 carriages at one time.[6] S. J. Claye and his manager G. H. Parke joined the ranks of the comparatively small group which stood at the head of affairs in Barrow, the former taking up residence in the town and becoming a councillor.[7]

Other firms of some consequence were establishing themselves in the district. Solomon Woodall, the owner of large works at Windmillend, Dudley, set up a boiler and girder works in Barrow in 1867, finding it more easy to carry out work for local industries in the town itself than to execute the former at his establishment in Staffordshire.[8] Woodall's firm erected the roofing for the Shipbuilding Company, and boilers for the Flax and Jute Company ; Westray and Copeland's (established 1866) erected engines for the F.R. group's steam corn mill ;[9] Stuart's Rope Works manufactured ropes for local mines and industries ;[10] Gradwell, as before, was engaged in large building contracts, and his men erected the steam corn mill mentioned ;[11] the type of work executed by Joseph Brigg's iron foundry consisted chiefly of " castings for the blast furnaces, steelworks, railway company, and general jobbing for the town and neighbourhood" ;[12] and the North Lancashire Brick and Tile Works of Woodhouse, Son and Andrews provided " the whole of the brickwork of the Old Gas Works, the Railway Station, the Iron and Steel works, and the Jute Works ".[13] But only two undertakings outside the F.R.-inspired group employed more than

[1]B. Her., 26.11.70. Claye's Long Eaton works were established in 1849, and developed with the establishment of Toton Sidings by the M.R. in 1855. " Claye's wagon works " are still a well-known feature in Long Eaton, Nottingham. The name of S. J. Claye is borne by a well-known wagon works at Horbury, Wakefield, but the firm has lost all connection (Co. file, Bush Ho.) with the family of that name. [2]Dir. Mins. (F.R.), 4.2.68, 23.6.69, 19.2, 7.11.72, 14.2, 9.8.73. [3]F.P. & P., II, 291. [4]Leach, op. cit., 82. [5]Loc. cit. [6]See description in F.P. & P., II, 291-2. [7]Op. cit., facing p. 291 ; Claye built Infield House, now a convalescent home. Parke also became a councillor. [8]Leach, op. cit., 81. [9]F.P. & P., II, 279, 288. [10]Ibid., and 254.[11] F.P. & P., II, 278. [12]F.P. & P., II, 286. [13]Leach, op. cit., 77.

500 men ; Gradwell's (750 in 1872) and the brickworks mentioned in the previous sentence (800 in 1872). The lesser engineering firms and manufactories all had fewer than 250 employees, with the possible exception of Westray and Copeland's.[1] But all establishments, large and small, had something in common ; they were utterly dependent upon the investments of the Furness Railway group, which was now filling its Hindpool Estate in more or less satisfactory fashion. The local industrial edifice still had a perilously narrow base.

The Barrow economy, too, was developing inner contradictions. It was not enough that (as a local newspaper editor somewhat savagely put it) the town's rulers were " connected with a dozen undertakings in the town, all dependent on each other for support " ;[2] other and lesser firms, owing to the very speed of the town's growth and the enormous demand for their products, tended to become more and more integrated. This tendency had been evident in the Barrow building trade for some time,[3] and certain firms like Woodhouse's not only manufactured their own bricks and joinery work and mass-produced mortar, but made their own carts and wheelbarrows " and other necessaries in that line ". Gradwell's establishment had been highly integrated before any of the others, and had now (1872) extended its brickmaking plant, acquired " large mortar mills, rooms for the manufacture of patent manures, and others fitted up with various descriptions of agricultural machinery, all driven by steam power ".[4] While such developments reflected the fire and drive of the principals of the firms concerned, it is more than arguable that they narrowed the field for other and smaller competitors, or even for those who might have established small businesses complementary to the main firms. Such self-sufficiency was of course a necessary consequence of the rapid development of an isolated district, in which even simple objects like wheelbarrows were not made in quantity.

After 1872 there was no great change in the number or variety of Barrow industries ; the town had reached saturation point in this respect. Nearly all subsequent major expansion took place in industries which, like the steelworks, were already established, or in the satellite industries of the F.R. group. The building trade remained under the control of the same personalities, Gradwell, Woodhouse, Rawcliffe and Garden, with the significant qualification that when an unprecedentedly vast new contract—for the erection

<hr/>

[1]Nos. of men employed are given in Leach, *op. cit.*, Ch. III, 47 sqq. Westray and Copeland's was originally Westray and Forster's (1866). A member of the Westray family afterwards founded the shipbroking firm of J. B. Westray and Co. Ltd., Leadenhall St., London, to one of whose directors, Mr. A. G. Fagg, I am indebted for most interesting information.   [2]*B. Her.*, 22.3.73.   [3]See p. 286 above.   [4]Leach, *op. cit.*, 79.

of no fewer than 800 houses in the Hindpool area—came along in 1873, it was let to the firm of London contractors, Yewdall and Hitchens.[1] Similarly, the erection of a large block of flats in Hindpool for the Haematite Steel Company (1871-2) was let to the Dundee firm of Smith and Caird,[2] possibly because it was felt that this firm knew how to erect flats " on the Scotch model ", and that Gradwell or Woodhouse—the former a man who had already tried his hand at nearly everything in the sphere of building, from mills and churches to cottages and railway stations—were not equal to the particular task.

The town was, indeed, now growing rapidly, and it may also be significant that the labour force now had to be accommodated vertically in boxes—the barrack-like stone flats which were, no doubt, considered an advanced form of working-class housing in their time, but which remained an eyesore until their demolition in 1956. The F.R. policy of industrial expansion created an appalling housing problem (dealt with in another chapter), and in April, 1873, a visiting customs inspector reported to his superior that " houses are taken as soon as the foundations are laid . . . it was told me (sic) that some of the beds in the lodging houses are never cool ".[3] Scaffolding, piles of bricks, deep mud and swarms of building workers were seen in every street. The Furness Railway Company and steelworks, chiefly under the direction and inspiration of James Ramsden, arranged for the building of more and more houses,[4] but the supply fell far short of the demand. Ramsden, Schneider, Smith, Gradwell and Wadham were members of the Barrow Council as well as industrial organisers. But the Duke of Devonshire, apparently on his own initiative,[5] caused " model buildings " to be erected on Barrow Island, near the junction of Island and Michaelson roads and in close proximity to the shipyard. Architecturally, these were a distinct advance on the " Scotch " tenements at Hindpool,[6] but their economic advantage, possibly their *raison d'etre*, was enormous ; as further blocks of flats were added, it became possible to achieve an average density of 69.85 structurally separate dwellings per acre, and by 1881, 3590 people of the parish of St. John (Old Barrow), nearly all flat-dwellers, occupied 392 inhabited houses covering less than seven acres.[7] These had replaced a colony of insanitary hutments erected by the Shipbuilding Company as a temporary expedient.

[1]*B. Times*, 18.10.73.   [2]*B. Her.*, 22.7.71 ; this firm also erected Barrow Island flats in 1873-4.   [3]*Inspections (Reports of Customs Inspectors, MS.)*, 1874, fol. 445 sqq., Customs and Excise Library, London.   [4]See Dr. Pollard's figures, *L. & C.*, LXIII, *cit.*, p. 110, Table 2.   [5]*MS. Diary*, 7.11.72. For a full description, *B. Her.*, 28.6.73.   [6]Again, *B. Her.*, 22.7.71.   In the Hind-pool flats, 264 families were accommodated on 1½ acres. They were in the Glasgow tradition, with stone stairs and landings, and are still (1956) an eyesore.   [7]Tyson, *Abstract, Dalton* etc. (*cit.*), Table D.

Francis Leach wrote in mid-1872 that the latter company had :
" . . . already entered into extensive contracts with the
Eastern Steamship Company, under which they are engaged in
building four first-class iron steam vessels each of 4000 tons burden
and 500 horse-power. Thousands of men are even now employed,
and Old Barrow Island—two years since quite a pleasant rural
nook, with fields of waving grain and blooming hedge-rows—has
been transformed with almost magic rapidity into a teeming hive
of industry . . . "[1]

The town of Barrow, like the island, was transformed in
appearance, and thanks to a book-length prospectus written by
Francis Leach,[2] we have a most detailed picture of the changes
that were taking place. The mighty iron and steel works have
been described ; otherwise, it is better to let Leach speak for himself.
A description of the Flax and Jute Works[3] will not be a mere formality, for the last remains of this once great establishment were
demolished a few years ago :

" The portion of these extensive works that is at present
finished is divided into two parts by a large central court-yard, the
buildings on the south being occupied for weaving, calendering,
packing &c., and on the north for spinning . . . The style of
architecture is an adaptation of Italian. The principal facade
faces the Hindpool-road, and overlooks the docks, the central feature
being a large block of buildings containing general offices, boardroom, store-rooms, mess-room, lodge, principal entrance &c. flanked
by two-storied buildings, terminated with three-storied pavilions
at the angles, used as warehouses, store-rooms &c."

Although the centre of the town lacked the great Town Hall
that is its most conspicuous landmark of the present day, the main
thoroughfares were beginning to impress. The Working Men's Club
and Institute, on Abbey Road, was, in Leach's words :

" This magnificent structure . . . one of the architectural
ornaments of the town . . . The ground plan consists of the
entrance vestibule ; hall, containing the principal staircase, lava-
tories &c. ; coffee-room, 36 ft. long by 24 ft. wide ; reading-room
and chessroom, each 24 ft. long by 17 ft. wide ; committee-room,
kitchen, offices, back staircase &c. The upper plan consists of
lecture rooms and billiard-rooms . . ."[4]

[1]Leach, *op. cit.*, 29. [2]Francis Leach, B.A., was brought to Barrow-in-
Furness by Joseph Richardson to assist in writing a history of the district,
Furness Past and Present. Leach became editor of the *Barrow Times*
(Richardson's former newspaper) and propagandist for the main industrial
group. [3]*Op. cit.*, 69. [4]*Op. cit.*, 119.

A short distance from the Institute lay Ramsden's swimming bath :

" The spaces between these two buildings . . . will be turfed and used one as a bowling green, and the other as a quoit ground. Seats are already provided under the colonnades for the convenience of spectators. When the entire design is carried out, the effect of the three detached buildings and the colonnades between them, presenting a frontage to the road of 360 ft., will be very handsome." [1]

This, however, was but one portion of Abbey Road. Shops and offices, in a more or less uniform architecture approved by Ramsden, were beginning to lend dignity to the town; the spire of St. James's church now arose from Hindpool terraces; and the prevailing newness of the brickwork and stonework at every corner never failed to impress visitors. The visible achievement was no less in the field of industry. When Ramsden escorted distinguished visitors from the railway offices to the steelworks by special train, they went to the station at St. George's Square, where " One of the most commodious carriage sheds in England " was pointed out to them :

" The shunting ground in which all trains are made ready is about a mile in length, and occupied in some places by sixteen sidings abreast. The line, which is crossed by a light lattice girder bridge, connecting the front of the pier with the town, is carried over a bridge, underneath which is the Middle Road to Barrow Island. Passing along, with the Dock Warehouses, new Corn Mill, and buildings containing the docks hydraulic machinery on the left, and Messrs. Waddington and Longbottom's Foundry, the Gas and Water Works, and Messrs. Westray and Forster's Foundry on the right, the line is carried over another bridge which spans the North Road to Barrow Island. The railway is then bounded on the left by the graving dock, Messrs. Ashburner's shipyard, and Messrs. Woodall's Boiler and Girder Works, and on the right by Mr. Gradwell's Saw Mills. From thence it passes through the heart of the Steel and Iron Works, and forms a junction with sidings, which communicate with these works." [2]

A new loop line between Salthouse and Hindpool (the present British Railways line) was then planned, and Leach made an imaginary journey along it, pointing proudly to more industries and establishments which then existed :

" . . . it passes to the left of Mr. Briggs's foundry and Mr. Gradwell's Salthouse brick works, underneath Greengate, by a

[1]Leach, *op. cit.*, 120.   [2]Leach, *op. cit.*, 47.

bridge spanning four lines . . . it passes close to the Cavendish-street brewery, through Mr. Gradwell's Dalton-road brickworks then under Abbey-road by a handsome iron bridge . . . "

It was, without question, almost impossible to believe that a mere village had occupied this place little more than a dozen years previously.

What of the men who were most associated with these achievements in the public mind ? H. W. Schneider continued to exert much influence over municipal affairs, and was the subject of not a little hero-worship. In 1872 it was expected that he would automatically become Mayor of Barrow in succession to James Ramsden, but—perhaps because he hoped, temporarily at least, to remain in the broader arena of parliamentary politics—he declined.[1] In 1869 he purchased a large residence at Belsfield, Bowness-on-Windermere[2]—a considerable journey from Barrow—and seems to have confined his local activities to visits to the monthly council meetings, and board meetings of the various Barrow companies with which he was associated ; the Shipbuilding Company, the Flax and Jute Company, the Rolling Mills Company and a Barrow Printing and Publishing Company, of which more will be said later. In 1872 he became a member of the Barrow School Board, and became also a Justice of the Peace for Westmorland. In the same year he caused a second residence to be built at Oak Lea " and resided there when busily engaged in Barrow ".[3] There can be little doubt that Schneider was as much responsible for the appearance and destiny of Barrow-in-Furness as any man of the period. He liked to play the paternal figure in his chosen sphere, and was described as " the most generous and liberal despot in Lancashire ",[4] heading subscription lists and giving advice whether it was really wanted or not.

Devonshire had far less interest in Barrow than Schneider. As we have seen, he was in the habit of entrusting the administration of the towns on his estates (Buxton and Eastbourne) to capable agents,[5] but in the view of a historian of Buxton, his maxim of government was " What is good for the community to have or to do, let the community carry into effect ".[6] In other words, he did not believe in or practise paternalism, as that word is usually applied and understood, and although he attended official functions in the Barrow district and in Furness, and still, throughout the years, acted as chairman of the Ulverston Guardians, it was only his ever-

[1]*B. Times*, 16.11.72.   [2]*MS. Diary*, 10.8.69.   [3]Casson, *A Few Furness Worthies*, 71.   Other details in *Co. files, cit.* and the press.   [4]Casson, *op. cit.*, 73.   [5]See p. 279 above.   [6]Heape, R. G., *Buxton Under the Dukes of Devonshire* (1948), 88.

growing investments in Barrow industries that frequently brought him into that town.[1]

The great uprising of the town was a realisation of James Ramsden's dream. Although Barrow itself was not of his making, he had controlled and directed its growth at every stage. In him, the functions of industrial organiser and civic administrator were combined. Not only had the Furness Railway grown partly under his guidance ; he was a director of the Haematite Steel Company, of the Shipbuilding Company, the Steam Corn Mill Company, the Flax and Jute works, the Linseed Company, the Barrow Rolling Mills Company, and the administrator of the Furness Railway's lands in Barrow. He was Mayor of Barrow continuously between 1867 and 1872, a local Justice of the Peace, a member of the Ulverston Board of Guardians, a member of the Barrow School Board (1872), the Colonel commanding the local Rifle Volunteers, a representative of the civic (and F.R.) interests in all parliamentary and public enquiries, patron of Barrow's theatre, President of its cricket club and Sanitary Association, and Vice-Commodore of its Yacht Club.[2] It is true that he derived much of his power from the Furness Railway board and from the Duke of Devonshire, who was still partly dependent upon him for advice and encouragement ;[3] but he was a clever and able man, diligent, sanguine and level-headed, endowed with as much energy as Schneider but very often even more effective in its use. He seems to have had little desire to stand for Parliament. Unfortunately, too much centred on him ; no man on earth could run a large, growing and turbulent town single-handed, yet that is what he tried at times to do.

He was lionised almost inordinately. In December, 1870, a meeting attended or supported by nearly every prominent citizen in Barrow decided to " provide some enduring record of the manner in which his services on behalf of the town of Barrow were appreciated by his fellow-townsmen ". A " Ramsden Statue Fund " was opened immediately after this meeting.

The statue—representing a man only fifty years of age, and still but little known to the world outside Furness—was unveiled on May 11th, 1872, amid a large attendance of magnates, lesser businessmen, townsfolk and mayors of other towns. Devonshire himself made the following comment :

[1]Dr. Pollard's article, *Barrow-in-Furness and the Seventh Duke of Devonshire* (*Ec.H.R.*, VIII, Dec., 1955), while factually sound, might tend to give the impression that Devonshire was " paternal " in his attitude to Barrow. He did, as Dr. Pollard shows, try to save its industries from ruin—but that is not the same thing. [2]The local press, *passim*, and Leach, *op. cit.*, 123, 128-9. [3]E.g., *MS. diary*, 22.3, 31.3, 25.5, 9.8.70; 4.1, 28.1, 8.8.71; 2.1, 8.2, 21.3, 10.5, 7.11.72 ; 14.1.73.

" . . . the surprising progress of Barrow, which is of interest to everyone connected with the town and neighbourhood, must be to you, upon whom the responsibility has chiefly rested, and who has borne the greater part of the labour to which this result is attributable, a source of just satisfaction and pride . . . "

The figure on the pedestal gazed towards the sea [1] (from which disappointments, as well as shipping, would soon come). The man himself lacked only a Smiles to expound his merits. The whole town watched, and a large part of it cheered ; but the first stage of the depression was only two years away, and the custom of erecting statues posthumously is based on good sense. On this brilliant May day, with Ramsden Square crowded and arranged as though for a coronation procession, the world seemed to hold limitless possibilities to speechifiers. The atmosphere of the time was well conveyed in a speech of the Bishop of Carlisle : [2]

" Some of my friends are in the habit of saying . . . that I am thoroughly a nineteenth-century man ; and I am not ashamed of being so accused . . . this wonderful town strikes me as being one of the miracles of our time, and I look upon it with the same sort of ignorant wonder with which some people regard the pyramids —how on earth it has been built, is being extended, and what is to become of it if it continues to go on as it is doing at present . . . "

LABOUR

So much for the main personalities. A town is not three men, or even thirty, [3] and Barrow contained thirty thousand souls a few months after Ramsden's statue had been unveiled. We are justified in asking where they came from, and what was likely to happen to them.

The population of the borough of Barrow reached 18,911 at the time of the 1871 Census. This total was sixfold the figure of the 1861 Census, [4] and was composed of 6170 males of twenty years and over, and 3777 females in the same category, with 8964 young persons and infants. Of the women, 3006 were " wives ", and it is reasonably safe to estimate that number of families, with well over twice as many children or dependents. Owing to the presence of a large group of single male immigrants, Barrow was predominantly a

---

[1] It has since been reversed, as an act of unconscious symbolism. Barrow still builds ships, but ocean liners return only for repairs. [2] Full account of the ceremony in Leach, *op. cit.*, Appendix to Chapter One. Ramsden was knighted on June 25th following. [3] Perhaps the maximum number of men who held real power or influence in Barrow and district. [4] See p. 281 above.

male town, with twice as many men as women.   It was a young town in a young district.   Out of a total male population in the Dalton registration sub-district (total population, 30,099, including Barrow with Dalton, Aldingham and Urswick) of 17,014, no fewer than 14,136, or 83.1 per cent., were under the age of forty.   Similarly, out of 13,085 females, 10,779 or 82.3 per cent. were under the same age.[1]

Many of the male immigrants had entered the district from afar.   There was still much short-distance movement towards Barrow, and the nearby villages were still making their contributions to the growth of industrial Furness.   It will be as well to deal with the extent (estimated only), of this contribution first of all :

Table 32

Estimated loss of population in Furness villages, etc.,[2] 1861-70

Registration sub-district	1861-71 increase or decrease	1861-70 excess of births over deaths	Estimated loss by emigration
Cartmel	384	774	390
Colton	— 75	474	549
Ulverston	415	1099	684
W. Broughton	6	390	384
Hawkshead	— 242	448	690
		Total	2697

Immigration

Dalton	18,806	4277 (gain) 14,529 *immigrants.*

Ten North Lonsdale parishes or townships experienced an absolute intercensal loss of population, and in a further twelve the total intercensal gain was only 1146.   The drift away from the countryside, therefore, was still general, and was not confined to any particular sub-district or villages.   Rather fewer people, however, seem to have left the fell hamlets and villages than in the previous decade,[3] and the Furness ironfield had long passed the stage when it could rely on the neighbouring countryside and counties for its supplies of workers.   It is true that some 52 per cent. (9493 persons) of the population of the borough of Barrow were Lancashire born in 1871, and it can be accepted as certain that

---

[1]1871 *Census, Vol. III, Ages and Occupations of the People.*   [2]Based on Census figs., and 24*th* to 33*rd Annual Report of the Registrar-General*, pp. 36, 72, and also 33*rd Report*, pp. 346-7, for the totals used in the above table. [3]See p. 238 above.

a large number of these were Furness people ;[1] but whereas 7,400 (or slightly over 20 per cent.) of the 1861 population of Furness and Cartmel had come from other counties, 7,428 of the inhabitants of 1871 Barrow alone (40.7 per cent.) had come from Staffordshire, Westmorland, Ireland, Cumberland, Yorkshire, Worcestershire and Scotland.   The magnitude of the contingents was graded in that order ; Barrow had no fewer than 1524 Staffordshire people in 1871, as compared with 197 in the whole of Furness ten years previously.[2]   The censal year mentioned, however, saw only the beginning of a phenomenal increase of population in the new town and Dalton-in-Furness combined, and although local estimates tend to be conjectural and are not fully reliable, the registration figures for Dalton sub-district[3] tell their own story :

Table 33

The population growth of Barrow-in-Furness and Dalton (Dalton sub-district)
as indicated by registration of births and deaths

Year	Births	Deaths	Excess	Remarks
1861	452	233	219 ⎫	*Population of sub-district*, 1861 ; 11,243
1862	462	309	153 ⎬	Effect of increased iron output, railway
1863	562	285	277 ⎭	traffic, iron ore mining etc.
1864	683	406	277 ⎫	Period of dock-building, Barrow
1865	854	364	490 ⎬	,, ,, ,,
1866	1000	576	424 ⎭	,, ,, ,,
1867	1035	482	553 ⎫	Population of Barrow almost stationary ;
1868	1120	516	604 ⎬	probably some net emigration from the
1869	1025	451	574 ⎭	town
1870	1180	474	706 ⎰	New constructional projects
1871	1350	702	648 ⎱	*Population of sub-district*, 1871 ; 30,099
1872	1775	818	957 ⎰	Period of phenomenal growth. Barrow
1873	2115	1022	1093 ⎱	population estimated at 30,000 (1873)

During the period 1873-4 the Barrow-in-Furness population reached an estimated 30-35,000 souls, and the 1881 Census revealed that the population of the town was 47,259 in that year.   The population of Furness and Cartmel, including Barrow, had then risen to 90,940 persons.   If we add the Dalton figure (1881) to that for Barrow, the sum of the two is 60,598; in other words, Furness was two-thirds urbanised and industrialised.   The population of its villages remained static or, as before, tended to decline.

To keep our eyes on Barrow : in 1871-2 its main groups of workers and main occupations were distributed as follows :

---

[1]Although the observation no doubt errs from the scientific standpoint, it might be added that directory lists of Barrow tradespeople and residents in 1865 are full of the old family stock names of Furness, dealt with in Part I (see esp. pp. 17-18 above).   [2]See Table 25, p. 239 above.   [3]*24th* to *36th Repts. of the Reg.-Genl.*

Table 34

Borough of Barrow-in-Furness ; numbers of workpeople by firms and occupations, 1871-2

Firm	Remarks	Men employed,[1] (approx.) (1871-2)	1871 Census[2] Occupation	No. in
Haematite Steel Co.		1000[3]	Steel manufacture	256
			Iron ,,	556
N. Lancs. Brick & Tile Works	Mass production of bricks	800	General labourers	1962
F.R. Engineering Wks		600	Engineering and	
Gradwell's	Joinery, bricks	750	machine workers	307
Barrow Shipbuilding Co.	1872 only	600	Carpenters and joiners	289
Westray's Eng. Wks.	Millwrights, etc.	250	Bricklayers	124
Woodall's Boiler Wks.	Jobbing engineers	150	Engine drivers,	
Waddington's	Pipes, genl. ironwk	150	stokers	178
S. J. Claye	Wagons for F.R.	100	Railway labourers,	
Cooke & Swinnerton	Wireworks	100	platelayers,	
Ashburner's Shipyd.	Small family firm	70	navvies	155
Messrs Fisher	Small shipbldg.	50	Marble masons	145
Stuart's Ropeworks	Ropes for mines, &c.	40	Seamen	261
Briggs' Foundry	Ingots, jobbing	90		
Beveridge's Foundry	Brasswork, moulding	50		
Others :				
Jute Works	Construction (est.)	200		
Rolling Mills (1872)	,, ,,	200		
Steam Corn Mill	Opened July, 1871	50		
	Total	5250	*Total*	4233

Total population, adult males within the Borough, 20 and over (1871) : 6170

The " professional " class in the town totalled (1871) only 115 persons, including doctors, lawyers, dentists and 12 school-masters (the latter face to face with an under-twenty population of 8301 and a potential school population of perhaps half that figure), and the " commercial " class about 800 persons.[4] In other words, the new town was an overwhelmingly proletarian place, with a comparatively small middle-class between its large groups of workpeople and the main employers. As the months passed by, it became even more so ; workers skilled and unskilled poured into the town, drawn into Furness by trade union circulars and reports that Barrow was experiencing boom conditions.

Many of these immigrants were trade unionists. Several examples will amplify the point. The General Union of Operative Carpenters' and Joiners' local branch could boast of only 30 members during 1869. By the end of 1871 there were 88 men in the lodge, and in the following August (1872) no fewer than 227.[5] Apple-

---

[1]Figs. in Leach, *op. cit.*, 74-83.　　[2]*Vol. III*, p. 430.　　[3]Broad est. only.
[4]This class includes ships' stewards, commercial clerks, pilots, pawnbrokers, salesmen, auctioneers and hucksters.　　[5]*G.U. Monthly Repts.*

356

garth's union, the rival A.S.C. & J., hitherto had a precarious footing in Barrow, but increased its membership from 22 in March, 1872, to 42 in December.[1] The Operative Bricklayers (Coulson's union) had a local branch at the same time, and were numerous enough to challenge the Haematite Company in the January of 1873.[2] The A.S.E., which in June, 1871, had only 81 members (whose secretary reported with Allan-like caution that trade was " moderate "), had 136 men in the local lodge by December, 1872.[3] As the Barrow shipyard commenced production, the Boilermakers and Iron and Steel Shipbuilders' Union established a local branch, which in 1873 became 157 strong.[4] The Iron-moulders had a branch, and the Painters appear to have been organised.[5] In 1872, Francis Leach listed the following " Trade Societies " as existing in the town : engine-drivers and firemen, blacksmiths, engineers, boilermakers, moulders, carpenters and joiners, bricklayers, masons, cordwainers and tailors.[6] It would appear that the total trade union membership figure was then moving towards 700, about 500 being definitely traceable.

As in 1865-6, the union leaven was capable of activising much wider sections of the population. In the earliest years of town-construction, the building workers had successfully administered numerous pinpricks to their employers. It will be remembered that in 1865, a year of " prosperity " and climbing prices, strike activity reached a peak ;[7] and then, as constructional work ceased, workers had drifted away and the membership of union lodges had declined. In 1871, one of the local grievances of 1865 was still alive, namely the system of monthly or fortnightly pays, which the Haematite Company in particular were reluctant to abandon. As the member-ship of the Barrow lodges increased once more, the engineers' branch stepped into the lead as the activising agency, stimulated in this case by the example of the Nine Hour movement on the north-east coast. The A.S.E. members commenced operations in the autumn of 1871 by organising a petition demanding the adoption of weekly wage payments. This was signed by 3367 people in Barrow, or a very high proportion of the town's working population. In this campaign they were joined by the Iron Moulders' and other societies, and a representative of the former declared that they were " perfectly in co-operation with the other society men in the town, with the non-society men and with the public at large on this subject ".[8] A public meeting was held at the Assembly Rooms and a deputation of 14 trade unionists was elected to meet the employers of the town, most of the members of the

[1]*A.S.C. & J. Monthly Reports.*   [2]*B. Her.*, 20.1.72 ;   *Executive Council Minutes, Operative Bricklayers' Society*, Jan., 1873.   [3]*A.S.E. Monthly Reports.* [4]*Boilermakers' Annual Reports*, 1872, 1873.   [5]*B. Her.*, 4.11.71, 13.4.72. [6]Leach, *op. cit.*, 116.   [7]See pp. 315-6 above.   [8]*B. Her.*, 4.11.71.

deputation representing the Ironmoulders and A.S.E.[1] As subsequent events show, very much more than the subject of weekly pays was discussed at this meeting ; not only was the nine hour day a topic of urgency, but so, too, was the formation of a trades council in Barrow.[2] On November 1st, 1871, shortly after the successful conclusion of the Newcastle struggles,[3] the Barrow deputation met an array of local employers at the Municipal Offices. Ramsden, in his capacity of Mayor of the town, took the chair in the ensuing discussion ; and on the employers' side were J. T. Smith, Gradwell, S. Robertson (manager of the Shipbuilding Co.), and Forster, Waddington, Longbottom and Briggs of the smaller engineering works.

It will therefore be seen that the embattled forces in the whole town were joining issue in preliminary argument. The trade union spokesmen put their case—in reasonable enough terms—without overmuch of the deference which was so often associated with " waiting upon " employers at this period, and succeeded in obtaining from Ramsden a recommendation in favour of weekly pays, with a reservation that rendered the statement virtually useless ; the Steelworks, the largest employer of labour, was to make its own arrangements. J. T. Smith yielded only so far as to promise to pay wages in weeks when other firms were not making wage payments, so that market and shops would not be swamped with buyers on a given day (a state of affairs that caused reiterated complaints from workers and their wives). Ramsden, meanwhile, assumed the role of arbitrator, with an impartiality perhaps more apparent than real.[4] When the matter of the nine hour day was introduced, he himself repeatedly returned to an arrangement whereby Leeds employers had granted a 54 hour week, but had offered payment at time and one-eighth for overtime instead of time and a half. Smith was left free to offer the most obdurate opposition to any reduction of hours, and the negotiations closed without result in this sphere ; but not before Lax, of the A.S.E. had informed the employers that a trades council was to be established, and asked Ramsden whether he would prefer to negotiate with that body.[5]

Ramsden, as arbitrator, had promised to withhold his decision *pro tem* ; but the Ironmoulders, perhaps anticipating what he would announce, did not wait for it, and struck, early in the New Year,

---

[1]*Ibid.* The engineers in the deputation were Geo. Lax (A.S.E.), Richard Towers (A.S.E.), James Ryder (do.), R. Pickthall, John Hope, James Myers,— Arbuckle, Thomas Kay (A.S.E.) ;others were Richards (Ironmoulders' Society), John Kurrin, Thos. Gill (ironworkers), E. Barnes, T. Taft (steelworkers), John Morris and George Carruthers of the *Barrow Herald.* This list (A.S.E.) members identified in auditors' lists) almost certainly includes some founders of the Barrow Trades Council. [2]*Ibid.* [3]Cf. Burnett, J., *A History of the Engineers' Strike . . . in* 1872. [4]See his remark to Devonshire, p. 359 below. [5]*Ibid.*

for the nine hours in three of the engineering works in the town.[1] In each case the employers had echoed Ramsden's offer of the Leeds concession, and on January 20th the Mayor himself was reported as having made his decision in favour of the time and one-eighth payment.[2] But his notion, whether designed as a delaying tactic or not, produced no fruitful result ; " labour troubles " were once more upon the scene on a grand scale. A. J. Woodhouse's brickmakers gave a strike notice demanding the nine hours ; the Operative Bricklayers tabled a demand for the Saturday half day and 3d. a day wage increase in view of " the present enormous prices of provisions and other commodities " ; and, meanwhile, there had been persistent trouble in the docks with labourers who, according to Devonshire, "earn(ed) high wages and ask for more ".[3] In the February the Hawcoat quarrymen were asking for shorter hours, and in the March the ironworkers were demanding an eight hour day (stating that they were, in some cases, having to work 24 hours at the weekend). In the same month, too, the dock workers struck for a 54 hour week, obtaining some concessions from the Furness Railway Company and an agreement to pay them at piece rates instead of time rates, as hitherto. In April, Ramsden reported to the Duke that he—the arbitrator—was " troubled by demands for higher wages in all departments ", and during the following months the painters, joiners, blacksmiths' strikers and even journeyman tailors demanded wage increases, shorter hours or both. In July, there was a strike of 400 miners at Roanhead and Greenscoe, for a minimum wage of 6s. a day ; and in the September the bricklayers and labourers engaged on an A. J. Woodhouse contract at the Steelworks made clear that they wanted the Saturday half-day.[4] J. T. Smith was resolutely opposed to this last concession, for rail production and steelworks expansion were gaining huge momentum, and in January, 1873, no less a person than the temperate but determined Edwin Coulson, of the O.B.S., visited Barrow to seek an interview with Smith, which was granted.[5]

It will be seen that the demand for nine hours, or less, spread through a variety of skilled and unskilled trades. On the other hand, the local employers would more readily grant a wage increase than allow a reduction in working hours. Rapidly climbing prices, of nearly all commodities, characterised the boom year of 1872, and this tendency explains the numerous demands for increased wages ; it would seem, however, that the worker valued leisure quite as

[1]B. Her., 6.1.72.   [2]B. Her., 20.1.72.   [3]B. Her., 3.2, 10.2.72 ; MS. Diary, 8.8.71.   [4]B. Her., 3.2, 17.2, 9.3, 23.3, 30.3, 13.4, 27.4, 4.5, 20.7, 7.9.72 ; Barrow Pilot, 27.4, 20.7.72 ; MS. Diary, 15.4.72 ; Report of Council, Mins. O.B.S., Jan., 1873 ; A.S.C. & J. Rept., Feb., 1872.   [5]Rept. of Council, O.B.S., cit., The encounter between two notoriously determined personalities produced little immediate result, and Coulson recommended the formation of a joint committee to carry on propaganda for the Saturday holiday.

much as money, and some appalling hours were worked in the iron and steel industries of the locality. The lack of a Saturday half-day was an old grievance.

Sociologists and social historians are naturally interested in the causes of strike activity or working-class unrest of any kind. It is sometimes argued, in defence of the employer, that his motives are not purely " materialistic " (i.e., concerned purely with profit or gain), and the same, of course, applies to the workman. The latter's environment inevitably influences his outlook. A workman entering Barrow, tramping on foot or bringing his family by train, found that living conditions in the town could be highly unpleasant ; houses and streets could be insanitary, overcrowding was rife, working hours were long, and there were, on the whole, comparatively few spare-time amusements (outside the public house) to the taste of the intelligent workman. The major personalities of the district, however, whose personal influence and prestige were great, were obviously extremely prosperous. Ramsden and Schneider were well known in Barrow (still a very small town in physical extent), and made frequent demonstrations of their interest in the town. But the lesser employers, represented on the Council and uncritical of the directing influences, sided with the major employers of labour. and the identification of a comparatively small, powerful and visible group with the interests of " capital " inevitably impressed itself on the minds of the more observant workers. Owing to the likelihood that trade unionists, through their society circulars, would be better-informed of developments (and opportunities for employment) in Barrow than other workmen, a great many of the former tended to congregate in the town, with the result suggested above—a distinct exacerbation of the wages struggle. Lest the account so far given may seem to exaggerate the element of class conflict, it should be added that when its comparatively small size is taken into full account, Barrow was one of the most strikebound towns in Britain during the eighteen hundred and seventies, and some interesting statistics prove the point. [1]

The town, then, was a discontented and turbulent one, and the discontent had numerous causes and a variety of effects. More or less acute outbreaks of drunkenness—not, as is sometimes thought, a manifestation of original sin among British workmen—were among these effects. In 1873 it was estimated that a Barrow population of 32,000 had no fewer than 30 public houses and 50 beershops at its

---

[1] *Vide* Bevan, G. P., *The Strikes of the Past Ten Years*, in *Journal of the Royal Statistical Society*, XLIII (1880), esp. list of towns and nos. of strikes therein, p. 45. Barrow was perhaps the fiftieth town in Britain in respect of population, and was yet *eighteenth* (with 29 strikes) in a list of fifty-five towns which experienced 10 to 85 strikes in the 1870's. Barrow, with an average population one-fifth that of Nottingham, came next to the latter.

disposal—that is, one place of refreshment to about 160 adults. The Congregationalist minister W. H. Fothergill alleged that £208,000 a year was spent on drink by local inhabitants—yet, he told a meeting in the town, licenses for 53 further public houses were now demanded![1] The police statistics[2] relating to drunkenness will show that in this short but decisive period, the number of such court cases increased faster than the population :

	1872	1873
Estimated population of Barrow :	24,000	32,000
Licensed victuallers convicted	1	4
Beersellers ,,	2	1
Persons convicted for selling without licence	1	35
,, apprehended for drunkenness	262	460
,, ,, for all offences	359	728
Cases before magistrate, all summonses	919	1530

Yet, although Hindpool steelworkers might be seen almost daily staggering along the streets, and although the so-called "Hindpool lambs" were given an unenviable reputation, the workman was not simply the demoralised, ignorant instrument of his employers. We have seen that he concentrated upon trade union organisation if a skilled artisan ; and the men who could take the initiative in circulating a petition demanding weekly pays, or who could bring their fellows together in a trades council, were also capable of organising other forms of protest. The Shipbuilding Company had caused a large number of its employees to be housed in insanitary rows of wooden huts on Old Barrow Island, and the conditions in this unhappy precursor of the modern prefabricated estate were such that the radical newspapers *Barrow Herald* and *Barrow Pilot* continually referred to them as a scandal.[3] But although George Carruthers, the editor of the first and the owner of the second, gave a lead to the inhabitants, the hut-dwellers themselves organised a protest meeting, at which it was alleged that the Shipbuilding Company received a clear rent (in excess of all expenses) of £2,278 *per annum* from the hut-dwellings, and yet proposed to raise the rents from 3s. to 3s. 6d. The great company flats on Old Barrow Island were, it is true, then being built, but the chairman of the meeting remarked that " It had been urged that the Shipbuilding Company were building houses, but he was of the opinion that three years would transpire before there would be sufficient ". Those present passed a resolution threatening to draw the attention of the Local Government Board to Old Barrow, " with a request

---

[1]*B. Her.*, 6.9.73.   [2]*B. Her.*, 13.9.73.   [3]E.g., *B. Her.*, 11.1.73 ; " hundreds of double-roomed wooden boxes have been placed on Barrow Island, where there is no drainage and but a solitary out-office for each row of habitations . . ."

that a special commissioner be sent down to inquire into the sanitary conditions of Old Barrow Island ".[1]

These, however, were the more vigorous outbreaks of rebellion. George Carruthers, who championed vigorously the cause of the local workpeople in 1871-3, despaired of " the air of stolid indifference on the part of the inhabitants of Barrow ",[2] yet a few weeks later, writing of a stormy meeting on the subject of the 1873 Barrow Corporation Bill (which the radical element opposed as a piece of window-dressing), said " It was a noticeable fact that few ratepayers . . . were present, and that the audience consisted chiefly of workmen, the majority of them not being entitled to a vote, and who, as is well known, tacitly subscribe to every movement initiated or supported by their leaders as a matter of self-interest rather than of judgment ". It would seem that in this case the trade unions, indifferent to the lesser ratepayers, had organised support for the Corporation Bill as productive of more employment ; and in a later case[3] a nomination meeting for council candidates, filled with workmen, was ribald and uproarious in the extreme as one stammering candidate after another was shouted down or cat-called. It cannot be assumed that the literate or self-educated artisan took no interest, and there are signs that his education, here and elsewhere, was being augmented.[4]

Until the early months of 1873 the *Barrow Herald* provided plenty of subject-matter for the radical-minded. Its editor, always sympathetic to the more moderate aspirations of trade unionism,[5] gave full prominence to all industrial disputes, was a member of the Nine Hours delegation of 1871,[6] and a ceaseless critic of the " meddling and muddling " of the Council and Corporation. His journalist colleague Joseph Richardson, formerly editor of the *Barrow Times*,[7] although conventional in his attitude to many matters, also became increasingly critical of the ruling group in the town. In early 1873 both Richardson and Carruthers were infuriated by the news that Ramsden, Schneider and Fell were to

---

[1]*Barrow Pilot*, 31.1.74.   [2]*B. Her.*, 8.2.73 ; and also *vide B. Her.*, 22.2.73.   [3]*B. Her.*, 25.10.73.   [4]The Chairman of the Old Barrow protest meeting, Joseph Lambert, told his listeners that " He was glad to know there was a movement on foot to do away with the qualifications for Councillor, for if working men were qualified to legislate in the House of Commons and sit on School Boards, surely they were able to sit in the Council . . . "
[5]See, e.g., p. 315 above.   [6]See p. 358 above.   [7]In 1870 Richardson had been induced to give up the editorship and proprietorship of the *Barrow Times*, and to sign an agreement " barring him from commencing another newspaper within seven years ". That newspaper continued to circulate with the financial aid of the F.R. group, and with Francis Leach as editor. It became, by mid-1872, " the only daily paper published in North Lancashire, Cumberland and Westmorland, and between Newcastle and Manchester ", with a weekly edition which claimed to be " the largest penny paper in the country ". It is not unfair to say that it was stodgy, colourless and sycophantic.

form a company to undertake publishing and printing on a large scale.[1] Carruthers attacked this venture in the strongest terms, and his remarks are worthy of quotation in that they exemplify a freedom of comment rarely met with in the locality before that time, and not often encountered in local newspapers even in the present century :

" It is usual for shareholders to elect their own directors ; but in this case the directors are self-elected. As only five directors are required, the self-election of four forms a decided majority. This is as it should be, because business will no doubt be directed into its proper channels. We have only one suggestion to make, and it is that the gentlemen who have already become shareholders of the ' Barrow Printing and Publishing Company ' should extend the sphere of their operations. It is not enough that they should be connected with a dozen undertakings in the town, all dependent on each other for support ; but they should start a company for the government of Barrow, taking care to constitute themselves the directors and fix their own salaries, and so spare the proviso that a general meeting shall be called to determine their remuneration . . . What guarantee there will be for the disinterested conduct of a newspaper where the gentlemen concerned on the directorate have such large vested interests, we leave the public of Barrow to judge . . ."[2]

This angry outburst was not unconnected with the then exclusion of the *Barrow Herald* reporter from official functions,[3] and the total exclusion of the press from Steel Company, Shipbuilding Company and Jute Company meetings.[4] Even afterwards, when the *Barrow Herald* had been sold to a joint-stock company and its policy had become milder, the onslaught was continued by Joseph Richardson in the pages of his newly-founded *Barrow Vulcan*,[5] and this fact may explain why H. W. Schneider opposed (in 1874) the admission of the press to meetings of council committees.[6]

The press not only reacted sympathetically to the discontent and turbulence of Barrow; it sometimes canalised and directed unrest into socially beneficial channels,[7] and it should not be supposed, on any account, that it was merely irresponsible. It is a measure of the value of British liberties that they have been fought for, and the local editors were only doing what many scores

---

[1]See p. 351 above.   [2]*B. Her.*, 1.2.73.   [3]*Ibid.*   [4]*B. Her.*, 22.3.73.
[5]First published 13.1.74 as a satirical weekly.   (*B.M.* file, Colindale and Barrow P.L.) Cf. his biography (*Joseph Richardson, cit.*) ; " In Barrow, nothing is allowed to succeed except under the auspices of certain magnates." (p. 14).   [6]*B. Her.*, 7.3.74.   [7]E.g., the Barrow huts protest, for which the *Vulcan* was thanked by those taking part.

of obscure journalists felt obliged to do. The intelligent workman or tradesman, meanwhile, was bound to be affected, if imperceptibly, by the disturbing atmosphere of the neighbourhood. There are signs that the latter eased in some measure during the summer and autumn of 1873, and only the A.S.E. and Boilermakers' Barrow branches reported any troubles in those months.[1] Trade union membership grew steadily, all industries remained fully occupied, and money wages appear to have reached their highest point for the time being. The steelworks refused to consider any shortening of hours in 1873 and 1874,[2] and there was no sharpening of industrial strife until the autumn of the latter year, when the unions were placed on the defensive.

The first reported mass trade union demonstration in the district, having a political rather than an economic objective, took place in Dalton on July 26th, 1873, when Alexander MacDonald, of the Miners' National Association, and Dixon of the West Yorkshire Miners' Association, addressed a large meeting called to protest against the Criminal Law Amendment Act and to demand the widening of the franchise. An ore miners' union in Dalton was then enrolling members, but the attempt ended, in consequence of the slump of 1874, in failure.[3]

The more stable working-class institutions, like the co-operative societies, continued to make progress, and that of Dalton-in-Furness still led the way ; in 1869-73 its total sales were nearly double the figure for the ten years 1861-70, while the " profits " amounted to £3 6s. 8d. per member.[4] Barrow had two such societies by 1870, the steelworkers of Hindpool having formed a separate one in the April of that year. Their progress, as before, was somewhat slower than that of the Dalton body, and only about one in 36 of the Barrow population traded at the " stores " in 1871.[5] As has been indicated, the proliferation of small shopkeepers in Barrow must have had a great deal to do with the unremarkable co-operative record there, and in 1871, for example, a local directory[6] indicates that there were no fewer than 116 small general stores or groceries out of a total of 310 shops in Barrow itself, each with an average clientèle of 163 persons, or perhaps fewer than 50 regular adult shoppers or representatives of families.[7]

Co-operation in Barrow, however, is distinguished by a pioneering enterprise in a somewhat unusual field. The housing shortage, together with the greed of property owners and land speculators,[8]

[1]*A.S.E.* and *Boilermakers'* reports ; *B. Pilot*, 8.11.73. [2]*O.B.S. Trade Circular*, Aug., 1874. [3]*B. Her.*, 2.8.73 and *passim*. [4]*B. Her.*, 21.2.74. [5]*B. Her.*, 1.5, 25.11.71 ; *B. Times*, 7.1, 4.2.71. [6]*Commercial Directory of Barrow* (1871), Barrow P.L. [7]Figs. from *Census* and directory, *cit.* 56 tea dealers and grocers are listed in the Census—others were obviously part-timers. [8]See p. 374 below.

forced housing rents to a high level, and the Barrow co-operators made an attempt to help themselves in face of the problem.   The Industrial and Provident Societies Act of 1871 [1] made it possible for a society registered under this Act to buy and sell land wholesale and retail as a body corporate, with none of the disadvantages of existing building societies, which had to sell through trustees and buy or sell land on the personal responsibility of directors.   No initial fee or charge of registration was now required, and artisans might club together to buy building land for themselves without recourse to a builder-controlled local society.   Rochdale, in the spirit of its Pioneers, was the first town in England to take advantage of this Act by forming a co-operative building society, and Barrow claimed to be the second.   An initial meeting was held in January, 1872, and the " Barrow Co-operative Building, Investment and Land Society Ltd." was formed in the March of that year.   Any legal or official connection with the co-operative stores was disclaimed, but the formation meeting was held in the Co-operative Rooms, and a moving spirit was John W. Webster, one of the founders of the movement in Barrow. [2]   C. F. Preston, the Town Clerk, was induced to give his advice regarding the rules of the new society, which began its career with 50 members, who had to have ten £1 shares to qualify for a dwelling, for which they then had to ballot.   In such circumstances it was obvious that the capital for more than a very few dwellings could not be raised at once.   Nevertheless, 13 houses, built co-operatively, were commenced in Hindpool in 1873, and others appear to have been built from time to time. [3]

The friendly societies continued to flourish.   By 1872, well over two thousand people in Barrow, or between 12 and 15 per cent of the adult population of the town, were members of these bodies, and about 1300 of these belonged to the non-temperance societies. Of the lodges in general, the Oddfellows (Barrow Lodge, 1855) had some 400 members each with an average deposit of £5 10s. ;   the Barrow Rangers had 239 members ;   the Free Gardeners had 140 with an average of £2 10s. each in deposits ;   the Ancient Order of Foresters had a comparatively large membership ;   and the Independent and United Orders of Mechanics together had about 140 members.   On the side of Temperance, the Rechabites were by far the strongest, with 490 members in 1872 ;   the Good Templars (300 in two lodges) followed;   and the Sons of Temperance claimed only 60 members in 1872.   The latter body, however, boasted of 379 members in mid-1873, and it is evident that the local movement

[1] 34 & 35 *Vict.*, *c*.80 ;   the 1871 enactment was an amending Act ;   *vide Halsbury*.   [2] See p. 310 above.   [3] *B. Her.*, 3.2, 24.2, 23.3, 8.6.72, 8.1, 9.8.73. The Hindpool Co-operative Society (Leach, *op. cit.* 116) had its own building society, and was probably responsible for the houses mentioned.   The Barrow society (*B. Her.*, 8.1.73) caused houses to be erected in Sutherland Street. *Vide* also *B.T.C. Mins .(Health Committee)*, 30.7.73.

as a whole was growing rapidly in the early 'seventies after a noticeable pause (involving, in some societies, loss of membership) in the late 'sixties. Deposits per member had not grown visibly larger by 1872. [1].

The success of friendly societies is often considered—reasonably, on the whole—to indicate an improvement of living standards among certain sections of the working-class. In the early 'seventies wages and prices were engaged in a neck-and-neck race upwards ; and, no doubt, some sections of the workers in the heavy industries benefited as compared with others. H. W. Schneider thought that local wages were high in 1874, and used this view in the course of an argument against the establishment of a public library in Barrow — workmen could afford to buy books for themselves, he urged. [2]

It may be significant that at the height of the boom conditions of 1872-3, 150 Barrow people decided to emigrate to Minnesota. An initial meeting " consisting entirely of the working-classes " was held in the January, and it was decided to establish a Furness colony there ; in the March, despite vigorous warnings in the press, the would-be emigrants were adamant ; and in the June, it was reported that they had arrived in their new home. The whole poignant story, up to this point, is in the yellowing newspaper sheets ; but it remains unfinished. [3]

[1]For comparative data, *Ulverston Mirror*, 17.6.65 ; *B. Her.*, 3.6.71, 17.5.73, 7.6.73 ; Leach, *op. cit.*, 111-15. The movement was of course flourishing in Dalton also. The Free Gardeners and Oddfellows seem to have lost members between 1865 and 1871. [2]*B. Her.*, 7.3.74. [3]*B. Her.*, 25.1, 1.3, 22.3, 14.6.73.

THE OVERCROWDED YEARS (II); LOCAL GOVERNMENT IN BARROW AND DISTRICT, 1870-4

THE SEPARATION OF BARROW

The year of rapid trade recovery, 1870, saw Barrow with a house still much out of order in the important matters of poor law relief, sanitation and sewerage, and disposal of the dead.

The extreme inconvenience of the town's position regarding registration, relief and medical treatment of the poor has already been mentioned. [1] The sick poor were the worst sufferers, and they tended to increase in numbers after 1867, as unemployment itself —almost unknown in the new town—appeared more obviously. In 1869, H. W. Schneider estimated that the number of Barrow paupers averaged 1,100 (this out of a population of about 16,000), and those of Dalton, 340. Of the Barrow paupers, 71 were sick, and in the following year it was alleged that pauper deaths in Barrow were four times as numerous as in Dalton, and that gross neglect was the cause. The medical officer to the Guardians, Dr. Hall, was said to visit pauper patients in Barrow only half as often as those in Dalton. [2] As in previous years, the unfortunate Hall was still covering a great area on horseback. Money relief to the families of sick persons was dispensed by the sub-registrar and relieving officer, Simpson, whose lack of liaison with Hall caused further suffering.

The meetings of the Guardians at this time were tinctured with (in Devonshire's word) " asperity ". Ramsden, Hannay and Schneider, led in this case by John Fell, commenced a campaign for the separation of Barrow's Poor Law administration from that of the rest of the Union. They did much canvassing beforehand, [3] but expected, and received, much opposition from the non-Barrow and Ulverston members, who quite understandably thought that some rate-evasion scheme was afoot. During the campaign, it was revealed that destitute persons, wandering into Barrow in search of work had been found in outhouses and even unused iron furnaces, where they huddled for warmth. In October, 1870, the Superintendent of the Lancashire Constabulary complained in a letter to Devonshire that his police officers in Barrow were unable to offer any relief or accommodation to these destitute wanderers, and were in fact obliged to turn the latter on to the streets. In face of

---

[1] See pp. 290-1 above.   [2] *Proc. Division of . . .* 1871 (pamph. in Barrow P.L.), 11-23 ; *B. Her.*, 14.1.71 ; also *B.T.C. Mins.*, 2.3.68, where the Guardians saw nothing greatly amiss with the registration arrangements.   [3] *Mins. Ulv. Gdns.*, 29.9.70, and *letter transcripts, f.*246, *Misc. Book, PUU*/11, Lancs. R.O.

such revelations, an enquiry could not be long forthcoming. At the Guardians' meetings, Fell, Ramsden, Schneider, Wadham and Montague Ainslie were successful in their motion asking for such an enquiry by the Poor Law Board, although a majority was still opposed to the separation of Barrow.[1] R. B. Cane, an inspector of the latter Board, took evidence from witnesses at Furness Abbey on January 10th, 1871, and the effect of a two-day hearing was to make the Barrow case unassailable.

On May 1st, 1871, the Ulverston Board of Guardians received notice of a provisional separation order of the Poor Law Board making Barrow, with Walney and other islands, a separate Poor Law district for relief purposes, repair of highways, the making and collection of parliamentary, county and parochial rates and taxes, the preparation of voters' and jury lists, the quartering of police and the appointment of magistrates.[2] The borough of Barrow was, however, to remain in the Ulverston union area and to have four Guardians on its Board, while Dalton had two. Thus ended nearly a decade of anomaly. Barrow could now bury its own dead (although the Corporation, by its 1868 Act, was empowered already to act as a Burial Board), elect its own overseers and churchwardens, and be better served by medical and relieving officers. As events were to show, these arrangements came not a day too soon.

By mid-1871 the cemetery battle, which had been carried on fitfully since 1862,[3] had been won by the Barrow faction. Schneider raised the question of a separate Barrow cemetery in April, 1868, shortly before the Corporation Act of that year took effect. But there was a difficulty ; the Dalton cemetery rate would not lapse immediately, while that of Barrow would not be less than 4½d., and an extra rate of 5¾d. (the Dalton rate was 1¼d.) was bad politics in a year of depression. It was estimated that the cost of a cemetery would be £10,000 at the lowest, casting an annual charge of £933 on the ratepayers of Barrow.[4] In consequence, Barrow dead, pushed along the miry road to Dalton, were crammed somehow into Dalton ground for another two years (i.e. until 1870). In early 1870 Dalton ratepayers were obliged to hold a meeting to consider, not surprisingly, the enlargement of their own cemetery, and the Barrow Council thereupon opened a vigorous correspondence with the Daltonians, stating that the Council had arranged for an enquiry to be held before an official—presumably a representative of the Burial Acts Office.[5]

[1]*Mins. Ulv. Gdns.*, 13.10, 20.10, 8.12.70 ; *B. Her.*, 10.9, 22.10.70 ; *B. Times*, 15.10.70 ; *Misc. MSS. of John Fell*, Z308/1, Barrow P.L. ; evidence of Rev. J. Bilsborrow in *Proc. . . . Div.*, 1871, for details of the plight of immigrants. [2]Tyson, *Abstract . . . Dalton* etc., 22, for P.L. Board Orders. [3]See p. 291 above. [4]*B.T.C. Mins.*, 27.4, 30.5.68 ; cf. also 1868 *Act*, Barrow Corpn., Clause XI. [5]*B.T.C. Mins.*, 4.4.70 ; Leach, *op. cit.*, 33.

The enquiry was duly held. On April 9th it was agreed that the Borough should provide its own burial ground, meanwhile joining with the rest of Dalton parish to pay off a debt of £3622 on the old Dalton cemetery.[1] It then remained to find a suitable site in or near Barrow. This was not as easy as might have been thought, and when the Council made enquiries about land at Roose, the cheapest portion was offered at £200 an acre, and nearby territory was priced at £500 an acre — in other words, local landowners were behaving in the approved fashion by charging what they thought a flourishing land market would bear. In the end, Devonshire offered land at Hawcoat " at a merely nominal price ",[2] and the work of planning, preparation and layout commenced before the end of 1870. This time, there were no half-hearted or halting measures, and Victorian respect for the dead produced, with the aid of the landscape gardener Kemp, a cemetery of which any town of less than 20,000 inhabitants could have felt proud.

These were basic necessities, travelling only a little distance towards a guarantee of tolerable living conditions for the majority who might hope to work at the new Barrow installations for a number of years without recourse to the services offered by the Cemetery Committee. The latter soon came to regard their Hawcoat burial ground as a most important source of corporation income, while money was constantly expended on its improvement ; more, indeed, than was spent on sanitation and highways up to 1874.[3]

The story of early experiments in sewerage is less clearcut and straightforward. The Barrow docks, strikingly enough, were originally regarded as a suitable place for a sewerage outfall, and the town's extension inland, to a distance of about half a mile, raised problems of gradient. The older portion of the town stood on a low eminence (over which passed Harrison and Greengate streets), and beyond this slight hill further development was already taking place in the early 'seventies—towards Salthouse Marsh to the north-east, and on both sides of Rawlinson Street. A sewer along Rawlinson Street could collect from a large area as the town extended, and the sewage would then flow towards the Marsh and thence into the sea or the docks as the latter were extended. The construction of such a sewer was commenced in 1869, together with an outfall at the Buccleuch dock entrance, but for reasons which are not clear (but which are suggested by later developments) the scheme proved unworkable.[4] Successive engineers, including McClean and Stileman, pinned their faith to a system by which

<hr>

[1]Leach, *op. cit.*, 34.   [2]*Op. cit.*, 35.   [3]The Cemetery Account was over £21,000 in 1874, while Scavenging and Highways (with current Sanitary Dept. expenditure) barely exceeded one-third of this sum in the same year ; *Treas. Accts*, 1873-4.   [4]*Wadham Diary*, 15.10, 2.12.69, 7.3.70.

the sewers were flushed by storm water in the higher localities and tide water in the lower. When a high tide coincided with heavy rains, effluvium and noxious matters poured out of street gratings and infectious gases were forced back into houses. The Corporation was in fact slow to achieve a satisfactory system ; McClean and Stileman, on whom the leading council officials and members leaned heavily, failed to provide a solution, and in 1875, there was strong criticism of this firm—the F.R.'s chief engineers—by Messrs. Brierley and Holt of Blackburn, who reported that " Barrow is by no means a difficult town to sewer on the best principles—the compact arrangements of the buildings and the uniformity of the streets afford special opportunities for a really good and comparatively inexpensive scheme ".[1]

It was maintained that McClean and Stileman had made a mistake in joining the sewage and rainwater outflow at the docks ; and the then (1875) Borough Surveyor, Arthur Jacob, was campaigning for an ambitious scheme of double sewers for the town against much opposition. The existing system was a mere patchwork, and made no allowance for new population areas.[2] In 1872, moreover, a year of peak expansion of population, little over £1000 was spent on construction of main sewers, yet the total expenditure of the Corporation had risen to £21,544, and it was possible in that year to transfer £5000 worth of profits from the Gas and Water Estate to the balance.[3] It was left to the *Barrow Herald* to state the obvious :[4]

" . . . If as much attention had been paid to sanitary matters as seems to have been paid to the construction of our vast establishments there would be less cause for complaint. But it is obvious that the capitalist has been able to look to himself, and that the workman has not. The Town Council, it is true, is doing something by way of justifying its appointment, but in the absence of any useful system of sewering, what the Council has done is mere meddling and muddling . . . "

Later, however, the double sewer system (by which storm water and sewerage filth were kept separate) established itself, as Dr. Pollard has put it, " as a successful precedent among sanitary engineers ".[5] Needless damage had been done by then.

---

[1]Copy of Rept. in *MS. Memo. Book of J. E. Swindlehurst*, 23.3.75, by courtesy of Barrow Corporation.   [2]*Ibid.*, and article by Jacob in *Proc. Ass. Municipal and Sanitary Engineers*, 1874, p. 144 ; *Barrow Vulcan*, 4.7.74. [3]*Treas. Accts.*, 31.8.71 to 31.8.72.   [4]*B. Her.*, 11.1.73.   [5]*L. & C.*, LXIII, 106.

The improvements in poor relief and disposal of the dead represented positive achievements ; the Corporation also, as will be seen, made considerable improvements in the local water supply during the early 'seventies. Against this record we must weigh poor sewerage, inefficient surface drainage of roadways, and inefficient scavenging. The *Barrow Herald* went on to add that " . . . Many of the public streets are a disgrace in a town like this ", while a correspondent in the same newspaper wrote about ashpits which were " brimful and reeking with filth and dirt ".[1] It is necessary, of course, to give full weight to the problems of a Victorian council, ill-equipped as well as parsimonious, trying to deal with the administrative requirements and social needs of a town which, every time it met, had grown by several hundreds of people or several scores of houses. Likewise, we shall not ignore that council's aspirations as expressed in local Acts of 1872 and 1873.

The preoccupation of the main industrialists, and of the council which reflected their outlook, was to get houses built. James Ramsden went so far as to say that :

" Up to the present time I have been, in fact, obliged to discourage persons who desired to settle, from the want of accommodation for their people. This (i.e., in 1873) is the only drawback to the doubling of the population tomorrow. I have no hesitation in saying that, if tomorrow houses could be found for 60,000 people, people could be found to fill the houses."[2]

There were 2950 dwellings in the borough in 1868, 4711 by 1873 and just short of 6000 by 1875. But the work of building, in face of an unparalleled emergency, was somewhat slow in getting under way. Only 50 houses were completed in 1868-9, 66 in 1869-70, 245 in 1870-1, 594 in 1870-2, and 806 in 1872-3. In 1873-4 the rate reached a record peak of 889 dwellings, a figure never afterwards reached in the history of the town, and probably unsurpassed by any town of similar size.[3] By that time, however, the population had risen to an estimated 35,000, giving approximately 6.5 persons per dwelling. As Dr. Pollard has shown,[4] the main F.R.-dominated firms owned increasing numbers of houses during these years, but whatever behind-the-scenes policies were adopted to speed the building programme, the latter was quite unable to keep pace with

---

[1]*Ibid.* [2]Ramsden's ev., B. in F. *Corporation Bill*, 1873 (1*st May*, 1873), Q. 49. [3]*Treas. Repts.* [4]*Op. cit.*, 110, Table 2 (the fruits of some revealing work on the Corporation Rate Books).

the unprecedented immigration rate, for which the expansion of the Barrow shipyard was mainly responsible in 1873-4. [1]

Necessarily, a continually mounting flood of building plans came before the council's Health Committee ; over 250 plans a month were passed by that body between June and August, 1872, mainly for houses in the " Marsh " and in Hindpool. [2] By the August, it was found that builders were infringing the by-laws of the Corporation as laid down in 1868, but few plans were in fact rejected. In the following year, A. J. Woodhouse, a major builder and brickmaker in the town and on this occasion a council candidate, claimed that " half the builders are on the Health Committee ", [3] and Dr. C. M. Deane, a reforming and successful candidate in that year, counted seven builders (or men directly connected with the building trade) on the Council itself. [4] Any supervision was exercised in dilatory fashion ; an occasional prosecution made local news, and Joseph Rawcliffe, another large builder who seems—like Woodhouse—to have been somewhat resentful in that he did not belong to the inner circle dominating Barrow affairs, complained that " the present monopoly " was holding up the growth of the town ; but he was nevertheless fined 40s. for blocking up a roadway with building materials, and thereby infringing the 1868 Barrow Corporation Act. [5] The prosecution was doubtless unfair—the town looked as though it had been bombarded [6]—and far keener supervision, fully provided for by local enactment, might well have been applied to the character of the houses themselves. The ever-watchful *Herald* went so far as to claim that " houses need propping up and repairing before they can be finished ", and that the town was " unequalled for its badly-built dwellings ". [7] This last charge, while undoubtedly made in good faith, was almost certainly unjustified; but it had the warmth of the controversies of the time. The integrity and skill of Barrow's building workers wavered so little before the demands placed upon them that most of the houses of this period are standing and occupied in the mid-twentieth century.

The erection of hundreds of new houses meant the provision of new carriage-ways and paving, and the Council awakened to this fact on March 4th, 1872, when it gave an order that no fewer than 103 streets, sections of streets, or back alleys were to be " freed from obstruction, drained, levelled, sewered, flagged, paved, macadamised or otherwise completed ". [8] The *Herald* of March 9th stated that numerous throughfares were in a " most deplorable state ",

[1] *Vide J.I.S.I.*, 1, 1874, xxi. By 1874 the works covered 55 acres, had a dozen launching slipways, large fitting, turning and erecting shops, and had built 25 vessels. [2] *B.T.C. Mins.*, 3.6, 1.7, 5.8.72. [3] *B. Her.*, 25.10.73 (rept. of local election meeting). [4] *Loc. cit.* [5] *B. Her.*, 29.3.73. [6] *B. Her.*, 23.9.71. [7] *B. Her.*, 1.2.73. [8] *B.T.C. Mins.*, 4.3.73.

with stagnant water in large pools, the footpaths improperly flagged (" in many cases not at all "), and that the roadways were " altogether in such a state that the passengers were compelled to wade ankle deep to cross from one side to the other ".[1]

At the height of the accommodation crisis, in 1872, the Council set about increasing its powers of control over the use of dwelling space and over sanitary matters connected thereto. The direct stimulus here is somewhat difficult to identify with certainty, but it was probably a severe shock administered by the smallpox epidemic of 1870-1, which raged throughout the north of England in the last quarter of 1870 and the first quarter of 1871.[2] This disease appeared intermittently in Barrow during the latter year,[3] to reappear with redoubled venom in the spring and summer months of 1872. From January to July, 1872, 730 cases were reported, of which 85 were fatal, the sufferers having occupied 449 rooms in 387 houses, according to which figures over one-twelfth of the houses in the town had been affected.[4] The epidemic was a concomitant of overcrowding and the lack of a suitable isolation hospital;[5] its victims did not die entirely in vain, for the Council secured authority to provide hospital accommodation and artisans' dwelling houses, these powers being embodied in the Barrow Corporation Extension and Amendment Act (1872).[6] The Corporation was empowered to raise £10,000 for a hospital, and a further £10,000 for " dwelling-houses for the working classes ". In fact it did neither, and this part of the Act remained a dead letter, but the intention, if not the deed, had historical significance. Section 26, which dealt with overcrowding, gave the Corporation power to fix " the number of persons who may occupy a house or part of a house which is let in lodgings or occupied by members of more than one family ". Houses could be whitewashed and " purified " by order of the Corporation, provided that they were certified dangerous to health by " any two physicians or surgeons ".[7] The remainder of the Act was more conventional in scope; it codified the extension of the boundary granted under the Poor Law Order of 1871, thereby making the borough coterminous with the Barrow Guardians' administrative area, and bringing Walney Island into the borough itself; it specifically allowed the Corporation to extend Duke Street,[8] across the untidy sprawl of buildings which marked the remnants of Barrow's old village, and into the Strand, and to widen

---

[1]*B. Her.*, 9.3.72.   [2]*34th* and *35th Annual Reports of the Registrar-General*.   [3]*B.T.C. Mins.*, 3.7.71.   [4]*B.T.C. Mins.*, 5.8.72. Cf. also *MS. Diary*, 21.1.72.   [5]Some feeble measures to erect a wooden hospital were taken in 1871 ; *B.T.C. Mins.*, 3.7.71.   [6]35 & 36 *Vict.*, c.113 (18th July, 1872). The power to erect dwellinghouses was not a new one, and had been embodied in Lord Shaftesbury's Act of 1851 (14 & 15 *Vict.*, c.34), but only Huddersfield and Liverpool had built municipal dwellings by 1870. (Inf. by courtesy of Dr. W. Ashworth.)   [7]Section 20 of the Act.   [8]This was mainly a matter of improving the appearance of the town centre.

Dalton Road between Fisher Street and Church Street ; and it gave the Corporation borrowing powers for the extension of the gas and water undertakings, the cemetery, more market space, slaughterhouses, sewers, new streets and general improvements, all to a total sum of £105,000, thus permitting a great widening of its operations. It is characteristic, nevertheless, that £65,000 was to be earmarked for gas and water and only £5000 for new streets and sewers. [1]

Only one provision of the Act threatened to invade the unsullied pastures of the local business community, that permitting the Duke Street extension ; it was resisted furiously, and led to a long enquiry, having envisaged a trespass on the property of one William Clayton of Blackburn, a leading land speculator in the town. [2] The printed record of this enquiry is a local historical document of some value, showing in detail the extent to which land prices had soared between the 'sixties and 1872-3. The rapid increase of land values naturally tended to discourage the Corporation from making large-scale purchases of territory, either for building or for street improvement. Some purchases were in fact made in the early 'seventies, and in 1874 the Corporation's Public Improvement Account [3] showed an expenditure of £12,248 (the cost of a few houses with attached land) and about one-quarter of that amount in moneys expended on land for general improvements.

As regards local land prices, the evidence of witnesses in the Duke Street enquiry was conflicting and necessarily highly interested ; but it appears, however, that land in the new shopping thoroughfares, like Dalton Road and Duke Street, could command up to £8 a yard, but that it could also be sold, near the same localities, for as little as 3s. 6d. a yard. Prices rose enormously after 1870 ; land at the corner of Buccleuch Street and Duke Street actually rose to the fantastic level of £11 a yard in 1872, having risen from £1 10s. in a few months, while in 1866, 779 square yards of land in the Cavendish Street-Duke Street area had been bought at 10s. a yard, and land in the immediate vicinity was being sold for between 30s. and £2 a yard in 1872. 7s. 6d. a yard, or rather less, was common in the town in the mid-'sixties, and it may be said that prices had risen between four and six times in four years. [4]

[1]Preamble to the 1872 Act. [2]For Clayton (who was one of the early birds in this field) see p. 284 above. The printed record, *Notes . . . on the Proceedings of an Enquiry etc.*, 1872, *July* 15th-19*th*, 1873, is in Barrow P.L. [3]*Treas. Accts.*, 1873-4, Pub. Improvemt. Acct., p. 43.

[4]*Notes . . . on the Proceedings*, 26, 30, 106, 114 and *passim*. It was revealed that the leading personalities of the Ratepayers' Protective Association were protecting themselves vigorously. John Poole claimed that he handled £200,000 worth of property in Barrow alone, and was then buying land in the Abbey Road area, to which the town was extending ; *Notes*, 135.

Much of the most vigorous and profitable speculation took place on land which had never been Furness Railway property. This was by no means always the case, however, and the attitude of the F.R. appears as somewhat ambiguous in these years. James Ramsden acted as chief land agent for the company, and possibly the extreme cheapness with which the Hindpool Estate had originally been bought, made it possible for him to sell parts of it at less than £2 a yard. By 1873 he had sold parts of Ramsden Square, which soon afterwards sold at £5 a yard, and there existed an arrangement by which purchasers of Hindpool Estate land should "pay into the hands of James Ramsden . . . a deposit of 20 per cent. as part payment of the same ".[1] The Mayor was not only left to dispose of land at his own personal profit, but also acted as a semi-private agent for the Corporation.[2] The Duke of Devonshire had been selling Abbey Road land to him, and in 1872 Ramsden was checked by the Furness Railway board for disposing of land which was to be used for the new Barrow railway station at Longreins.[3] A man in Ramsden's position must have been beset by manifold temptations, and the real point of these comments is that the Corporation and Furness Railway Company, although enjoying an extremely close underlying association, had no unified land policy in the town. Important decisions were left to individuals.

Nevertheless, the growth of the town continued, with some modifications, to follow the plan that Ramsden had laid down,[4] and, indeed, there were positive achievements in the sphere of corporation planning. In 1873 the Duke of Devonshire made a large tract of land to the north of Abbey Road available for building ; 100,000 square yards were laid out to accommodate between 700 and 800 houses—i.e., at a density of about 35 houses an acre—with main streets up to 60 feet wide and back streets 30 feet.[5] These widths were becoming standard in Barrow, and, with variations, were ordered in a local Act of 1875.[6] By 1881 this area, an extension of Hindpool, was almost completely filled in. A specially constructed railway line was used for carrying material to the building sites, just as sandstone from the Hawcoat quarries was carried by rail direct to Old Barrow Island during the erection of the flats there. These flats and the newer Hindpool houses showed a distinct advance on the earlier cottage dwellings of the town, and the terrace houses built by the London contractors Yewdall and Hitchens in Hindpool were often supplied with a third bedroom, which in the twentieth century was sometimes available for conversion into a bathroom.[7]

[1]*Notes*, 120. [2]*Treas. Reports*, 1873-4 ; Pub. Improvement Acct. [3]*Dir. Mins.* (*F.R.*), 8.8.72. Cf. also Dr. Pollard's comments, *L. & C.*, LXIII, 111. [4]*B. Her.*, 2.3.72. [5]*B. Times*, 18.10.73. [6]The Barrow Corporation Act (1875), 38 & 39 *Vict.*, c.204 (Aug. 11th, 1875), Sec. 42-3. Main through-fares were to be 80 feet wide, main carriage-roads 60 feet, and back streets not less than 20 feet. [7]*Basic Survey Schedule*, Barrow Corporation.

Such examples as the foregoing might give the impression that the F.R. group had in fact conducted a vast building operation in order to house its workpeople. In 1873-4, at the height of the building drive, 1487 houses with a total rateable value of £12,551 [1] were owned by the ruling syndicate (F.R., Haematite Co., Ship-building Co., Jute Co.) when the total number of dwellings in the town was 5600, and the total rateable value of the borough was £102,231. It will therefore be seen that most of the houses were owned by private individuals or firms. Nor did the dominant elements carry an exorbitantly heavy rate burden. In the late months of 1873 it was revealed that the Furness Railway and Steel-works had not been assessed for two years, and that the rateable value of the Furness Railway in the borough was some £6,500; but the London and North Western Railway's assessment in Preston was £17,100 for the same track-mileage. [2]

What of the councillors and corporation officials? Between 1868 and 1872 the council membership showed little change, most of its leading personalities having been confirmed in their positions by election. [3] The year 1873 brought an infusion of new blood in the persons of Dr. C. M. Deane (a bitter critic of the insanitary state of the borough), and J. P. Bell, a shopkeeper. Benjamin Fish, of the Ratepayers' Protective Association, had also reached the council chamber. The aldermanic bench was still solidly syndicate (Schneider, Wadham and Ramsden), and J. T. Smith had become Mayor in succession to Ramsden. There was still, as in 1867, only 12 councillors and four aldermen—16 representatives for a popula-tion rapidly approaching 35,000, and it was pointed out that Burnley, Warrington, Lancaster, Bootle and Clitheroe all had more than twice as many council representatives per head of population. [4] The 1875 Corporation Act, however, brought a complete reconsti-tution; 24 councillors representing eight wards (Walney, Hindpool, Ramsden, Central, Salthouse, Hawcoat, Newbarns and Yarlside), and eight aldermen. There were then 5612 local government voters in a population of 37,000, and democracy was on the way; or so it appeared.

By 1870 it had become fairly clear to the Council that competent full-time officials were required, and when, in that year, it advertised for a competent surveyor, there was no dearth of applicants. It secured the services of Howard Evans, formerly Chief Assistant Surveyor of Salford, at £200 *per annum*. The latter obtained some much needed assistance, in the form of a sur-veyor's foreman, in February 1871, at 35s. a week. [5] A month later

[1]Dr. Pollard's calculation from the Corporation Rate Books. [2]*B. Her.*, 25.10.73. [3]Robert Hannay and Kennedy had retired. [4]Dr. Deane's analysis of the Council, *B. Her., loc. cit.* [5]*B.T.C. Mins.*, 9.11.70, 6.2.71.

Ramsden recommended the appointment of Joseph Allison—already a member of the Council—as Medical Officer of Health, thus anticipating the requirements of the Act of 1872 (35 & 36 *Vict.*, c.79), which made the appointment of such an official compulsory. Allison, outstanding among the councillors as a man of integrity and self-sacrifice, took over the post immediately.[1] Meanwhile, the councillors had ratified an even more notable appointment, that of C. F. Preston as Town Clerk ;[2] he remained in his post for a generation, and saw, and was responsible for, many great improvements in the administration of the borough of Barrow-in-Furness. The Corporation still needed the services of a capable and experienced sanitary engineer who could plan and organise without recourse to the advice of the F.R. engineers ; such an official, Arthur Jacob, became Borough Surveyor in succession to Evans, and he was provided with an assistant in 1874.[3] But in spite of the undoubted ability of these individuals, the corporation staff was still hopelessly small, and could not hope to deal satisfactorily with the problems which faced it month by month.

There was one fairly satisfactory achievement in an otherwise mixed and indifferent record. Owing to the existence and needs of the iron and steel works within its boundaries, Barrow had for some time had comparatively good piped water supplies. But the water supply, as existing in 1872, proved to be completely inadequate. It is true that the demands on the water supply system had quickened enormously, as the following figures show :[4]

Year	Inhabitants of Barrow	Gallons per day	Gallons per head per day (including works)
1864	7000	115,000	$16\frac{1}{2}$
1872	30,000	1,124,000	$37\frac{1}{2}$

In 1870-74 the number of water consumers doubled, from 3250 to 6550, an increase of 3300. The Poaka Beck reservoir could, in 1872, yield one and a half million gallons a day, and in 1871 the Haematite Steel Company erected a service reservoir of 60 million gallons ; the town therefore had a water reserve of 236 million gallons, or 190 days' supply. But the system of distribution was still far from perfect, especially when the vast demands of the Hindpool steelworks coincided with drought conditions.[5] The Corporation therefore sought for a new Reservoir at Pennington Beck, which was to be linked with Poaka Beck by an aqueduct,

[1]*B.T.C. Mins.*, 6.3.71, 2.6.73.   [2]*B.T.C. Mins.*, 5.12.70. Manclarke, who resigned, was of course a part-time official.   [3]*B.T.C. Mins.*, 6.5.72, 2.3.74. Jacob fought for a system of " double " sewering.   [4]Details in *H. of C. Cttee, Barrow Corporation Bill,* 1873, 3-4, 38, etc.   [5]*Barrow Vulcan,* 26.6.74 ; *B.T.C. Mins.*, 7.7.73, 6.7.74 ; *B. Her.,* 12.7.73 ; *H. of C. Cttee, cit.* Q. 291.

and which would therefore use the same pipe system into Barrow. It was a reasonable idea, but the Ulverston Waterworks Company felt that its interests were affected, and the 1873 Barrow Corporation Bill proceedings (the Corporation had opted to spend up to £28,000 on new water supplies) were much protracted with wearisome argument. The Ulverston company got its own water from Pennington Beck, and it eventually received a compensation of 400,000 gallons *per diem* free of charge, and 200,000 more at reduced price. The Barrow councillors and officials continued to build up the Poaka Beck system, and the latter served the town of Barrow, Dalton and Askam in succeeding years ; Ulverston, as has been shown, also benefited.

INSTITUTIONS

Barrow's first hospital has already been mentioned.[1] Its further career, in the years following 1870, can be dealt with briefly. It was decided, at a public meeting held in January, 1870, to form a council of management " consisting of representatives from the various works and mines " to " enlarge its usefulness and increase its funds ". Penny subscriptions were obtained from all the workmen in the town, " supplemented by contributions to an equal amount by the employers ". In 1875, new and better presmises were secured in School Street, containing 25 beds.[2] There was, for a time, a possibility that the Corporation would take over the running of this institution, but any plans (like those for municipal housing schemes) were set aside. But the end of the century saw the North Lonsdale Hospital as an important institution.

The Barrow School Board demands some attention, if only by virtue of the vast problems which faced it. Formally constituted in 1872, it held its first meeting on January 2nd, 1873, with Lord Frederick Cavendish in the chair, and a membership which included five clergymen of the different denominations, Sir James Ramsden, John Fell and William Ashburner. In Lord Frederick's words : " The work before the Board is very onerous and considerable, and has been delayed a little too long, but that is due to exceptional circumstances ". There were some 5000 children requiring school places in the borough ; in the January a census of school accommodation revealed that 2084 children were attending Barrow schools, including the National Schools of St. George (306) and St. James (782), and the St. Mary's Roman Catholic School on Newland Street (501). The deficiency of places amounted to 3059. The Board's teething troubles then started. The council was slow and

---

[1]See pp. 323-5 above.   [2]*F. P. & P.*, II, 313. This institution was as necessary as ever ; there was still, as a rough average, an accident a week at the steelworks ; for details, the Barrow press for 1875, *passim*.

unco-operative in applying a precept for the School Board ; there was the usual inter-denominational distrustfulness (the Rev. W. H. Fothergill even went so far as to advocate secular schools as the price of peace) ; and the members had to search for temporary school presmises to hire, and to consider how they might cause temporary school buildings to be erected. With the consent of the Education Department, temporary schools were erected at Rawlinson Street and Old Barrow, the former (about 400 pupils) on July 14th, 1873. A small school was also established in the customs house at Roa Island, which was soon afterwards reported to be " unruly ".[1] Arrangements were made, meanwhile, to build a permanent school at Holker Street,[2] and the Island Road School, Old Barrow, was built during 1873. By 1877, eight schools had been built with a total of 3896 places ;[3] 5097 were " making a pretence of going to school " (including, presumably, those attending the older church schools and private schools) ; and there were 8000 children of schoolgoing age in the town. The result was that the town lost £2000 in school pence and government grants, although (according to the then Mayor) £40,000 had been spent on school accommodation, and the School Board's rate had risen to the ostensibly frighten-figure of 3½d. in the pound.[4]

---

[1]The detailed early story of the Board may be followed in *B. Her.*, 4.1, 18.1, 21.1, 8.3, 29.3, 10.5, 5.7, 19.7, 9.8, 20.9.73.   [2]Opened in November, 1875 ; *vide B. Her.*, 25.11.75.   [3]Full table in *F.P. & P.*, II, 312.   [4]*Vide* rept. in *B. Her.*, 10.11.77 ; also *B. Times*, 9.3.78.

CHAPTER XVIII

YEARS OF ANTI-CLIMAX

Professor Rostow has identified 1874 as the first full year of the Great Depression.[1] For the twenty years following that date, Britain is said to have suffered considerable economic setbacks and long periods of crisis, the heavy industries (as in Barrow) having been most affected. More recently, however, it has become fashionable to treat the notion of " depression " with a measure of reserve, and economic historians have pointed out that through the period mentioned, British industrial progress went on much as before. Yet, as the local historian soon becomes aware, the glib or fashionable generalisation may help to set the minds of students at rest, but it helps the investigator little or not at all. The statistician, the individual industrialist and the individual workman are all too likely to have different ideas as to what constitutes a depression.

If by economic progress we mean growing production and continued construction and use of new plant, then the Furness district could boast of such progress between 1874 and the end of the century. Local industrialists did not think in such terms ; they thought rather of the heady days and vast plans of 1871-3, and to them the following years represented what was indeed a period of anti-climax. It represented falling prices and profits, and to the workman it often meant unemployment, wage reductions and longer hours. Nevertheless, investment of various types continued locally, and it may be significant that during the first observable period of depression and recovery (1874-7) a new enterprise, the North Lonsdale Iron and Steel Company, constructed an ironworks of three furnaces at South Ulverston, on level ground near the Ulverston Canal and the shore of the Leven Estuary.

This venture is interesting in that a comparatively large number of local people invested in it; in 1874 the company had some 219 shareholders (compared with fewer than half that number in the Haematite Steel Company), of whom 65 belonged to the Ulverston district, 20 to Barrow and 46 to other parts of Furness. Over 50 of these were shop and hotel keepers, who had invested a total of £17,600 in the new project, while farmers, maltsters, shoemakers and clerks also held shares in it. The major shareholders were the Ainslies (£20,000) and Myles Kennedy (£15,000),[2] and as is indicated by the names mentioned, the company was a somewhat belated result of capital accumulation on the part of leading ore merchants.

[1]Rostow, W. W., *British Economy in the Nineteenth Century*, 202.
[2]*File* 7730, Reg. J. S. Cos., London ; lists dated Oct. 18th, 1873, and Feb. 30th, 1874.

Meanwhile, Barrow was recognised as the focal point of an important and growing iron district when, on April 13th, 1874, the North Lancashire and Cumberland Iron Exchange was opened in the town ; it was, as William Crossley put it, " a kind of halfway house between the Cumberland and Furness districts and users of haematite iron and haematite ore ".[1] The users met in the Town Hall at first, and there were 167 members in the February of the following year (1875).[2] But within a few months of the formation of this body, the members were retailing bad news.

Monthly trade reports tell the story, and fully supplement what Professor Rostow has to say in his well-known study of the period.[3] " The request for Bessemer iron is restricted ", reported *Iron* in August, 1874, and business was thereafter slow on the Barrow Exchange ;[4] although the profits of the Hindpool steelworks remained high until February, 1875, when the Duke of Devonshire complained to himself that the dividend was only 15 per cent. and that no bonus was possible.[5] Stocks of pig were then accumulating and large debts were outstanding.[6]

The steelworks proved to be a central bastion of Barrow hopes, but even that great enterprise did not represent the proudest aspiration on the part of the local captains. Work on the vast dock installations was carried on continually. In the boom year of 1873 a customs inspector remarked that " The Bonded Vault is at least ten times as large as necessary and although a great number of Casks of Wine are deposited in it they were quite lost ".[7] Ships, too, were almost lost in the great dock basins. In these years a new dock, the Ramsden, was under construction in the south-west corner of Barrow Island, and in respect of accommodation the port of Barrow (which had been separated from Lancaster and constituted a port of independent standing by Treasury Order in 1872) was now among the half-dozen largest in the British Isles. Yet the average tonnage of all the visiting vessels using Barrow in 1873 was a mere 179 tons, as compared with 418 tons at Liverpool and 180 tons at Grimsby[8]—in other words, the mighty Devonshire and Buccleuch docks were habitually filled with ships little larger than those which entered the Lincolnshire fishing port. Moreover, more than two-thirds of the Barrow visitors were still sailing vessels (of which Liverpool had seven to eight times as many), while Grimsby, another railway-inspired port, handled twice the Barrow tonnages entered and cleared in 1873. Indeed, out of thirteen main English ports,[9] Barrow had the smallest tonnage and trade in both 1873 and 1883.

[1]Rept. in *B. Pilot*, 18.4.74.   [2]*Iron & Coal Trades Review*, X, 12.2.75, 167.   [3]*Op. cit.*, 180, 202-3.   [4]*B. Pilot, passim.*   [5]*MS. Diary*, 16.2.75.   [6]*MS. Diary*, 10.6, 10.8.74.   [7]*Reports of Customs Inspectors, loc. cit.*   [8]Vernon-Harcourt, L. F., *Harbours and Docks* (1888), I, Appx. VII.   [9]*Op. cit.*, I, Appx. V.

Nor was the trade at the Barrow docks an adequately varied and balanced one. In the years 1873-5 inclusive, timber was by far the largest import, mainly fir wood from Russia, Sweden, Norway, Canada, Germany and the U.S.A. For the rest, steel rails (bound for Canada) and iron ore were major exports, but iron ore from Bilbao and pig *via* Rotterdam and Stettin were also imported to help in the rail manufacture.[1] It is worth noting that Spanish haematite (13,874 tons in 1873) was brought into Barrow long before the local iron mines reached peak production, although some were of course giving out at that date ; and the Spanish ores, judging by their recorded customs values, were in 1873-4 scarcely cheaper (and indeed, in terms of local mineral statistics, much dearer) than the Furness haematite they were intended to supplement.[2]

A further important commodity brought from abroad was of course jute from Bengal, of which nearly 205,000 cwt. entered the port in 1873 prior to absorption and use in the F.R. syndicate's Flax and Jute Works at Hindpool. Even here, however, the figures for the two succeeding years tell a sad story—rather over 100,000 cwt. imported in 1874, and a mere 47,000 in 1875.[3] Due mainly to the diminution in imports of timber and jute, the trade of the port fell almost catastrophically in 1874-5. Had this meant simply a loss in Furness Railway traffic, the result would no doubt have been a disturbing one ; but, of course, local industries were directly affected, and the Jute Works, whose fortunes are only too clearly portrayed in these pages, was in desperate straits during 1875 and losing money continually.[4] This, however, was but one aspect of the local crisis which steadily developed in that year, and it will be as well to trace the former in some detail.

The railway company and the steelworks proved themselves to be comparatively seaworthy in the general crisis. In June, 1874, Ramsden reported to his fellow-directors that the traffic of the railway had fallen off considerably, and that the dividend would probably be reduced to no more than six per cent.[5] A fall in loco coal prices in 1873-4, and a reduction in working expenditure over the same period did not, psychologically at least, counterbalance apparently toppling general merchandise receipts—from £105,433 in 1874 to £81,473 in 1875.[6] This was partly due to the lagging dock traffic ; the Jute Company, as has been implied, was in a depressed state (it was unable to pay any dividend in the August of 1874),[7] and the import of that commodity fell sharply. The

---

[1] *P.R.O., Abstracts of Imports and Exports, etc., Customs* **23 and** 24 ; *Reports of Customs Inspectors, loc. cit.* [2] *Customs* **23,** *etc., ibid.* Welsh steelmakers found that Spanish ores could be used in the early 'seventies ; Burn, *Economic History of Steelmaking,* 23. [3] *Customs* 23, *ibid.* [4] For the whole group of Barrow companies and their misfortunes, *vide MS. Diary,* 28.5, 11.6, 16.7, 9.8. 10.8.1875. [5] *Dir. Mins.* (*F.R.*), 9.6.74. [6] *Bd.* of *Tde. Returns.* [7] *MS. Diary,* 11.8.74.

Duke, with such facts pressing on his mind, took the unusual step of personally addressing the F.R. shareholders in the general meeting of the same month, and explaining to them the reason for the reduction of dividends.[1] For obvious reasons, and without reference to the Duke's personal integrity, many things must have remained unsaid. Not only was the Jute Company in trouble, but much remained to be done in the way of further construction at the shipyard, which was engaged in a not very large building programme devoted chiefly to sailing vessels ; moreover, the yard was not well managed and Robertson, the Shipbuilding Company's manager, was held accountable for heavy losses and dismissed early in the following year.[2] Nor was this all. The railway company was spending some £10,000 a month on the improvement of Barrow docks (adjacent to which, of course, the shipyard was situated) by mid-1874,[3] and this consideration, too, must have weighed on the minds of directors and shareholders.

Yet the position of the railway company was not unsound. The fall in its total receipts was less than 5 per cent. in 1874-5, and its net receipts showed a small but steady increase during these early recession years of 1874-6.

The almost catastrophic drop in haematite prices was far more productive of troubled minds ; Furness ore production (in fact 926,497 tons in 1873) was reaching out to the million mark, and comfortably exceeded that level in annual value in 1871-4, but the fall in the value of the produce to £626,000 in 1875 must have seemed disastrous to the business community of the time. A slump in exports of Bessemer iron was of course at the root of the crisis.[4] It is all the more striking, therefore, that the Haematite Steelworks dividend could stand at 15 per cent. in early 1875, and it is a bizarre reflection that this figure could be considered low even by persons who had purchased shares at market values grossly inflated by much higher dividends.[5] The steelworks and railway together appeared well capable of riding the storm, but their captains were busily engaged in trying to steer much less buoyant vessels into harbour.

It is a measure of their desperation by April, 1875, that they were even considering the sale of the Furness Railway Company, and Ramsden was instructed to approach the Midland and London and North Western railways with this in mind.[6] H. W. Schneider, meanwhile, proposed that the Duke of Devonshire should spend some £630,000 at once—with no immediate return—in order to save the shipyard.[7] The F.R. was not sold, but Devonshire, as has been

---

[1]MS. Diary, 26.8.74.   [2]MS. Diary, 17.2.75.   [3]Dir. Mins. (F.R.), 8.5.74.
[4]Cf. Burn, op. cit., 27 ;   J.I.S.I., 1874, 278-9 ;   Iron, 8.8.74.   [5]Barrow Times, 29.6.78, states that the dividend was generally 20 per cent. or more. For a 30 per cent. example, see p. 270.   [6]MS. Diary, 29.4.75.   [7]MS. Diary, loc. cit.

explained in a recent article,[1] was obliged eventually to increase on a very large scale his holdings in local companies. The Jute Company and Shipbuilding Company losses went on during 1875, and it says much for Devonshire's acceptance of responsibility that the Jute Works remained working until well into the following year.[2] This responsibility was vast as well as onerous, for the Barrow enterprises controlled by the F.R. group were heavily in debt to banks in mid-1876, and the London and Westminster Bank refused to extend further credit to the main local firms. This, of course, threw a still greater burden upon Devonshire, who would not have doubted that a depression was in progress.

During the autumn of the same year there were signs of returning trade, although the Shipbuilding Company still tottered. In March, 1877, Devonshire noted that " It will clearly be necessary for me to find a great deal of money to prevent a smash ", and the shipyard directors resolved to raise £200,000 by shares and half the sum by debentures. Devonshire took the new shares in their entirety and further increased his existing holdings, with the result that Devonshire and his family, together with Ramsden, made a total contribution of £300,000.[3] Such an action implied a profound confidence in the future of Barrow, and although the Duke would not have wanted himself to be sentimentalised by historians in a later age, there was a solid philanthropy and humanitarianism in these actions. The Jute Works, as is noted in the foregoing paragraph, remained working during black days ; and in 1875 the Jute Company, too, increased its loan capital considerably, Devonshire later taking an ever larger proportion of the total shares.[4]

This part of the story has been well told by Dr. Pollard.[5] The first stage of depression had several salutary consequences, not the least of these being an improvement in the technological efficiency of the steelworks. The easy profits and inflated dividends of the boom years had caused even J. T. Smith to overlook the extreme wastefulness of transferring molten iron a distance of one and a half to two miles *en route* from furnaces to steel sheds, causing the cooling of the iron and making obligatory its re-heating in a cupola.[6] By 1876, however, Smith was telling the members of the Iron and Steel Institute of his conversion to the direct or heat-conserving process, and Schneider said frankly that " . . . in 1874 steel rails were very much higher in price than they are now. The decrease in the price of iron and steel has sharpened the Barrow wits more than anything else ".[7] The prominent iron technician William Menelaus agreed that the check to large profits had enforced a cheapening of production.[8]

[1]Pollard, S., in *Ec. H. R.*, Dec., 1955.   [2]*B. Times*, 12.2.76.   [3]*MS. Diary*, 12.3, 13.3.77.   [4]Pollard, *op. cit.*, 218.   [5]*Ibid.*   [6]*J.I.S.I.*, 1876, 13 and ff. [7]*Ibid.*   [8]*Op. cit.*, p. 41.

Another and well-tested method of cheapening production had already been tried, with unfortunate results in the locality. The trade unionists of Barrow, who had been organised through the Trades Council since 1872,[1] had obtained, in certain cases, a nine-hour day agreement in the agitations of the previous year. In fact, a ten-hour day was customary, but according to the *Barrow Pilot*, all hours over nine were paid for.[2] This generalisation of course relates to an organised minority consisting chiefly of A.S.E. men. According to the same source, labourers in the Steelworks had never had the benefit of the nine hours movement as in other parts of the country. By December, 1874, the A.S.E. local secretary reported to his headquarters that Barrow trade was " Bad ".[3] Implied in this bald statement was a proposed wage reduction of 5 per cent.—which seems to have affected all classes of labour in the Steelworks—as well as an increase in the working week for the organised section, from 54 to 57½ hours. The A.S.E. men regarded the lengthening of hours as more detrimental to their interests than the reduction in wages, and after representations had been made, J. T. Smith caused the steelworks engineers to be given notice. A somewhat similar move took place in the shipyard, where a possible reduction in wages was announced, but the public notices to this effect were soon afterwards withdrawn.[4] Plainly enough, it was hardly a feasible proposition to lock out a majority of the skilled men in the town, and consequently the experiment was confined to the steelworks.

The ensuing lock-out of engineers was a painful affair which exacerbated animosities in the town. At least one school of thought might have contended that advantages gained in boom conditions, when the employer is at a disadvantage, should be surrendered when the latter is facing unfavourable trade. The counter-attack of the employers, however, was not directed solely against those labour aristocrats who had gained advances and shorter hours in 1871-2 ; it was also according to the radical *Pilot*, turned against labourers earning 21s. a week, and against gasfitters who earned the same wage but who paid 6s. 3d. a week for their occupation of company houses.[5] These were expected to accept a 5 per cent. reduction, and apparently many of them did.

The lock-out of the A.S.E. men lasted from January 8th, 1875, until September 12th of the same year ; a period of nine months. The men affected were sustained by donations from other parts of the country, and by 25s. a week strike pay. The Lock-out Committee's funds were also used to help workers at Messrs. Westray and Copeland's who were striking against a 2½ per cent. reduction.

---

[1]Or, perhaps, since the winter of 1871-2 ; see p. 358 above.　[2]*B. Pilot*, 16.1.75.　[3]*A.S.E. Monthly Repts.*　[4]*B. Pilot, loc. cit.*　[5]*Ibid.*

The engineers concerned were in fact handsomely supported by press and publicists, the radical hatter of Duke Street, Samuel Swindlehurst, taking a prominent part in this sphere ; and it may well be that many of the locked-out men did not suffer more than was usual. But the affair had an ugly side, shown when occupants of steelworks houses were ejected in the February and March. The steelworks management could afford to wait, and the engineers ultimately returned to work at reduced pay if not extended hours. During the entire period that they were out of the works, it was understood that they were engaged in a fight for principle and on behalf of others.[1] Perhaps, too, the management made an astute move in forcing the Amalgamated Society of Engineers to pay the wages of part of their staff for nine months.

Whatever the truth, and whatever the extent to which technical reorganisation and lower wage bills may have benefited the steelworks directorate, the Steel Company was able to record a profit of over £100,000 in the accounting year 1876-7.[2] This was not all the story, and the company was heavily overdrawn at the bank, [3]but at least some success was evident. Nevertheless, the directors were unable to enjoy these reassuring crumbs, for the shipyard's building programme was a wretched 400 tons in 1876, the situation at the Jute Works became almost daily worse, and the dock traffic showed little sign of improvement during that year. It is true that the iron ore trade recovered slightly, and that it went on to achieve, in the following year, a record output figure for the history of the locality ; and it cannot be too strongly emphasised that work and production tended to go on much as before. On behalf of the small group of presumably non-manual workers who had a direct interest in the profits made from local industry, Devonshire recorded in his notebook, a year or two afterwards, that there was no grumbling at any of the general meetings held in connection with the major companies.[4] The Furness Railway dividend climbed, as if warily, back to a frugal but respectable 8 per cent. in 1877, and for a time the clouds seemed to move away from the sun.

There was, of course, a natural tendency to grumble on the part of those manual workers whose wages were reduced. The *Barrow Pilot* of August 28th, 1875, was convinced that trade was in a sorry state. Local trade union secretaries tended to agree with the press —" Bad " was the adjective used by the A.S.E.'s representative— and there was short time at the wire works (Messrs. Cooke and Swinnerton's) in the month mentioned, another strike at the steelworks in the November, and a 5 per cent. reduction for the Bessemer men in the following February.[5] There were even a few unhappy

---

[1]*B. Pilot,* 16.1, 13.2, 20.2, 6.2, 6.3, 20.3, 27.3 ; *B. Her.,* 27.3, 18.9.75.
[2]*MS. Diary,* 7.8.77. [3]*MS. Diary,* 15.6.76, 21.5.78. [4]*MS. Diary,* 23.9.78. [5]*A.S.E. Monthly Repts.* ; *B. Pilot,* 25.3.76 ; *B. Times,* 5.2, 12.2.76.

episodes among other minor firms of the neighbourhood ; Messrs. Westray and Forster dissolved their partnership in early 1875, and S. J. Claye, the Salthouse wagon-builder, abandoned a project for the manufacture of rails—although, even in that year, he still had large rolling stock orders in " gratifying contrast to the depression ".[1]

The Jute Company still limped desperately, and was facing a crisis in the summer of 1877, when, in the July, the weaving department was standing idle as the womenfolk employed there resisted considerable wage reductions (amounting in some cases, to four shillings a week).[2] That these women struck at all is a matter of much sociological interest, and it seems that they, too, had been affected by the prevailing local atmosphere. It should be made clear that the Jute Works (as is already implied by references on another page[3]) was a vast enterprise of its kind, with a maximum labour force of 1700, an elaborate system of production, and (in 1881) an average output of 140 tons of fabric a week. A product upon which its directors placed much reliance, as a means of extending the market, was a high-quality fabric known as " Kalameit ".[4] In respect of its actual and potential addition to the national wealth, undoubtedly the Barrow Jute Company deserved to succeed. The conditions of work in the factory cannot now be easily analysed ; the interior seems to have been more pleasant than was usual in textile works, but the atmosphere was heavily charged with fluff, and no doubt the work, mainly machine-minding, was monotonous in the extreme. It is a matter for regret, too, that we do not know more about the effect of this employment upon local social life. It is not clear, for instance, whether Sir James Ramsden intended that the work should appeal mainly to married women in the town (thus giving some families a sense of prosperity, if an absence of family life), or whether he had allowed for the possibility that large numbers of younger women might migrate into the vicinity. (It should be added that the Jute Works provided inducements for entire families from outside to settle in Barrow, for in the ordinary way of things, and in view of a severe shortage of accommodation in periods of full employment, the fathers of families tended to enter the town in advance guard ; in 1881, for example, it was estimated that £1000 per week were sent out of Barrow by such workers to their distant relatives[5]).

If the affairs of the Jute Company were unhappy, those of the Barrow Shipbuilding Company were scarcely less so. In May, 1875, the latter came under the management of James Humphrys, who may indeed have battled against adverse circumstances (including

[1]*Iron and Coal Trades Review*, Feb. 12th, 1875, 41 ; April 9th, 1875, 422. [2]*Barrow Vulcan*, 10.7.1877 ; *B. Her.*, 14.7.77. [3]See p. 349 [4]Cf. account in. *Trans. Mechanical Engineers* (1881), pp. 380, 480. [5]*B. News*, 12.4, 8.7.1881.

that of an inexperienced directorial board) but whose influence on labour-management relations was anything but beneficial. An A.S.E. Report of 1879 observed that " The relations of employers and employed have not always been of the most amicable character, and in the August of 1878 a series of disputes commenced, which continued in some form or another for many months, and caused a great deal of unpleasantness or inconvenience to our members . . . to the petty tyranny of the manager (of the Shipbuilding Company) the disturbances . . . were chiefly due ". Humphrys introduced a system of comparatively heavy fines for minor infringements of punctuality, and subsequently attempted to restrict the use of the shipyard closets to seven minutes per day per man ; a " more or less general strike " followed, led by the A.S.E. members, in answer to which the company imported blackleg labour. Some form of settlement resulted, but this in turn was nullified by a series of victimisation cases for which the A.S.E. blamed Humphrys. These cases were accompanied by wage cuts varying from 5 to 15 per cent., and after an approach to Sir James Ramsden had brought little success, " all our members (of the A.S.E.) were withdrawn from the establishment ". Yet later, an interview took place between trade unionists and the board of directors, " and it was arranged that in future the management would make no distinction between society and non-society men in their employ ". The strike, which lasted three or four weeks, then terminated. (While it was " transpiring " there were further disputes at Claye's Wagon Works and at the Furness Railway Works, involving wage reductions and extensions of the working week.) [1]

This agreement did not mark the end of Humphrys's misfortunes. The Shipbuilding Company successfully completed a series of vessels under his management ; for the Royal Navy, the gunboats *Foxhound* and *Forward* in 1879, and the *Banterer*, *Espoir*, *Grapple*, *Wrangler* and *Wasp* in 1880 ; and for the Merchant Navy, the *Earl of Ulster* in 1877, the *Circassia* in 1878, and the *Furnessia* and *City of Rome* in 1880-1. The last of these was to blight Humphrys's career much as the ill-fated Tay Bridge did that of Thomas Bouch. The Inman Line wanted a sister ship to the *City of Berlin*, itself second only to the *Great Eastern* in size ; this was to be a vessel for the Liverpool—New York passenger traffic, capable of attaining high speed and yet providing " comfort such as can be found only in the most completely appointed modern hotels ". " After the most careful deliberation " the Barrow Shipbuilding Company decided to construct a vessel of at least 8000 tons, with an overall length of 600 feet, and engines of 8000 horse-power. In August, 1880, several months before the vessel was ready,

---

[1]*A.S.E.*, *Abstract Report of the Council's Proceedings, June 30th, 1878, to Dec. 31st, 1879*, pp. 22-3.

Humphrys's constructional plans were subjected to a most detailed and critical scrutiny by the Institute of Mechanical Engineers, whose members focussed their criticisms on the boilers, the engine-arrangement and crankshafts, and the company's use and non-use of steel. Several engineers were particularly critical of the *City of Rome*'s iron boilers—steel was coming into more general use in shipbuilding at this period—but Humphrys pointed out that while steel was undoubtedly superior " it was a matter of pounds, shillings and pence. The shipowner was a merchant, and he regarded his ship as a machine for bringing him a return for the capital invested on it ".[1] Earlier in the discussion, Daniel Adamson of Manchester had pointed out that it was the purchaser who was the important person in matters of specification.[2]

Accordingly, it may well be that Humphrys was the victim of circumstances at a time of rapidly advancing ship-building technique ; during the 'seventies the total tonnage of British steam-shipping nearly doubled, and there was much that was experimental in contemporary naval architecture. Somebody had to pay the price of failure from time to time. Whatever the particular case, the *City of Rome*—an achievement in constructional engineering if nothing else—appears an outlandish vessel in retrospect, lying long and low in the water, with four masts and three slim funnels, and a figurehead of one of the Roman Caesars dressed in the imperial purple. She had hardly any superstructure by modern standards, and must have shipped heavy seas in Atlantic gales. Her single screw plainly reduced her manoeuvrability.

This great new liner (for the vessel, with accommodation for 1500 emigrants, was certainly entitled to this description) was launched on June 14th, 1881, in view of a large crowd and the usual concourse of prominent personages, including a representative of the Inman family. As though in grim justification of the remarks proffered at the engineers' conference a few months previously, a boiler exploded as the vessel moved down the slipway, killing several men.[3] Her subsequent career was not a happy one ; the liner was so disappointing in performance that the Inman line threatened an action against the Barrow Shipbuilding Company for breach of contract, an event unparalleled in British ship-building history.[4] As a result the *City of Rome* had to be re-purchased by the Barrow firm, and fitted out by the latter for use by Barrow-associated lines ; in 1891, for instance she was working for the Anchor Line (Messrs. Henderson). Even before the launching, however, Humphrys had received notice of his dismissal—one can only conjecture the misgivings and head-shakings at

---

[1] *Trans. Inst. Mech. Eng.*, 1881, **336** ff. [2] *Op. cit.*, 352. [3] *B. Times*, 18.6.1881. [4] I owe this information to Dr. Pollard.

directorial meetings, and the degree of gloom as the 14th of June drew near [1]—and William John, a particularly skilful and respected naval architect, was appointed in his stead. During Humphrys's reign the Shipbuilding Company had sustained a loss of £170,000, due, it was thought, to wasteful use of labour and materials. [2] Certainly the man in question was not good at handling workers in the yard ; in looking back, however, we must also remember that the inexperience of the board of directors, and the insistence of the Inman line on a certain type of design, must bear a share of the blame.

It is a striking feature of Barrow history that after Schneider's brilliant stroke in the appointment of J. T. Smith to the management of local iron production, the directing group showed inability to appoint any other technician of equal skill ; and as their failure in this respect grew more apparent, so did they become more prone to make scapegoats of their managing officials. The first shipyard manager, Robertson, was dismissed in 1874 ; Finlayson, the manager of the Jute Works, was dismissed in 1875, when the works began to show heavy losses ; in 1880, a committee of shareholders threatened to dismiss William Fleming, the second Jute Works manager ; and, as we have seen, the later shipyard manager left his employ in 1881. By 1878, indeed, the chief personalities were beginning to blame each other, and in that year the Duke of Devonshire noted that new organisational arrangements of the main works " will . . . leave less power in Ramsden's hands ". Some months later, Devonshire reflected that " What we really want are people of experience in the jute and shipbuilding business ". [3]

Devonshire was undoubtedly right ; but, in fairness to the Duke and his associates, it should be recognised that they had other and even more far-reaching schemes under consideration. Barrow was not only to construct ocean liners, but to control a fleet of them, thereby bringing passengers and merchandise to local wharves and on to Furness Railway wagons. This vision had been born in the days of 1871-2, and seems to have been elaborated in the brain of the pushful Richard Potter. [4] His daughter, Beatrice Webb, referred affectionately to her father's part in a scheme " to make a Grand Canal through Syria to compete with the Suez Canal ; an enterprise abandoned on the report of the engineers that such a canal would not only submerge the Holy places—a small matter— but take forty years to fill ". After this it was not surprising that such an imagination could conceive " another scheme for a live-cattle trade between Barrow-in-Furness and the United States,

---

[1] On the day of the launch, Sir James Ramsden left the ceremony early, on the grounds that a train could not be made to wait for him ; *B. Times, cit.* [2] *MS. Diary*, 17.2.1875 to 6.3.1883, *passim.* I am indebted to Dr. Pollard for several of these references. [3] *Ibid.* [4] See pp. 344-5 above.

balked by Privy Council orders against cattle disease, or, as my father complained, against free trade in food ".[1] In fact the cattle-importing plan grew, and its execution was attempted, over a considerable period. It was originally broached by Garnett of the Baltimore and Ohio Railway, and taken up by Potter and his timber-importing firm at Barrow ; but not before a line from New Orleans was projected (at the end of 1877) by the Liverpool ship-owner Fernie, with the aim of bringing cattle, wheat and Indian corn to the Furness port. Early in 1878, Ramsden entered into a provisional agreement with the Merchant Trading Co. of Liverpool, by which the F.R. were to build cattle sheds in the newly-construct-ing Ramsden docks. Accordingly the Furness Railway Company found themselves facing yet another instalment of heavy expendi-ture.[2] The Ramsden docks were opened in 1879, and vessels sailing under the flag of the Anchor Line (Messrs. Hendersons) used them ; by that time, about £300,000 had been spent on the Barrow dock accommodation, and Vernon-Harcourt was soon afterwards to observe in wonderment that (1883) " there were 234 acres of docks, inferior only in this respect to London or Liverpool ".[3] Not content with this, Barrow's rulers invested in a floating dry dock capable of raising a vessel of 3200 tons, the third of its type in the world.[4] Barrow trade did in fact improve considerably in 1878-80, the value of total exports doubling, and the value of imports nearly doubling, between these two dates. The dock figures, however, seem merely to have reflected the general trade recovery, reacting from a boom in American and world railway building, in turn sweeping the British iron and steel export " breathlessly up to its nineteenth century zenith in 1882 ".[5] Furness and Cumber-land iron ore and pig production went up in striking fashion between 1879 and the last-mentioned date.[6] Sir James Ramsden was " sanguine " (his favourite word in public addresses) during this period, but there is no indication that the cattle and dock plans in themselves played any significant part in the local recovery. He had, of course, exerted much influence on behalf of both. The shipyard, as we have seen, had a greatly improved building pro-gramme during the period, but suffered from managerial, labour and technical troubles ; the Furness Railway Company, having more goods to carry, was able to raise its dividend from 3½ per cent. (1879) to 7¼ per cent. (1881) ; and in February, 1881, the *Barrow Times* was able to report that " the output of the (local) furnaces is not much below its maximum, and the steel mills are fully employed. Shipbuilders and engineers are exceptionally busy "[7]. The *New-castle Chronicle* remarked that " . . . the receipts of the Furness Railway are the best trading barometer . . . of the north-west . . .

[1]Webb, *My Apprenticeship* (Pelican Ed.), i, 22.   [2]*MS. Diary*, 19.10, 5.12, 24.12.77, 25.1, 11.9.78, 27.3, 20.5.79 ; *Dir. Mins.* (*F.R.*), 12.2.78, 20.5.79, 25.11.79.   [3]*Harbours and Docks*, cit., i, 553.   [4]*Op. cit.*, i, 463.   [5]Burn, *op. cit.*, 73.   [6]*Min. Stats. U.K.*, also *V.C.H. Cumberland*, ii, 390.   [7]*B. Times*, 26.2.81.

Its shares have risen more in market value than any other line ; its traffic shows one of the largest proportionate increases ".[1] Normally sober trade union reports, too, acknowledged that there had been a recovery.

Nevertheless, labour troubles continued, and it seems that an important section of the Barrow labour force had not received a fair share of the fruits, for the *Barrow Vulcan* of May 10th, 1881, stated editorially that " We are very glad the shipyard directors have conceded a slight rise to the men. 18s. a week is really too little for a poor fellow to exist on, and by the time he has paid for fuel and rent, and then provided his children with bread, there is very little left for him to get nourishment . . . to do his daily toil upon ". This observation referred to the shipbuilding labourers, who soon afterwards made their small contribution to trade union history by forming a branch of the National Amalgamated Union of Labour,[2] a pioneering organisation of the unskilled.

It is very noticeable that strike activity and union branch formation, in local history as elsewhere, appeared usually in the upswing of a boom ; the more tightly organised unions of the highly skilled would be the first to react when profits were high and the demand for labour keen, and other unions followed. Information was disseminated through the now active and regularly meeting Barrow Trades Council, at which the A.S.E., Steam Engine Makers, Iron Moulders, Iron Dressers, Painters, Printers, Tailors, Coach Builders, Cabinet Makers and General Union of Joiners were represented.[3] The generality of member organisations were still the highly skilled or specialised unions ; their total membership, as represented at the 1883 Nottingham T.U.C., was in the region of 600[4], a figure which was outstripped by a newly formed branch of the unskilled. These small and select groups, like the Pattern-makers (whose Barrow branch was formed in 1875) were often able to wrest advantages from boom conditions, and the latter (1880) were receiving an average wage of 33s., at least 2s. higher than was usual in that trade, while in 1882 the Barrow members won a further 1s. 6d.[5] But gains of this kind were often only temporary, and the unorganised and unskilled tailed far behind, sometimes offering support to their skilled brothers during strikes, but receiving or winning little in the way of a durable advance. Commodity prices were tending to fall in this period (often very substantially) and there was consequent improvement in real wages for those who

---

[1]Quoted *B. Times, loc. cit.* [2]*B. Her.*, 4.6, 27.8.1881. This union had been formed as the result of a strike, and soon had 630 members locally. [3]For refs. to Trades Council, *vide* (e.g.) *B. Times*, 20.7, 10.8.1878, 12.9, 12.10, 16.11.78. [4]List of represented trades councils in *Nottingham Jnl.*, 11.9.1883. N. Gorrie was the Barrow delegate. [5]Mosses, W., *Hist. of the United Patternmakers* (1922), and infn. courtesy Mr. W. Beard.

managed to hold their money earnings at the same level. It is of course very hard to say whether the position of local workpeople was greatly ameliorated in the period ; there was short-time working and unemployment to drain away savings, and rents in Barrow itself remained high, while the skilled workers, the labour " aristocrats " who feature so largely in these pages, were of course in a minority. Perhaps, as improvements in local government and social services made themselves felt (although there was still occasional need for soup kitchens), and as a few new social amenities appeared, existence had a little more to offer to the generality of folk. Discontent, without which there can be no human amelioration, was there in plenty, but it would be totally wrong to imagine there were no real advances.

Yet it remained a period of anti-climax ; not only because of Ramsden's (and Barrow's) failure to eclipse Dundee and Glasgow as well as Sheffield and Liverpool—or, more accurately, to make Barrow into a combination of all these—but because even those industries truly basic in the local economy began to show signs of strain, and because the population growth of the district fell away seriously. The latter phenomenon is dealt with more fully below. [1] The basic industries, ore-mining, iron and steel, continued to make resounding progress in productive terms. In 1870, some 872,000 tons of ore had been raised in North Lancashire, of which rather less than three-quarters had gone into local furnaces. By 1881 the total tonnage of ore raised was comfortably past the million mark, although it was rather lower than the 1880 figure (1,266,000 tons) or that of 1882, (1,408,000 tons). In 1881 a good seven-eighths of the total ore output was going into local furnaces, a measure of considerably increasing pig and steel production, and even in 1885, a year of comparatively poor trade, the Furness pig-iron output (from the furnaces at Barrow, Ulverston, Askam and Carnforth) was in the region of 550,000 tons, or about one-half of the tonnage of ore extracted in the district. The number of iron ore pits operating in Furness increased from 26 in 1870 to 34 in 1881. [2] Of the latter, about twenty were pits of real consequence.

Although the Barrow Haematite Steel Company had its problems during the mid-'seventies, its profitability remained as durable as ever. Its massive sales of steel products, mainly rails, and equally massive income, flowed like arterial and veinous blood in a strong and vigorous heart ; and it was indeed the heart of the local economy, without which the latter would not easily have lived in the first place, and without which it could not have continued to grow. During the first eleven years of the Haematite Company's existence, its rate of profit averaged 20 per cent. ; the

[1]See p. 407. [2]*Min. Stats. U.K.* ; for some 1885 estimates, Schneider in *Trans. C. & W. Assn. Adv. Lit. & Science* (1884-5), X, p. 107.

highest rate of profit in any one year would seem to have been in 1873, when, on a paid-up capital of £800,000, of which £300,000 was accumulated, the annual profit of the enterprise was £370,000, or 72 per cent. There was a fall in succeeding years—hardly surprisingly—and in 1877, on a paid-up capital of £1,550,000, the year's net profit was a mere £125,000.[1] Between that year and 1879, Edward Wadham was acting as an agent for the Company in Ireland, attempting to obtain orders from Irish railway companies[2] —the directors' eyes were turning restively to any market they could find—and Schneider, normally ebullient and sanguine, was uneasy because Russian firms were heavily in debt for Barrow steel.[3] Exports to the U.S.A. remained considerable.

The increasing use of Spanish haematite by British firms was troubling all the Furness iron enterprises in 1878-9, and the Millom, Askam, Carnforth and North Lonsdale iron companies asked the Furness Railway for a 10 per cent. reduction in tolls, and another reduction in coke and pig rates, in September, 1878. Fortunately the leading F.R. directors were also ironmasters, and a 7½ per cent. reduction was granted in order that they could meet the increasing competition of Spanish ores in Cleveland and South Wales. Late in 1878 the Furness Iron and Steel Company of Askam was in process of liquidation—although it was reconstituted, to remain in production—and it was found that it owed the F.R. more than £13,000 in unpaid tolls.[4]

Meanwhile (1875-8) Sidney Gilchrist Thomas had developed the " basic " process of steel manufacture, which meant that Bessemer steelmakers were no longer dependent on haematites or non-phosphoric ores, or on supplies of " acid " pig ; and on May 20th, 1879, the directors of the Furness Railway recognised that the successful demonstration of the Gilchrist Thomas process implied a serious threat to the local economy.[5] They were right. In the words of Mr. D. L. Burn and *The Economist*, Thomas had " dealt a blow . . . at the supremacy of English haematite steel ",[6] and the latter had made possible the use of minette (phosphoric) pig on the continent of Europe, thereby exposing English steelmakers to the full blast of competition. Yet Furness haematite ore production, in spite of depressions and new inventions, was at its highest in the early and middle 'eighties, and the " depression " was felt more in boardrooms than in terms of productive activity. By 1881 the Haematite Steel Company's dividend was reduced to 5 per cent.—this in a year of comparative prosperity—and it was

[1]A full statement is in (e.g.) *Barrow Vulcan*, 2.10.1877 and in local and national press of approx. date ; other infn. in *Co. file* (Reg. J/S. Cos.), *MS. Diary*, 7.8, 8.8.77. [2]*Wadham Diary*, 8.2, 19.2, 25.4, 16.7.77 ; 15.2, 23.2, 16.6, 14.9.78. [3]*MS. Diary*, 18.5.1878. [4]*Dir. Mins.* (*F.R.*) 24.9.78, 20.5, 30.8.79. [5]*Dir. Mins.* (*F.R.*) for date. [6]*Economic History of Steelmaking*, 77, quoting *Economist*, Supplement, 9.1.1886.

found necessary to appoint a committee of enquiry into the management, consisting of Lowthian Bell, Menelaus and Monkhouse. But even this battery of experts could find little at which to cavil, and J. T. Smith, in company with Bell and Sir Meysey Thompson, was added to the board of directors.[1]

The Haematite Company, which had written off most of its capital in the booming days of 1870-74, was in a much better position than firms which had piled up their liabilities by costs of erection at peak prices.[2]   Yet, although it remained able to sell its wares, and produced about 300,000 tons of pig in the recession year of 1885, it was unable to recompense its shareholders on anything like the scale of previous years.   The 'eighties were unprofitable for owners of " Barrows "—Schneider was given to announcing, before his death in 1887, that he had not had a penny piece out of local industries for several years—and news was made by an announcement in March, 1891, that the Haematite Steel Company had declared a dividend.   The *Financial News* remarked that " For years no profit has been made on its transactions, and interest on the preference shares had fallen into arrears to the very considerable amount of £57,000 ".[3]   This statement is to be regarded with care, and there had certainly been profits in previous years ; but they were not of the type that made possible twenty, or even fifteen per cent. dividends.   The £158,000 profit of 1890 was thought to render feasible a division of two-and-a-half per cent.[4]   Thus was the anti-climax complete : for, during the 'eighties, Furness remained one of the Bessemer steel strongholds of Britain, and produced, as has been implied, more haematite and pig than ever before.   The directors of Barrow industries were not ruined, but they were disillusioned men, and even if the Great Depression is a myth, a mere plaything or paradox for professional economic historians, it stalks through the Duke of Devonshire's diary.

Throughout the 'eighties the latter bore the heaviest responsibilities, and had by far the heaviest investments, of any of the Barrow capitalists.[5]   He had made vast sums of money when the district seemed to prosper, and could not very well withdraw from his commitments when it seemed to be stricken by depression.   As need hardly be said, the moral challenge which was offered by Barrow's plight was readily and characteristically faced by Devonshire, although it is also certain that he would have been much happier had the Midland Railway offered to purchase the Furness railway system and docks, just as he was greatly relieved when the Barrow shipyard was brought under the control of an outside group in 1888.   There are, of course, several ways of regarding his

[1]*MS. Diary*, 23.3, 28.6, 20.7, 18.12.1881.   [2]I am grateful to Dr. Pollard for drawing my attention to this point.   [3]*B. Her.*, 21.3.1891.   [4]*Ibid.* [5]Pollard, *passim.*

experiences and fortunes ; because wealth in itself meant very little to him personally, and because he was at heart a recluse and a hater of public activity, he was also an intelligent amateur in business matters—and for an amateur he had done extremely well. In purely business terms he undoubtedly gained far more than he lost, even though large sums of money appeared on both sides of the account books ; in other words, the Shipyard and the Jute Works cost him dear, but it must also be remembered that according to Schneider's calculation, the Park Mine alone produced ores on which £80,000 an acre was paid in royalties to the Duke in the period 1851-85.[1] Such windfall gains were the result of good fortune rather than calculation, and—when full allowance is made for his clarity of thought and intellectual grasp—many more gifted, passionate and persistent investors and industrialists emerged from their adventures, even when conducted on the Barrow scale, with far less.

Yet he was not personally a lucky man, and certainly he was not a happy one. The death of his wife had haunted him for twenty years, although as the anniversaries passed, time softened the recurrent unhappiness ; his accession to the Dukedom brought new worries and responsibilities, and it was his desire to acquit himself well in his station, and to put the Cavendish estates on a sound foundation for his family, that led to his vast and seemingly risky industrial enterprises. The latter led in turn to worry and disillusionment. A shattering blow came with the assassination of his son Lord Frederick Cavendish in Phoenix Park, Dublin, in May, 1882 ; the son had shared his father's interests and attitudes, and had more of his moral fibre and intellect than the older Marquess of Hartington. Grim and tired, and pushed into the arms of Unionism by the assassination, the Duke went on to outlive his third son, Lord Edward Cavendish.

This is not so much local history, as history in which local people shared. The death of Lord Frederick, who was held in very real esteem, stirred the town of Barrow. It will in no way minimise the tragedy of the Duke's life if we recall that a justification for the study of local history is that it brings us nearer to the humble workman. We shall not forget that the latter esteemed the Duke and Lord Federick because they appeared to show, from time to time, some interest in him ; and that this interest, in turn, was an expression of their sense of responsibility for the town and its troubles. We shall also face the fact that they could do very little about these troubles, except make philanthropic gestures, and that those men who toiled in the heat and danger of the steelworks were

[1]Schneider, *op. cit.*, 107-8. It may be relevant to add that Devonshire's will, dated July 29th, 1891, provided for an estate of £1,790,871 ; Gibbs, *The Complete Peerage*, 350.

labouring on a corner of the Cavendish estates with far less consideration and security than farming tenants enjoyed on the lands which could truly be called by this title. In other words, we shall not forget the twenty-three persons a year who were killed in local industrial accidents in the late 'eighties ; nor the men who developed pneumonia and bronchitis from the working conditions in the steelworks ;[1] and neither need we forget Thomas Turner, who was one of many hundreds of local unemployed in 1878, and who had been out of work for 39 weeks. During this time he had had a death in the family, and his wife had been confined. The Duke was not able to help him, but his union (the A.S.E.) did.[2] This, too, was one of the usually invisible particles of human tragedy which help to make history, and, in the end, to determine historical attitudes.

Nevertheless, the Duke's decisions helped to map out the short-term course of events in given cases. He was not responsible for booms and depressions, but he provided the Jute Company with capital and enabled it to go on working at a loss ; and it is now clear that his investments in the Barrow Shipbuilding Company had the same effect. The entry in his diary dated March 13th, 1877, is indicative : " It will clearly be necessary for me to find a great deal of money to prevent a smash." Not only did the duke find a great deal of money ; he was the major, and almost the sole, shareholder of consequence (in both the Jute and Shipbuilding companies) within a few years. But although the shipyard executed a fair building programme between 1877 and 1886—1881 and 1882 were the best years in that period—tonnages generally tended to tail off up to 1887. Between 1884 and that year the A.S.E. secretaries' reports to headquarters, giving their warning signals to the tramping artisan, began to describe local trade as " Bad " once more. In 1886 the ominous word " Discharging " appears, and Devonshire's resigned diary entry puts the point of view of the general in the field : " . . . unless matters improve shortly, a catastrophe cannot long be averted ".[3] Some of the Barrow difficulties, however, arose from the Shipbuilding Company's semi-concentration on the building of merchant vessels, a risky and unpredictable trade ; and although Devonshire himself, ageing and worn, was perhaps not fully aware of the future course of events, that course was clearly marked out in ensuing months.[4] An approach was made to the submarine designer Nordenfelt and to Bryce Douglas, who were to exert, respectively, their skill and influence in forming a powerful company to build men-of-war and submarines and in

[1]Medical Officer's report, *B. Her.*, 25.5.89.   [2]*A.S.E., Abstract Rept. of the Council's Proceedings*, 1878-9, p. 69. Devonshire was of course fully aware of the distress in the district ; *MS. Diary, passim.*
    [3]*MS. Diary*, 26.7.1886.   [4]*MS. Diary*, 12.11.86, 18.1, 20.7, 10.8, 5.11.87, 23.2.88 ; *MS. Letter to the Marquess of Hartington*, 30.1.87.

attracting new orders for such engines of destruction. The competitive battle between nations, paradoxically enough, was expressed not only in statistics of coal, iron and steel produced ; it was beginning to find its expression in the gunboat, and that which threatened to kill Furness industry gave forth ultimately the means of its further existence. Barrow was to labour in filling the armoury of the late Victorian imperialist.

Thorsten Nordenfelt was the outstanding European submarine designer of his period. He was not strictly original—he had borrowed from the designs of a Liverpool curate—but his underwater craft were good enough to find markets in several European countries, and had been tried out with success at Stockholm, Constantinople and Southampton in 1886-7. Nordenfelt's boats contained one serious weakness in design ; they had to be forced under the surface by vertical propellors.[1] Nevertheless, at least two individuals closely associated with the Admiralty became interested in the projected Barrow company, including Admiral Henry Boys, a former Director of Naval Ordnance. Two of the Nordenfelt submarines were built at Barrow before the incorporation of the Naval Construction and Armaments Company, in February 1888, with the Marquess of Hartington as chairman, and a board which included Lord Brassey and Bryce Douglas. Hartington, who was now taking over more of his father's Barrow responsibilities, was of course a powerful attraction to would-be investors, and the new body was constituted to allot 120,000 shares of £5 each. They were subscribed for vigorously. The freehold property of the Barrow Shipbuilding Company, valued at £320,000 was taken over with stores and stocks worth £65,000, and the company also had the aim of opening a branch establishment at Bilbao, whence quantities of non-phosphoric iron ore now came to Britain, and where ships were now to be built for the Spanish government.[2] Messrs. Joseph Whitworth and Company were to supply large guns and carriages, and the Nordenfelt Guns and Ammunition Company was to provide quick-firing guns and ammunition.

The formation of the N.C. & A.C. did not pass entirely without repercussions ; within a few days of the advertisement of the sale of shares, a sharply-worded letter (signed " An Englishman ") appeared in the London *Times* expressing astonishment at some of the names that were listed on the company prospectus. " Can anything be more anomalous," it demanded, " than that our ex-

---

[1]In matters of design, Nordenfelt was surpassed by the American designer John P. Holland, who built the first of several submarines in 1875. Here the American-biassed and misnamed *Encyclopaedia Britannica*, Vol. 21, 492, seems to be on safe ground. See also the better account in *Chambers's Encyclopaedia*, XIII, 244, and Kemp, P. K., *H.M. Submarines*, esp. 29. [2]Details of company formation in London *Times*, 21.2.88 (p. 13), and *B. Her.*, 25.2.88.

Ministers and officials should, for the sake of lucre, be building ships of war for Spain, perhaps to be used to turn us out of Gibraltar, if they can ? It almost passes belief."[1] It is an irony that after a gun-bristling prospectus and allegations of defective patriotism, the new company at first concentrated largely on the building of passenger steamers ; Bryce Douglas quickly secured several contracts from the Pacific Steam Navigation Company and Messrs. Elder, Dempster and Company of Liverpool, and the quickly modernised and extended Barrow yard also built three large " Empress " steamers (of India, of China, and of Japan) for the Canadian Pacific.[2] Nevertheless, a contract for three cruisers in 1889 was the first considerable Admiralty order, and the N.C. & A.C. also built H.M.S. Powerful, the largest cruiser in the world, a year or two later. During the nine years of the company's existence, and until the completion of the First World War, Barrow's fortunes followed the course dictated by international naval rivalries ; and those fortunes were reflected in a more or less steadily increasing output of naval craft and in diminishing yard-space devoted to merchant vessels.

The Daily Telegraph had suggested that the N.C. & A.C. might be " the salvation of Barrow ",[3] and other persons in the locality hoped as much. Salvation, of course, can take manifold forms ; 1889 was a year of comparatively good trade and brought numerous wage advances, as well as bickering between the A.S.E. and A.S.C. & J. over matters of demarcation in the shipyard.[4] By 1892 trade was again " Bad " for the local engineers, and it remained so throughout the ensuing year.[5] There should be no misunderstanding of what was connoted here ; a bad year was still terrifying in the way it sought out the weak and defenceless. According to the local press there was actual starvation in the April of 1892, and a meeting at the Town Hall led to the opening of a relief fund and the establishment of soup kitchens during the early spring. Depression in the Shipyard coincided with striking and unemployment at the Steelworks.[6] The situation improved little in the next eighteen months, even for the craftsmen ; highly skilled trade unionists complained of attempted wage reductions and short time.[7]

In 1894, however, it was reported that a good building programme was occupying the shipyard workers of the area, that the N.C. & A.C. was a " fair shop ", but that in many departments of that firm " the proportion of boys to men (was) beyond all reason

[1]London Times, 24.2.88 (p. 13).   [2]Cf. Obituary of Bryce Douglas, B. Her., 7.4.91.   [3]D. Telegraph, 21.2.88.   The Naval Defence Act of 1889 naturally made a difference to the Barrow shipbuilding programme.   [4]A.S.E. Repts., passim. But 1890 saw strikes in the shipyard, by shipjoiners, plumbers and engineers. See Report of Strikes and Lockouts, B.P.P., LXXVIII (1891), Appx. I. [5]A.S.E. Repts. [6]B. Her., 2.4, 12.4, 16.4, 19.4, 23.4, 26.4.92 ; see also B. Her., 10.2.94, regarding the organisation for providing free meals for children. [7]A.S.E. Repts.

. . . the desire of employers to crowd their shops with boys is not apparently tempered by the least consideration of what is to be the future of their apprentices ". Nevertheless, the A.S.E. Divisional Organiser looked forward to " substantial improvement in conditions and wages " in the Furness district. By the middle of 1894 the A.S.E. had succeeded in making the Barrow Shipyard " a society shop ". But there were still unemployed engineers in the locality, and there was a vigorous campaign on the part of the union against the use of unskilled men on machines.[1] ·The atmosphere of this phase was expressed in fights over dilution and demarcation, which originated less in the wrong-headedness of the workmen than in the increasing technological complexity of engineering and shipbuilding.[2] Side by side with the craft-consciousness of the fitter, the boilermaker and the shipwright was growing an interest in working-class politics, expressed in frequent allusions to the formation of " a party of labour " and at meetings of the Barrow Fabian Society and Independent Labour Party.[3] Local trade unionism made its greatest strides in these years, in both magnitude and extent of support. In 1896 the Barrow Trades Council had 2,873 subscribing members belonging to 21 affiliated societies,[4] as compared with about 600 members in 1883, while the main unions had branches at Ulverston, Dalton and Askam. The iron ore miners now had their union (the Dalton and District United Workmen's Association) with branches at Dalton, Askam, Ulverston, Roose, Hawcoat, Kirkby, Gleaston, Marton, Stainton, Urswick and Newton.[5] Perhaps one-quarter of the workpeople (male) of Barrow and District were now in unions ; certainly most of the skilled men, and a small but growing proportion of the unskilled. On the part of the latter, the Gasworkers' and General Labourers' Union had a Barrow branch by March, 1894.

Of wages and hours ; the house carpenters, who had been fighting for their 26s. a week in the mid-'sixties, were getting locally between 32s. and 33s. in 1889-90. This rise is a representative one, but it can mislead nevertheless, and the greater part of it took place in the early 'seventies. Hence the Barrow pattern-makers were receiving 33s. in 1880, 32s. in 1887, and 36s. in 1889. Iron ore miners, who sometimes in the mid-'sixties earned 27s. a week if they worked for H. W. Schneider, were receiving an average of 23s. 7d. in 1885. By contrast, a number of the skilled grades exhibit quite princely sums in 1889-90 ; shipwrights 36s., cabinet-

---

[1]*Ibid.* (Divisional and Executive Council repts.) ; the general trends are also exemplified by the reports of the Associated Shipwrights, and Boilermakers.   [2]See in this connection Jefferys, J., *The Story of the Engineers.* [3]Barrow press, *passim*, and Mowat, J., and Power, A., *Fifty Years . . . of the Labour Party in Barrow* (1949). The local I.L.P. was founded on October 16th 1892, at one of Keir Hardie's meetings.   [4]*Annual Reports* of the Barrow Trades Council.   [5]*Prospectus* of the Association, *cit.*

makers up to 35s., engineers (early 1891) 33s. to 36s., and iron-founders 34s. Each of these wage rates relates specifically to Barrow-in-Furness. Iron ore miners' labourers and general labourers, a large section of the working force, were the men who (in 1889-90) were still expected to bring up a family on 21s. a week, and it is not surprising that these workers and their wives saved little for days of unemployment.[1] John Myers, the secretary of the Furness ore miners' union, wrote of the days off work in winter when there was flooding or freezing in the mines.[2] Pauperism in the locality was never of great magnitude, as the figures for industrial districts went at this period, and was sometimes little more than one per cent. of population ; but the pauperism returns[3] bear no direct relation to unemployment, and were also affected by the readiness with which workless men migrated from the district. It was stated, for instance, that in the mid-September of 1891, about 4000 men were discharged from the works of the neighbourhood.[4] These were both skilled and unskilled men, the former going " on dona-tion " in their unions or moving from the area ; but such breaks in employment must be taken into account when wage-levels are examined.

Working hours likewise were apt to vary, and there was resist-ance to overtime by the shipyard engineers (1892), who obtained an agreement restricting it to eleven hours a week.[5] But since the typical working week in most local trades was 54 hours[6] (1890— a period mostly unaltered since 1872), it is obvious enough that some Barrow craftsmen were taking over 60 at busy times and were out of work at very bad ones. Averages do not, of course, show the physical and nervous strains accompanying fluctuations of this kind. An attempt to impose extended overtime on the part of the N.C. & A.C. was sharply resisted by the A.S.E. and Steam Engine Makers in 1896.[7]

We must continue to take rents in account in any estimate of possible improvement of living standards. It may be signifi-cant that Pete Curran, Barrow's first socialist parliamentary candidate (1895) isolated two special objects of assault ; royalty payments, and high rents. He felt " bound to say that rents in Barrow, compared with such industrial centres as Bradford, Leeds, Birmingham, Liverpool and Manchester . . . were . . . 2s. to

---

[1] *Rept. on Strikes & Lockouts, cit.*, Appx. VI ; Mosses, *Hist. of the Pattern-makers, passim,* and infn. from the Society by courtesy of Mr. W. Beard ; *Return of Wage Rates in Mines and Quarries* (1891), B.P.P., LXXVIII. [2] *Prospectus, cit.* The statement is correct in its implications. See *B. Her.,* 5.1.97, for instance, where several hundred Furness miners are out of work owing to flooding. [3] In local press. [4] *B. Her.,* 12.9.91 (a computation representing about one-third of the Barrow labour force). [5] *A.S.E. Repts.* [6] *Rept. on Strikes & Lockouts, cit.* [7] *A.S.E. Repts.*

2s. 6d. higher . . ."[1] The facts need further examination, but the choice of ground may be noted. There had been new building in the locality in the 'eighties, and the character of the accommodation must be dealt with in a further chapter. The ebb and flow of workpeople caused occasional overcrowding still ; a district delegate of the Shipwrights reported in 1899 that " So many workmen are at present employed at Barrow that the town cannot accommodate them with lodgings, and . . . they are fitting up an old ship to lodge them on board ".[2]

By then a new industrial organisation, Messrs. Vickers, had taken over the Barrow shipyard (1896-7). The history of this firm is in other hands, and it is as well that the narrative should conclude—as regards Barrow industries at least—in those years. The period of anti-climax was already over, and a new phase in the story was beginning.

The full story of anti-climax, however, is not yet complete. The group of men who had assisted at the birth of Barrow, and who had ruled it in its eventful early days—they have been well called a syndicate—had ceased to exert any direct influence by 1888. By the mid-'eighties these men—Schneider, Devonshire, Ramsden, John Fell and J. T. Smith—had grounds for knowing that their efforts to put Barrow at the centre of a web of world trade had met with conspicuous failure. The ultimate failure was compounded of numerous smaller ones, and some aspects of the latter have already been described. The disastrous story of the Jute Works was punctuated by two destructive fires, one occurring in 1879 and the other in 1892. The venture was, of course, foundering before the first of these dates, unable to compete with the established Dundee trade ; but there were attempts to re-start it, associated with Thomas Briggs and others, and one of these was in progress in 1897.[3] The difficulty was not simply one of geographical position or natural advantages—this fact, at the present day, cannot be too strongly emphasized—but arose from the incidental problems of competition with an already established industry and from the inability of the rulers of Barrow to find suitable managers, added to the unfortunate timing of their experiments—the beginning of a serious depression is not the best of times to develop new industrial enterprises. The Barrow Shipbuilding Company faced much the same problems ; while a lesser enterprise of the local syndicate, the Barrow Steam Corn Mill Company, was wound up in 1880, being

[1]*Barrow News* and *B. Her.*, 9.3.95.   [2]*Reports* of the *Associated Society of Shipwrights.*   [3]See (e.g.) *B. Her.*, 1.6.97, when Lancaster investors acquired the property.

afterwards taken over by Messrs. Walmsley and Smith. This venture, too, had suffered from management difficulties. There was in fact no reason whatever why lighter industries should not have prospered in the long run ; corn and flour continued to be handled and processed at Barrow, the steady importation of timber led to the establishment of a local paper pulp industry in 1889—a consequence of the cheap popular press—and there was an increasing amount of space devoted to petroleum storage.

All these gains, however, were obtained at the price of vast and largely empty docks. There was no great mystery here ; goods passing in and out of England were consigned by the shortest route, and too often the latter pointed in the direction of Liverpool, which was more conveniently sited for the industrial districts of Lancashire and the West Riding. Likewise Barrow was 264 miles from London by rail, as compared with Liverpool's 201 miles. On the other hand, Barrow was nearer to Belfast than Liverpool, and was well situated for the Irish trade, although its shipping remained affected by the tide ; this inevitably affected the co-ordination of rail and steamer services.[1] This, however, is only a temporary judgment of history, and of a given social order. Barrow docks may not have been used to the full, but they are not useless to a Britain which still depends on ships for its life.[2]

Sir James Ramsden was never to live to see them filled with vessels. Having involved the Furness Railway Company in vast dock investments which grew yearly, he could do little other than defend his actions to the best of his ability. In 1882, after three years of considerably increased traffic, he was able to answer a questioning F.R. shareholder's importunity on the subject of dock expenditure by pointing out that these installations were responsible for the favourable traffic enjoyed by the railway system as a whole; in 1889, however, when the company dividend was down to $3\frac{1}{2}$ per cent., and when £2,149,000 had been spent on the docks, he could only hedge at a similar question.[3] No doubt the share-

---

[1] *Proc. Inst. C. E.*, CLIV, Suppt., 1903, pp. 131-8, for some technical and statistical details of north-western ports.   [2] Certainly not for goods which require storage, like petroleum, oil, timber, grain, hides or fibrous materials.   [3] *B. Times*, 19.8.82, 31.8.89 (half-yearly meeting reports). In the second case Mr. Hamilton of Manchester wanted to know why separate dock accounts were not made available. Sir James replied " that the accounts of the company did not admit of that being given ". The dock traffic of the period, according to *B.P.P.*, *Trade and Navigation of the U.K.*, was (Barrow only) :

	£ Value Exports	£ Value Imports		£ Value Exports	£ Value Imports
1877	531,164	447,501	1882	1,502,155	635,994
1878	617,035	445,932	1883	878,540	532,207
1879	869,853	476,743	1884	465,080	351,429
1880	1,201,021	790,916	1885	439,683	380,629
1881	1,173,716	678,212	1886	612,313	368,718
			1887	608,968	388,967

holders felt within their rights in harrying the weary father-figure of the F.R., but they did not feel his keen disappointment. They were merely prevented from receiving the money which they thought was their due ; he was seeing the fading of a dream.[1] Nevertheless, he retained his faith in the future of Barrow docks to the last, and handed on something of the same optimism to Alfred Aslett, who became Secretary and General Manager of the F.R. in August, 1895.

By the time Aslett took his post, however, the policy of the Furness Railway Company was due for a transformation. It remained substantially a ducally-orientated enterprise, the Marquess of Hartington having succeeded his father in the chairmanship in 1887. After the death of the Duke of Buccleuch in 1884, Edward Wadham became a director and thereby ensured a representation of Buccleuch interests on the board.[2] The entire period from 1883 to 1895 was one of wretchedly low dividends—by the previous standards of the F.R. if not by those of other companies— and as long as James Ramsden was able to exert an influence on a board which was still largely composed of amateurs, Hartington and his colleagues turned their eyes expectantly towards Barrow traffic and industries. Passenger facilities had not altered or improved greatly since the early 'seventies, when the F.R. had become the subject of sarcastic comment ; and in March, 1881, when a Cambridge lecturer in political economy was giving an extension lecture in the town (thereby helping to lay the foundation of the modern adult education movement), he had only to remark meaningly that " When a railway keeps the monopoly of a district, you see the manner in which the district is served ", to call forth laughter and applause.[3] The early 'seventies had seen an increase in passenger traffic which was itself a consequence of growing population ; but since the population of Barrow and district grew but slowly after 1875, there seemed little hope of more satisfactory receipts from that quarter.

In 1891, however, there was an " increase in passenger traffic on branch lines of the company ".[4] As though to compensate very slightly for the loss of the easy profits of a generation before, that now solidly established institution, the annual family holiday, promised to rescue the F.R. shareholders and directors from their plight. No longer were the Lakeland dales a preserve of the leisured or the comfortably-placed sections of society, to be visited by proletarian excursionists only on Bank Holidays ; ever wider

---

[1]Mr. Gradon, in a competent account of the F.R. in this period, also deals with the baiting of Ramsden ; *Hist. of the F.R.*, cit., 41, 42. [2]*Div. Mins.* (*F.R.*), 13.5.84, 18.6.84. [3]*B. Times*, 5.3.81. [4]Pettigrew, W. F., *Proc. Inst. Mech. Eng.* (1901), iii, 734. This informative article deals with the rolling stock of the F.R.

sections of the British public were beginning to find the value of walking shoes, bicycles and climbing tackle, and those who were tied by family commitments could still pay decorous visits to Windermere or Ambleside. As has been made clear throughout the story of the Furness Railway, the directors had long had an eye to the attraction of tourists, but they had been diverted by much greater aims for a period almost equally long ; now, under Alfred Aslett's competent rule, the company concentrated fully upon tourist traffic for the first time in its history. The process of concentration took a little time, and did not really belong to the last years of James Ramsden's lifetime. In 1895, a year before that remarkable man passed away, there were further strikes and unemployment in Barrow, and the town and railway were both in an unusually depressed state ; and the directors,[1] weary of years of sustained stagnation, decided on the new policy.

Within three years, Aslett and his men had achieved a twelve per cent increase in passenger traffic, had " completely revolutionised " the F.R.'s carriage stock, and had decided to lay heavier rails and obtain more powerful engines.[2] They had arranged no fewer than twenty separate Lakeland tours for visitors, who might vary their journey by use of the company's Windermere steam yachts, and even the Carnforth-Barrow service, for years regarded as the worst part of any journey to or from the rest of England, was allocated 10 passenger trains daily in winter and 15 in summer. In its overtures to the tourist, the F.R. started with several advantages, one of which was to be found in its " exceedingly well built " stations. The latter, as Aslett reminded the readers of the *Railway Magazine*, dated from a time when the F.R. " paid a very handsome dividend " ; and in making this observation he was in fact commenting on an important phase in social history and railway architecture alike. Other advantages—a new General Manager and a superb Lakeland background—need no further comment. Aslett's reign of 18 years brought no fortunes to F.R. shareholders, but did bring an increase of passenger traffic of more than 100 per cent. During this final stage of its history the Furness Railway ceased to be a mineral line which carried passengers almost on sufferance, and became instead one of the most valuable amenities of the southern Lake District.

By the mid-'eighties the Furness haematite-mining industry was passing its period of maximum output. Soon the latter would decline rapidly. Intensive exploitation had carried total annual tonnages for the district within a comparatively small distance of the normally greater Cumberland production figures in 1880-4.

---

[1]In addition to Hartington and Wadham, the directors were Lord Muncaster, Victor C. W. Cavendish, W. B. Turner and James Little. [2]Aslett in *Railway Magazine*, Aug. 1898, 121 and sqq.

The late 'eighties saw a slight fall of output in both fields ; thereafter Cumberland held its annual averages above the million-ton level while the Furness figures plunged rapidly downwards. [1]

A number of local reports of the early and middle 'eighties [2] show that the dangers facing the non-phosphoric ore market were fully appreciated ; " the value of the ore (would decline) owing to constant improvements which are going on in Steam Navigation, cheapening the cost of similar ore delivered from Foreign countries " [3]. The use of the Gilchrist-Thomas process, it was reported to the Barrow Haematite Steel Co. in 1883, meant that East Coast iron was used in steelmaking, while in the following year J. T. Smith drew attention to the cheapness and quantity of the ore shipped from Bilbao to South Wales and Middlesbrough. [4] In 1890 Edward Wadham estimated that four million tons of Spanish haematite were imported annually into the country. [5]

Wadham, however, pointed out that the competition of the Spanish ores was a less important factor than the " exhaustion of (Furness) mines and extra pumping due to deeper working ". [6] The local mines were in fact being rapidly worked out, and as this authority stated, many had had to be abandoned because of the poor quality of the ores which remained. [7] In spite of more scientific and judicious working of the larger mines, [8] the average annual production per man fell from 258 tons in 1895-9 to 212 tons in 1905-9, while the number of men employed in local iron mining declined more sharply. Nevertheless, nearly 3000 men were employed in Furness pits in the late 'nineties, and their wages at the commencement of that decade were given by Wadham as 4s. to 5s. 2d. a day, although, as he said, the wages still varied " at every mine ".

By 1900-4 the Furness output (averaging 474,845 tons) was only about one-third of that for the mid-'eighties—a shrinkage indeed. Nature's riches had been seized all too quickly. Throughout the world, steel railway lines glistened ; in Furness, a disfigured countryside and abandoned tramroads and buildings were soon to be all that remained.

---

[1]Cf. the useful table in Jewkes, J., and Winterbottom, A., *An Industrial Survey of Cumberland and Furness* (1933), 107. [2]*Reports of Barrow Haematite Steel Co. re Royalty Reduction* (ctsy. Boughton Estates Ltd.). [3]*Report* of 20.11.83.
[4]*MS. letter to E. Wadham*, 21.1.84. [5]In evidence before *R. Comm. Min. Royalties*, 1890-3, 2nd Report, Q. 13527. [6]*R. Comm., cit.*, Q. 13430. [7]Q. 13499. For the general background to the haematite trade at this time, *vide* Flinn, M. W., *Ec. H.R.*, Vol. VIII, No. 1, 1955, pp. 85-7, 89. [8]For techniques, *Trans. Inst. Mech. Eng.*, 1880, 365 sqq.

CHAPTER XIX

TOWN AND COUNTRY, 1870-1900 ;
WITH AN EPILOGUE

The period 1875-1911 was one of steady migration out of the Furness area. This movement was less an anti-climax than a return to normal, if we make the qualification that the numbers of emigrants far exceeded those for any previous period, whether in terms of absolute totals or percentages of total population. The population of Barrow continued to grow, from 47,429 in 1881 to 57,712 in 1891, but was enabled to do so only by virtue of a high rate of natural increase. The presence of large numbers of young artisans and their wives ensured a high birth-rate (even though this rate could be depressed during periods of peak emigration[1]), and the predominantly youthful populace had far more use for cribs than for coffins. In 1879, a depression year locally, Barrow's birth-rate per 1000 souls living was 41.8 (as compared with a 35.6 average rate for 50 towns), and the death-rate was 18.8 (as compared with an average 21.3 for 50 towns). [2]

There can be little doubt that Barrow's superior sewerage system was beginning to have some effect by that date, although it would be unwise to give much weight to this effect before the mid-'eighties. Barrow's death-rates for seven zymotic diseases (1876-9) were little different from those for 14 other Lancashire urban districts, [3] while the same local rate for the year 1879 was decidedly above the national urban average[4] in spite of the low general death-rate in Barrow itself. Likewise the death-rate of children under one year per 1000 births was slightly above the average for fifty towns in 1879. [5] The general Barrow death-rate remained a little in excess of 18 during the late 'seventies, reached 19.2 in 1880, but remained below that figure during the following decade. In 1888 it sank to the lowest level since the incorporation of the borough, and was a mere 14.18 per 1000 persons living, chiefly by virtue of a decline in infant mortality. The Medical Officer of Health blamed the ignorance of mothers for the many infant deaths[6], and no doubt it was his job, as a participant in the process of public education, to be censorious ; but the historian, looking back over more than half a century, may justifiably conclude that if ignorance in matters of hygiene had been responsible for the slaughter of the innocents, then defects in the educational system were responsible for the ignorance. Once these defects were overcome, Barrow—with the rest of urban Britain—went a long way towards achieving a death-rate consonant with twentieth-century

---

[1]M. o. H. rept. in *B. Her.*, 25.5.89.   [2]*42nd Annual Report of the Registrar-General*, cxiv.   [3]*Op. cit.*, cxiii.   [4]*Op. cit.*, cxiv.   [5]*Ibid.*   [6]*B. Her.*, 25.5.89.

standards. Medical practitioners, it is true, were learning more effective techniques in preventive medicine, but their work was one very important aspect of the general enlightenment. We may judge the latter in terms of fewer children " overlain " or dosed with laudanum, and in terms of more intelligent choice of diet for the very young. There is little proof that sound drainage and sewerage techniques led to any sudden drop in the death-rate, but, of course, they enabled town authorities to keep the latter at a humane level.

Certainly the Barrow Town Council was not inactive during the late 'seventies and 'eighties. The 1875 Barrow Corporation Bill provided for a great accession of borrowing power to the Corporation, amounting to more than £543,000, or an increase of some £270,000. The Act itself (38 & 39 *Vict.*, *c. CCIV*) carried powers to regulate materials and workmanship in buildings, and laid down that 150 square feet of open space must be attached to any dwelling house " free from any erection ", provided that every room of 125 square feet should have at least one window, and made the situating of a sleeping room over a midden or cesspool a punishable offence. There was no direct reference to overcrowding *in rooms*, and the Act observed vapidly that " No cesspool shall be allowed except when unavoidable ".[1] Nevertheless, the successive Barrow acts gave its Corporation a formidable armoury of powers ranging from summary jurisdiction and police organisation to evacuation of uninhabitable dwellings and the inspection and destruction of food, and they were thoroughly in accordance with the spirit of Cross and Joseph Chamberlain. The 1875 Act, too, gave the town a much more democratic constitution, and from that year onwards its citizens could really hope to run their own affairs.

The element of planning, which had governed the placing of streets and houses from the earliest days of the town, and to the furtherance of which the leading industrialists and councillors were committed, received what was perhaps an unconscious testimony from Edward Wadham, the Conservative Barrow alderman, in 1875 : " Our experience . . . has been, that we have no difficulty whatever in making sanitary arrangements in the new part of the town, but where the town has got huddled together, we have difficulties in carrying out such arrangements as are satisfactory to the sanitary authority ".[2] Perhaps " difficulties " of the kind Wadham had in mind explained the faulty drainage in Hindpool in 1889, the polluted sewers which could still annoy the Medical Officer of Health in that year, and a general dilatoriness in enforcing local bye-laws ; the fact remains that progress was made, and that Barrow spent £67,840 on its main drainage between 1867 and 1889.

---

[1]Text of the *Barrow Corporation Act of* 1875, secns. 57-61, 64-5, 69-71, 79, 82. [2]*Select Committee on Private Bills* (*Barrow Corporation Bill*), H. of Commons, *July* 22nd, 1875, Q. 190.

This was still less than was spent on the new Town Hall, Police Courts and Markets in the same period (£94,150), and of course less than was spent on the much-prized Gas and Water Departments (£282,517). Some £48,977 were spent on new streets and general improvements, the foregoing items making up the greater part of the Corporation's total expenditure (£625,056) in the course of 21 years.[1] The expenditure per head of population during this period amounted to roughly 15s. *per annum*, a figure which shows how cheaply a new industrial town could be rendered habitable, and which at the same time indicates the distance still to be travelled towards the large-scale welfare services of mid-twentieth-century local government. The quality of life—or the quality of mercy—cannot be satisfactorily analysed in purely economic terms, although its analysis cannot be attempted historically without a foundation of measurable data ; and it may or may not be fair to suggest that Victorian concern for social welfare can be gauged by comparing the total expenditure on all town services and improvements with the sums of money spent on, or made from, the industries of the locality. Four or five years' profits at the Steelworks would have met the entire cost of 21 years' local government activity in Barrow (excluding, of course, the work of the School Board and the Guardians) ; the Furness Railway Company spent on its docks more than three times the sum expended on civilised arrangements by the town's fathers in those same years ; and there is no possible doubt that in purely monetary terms the cost of running this large community was almost negligible if we take into account the receipts of all the local industrial undertakings. After all, it was a question of the health and welfare of the men and women who worked in them.

The time of men like Ramsden, John Fell, Wadham and Schneider, however, was still money ; and they gave liberally of that time. Schneider was chairman of the Finance and Estate Committee from the mid-'seventies to the year of his death (1887), and was able to give that Committee the benefit of his considerable financial *expertise* in equalising the payment of interest on loans ; he served as Chairman of the local Guardians to the time of his death ; he was for some time a member of the Barrow School Board and of the similar body at Dalton-in-Furness ; and he contrived to serve as the Chairman of the Bowness-on-Windermere Local Board in addition. John Fell was at various times a prominent member of the Ulverston Board of Guardians, a chairman of the Ulverston Sanitary Authority,[2] and a leading Barrow alderman ; and Edward Wadham played a prominent part in Barrow local government for a generation. Ramsden's manifold

[1]Details in *B. Her.*, 27.7.89.   [2]His comment before the *Select Committee on the* 1875 *Barrow Corporation Bill, cit.*, Ques. 223, is revealing ; " Yes, I was chairman (of the Ulverston Rural Authority) until last year when I was obliged to give it up as I had so **many** engagements that I could not retain it "

offices and points of influence have already been described. Each of these men gave many thousands of hours to the ordering and governance of their town and district, and it is perhaps platitudinous and irrelevant to add that they were in no way obliged to do so, and rather more to the point to remind oneself that many thousands of local councillors have devoted life-times to the service of others with no more initial stimulus than these pioneer-figures of modern Furness.

When sentimentalities are firmly eschewed, the really striking characteristic of these Victorian worthies is their almost incredible energy and self-confidence, not to say administrative competence and ability to focus their minds on a dozen different problems over a comparatively short period. They are not by any stretch of imagination to be envied, and they lived in a world very different from that of the modern councillor or industrialist—it was a world which they had helped to create, and which carried them forward with its own momentum, calling forth all their active and latent abilities but presenting them with ever more complex and—by their standards—insoluble problems. It was not a world in which a sensitive man could flourish, and the 7th Duke of Devonshire, who was perhaps alone in meriting this description among the key figures of the time and place, was spared the hurly-burly of local politics. His Furness associates were in any case faced with a serious dilemma ; they felt themselves to be indispensable as the " bread-providers " of the district, and seemed obliged to be present to give advice on almost any important body, while at the same time local industrial problems demanded more and more of their energies. There seemed to be nobody who could understudy them—one of the unfortunate consequences of the lionisation of Schneider and Ramsden—and their contributions to local development had their positive and negative aspects ; positive, in their demonstration of administrative efficiency and purpose, and negative in that the cult of the individual encouraged the second-rater and the sycophant. It should be added that no crude theory of " material " influence and interest will explain the individual actions and preoccupations of these men (they did not " represent " the interests of local industry, for they were local industry personified) ; but their very embodiment of industrial power reacted upon the behaviour of other men. Above all, they were unlikely to give full play to that healthy and open conflict of private and public interest which is essential to the conduct of a truly democratic society. This is not to suggest that these local politicians were in league against the wider public. They were mutually suspicious and sometimes openly jealous and critical.[1] It is no cynicism to

[1]Wadham's acid (although not vindictive) comments on Ramsden and Schneider are occasionally revealing, while Schneider openly jeered at Ramsden's " handle ". The Duke of Devonshire and the Marquess of Hartington were not particularly cordial towards Schneider.

point out that great compensations lay in the rôle of local lion ; there was almost limitless fuel to feed the fires of self-esteem, and publicly expressed admiration and approbation (broken occasionally by onslaughts from journalists like Joseph Richardson) was almost continuous. In any case, right or wrong, the subject of these comments was perpetually in the public eye.

With extraordinary confusion of public and private interests, intrigue followed as a matter of course. The historian can unearth very few of the more unsavoury undercover schemes of a past century, and for the most part he does not wish to do so. Occasionally there is a hint of what lay beneath the surface, as in the case of a corporation printing contract of 1876 which went to a company in which town councillors had an interest ; the council discussion of this matter was cut short by the Mayor himself on the ground that it would be " damaging to certain parties " if it was carried on in the press.[1] Over other actions of the council and its dominating personalities, a question-mark must hang more or less indefinitely ; official records, for all their wealth of fact, are usually silent at some essential point. One well-known episode in the history of modern Barrow, that of the " annexation " of Biggar Bank, may be thought to come within such a category—a great deal is known about it, but the identification of the persons who wielded real influence at given and crucial moments is left open to guesswork.

The general aspects of the story have been outlined elsewhere,[2] and the briefest of summaries will suffice here. Barrow had no public park during the 'seventies, and its inhabitants occasionally crossed the fords to Walney Island and used the Biggar High Bank, then used as a common pasture by the Biggar tenement-holders, as a place of recreation. Here, in the words of a local journalist, " the Barrovian loved to smoke the pipe of peace . . . nose and toes turned heavenwards ",[3] or played football or the steelworkers' version of golf. As the flood of trespassers grew almost monthly, the Walney farmers became alarmed at the threat to their property, and early in 1876 it was reported that they were forcefully ejecting people from the Bank. Soon afterwards one " J.F."[4] wrote to the press pointing out that it was essential that Barrow had a pleasure ground, and that it might be necessary to pay an inflated

---

[1] *B. Pilot*, 8.1.76 ; cf. also Dr. Pollard, *L. & C.*, LXIII, 105, n.67. [2] Articles by the writer, *N. Western Evening Mail*, 9.9, 16.9, 23.9.49.   [3] *B. Pilot*, 18.3.76. The controversy may be followed through these sources ; Pearson, H. G., *C. & W.* (NS), XI, 194 ff. ; *B. Her.*, 9.10.75, 18.3, 25.3, 1.7.76, 3.2, 14.7, 4.8, 11.8, 27.10.77 ; *B. Times*, 12.2, 26.2, 13.3.76 and *passim*, 10.8, 30.3, 29.6, 3.7, 13.7.78 ; *MS. Notebook (No. 1)* of the late Harper Gaythorpe, Barrow P.L. ; *Treasurers' Reports*.   [4] This could conceivably have been Ald. John Fell, a point of considerable importance in the light of the rest of the story.

price for the land if prompt action was not taken. The local radical press took the cue and went on to attack the Walney " landowners " (mostly holders of small tenements) ; " Biggar, with its grand hotels, grand shops and odoriferous pig-styes," sneered the *Barrow Pilot* of March 18th. On March 13th, 1876, several hundred men from the Steelworks invaded Biggar Bank in orderly and good-humoured fashion and proceeded to dismember the fences which the tenement-holders had erected to protect their pasture. A police inspector and six constables " witnessed the proceedings ", which were evidently organised at the works, and the " riot " passed off without serious occurrence. A pulsating legal wrangle then ensued. The farmers fought back in the following winter and succeeded in prosecuting a man for trespass on the Bank ; a Biggar Bank Defence Association was formed " to ascertain what are the real rights of the farmers of Biggar, and whether the public have a right in law to the use of the Bank as a place of recreation " ; and the *Barrow Herald* claimed that the farmers had no clear right of enclosure, and that they should have received the sanction of the Land Enclosure Commissioners. In the March of 1877 the Council made an amicable approach to the farmers and obtained a lease of the Bank for 21 years ; Joseph Richardson and the *Vulcan* (which remarked in the May that it was time that Barrow became a watering place with a decent esplanade) would have none of this, and claimed an absolute public right to the Bank. Richardson imported into the town the fiery John de Morgan of the Commons Preservation Society, who addressed a series of demonstrations designed to deter the councillors from making the final arrangements for the lease. Richardson and de Morgan were successful in achieving the right degree of deterrence, and thereafter the public were allowed to grow tired of the whole business.

Nevertheless, the Furness Railway Company opened its Walney Steam Ferry on July 1st, 1878, and shortly afterwards Edward Wadham commenced agitating on the Council for the construction of a road over the Bank. In the following year the Corporation made the first step towards its purchase, and in 1881-3 the former spent upwards of £4000 on turning it into a place of recreation. The land was obtained very cheaply indeed—at about £30 an acre[1]—and Alderman Fell opened the new public recreation ground on Good Friday, 1883, some 20,000 people visiting the Bank on that day. While present-day citizens of Barrow have excellent reason for thanking early fathers for this acquisition, the lengthy and involved events which culminated in its purchase must

[1]*Barrow News*, 14.5, 19.5.83. The Duke of Buccleuch received a small sum for the " enfranchisement of Biggar Bank ", and it is astonishing that the men who attacked the mediaeval customs of Biggar saw little that was inconsistent in paying this money ; *Treasurers' Accts.*

remain a matter for wonderment, and the part played by masters—as well as men—at the Steelworks, and in the council chamber, must likewise remain open to speculation.

Another development in Barrow municipal history had a less happy and beneficial outcome. As has been shown, the Barrow Corporation Act of 1872 was one of the earliest to permit a local authority to " erect and fit up improved dwelling houses for mechanics ". For some reason the municipality (which, as Joseph Richardson said, was run by men of sound business habits) was never permitted or inspired to earn the distinction of having undertaken the pioneering scheme of public enterprise promised by the Act. Nevertheless, housing remained a problem, and in spite of the sharp deceleration of population growth after 1874, there were periodic complaints of overcrowding and concomitant high rents.[1] In an attempt to provide additional housing accommodation as cheaply as possible, the directorate of the Furness Railway engaged the services of Messrs. Caird to build further flats on Old Barrow in the early 'eighties.[2] In this way appeared the vast and barrack-like erections adjoining the shipyard at the western end of Michaelson Road. Let nobody suppose that the directors of the Furness Railway Company looked at them in this light ; they were regarded as the most advanced type of working-class housing that was possible in the circumstances. A memorandum of Sir James Ramsden shows that they were a conscious attempt to outstrip the building organisations of George Peabody and Sir Sydney Waterlow (both pioneers of semi-philanthropic companies for building dwellings for the " working classes ") in cheapness of erection if nothing else. By 1884, for instance, Ramsden estimated that the various Peabody buildings had cost £75 per room without land, with an average rental of 2s. for each room ; the Barrow buildings, however, cost only £49 10s. per room and demanded a rental of only 1s. 6d.[3] By that year 37 blocks had been erected on the Island. This was a tragedy in every way, the flats, with their repellent exterior railed landings, were well enough built to give people the Hobson's choice of living in them in the twentieth century. Secondly, they were erected when the standard of terrace housing was improving visibly in the town and country at large, and, moreover, in a borough which embraced a greater area of non-urban land than any similar town in England. The determining factor was, of course, the Railway Company's ownership of Barrow Island, and the people of the town ultimately paid for its enterprise.

The F.R. was also responsible for another well-known landmark in modern Barrow, the High Level Bridge,[4] which was first en-

[1]E.g., *B. Her.*, **28.2**, 7.3.91.   [2]*Dir. Mins.* (*F.R.*), 20.5.79, 11.2.81. [3]*Memorandum Book* of Sir James Ramsden (kept in connection with the Furness Railway), 1.2.84 ; infn. by courtesy of Dr. Pollard.   [4]*Dir. Mins.* (*F.R.*), 9.8.1880.

visaged in 1880 and which afterwards became Corporation property to the value of £58,000. Indeed, by the end of the 'eighties most of the familiar landmarks of modern Barrow were there ; the great Balmoral Gothic Town Hall (1887) dominated the town centre, nearly all the present streets in the main body of the built-up area were to be seen, and in any real or mental photograph only the white dust of the streets, the municipal steam trams (1884) and the horse-vehicles would suggest another age.

The life that went on in this environment, however, is a very different matter. As far as industrial Furness was concerned, the 'eighties constituted a watershed between one age and another, the period of the industrial captains and father-figures and a more democratic and impersonal one. During that decade, and even before it, the dominant personalities died, met reverses or were otherwise scattered. J. R. McClean and Robert Hannay were among the first to go ; McClean in 1873[1] and Hannay on September 30th of the following year. Hannay, according to one of Wadham's notes, died of a " broken heart ". He had invested a large part of his fortune in the great Blochairn works of Glasgow, an enterprise which failed disastrously.[2] William Gradwell died in 1882,[3] but the business bearing his name, and a son of the same name, remained in existence. Alexander Brogden was plunged into a sensational bankruptcy then or soon afterwards,[4] while the 5th Duke of Buccleuch, whose family fortunes had benefited so much from the rise of local industry, died in 1884.[5] The most severe blow to the dominant powers came in 1887, when H. W. Schneider passed away ;[6] the thousands of people who lined the streets at his funeral were in reality marking the end of much more than one human being. J. T. Smith left Barrow in the same year, to live in semi-retirement at Stratford-on-Avon,[7] and the 7th Duke of Devonshire withdrew from active direction of the F.R. and of local industry, to die at Holker Hall in 1892.[8] F. C. Stileman died in 1889,[9] and James Ramsden, who continued to outlive so many of his colleagues until 1896,[10] was a tired old man, a pathetic shadow of the jaunty industrial missionary and town-builder of a generation before. Among the notable mid-Victorians who survived the disillusionments of the 'eighties and 'nineties were Edward Wadham, twice Mayor of Barrow before his death in 1913, and John Fell, Mayor in 1882-5, who died, in 1910. Perhaps the most remarkable survival of all was that of Colonel W. J. A. Baldwin, of the same family as the eccentric Georgian Vicar of Aldingham, who was one of the original Barrow councillors of 1867 and who was still an active magistrate in the second decade of the twentieth century.

[1]*B. Her.*, 19.7.73.   [2]*Proc. Inst. C.E.*, xl, 261.   [3]*Barrow News*, 9.9.82. [4]According to a local newspaper report noted by the writer (*Nottingham Daily Express*, 21.1.84), Brogden's liabilities at that time were £723,630 !   [5]*D.N.B.* [6]*B. Her.*, 12.11.87.   [7]*J.I.S.I.*, i, 1906, 269.   [8]See various memoirs, *cit.* [9]*B. Her.*, 1.8.89.   [10]*B. News*, 20.10.96.

The passing away of so many key figures naturally affected the conduct of affairs in the town and district. In October, 1886, the aldermen and councillors were present at a farewell meeting in honour of Joseph Richardson, who left the town on December 16th in the same year, after a stay of 21 years. This courageous and rather quixotic personality, antiquarian, printer, newspaper pioneer and journalist, was a type of local character which was also disappearing—a flagellator if not unmaker of councils, a projector of schemes, and a man fired with local patriotism by the town he had adopted; a man, too, who could always make (if not always keep) friends in high places. The councillors who assembled to say farewell to him included Benjamin Fish, once assailed by Richardson as a member of the anti-Ramsdenite " Cabal " and later (1897-8) the respected Mayor of Barrow ; and Benjamin Townson, another pioneer in local government circles. These were of the old brigade already, and a new generation of councillors was arising. Whatever Joseph Richardson may have done or not done (and he was apt to make exaggerated claims for the results of his own agitations) he taught the newer men to qualify and modify their respect for the high and mighty, and they appreciated it.[1] Party-political affiliations, however, still meant very little, and did not receive a significant stimulus until November 1st, 1892, when an Independent Labour candidate, Nicholson, was successful in a Hindpool Ward election,[2] and another such candidate, Cross, nearly successful in Yarlside. Thus commenced a phase of local history which continues to develop.

The 'eighties, however, were not without political excitement. On the passing of the Redistribution of Seats Bill in 1885, Barrow was granted a separate parliamentary representation. The political temperature rose almost immediately. An influential group of citizens felt that Sir James Ramsden deserved the seat automatically, but H. W. Schneider claimed publicly that he had ten times the right to be Barrow's representative, and that his colleagues would not have been in Barrow at all but for his exertions.[3] But Barrow was strongly Liberal in inclination, and as one Furness newspaper put it, Schneider was " unmistakeably popular apart from his political views ".[4] A committee of radicals, determined to oppose Schneider at all costs, invited the Liverpool shipowner David Duncan to contest the seat (perhaps hoping to remind

---

[1]See his *Farewell Address* and the biographical pamphlet, *cit.* ; and the *Barrow Vulcan, passim*. Richardson had no political affiliation or consistency in his later years. He supported H. W. Schneider in his candidature for parliament, and both men were " independents " with a conservative leaning.
[2]*B. Her.*, 22.10, 29.10, 5.11.92. [3]See the reported speech in *Ulv. Adv.*, 24.9.85, in which he referred jibingly to Ramsden's " handle ". Elsewhere he threatened to bring a libel action against the " radicals ". [4]*N. Lonsdale Express*, 21.8.81. Schneider had earlier summarised his views by saying that " he was not a conservative, and neither was he a democrat ".

Schneider of the Lancaster debâcle of twenty years before), and the atmosphere of virulence thickened. But if Barrow was a Liberal-radical stronghold, the rest of Furness was decidedly Conservative in leaning, and when the election came (1886), the district Conservative organisation was able to throw its weight behind Schneider and provide (according to a witness, Ald. Park) three times as many transport conveyances as the Liberals. Duncan, who was a rich man and willing to take risks in face of the much-needed and severe Corrupt Practices Act of 1883, riposted by large-scale treating ; and although successful at the poll, he was one of the first M.P.s to be unseated under the terms of this Act. He was in fact deprived of his seat for illegal employment of election workers rather than for treating or bribery,[1] although Barrow tradition has it that sovereigns were found in certain meat pies. Schneider, meanwhile, had revenged himself for Lancaster (the Marquess of Hartington, his one-time party leader, supported Duncan in this election[2]), and declined to contest the seat any further. The latter was afterwards occupied (1886-90) by W. S. Caine. Caine, however, who was well right of centre in his party, was too liable to be seduced by Unionism to satisfy Barrow tastes—Barrow, it was argued, was pro-Home Rule[3]—and when the aged Duke of Devonshire and Lord Edward Cavendish swung to Unionism in 1889, Caine's unpopularity was a function of his conversion.[4]

During the 'eighties there was a fairly vigorous Conservative and Primrose League movement in Furness, represented and led by W. G. Ainslie (whose family were associated with the North Lonsdale Iron Company) and Edward Wadham. The movement was not without connections in Barrow—there was a Conservative Workmen's Association there in 1877[5]—and it could rally considerable forces in the course of an election, as has been seen. But the time of the modern political party, with its continuous organisation and propaganda at all levels, was not yet. As many as 4000 Barrow " Liberals " turned out to hear the Earl and Countess of Aberdeen in 1889, but in 1891 the Barrow Liberal Association could count only 250 members ;[6] and the followers of this creed and party were thought to carry all before them. Continuous local party struggles, as has been implied, did not really commence until the political Labour movement was firmly established.[7]

The foregoing remarks broadly dispose of several aspects of Barrow history which have appeared to need treatment in isolation. But nearly half the population of Furness lived outside Barrow in 1881-91, and although it has been necessary to deal with the latter's

---

[1]*B. Her.*, 13.3, 20.3.86 ; London *Times*, 18.3, 19.3, 20.3, 22.3, 24.3.86.
[2]See paper by the writer, *L. & C.*, LXIII, 117 sqq., for the significance of this.
[3]*B. Her.*, 22.6.89.   [4]*Ibid.*, and 14.9.89.   [5]*B. Vulcan*, 15.5.77.   [6]*B. Her.*,
7.3.91.   [7]For the story of its development, Mowat and Power, *passim*.

industries and institutions in some detail, they are not (nor are they meant to be) the only important features in the tale. Numerous administrative developments, for instance, are best studied by viewing the district as a whole, and such an approach gives a sense of proportion more chance to operate.

Ulverston obtained its local government board, after a long and fluctuating struggle, on January 27th, 1871.[1] This was a fortunate and timely event, for, with the establishment of the North Lonsdale Ironworks at South Ulverston in 1874, the town ceased to stagnate and commenced to grow in population once more. In 1871-81 it increased by 370 houses, or one-sixth of the 1871 total, and the population was greater by 2401 in 1881. Two years later (1873) a rural sanitary authority for the Ulverston Union district was constituted and appointed.[2] Meanwhile Dalton also sought its local board, primarily (it was believed) because a number of its most active inhabitants who were also ratepayers wished to prevent the possible absorption of the town and locality into the Borough of Barrow, and thereby to avoid any possible increase of the rates that might be entailed in such an event.[3] The Local Government Act was duly adopted at Dalton on August 15th, 1872, and the Act came into force on April 25th of the following year.

The 'seventies brought another considerable increase in the Dalton population, and here, too, it was fortunate that a more advanced form of local government organisation had supplanted the Four and Twenty and the Guardians. The number of dwellings increased by about 40 per cent in that decade, and the population by nearly 50 per cent. The new authority was not only responsible for the metalling of the Dalton streets and the sewers there, but had a similar set of tasks in the satellite townlet of Askam. Happily some of this work had already been performed in Askam by the Furness Iron and Steel Company (whose manager, William Crossley, was a leading Dalton Local Board member), and this company and the ore merchants, including the former Barrow councillor Joseph Rawlinson, naturally exercised some influence over the destiny of the new body. It was aided in its work by one very fortunate circumstance : owing to the operation and effect of the rating of the local ore mines in 1874-5, the rateable value of the locality rose from £39,529 in 1874 to £116,275 in the following year. By 1876 the Board's income had doubled, while the total Dalton district rate in the pound fell to nearly half that paid by Barrow inhabitants. Until 1888 the Dalton district rate averaged only 2s. 5d. ; those who had resisted absorption could well preen themselves, for the occupants of the neighbouring borough continued to

<hr>

[1] *B. Times*, 18.1.71 ; *B. Her.*, 28.1.71. [2] *B. Times*, 18.1.73. This authority was established in pursuance of the Public Health Act of 1872. [3] *B. Her.*, 13.4.72.

pay roughly half as much again. Nor was the tale merely one of the Podsnap-parsimony too common among those who had rated property ; after 13 years the Board had spent some £10,000 on much-needed improvement of the highways in Dalton, Askam, Ireleth, Lindal and Newton, had made a determined attempt to tackle the sewerage problems of the first two places, and had spent —under all heads—£109,970 on local government by 1887, or an average of £1 per head of population *per annum* over the preceding 13 years.[1] It will be observed that Dalton was able to spend proportionately more on the common weal than Barrow, although it is to be doubted whether local politicians have ever used the fact in arguments against derating.

Dalton seems to have experienced few serious public health problems. It had an average death rate of 18.6 over the 17 years 1870-86, and an average birth rate of 44.2 ; both figures very close to those for Barrow. The former suffered from occasionally severe overcrowding ; the cottage houses were small, and the average number of persons per inhabited house varied from 5.5 to 5.75 during the whole of this period.[2] A healthy situation, added to the youthfulness of the population, kept the death rates at a reasonable level for the period ; here again, the age-composition of the local populace[3] seems to have had far more direct relationship to the rates of mortality than improvement in drains and sewers, although undoubtedly a great many factors combined to bring those rates down as the new century approached. Furness remained a healthy district, just as it had been in the eighteenth century, and once the main problems of sanitation were suitably attacked there would be no reason to expect abnormal mortality.

Sanitation was certainly not an irrelevance. Ulverston remained the black spot of Furness, and in the early 'eighties its death-rate was still around 20. In 1886 its Medical Officer of Health had no doubt as to the cause ; " The scavenging of the town is still open to considerable improvement . . . Many ashpits are still uncovered (and) are sunk below the level of the surrounding ground ".[4] He was able to welcome a reduction of the death-rate to 19.4, and not many years would elapse before this quiet, clannish little town would present a bill of health no better or worse than a thousand other places, and immensely improved in the light of its previous history.

Administratively, there were many alterations and reforms in Furness before the end of Victoria's reign. By orders of the Local Government Board dated February 7th and March 6th, 1876,

---

[1]Tyson, *Abstract of . . . Dalton, cit.*, 33 sqq., Tables 1 to 5 ; rating tables, pp. 31-33. [2]*Op. cit.*, population tables A and B. [3]There seems to have been comparatively little loss by migration from Dalton at this period. [4]*N. Lonsdale Express*, 3.7.86.

Barrow was separated completely from the Ulverston Union district for Poor Law purposes.[1] (The result was a marked reduction in the poor rate paid by Barrow people.) The relief of the poor in Barrow was to be administered by a Board of twelve elected Guardians and the Justices of the Peace resident in the parish, and after local paupers had been accommodated temporarily in a building in Dalkeith Street, the Roose workhouse was erected in 1879 with space for 300. Although the administration of the Poor Law became more humane, there is no reason to believe that the public attitude to this institution altered in any way. As far as Barrow was concerned, meanwhile, the last step towards complete autonomy was taken on August 1st, 1881, when the town police ceased to be administered by the county constabulary and the police force was instead controlled by the borough.

The next major development, in the district as a whole, followed on the Local Government Act of 1888, which decreed that County Councils should be formed in every administrative county. Under this Act, Furness was divided into four electoral divisions, High Furness, Low Furness, Ulverston and Dalton, Cartmel constituting a separate division. Each returned a county councillor. These councillors were entrusted with the business hitherto transacted by the magistrates in Quarter Sessions. In accordance with the 1885 Redistribution of Seats Act, the County Constituency of North-West Lancashire was divided into four parliamentary divisions, of which North Lonsdale was one. Barrow, as has been seen, was made a separate constituency. Meanwhile, agricultural workers had received the parliamentary vote in 1884. The parish and District Councils Act, passed ten years later, enacted that every rural parish of 300 or more people should have the right to elect its own parish council—it was an apparent strengthening of the democratic roots of English society which, generally speaking, led to much disappointment on the part of the village enthusiasts who discovered the financially conditioned limitations of parish powers. The formation of the Urban District Councils of Ulverston and Dalton also followed, and the stage was set for the much more complex local government organisation of the twentieth-century. These developments, however, were preliminaries—the preparation for something new as much as the logical consequences of what had gone before—and for a generation the local School Boards carried the incalculable responsibility implied in the training and conditioning of the mature men and women of the early twentieth century. The Barrow Board, as has been seen, had faced some severe disadvantages, and in 1877 many children were evading school. By 1890 the worst difficulties had been overcome ; the Board then had twelve schools accommodating 7,136 pupils, and was spending £6,400 a year as against £1,300

---

[1]The orders were made effective on April 19th.

in 1873.[1] The story was not one of uninterrupted progress, and until the mid-'eighties much of the school accommodation offered was poor in the extreme, temporary buildings having to serve too long for too many. Between 1883 and 1887, permanent schools were erected at Barrow Island, Roose, Oxford Street and Thwaite Street, while the Higher Grade School (which originated in 1879) found a permanent home in Duke Street ten years after its formation. Between 1887 and 1894 there was a slackening of building operations, only two new schools (replacing temporary structures at Hawcoat and Roa Island) then appearing ; in the latter year, however, extensive additions were made to Holker Street and Rawlinson Street Schools. The School of Science and Art, which had its genesis in some classes of 1874, had a somewhat chequered and wandering existence—typical of the inability of English people to face up to the need for scientific education—until 1891, when the management of the School was assumed by the Corporation. The erection of the present Technical School was commenced—perhaps symbolically—at the turn of the century. It may be added, without further comment, that churches and chapels appeared more readily than adequate schools in nineteenth-century Barrow, and probably absorbed quite as much labour and building material, a consideration that has to be borne in mind when the contribution of religious bodies to educational development is examined. Inns and beer-houses, of course, appeared more readily than any of these.

Dalton's School Board was established in 1876, the first board election taking place on July 10th of that year. H. W. Schneider added to his already considerable commitments by serving on this body. The rating of the iron mines—which he had opposed a generation before—indirectly aided the erection of five Dalton and Askam schools between 1876 and 1887, with space for 1736 children. But only 1455 were on the rolls in September, 1887, and the reason for the empty places must be sought elsewhere. Ulverston's School Board was formed in 1875, and was able to carry out its work, for the most part, with existing church and chapel school premises, the Church Walk Infant School being built in 1896. Ulverston did however make an important contribution to local educational advance by the opening of the Victoria Grammar School in 1900, thus carrying forward, in twentieth -century terms, the tradition of the old Town Bank Grammar School of previous centuries. In the Furness villages, during the closing years of the old Queen's reign, the schools which had been built in the 'fifties and 'sixties were still in use by teachers and taught, and were often likely to remain so for many years to come.

[1]Barnes, *Barrow and District*, 134. Other facts in this section are drawn from the same most useful source.

There was much that was ugly in the industrial civilisation that was now firmly seated at the tip of the Furness peninsula, and yet there was a soul within it. Barrow's Public Library was opened on September 18th, 1882, and was housed—like too many of the schoolchildren—in a temporary " iron " building, being transferred to the great new Town Hall in 1887. During the 'eighties the issue of volumes nearly doubled, and the increase went on more slowly in following years ; in the decade mentioned 68 per cent of the books borrowed were fiction, and perhaps many of the rest indicated the growing thirst for knowledge which found expression in attendance at University extension lectures, or meetings addressed by Mrs. Besant or other controversial figures like Keir Hardie. Dalton obtained its Carnegie Free Library in 1903.

Many of the children who had the three R's drilled into them in Furness board schools were not to root their lives in the locality. An exhaustive story of Furness people would follow them all over the world—to Africa, North America and almost anywhere marked red on the map. A century before, the majority of local people had not moved far, although a scattering of eighteenth-century stalwarts had been pressed into the navy or adventured in trading vessels. Barrow acted as a reception centre for people who were already uprooted—families from the iron districts of Staffordshire and Worcestershire, and Scotsmen from the Clyde. By 1911 Barrow had more Scots-born inhabitants than any county borough in England.[1] But the Cornish miners who worshipped at the Chapel of St. Perran at Roose had often gone far away by that date, and so had many of the younger sons of Furness villagers, forced to leave their dales during years of agricultural depression.

The movement was no longer from High Furness parishes into the iron-mining foot of the peninsula. But just as Barrow's natural excess of births over deaths was siphoned off by migration, so the Furness villages were losing proportionately more people by the same process. Several parishes were actually declining in population in spite of the strong tendency to natural increase ; Church Coniston, Kirkby Ireleth, the hamlets of the Crake Valley, and Colton. Others, like Broughton and Dunnerdale or Hawkshead, were increasing only slowly or stagnating. It will be noticed that these are High Furness parishes. Plain Furness agricultural parishes like Urswick and Pennington showed a substantial population increase towards the end of the century.

[1]Bainbridge, T. H., in *Economic Geography* (Clark University, U.S.A.), Vol. 15, No. 4, 1939, 380.

The explanation for this movement may lie not so much in the effects of iron-mining (which was declining in any case by 1901) as in the varied results of the depression which affected national agriculture in the last quarter of the nineteenth century.[1] It is not possible to give here a fully detailed account of Furness agriculture during these years, but the comments which follow might serve as the starting point for the exhaustive study which will one day be needed. An account of Furness agriculture in 1870[2] shows that it had probably made some progress during the years of industrialisation ; viz., mechanical mowing and reaping were common in that year, and it was stated that the competition of the iron mines for labour had had the effect of forcing up agricultural wages. The farms remained small in Low Furness (80-120 acres), and rentals in the same district were in the 30-35s.[3] range, as compared with Garnett's 15-32s. an acre in 1849. The proportion of arable land, as high as 85 per cent. on each farm, is in line with earlier details for the Dalton district. In High Furness, the emphasis was on sheep and dairy farming (the milk being sold in Ulverston), and mowing machines were common.

The description for 1870 gave half-yearly farm servants' wages as £13 to £15 ; this may be compared with the £15 to £17 for the *full* year which was Binns's figure for 1850. By 1877, however, wages were down to £15 to £20 yearly,[4] and the temporarily intense demand for unskilled labour had of course slackened. The labourer could no longer threaten to move to Barrow or the Dalton mines—he now had to go farther afield if he wished to " better himself ". Nevertheless, the country folk circulating at one of the Ulverston hiring fairs in 1877 appeared reasonably prosperous, and were " dressed in good, well-fitting suits of tweed ".[5] In 1886, nobody attempted to disguise the fact that farming was in an unhappy state. The Ulverston Martinmas hiring fair " was about as dull a one as has been known for many years . . . The wages which were offered and accepted in most cases were small, the general complaint of the farmers being that they were unable to pay big wages owing to the depressed state of trade ".[6] In the same year Lord Edward Cavendish, at the Cartmel Show, " regretted that the farmers had had to contend for so long against falling prices and bad seasons ".[7] It has been stated that towards the end of the century, rents in the Hawkshead district—and in other parts of North Lancashire—fell as much as forty per cent., although the fall was checked near the turn of the century.[8]

---

[1]For which see Lord Ernle, *English Farming Past and Present*, 374 sqq. [2]Particulars of John Fell repr. in *F. P. & P.*, I, 30 ff. [3]*The Return of Owners of Land* (1873) gives rentals lower than this. [4]*Barrow Vulcan*, 31.7.77. [5]*Ibid.* [6]*N. Lonsdale Express*, 13.11.86. [7]*N. Lonsdale Express*, 18.9.86. [8]*V.C.H. Lancs.*, II, 436.

An important feature of the depression was the widespread reduction in arable land which took place in many counties, and a corresponding increase of pasture area. Cumberland, and to a lesser extent Westmorland, both experienced such a reduction, although in the case of Lancashire as a whole the proportions of arable and permanent pasture were not much altered.[1] Plain Furness, agriculturally speaking, had more in common with the Cumberland coastal strip than with the smallholdings of the County Palatine, and seems to have suffered the decline in arable that might be expected. According to a calculation based on the 1905 Board of Agriculture Returns,[2] the proportion of arable to all agricultural land in Urswick, Bardsea, Aldingham and Dalton was 47 per cent.— indicating a fall of about 40 per cent. since 1870. But since there was still an element of spirited farming in Plain Furness, notably on the Cavendish estates,[3] and since its farms were situated near large urban areas with some demand for milk, vegetables and dairy produce, there was no wholesale exodus of agricultural population near the towns.

In the fells, as we have seen, the story was a very different one. It should be emphasised once more that local agricultural wages were not low by contrast with other areas, particularly those in the south of England; but they were on the low side by contrast with wages paid in urban occupations, and the stagnation in farming and lack of prospect in the moorland hamlets caused migration of those who had no deep roots or commitments.[4] A comparison of the numbers of farmers listed in the 1866 Mannex directory of North Lonsdale, and those in Bulmer's 1911 directory for the same area, shows a slight increase in the numbers of names and farmsteads listed. This increase occurs in both High and Plain Furness, and it is probable that there was little throwing together of farms. On the other hand, there were still fewer independent landowners, if the numbers of " yeomen " (or statesmen) are any guide. The 1873 *Return of Owners of Land* confirms the impression that land was coming into fewer hands in the late nineteenth century, and provides at least 22 cases of Furness estates of over 500 acres and nine over 1000. Of these, 15 were on poor and low-rented fell territory. The late H. S. Cowper's reference to " rich manu-facturers . . . on the margin of Windermere " who " absorbed " the estates of the dalesmen[5] is not to be dismissed as fiction, although the process of absorption occupied a considerable period.

[1]Bainbridge, T. H., *C. & W.* (NS), XLIV, 92 ; *V.C.H. Lancs*, II, 434-5. [2]*V.C.H., Lancs*., VIII, 321, 329, 307. See also Table 6, p. 77 above. [3]According to indentures examined by the writer, efficient farming standards were insisted upon in leases. The 7th Duke of Devonshire remained a famous agriculturist during his lifetime, and his shorthorns were world-famous. [4]Agricultural wages appear to have remained under the urban labourer's 18s. until the end of the century. [5]*History of Hawkshead*, 209.

Nevertheless, it would be misleading to paint a picture of unbroken gloom. The families of the farmers and " yeomen " who weathered the storm were finding that there were opportunities in the tourist trade ; ever more visitors came to the Furness Fells and to Hawkshead (carried by the F.R.'s improved services), and if the slate trade at Coniston had its dull days, " Apartments and Lodgings " were offered there instead. The appearance of institutes in the villages (as at Broughton and Coniston),[1] and a slow improvement in amenities, did something to counteract the disappearance of the vigorous bucolic life of an earlier century.

[1] *Vide* Bulmer's *Directory of Furness and Cartmel* (1911), 178, 320.　There were village co-operative societies at Broughton, Hawkshead and Coniston, which await their historians.　The Hawkshead society was there in 1881 (*B. Times*, 26.3.81) and doubtless earlier.

EPILOGUE

It was not an easy task to decide upon a date at which this study should end. As we have seen, the age of the prominent industrialists ended in the 'eighties ; the political labour movement was awakening in the 'nineties ; and 1897 saw the commencement of the Vickers' association with Barrow. Thereafter the town became increasingly dependent upon shipbuilding for its livelihood, and, naturally enough, any future history of the district will have to deal largely with the fortunes and the vicissitudes of the ship-building industry.

Yet no balanced history of any locality can be constructed from business records. The story so far has been complex enough in all conscience, and has called for the use of municipal, industrial and trade union sources ; of railway records, parliamentary reports and committees, and private diaries. But it may be doubted whether the foregoing narrative has taken us very far into the minds and hearts of men. The labourers and artisans of mid-Victorian times remain shadowy figures, as firmly embedded in another and at times impenetrable age as the industrialists who utilised their services.

But the early twentieth century is not the middle railway age ; it is still within living memory. We may yet hope to probe rewardingly into a phase of social history which ended in 1914, and which seems as far removed from the mid-twentieth century as the earlier periods which have been covered in this book. If a history of the Furness district can be carried through the last fifty years, the historian will enjoy at least one great advantage—he will, if he hurries, be able to use living memories as his sources, and can to that extent avoid the frustration of finding only the occasional diary and personal reminiscence to support him in his attempts to burrow beneath the surface. His subject, if he is to write a worthwhile local history, will be the quality of life ; he will not be obliged to build upon quantities only. While changes in shipbuilding technique must occupy him, he will show the effects of those changes upon human beings ; the welder replaces the riveter, and they are different men.

As the new century unrolls, trade unionism becomes a bigger and better-documented subject. Historians will need an account of the effect of premium bonus payments—even those who do not know what the term means. Sociologists will find much of interest in the story of social and psychological stresses in a town and district dependent upon one major industry. The student who wants to investigate strain and conflict need not confine his enquiries to Victorian years; the First World War is a subject redolent of perpetually warm beds and overcrowding of human bodies. The narrator will deal with Vickerstown, which arrived twenty years too late—the flats had already gone up—and no balanced historian should mention model housing without also mentioning the boarded-up and empty houses which appeared within the same social framework. The analyst of social trends may care to examine the evolution of welfare services and relief schemes, from the system of poor relief of Victorian times (which appears to have encouraged artisans to move away from the locality as quickly as possible) to the organisations of a more recent time, when unemployed folk stayed in the district and were engaged on public works.

Yet the story need not be a pessimistic one. The Furness district, which in spite of its manufacture of engines of destruction has contributed so largely to the real wealth of the world, has suffered more than its fair share of vicissitudes. The labours and sacrifices of past generations cannot be repaid. Countless thousands of hours of labour, when solidified in docks that are largely empty, appear as a reproach. In fact, Ramsden's (and McClean's) dock basins have proved exceedingly valuable for the fitting out of large vessels by the modern shipbuilding industry, resilient national and international economies have assured fairly regular orders for such vessels in recent years, and the development of new industrial techniques has led to the appearance of light industries in an area which once depended solely on the heavy ones. Nor has James Ramsden's town planning been wasted. A century after that energetic man put his wide thoroughfares on paper for the first time, an enlightened corporation—incidentally assisted by the work of Nazi bombs—is making the best of those broad and spacious approaches and vistas which allowed cold winds to lash inadequate clothing and undernourished bodies for so long. The winds are still cold, but the suffering has gone. In recent years, too, there have been signs that the spirit of John Wilkinson, George Stephenson and John Hague has not been dissipated for ever; brave schemes envisaging the reclamation of Morecambe Bay, the establishment of hydro-electric stations and the construction of an embanked motor road have once more awakened vigorous discussion. The Industrial Revolution, still in progress, may yet show that nothing is impossible, though the threat of uncontrolled radioactivity warns a later generation to be vigilant.

ADDITIONAL NOTES

Page number :

56—57   Land tax assessments : in the area around Lancaster, for which the sums levied were similar to those collected in Furness, this tax was collected " at about 1½d. in the pound on the net rental." Eden, *State of the Poor* (1797), ii, 302.

61   Agriculture and the colonial trade ; it should be noted that the latter had earlier affected the local iron industry — see also p. 31.

118   (Footnote 7). Should read *op. cit.* p. 17. cf. *Antiquities*, 1774, p. xvii.

120   Average death ages in Preston and elsewhere ; it should be borne in mind that far more young children were exposed to risk in an industrial town. Later in the 19th century however, Dr. Farr's death-rate calculations make it clear that — in spite of the preponderance of young people in the towns — death-rates were higher in the latter than in the country.

125   (Footnote 1). See Drummond, J., and Wilbraham, A., *The Englishman's Food* (London, 1939), 390.

147, 152   Hawkshead Grammar School ; see Ben Ross Schneider, jnr., *Wordsworth's Cambridge Education* (1957), 4—6, which argues that Hawkshead was " one of the best schools in England " in the late 18th century. Its curriculum was designed to keep abreast of Cambridge mathematics and natural philosophy. Mr. Schneider also gives (pp. 6—7) a list of distinguished men produced by Hawkshead School.

296   Child mortality (under fives) ; this should be given as a percentage of births as well as deaths. Percentages of births in the Ulverston registration district also show a worsening in 1856—60, 1861—65, and 1866—70, going from 18 per cent to 22 per cent and then to 23 per cent. The case therefore remains valid. Regarding similar calculations on p. 119, a table of percentages is given in my thesis, p. 140. They support a low, if not downward, rate of child mortality in the late 18th century.

LOCAL NEWSPAPERS, AND BIBLIOGRAPHIES

The local press provides a rich source of information for the investigator. Although it has been used extensively in the foregoing work, much material remains to throw light on topics touched upon in these pages. There is an almost complete collection of local newspapers at the British Museum Newspaper Library, Colindale, N. London, and full details of the collections existing at Barrow and elsewhere are given in *Handlist of Newspapers Published in Cumberland, Westmorland, and North Lancashire,* by F. Barnes, B.A., F.L.A., & J. L. Hobbs. (C. &. W. A. & A. Soc. Tract Series, No. XIV. 1951). It should be noted that no newspaper appeared in the Furness district before 1847, but earlier material may be found in :
Westmorland Advertiser & Kendal Chronicle (1811) ; *Westmorland Gazette & Kendal Advertiser* (1818) ; *Cumberland Pacquet* (1774) ; *Lancaster Gazette* (1801) ; *Lancaster Guardian* (1837).

No district Bibliography has been published, but the catalogue of the excellent Local Collection at the Barrow Public Library, (Reference Dept.), will be found to be of great assistance.

Addenda and corrigenda to 1981 reprint.

p.65, note 2.	The correct source is W. H. Chaloner, 'The Agricultural Activities of John Wilkinson, Ironmaster', *Agricultural History Review*, V, (1957), 48 ff.
p.70, para. 1.	Silberling is a very out of date source for price movements, and an unreliable one. The student will find much more reliable guidance in B. R. Mitchell and Phyllis Deane, *Abstract of British Historical Statistics* (Cambridge, 1962), especially pp. 338 and ff. It should be noted that regional indices are lacking.
p.80.	Table 7. See the foregoing note. More recent wage data do not invalidate the argument.
p.86, note 7.	This should be 'p.33 above'.
p.199, line 13.	The former Barrow St. George's school is still standing (1981), notwithstanding alterations.
p.206, line 6.	This is a misprint for C. S. Kennedy.
p.209, note 3.	This should read 'the late Professor D. H. Pike'.
p.219 11 up.	Coniston Station is now demolished.
18 up.	The line is of course lifted.
p.264, line 13.	Lord Lonsdale was essentially a coal magnate.
p.286 12 up.	The Paxton Terrace housing is demolished.
p.415, para 1	Joseph Richardson's work as a local editor is dealt with by Mr. P. J. Lucas in 'Provincial Culture and the ''Penny Brotherhood''' in *Transactions of the Cumberland and Westmorland Antiq. and Archaeological Soc.*, LXXVIII, (1978), pp.187 – 198. See also the same author, on the Barrow press: 'Publicity and Power; James Ramsden's Experiment with Daily Journalism', the same *Transactions,* LXXV, (1975), pp.352 – 75.
p.425, para 3.	Dr Elizabeth Roberts, in her *Working Class in Barrow and Lancaster* (Lancaster, 1976) has much developed the type of enquiry suggested here.

Abbots Wood 226, 297
Above Town (Dalton) 4, 10, 128
Accidents (industrial) 308, 322–4, 397
Account Book of Sarah Fell 124
Adgarley 10, 23
Adult Education 329, 404
Agriculture 55 ff.
  (crop rotations) 63, 78
  (land utilisation) 77
  (landholders) 5—6
  (landholding families) 10–11, 73–4,
    164, 423
  (rents) 68, 246, 422
  (town fields) 11–13, 130
  (wheat growing) 55, 61
  See also *Arboriculture, .Rents*
    (manorial), Reeans, Sheep-
    raising, Wages, Wartime Wheat
    Boom, Wood Conservation, etc.
Ailesbury, Marchioness of, 178
Ainslie, Aymer, 380.
Ainslie, Montague, 178, 194, 368, 380.
Ainslie, W. G., 416.
Aldingham, 3—6, 14, 97, 119–20, 122,
  129, 140, 235–7, 354, 423.
  (workhouse at) 137
Allen line, the, 344
Allison, Joseph, 299, 323, 334, 377
Allithwaite, Upper, 10, 137
Allotments, 287
Allowance System, 136
Allport, James, 253, 262.
Amalgamated Soc. of Carpenters and
  Joiners (see *Trade Unions*)
Amalgamated Society of Engineers
  (See *Trade Unions*)
Ambleside, 49, 83
Anchor line, the, 389, 391
Angerton, 129–30
Appleby, 171
Applegarth, Robert, 313
Apprentices (factory), 52–3, 149–50
Apprenticeship (parish), 137
Arboriculture, 59–60
Arnside, 85–6
Arnside & Hincaster railway, 268
Arrad Foot, 167–8
Ashburner, G. B., 206, 257, 334.
Ashburner, Margaret, 124, 168
Ashburner, Wm., 275, 299, 304, 350,
  356, 378
Ashton, T. S., 30, 50
Askam-in-Furness, 13, 193, 203, 255,
  317, 337, 340, 393, 400, 417.
Aslett, Alfred, 404–5
Atkinson, Edmund, 161

Backbarrow
  (cotton mills) 50–3, 111, 149–50
  (furnace), 20, 22, 30, 194, 222, 250
  (Iron Company) 20 ff., 33, 47, 83,
    107, 156
Backhouse, James, 29
Baldwin, Dr. Roger, 118, 160
Baldwin, W. J. A., 299, 414
Baltimore & Ohio Railway, 391
Banking, 28, 156 ff., 384
Baptists, 103, 331
Bardsea, 10–11, 117, 423.
  (school at), 146–8
Bardsley, Canon C. W., 15
Barfoot and Wilkes, 50
Barley trade, 68
Barnsley, 343
Barratt, J. and W., 222–3
Barrett, Rev. T. S., 323–4

Barrow Building Society, 198, 200, 229,
  284
Barrow Corporation Acts (1868) 301–3,
  326, 368, 372; (1872) 371, 373–4, 413;
  (1873) 362, 371, 378; (1875) 408.
Barrow Flax and Jute Co., 338–43, 346,
  349, 351–2, 363, 376, 382–4, 386–7,
  396, 402.
Barrow Haematite Steel Co., 249, 251,
  261, 269–70, 297, 323, 336, 339, 341–3,
  345–6, 348, 350–2, 357–8, 363, 375,
  377, 380–3, 386, 393–5, 406, 409–13.
Barrow Harbour Commissioners, 197,
  215, 225.
Barrow Herald, 288–9, 292, 294, 314–16,
  322–3, 361–3, 370–2, 412.
Barrow I.L.P., 400, 415.

BARROW-IN-FURNESS ; see also
  Cocken, Hawcoat, Hindpool,
  Hindpool Estate, Newbarns,
  Rampside, Salthouse etc.
  (Burial Board), 302, 368.
  (churches and chapels), 281, 292,
    330–3.
  (docks and harbour), 245, 253,
    261–5, 269, 272 ff., 381–3, 391,
    403–4.
  (early port, harbour and village),
    88, 92–3, 95, 122, 148, 173 ff., 166,
    168, 189, 193, 198, 208, 211–12,
    227–8.
  (education in), 199, 282, 332–4,
    378–9, 409, 419–20.
  (gas and water supplies), 282, 288,
    292, 300, 346, 370, 377, 409.

(general refs. to), 250, 263, 277, 278, 281, 289, 294, 302, 321, 327, 352, 368, 413–4.
(Guardians for), 373, 409, 419.
(local government in), 278, 288 ff., 291, 293, 296 ff., 302 ff., 371, 376 ff., 408 ff., 415.
(pauperism and unemployment in), 290, 367, 397, 399–401, 405, 419.
(population of), 198, 201, 281, 284, 287, 324, 354–6, 371–2, 407.
(public health in), 289, 397, 407–8.
(sanitation in), 289–90, 298, 304, 369–71, 373, 407–8.
(shipping lines based on), 334, 340, 343–5.
(theatres, clubs, institutes, societies in), 199, 319, 326–7, 329, 349, 352, 400.
(town planning in), 228–33, 282–7, 322, 408.

Barrow Island, 273, 276, 281, 340, 348-9, 361–2, 379, 381, 420.
Barrow Pilot, 361, 385–6, 412.
Barrow Printing and Publishing Co., 351–3, 363.
Barrow Rolling Mills Co., 342, 344–5, 351–2, 356.
Barrow School Board, 334, 351–2, 378–9, 409, 419–20.
Barrow Shipbuilding Co., 339, 342–6, 348, 351, 356, 361, 363, 376, 384, 387–9, 390, 396–8, 402.
Barrow Steam Corn Mill Co., 339–40, 342, 356, 402.
Barrow Times, 287, 296, 301, 303–5, 321, 323, 335, 338–9, 362, 391.
Barrow Trades Council, 358, 392, 400.
Barrow Vulcan, 363, 392, 412.

Barton (Westmorland), 120
Beerhouses and taverns, 95, 164, 327, 360–1.
Beetham, 84
Belfast, 277, 403
Bell, Lowthian, 343, 395
Bernard, J. A., 294
Bersham, 36
Bessemer, (Sir) Henry, 250
Bessemer Steelmaking, 184, 251 ff., 342, 383, 394–5,
Beveridge, Thomas, 234, 275, 356.
Bewdley, 25, 27.
Bierleys, 4, 128
Biggar, 12, 122, 130, 167, 306
(Bank), 411–13.
Biggins, 121
Bigland, George, 65
(family), 128
Bilbao, 382, 398, 406.
Binns, Jonathan, 78, 238, 241

Bintley, Job, 175–6, 228.
Birch, Robinson & Walmsley, 50, 52–3, 89, 149.
Birkenhead, 263, 313
Birkrigg, 130
Birmingham, 401
Black, Peter, 304
Blackburn, 69, 108
Blackpool, 173, 245
Blamire, William, 74, 157
Blawith, 59, 107–8, 128–9, 159–60, 165, 235–7.
(school at), 146
Blochaim works, 342–3.
Bloomeries, 16, 19.
Bloomery forges, 10
Bobbin mills, 54, 237
Bolton, 108, 136
Bolton-in-Furness, 12, 207
Bolton, Col. John, 153
Bolton, John, 154–5
Bootle (Cumb.), 83, 108, 239
Bootle (Lancs.), 376
Borrowdale, 23
Borwick Rails, 265, 270
Bowness, 351, 409
Boyle, Alexander, 226, 278
Boyle, Robert, 184
Braddyll family, 11, 62
(Col. T. R. G.), 74, 155
Bradford, 401
Brassey, Thomas, 252–3, 265, 273–4, 314, 316, 318.
Briggs, Joseph, 346, 350, 356, 358.
Briggs, Thomas, 402.
Brighton, 52, 149
Bristol, 17, 21, 27
Bristol Brass & Copper Co., 47
Brogden, Alexander, 204–5, 216, 218, 221, 327, 333, 414.
Brogden, John sen., 153, 181, 204–5
Brogden family, 194, 204–6, 211–2, 215–8, 257.
Brougham (Westmorland), 120
Broughton, East (school at), 147
Broughton-in-Furness, 3, 5–8, 12, 49-50, 58, 67, 83, 97, 110, 113, 118, 120–2, 130, 140, 153, 165–6, 181, 189–91, 212, 219, 235–7, 295, 354, 421, 424.
(manor of), 8
(schools), 146, 333
(workhouse), 137
Brooke, Lord, 178
Brow Edge, 151
Brown, John (Sheffield), 250, 252
Brunlees, James, 216–7
Buccleuch, 5th Duke of (and family), 73, 174 ff., 185, 193, 195, 200, 205, 207, 217, 220, 278, 299, 332, 335, 404, 414.

430

Building industry, 123, 240, 286–7, 347, 371–2.
Building societies, 198, 200, 284–5, 365
Burges, Alfred, 175
Burlington, Earl of, (see 7th Duke of Devonshire),
  171, 174 ff., 184–6, 200, 203–4, 207–8, 216, 220, 224, 228, 238.
Burn, D. L., 221, 394.
Burton, Myles, 157, 195
Bury, 313
Bury, Edward, 183, 200.
Buxton, 225, 279, 351.

Caernarvon, 108–9
Caine, W. S., 416
Calcutta, 338, 344
Caldbeck, 21, 47
Canal mania, 89
Carlisle, Bishop of, 353.
Carnforth, 68, 215, 255 ff., 393, 405.
Carnforth Haematite Co., 255, 394
Carruthers, George, 288, 315–6, 323, 358, 361–3.
Carruthers, James, 255
Cartmel, 1, 10–11, 65–7, 118, 127–9, 132–3, 135, 137–8, 141, 158, 227, 234–5, 238, 242, 295, 333–4, 354–5, 422.
  (commons and enclosure at), 52, 65–6, 122
  (schools at), 144–5, 147, 333.
Castle Head, 64–5
Catholics, 103, 317, 331–3
Cavendish family, the, 10, 46, 62, 73, 157, 184–5, 224, 245, 280, 343–4, 397.
  (Henry Cavendish), 184
  (Lord Edward), 396, 416, 422
  (Lord Frederick), 65
  (Lord Frederick C.), 252, 332, 339, 378, 396.
  (Lord George), 161
  (Lord George A.), 45, 63, 184–5
  (Lord John), 43–5
  See also Devonshire, Dukes of
    Burlington, Earl of
    Hartington, Marquess of
Cemeteries and burial grounds, 103, 291, 368–9
Census enumerations, 235, (1801–31) 66, 72–3, 78, 96, 109–11, 135, 240, (1851) 242, (1861) 78, 238, 240, 242, 244, 281, 353, 355, (1871) 323, 353–5, (1881) 407, (1891) 407, (1911) 421.
Chamberlain, Joseph, 408
Champions of Bristol, the, 21, 25, 47
Chapmen, 7, 50
Charcoal, (pool), 23–4, 33–4, (prices), 22, 34.
Chatsworth, 184, 225

Cheadle, 48
Check Manufacture, 50, 53
Chepstow, 47
Cheshire, 19–20, 36, 82
Child mortality, 53
China, 344
Claife, 9–10, 60, 132
Clapham, 262
Claye, S. J., 340, 345–6, 356, 387–8.
Clayton, William, 284
Clergy, 159 ff.
Cleveland, 220, 249
Cliburn, 120
Clitheroe, 376
Clock (makers), 125, (smiths), 51
Close, William, 61, 66, 69, 88, 109, 118
Closed vestries, 4, 127 ff.
Clothing, 124
Clyde, the, 273
Coalbrookdale, 22
Coalminers, 163
Coastal road schemes, 64
Coastal shipping, 32, 86–7, 90 ff., 187–8, 197.
Cocken, 12, 13, 151
Cockermouth, 151
Cockermouth & Workington Rly., 268
Cockermouth, Keswick & Penrith Railway, 268
Coke-smelting, 26, 29
Collingwood, W. G., 222
Colthouse, 103, 162
Colton (parish), 3, 5, 9–10, 14, 51, 58, 62, 97, 103, 107, 110–1, 116–9, 120, 133, 135, 137, 140, 160, 165, 295, 354, 421.
  (schools at), 145, 148
Combination (ironmasters'), 33
Company of Mines Royal, 15
Competition for fuel, 24
Congregationalists, 103, 162
Conifer planting, 60
Coniston (chapelry of Church Coniston) 2, 8, 13–15, 17, 21, 42, 45, 47–9, 75, 121, 128–9, 139, 189, 223, 236–7, 333, 421, 424. (manor of), 8, (Water), 2.
Coniston Mining Company, 223
Coniston Railway Co., 219, 225.
Conservative Party, the, 334, 416.
Cooke & Swinnerton, 340, 356, 386.
Co-operative societies, 309–11, 364–5, 429.
Copper mining, 47 ff., 75, 219, 223
Cornwall & Cornishmen, 192, 209, 223, 239, 421.
Corrupt Practices Act (1883), 416
Cost of living, 79, 161, 311–2, 359, 366, 401.
Cottagers, 56, 70–1.
Cotton, Daniel & Thomas, 20
Cotton manufacture, 50 ff.
Coulson, Edwin, 359

Cranke family, the, 75–7, 152
  (John), 228, (William), 75.
Crossfield (Stephen), 20, (William), 29
Crossgates, 23, 35
Crosthwaite, 108
Cumberland, 1, 15, 17, 136, 139, 149,
  163, 181, 206, 218, 220, 223, 235, 239,
  242, 259, 336, 338–9, 355, 391, 405–6,
  422.
Cumberland Iron Mining & Smelting
  Co., 256, 394
Cunsey, 15, 29
Cunsey Company, 20, 29.
Curran, Pete, 401–2.
Currey family, 181, 185, 190, 208,
Currey, Benjamin, 177–9, 190.
Currey, William, 297, 339, 343.

Dalton-in-Furness, 2–3, 5, 16, 70, 74–5,
  77–8, 83, 108–10, 117–9, 121–2,
  127–9, 132, 136, 138–40, 144–6, 148,
  151, 158, 166, 175, 180, 189, 195, 227,
  229, 235–8, 241–3, 245, 281, 287–9,
  291, 293, 297–8, 309–11, 333, 354–5,
  364, 368, 400, 417–8, 423, (divisions
  of), 128–9, (registrar), 294, (relieving
  officer), 290, (schools), 144–6, 148–9,
  333, 409, (School Board), 420,
  (workhouse), 137.
Darby, Abraham the first, 20, 24, 26–7.
Davis, James, 193, 205
Deane, Dr. C. M., 372, 376
Debentures, 190, 269–70
Dendron, 5, 7, 12, (school), 145, 148.
Derby, Earl of, 207, 334
Devonshire, 4th Duke of, 184
Devonshire, 7th Duke of, (See also
  Burlington, Earl of), 185, 200, 220,
  224–6, 251–4, 262–3, 265, 278–80, 283,
  285, 297–9, 324–5, 327, 332–3, 339,
  341–5, 348, 351–2, 367, 375, 381–3,
  386, 390, 395–7, 402, 410, 414, 416.
Devonshire, 8th Duke of, 185, (See also
  Cavendish family, and *Hartington,
  Marquess of*).
Dickson, R. W., 37, 44, 62–3, 66, 70.
Disease, 116–20, 294–6, 298, 407,
  (occupational do.), 296, 397.
Donnelly, Capt. R. E., 297
Douglas, Bryce, 397–9
Dowthwaite, Robert, 25.
Duddon Bridge, 83, (See also *River
  Duddon*).
Duddon Company, 30, 32–3, 156,
  (furnace), 32–8.
Duddon crossing scheme, 267 ff.
Duncan, David, 415.
Dundee, 344, 348, 393, 402.
Dunnerdale (with Seathwaite), 58,
  235–6, 421.
Duopoly, 19
Durham, 220, 249–50, 254, 264, 277.

Eastbourne, 225, 279, 351
Eastern Steamship Co., 344, 349.
Eddy, Capt. Stephen, 226, 245.
Eden, Sir F. M., 123–4, 158.
Eden Valley railway scheme, 220
Education, 143 ff., 332 ff., 378–9, 419 ff.
Egton-cum-Newland, 48, 128–9, 237,
  (enclosure), 67.
Electoral divisions, 334, 376, 419
Elder, Dempster & Co., 399
Emigration (see *Population*).
Enclosures (parliamentary), 65–8, 81,
  122, (private), 13, 55, 58, (of sands),
  63 ff., (of woodland), 58.
Encroachments on common, 59
English and Australian Copper Co.,
  202–3, 209, 225.
Epidemics, 16, 116–7, 298, 373.
Evans, Howard, 376.
Exportable food surplus, 68.

Fell, Alfred, 22, 41.
Fell, Burton & Co., 157.
Fell, John (d. 1910), 157, 290, 327, 334,
  339, 362, 367–8, 378, 409, 411–2, 414.
Fell, J. B., 181, 189, 191, 214.
Fell, Margaret, 20
Fells of Ulverston, the, 156–7.
Field drainage, 11, 75–6.
Finsthwaite, 14, 51, 53, 111, 149,
  (school at), 145, 147–8
Fire Prevention, 292–3.
Firth, Mark, 252.
Fish, Benjamin, 285, 376, 415.
Fisher (James) 299, 356, (Joseph) 94,
  203, (Thomas) 94, 193, 198, 203.
Flan sports, 167.
Flats in Barrow, 348, 413. (See also
  Housing conditions etc.)
Flax industry, 50, 52–3.
Fleetwood, 173, 182, 188–9, 207, 245
Fleming family (of Rydal and Coniston),
  27, 43, 130, 219.
Fleming, William, 390
Flookborough, 134, 168, (poorhouse),
  137.
Food and nutrition, 121, 123–5, 312.
Force Forge, 15, 20.
Ford, Richard, 29
Forest of Dean, 36
Forshaw, Jabez, 286, 334
Foster, Sir William, 225
Fothergill, Rev. W. H., 361, 379.
Four and Twenties, 4, 127–8, 132, 137,
  144, 291–2, 306.
Foulis, William, 284
Fox, George, 20, 25, 103, 162.
Fresh, Thomas, 74, 153
Friendly societies, 158, 246, 309, 327,
  365–6.

Furness Abbey, 2, 4, 12, 131, 176, 180, 188, 226, 330, (rental of), 12.
Furness & S. Cumberland Building Soc., 284.
Furness deanery, 6.
Furness Gas and Water Co., 292, 300–1.
Furness Iron and Steel Co., 255, 271, 340, 394, 417.
Furness " Manor ", 10
Furness Railway Company, 92–4, 96, 142, 174 ff., 209 ff., 215 ff., 224–5, 229, 244, 251, 258 ff., 274, 282–3, 284, 299–301, 305, 319–20, 327, 332, 337, 339–41, 343, 346, 348, 352, 375–7, 383 ff., 391, 403–5, 409, 412, (passenger traffic), 188, 191, 210, 277, 338, 404–5, (politics of), 216 ff., 261 ff., 277, 383, (statistics of), 209–11, 259–60, 269–72, 276, 337–8, 391–2.
Furness Railway–Midland Railway joint line, 255, 263 ff., 270–2, 344.

Gaitswater, 42
Gales of Bardsea, the, 74
Galloway, Messrs. W. & J., 216–17
Garden, James, 287, 347.
Garnett, W. J., 75
Garstang, 239
Gastrell, Bishop, 159
Gasworks, 245, 300, (see also Barrow-in-Furness).
Gawthwaite, 45
General Board of Health, 120, 143, 290
" Gentlemen Ironmasters ", 38, 166.
Geography of Furness, 1–3
Geology of Furness, 2–3
Germany, 382
Gibson, A. Craig, 45, 162, 223
Gibson, William, 154
Gilboy, Dr. E. W., 39–40
Gilchrist-Thomas process, 254, 394, 406
Gladstone, W. E., 274, 298
Glasgow, 207, 393
Gleaston, 5, 10, 68, 148, 400
Gloucester, 276
Goatfield, 34, 37
Goldney (Margery), 20, (Thomas), 21.
Gradwell, William, 234, 275, 284–6, 292, 299, 304–5, 314, 317, 334, 346–8, 350–1, 356, 358, 414.
Grand Trunk Railway of Canada, the, 336, 345
Grange-over-Sands, 333
Granges (monastic), 12
Gravewicks, 131
Gray, Thomas, 17, 60
Great Depression, the, 380 ff.
Great Eastern, the, 388
Great Northern Railway, 277
Greenodd, 46, 48, 84–6, 188, 208, 269–70

Griffiths, Samuel, 342
Grimsby, Great, 276, 381
Guano, 76, 78
Guardians of the Poor (see Ulverston, Barrow-in-Furness).
Gummer's How, 83

Hacket, 15
Hague, John, 171, 176
Halifax, 313
Hall, Dr. Edward, 290, 367
Hall, Edward & Co., 20 ff.
Halton Company, the, 33
Hannay, Robert, 194, 205, 212, 217, 220–2, 227, 252–3, 278, 299, 327, 330, 334, 342, 367, 376, 414.
Harecastle, 313.
Harrington ironworks, 222
Harrison, Ainslie & Co., 186, 193–4, 205–8, 229, 246, 257, 308. (See also Newland Co.)
Harrison, Benson, 178, 194
Harrisons of Coniston Waterhead, the, 38
Harrison, William, 300, 304
Hart & Ashburner, 95
Hartington, Marquess of, 334, 396, 398, 404, 416
Hartley, Philip, 53
Haverthwaite, 9, 51, 83, 111, 147
Hawcoat, 10, 13, 128, 130, 140, 273, 286, 292, 297, 306, 316, 322, 369, 375–6, 400, 420.
Hawkfield Farm, 76–7
Hawkshead, 3–4, 14, 48–9, 50, 68, 75, 111, 118, 122, 127, 130, 136, 138–9, 235–8, 295, 354, 421, 424, (grammar school), 144–5, 147–8, 151, (poorhouse), 137.
Heaf, the, 13
Heaning Wood, 23
Heathwaite, 13
Heriots, 130
Hindpool, 12, 77, 198, 222, 227–8, 281–3, 310–1, 314, 322–3, 332, 336, 348, 350, 361, 364–5, 372, 376, 381, 388, 408. (See also Barrow-in-Furness).
Hindpool Estate, 229, 285, 287, 290, 292, 304, 326–7, 375.
H.M.S. Powerful, 399.
Hodbarrow, 223, 253, 255, 270
Hodgson, J. K., 245, 299
Holborn Hill, 257
Holker Hall, 185, 274, 279
Holker (Upper), 122, 238, (Lower), 129, 134, 136, 138, 238, 333.
Holt, John, 43, 61.
Hordley, Ralph, 199
Hound trailing, 168
House prices, 182, 286–7

Housing conditions, 121–2, 242–4, 287, 371–3, 402. (See also *Rents, housing*).
House construction, 121–3, 286–7, 348, 372, 375, 408, 413, 417.
Howard, F. J., 178, 226
Howard, Lady Blanche (Countess of Burlington), 185
Huddleston, George, 195–6
Hudson, George, 190
Hull, 313
Humphrys, James, 387–90
Hunt, John, 299
Hunter, T. C., 215, 314
Hutchinson, W. E., 262, 277.

Illegitimate births, 112, 165
Immigration (see *Population*)
Improving farmers, 62–3, 245, 422.
Independents, 103, 331
India, 344
Industrial and Provident Societies Act (1871), 365
Infields, 10
Inman Line, the, 388–90
Institute of Mechanical Engineers, the, 389
Integration, 24, 286, 347
Interest rates, 27, 156, 196, 300.
Invergarry, 28
Ireland and the Irish, 105–8, 111, 239, 246, 314, 355.
Ireleth, 282, 418, (and Angerton), 92–3, 174, (Free School), 144, (Lane End), 83.

Iron, 338
Iron and steel industry of Furness, (charcoal iron manufacture), 19ff.
(costs and profits), 22, 28, 33–4, 207–8, 211, 250, 257–8, 393–4, (customers), 37, 250, 254, 336, 394 (output and statistics), 35, 194, 204–7, 251, 257, 275, 336–7, 393, 395.
Iron and Steel Institute, 343, 384
Iron forges, 17–18, 22, 25, 28.
Iron ore merchants, 94, 179, 192–5, 204–9, 211–12, 223, 257.
Iron ore mines, 193–4, 204, 206, 223, 257–8, 308, 336, 406, 422.
Iron ore trade and markets, 33, 36–7, 206, 251, 257–8, 308, 393, (See also, *Leases, Royalties*).
Ironworks of Schneider and Hannay, 221, 249 ff., 282, 288, 330, (see also *Barrow Haematite Steel Co.*)
Irton, 7.

Jackson, Rev. Edward, 83, 160–2, 166
Jacob, Arthur, 370, 377
Jenkinson, John, 64–5.

Jenner, Edward, 118
John, William, 390
Jordan, M. Samson, 249
Jute Industry, 339 ff. (see also *Barrow Flax & Jute Co.*).

Kelly, P. V., 12
Kendal, 2, 7, 49, 82–4, 89, 123, 146, 156, 228.
Kendal–Arnside railway plan, 263–4
Kendall, Edward, 29
Kendall, Henry, 32
Kendall, W. B., 11–12, 61, 285
Kennedy & Eastwood, 275
Kennedy Bros., 255, 257
Kennedy, C. S., 94, 194, 196, 205–6.
Kennedy, Charles B., 94.
Kennedy, Henry, 205–6.
Kennedy, Myles, 94, 299, 376, 380.
Keswick, 15, 21, 47, 82
King, Joshua, of Lowick, 154
Kirkby-in-Furness, 42, 75, 190.
Kirkby Ireleth (manor of), 8–9, 43, (parish), 3–5, 8–9, 47, 83, 97, 110–11, 113, 127, 235–7, 333, 400, 421 (poorhouse), 137, (slate quarries), 42 ff., 84, 174, 180, 193.
Kirkby (Pool), 46, 92, (Foot), 175.
Knott family, the, 38, 84.
Krupps, 342.

Labour " aristocrats " 39, 313, 393
Labour costs, 41, 208, 250
Labour migration (see *Population*)
Labour, " party of ", 400.
Labour shortage, 69, 75, 78–9, 179–80, 216, 251.
Labour supply (see *Population*).
Lancashire & Yorkshire Railway, 190
Lancaster, 3, 17, 21, 82, 86, 93, 181, 239, 262, 313, 322, 334, 376, 381, 416 (Banking Co.), 157, (Canal Co.), 77, 89, (Castle), 262, (creeks of), 85, 197, (port of), 31–2, 264–5.
Lancaster and Carlisle Railway, 181, 212, 263, 267, 277.
Landing places (coastal), 85
Land reclamation, 61, 63 ff., 84
Land tax assessments, 5–7, 56–7, 71–2.
Land values, 63, 200, 229, 284, 301, 341, 369, 374.
Langdale, Great, 13.
Last, Robert, 313, 317
Latham family, the, 29
Latham, William, 29, 156
Law of Master and Servant, 315–6
Law of Settlement, 138
Leach, Francis, 349

Leases, 9, 284,
  (copper), 47–8,
  (iron mining), 205.
Le Creusot, 221, 342
Leece, 5, 7, 148.
Leeds, 181, 313, 401
Leighton furnace, 22, 26
Leighton Wood, 60
Levens Bridge, 84
Liberal Party, the, 334–5, 415–16
Libraries, 150, 366, 421
Lindal, 83, 179, 191, 196, 205, 208, 287,
  418, (Cote), 35, (Moor), 35, 94, 258.
Literacy, 149, 247–8, 332–3
Little, James, 340, 343–4
Little North-Western line, 262
Liverpool, 32, 52, 69, 78, 167, 173, 189,
  193–4, 207, 245, 261, 263, 274–5, 334,
  344, 381, 391, 393, 401, 403.
Llanelly, 202, 212
Llanrhychwyn, 108
Loan capital, 27, 156
Local Government Act (1858), 293, 300,
  (1888), 419.
Loch Garry, 28
London, 167, 192, 391, 403.
London & Birmingham Railway, 183.
London and North-Western Railway,
  183, 261–2, 264, 267–8, 272, 277–8,
  376.
Long Eaton, 345–6
Lonsdale, Earl of, 174, 264, 267.
Lorn furnace, 34
Lowick (manor), 8, (parish), 107, 128,
  159, (quarries), 47, (school), 333.
Lowther of Marske and Holker, 10, 128
Lowwood Gunpowder Works, 238.
Loxham, Robert, 334.
Lumley, R. W., 178–9
Lund Beck, 54
Lytham, 245.

Macclesfield Copper Co., 47–8.
Machell family, 11, 20 ff., 30, 84, 161.
Machell, John, 19 ff.
Machell, Thos. M., 65.
McClean, Frank, 279, 343.
McClean, J. R., 178–9, 190, 215–6, 224,
  262, 265, 278–9, 343, 369–70, 414.
Malt trade, 68.
Manchester, 136, 167, 245, 282, 316,
  327, 401.
Manclarke, W. T., 300, 334.
Mansriggs, 128–9, 238
Mariners in local records, 85–6, 126.
Marriage ages, 113.
Marton, 109, 287, 400.
Master General Builders' Association,
  317.
Mault, Alfred, 317.

Mayor hunts, 166.
Menelaus, William, 384, 395.
Methodists
  (Primitive), 331.
  (Wesleyan), 103–4, 162, 331, 333.
Meysey-Thompson, H., 343, 395.
Mexican and S. American Co., 192.
Middlesbrough, 222, 255, 320, 324, 406.
Midland Counties Railway, 183.
Midland Railway, 261–2, 267, 272–3,
  278, 395.
Milburn (Westmld.), 120.
Millom, 223, 337
  (Sands), 82–3.
Milner, Samuel, 25, 27, 47.
Milnthorpe, 85.
Milnthorpe and Arnside line, 263.
Miners' National Association, the, 364.
Mines Royal, 15, 47.
Minnesota, 366.
Molyneux, Lord, 10.
Montagu, Duke of, 111.
Montagu family, 45.
Morecambe (Poulton), 263, 294.
Morgan, John de, 412.
Muchland, Manor of, 8, 129.
Multiplier, use of, 100.
Muncaster, Lord, 74, 176, 207.
Myers, John, 401.

Naval Construction & Armaments Co.,
  398–9, 401.
Newbarns, 121, 130, 297, 306, 332–3,
  376.
Newby Bridge, 24, 83, 269–72, 277.
Newland Beck, 194, 208.
Newland Company, 29–30, 33–4, 37,
  88–9, 93–4, 156, 182.
New Orleans, 391.
Newton, 400, 418.
Nibthwaite, 9, 33.
Nicholl, F. I. and J. I. 178–9, 226, 252,
  343.
Nine Hour Movement, 357, 362.
Nordenfelt Guns & Ammunition Co.,
  398.
Nordenfelt, Thorsten, 397–8.
North-Eastern Railway, 345.
North Lancashire & Cumberland Iron
  Exchange, 381.
North Lonsdale Agricultural Society,
  63, 78.
North Lonsdale Hospital, 322 ff., 378.
North Lonsdale Iron & Steel Co., 380,
  394, 417.
North Scale, 122.
Norway, 382.
Nutrition, 123 ff., 408.

Oatmeal, use of, 123.
Oats (cultivation), 61–2.
(trade), 68.
Occupations, (see *Population, Mariners in Local Records, Weavers*, etc.)
Oddie, H. H., 178.
Old Barrow (see *Barrow Island*).
Oligopoly, 23, 33.
Olivant, John, 20.
Osmotherley, 47, 128–30, 328
(school), 146–8.
Overcrowding, 287, 321, 371, 408, 418.
Owner-occupiers, 58, 66, 72–4, 423.

Pacific Steam Navigation Co., 399.
Painlookers, 131.
Park, James, 195.
Park Mine, 203–5, 211, 251, 253–5, 396.
Parke, G. H., 346.
Parliamentary representation, 415–6, 419.
Parochial divisions, 3–4.
Parys Mine, 48.
Patent Copper Company, 202.
Pauperism in Furness, 132 ff., 164, 290–1, 367–8, 401.
Peabody, George, 413.
Pease, Henry, 217.
Pease and Co., 272.
Pennant, Thomas, 11, 61, 83.
Pennington, 3, 8, 14, 37, 77, 82, 130–1, 135–7, 207, 235–8, 421,
(poorhouse at), 137.
Pennington, Sir Isaac, 154.
Penny Bridge, 14, 52, 58, 83, 166, 333,
(furnace), 30, 33,
(Wood Articles), 33,
(mill), 52–3.
Penny family, the, 84, 161.
Penrith, 20, 171.
Pensioners, 138.
Petty and Postlethwaite, 157.
Petty, Thomas, 195.
Piel of Fouldrey, 2, 17, 85–6,
(Bar), 198,
(Harbour), 173, 175, 182, 188, 212, 245, 297,
(Pier), 189, 277.
Pitt, William, 44, 153.
Plague, bubonic, 16.
Plumb, Dr. J. H., 159.
Plumpton, 270.
Plymouth, 327.
Pococke, Dr., 61.
Police, 314, 408, 412, 419.
Political campaigns, 334–5, 362, 415–6.
Pollard, Dr. S., 370–1, 384.
Poole, John, 297, 301, 374.
Poor Law Amendment Act (1834), 140-1
Poor Law Board, the, 368.
Poor Law Commissioners, 128, 142–3.

Poor rates and expenditure, 133–6, 139, 142–3, 304, 368, 419.
Population of Furness : (birth and death rates), 114–5, 243, 289, 293–5, 321, 407, 418, (emigration), 15, 109–12, 235, 238, 240, 316, 320, 366, (general growth), 97 ff., 234 ff., 295, 333, 353 ff., 417, (immigration), 15, 104–9, 234, 238, 313, 353–5, 387, (mortality years, ages), 116 ff., 243–4. (occupations), 4 ff., 126, 164, 240, 356,

Potatoes, 62, 242.
Potter, Richard, 276, 344–5, 390–1.
Pratt, J. Tidd, 328.
Presbyterians, 103, 331.
Presow, Richard, 308.
Preston, 89, 120, 245, 282.
Preston, C. F., 365, 377.
Price movements and the trade cycle, 22, 30–31, 43–4, 68–70, 79–81, 91, 135, 144, 157, 190, 210, 218–9, 270–1, 311–2, 321, 336, 359, 383, 391, 395, 403.
Price, Potter, Walker & Co., 276, 340, 344.
Public health, 115 ff., 122, 165, 244, 289–90, 294–5, 373, 397, 407–8.
Public Health Act (1875), 302.
Punch, 326, 328.

Quakers, 20–1, 25, 27, 103, 146, 162.
Quarrymen, 43, 44, 46–7.

Railway " mania " of 1845–6, 179.
Raistrick, Dr. A., 21, 27.
Rampside, 85, 152, 173, 175, 177, 189, 281, 292.
Ramsden, (Sir) James, 182–3, 186–7, 198–9, 200, 215, 221, 224–6, 227–9, 233, 243, 245, 251–3, 262–5, 278–9, 282–3, 285, 288, 290, 292–3, 296–7, 299–302, 305, 324–5, 327–9, 330–2, 334, 338, 343–5, 348, 350–3, 358–60, 362, 367–8, 375–6, 378, 382, 384, 387–8, 390–1, 402–4, 409–10, 413–5.
Rateable values, 143, 291, 302–3, 376, 417.
Ratepayers' Protective Association, 305, 376.
Ravenglass, 82.
Rawcliffe, Joseph, 347, 372.
Rawlinsons of Graythwaite, the, 11, 20 ff., 38, 74, 222.
Rawlinson, Joseph, 94, 195, 205–6, 255, 257, 287, 299, 417, (see also *Town & Rawlinson*).
Rawlinson, William (d. 1734), 20 ff., 38, 222.

Rea, William, 29.
Reeans (reins), 12.
Redistribution of Seats Act, (1885), 419.
Registrar-General, the, 120, 293–4.
Relph, William, 334.
Rennie, John, 89.
Rents (housing), 70, 80, 154, 287, 311–2, 321, 342, 385.
Rents, (manorial), 8 ff., 131. (See *Agriculture* for other rentals).
Retail traders, 125, 240, 311, 364.
Return of Owners of Land (1873), 423.
Richardson, Joseph, 296, 305, 315, 321, 323–4, 334, 338–9, 362, 411–3, 415.
Richmond Wills, 6, 86.
Rigg, Thomas, 29.
Rigge, Thomas, 43–4, 46.
Rigge, William, 43.
Riggs, 12.
River Clyde, 273, 421.
River Crake, 14, 48, 54.
River Duddon, 1, 64, 174–5, 180, 203, 255, 265, 267.
River Kent, 64, 218.
River Leven, 1, 46, 52, 54, 64–5, 90, 218, 380.
River Lune, 64.
River Mersey, 263, 273.
Roads, 82 ff., 196, 292, 418.
Roanhead, 257.
Robertson, S., 343, 358, 383, 390.
Robinson, J. N., 43.
Robinson, Richard, 74.
Rochdale, 365.
Rock Assurance Company, 300.
Romney, George, 151, 156.
Roose, 12, 180, 400, 420–1, (Cote), 286.
Roper, Richard, 178.
Roper, Thomas, 194, 198, 200, 220, 229, 246, 318–9.
Rose, George, 158.
Rostow, Prof. W. W., 380–1.
Rotations (woodland), 24, 28, 58. (See also *Agriculture*).
Rotterdam, 382.
Royal Commission on Trade Unions, (1867), 316.
Royal Geographical Society, 154.
Royal Mines Copper, 47.
Royalties (copper), 48, (iron ore), 35–7, 204, 251, 258, (slate), 45–6.
Run-rig, 10.
Rusland, 111, 333, (school), 146.
Russia, 382, 394.

St. Helens, 78.
Salford, 376.
Salt, Titus, 321.
Saltaire, 283, 321.
Salthouse, 12–13, 67, 121, 124, 130, 180, 182, 200, 228, 243, 274, 281–3, 289, 306, 346, 350, 369, 372, 376.
Sandys, Archbishop Edwin, 144, 155.
Sandys family, the, 11, 74, 160.
Sandys, Myles, jun., 128.
Satterthwaite, 139, 236–7, 333.
Sawreys of Broughton, the, 11, 73–4.
Sawrey school, 146–8.
Schneider, H. W., 95, 155, 173–5, 185–6, 192–3, 195–6, 202, 205–6, 208–9, 211–2, 217, 220–2, 224–5, 227, 238, 246, 252–3, 278, 288, 290–1, 297–9, 308–9, 314, 325, 327–9, 330, 332, 334, 339, 342–3, 345, 348, 351–2, 360, 362–3, 366–8, 376, 383, 394–5, 400, 402, 409–10, 414–6, 420.
Schneider, John, 192.
Scotland (immigration from), 239, 355, 421, (ironworks in) 28–9, 34, (trade with), 78.
Seathwaite, 58, 156.
Seaton ironworks, 222.
Sedgwick, Adam, 154–5.
Settle, 83.
Settle–Carlisle line, 267, 277.
Severn ports, the, 21, 36–7.
Shap, 120.
Shaw, Rev. S. S., 17, 163.
Sheep-raising, 11, 58–9.
Sheffield, 194, 250, 261, 393.
Shipbuilding, 8, 16, 39, 85–6, 95, 234, 273, (see also *Barrow Shipbuilding Company*).
Simpson, George, 290, 367.
Skelwith Bridge, 83.
Skipton, 83, 181, 262.
Slate (grades of), 43, (taxation of), 44, (trade in), 16, 42 ff., 75, 223, (uses), 46–7, 121.
Smallpox, 116–7, 373.
Smiles, Samuel, 353.
Smith & Caird, 348.
Smith, J. T., 221–2, 249, 251, 253, 292, 299, 303, 319, 334, 343, 348, 358–9, 376, 384, 390, 395, 402, 406, 414.
Smith, John Abel, 173, 176–7, 182, 186, 189, 198.
Smith, Richard, 195.
Social morality, 164–5, 361.
Soulby, John and Stephen, 150.
South Durham and Lancashire Union Railway, 216, 249.
Southport, 216.
South Wales, 191, 209, 212, 251.
Spain, 382, 394.
Spark Bridge (forge), 33.
Speenhamland, 136.
Spinning jennies, 51.
Staffordshire, 191, 206, 239, 251, 281, 331, 346, 355.
Stainton, 10, 123, 211, 253, 269, 400.
Stank, 336.
Stanley, the Hon. F., 335.

Statesmen, 9–10, 55, 59, 74, 423.
Staveley (Cartmel), 10.
Steam power, 50–1, 53–4.
Stileman, F., (d. 1904), 279.
Stileman, F. C., 215–6, 278, 343, 369–70, 414.
Steamer services, 96, 277, 391, 403.
Stephenson, George, 171, 176, 426.
Stephenson, Robert, 188.
Stinting, 13.
Stockdale, James, 62, 65, 134–5, 238.
Storey, John, 282.
Stout, William, 21–2, 25, 39.
Stockton and Darlington Railway Co., 217, 220.
Subberthwaite, 13.
Submarines, 397–8.
Suez Canal, the, 338, 344, 390.
Summer fallows, 61.
Sunbrick, 103, 162.
Sunday school movement, 150.
Sunderland family, the, 30, 160,
Sunderland, Rev. John, 160.
Surgeons and medical treatment, 117–8, 321, 323, 407–8.
Surnames of Furness, 14, 104–7.
Surveyors of highways, 129, 292.
Swainson, Isaac, 154.
Swansea, 192.
Swaledale, 83.
Swarthmoor, 103, 162, 309,
      (school), 145–6.
Sweden, 382.
Swindlehurst, Samuel, 386.
Syria, 390.

Taylors of Finsthwaite, the, 11, 74.
Taylor, the Rev. William, 152.
Tebay, 264.
Temperance, 327–8, 365.
Tenant farmers, 10–11, 62–3, 72–3, 77, 245–6.
Textile industries (domestic), 49–50.
Thackeray and Co., 50.
Theatres, 150, 329–30.
Thompson, H. S., 252–3, 278, 343, 345.
Tilberthwaite, 42, 45, 48.
Tillotson, Archbishop, 160.
Timber trade, the, 60, 258, 275–6, 337, 382, 403.
Tissington, Anthony, 48.
Tithe commutation, 7.
Tithes, 64.
Titley, Joseph, 25.
Todmorden, 313.
Torver, 4–5, 7–8, 13, 14–15, 45, 47, 59, 108, 128–9, 160, 235–7.
Town, Robert, 195.
Town and Rawlinson, 196.
Townson, Benjamin, 275, 285, 334, 415.

Trade unions and combinations :
      (blacksmiths'), 357, (boilermakers'), 357, 364, (bricklayers'), 313, 357, 359, (cabinet makers'), 392, (carpenters'), 313–7, 320, 356–7, 392, 399, (coach-builders'), 392, (engineers'), 247, 313, 320, 357–8, 364, 385–6, 388, 392, 397, 399–400, (gasworkers'), 400, (iron-founders' and moulders'), 319, 357–9, 392, (iron ore miners'), 246, 307–8, 359, 364, (labourers'), 392, 400, (painters'), 313, 357, 392, (pattern-makers'), 392, (printers'), 392, (rail-waymen's), 316, 319, 357, (shoe-makers'), 316, 357, (stone-masons'), 313, 316, 357, (tailors'), 357, 392.
      (See also *Working hours*).

Tramways, 45, 94, 196, 258, 414.
Turner, Thomas, 397.
Turnips, 62–3, 75–6.
Turnpike trusts, (Carnforth), 84.
      (Kendal), 83,

Ulverston : (Canal), 84, 89–93, 155, 173, 187, 196, 207, 218, (Highway Board), 294, (Registration District), 114, 244, 296, (schools in), 144–5, 148, 150, 153–4, 171, 420, (town, manor and parish), 3–4, 8, 14, 49, 52–4, 60, 65, 67–9, 77, 82–6, 93, 95, 111, 113, 116–8, 122 ff., 127–9, 130, 135, 138, 158, 162, 165–8, 175, 177, 180, 188, 215, 238, 242–4, 267, 282, 288, 291–4, 309, 317, 327, 329, 333, 354, 367, 393, 400, 417–8, (Urban District Council), 419, (Waterworks Company), 378, (workhouse), 137, 139–40.

Ulverston Advertiser, 229, 312.
Ulverston and Lancaster Railway Co., 217–8, 239, 251, 259, 262.
Ulverston Mining Co., 77.
Ulverston Mirror, 294, 308, 316.
Ulverston Savings Bank, 39, 158.

Unemployment, 135–6, 320, 397, 399–401, 405.
Urswick, Great and Little, 129, 152, 154, 159, 235–7, 290, 354, 400, 421–2, (poorhouse), 137, (school), 144–8.
United States, the, 382, 390, 394.

Vaccine inoculation, 118.
Vaughan, John, 217.
Vestries, (closed), 4, 127–9, (Select), 138–9.
Vickers-Maxim, 402.
Vickerstown, 426.

438

Waddington, Andrew, 275.
Waddington & Longbottom, 257, 350, 354, 358.
Wadham, Edward, 35, 220, 245, 299, 335, 348, 368, 376, 394, 404, 406, 408–9, 414, 416.
Wages : (agricultural), 69–70, 79–81, 241–2, 422, (bricklayers'), 179, 359, (cabinet-makers'), 401, (carpenters'), 179, 317, 400, (engineers'), 313, 388, 401; (general), 311, 359, (general labourers'), 40, 140, 311, 385, 392, 401, (ironworkers'), 40–41, 250, 401, (masons'), 179, (miners' and quarry-men's), 36, 41, 48, 208, 237, 242, 308, 316, 359, 400, 406, (patternmakers'), 401, (railway), 179, 242, (ship-wrights'), 400, (weavers'), 140.
Wakefield, Crewdson & Co., 157, 217.
Wakefield, John, 217.
Walker, James, 174–6, 178, 180, 226.
Walker, Rev. Robert, 156, 160, 163, 165, 168.
Wallas, Robert, 300.
Walney, 3–4, 61, 66, 84, 122, 144, 167, 198.
    (Channel), 228, 273,
    (land reclamation at), 66, 292, 306, 330, 333, 368, 376, 411–3.
War demand (for charcoal), 60, (for iron), 31, (for softwood), 60, (for wheat etc.), 62 ff.
Warhurst partnerships, the, 51.
Warrington, 21, 376.
Warsash (Hants.), 194.
Waterlow, Sir Sydney, 413.
Water-power, 2, 19, 50–2, 54.
Weavers, 8, 49–50, 126, 140.
Webb, Beatrice, 276, 390.
Webster, John W., 365.

Wennington, 262.
Wesley, John, 82–3.
West, Thomas, 58–60, 102, 161, 163, 165
Westmorland, 15, 97, 99, 149, 235, 242, 239, 351, 355, 422.

Westray & Copeland, 346–7, 356, 385,
Westray & Forster, 275, 347, 350, 387.
Westray, John, 299, 305.
Whinfield Farm, 77, 180.
White, William, 95.
Whitechapel, 52.
Whitefield, George, 161–2.
Whitehaven, 3, 25, 32, 82–3, 196, 270–1, (Provisional Committee), 171.
Whitehaven and Furness Junction Railway, 167, 181, 188, 212, 259, 267–8, 291.
Whitehaven, Cleator & Egremont Railway, 259, 268–9.
Whitehaven Haematite Iron Company, 222.
Whitehaven Junction Railway, 211, 268
Whitworth, Joseph, & Co., 398.
Wilkinson, John, 36–8, 50, 64–5, 171, 176.
Wilson House, 84.
Wilsons of Bardsea, the, 11.
Windermere, 1, 23–4, 189, 269, 405.
Winder Moor, 67.
Wolverton, 183, 200.
Wood agreements, 33–4.
Wood conservation, 58.
Woodall, Solomon, 275, 346, 350, 356.
Woodburne, Thomas, 223.
Woodhouse, A. J., 275, 286, 314–5, 334, 347–8, 359, 372.
Woodhouse, Son & Andrews, 346.
Worcestershire, 355.
Wordsworth, John, 151.
Wordsworth, William, 1, 7, 71, 151–2, 156, 180.
Workhouses, 136–9, 140, 142.
Working hours, 48, 52–3, 314–6, 318–9, 359–60, 364, 399, 401.

Yarlside, 10, 128, 376.
Yeomen, 6 ff., 76, 78, 423.
Yewdale, 45.
Yewdall & Hitchens, 346, 375.
Yorkshire, 17, 56, 264, 355.